D0817827

Hacking RSS and Atom

Leslie M. Orchard

WILEY

Wiley Publishing, Inc.

Hacking RSS and Atom

Published by
Wiley Publishing, Inc.
10475 Crosspoint Boulevard
Indianapolis, IN 46256
www.wiley.com

Library of Congress Cataloging-in-Publication Data:

Orchard, Leslie Michael, 1975-
  Hacking RSS and Atom / Leslie Michael Orchard.
    p. cm.
  Includes index.
  ISBN-13: 978-0-7645-9758-9 (paper/website)
  ISBN-10: 0-7645-9758-2 (paper/website)
  1. Computer security. 2. File organization (Computer science) 3. Computer hackers. I. Title.
  QA76.9.A25O73 2005
  005.8--dc22
                              2005016634

About the Author

Leslie M. Orchard is a hacker, tinkerer, and creative technologist who works in the Detroit area. He lives with two spotted Ocicats, two dwarf bunnies, and a very patient and understanding girl. On rare occasions when spare time comes in copious amounts, he plays around with odd bits of code and writing, sharing them on his Web site named 0xDECAFBAD (`http://www.decafbad.com/`).

Credits

Acquisitions Editor
Chris Webb

Development Editor
Kevin Shafer

Technical Editor
Brian Sletten

Production Editor
Felicia Robinson

Copy Editor
Kim Cofer

Editorial Manager
Mary Beth Wakefield

Production Manager
Tim Tate

Vice President & Executive Group Publisher
Richard Swadley

Vice President and Publisher
Joseph B. Wikert

Project Coordinator
Erin Smith

Graphics and Production Specialists
Denny Hager
Stephanie D. Jumper
Ron Terry

Quality Control Technicians
John Greenough
Leeann Harney
Jessica Kramer
Carl William Pierce
Charles Spencer

Proofreading and Indexing
TECHBOOKS Production Services

Acknowledgments

Alexandra Arnold, my Science Genius Girl, kept me supplied with food, hugs, and encouragement throughout this project. I love you, cutie.

Scott Knaster, in his book *Hacking iPod + iTunes* (Hoboken, N.J.: Wiley, 2004), clued me into just how much the iPod Notes Reader could do—which comes in quite handy in Chapter 5.

Mark Pilgrim's meticulously constructed contributions to handling syndication feeds (and everything else) in Python and with XPath made my job look easy.

Dave Winer's evangelism and software development surrounding RSS feeds and Web logs are what got me into this mess in the first place, so I'd certainly be remiss without a tip of the hat his way.

This list could go on and on, in an effort to include everyone whose work I've studied and improvised upon throughout the years. Instead of cramming every name and project into this small section, keep an eye out for pointers to projects and alternatives offered at the end of each chapter throughout the book.

Contents at a Glance

Contents

Part I: Consuming Feeds

Part III: Remixing Feeds

Introduction

As you'll discover shortly, regardless of what the cover says, this isn't a book about Atom or RSS feeds. In fact, this is mainly a book about lots of other things, between which syndication feeds form the glue or enabling catalyst.

Sure, you'll find some quick forays into specifics of consuming and producing syndication feeds, with a few brief digressions on feed formats and specifications. However, there are better and more detailed works out there focused on the myriad subtleties involved in working with RSS and Atom feeds. Instead, what you'll find here is that syndication feeds are the host of the party, but you'll be spending most of your time with the guests.

And, because this is a book about hacking feeds, you'll get the chance to experiment with combinations of technology and tools, leaving plenty of room for further tinkering. The code in this book won't be the prettiest or most complete, but it should provide you with lots of practical tools and food for thought.

Who Is This Book For?

Because this isn't a book entirely devoted to the basics of syndication feeds, you should already have some familiarity with them. Maybe you have a blog of your own and have derived some use out of a feed aggregator. This book mentions a little about both, but you will want to check these out if you haven't already.

You should also be fairly comfortable with basic programming and editing source files, particularly in the Python programming language. Just about every hack here is presented in Python, and although they are all complete programs, they're intended as starting points and fuel for your own tinkering. In addition, most of the code here assumes you're working on a UNIX-based platform like Linux or Mac OS X—although you can make things work without too much trouble under Microsoft Windows.

Something else you should really have available as you work through this book is Web hosting. Again, if you have a blog of your own, you likely already have this. But, when you get around to producing and remixing feeds, it's really helpful to have a Web server somewhere to host these feeds for consumption by an aggregator. And, again, this book has a UNIX-based slant, but some attention is paid in later chapters to automating uploads to Web hosts that only offer FTP access to your Web directories.

What's in This Book?

Syndication feed technology has only just started growing, yet you can already write a full series of articles or books about any one of a great number of facets making up this field. You have at least two major competing feed formats in Atom and RSS—and there are more than a half-dozen versions and variants of RSS, along with a slew of Atom draft specifications as its development progresses. And then there are all the other details to consider—such as what and how much to put into feeds, how to deliver feeds most efficiently, how to parse all these formats, and how to handle feed data once you have it.

This book, though, is going to take a lot of the above for granted—if you want to tangle with the minutiae of character encoding and specification hair-splitting, the coming chapters will be a disappointment to you. You won't find very many discussions on the relative merits of techniques for counting pinhead-dancing angels here. On the other hand, if you'd like to get past all that and just *do stuff* with syndication feeds, you're in the right place. I'm going to gloss over most of the differences and conflicts between formats, ignore a lot of important details, and get right down to working code.

Thankfully, though, a lot of hardworking and meticulous people make it possible to skip over some of these details. So, whenever possible, I'll show you how to take advantage of their efforts to hack together some useful and interesting things. It will be a bit quick-and-dirty in spots, and possibly even mostly wrong for some use cases, but hopefully you'll find at least one hack in these pages that allows you to do something you couldn't before.

I'll try to explain things through code, rather than through lengthy exposition. Sometimes the comments in the code are more revealing than the surrounding prose. Also, again, keep in mind that every program and project in this book is a starting point. Loose ends are left for you to tie up or further extend, and rough bits are left for you to polish up. That's part of the fun in tinkering—if everything were all wrapped up in a bow, you'd have nothing left to play with!

How's This Book Structured?

Now that I've painted a fuzzy picture of what's in store for you in this book, I'll give you a quick preview of what's coming in each chapter:

Part I: Consuming Feeds

Feeds are out there on the Web, right now. So, a few hacks that consume feeds seems like a good place to start. Take a look at these brief teasers about the chapters in this first third of the book:

- *Chapter 1: Getting Ready to Hack*—Before you really jump into hacking feeds, this chapter gives you get a sense of what you're getting into, as well as pointing you to some practical tools you'll need throughout the rest of the book.

- *Chapter 2: Building a Simple Feed Aggregator*—Once you have tools and a working environment, it's time to get your feet wet on feeds. This chapter offers code you can use to find, fetch, parse, and aggregate syndication feeds, presenting them in simple static HTML pages generated from templates.

- *Chapter 3: Routing Feeds to Your Email Inbox*—This chapter walks you though making further improvements to the aggregator from Chapter 2, adding persistence in tracking new feed items. This leads up to routing new feed entries into your email Inbox, where you can use all the message-management tools there at your disposal.

- *Chapter 4: Adding Feeds to Your Buddy List*—Even more immediate than email is instant messaging. This chapter further tweaks and refines the aggregator under development from Chapters 2 and 3, routing new feed entries direct to you as instant messages. Taking things further, you'll be able to build an interactive chatbot with a conversational interface you can use for managing subscriptions and requesting news updates.

- *Chapter 5: Taking Your Feeds with You*—You're not always sitting at your computer, but you might have a Palm device or Apple iPod in your pocket while you're out. This chapter furthers your aggregator tweaking by showing you how to load up mobile devices with feed content.

- *Chapter 6: Subscribing to Multimedia Content Feeds*—Finishing off this first part of the book is a chapter devoted to multimedia content carried by feeds. This includes podcasting and other forms of downloadable media starting to appear in syndication feeds. You'll build your own podcast tuner that supports both direct downloads, as well as cooperative downloading via BitTorrent.

Part II: Producing Feeds

Changing gears a bit, it's time to get your hands dirty in the details of producing syndication feeds from various content sources. The following are some chapter teasers for this part of the book:

- *Chapter 7: Building a Simple Feed Producer*—Walking before you run is usually a good thing, so this chapter walks you though building a simple feed producer that can process a directory of HTML files, using each document's metadata and content to fill out the fields of feed entries.

- *Chapter 8: Taking the Edge Off Hosting Feeds*—Before going much further in producing feeds, a few things need to be said about hosting them. As mentioned earlier, you should have your own Web hosting available to you, but this chapter provides you with some pointers on how to configure your server in order to reduce bandwidth bills and make publishing feeds more efficient.

- *Chapter 9: Scraping Web Sites to Produce Feeds*—Going beyond Chapter 7's simple feed producer, this chapter shows you several techniques you can use to extract syndication feed data from Web sites that don't offer them already. Here, you see how to use HTML parsing, regular expressions, and XPath to pry content out of stubborn tag soup.

- *Chapter 10: Monitoring Your Server with Feeds*—Once you've started living more of your online life in a feed aggregator, you'll find yourself wishing more streams of messages could be pulled into this central attention manager. This chapter shows you how to route notifications and logs from servers you administer into private syndication feeds, going beyond the normal boring email alerts.

- *Chapter 11: Tracking Changes in Open Source Projects*—Many Open Source projects offer mailing lists and blogs to discuss and announce project changes, but for some people these streams of information just don't run deep enough. This chapter shows you how to tap into CVS and Subversion repositories to build feeds notifying you of changes as they're committed to the project.

- *Chapter 12: Routing Your Email Inbox to Feeds*—As the inverse of Chapter 3, this chapter is concerned with pulling POP3 and IMAP email inboxes into private syndication feeds you can use to track your own general mail or mailing lists to which you're subscribed.

- *Chapter 13: Web Services and Feeds*—This chapter concludes the middle section of the book, showing you how to exploit Google, Yahoo!, and Amazon Web services to build some syndication feeds based on persistent Web, news, and product searches. You should be able to use the techniques presented here to build feeds from many other public Web services available now and in the future.

Part III: Remixing Feeds

In this last third of the book, you combine both feed consumption and production in hacks that take feeds apart and rebuild them in new ways, filtering information and mixing in new data. Here are some teasers from the chapters in this part:

- *Chapter 14: Normalizing and ConvertingFeeds*—One of the first stages in remixing feeds is being able to take them apart and turn them into other formats. This chapter shows you how to consume feeds as input, manipulate them in memory, and produce feeds as output. This will allow you to treat feeds as fluid streams of data, subject to all sorts of transformations.

- *Chapter 15: Filtering and Sifting Feeds*—Now that you've got feeds in a fluid form, you can filter them for interesting entries using a category or keyword search. Going further, you can use machine learning in the form of Bayesian filtering to automatically identify entries with content of interest. And then, you will see how you can sift through large numbers of feed entries in order to distill hot links and topics into a focused feed.

- *Chapter 16: Blending Feeds*—The previous chapter mostly dealt with reducing feeds by filtering or distillation. Well, this chapter offers hacks that mix feeds together and inject new information into feeds. Here, you see how to use Web services to add related links and do a little affiliate sponsorship with related product searches.

- *Chapter 17: Republishing Feeds*—In this chapter, you are given tools to build group Web logs from feeds using a modified version of the feed aggregator you built in the beginning of the book. If you already have Web log software, you'll see another hack that can use the MetaWeblog API to repost feed entries. And then, if you just want to include a list of headlines, you'll see a hack that renders feeds as JavaScript includes easily used in HTML pages.

- *Chapter 18: Extending Feeds*—The final chapter of the book reaches a bit into the future of feeds. Here, you see how content beyond the usual human-readable blobs of text and HTML can be expanded into machine-readable content like calendar events, using microformats and feed format extensions. This chapter walks you through how to produce extended feeds, as well as how to consume them.

Part IV: Appendix

During the course of the book, you'll see many directions for future development in consuming, producing, and remixing feeds. This final addition to the book offers you an example of one of these projects, a caching feed fetcher that you can use in other programs in this book to speed things up in some cases. For the most part, this add-on can be used with a single-line change to feed consuming hacks in this book.

Conventions Used in This Book

During the course of this book, I'll use the following icons alongside highlighted text to draw your attention to various important things:

Points you toward further information and exploration available on the Web.

Directs you to other areas in this book relating to the current discussion.

Further discussion concerning something mentioned recently.

A few words of warning about a technique or code nearby.

Source Code

As you work through the programs and hacks in this book, you may choose to either type in all the code manually or to use the source code files that accompany the book. All of the source code used in this book is available for download at the following site:

www.wiley.com/compbooks/extremetech

Once you download the code, just decompress it with your favorite compression tool.

Errata

We make every effort to ensure that there are no errors in the text or in the code. However, no one is perfect, and mistakes do occur. Also, because this technology is part of a rapidly developing landscape, you may find now and then that something has changed out from under the book by the time it gets into your hands. If you find an error in one of our books, like a spelling mistake, broken link, or faulty piece of code, we would be very grateful for your feedback. By sending in an errata you may save another reader hours of frustration and at the same time you will be helping us provide even higher quality information.

To find the errata page for this book, go to `http://www.wiley.com/` and locate the title using the Search box or one of the title lists. Then, on the book details page, click the Book Errata link. On this page you can view all errata that has been submitted for this book and posted by Wiley editors. A complete book list including links to each book's errata is also available at `www.wiley.com/compbooks/extremetech`.

Consuming Feeds

part

Getting Ready to Hack

What are RSS and Atom feeds? If you're reading this, it's pretty likely you've already seen links to feeds (things such as "Syndicate this Site" or the ubiquitous orange-and-white "RSS" buttons) starting to pop up on all of your favorite sites. In fact, you might already have secured a feed reader or aggregator and stopped visiting most of your favorite sites in person. The bookmarks in your browser have started gathering dust since you stopped clicking through them every day. And, if you're like some feed addicts, you're keeping track of what's new from more Web sites and news sources than you ever have before, or even thought possible.

If you're a voracious infovore like me and this story *doesn't* sound familiar, you're in for a treat. RSS and Atom feeds—collectively known as *syndication feeds*—are behind one of the biggest changes to sweep across the Web since the invention of the personal home page. These syndication feeds make it easy for machines to surf the Web, so you don't have to.

So far, syndication feed readers won't actually read or intelligently digest content on the Web for you, but they will let you know when there's something new to peruse and can collect it in an inbox, like email.

In fact, these feeds and their readers layer the Web with features not altogether different than email newsletters and Usenet newsgroups, but with much more control over what you receive and none of the spam. With the time you used to spend browsing through bookmarked sites checking for updates, you can now just get straight to reading new stuff presented directly. It's almost as though someone is publishing a newspaper tailored just for you.

From the publishing side of things, when you serve up your messages and content using syndication feeds, you make it so much easier for someone to keep track of your updates—and so much more likely that they will stay in touch because, once someone has subscribed to your feed, it's practically effortless to stay tuned in. As long as you keep pushing out things worthy of an audience's attention, syndication feeds make it easier to slip into their busy schedules and stay there.

Furthermore, the way syndication feeds slice up the Web into timely capsules of *microcontent* allows you to manipulate, filter, and remix streams of fluid online content in a way never seen before. With the right tools, you *can* work toward applications that help more cleverly digest content and sift through the firehose of information available. You can gather resources and collectively republish, acting as the editorial *newsmaster* of your own personal news wire. You can train *learning machines* to filter for items that match your interests. And the possibilities offered by syndication will only expand as new kinds of information and new types of media are carried and referenced by feed items.

But that's enough gushing about syndication feeds. Let's get to work figuring out what these things are, under the hood, and how you can actually do some of the things promised earlier.

Taking a Crash Course in RSS and Atom Feeds

If you're already familiar with all the basics of RSS and Atom feeds, you can skip ahead to the section "Gathering Tools" later in this chapter. But, just in case you need to be brought up to speed, this section takes a quick tour of feed consumers, feed producers, and the basics of feed anatomy.

Catching Up with Feed Readers and Aggregators

One of the easiest places to start with an introduction to syndication feeds is with feed aggregators and readers, because the most visible results of feeds start there. Though you will be building your own aggregator soon enough, having some notion of what sorts of things other working aggregators do can certainly give you some ideas. It also helps to have other aggregators around as a source of comparison once you start creating some feeds.

For the most part, you'll find feed readers fall into categories such as the following:

- Desktop newscasts, headline tickers, and screensavers
- Personalized portals
- Mixed reverse-chronological aggregators
- Three-pane aggregators

Though you're sure to find many more shapes and forms of feed readers, these make a good starting point—and going through them, you can see a bit of the evolution of feed aggregators from heavily commercial and centralized apps to more personal desktop tools.

Desktop Headline Tickers and Screensavers

One of the most common buzzwords heard in the mid-1990's dot-com boom was "push." Microsoft introduced an early form of syndication feeds called Channel Definition Format (or CDF) and incorporated CDF into Internet Explorer in the form of Active Channels. These were managed from the Channel Bar, which contained selections from many commercial Web sites and online publications.

A company named PointCast, Inc., offered a "desktop newscast" that featured headlines and news on the desktop, as well as an animated screensaver populated with news content pulled from commercial affiliates and news wires. Netscape and Marimba teamed up to offer Netcaster, which provided many features similar to PointCast and Microsoft's offerings but used different technology to syndicate content.

These early feed readers emphasized mainly commercial content providers, although it was possible to subscribe to feeds published by independent and personal sites. Also, because these aggregators tended to present content with scrolling tickers, screensavers, and big and chunky user interfaces using lots of animation, they were only really practical for use in subscribing to a handful of feeds—maybe less than a dozen.

Feed readers of this form are still in use, albeit with less buzz and venture capital surrounding them. They're useful for light consumption of a few feeds, in either an unobtrusive or highly branded form, often in a role more like a desktop accessory than a full-on, attention-centric application. Figure 1-1 offers an example of such an accessory from the K Desktop Environment project, named KNewsTicker.

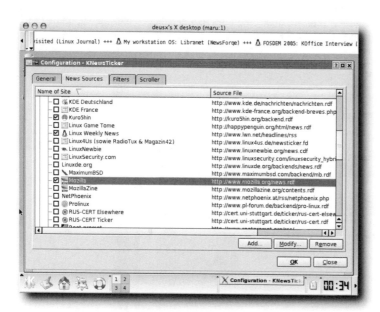

FIGURE 1-1: KNewsTicker window

Personalized Portals

Although not quite as popular or common as they used to be, personalized portals were one of the top buzzworthy topics competing for interest with "push" technology back before the turn of the century. In the midst of the dot-com days, Excite, Lycos, Netscape, Microsoft, and Yahoo! were all players in the portal industry—and a Texas-based fish-processing company named Zapata even turned itself into an Internet-startup, buying up a swath of Web sites to get into the game.

The idea was to pull together as many useful services and as much attractive content as possible into one place, which Web surfers would ideally use as their home page. This resulted in modular Web pages, with users able to pick and choose from a catalog of little components containing, among other things, headline links syndicated from other Web sites.

One of the more interesting contenders in this space was the My Netscape portal offered by, of course, Netscape. My Netscape was one of the first services to offer support for RSS feeds in their first incarnations. In fact, the original specification defining the RSS format in XML was drafted by team members at Netscape and hosted on their corporate Web servers.

Portals, with their aggregated content modules, are more information-dense than desktop tickers or screensavers. Headlines and resources are offered more directly, with less branding and presentation than with the previous "push" technology applications. So, with less window-dressing to get in the way, users can manageably pull together even more information sources into one spot.

The big portals aren't what they used to be, though, and even My Netscape has all but backed away from being a feed aggregator. However, feed aggregation and portal-like features can still be found on many popular community sites, assimilated as peripheral features. For example, the nerd news site Slashdot offers "slashbox" modules in a personalizable sidebar, many or most drawn from syndication feeds (see Figure 1-2).

FIGURE 1-2: Slashdot.org slashboxes

Other Open Source Web community packages, such as Drupal (http://www.drupal.org) and Plone (http://www.plone.org), offer similar feed headline modules like the classic portals. But although you could build and host a portal-esque site just for yourself and friends, this form of feed aggregation still largely appears on either niche and special-interest community sites or commercial sites aiming to capture surfers' home page preferences for marketing dollars.

In contrast, however, the next steps in the progression of syndication feed aggregator technology led to some markedly more personal tools.

Mixed Reverse-Chronological Aggregators

Wow, that's a mouthful, isn't it? "Mixed reverse-chronological aggregators." It's hard to come up with a more concise description, though. Maybe referring to these as "blog-like" would be better. These aggregators are among the first to treat syndication feeds as fluid streams of content, subject to mixing and reordering. The result, by design, is something not altogether unlike a modern blog. Content items are presented in order from newest to oldest, one after the other, all flowed into the same page regardless of their original sources.

And, just as important, these aggregators are *personal* aggregators. Radio UserLand from UserLand Software was one of the first of this form of aggregator (see Figure 1-3). Radio was built as a fully capable Web application server, yet it's intended to be installed on a user's personal machine. Radio allows the user to manage his or her own preferences and list of feed subscriptions, to be served up to a Web browser of choice from its own private Web server (see Figure 1-4).

FIGURE 1-3: The Radio UserLand server status window running on Mac OS X

FIGURE 1-4: The Radio UserLand news aggregator in a Firefox browser

The Radio UserLand application stays running in the background and about once an hour it fetches and processes each subscribed feed from their respective Web sites. New feed items that Radio hasn't seen before are stored away in its internal database. The next time the news aggregation page is viewed or refreshed, the newest found items appear in reverse-chronological order, with the freshest items first on the page.

So for the first time, with this breed of aggregator, the whole thing lives on your own computer. There's no centralized delivery system or marketing-supported portal—aggregators like these put all the tools into your hands, becoming a real personal tool. In particular, Radio comes not only with publishing tools to create a blog and associated RSS feeds, but a full development environment with its own scripting language and data storage, allowing the user-turned-hacker to reach into the tool to customize and extend the aggregator and its workings. After its first few public releases, Radio UserLand was quickly followed by a slew of inspired clones and variants, such as AmphetaDesk (`http://www.disobey.com/amphetadesk/`), but they all shared advances that brought the machinery of feed aggregation to the personal desktop.

And, finally, this form of feed aggregator was even more information-dense than desktop newscasters or portals that came before. Rather than presenting things with entertaining but time-consuming animation, or constrained to a mosaic of on-page headline modules, the mixed reverse-chronological display of feed items could scale to build a Web page as long as you could handle and would keep you constantly up to date with the latest feed items. So, the number of subscribed feeds you could handle was limited only by how large a page your browser could load and your ability to skim, scan, and read it.

Three-Pane Aggregators

This family of feed aggregators builds upon what I consider to be one of the chief advances of Radio UserLand and friends: feeds treated as fluid streams of items, subject to mixing, reordering, and many other manipulations. With the bonds of rigid headline collections broken, content items could now be treated like related but individual messages.

But, whereas Radio UserLand's aggregator recast feed items in a form akin to a blog, other offerings began to look at feed items more like email messages or Usenet postings. So, the next popular form of aggregator takes all the feed fetching and scanning machinery and uses the familiar user interface conventions of mail and newsgroup applications. Figure 1-5, Figure 1-6, Figure 1-7, and Figure 1-8 show some examples.

In this style of aggregator, one window pane displays subscriptions, another lists items for a selected subscription (or group of subscriptions), and the third pane presents the content of a selected feed item. Just like the mail and news readers that inspired them, these aggregators present feed items in a user interface that treats feeds as analogous to newsgroups, mailboxes, or folders. Extending this metaphor further, many of these aggregators have cloned or translated many of the message-management features of email or Usenet clients, such as filtering, searching, archiving, and even republishing items to a blog as analogous to forwarding email messages or crossposting on Usenet.

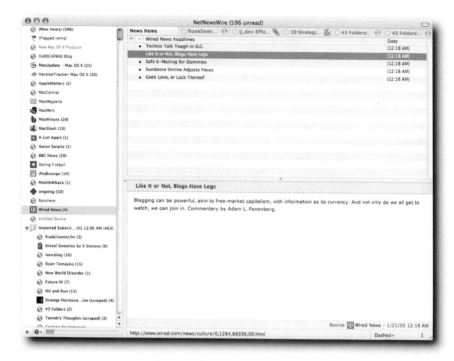

FIGURE 1-5: NetNewsWire on Mac OS X

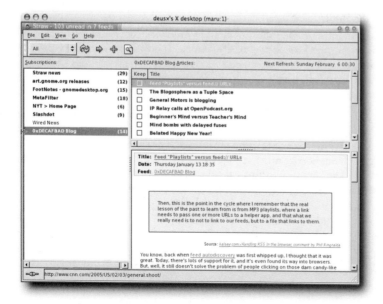

FIGURE 1-6: Straw desktop news aggregator for GNOME under Linux

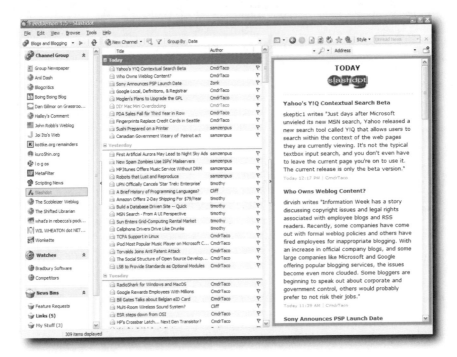

FIGURE 1-7: FeedDemon for Windows

Aggregators from the Future

As the value of feed aggregation becomes apparent to more developers and tinkerers, you'll see an even greater diversity of variations and experiments with how to gather and present feed items. You can already find Web-based aggregators styled after Web email services, other applications with a mix of aggregation styles, and still more experimenting with novel ways of organizing and presenting feed items (see Figure 1-9 and Figure 1-10).

In addition, the content and structure of feeds are changing, encompassing more forms of content such as MP3 audio and calendar events. For these new kinds of content, different handling and new presentation techniques and features are needed. For example, displaying MP3 files in reverse-chronological order doesn't make sense, but queuing them up into a playlist for a portable music player does. Also, importing calendar events into planner software and a PDA makes more sense than displaying them as an email inbox (see Figure 1-11).

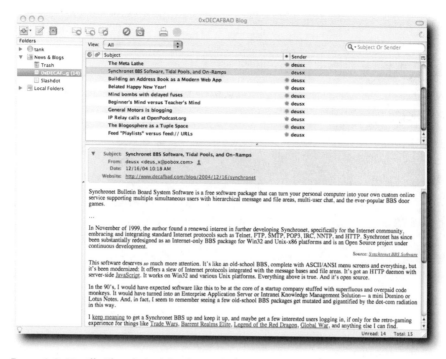

FIGURE 1-8: Mozilla Thunderbird displaying feed subscriptions

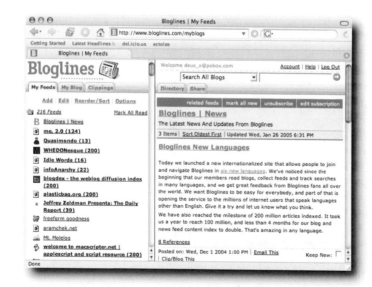

FIGURE 1-9: Bloglines offers three-pane aggregation in the browser.

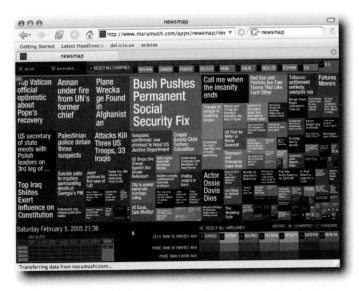

Figure 1-10: Newsmap displays items in an alternative UI called a treemap.

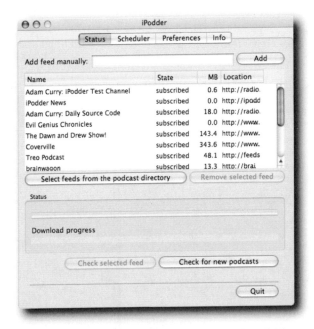

Figure 1-11: iPodder downloads podcast audio from feeds.

The trend for feed aggregators is to continue to become even more personal, with more machine smarts and access from mobile devices. Also in the works are aggregators that take the form of intermediaries and routers, aggregating from one set of sources for the consumption of other aggregators—feeds go in, feeds come back out. Far removed from the top-heavy centralized models of managed desktop newscasts and portal marketing, feeds and aggregators are being used to build a layer of plumbing on top of the existing Web, through which content and information filter and flow into personal inboxes and news tools.

Checking Out Feed Publishing Tools

There aren't as many feed publishing tools as there are tools that happen to publish feeds. For the most part, syndication feeds have been the product of an add-on, plug-in, or template used within an existing content management system (CMS). These systems (which include packages ranging from multimillion-dollar enterprise CMS systems to personal blogging tools) can generate syndication feeds from current content and articles right alongside the human-readable Web pages listing the latest headlines.

However, as the popularity and usage of syndication feeds have increased, more feed-producing tools have come about. For example, not all Web sites publish syndication feeds. So, some tinkerers have come up with scripts and applications that "scrape" existing pages intended for people, extract titles and content from those pages, and republish that information in the form of machine-readable syndication feeds, thus allowing even sites lacking feeds to be pulled into your personal subscriptions.

Also, as some people live more of their time online through aggregators, they've found it useful to pull even more sources of information beyond the usual Web content into feeds. System administrators can keep tabs on server event logs by converting them into private syndication feeds. Most shipping companies now offer online package tracking, so why not turn those updates into feeds? If there are topics you're interested in, and you often find yourself repeating the same keywords on search engines, you could convert those searches and their results into feeds and maintain a continually updating feed of search results. And, although it might not be the brightest idea if things aren't completely secure, some tinkerers have filtered their online banking account statements into private feeds so that they stay up to date with current transactions.

Another form of feed publishing tool is more of a filter than a publisher. This sort of tool reads a feed, changes it, and spits out a new feed. This could involve changing formats from RSS to Atom or vice versa. The filter could insert advertisements into feed entries, not unlike inline ads on Web pages. Or, rather than ads, a filter could compare feed entries against other feeds and automatically include some recommendations or related links. Filters can also separate out categories or topics of content into more tightly focused feeds.

Unfortunately, feed publishing tools are really more like plumbing, so it's hard to come up with many visual examples or screenshots that don't look like the pipes under your sink. However, these tools are a very important part of the syndication feed story, as you'll see in future chapters.

Glancing at RSS and Atom Feeds

So, what makes an RSS or Atom feed? First off, both are dialects of XML. You've probably heard of XML, but just in case you need a refresher, XML stands for Extensible Markup Language. XML isn't so much a format itself; it's a framework for *making* formats.

For many kinds of data, XML does the same sort of thing Internet protocols do for networking. On the Internet, the same basic hardware such as routers and hubs enable a wide range of applications such as the Web, email, and Voice-over-IP. In a similar way, XML enables a wide range of data to be managed and manipulated by a common set of tools. Rather than reinvent the wheel every time you must deal with some form of data, XML establishes some useful common structures and rules on top of which you can build.

If you have any experience building Web pages with HTML, XML should look familiar to you because they both share a common ancestry in the Standard Generalized Markup Language (SGML). If anything, XML is a cleaner, simpler version of what SGML offers. So, because both RSS and Atom are built on XML technology, you can use the same tools to deal with each.

Furthermore, because RSS and Atom both describe very similar sets of data structures, you'll be able to use very similar techniques and programming for both types of feeds. It's easier to show than tell, so take a quick look at a couple of feeds, both containing pretty much the same data. First, check out the sample RSS 2.0 feed in Listing 1-1.

Listing 1-1: Example RSS 2.0 Feed

```xml
<?xml version="1.0"?>
<rss version="2.0">
  <channel>
    <title>Testing Blog</title>
    <link>http://example.com/blog/</link>
    <description>This is a testing blog!</description>
    <WebMaster>john@example.com</WebMaster>
    <item>
      <title>Test #1</title>
      <link>http://example.com/blog/2005/01/01/foo.html</link>
      <pubDate>Tue, 01 Jan 2005 09:39:21 GMT</pubDate>
      <guid isPermaLink="false">tag:example.com,2005-01-01:example.001</guid>
      <description>
        This is an example blog posting. &lt;a href="http://www.
        Example.com/foobarbaz.html"&gt;Foo Bar Baz&lt;/a&gt;.
      </description>
    </item>
    <item>
      <title>Test #2</title>
      <link>http://example.com/blog/2005/01/02/bar.html</link>
      <pubDate>Tue, 02 Jan 2005 12:23:01 GMT</pubDate>
      <guid isPermaLink="false">tag:example.com,2005-01-01:example.002</guid>
      <description>
        This is another example blog posting.
      </description>
    </item>
  </channel>
</rss>
```

The anatomy of this feed is pretty basic:

- `<rss>` opens the document and identifies the XML data as an RSS feed.

- `<channel>` begins the meat of the feed. Although I'll continue to refer to this generically as the feed, the RSS specification refers to its contents as a "channel." This terminology goes back to the origins of RSS in the days of portal sites.

- `<title>` contains the title of this feed, "Testing Blog."

- `<link>` contains the URL pointing back to the human-readable Web page with which this feed is associated.

- `<description>` contains some human-readable text describing the feed.

- `<WebMaster>` provides the contact email of the person responsible for the channel.

- Next comes the `<item>` tags. Again, here's a terminology shift. I'll refer to these as feed entries, while the official RSS terminology is "channel item"—same idea, different terms, but I'll try to stay consistent. Each `<item>` tag contains a number of child elements:

    - `<title>` contains the title of this feed entry.

    - `<link>` contains the URL pointing to a human-readable Web page associated with this feed entry.

    - `<pubDate>` is the publication date for this entry.

    - `<guid>` provides a globally unique identifier (GUID). The `isPermalink` attribute is used to denote that this GUID is not, in fact, a URL pointing to the "permanent" location of this feed entry's human-readable alternate. Although this feed doesn't do it, in some cases, the `<guid>` tag can do double duty, providing both a unique identifier and a link in lieu of the `<link>` tag.

    - `<description>` contains a bit of text describing the feed entry, often a synopsis of the Web page to which the `<link>` URL refers.

- Finally, after the last `<item>` tag, the `<channel>` and `<rss>` tags are closed, ending the feed document.

If it helps to understand these entries, consider of some parallels to email messages described in Table 1-1.

Table 1-1 Comparison of RSS Feed Elements to Email Messages

Email message	Feed
Date:	`<rss>` ⇨ `<channel>` ⇨ `<item>` ⇨ `<pubDate>`
To:	None in the feed—a feed is analogous to a blind CC to all subscribers, like a mailing list.

Continued

Table 1-1 *(continued)*

Email message	Feed
From:	`<rss>` ⇨ `<channel>` ⇨ `<Webmaster>`
Subject:	`<rss>` ⇨ `<channel>` ⇨ `<item>` ⇨ `<title>`
Message body	`<rss>` ⇨ `<channel>` ⇨ `<item>` ⇨ `<description>`

In email, you have headers that provide information such as the receiving address, the sender's address, a subject line, and the date when the message was received. Now, in feeds, there's not usually a "To" line, because feeds are, in effect, CC'ed to everyone in the world, but you can see the parallels to the other elements of email. The entry title is like an email subject, the publication date is like email's received date, and all of the feed's introductory data is like the "From" line and other headers in an email message.

Now, look at the same information in Listing 1-2, conveyed as an Atom 0.3 feed.

Listing 1-2: Example Atom 0.3 Feed

```
<?xml version="1.0" encoding="utf-8"?>
<feed version="0.3" xmlns="http://purl.org/atom/ns#">
  <title>Testing Blog</title>
  <link rel="alternate" type="text/html"
      href="http://example.com/blog/" />
  <tagline>This is a testing blog!</tagline>
  <modified>2005-01-13T12:21:01Z</modified>
  <author>
    <name>John Doe</name>
    <email>john@example.com</email>
  </author>
  <entry>
    <title>Test #1</title>
    <link rel="alternate" type="text/html"
        href="http://example.com/blog/2005/01/01/foo.html" />
    <issued>2005-01-01T09:39:21Z</issued>
    <modified>2005-01-01T09:39:21Z</modified>
    <id>tag:example.com,2005-01-01:example.001</id>
    <summary type="text/html" mode="escaped">
      This is an example blog posting. &lt;a href="http://www.
      Example.com/foobarbaz.html"&gt;Foo Bar Baz&lt;/a&gt;.
    </summary>
  </entry>
  <entry>
    <title>Test #2</title>
    <link rel="alternate" type="text/html"
        href="http://example.com/blog/2005/01/02/bar.html" />
    <issued>2005-01-02T12:23:01Z</issued>
```

```
    <modified>2005-01-02T12:23:01Z</modified>
    <id>tag:example.com,2005-01-01:example.002</id>
    <summary type="text/plain" mode="escaped">
      This is another example blog posting.
    </summary>
  </entry>

</feed>
```

As you can see, with respect to RSS, other than the naming of tags used in this Atom feed and some small changes in structure, just about all of the information is the same:

- `<feed>` opens the Atom feed, as compared to `<rss>` and `<channel>` in RSS.

- `<title>` contains the title of this feed, "Testing Blog."

- `<link>` has an attribute named `href` that contains the URL pointing back to human-readable Web page with which this feed is associated. Atom differs from RSS here in that it specifies a more verbose linking style, including the content type (`type`) and relational purpose (`rel`) of the link along with the URL.

- `<description>` contains some human-readable text describing the feed.

- `<author>` provides the contact information of the person responsible for the channel. Again, Atom calls for further elaboration of this information:

    - `<name>` contains the name of the feed's author.

    - `<email>` contains the email address of the feed's author.

- In Atom, the feed entries are contained in `<entry>` tags, analogous to RSS `<item>` tags. Their contents are also close to RSS:

    - `<title>` contains the title of this feed entry.

    - `<link>` points to a human-readable Web page associated with this feed entry. And, just like the feed-level `<link>` tag, the entry's `<link>` is more verbose than that of RSS.

    - `<issued>` and `<modified>` specify the date (in ISO-8601 format) when this entry was first issued and when it was last modified, respectively. The `<pubDate>` tag in RSS is most analogous to Atom's `<issued>`, but sometimes `<pubDate>` is used to indicate the entry's latest publishing date, regardless of any previous revisions published.

    - `<id>` provides a GUID. Unlike `<guid>` in RSS, the `<id>` tag in Atom is never treated as a permalink to a Web page.

    - `<summary>` contains a description of the feed entry, often a synopsis of the Web page to which the `<link>` URL refers.

- Finally, after the last `<entry>` tag, the `<atom>` tag is closed, ending the feed document.

In general, the differences between RSS and Atom can be summed up like so:

- RSS stands for "Really Simple Syndication," according to the RSS 2.0 specification, and this describes its aims—the format and structure are meant to remain simple and easy to use.

- Atom places more of an emphasis on a more finely detailed model of feed data with a greater attention to well-defined specifications and compliance to the specs.

The more subtle and specific differences between RSS and Atom are subject to debate—even the trivial summary presented here might be heavily disputed, and some of the less-civilized discussions online have become legendary. For practical purposes, though, this book treats RSS and Atom feed formats as mostly equivalent and highlights any differences when they come up and as they affect your tinkering. The important thing is to get you working with feeds, not debating the finer points of specifications.

Gathering Tools

Before you start digging into what you can do with RSS and Atom feeds, it would help to assemble a toolkit of some useful technologies. It also wouldn't hurt if you could get these tools for free on the Web. With this in mind, this section briefly introduces you to Open Source packages such as the following:

- UNIX-based command shell tools
- The Python programming language
- XML and XSLT technologies

Although this chapter won't make you an expert in any of these technologies, it should point you in the right directions to set yourself up with a decent working environment for hacking RSS and Atom feeds in the next chapters.

Finding and Using UNIX-based Tools

First off, you should get yourself a set of UNIX-based tools. Though most of the hacks you explore here can be done in many environments (for example, using the Command Prompt on Windows XP), things go more smoothly under a UNIX-based environment. So, the examples in the following chapters assume you have these tools at your disposal.

Using Linux

If you're a Linux user, you're probably already familiar with command shells, as well as how to install software packages. Rather than trying to cover all the available distributions and variations of Linux, this book focuses on the Debian Linux distribution. The Advanced Packaging Tool used by this distribution makes installing and updating software packages mostly painless, so you can get up and running quickly.

If you have another favorite Linux distribution, you should be able to use whatever method is required by that distribution to get tools installed and configured.

In any case, you'll want to be sure that your Linux installation has been installed with the full set of developer packages (for example, GCC, editors, and so on). Other than that, you should be ready to continue on.

Using Mac OS X

If you're using Mac OS X, you may not yet be familiar with the UNIX-based foundation on which OS X is built. Thanks to that foundation, though, you already have most of the tools you'll be using. You may need to find and check a few things, however.

You're going to be using the Terminal application a lot under OS X, so one of the first things you should do is find it and get acquainted with it. You can find the Terminal application at Applications ➪ Utilities ➪ Terminal. You might want to drag it to your Dock to be able to find it quickly in the future.

A full tour and tutorial of the UNIX-based underpinnings available to you via the Terminal application would take up a book all on its own, but this at least gives you a way to begin hacking.

Using Windows

Working under Windows to build the projects in this book is not quite as nice an experience found under Linux and OS X, but it is still workable. Because you'll be doing just about everything from the Command Prompt, you'll want to locate it first thing. On Windows XP, you'll find it under Start Menu ➪ Accessories ➪ Command Prompt. You may want to make a shortcut to it on your Desktop or Quick Launch bar, if you haven't already.

You may also want to install some UNIX-based tools, if the Command Prompt proves too cumbersome. Most of the programs you build in this book will work using the Command Prompt, but occasionally an example here may not quite work in this context. A lot of options are available to get working UNIX-based tools on Windows, but my favorite is called Cygwin.

With Cygwin (http://www.cygwin.com), you get a "Linux-like environment for Windows" where you can use the sorts of command shells found on Linux, and you can run many UNIX-based tools in the Windows Command Prompt. Cygwin is a sort of compromise between Windows and UNIX, giving you much of what you need. It's not the same as an actual Linux environment, but it's usually close enough.

Check out the documentation on the Cygwin site if you'd like to install it and try it out.

Installing the Python Programming Language

Python is an extremely useful and flexible object-oriented programming language available for just about every operating system, and it comes with a lot of power you'll need, right out of the box.

Installing Python on Linux

Under Debian Linux, you can install Python by logging in as root and using apt:

```
# apt-get install python python-dev
```

This should grab all the packages needed to get started with Python.

Installing Python on Mac OS X

Python is another thing that Mac OS X already provides, so you won't need to do anything to get started.

Well, actually, there is one thing you should do. For some reason, Python on OS X doesn't come with readline support enabled, and so line editing and command history won't work unless you install it. You can do this by opening a Terminal and running this command:

```
# python `python -c "import pimp; print pimp.__file__"` -i readline
```

What this does is install readline support using a Python package manager that comes with OS X. (Thanks to Bill Bumgarner for this tip at `http://www.pycs.net/bbum/2004/1/21/#200401211`.)

Installing Python on Windows

For Windows, you can use an installer available at the Python home:

1. Visit the Python download page at `http://www.python.org/download/` and click to download the Python Windows installer, labeled "Windows binary -- does not include source."

2. After the download completes, double-click the installer and follow the instructions. This should result with Python installed as `C:\Python24`, depending on which version you install.

You may want to visit the Python Windows FAQ at `http://www.python.org/doc/faq/windows.html` to read up on how to run Python programs and other Windows-specific issues.

Installing XML and XSLT Tools

RSS and Atom feeds are XML formats, so you should get your hands on some tools to manipulate XML. One of the most useful and most easily installed packages for dealing with XML in Python is called 4Suite, available at:

```
http://4suite.org/
```

At that URL, you'll be able to find downloads that include a Windows installer and an archive for installation on Linux and Mac OS X. You'll see this package mentioned again a little later, but it's worth installing right now before you get into the thick of things.

Installing 4Suite on Windows

As of this writing, this is a URL to the latest version of the Windows installer:

```
ftp://ftp.4suite.org/pub/4Suite/4Suite-1.0a3.win32-py2.3.exe
```

Once downloaded, simply double-clicking the installer will get you set up. However, if you want to be guided through the process, check out this Windows installation HOWTO:

```
http://4suite.org/docs/howto/Windows.xml
```

Installing 4Suite on Linux and Mac OS X

For Linux and Mac OS X, you'll want this archive:

```
ftp://ftp.4suite.org/pub/4Suite/4Suite-1.0b1.tar.gz
```

Once downloaded, check out this UNIX installation HOWTO:

```
http://4suite.org/docs/howto/UNIX.xml
```

You can install this package with a series of commands like the following:

```
$ tar xzvf 4Suite-1.0b1.tar.gz
$ cd 4Suite-1.0b1
$ python setup.py install
```

Depending on what account you're logged in as, that last command may need root privileges. So, you may need to login as root or try something like this (particularly under Mac OS X):

```
$ sudo python setup.py install
```

It's worth noting that just about every Python package used later in the book follows this same basic installation process—that is, download the package, unpack the archive, and run `setup.py` as root.

Summary

After this chapter, you should have the "50,000-foot view" of syndication feeds and feed aggregation technology in terms of the sorts of tools you can find and the number of feeds you can manage. In the coming chapters, you'll have the opportunity to build working versions of many of the things mentioned here.

Also, you should have a start at a working environment used in this book, with Python and XML tools at your disposal. You might want to read up on these tools, because this book won't be spending much time explaining basic Python or XML concepts. Instead, you'll be jumping right into writing working code, so it might help to have at least gotten past the "Hello World" stage first.

So, with that, continue on to Chapter 2, where you'll be building your first simple feed aggregator!

Building a Simple Feed Aggregator

This chapter walks you through the building of a basic syndication feed aggregator. This serves as the base platform for a few hacks in chapters yet to come, so you should get a lot of use out of this little thing.

The main idea here is to get something up and running, so this chapter won't spend too much time fussing with specifications or fine points. However, it does let you see a few of the issues authors of feed aggregators face in dealing with the variety of feeds "in the wild," how some of them diverge from the standards, and how some of them fall into gaps left by fuzzy areas in (or fuzzy understanding of) the specifications.

By the end of the chapter, though, you should have something cobbled together that deals reasonably well with just about anything you could throw at it during daily use.

Finding Feeds to Aggregate

When putting together a feed aggregator, one of your first challenges is finding feeds to aggregate in the first place. Most of the time, the situation is one in which you know the URL of the site you're interested in tracking, but you don't know whether or not it has an associated feed—and you'd like to find it and subscribe to it if it does.

On many Web sites and blogs, feeds are easy to find somewhere on the page—just look for one of the following (see Figure 2-1):

> ➤ A ubiquitous "XML" button link

> ➤ One of the more stylized "RSS 2.0" or "ATOM 0.3" mini-button links

> ➤ Any hyperlink with a direct mention of "RSS" or "Atom" feeds

> ➤ A hyperlink that reads "Syndicate this Site," (particularly on Movable Type blogs)

FIGURE 2-1: A few examples of
links to feeds on Web sites

Publishers link to their feeds in a dizzying variety of ways. Bloggers and Web publishers are creative sorts, so every site can be different—even if many do follow similar templates. But, for the most part, site owners publishing feeds want you to find them, so they're not too hard to spot if you're looking for them.

However, feeds are about letting machines do the work for you, and they're not really smart enough to dig through the context of a Web page and figure out where the feed links are. And then, even if you do the work of finding the feed for the machine, you still have to go through the process of copying the feed's URL from your browser and supplying it to the application somehow (usually, just clicking the feed link gives you a screenful of XML). Wouldn't it be nice to just click a button or point the aggregator at one of your favorite sites and take it from there?

Well, it just so happens that some work has been put into solving this problem, from several different approaches:

- Clickable feed buttons that launch a helper application or the aggregator itself
- Feed autodiscovery, enabled by metadata embedded in HTML
- Feed directories with Web services to help locate feeds

Clickable Feed Buttons

Usually, when you click a feed URL, you just get a screenful of XML thrown at you. There must be a way to coax your computer to do something more intelligent. For example, when you click a streaming audio or video link, you usually get either an in-browser player, or an external media player is launched. It would be nice if this worked the same way for syndication feeds.

Unfortunately, this isn't quite yet a solved problem. However, two approaches have enjoyed a lot of debate:

- Appropriate MIME-types in Web server configuration
- The `feed:` Universal Resource Identifier (URI) scheme in feed URLs

Configuring Apache with Feed MIME Types

When a document is served up over HTTP by a Web server, one of the pieces of information supplied in the header of the response is the MIME content-type. For example, HTML pages are usually identified by something like `text/html`, whereas JPEG images come up as `image/jpeg`. In most cases, the browser handles the content, loading up a page or embedding an image into a page layout.

However, in some cases, the browser encounters a MIME type it doesn't know how to handle. This is where helper applications come into play. Sometimes the browser prompts you to save a file somewhere, but sometimes the browser has established a mapping between a content-type and an external application on your system. For example, MP3 links are usually served up with a MIME type of `audio/x-mp3` and browsers can launch an external media player to handle these.

In Apache, you can configure what MIME type is used for feeds with something like this in the configuration file (or an `.htaccess` file):

```
AddType application/atom+xml .atom
AddType application/rss+xml .rss
```

With this configuration, Apache serves up files with `.atom` and `.rss` extensions with Atom and RSS content-type headers, respectively.

Unfortunately, as of this writing, this doesn't work yet. You see, what I said about MP3 links earlier was a bit off track: What I should have been talking about are *streaming* MP3 links. When you click a link that leads to content to be handled by a helper application, the browser downloads *all of the data* at that URL and hands that data off to the helper application as a file.

Now, of course, this won't work for streaming MP3 links, because if you were to attempt to download the whole stream before handing it off to a player, the download would never end and the player would never start playing. Instead, what streaming audio stations tend to do is serve up *playlist files*.

Playlists for MP3 use formats called M3U and PLS, with content types of `audio/x-mpegurl` and `audio/x-scpls`, respectively. These files don't contain any sound data, but what they do contain are URLs pointing where the audio can be found. So, links to streaming audio tend to point at playlists, which are downloaded when clicked and handed off to a helper application, which then extracts the streaming audio URLs and starts playing.

The problem with MIME types and syndication feeds is similar: When a feed link is clicked, the feed itself is served up and handed to a helper application. Now, unlike an unending streaming MP3 download, a feed download won't go on forever. But, the problem for aggregators is that, to set up a subscription, the aggregator wants to feed the URL first, rather than the feed data itself. And, unfortunately, pending changes to feed formats, the feed data doesn't contain any information like a playlist pointing at the URL it came from.

So, until someone introduces a *feed playlist* format, or embeds the URL of the feed into itself, correct MIME types for feeds won't help with aggregator subscriptions. As of this writing, neither of these things has come about, but this topic has been under active debate for some time now.

Using the feed: URI Scheme

An alternative to MIME types that has been proposed involves altering the URLs themselves used to link to feeds. This approach introduces a new URI protocol scheme of `feed:`. For example, instead of your usual URL beginning with `http`, you'd use a URL like this for a feed link:

```
feed://www.decafbad.com/blog/atom.xml
```

As with MIME types, most browsers and operating systems allow for a mapping between URI protocol schemes and helper applications. Just as `http` is most often associated with a Web browser, and `ftp` is sometimes associated with a file-transfer program, `feed` can be associated with a feed aggregator.

Where this approach differs from using MIME types, though, is that the program registered to handle the `feed` pseudo-protocol is supplied with the URL to the feed, rather than the data. So, this would seem to solve the feed contents versus feed location problem with the MIME-type-dependent subscription explained earlier.

However, establishing a relationship between the `feed` URIs and a helper application can be a bit complex, depending on your operating system. So, this chapter won't dive into a deep discussion on how to configure your system to do this. Also, this approach continues to be debated, because `feed` isn't really a new "protocol" on the Internet per se, and so some would say that this is too much of a hack.

Nonetheless, some aggregators support this method, so it may have some staying power.

Feed Autodiscovery

Another approach to finding feeds is to take all those buttons and links to feeds embedded in a Web page and turn them into metadata in an easily located spot in HTML. The conventional place to do that is in the `<head>` tag in an HTML document, where Web page authors already place things such as the page title, keywords, descriptions, and other resources (such as pointers to associated CSS files and JavaScript sources).

For example, a Web page might start off with a preamble like this:

```
<html>
  <head>
    <title>This is a web page</title>
    <meta http-equiv="Content-Type" content="text/html; charset=UTF-8" />
    <script type="text/javascript" src="/js/utils.js"></script>
    <link rel="stylesheet" title="Default Style"
          href="/css/main.css" type="text/css" />
    <link rel="shortcut icon" href="/favicon.ico" />
    <link rel="start" href="/" title="Home" />
    <link rel="prev" href="/foo" title="Previous page" />
    <link rel="next" href="/bar" title="Next page" />
```

In particular, notice all the `<link>` tags in the HTML header. These establish various linking relationships between this HTML page and other resources on the Web. Each of these tags contains the following attributes:

- `rel`—This specifies the kind of relationship this link represents. A CSS file for the page is denoted by a value of `stylesheet`, whereas the page's `favicon` is linked with `shortcut icon`.

- `title`—This offers a human-readable title for the link, in cases where the page's links will be presented to a user browsing to the page.

- `href`—This contains the actual URL to the linked resource.

- `type`—This provides the MIME content type of the resource being linked.

This, then, would be a natural place to establish pointers to associated feeds. So, on many pages with feeds, you'll find an *ad hoc* standard with links like the following:

```
<link rel="alternate" type="application/rss+xml"
      title="RSS" href="/index.rss" />
<link rel="alternate" type="application/atom+xml"
      title="Atom" href="/atom.xml" />
```

These links appear in the HTML header and provide details to find feeds associated with the page. The `alternate` relationship serves to claim that these feeds are alternate representations of the current page, and the `href` attribute points to the feeds, `type` establishes the feed format type, and `title` gives a description for the feed.

Although this convention isn't an "official" standard, it has been accepted by many publishers on the Web, and has even received support in a few Web browsers and feed aggregators. Figure 2-2 shows an example.

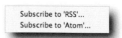

FIGURE 2-2: Autodiscovered
feed links displayed by Firefox

So, how to get to this metadata? Well, Python just happens to have all the tools you need in the standard library:

- `urllib2.urlopen`—Used for fetching data from a URL

- `urlparse.urljoin`—Used for resolving relative URLs into absolute URLs

- `HTMLParser`—Used for parsing HTML and extracting data

Here you start building a module that uses these tools. Start off with this in a file named `minifeedfinder.py` in your project directory, as shown in Listing 2-1.

Listing 2-1: minifeedfinder.py (Part 1 of 5)

```
#!/usr/bin/env python
"""
minifeedfinder.py

This module implements a simple feed autodiscovery technique using
HTMLParser from the standard Python library.
"""

import sys
from urllib2    import urlopen
from urlparse   import urljoin
from HTMLParser import HTMLParser, HTMLParseError
```

This is the brief preamble for the module. Start off with the initial comment, which identifies this as a Python program to a shell (more on that in a bit). Then describe what the module is for and import the tools you'll be using.

Next, start defining a class named `FeedAutodiscoveryParser` (the workhorse of this module), as shown in Listing 2-2.

Listing 2-2: minifeedfinder.py (Part 2 of 5)

```
class FeedAutodiscoveryParser(HTMLParser):
    """
    This class extracts feed candidate links from HTML.
    """

    # These are the MIME types of links accepted as feeds
    FEED_TYPES = ('application/rss+xml',
                  'text/xml',
                  'application/atom+xml',
                  'application/x.atom+xml',
                  'application/x-atom+xml')

    def __init__(self, base_href):
        """
        Initialize the parser
        """
        HTMLParser.__init__(self)
        self.base_href = base_href
        self.feeds     = []
```

This class inherits from HTMLParser, which is (oddly enough) useful for parsing HTML.

On the Web

If you want more information about the HTMLParser class in Python, check out the Standard Library documentation found here:

http://docs.python.org/lib/module-HTMLParser.html

One of the first things defined in the class is the FEED_TYPES constant, which is a list of MIME types associated with feed formats found in autodetection header links. Then, the class initialization method is defined, which calls the HTMLParser's initializer and sets up the base URL and an empty list for found feeds. The base URL is important, because relative URLs can be found in autodetection links, and these must be resolved to absolute URLs later on.

Now, on to the meat of this class. Listing 2-3 shows how the autodetection links are found and handled.

Listing 2-3: minifeedfinder.py (Part 3 of 5)

```python
def handle_starttag(self, tag, attrs_tup):
    """
    While parsing HTML, watch out for <base /> and <link /> tags.
    Accumulate any feed-candidate links found.
    """
    # Turn the tag name to lowercase for easier comparison, and
    # make a dict with lowercase keys for the tag attributes
    tag   = tag.lower()
    attrs = dict([(k.lower(), v) for k,v in attrs_tup])

    # If we find a <base> tag with new HREF, change the current base HREF
    if tag == "base" and 'href' in attrs:
        self.base_href = attrs['href']

    # If we find a <link> tag, check it for feed candidacy.
    if tag == "link":
        rel   = attrs.get("rel", "")
        type  = attrs.get("type", "")
        title = attrs.get("title", "")
        href  = attrs.get("href", "")

        # Check if this link is a feed candidate, add to the list if so.
        if rel == "alternate" and type in self.FEED_TYPES:
            self.feeds.append({
                'type'  : type,
                'title' : title,
                'href'  : href
            })
```

This method, named `handle_starttag`, is called by the `HTMLParser` each time it encounters the start of a new tag during HTML parsing. The parameters it receives are the name of the tag and the attributes set on that tag. The first thing it does is change the tag name to lowercase (because you want to make case-insensitive matches, and the list of tag attributes is turned into a dictionary with lowercase key names).

Next, the method checks whether the current tag is the `<base>` tag, which is used to establish a new base URL for the page. This must be tracked to properly resolve relative-link URLs later on.

Then, the method checks if this is a `<link>` tag. If so, it extracts the expected set of attributes (`rel`, `type`, `title`, and `href`). It then checks to see if the link's relationship is `alternate` and its type matches one in the set of accepted feed types in the `FEED_TYPES` list constant defined earlier. If this is true, this `<link>` tag's details are appended to the list of feeds found.

Next, go ahead and make something useful, as shown in Listing 2-4.

Listing 2-4: minifeedfinder.py (Part 4 of 5)

```
def getFeedsDetail(url):
    """
    Load up the given URL, parse, and return any feeds found.
    """
    data   = urlopen(url).read()
    parser = FeedAutodiscoveryParser(url)

    try:
        parser.feed(data)
    except HTMLParseError:
        # Ignore any parse errors, since HTML is dirty and what we want
        # should be early on in the document anyway.
        pass

    # Fix up feed HREFs, converting to absolute URLs using the base HREF.
    for feed in parser.feeds:
        feed['href'] = urljoin(parser.base_href, feed['href'])

    return parser.feeds

def getFeeds(url):
    return [ x['href'] for x in getFeedsDetail(url) ]
```

Two module-level functions are defined here: `getFeedsDetail()` and `getFeeds()`.

The `getFeeds()` function is just a convenience that simplifies usage of `getFeedsDetail()`, returning only the URLs to feeds found by autodiscovery. The `getFeedsDetails()` function is where the work happens.

In `getFeedsDetail()`, the first and only parameter expected is the URL of the HTML page to be searched for feed links. The data at the URL is loaded using `urlopen()`, and an instance is created of the parser class defined earlier, with the page URL supplied as the initial base URL for feed links.

 If you want more information about the `urlopen()` module in Python, check out the Standard Library documentation found here:

> `http://docs.python.org/lib/module-urllib.html#12h-3170`

Then, the HTML data is fed to the parser. Any exceptions that may happen during the parsing process are ignored because, as the comments in the code mention, you don't need to successfully parse the whole HTML document. You just need to extract the `<link>` tags found near the start of the document in the `<head>` section.

After parsing completes, any feed links found are resolved from relative to absolute using `urljoin()` and the final base URL found for the page. Then, the list of feed details is returned.

 If you want more information about the `urljoin()` module in Python, check out the Standard Library documentation found here:

> `http://docs.python.org/lib/module-urlparse.html#12h-3530`

Finally, wrap up this module with a small test function, as shown in Listing 2-5.

Listing 2-5: minifeedfinder.py (Part 5 of 5)

```
def main():
    url   = sys.argv[1]
    feeds = getFeedsDetail(url)

    print
    print "Found the following possible feeds at %s:" % url
    for feed in feeds:
        print "\t '%(title)s' of type %(type)s at %(href)s" % feed
    print

if __name__ == "__main__": main()
```

Thanks to a Python trick used in the last line of the listing, this code is written as both an executable program and a reusable module you can call upon later in future programs. You can use this from the command line like so:

```
# python minifeedfinder.py http://www.decafbad.com

Found the following possible feeds at http://www.decafbad.com:
        'RSS' of type application/rss+xml at http://www.decafbad.com/index.rdf
        'Atom' of type application/atom+xml at http://www.decafbad.com/atom.xml
```

```
# python minifeedfinder.py http://slashdot.org

Found the following possible feeds at http://slashdot.org:
        'Slashdot RSS' of type application/rss+xml at
http://slashdot.org/index.rss
```

Notice that some pages will link to multiple feeds. These feeds can be of different formats (that is, RSS and Atom), or for different purposes. Some blogs have feeds devoted to individual categories of entries, comments made on entries, and running lists of links to interesting sites. Usually, the feed links tend to provide sensible titles you can use to decide which ones are interesting.

This module is written for simplicity and clarity of code, not for robustness, so it's likely to break in some particularly bad situations—such as pages not found and *very* broken or strange HTML. But, it's left as an exercise for you to continue bullet-proofing and improving this code as you run into things.

Feed Directories and Web Services

If all else fails and you just can't find any feeds for a site, linked from buttons, metadata, or otherwise, it might be time to call out for help. One of the most comprehensive directories of syndication feeds on the Web is called Syndic8 (http://www.syndic8.com). As shown in Figure 2-3, Syndic8 offers a rich set of tools for humans to use in finding and describing subscriptions and feeds, as well as a number of Web service methods for use by machines.

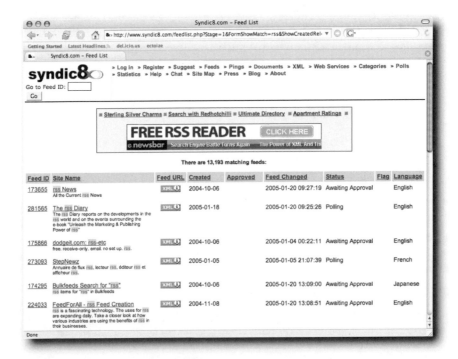

FIGURE 2-3: A listing of feeds at Syndic8.com

Again, Python has a tool in its standard library (xmlrpclib) to make accessing Syndic8 Web services easy. Use it for accessing XML-RPC Web services in a python-idiomatic way.

You can find the documentation for xmlrpclib in the Python standard library here:

```
http://docs.python.org/lib/module-xmlrpclib.html
```

XML-RPC is an early Web services standard, providing for some fairly rich and easy-to-implement remote-procedure-style interactions between server and client programs. You can find more details about XML-RPC itself here:

```
http://www.xmlrpc.com
```

The module shown in Listing 2-6 queries Syndic8 for feeds associated with a given URL.

Listing 2-6: syndic8feedfinder.py (Part 1 of 3)

```python
#!/usr/bin/env python
"""
syndic8feedfinder.py

This module implements a feed search using web services available
at Syndic8.com
"""

import sys, xmlrpclib

FEED_TYPES = { 'RSS'  : 'application/rss+xml',
               'Atom' : 'application/atom+xml' }
```

This is another familiar module preamble, with the module description and import statements pulling in the sys and xmlrpclib modules. It also defines a constant named FEED_TYPES, which maps feed format names to MIME types, for compatibility with the previous minifeedfinder.py module.

Next, on to the Web service calls, as shown in Listing 2-7.

Listing 2-7: syndic8feedfinder.py (Part 2 of 3)

```python
def getFeedsDetail(url):
    feeds    = []
    server   = xmlrpclib.Server('http://www.syndic8.com/xmlrpc.php')
    feedids  = server.syndic8.QueryFeeds('siteurl', 'like',
                   url+'%', 'headlines_rank')
    infolist = server.syndic8.GetFeedInfo(feedids,
                   ['status','sitename','format','dataurl'])
```

Continued

Listing 2-7 *(continued)*

```
for f in infolist:
    if f['status'] != 'Dead':
        feeds.append({
            'type'  : FEED_TYPES.get(f['format'], "unknown"),
            'title' : f['sitename'],
            'href'  : f['dataurl']
        })

return feeds
```

Like the `minifeedfinder` module, this module defines a `getFeedsDetail()` function that accepts the URL to a Web page for which feeds should be located.

The `xmlrpclib` module is used to access the Syndic8 Web service. This XML-RPC Web service is wrapped in a `Server` proxy object instance, which is used like a somewhat normal Python object: You can make method calls that return values—but everything is translated into Web service calls transparently.

On the Web

All of the Web service methods made available by Syndic8 are documented here:

> `http://www.syndic8.com/web_services/`

So, the first call made to Syndic8 is the `QueryFeeds` method, which accepts a field name, a relational operator, a search term, and a field on which to sort results.

In this program, a search is made on the `siteurl` field using the `like` operator with the given URL, along with an appended `'%'` wildcard to catch subdirectories of the site. You can remove this if you like, but it helps to catch variations of a URL, such as trailing slashes and deeper directories (that is, `/blog/` or `/mt/`). Once the results are returned, they're sorted in order of most relevant in terms of Syndic8 rankings.

The return value from the `QueryFeeds` method is a list of Syndic8 feed IDs. So, the next Syndic8 call is to a method called `GetFeedInfo()`. This method accepts feed IDs and a list of fields, returning a record containing those fields for each of the feeds identified.

After getting the list of feed details, the method loops through the records. For each feed that doesn't come up as `Dead` in status, the record fields are added to the list of feeds found as dictionaries compatible with those used in the `minifeedfinder` to the list of feeds.

Note

By the way, if you'd like to know what the possible values are for the "status" field in feed records, try calling the `GetFeedStates()` method of the Syndic8 API. Likewise, you can call `GetFeedFields()` to get a list of what fields are tracked for every feed.

Now, the code shown in Listing 2-8 finishes this module.

Listing 2-8: syndic8feedfinder.py (Part 3 of 3)

```
def getFeeds(self, url):
    return [ x['href'] for x in getFeedsDetail(url) ]

def main():
    url    = sys.argv[1]
    feeds  = getFeedsDetail(url)

    print
    print "Found the following possible feeds at %s:" % url
    for feed in feeds:
        print "\t '%(title)s' of type %(type)s at %(href)s" % feed
    print

if __name__ == "__main__": main()
```

The rest of the module is the same as `minifeedfinder.py`. Using this module or `minifeedfinder.py` is done in same way, both at the command line and in your code. Here's an example session with the Syndic8 client:

```
# python syndic8feedfinder.py http://www.decafbad.com

Found the following possible feeds at http://www.decafbad.com:
        '0xDECAFBAD Links' of type application/rss+xml at http://www.decafbad.
com/links/index.rdf
        '0xDECAFBAD Blog' of type application/rss+xml at http://www.decafbad.
com/index.rdf
        '0xDECAFBAD Links' of type application/atom+xml at http://www.decafbad.
com/links/atom.xml
        'DecafbadWiki.Main' of type application/rss+xml at http://www.
decafbad.com/twiki/bin/view/Main/WebRss?amp;amp;skin=rss&contenttype=text/xml
        '0xDECAFBAD Blog' of type application/atom+xml at http://www.decafbad.
com/atom.xml
        '0xDECAFBAD Blog' of type application/atom+xml at http://www.decafbad.
com/blog/atom.xml
        'DecafbadWiki.Main' of type application/rss+xml at http://www.decafbad.
com/twiki/bin/view/Main/WebRss?skin=rss
        '0xDECAFBAD' of type application/atom+xml at http://www.decafbad.com/
blog/index.atom
        '0xDECAFBAD' of type application/rss+xml at http://www.decafbad.com/
newslog.xml
        '0xDECAFBAD' of type application/rss+xml at http://www.decafbad.com/
blog/index.rss
        'l.m.orchard's Spirit of Radio' of type application/rss+xml at http://
www.decafbad.com/deus_x/radio/rss.xml
        '0xDECAFBAD Blog' of type application/rss+xml at http://www.decafbad.
com/blog/index.rdf
```

```
            'DecafbadWiki.Main' of type application/rss+xml at http://www.decafbad.
com/twiki/bin/view/Main/WebRss?contenttype=text/xml&skin=rss

# python syndic8feedfinder.py http://slashdot.org

Found the following possible feeds at http://www.slashdot.org:
            'Slashdot: BSD' of type application/rss+xml at http://slashdot.org/
bsd.rdf
            'Slashdot: Book Reviews' of type application/rss+xml at http://
slashdot.org/books.rdf
            'Slashdot: Your Rights Online' of type application/rss+xml at http://
slashdot.org/yro.rdf
            'Slashdot: Science' of type application/rss+xml at http://slashdot.org/
science.rdf
            'Slashdot' of type application/rss+xml at http://slashdot.org/
slashdot.rdf
```

As you can see, this code can come up with quite a number of feeds for a given URL. In particular, `decafbad.com` has had quite a few feeds submitted to the Syndic8 catalog for various blog categories, a wiki, even an older defunct version of the blog. Also, Slashdot appears many times with feeds taken from a few topic sections.

Anyway, if you want to choose between the `minifeedfinder` and `syndic8feedfinder`, the rest of your code should be able to remain unchanged, thanks to the similar function calls making up their respective APIs. In fact, if you want to improve things, try combining both of them.

Using the Ultra-Liberal Feed Finder Module

Now that you've played with your own code for finding feeds, you might be disappointed (or relieved) to learn that you've been reinventing the wheel a bit.

In his "Ultra-Liberal Feed Finder" module, Mark Pilgrim has implemented something like the previous two techniques and thrown in a few more to dig feed links out of hyperlinks and buttons on HTML pages. I know, I said that the computer wasn't smart enough to do that, and that's mostly true, but the Ultra-Liberal Feed Finder has a few tricks up its sleeves that are easier to use than explain.

So, go ahead and use it—you can find Mark Pilgrim's feed finder module here:

```
http://diveintomark.org/projects/feed_finder/
```

Just click the download link and stash a copy in your project directory. Like `minifeedfinder.py` and `syndic8feedfinder.py`, this module can both be used in other programs and be run from the command line as a program itself.

Here's an example session:

```
# python feedfinder.py http://www.decafbad.com
http://www.decafbad.com/index.rdf
http://www.decafbad.com/atom.xml
```

One difference between the Ultra-Liberal Feed Finder and the other two modules in this chapter is that `feedfinder.py` only offers a `getFeeds()` method, and lacks the `getFeedsDetail()` provided by `minifeedfinder` and `syndic8feedfinder`. Unless you feel like improving the Ultra-Liberal Feed Finder to implement a `getFeedsDetail()` method, using only the `getFeeds()` method from each of these three feed-locator modules should allow you to freely switch between them in your own programs.

Fetching and Parsing a Feed

Now that you've found a feed, the next step is to fetch the feed data and parse it. In this section, you learn how to start building your own feed handler and then see a more ready-made solution you can use if you don't feel like maintaining your own.

Building Your Own Feed Handler

Although it may seem obvious, there are two parts to handling feeds:

- Fetching the feed data from a URL
- Parsing the feed data into useful data structures

Both of these aspects of syndication feeds have received quite a bit of attention on their own, with issues of bandwidth usage and HTTP standards involved in the fetching, and various competing feed formats tangled up in the parsing. Here, though, you get straight to some useful tools and hopefully roll in some of the better things to come out of debates and efforts online.

Fetching Feed Data using httpcache.py

You could just use the HTTP modules that come with Python to fetch syndication feed data from a given URL. However, these modules are lacking a few features that can make feed consumption easier, both on you and on the publishers of feeds. A few of these include the following:

- Feed data caching
- Conditional HTTP GET
- HTTP gzip compression

Because syndication feeds operate on the basis of subscribers polling feeds for updates by downloading them on a periodic basis and checking for new entries (which could amount to more than a hit per hour, multiplied by the number of subscribers, occurring 24 times a day), a little conservation can go a long way. One way to get these features with an easy-to-use interface is with Joe Gregorio's `httpcache` module.

You can get the latest version of httpcache here:

```
http://bitworking.org/projects/httpcache/
```

Look for the download link to httpcache.py and stash a copy in your project directory. Using the module is pretty simple. Listing 2-9 shows a quick program to demonstrate it.

Listing 2-9: feed_fetch.py

```python
#!/usr/bin/env python

import sys
from httpcache import HTTPCache

feed_uri     = sys.argv[1]
cache        = HTTPCache(feed_uri)
feed_content = cache.content()

print feed_content
```

And a sample session with this program might look like this:

```
# python feed_fetch.py
http://feedparser.org/tests/wellformed/rss/aaa_wellformed.xml
<!--
Description: wellformed XML
Expect:      not bozo
-->
<rss version="2.0">
</rss>
```

One thing to notice is that, after running a program that uses httpcache, a new directory named .cache is created in your current directory. The httpcache module stashes downloaded data here, along with HTTP headers, in order to facilitate its caching features. Because everything downloaded using httpcache ends up here, you should make sure your programs have access to it and be able to delete things from it if you need to clear up disk space or need to troubleshoot any downloads.

Parsing Feed Data using SGMLParser

After fetching feed data, your next step is to parse the feed and extract the data into a form you can use in the rest of your aggregator. There are some challenges here in store for you, though. Not only will you encounter feeds based on the Atom format and a handful of different revisions of RSS (at least one of which is maintained by an entirely different group than the others); you'll also have to deal with variations in interpretation of all the above. Handling all of this complexity could easily take up a book in and of itself, so scope is limited here to a few types of feeds:

- RSS 1.0—This is an RDF-based syndication feed format based on earlier work at Netscape. It is documented at `http://purl.org/rss/1.0/spec`.

- RSS 2.0—This is roughly compatible with RSS versions 0.91 through 0.93. It is documented at `http://blogs.law.harvard.edu/tech/rss`.

- Atom 0.3—This is a newer syndication format. It is documented at `http://www.atomenabled.org/developers/syndication/atom-format-spec.php`.

Parsing for these three formats should cover a good majority of available feeds out there, or at least yield some usable results from feeds closely based on these methods.

 Rather than using a pure XML parser, using SGMLParser will help smooth over some common problems found in syndication feeds. The code you'll see in this parser originated with an article named "Parsing RSS at All Costs" by Mark Pilgrim in his XML.com column, "Dive into XML," found here:

> `http://www.xml.com/pub/a/2003/01/22/dive-into-xml.html`

Although the feed parser presented in this section has been expanded to support a few more feed formats, many of the details and considerations surrounding the parsing techniques from the original article still apply.

Okay, get into writing the parser module. Create a new file in your project directory named `minifeedparser.py` and start off with the code shown in Listing 2-10.

Listing 2-10: minifeedparser.py (Part 1 of 8)

```
"""
minifeedparser.py

A feature-light multi-format syndication feed parser, intended to do
a reasonable job extracting data from RSS 1.0, RSS 2.0, and Atom 0.3 feeds.
"""
from sgmllib   import SGMLParser
from httpcache import HTTPCache

def parse(feed_uri):
    """
    Create a throwaway parser object and return the results of
    parsing for the given feed URL
    """
    return MiniFeedParser().parse(feed_uri)
```

This shows nothing exciting so far—the module starts with a descriptive docstring comment, imports a few modules (namely SGMLParser and HTTPCache), and defines the first module-level function named parse(). This is a convenience function that (as its description claims) creates a temporary instance of a yet-to-be-defined class named MiniFeedParser and calls its parse() method with the feed URI passed in as a parameter.

Continuing on, you can begin defining the MiniFeedParser class, as shown in Listing 2-11.

Listing 2-11: minifeedparser.py (Part 2 of 8)

```
class MiniFeedParser(SGMLParser):

    def parse(self, feed_uri):
        """Given a URI to a feed, fetch it and return parsed data."""

        cache        = HTTPCache(feed_uri)
        feed_content = cache.content()

        self.reset()
        self.feed(feed_content)

        return {
            'version'  : self._version,
            'feed'     : self._feed,
            'entries'  : self._entries
        }
```

MiniFeedParser is a defined as a subclass of SGMLParser, as discussed earlier.

The next definition is for the parse() method. It accepts a feed URI and does the following:

- Feed data is fetched using an HTTPCache object.
- The reset() method is called and then parsing is begun by passing the feed data to the feed() method. Both the reset() and feed() methods are inherited from SGMLParser.
- Finally, data resulting from the parsing process is returned in a dictionary containing the feed format version, feed-specific information, and all of the entries found in the feed, using the keys version, feed, and entries, respectively.

The next thing is to get the MiniFeedParser prepared to parse feeds, as shown in Listing 2-12.

Listing 2-12: minifeedparser.py (Part 3 of 8)

```
    def reset(self):
        """Initialize the parser state."""
        self._version = "unknown"
        self._feed    = {
            'title'    : '',
```

```
            'link'    : '',
            'author'  : '',
            'modified' : '',
        }
        self._entries = []

        self.in_entry     = False
        self.current_tag  = None
        self.current_attrs = {}
        self.current_value = ''

        SGMLParser.reset(self)
```

SGMLParser is event-driven, meaning that as the parser works its way through the data, it attempts to call handler methods on itself when it encounters start and end tags and character data found inside tags.

On the Web You can find the documentation for SGMLParser in the Python standard library here:

> http://docs.python.org/lib/module-sgmllib.html

This feed parser subclass works as a *state machine*. In the course of parsing, it tracks things such as whether it is currently within an entry tag, what the current tag is, the attributes, and the value data gathered inside the currently open tag.

The reset() method defined here clears the state of the parser, and is called when parsing starts. The first part of this method initializes the data structures for the feed version, feed description, and entries in the feed.

So, continuing on the theme of event-driven parsing, the code shown in Listing 2-13 handles events corresponding to the opening tags used by each of the syndication feed formats the class will handle.

Listing 2-13: minifeedparser.py (Part 4 of 8)

```
    def start_rdf(self, attrs_tuples):
        """Handle RSS 1.0 feed start tag."""
        self.in_feed  = True
        self._version = "rss10"

    def start_rss(self, attrs_tuples):
        """Handle RSS 2.0 feed start tag."""
        self.in_feed = True

        # Attempt to verify that this is an RSS 2.0 feed.
        attrs = dict(attrs_tuples)
```

Continued

Listing 2-13 *(continued)*

```
        if attrs.get('version', '???') == '2.0':
            self._version = "rss20"
        else:
            self._version = "rss??"

    def start_feed(self, attrs_tuples):
        """Handle Atom 0.3 feed start tag."""
        self.in_feed = True

        # Attempt to verify that this is an Atom feed.
        attrs = dict(attrs_tuples)
        if attrs.get('version', '???') == '0.3':
            self._version = "atom03"
        else:
            self._version = "atom??"
```

Each of the three major feed formats targeted for parsing by this module start off with a different initial XML tag:

- `<rdf>` for RSS 1.0
- `<rss>` for RSS 2.0
- `<feed>` for Atom 0.3

Accordingly, event handler methods named `start_rdf`, `start_rss`, and `start_feed` are defined, to be called by the parser when one of these starting tags is encountered. Although there are other indicators of syndication feed version, watching for the opening tag is the easiest way to get started here.

Next, you can define the methods to handle parsing events for feed entries, as shown in Listing 2-14.

Listing 2-14: minifeedparser.py (Part 5 of 8)

```
    def start_entry(self, attrs):
        new_entry = {
            'title'   : '',
            'link'    : '',
            'modified': '',
            'summary' : '',
            'content' : '',
        }
        self._entries.append(new_entry)
        self.in_entry = True
```

```
def end_entry(self):
    # OK, we're out of the RSS item
    self.in_entry = False

start_item = start_entry
end_item   = end_entry
```

This code defines the following four methods: start_entry, end_entry, start_item, and end_item.

The first two methods handle the <entry> tag, used by the Atom format. However, because the handling of the <item> tag used by both versions of RSS is the same as for <entry>, you can just point the <item> handlers at the <entry> handlers, rather than defining completely new ones—one of the niceties of using Python is that you can do this simply.

The feed start tag event handler sets up a new, empty dictionary structure for the new entry and adds it to the list of entries found. Then, it sets the state flag indicating that further parsing is taking place inside an entry. And finally, the end feed tag event handler sets the state flag for entry parsing to false.

Now that you've implemented parsing as far as the opening feed tags, you can continue on to handling tags inside the feeds, as shown in Listing 2-15.

Listing 2-15: minifeedparser.py (Part 6 of 8)

```
def unknown_starttag(self, tag, attrs):
    self.current_tag   = tag
    self.current_attrs = dict(attrs)

    if 'atom' in self._version:
        if tag == 'link':
            current_value = self.current_attrs.get('href', '')
            if self.in_entry:
                self._entries[-1]['link'] = current_value
            else:
                self._feed['link'] = current_value

def handle_data(self, data):
    # buffer all text data
    self.current_value += data

def handle_entityref(self, data):
    # buffer all entities
    self.current_value += '&' + data + ';'
handle_charref = handle_entityref
```

The first method defined here, unknown_starttag, is a catch-all tag event handler that takes care of all tags not otherwise handled in this parser. For the quick-and-dirty parsing purposes of this module, everything that's not the feed start tag or an entry start tag gets handled here. In this start tag handler, the current open tag and its attributes are stowed away in the parser state variables.

The one interesting thing done here in unknown_starttag is that, if the feed format is Atom, the current tag is the <link> tag, and the href attribute is squirreled away into current entry data if you're currently processing an entry, or into the overall feed description if you're not. The <link> tag is handled this way because it is a bit of an exception. Whereas the relevant information in most other feed elements is contained in character data within opening and closing tags, the link data is contained in attributes, which are most easily handled at this phase of parsing.

The final two methods defined here handle the accumulation of character data found inside tags. For any given open tag, there can be more than one event in a stream of character data, including plain characters, entities (such as & and "), and character references (such as ”). The data from these events is just concatenated together in a running state variable, to be processed once the current tag ends.

This brings you to handling the events generated by closing tags, as shown in Listing 2-16.

Listing 2-16: minifeedparser.py (Part 7 of 8)

```python
def unknown_endtag(self, tag):
    current_value     = self.decode_entities(self.current_value.strip())
    current_prop_name = self.translate_prop_name(tag)

    if self.in_entry:
        self._entries[-1][current_prop_name] = current_value
    else:
        self._feed[current_prop_name] = current_value

    self.current_value = ''
```

This method, unknown_endtag, is the opposite to the previous event handler: This handles tags when they close. At this point, you've accumulated all the character data available for this tag, so you can figure out where it needs to go, and put it there.

The first thing that happens here is that the character data accumulated in parsing this tag is cleaned up and many entities found in the data are converted to normal text. Next, you convert from a tag name to a data structure name, but you see how that's done in just a minute. Then, if you're currently parsing a feed entry, the character data from the tag is put into the entry data under the translated property name. If you're not processing an entry, this data is put into the appropriate overall feed data structure. And, finally, the state variable containing character data during parsing is cleared.

Now, wrap up the loose ends in this class, as shown in Listing 2-17.

Listing 2-17: minifeedparser.py (Part 8 of 8)

```python
    def decode_entities(self, data):
        data = data.replace('&lt;', '<')
        data = data.replace('&gt;', '>')
        data = data.replace('&quot;', '"')
        data = data.replace('&apos;', "'")
        data = data.replace('&amp;', '&')
        return data

    def translate_prop_name(self, name):
        map = self.PROP_MAPS[self._version]
        if self.in_entry and map.has_key('entry'):
            return map['entry'].get(name, name)
        if not self.in_entry and map.has_key('feed'):
            return map['feed'].get(name, name)
        return name

    PROP_MAPS = {
        'rss10' : {
            'feed'  : {
                'dc:date'        : 'modified',
                'webmaster'      : 'author',
                'managingeditor' : 'author',
                'guid'           : 'id',
            },
            'entry' : {
                'dc:date'        : 'modified',
                'description'    : 'summary',
                'guid'           : 'id',
            }
        },
        'rss20' : {
            'feed'  : {
                'pubdate'        : 'modified',
                'webmaster'      : 'author',
                'managingeditor' : 'author',
                'guid'           : 'id',
            },
            'entry' : {
                'pubdate'        : 'modified',
                'description'    : 'summary',
                'guid'           : 'id',
            }
        },
        'atom03' : {
        },
    }
    PROP_MAPS['atom??'] = PROP_MAPS['atom03']
    PROP_MAPS['rss??']  = PROP_MAPS['rss20']
```

Two new methods are defined here, along with a data structure defined as a constant.

The first method, decode_entities(), is what's used to clean up character data during parsing, converting a limited set of XML/HTML entities to common text.

The second method, translate_prop_name(), translates from a current tag name to the name of the corresponding key in the data structures collecting feed and entry data. Associated with this method is a static structure named PROP_MAPS. This structure associates a decision tree from feed version, to whether the data is meant for the feed or an entry in the feed, to the name of an XML tag with the corresponding data structure key to be used.

For example, if the feed is in RSS 2.0 format, and a <Webmaster> tag is encountered in a feed, the data inside that tag ends up in the 'author' property for that feed's description data. And, if the feed is in RSS 1.0 format, and a <dc:date> tag is encountered in a feed entry data, that tag's contents end up in the entry's 'issued' property. This technique is far from perfect, but it does help blur the differences between the feed formats, settling on the Atom format's teminology for most things.

Trying Out the minifeedparser

Unlike the feed location modules, this parser hasn't been written as an executable program, so you'll need a testing program to try it out.

Listing 2-18 shows a quick program to pretty-print the results of the minifeedparser, called feed_reader.py.

Listing 2-18: feed_reader.py

```python
#!/usr/bin/env python

import sys
import minifeedparser as feedparser

if __name__ == '__main__':
    feed_uri  = sys.argv[1]
    feed_data = feedparser.parse(feed_uri)

    print "==========================================================="
    print "'%(title)r' at %(link)r" % feed_data['feed']
    print "==========================================================="
    print

    for entry in feed_data['entries']:
        print "-----------------------------------------------------------"
        print "Date:  %(modified)r" % entry
        print "Title: %(title)r" % entry
        print "Link:  %(link)r" % entry
        print "-----------------------------------------------------------"
        print
```

This program imports the `miniparser`, fetches and parses a feed from a URL given on the command line, then formats and prints a few selective elements extracted from the feed and its entries.

An example session running this test program might look like this:

```
# python feed_reader.py http://www.boingboing.net/atom.xml


============================================================
'Boing Boing' at http://www.boingboing.net/
============================================================


------------------------------------------------------------
Date:  2005-01-18T13:38:05-08:00
Title: Cory NPR interview audio
Link:  http://www.boingboing.net/2005/01/18/cory_npr_interview_a.html
------------------------------------------------------------


------------------------------------------------------------
Date:  2005-01-18T13:12:28-08:00
Title: Explanation for region coded printer cartridges?
Link:  http://www.boingboing.net/2005/01/18/explanation_for_regi.html
------------------------------------------------------------
```

Finding Room for Improvement with minifeedparser

This quick-and-dirty parser is pretty haphazard in what it extracts from feeds, so you may need to play with it and see what various feeds produce. Although you're very likely to see several feed entry properties parsed out, the only feed entry elements this code makes any effort toward normalizing are the following:

- `title`
- `link`
- `issued`
- `summary`

This feed format normalization technique could certainly do with some improvements.

Another thing worth pointing out is that *this parser does nothing with date values.* This might seem like a small thing, but between feed formats and even between individual feeds "in the wild," the way dates are expressed varies wildly. This means that, for example, if you wanted to aggregate several feeds together and place them in mixed reverse-chronological order, you'll need to put some work into this parser to normalize date formats before you'll be able to compare dates between various feeds.

For example, here are a few date formats I've seen in feeds:

- 2003-12-31T10:14:55Z
- 2003-12-31 10:14:55.0

- Thu, 31 Dec 2003 10:14:55 GMT
- Sun Dec 31 10:14:55 PST 2003
- Mon, 31 December 2003 10:14:55 PT

And these examples don't include some particularly broken, arbitrary, or regional timekeeping variations. Should you decide to tackle date handling in your own parser, you hopefully won't run into too much date weirdness, but you should know what you could be in for.

Finally, this `minifeedparser` doesn't make many allowances for broken feeds. It is likely to perform pretty well on the most common cases of breakage, but in a few cases it may return strange data. So, again, keep in mind that this parser is quick and dirty, and works mostly, but has lots of room for improvement.

Using the Universal Feed Parser

So, handling feeds can quickly become a challenge. Wouldn't it be nice if you could build upon the well-tested work of someone else who has already gone through all the hairpulling and trouble to get feeds turned into usable data?

Well, you're in luck. Mark Pilgrim (who wrote the Ultra-Liberal Feed Finder introduced earlier, as well as the article discussing the `SGMLParser` technique used in the `minifeedparser`) has built a Universal Feed Parser in Python. (I know, I know, with all of the material I've featured from Mark Pilgrim, I could have just as easily named this chapter "Parsing Feeds with Pilgrim." But the guy has contributed a lot of code toward handling syndication feeds in Python.)

The Universal Feed Parser supports almost a dozen feed variants and, with around 2,000 unit tests and plenty of users, this module certainly qualifies as well-tested. In addition, this module incorporates a raft of other features and best practices for feed fetching and parsing, including some effort toward cleaning up broken feed content, properly handling Unicode strings, and filtering out potentially malicious bits of HTML and Javascript.

Also, this parser turns every format of feed into the same data structures in Python, so ultimately you don't need to worry about feed formats because they all look alike to your code. The `minifeedparser` made some effort toward this goal, but the Universal Feed Parser takes the concept quite a bit further.

And best of all, the Universal Feed Parser handles about 25 different variations of date format and normalizes them all into a single form easily used in Python.

 For a more in-depth discussion of date formats in feeds, check out the Universal Feed Parser documentation here:

>   http://www.feedparser.org/docs/date-parsing.html

You can download the Universal Feed Parser here:

http://feedparser.org/

As of this writing, the latest version was 3.3.0. The interface for this module has been pretty stable for a while, so everything here should work with future versions of the module. When in doubt, though, check the version.

After you've downloaded the Universal Feed Parser, unzip the archive it comes packed in. Along with some documentation and an installer script, everything you're interested is all in one module file named `feedparser.py`. You can use the installer script, but it's also just as easy to copy the module into your project directory alongside the rest of your scripts and modules.

Having obtained the parser, why not try it out? You can reuse the test program written for the `minifeedparser` (with just one small change to the beginning) to use the Universal Feed Parser. Locate the following line in `feed_reader.py`:

```
import minifeedparser as feedparser
```

Change it to this:

```
import feedparser
```

Again, a session with this script should look much like it did for the `minifeedparser`, although it may produce a bit more content from the feed:

```
# python feed_reader.py http://www.boingboing.net/atom.xml


============================================================
'Boing Boing' at http://www.boingboing.net/
============================================================


------------------------------------------------------------
Date:  u'2005-01-19T12:15:19-08:00'
Title: u'Does the world need wireless robots'
Link:  u'http://www.boingboing.net/2005/01/19/does_the_world_need_.html'

u'<strong>Mark Frauenfelder</strong>: . . .'
------------------------------------------------------------
```

The remainder of the programs in this book use the Universal Feed Parser, but you can continue working with the `minifeedparser` if you'd like to tinker further with feed parsing.

Aggregating Feeds

At this point, you have the tools to help you find feeds, and tools to help you get information out of feeds once you find them. Now it's time to combine the tools and start bringing feeds together in one place with an aggregator.

Subscribing to Feeds

The first part of the aggregator is subscribing to feeds. To keep thing simple, just maintain a list of subscriptions in a text file named `feeds.txt` with one feed URI per line.

Using a `feedfinder` module, you can write a program to add feed subscriptions like the code shown in Listing 2-19.

Listing 2-19: agg01_subscribe.py

```
#!/usr/bin/env
"""
agg01_subscribe.py

Given a URI, try to find feeds there and subscribe to one.
"""
import sys, feedfinder

FEEDS_FN = "feeds.txt"

uri = sys.argv[1]

try:
    feeds = feedfinder.getFeeds(uri)
except:
    feeds = []

if len(feeds) == 0:
    print "No feeds found at %s" % uri

elif len(feeds) > 1:
    print "Multiple feeds found at %s" % uri
    for feed_uri in feeds:
        print "\t%s" % feed_uri

else:
    feed_uri = feeds[0]
    try:
        subs = [x.strip() for x in open(FEEDS_FN).readlines()]
    except:
        subs = []

    if feed_uri in subs:
        print "Already subscribed to %s" % feed_uri
    else:
        subs.append(feed_uri)
        open(FEEDS_FN, "w").write("\n".join(subs))
        print "Subscribed to %s" % feed_uri
```

This program first uses the `feedfinder` with a URI given at the command line to locate feeds. This search produces three possible outcomes, and here's what the program does for each:

- *Zero feeds found*—Print a message indicating no feeds found and exit.

- *Multiple feeds found*—Print a message that multiple feeds were found, list them, and exit.

- *One feed found*—If this feed is already in the list of subscriptions, report this and exit. Otherwise, add the feed URI to the subscriptions and write out the file.

This program doesn't make guesses about to which feed you want to make a subscription, which is why multiple feeds result in only a printed message. Here's a sample session with the program:

```
# python agg01_subscribe.py http://www.example.com
No feeds found at http://www.example.com

# python agg01_subscribe.py http://www.decafbad.com
Multiple feeds found at http://www.decafbad.com
        http://www.decafbad.com/index.rdf
        http://www.decafbad.com/atom.xml

# python agg01_subscribe.py http://www.decafbad.com/blog/atom.xml
Subscribed to http://www.decafbad.com/blog/atom.xml

# python agg01_subscribe.py http://www.decafbad.com/blog/atom.xml
Already subscribed to http://www.decafbad.com/blog/atom.xml
```

This program doesn't handle it, but unsubscribing from a feed is much simpler: You just delete the line from `feeds.txt` and save the file. You could improve this subscription program to include unsubscribe functionality, but that's left up to you.

After playing with this program for a bit, you should have a list of subscriptions in `feeds.txt`, something like the one shown in Listing 2-20.

Listing 2-20: feeds.txt

```
http://xml.metafilter.com/atom.xml
http://slashdot.org/index.rss
http://rss.cnn.com/rss/cnn_topstories.rss
http://news.bbc.co.uk/rss/newsonline_world_edition/front_page/rss091.xml
http://www.nytimes.com/services/xml/rss/nyt/HomePage.xml
http://rss.news.yahoo.com/rss/tech
http://www.wired.com/news_drop/netcenter/netcenter.rdf
http://www.decafbad.com/blog/atom.xml
```

Caution

Something to note about this `feeds.txt` file that might not be apparent at first glance: It's composed of feed URLs, one per line—and that's all. Anything else, such as extraneous blank lines, or really any lines that aren't feed URLs, will probably cause a few strange errors. The programs consuming `feeds.txt` in this book won't include any error checking, opting for a quick-and-dirty approach to loading up the feed URLs. You may want to play with improving this behavior in your own tinkering.

Aggregating Subscribed Feeds

After you've gone through some of your favorite sites and gathered some subscriptions, it's time to start aggregating the data from those feeds. So, here you learn how to build a simple mixed reverse-chronological feed aggregator using the feed parser covered earlier.

Start a new program file, named agg01_pollsubs.py, like the one shown in Listing 2-21.

> **Listing 2-21:** agg01_pollsubs.py (Part 1 of 7)

```python
#!/usr/bin/env python
"""

agg01_pollsubs.py

Poll subscriptions and create an aggregate page.
"""
import sys, time
import feedparser

FEEDS_FN    = "feeds.txt"
HTML_FN     = "aggregator.html"
UNICODE_ENC = "utf-8"

def main():
    """
    Poll subscribed feeds and produce aggregator page.
    """
    feeds = [ x.strip() for x in open(FEEDS_FN, "r").readlines() ]
    entries = getFeedEntries(feeds)
    writeAggregatorPage(entries, HTML_FN)
```

Like the other Python programs written so far, this one starts off with a description and a series of import statements that pull in tools you'll be using. Next up are a series of constants:

- FEEDS_FN—Contains the filename of your list of subscriptions

- HTML_FN—Contains the filename to which the HTML produced by the aggregator will be written.

- UNICODE_ENC—Contains the Unicode encoding to use in the HTML, though you shouldn't need to change this.

And then, the main() function is defined; this is the main driver for the aggregator. It loads up the list of subscribed feeds, using a quick Python one-liner to get a list of strings from the file named in FEEDS_FN. Again, note that there's no error checking here: The aggregator assumes that all the lines of this file are to be interpreted as feed URLs, possibly doing strange things with anything that's not a feed URL.

After loading up this list of feed URLs, a function named getFeedEntries() is called to get entries for all the feeds. This is followed by a call to writeAggregatorPage() to produce the page of aggregated feed entries.

Define the getFeedEntries() function next, as shown in Listing 2-22.

Listing 2-22: agg01_pollsubs.py (Part 2 of 7)

```
def getFeedEntries(feeds):
    """
    Given a list of feeds, poll each feed and collect entries found, wrapping
    each in an EntryWrapper object.  Sort the entries, then return the list.
    """
    entries = []
    for uri in feeds:
        print "Polling %s" % uri
        try:
            data = feedparser.parse(uri)
            entries.extend([ EntryWrapper(data, e) for e in data.entries ])
        except:
            print "Problem polling %s" % uri

    entries.sort()
    return entries
```

This function, getFeedEntries(), accepts a list of feed URIs. It iterates through each of those and uses the feed parser to extract the data for the feed. If there's any problem in fetching or parsing the feed, a message will be printed (although, in this program, the error message is not very descriptive).

For each entry found in the feed, the data from the feed parser is wrapped up in an instance of the EntryWrapper class, which is defined shortly. Finally, once every subscribed feed has been polled, the collected list of feed entries is sorted and then returned.

Continuing on, define the writeAggregatorPage() function, as shown in Listing 2-23.

Listing 2-23: agg01_pollsubs.py (Part 3 of 7)

```
def writeAggregatorPage(entries, out_fn):
    """
    Given a list of entries and an output filename, use templates to compose
    an aggregate page from the feeds and write to the file.
    """
    out, curr_day, curr_feed = [], None, None
```

Continued

Listing 2-23 *(continued)*

```
for e in entries:
    # If this entry's date is not the current running day, change the
    # current day and add a date header to the page output.
    if e['date'] != curr_day:
        curr_day = e['date']
        out.append(DATE_HDR_TMPL % curr_day)

        # Oh yeah, and output a reminder of the current feed after the
        # day header if it hasn't changed.
        if e.feed.title == curr_feed:
            out.append(FEED_HDR_TMPL % e)

    # If this entry's feed isn't the current running feed, change the
    # current feed and add a feed header to the page output.
    if e.feed.title != curr_feed:
        curr_feed = e.feed.title
        out.append(FEED_HDR_TMPL % e)

    # Add the entry to the page output.
    out.append(ENTRY_TMPL % e)

# Concatenate all the page output collected, fill the page templage, and
# write the result to the output file.
open(out_fn, "w").write(PAGE_TMPL % "".join(out))
```

This `writeAggregatorPage()` function accepts a list of `EntryWrapper` objects and an output filename, and it produces an aggregated page of all the entries written to the output file. In the course of producing the output, this function uses several template strings:

- `DATE_HDR_TMPL`—Used to insert a date when a new day is encountered in the list of entries.

- `FEED_HDR_TMPL`—Used to insert a new feed header, consisting of the title linked to the feed's HTML version, when entries from a new feed are encountered.

- `ENTRY_TMPL`—Used to render each individual feed entry.

- `PAGE_TMPL`—This is the overall page template, into which the rest of the content is inserted.

On the Web For more information about string formatting used in these templates, check out this documentation:

> `http://docs.python.org/lib/typesseq-strings.html`

In short, these templates are used with the `'%'` operator, passing in a value, or a dictionary/map-like object, depending on how the template is constructed. The templates mentioned here are defined at the end of the program, so you'll see how they're made.

This function runs through all the entries supplied to it, inserting each into the page to be produced. In the course of iterating through the entries, date headers and feed headers are inserted whenever a change in day or a change in feed is encountered. This applies a sort of blog-like appearance to the list of aggregated entries.

Now, to fill in another foreshadowed detail, define the EntryWrapper class, as shown in Listing 2-24.

Listing 2-24: agg01_pollsubs.py (Part 4 of 7)

```
class EntryWrapper:
    def __init__(self, data, entry):
        """
        Initialize the wrapper with feed and entry data.
        """
        self.data  = data
        self.feed  = data.feed
        self.entry = entry

        # Try to work out some sensible primary date for the entry, fall
        # back to the feed's date, and use the current time as a last resort.
        if entry.has_key("modified_parsed"):
            self.date = time.mktime(entry.modified_parsed)
        elif entry.has_key("issued_parsed"):
            self.date = time.mktime(entry.issued_parsed)
        elif self.feed.has_key("modified_parsed"):
            self.date = time.mktime(self.feed.modified_parsed)
        elif self.feed.has_key("issued_parsed"):
            self.date = time.mktime(self.feed.issued_parsed)
        else:
            self.date = time.time()

    def __cmp__(self, other):
        """
        Use the entry's date as the comparator for sorting & etc.
        """
        return other.date - self.date
```

The purpose of the EntryWrapper class is to simplify the aggregation and sorting of feed entries, and the production of the output page using template strings.

First, the __init__() method is defined, which accepts the entire parsed feed and a single entry from the feed. These data structures are tucked away in instance variables. Next, a hackish attempt is made to make some sensible choice of publication date for the entry—some feeds offer modified dates for every entry, whereas others offer only an issued date, and then some feeds only offer a date at the top level of the feed itself. The last-ditch fallback is to just use the current time as this entry's datestamp, which is not so great, but is better than nothing.

The dates become important with the definition of the __cmp__() method, which is used during sorting and other operations to determine the relative order of two EntryWrapper objects. This enables the list of feed entries to be sorted into reverse-chronological order, back in the getFeedEntries() function.

One more method to define in this class is shown in Listing 2-25.

Listing 2-25: agg01_pollsubs.py (Part 5 of 7)

```
def __getitem__(self, name):
    # Handle access to feed data on keys starting with "feed."
    if name.startswith("feed."):
        return self.feed.get(name[5:], "").encode(UNICODE_ENC)

    # Handle access to entry data on keys starting with "entry."
    if name.startswith("entry."):
        return self.entry.get(name[6:], "").encode(UNICODE_ENC)

    # Handle a few more special-case keys.
    if name == "date":
        return time.strftime("%Y-%m-%d", time.localtime(self.date))
    if name == "time":
        return time.strftime("%H:%M:%S", time.localtime(self.date))
    if name == "content":
        if self.entry.has_key("content"):
            return self.entry.content[0].value.encode(UNICODE_ENC)
        return ""

    # If all else fails, return an empty string.
    return ""
```

The __getitem__() method is what facilitates using feed entries in template strings. The template strings require map-like objects, which is what this specially named method emulates. With this method, an EntryWrapper object can be used like a Python dictionary to access feed and entry values.

For example, given some EntryWrapper object in a variable named entry:

- entry['feed.title'] gives the title of an entry's feed.
- entry['entry.link'] gives the link associated with an entry.
- entry['date'] gives a formatted string representation of just the date of an entry's published datestamp.

This method also uses the UNICODE_ENC constant defined at the beginning of the program to encode any special characters found in various fields in the feed and entries.

And that's the end of the `EntryWrapper` class. You're just about done—it's time to define the output templates, as shown in Listing 2-26.

```
# Presentation templates for output follow:

DATE_HDR_TMPL = """
    <h1 class="dateheader">%s</h1>
"""

FEED_HDR_TMPL = """
    <h2 class="feedheader"><a href="%(feed.link)s">%(feed.title)s</a></h2>
"""

ENTRY_TMPL = """
    <div class="feedentry">
        <div class="entryheader">
            <span class="entrytime">%(time)s</span>:
            <a class="entrylink" href="%(entry.link)s">%(entry.title)s</a>
        </div>
        <div class="entrysummary">
            %(entry.summary)s
            <hr>
            %(content)s
        </div>
    </div>
"""
```

These are three of the four output templates used by the `writeAggregatorPage()` function:

- The `DATE_HDR_TMPL` template string is pretty simple. It uses an `<h1>` tag with a CSS class of `dateheader` to wrap a single date passed to it.

- The `FEED_HDR_TMPL` template string is a little more involved. It expects to be used with an `EntryWrapper` object and produces an `<h2>` with CSS class `feedheader`, containing a link of the feed title pointed to the feed's HTML version.

- The `ENTRY_TMPL` template string uses more of the keys available from an `EntryWrapper` object to produce a display of a feed entry, which includes a link to the entry on its title, along with the summary and content of the feed entry.

Finally, to wrap up the whole program, define the overall page template, as shown in Listing 2-27.

Listing 2-27: agg01_pollsubs.py (Part 7 of 7)

```python
PAGE_TMPL = """
<html>
    <head>
        <style>
            body {
                font-family: sans-serif;
                font-size: 12px;
            }
            .pageheader {
                font-size: 2em;
                font-weight: bold;
                border-bottom: 3px solid #000;
                padding: 5px;
            }
            .dateheader   {
                margin: 20px 10px 10px 10px;
                border-top: 2px solid #000;
                border-bottom: 2px solid #000;
            }
            .feedheader   {
                margin: 20px;
                border-bottom: 1px dashed #aaa;
            }
            .feedentry    {
                margin: 10px 30px 10px 30px;
                padding: 10px;
                border: 1px solid #ddd;
            }
            .entryheader {
                border-bottom: 1px solid #ddd;
                padding: 5px;
            }
            .entrytime {
                font-weight: bold;
            }
            .entrysummary {
                margin: 10px;
                padding: 5px;
            }
        </style>
    </head>
    <body>
        <h1 class="pageheader">Feed aggregator #1</h1>
        %s
    </body>
</html>
"""

if __name__ == "__main__": main()
```

This template is the longest, but it's the simplest. It establishes the enclosing HTML wrapper for all of the page content and provides CSS to style all the other elements inserted into the page. You can tweak this into whatever format you like, but this is a good set of styles to start with.

The final line, again, is a trick to make Python call the `main()` function at the beginning when this file is run as a program. Here's what a sample run of the program looks like:

```
# python agg01_pollsubs.py
Polling http://xml.metafilter.com/atom.xml
Polling http://rss.cnn.com/rss/cnn_topstories.rss
Polling http://news.bbc.co.uk/rss/newsonline_world_edition/front_page/rss091.xml
Polling http://www.nytimes.com/services/xml/rss/nyt/HomePage.xml
Polling http://rss.news.yahoo.com/rss/tech
Polling http://www.wired.com/news_drop/netcenter/netcenter.rdf
Polling http://www.decafbad.com/blog/atom.xml
Polling http://slashdot.org/index.rss
```

When it's all done, you should end up with an HTML page named `aggregator.html`. Open this up in your Web browser to see all of the feeds' entries pulled together, as shown in Figure 2-4.

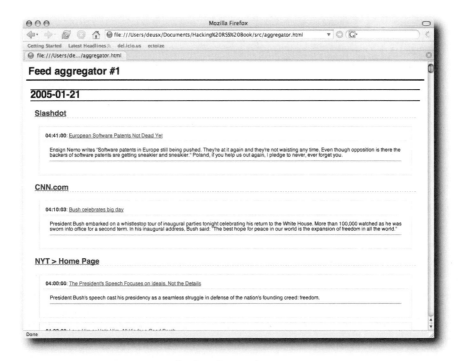

FIGURE 2-4: `aggregator.html` **displayed in Firefox**

Using the Simple Feed Aggregator

Now, how do you use this aggregator? Well, the best thing to do is set it up as a scheduled task on your system—run no more than once an hour—so that when you load up the HTML page it produces, you'll automatically have the latest entries updated.

Scheduling Aggregator Runs

You could run the program by hand at points throughout the day, but after you accumulate a dozen or so feeds, you'll find that this program takes quite some time to finish its job.

Using cron on Linux and OS X

Under Linux and Mac OS X, you can use the cron scheduler to fire off periodic runs of the aggregator. You may want to read up on cron and crontab, but in short, you can set up an hourly recurring run of the aggregator with something like this:

```
# crontab -l > curr_crontab
# echo "50 * * * * (cd $HOME/devel/aggregator; python agg01_pollfeeds.py)" >>
curr_crontab
# crontab curr_crontab
```

These commands do the following:

- List your current cron schedule out to a file named curr_crontab.

- Append a new schedule entry, which calls your aggregator at ten minutes before every hour.

- Replace the cron schedule with this new version.

Note that this assumes that your project directory is under devel/aggregator in your home directory—tweak according to your local setup.

Alternatively, you can use crontab -e to do all of the above within a text editor. Again, check out some documentation for cron and crontab (that is, using the man cron command) for more information. You'll want to be careful with this, because you don't want to wipe out any existing crontab entries.

Using a Scheduled Task on Windows XP

On Windows, you can add scheduled tasks through the Control Panel. Click your Start button, then navigate through Settings ➪ Control Panel ➪ Scheduled Tasks ➪ Add Scheduled Task. You can step through the wizard dialog provided here to schedule runs of your aggregator program from here.

Unfortunately, it seems that this method is limited to daily repeating tasks, so running this aggregator once per hour in this method would involve a tedious process of creating a daily repeating task for every hour in the day.

You may want to check out an alternative scheduler for Windows, such as VisualCron, available here:

`http://www.visualcron.com`

Checking Out Other Options

The simple feed aggregator built in this chapter, although it's very light on features, can be pretty useful and is a good introduction into the guts of feed aggregation. The rest of the chapters in this book provide further tweaks, improvements, and new programs built on top of the code used here. However, if you'd like to see some different or more powerful examples of syndication feed aggregators, this section contains a few suggestions.

Using spycyroll

Another feed aggregator in Python is called `spycyroll`, originally written by Vattekkat Satheesh Babu. It's been out of active development for quite a while, and uses a very early version of the Universal Feed parser, but it's worth checking out. You can find it on SourceForge here:

`http://spycyroll.sourceforge.net/`

This aggregator is based another older aggregator named `blagg`, written in Perl by Rael Dornfest, along with the `blosxom` blogging package. The general idea for this aggregator is that feed entries are stored as files to keep track of what's already been seen from feeds. Although you'll see some tweaks to the aggregator built in this chapter, this isn't a feature it has yet.

Using Feed on Feeds

Feed on Feeds, written in PHP by Steve Minutillo, offers a full-featured Web-based feed aggregator. You can find a download for this software here:

`http://minutillo.com/steve/feedonfeeds/`

This aggregator uses a PHP-based cousin to the Universal Feed Parser, named MagpieRSS, to load feed entries into a MySQL database. Through the Web interface, you can manage feed subscriptions, flag entries and mark them as read, as well as a host of other features.

Figure 2-5 shows an example view from Feed on Feeds.

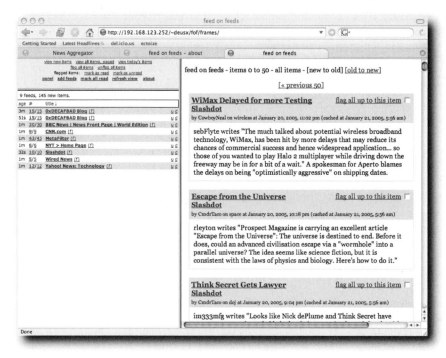

FIGURE 2-5: Feed on Feeds displayed in a Firefox window

Using Radio UserLand under Windows and OS X

The granddaddy of all modern desktop aggregators, Radio UserLand, is available for both Windows and Mac OS X from UserLand Software here:

```
http://radio.userland.com/
```

Figure 2-6 shows a quick peek at the feed aggregator in Radio UserLand:

FIGURE 2-6: Radio UserLand aggregator displayed in a Firefox window

Using NetNewsWire under OS X

For the Mac OS X platform, one of the premier feed aggregators is Ranchero Software's
NetNewsWire, found here:

```
http://ranchero.com/netnewswire/
```

NetNewsWire is a three-pane styled aggregator that runs as a desktop application—instead of
using the aggregator in your Web browser, NetNewsWire treats your feed entries more like
email and incorporates a Web browser into itself.

Figure 2-7 shows NetNewsWire in action.

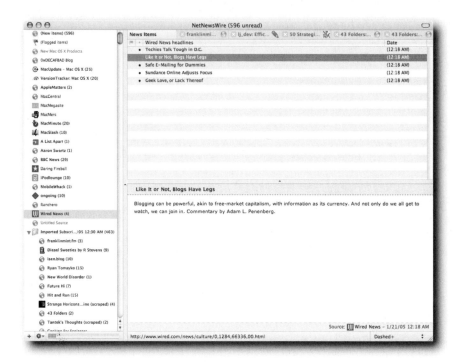

FIGURE 2-7: NetNewsWire running on OS X

Using FeedDemon under Windows

On the Windows platform, FeedDemon by Nick Bradbury is one of the best options around. You can check it out at this URL:

```
http://www.bradsoft.com/feeddemon/
```

FeedDemon is another desktop aggregator, loosely three-pane based, but it offers a lot of different configurations and customization options. It also embeds a Web browser within its interface, so you can do all of your feed reading there.

Figure 2-8 shows an example configuration of FeedDemon.

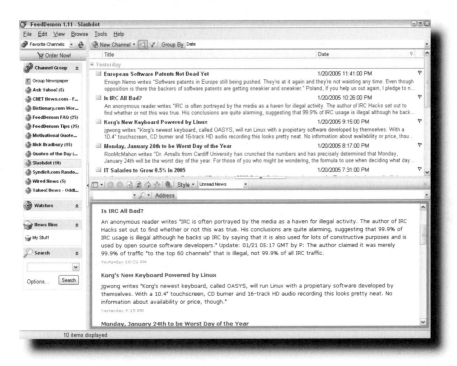

FIGURE 2-8: FeedDemon running on Windows

Summary

So that's it, you've built your first mixed reverse-chronological feed aggregator. There's not much to it yet, and it's certainly not fit for use with a large number of subscriptions, but you'll be building on it and improving it in the coming chapters.

Until then, though, there are a few improvement projects you could pursue:

- Check out templating packages for Python and replace the simple formatting string technique used at present. The book uses this approach to keep things relatively simple and to minimize the number of Python packages you need to install. However, something a bit more fully featured can help you come up with much more advanced feed entry presentation schemes.

  For example, you might want to take a look at Cheetah (`http://www.cheetah template.org`) for a mature and easy-to-use text-based templating mini-language. Alternatively, check out Kid (`http://kid-template.sourceforge.net`) for a relatively new but advanced XML-based templating package that uses an API very similar to that of Cheetah.

- Separate feed scanning from the production of the output page and store the results of scans in between program runs. You can play with this to spread out scans of a large number of feeds over time, and play with tweaking the aggregator HTML output separately from running lengthy feed scans.

- Turn the feed scanning program into a long-running process with its own built-in scheduler. That way, you won't need to depend on `cron` or some other task scheduling application for your operating system.

- Figure out how to turn the feed subscription program into a helper application for your browser when you click feed links, to automatically add new subscriptions to `feeds.txt`.

In Chapter 3, you continue improving on this aggregator. You reorganize your code a bit into some reusable modules, and you see how to add some persistence, in order to figure out what entries have been seen before in feeds. And then, you jump out of the browser window and start routing feed entries to your email inbox, where you can use the full range of message management facilities offered by your inbox but lacking in a static page in your browser.

Routing Feeds to Your Email Inbox

I n this chapter, you improve upon the simple feed aggregator you built in Chapter 2 and, among other things, enable it to provide you with regular email updates from your subscribed feeds.

You may find that bridging the gap between the inbox *metaphor* of aggregated feeds and the tools provided by your *real* inbox can give you many powerful capabilities (such as filtering and archival of feed entries). Reading feeds this way can also offer some simple things you'd take for granted with email messages (such as keeping track of what you've read and what's new).

Giving Your Aggregator a Memory

One of the first improvements you can make to your aggregator is to give it a memory. At the end of Chapter 2, your aggregator was polling feeds and assembling an HTML page of all the entries from all subscribed feeds. However, every time it ran, it aggregated *every* entry found in *every* feed, not just the entries that had appeared since last it checked. Also, because it had no recollection of what happened the last time it polled a particular feed, it had no way of knowing whether the feed might have actually changed at all before downloading the whole thing.

This sort of memory becomes an important feature in an aggregator— particularly if you want it to deliver reports by email, and you don't want it to flood you with lots of information you've seen already. Downloading the full content of feeds that haven't changed might not seem like a big deal, but not only will it slow down your process of checking for new entries across all your subscriptions, it will also waste bandwidth for the person hosting the feed.

To keep track of things, some aggregator authors use a full-blown SQL database such as MySQL, or even the more lightweight SQLite. For the purposes of your aggregator at this point, though, you don't need to get that fancy. In fact, you can get by for now by just using the shelve module that comes with Python. This module gives you a simple dictionary-like inter-face on top of an on-disk database that can store most native Python objects and data structures.

On the Web

You can find the documentation for `shelve` in the Python standard library here:

```
http://docs.python.org/lib/module-shelve.html
```

To get started, make a copy of `agg01_pollsubs.py` and call it `agg02_pollsubs.py`. It's smart to leave your work from Chapter 2 as-is, in case you want to go back to it, or compare it with the changes you'll make in this and future chapters.

Now, open up `agg02_pollsubs.py` in your editor and make some changes to the beginning of the file, as shown in Listing 3-1.

Listing 3-1: agg02_pollsubs.py Modifications (Part 1 of 8)

```
#!/usr/bin/env python
"""
agg02_pollsubs.py

Poll subscriptions and create an aggregate page, keeping track
of feed changes and new/old items.
"""
import sys, time, feedparser, shelve, md5, time

FEEDS_FN     = "feeds.txt"
HTML_FN      = "aggregator-%s.html"
UNICODE_ENC  = "utf-8"

FEED_DB_FN   = "feeds_db"
ENTRY_DB_FN  = "entry_seen_db"
```

The first change is in the docstring introducing the program—notice that the additions to the original program are presented in bold. Although not mandatory or having anything to do with the operation of the program, it's a good idea to keep an updated description of your program for when you come back to it later. It's easy to forget just what any particular program does if you've walked away from it for a while.

Notice that a few new modules are imported this time:

- `shelve`—This module facilitates access to on-disk databases as Python dictionaries.

- `md5`—This module provides functions for creating unique hashes from arbitrary data.

- `time`—This module gives you a set of functions dealing with dates and times.

Next up are a few changes and additions to the configuration constants—namely HTML_FN, FEED_DB_FN, and ENTRY_DB_FN. The HTML_FN constant is now a template string, which will be used shortly to insert a datestamp into the filename. This will enable your aggregator to generate pages containing only the new items for that particular program run, without over-writing the results of past runs. The FEED_DB_FN and ENTRY_DB_FN constants foreshadow the work you'll be doing with the on-disk databases for feed and entry data. These filenames will be used to create the database files.

Continuing forward, you need to replace the main() function definition, as shown in Listing 3-2.

Listing 3-2: agg02_pollsubs.py Modifications (Part 2 of 8)

```
def main():
    """
    Poll subscribed feeds and produce aggregator page.
    """
    feed_db, entry_db = openDBs(FEED_DB_FN, ENTRY_DB_FN)

    feeds   = [ x.strip() for x in open(FEEDS_FN, "r").readlines() ]

    entries = getNewFeedEntries(feeds, feed_db, entry_db)

    if len(entries) > 0:
        out_fn = HTML_FN % time.strftime("%Y%m%d-%H%M%S")
        writeAggregatorPage(entries, out_fn)

    closeDBs(feed_db, entry_db)
```

Starting off this new main() function, call the yet-to-be-defined openDBs() function, which will use the shelve module to open the two databases that will be used for keeping track of feeds and entries.

Next, as in the previous program, the list of subscribed feeds is read in. Then, a new function named getNewFeedEntries() is called with the list of feeds and the two databases. This will work much like getFeedEntries() did in Chapter 2's program, but with a lot of extra logic to return only the new entries since the last program run.

After getting the set of new feed entries, the program writes the HTML output. First, it checks to see whether, in fact, there were any new entries. If there weren't any, there's no sense in writing out an empty page. Otherwise, the program comes up with a filename for the new HTML page it's about to output, using the template string defined earlier with a current datestamp inserted. This results in a filename that looks something like this:

```
aggregator-20050130-134502.html
```

On the Web If you want to modify the format used for the datestamp in the filenames generated by this program, check out the documentation on time format strings, under strftime(), in the Python documentation:

```
http://docs.python.org/lib/module-time.html
```

Once the filename is worked out, the `writeAggregatorPage()` function is called, generating the HTML listing all of the new feed entries. Lastly, in the `main()` function, the databases opened at the beginning are closed with the `closeDBs()` function. Although the `shelve` module will close databases opened with it after a program has ended, it's always smart to close what you've opened and clean up everything when you're done.

Having established the new driving code for the aggregator, you can start to fill in some details with two new functions in Listing 3-3. Insert this new code directly after your new `main()` function, but before the `getFeedEntries()` function definition.

Listing 3-3: agg02_pollsubs.py Modifications (Part 3 of 8)

```
def openDBs(feed_db_fn, entry_db_fn):
    """
    Open the databases used to track feeds and entries seen.
    """
    feed_db  = shelve.open(feed_db_fn)
    entry_db = shelve.open(entry_db_fn)
    return (feed_db, entry_db)

def closeDBs(feed_db, entry_db):
    """
    Close the databases used to track feeds and entries seen.
    """
    feed_db.close()
    entry_db.close()
```

In Listing 3-3, two new functions are defined: `openDBs()` and `closeDBs()`. These, as their names suggest, respectively open and close the databases used in the rest of the program using the `open()` function provided by the `shelve` module.

After this, you can define the `getNewFeedEntries()` function, which represents the meat of the new functionality added to your aggregator. Start the function definition with Listing 3-4, entering the new code directly after the definition of the `closeDBs()` function (the order doesn't *really* matter, but this seems as good a place as any to put it).

Listing 3-4: agg02_pollsubs.py Modifications (Part 4 of 8)

```
def getNewFeedEntries(feeds, feed_db, entry_db):
    """
    Given a list of feeds, poll feeds which have not been polled in
    over an hour.  Look out for conditional HTTP GET status codes
    before processing feed data.  Check if we've seen each entry in a
    feed, collecting any entries that are new.  Sort the entries, then
    return the list.
```

```
"""
entries = []
for uri in feeds:
    print "Polling %s" % uri
    try:
        # Get the notes remembered for this feed.
        feed_data = feed_db.get(uri, {})
        last_poll = feed_data.get('last_poll', None)
        etag      = feed_data.get('etag', None)
        modified  = feed_data.get('modified', None)
```

This getNewFeedEntries() function starts off much like the previous getFeedEntries() function, creating an empty list for entries and iterating through the list of subscribed feeds passed in as a parameter.

However, what it does next is new. The feed database (passed in as a parameter named feed_db) is used, via the get() function, to retrieve a record stored using the feed's URI as a key. The get() function allows for a default value to be supplied, so if there is not yet a record for this feed, an empty dictionary is used for the feed's record. This default value will be used, for example, when a newly subscribed feed is polled for the first time—or when you run this new aggregator for the first time with an entirely empty feed database.

From this dictionary record, the code attempts to extract three values:

- last_poll—This is the UNIX epoch time (in seconds since January 1, 1970) when this feed was last polled for entries.

- etag—The ETag for a feed, used in facilitating conditional HTTP GET, is supplied in HTTP headers by the Web server from which the feed was downloaded.

- modified—Similar in use for conditional HTTP GET to the ETag, some Web servers supply a literal last-modified datestamp in HTTP headers for resources accessed.

For each of these, a default value of None is used in case the record doesn't contain one or more of these (or in case it's a brand-new empty record).

Moving on, you can continue writing getNewFeedEntries() and use these pieces of information, as shown in Listing 3-5.

Listing 3-5: agg02_pollsubs.py Modifications (Part 5 of 8)

```
        # Check to see whether it's time to poll this feed yet.
        if last_poll and (time.time() - last_poll) < 3600:
            print "\tFeed already polled within the last hour."

        else:
```

Continued

Listing 3-5 *(continued)*

```
# Fetch the feed using the ETag and Last-Modified
# notes.
feed_data = feedparser.parse(uri, etag=etag,
                                  modified=modified)

# If the feed HTTP status is 304, there was no change.
if feed_data.status == 304:
    print "\tFeed unchanged."
```

The code in Listing 3-5 first checks if there was a value retrieved for the feed's last-polled date-stamp. If so, it compares the value against the present time to see if an hour has passed since the last poll. (Note that an hour is 3,600 seconds, being the result of 60 seconds multiplied by 60 minutes.) It's kind of an established convention among feed publishers and aggregator authors to refrain from checking feeds more than once per hour, so this code enforces that convention.

But, if the feed's last poll was more than an hour ago, you can poll the feed again using the feedparser module. This works much like as in the previous incarnation of your aggregator, but this time the etag and modified values retrieved from the feed database are passed in as named parameters. This causes the feedparser to supply these values (if they're not None) as HTTP headers named ETag and Last-Modified to the Web server from which it will download the feed data.

The consequence of using the ETag and Last-Modified headers is that the Web server may report that the feed you're trying to download hasn't changed since the last time it issued the given values for ETag and/or Last-Modified. This is part of conditional HTTP GET, and will save time and bandwidth, because the feed data will not be transferred when this occurs. You can check for this outcome by looking at the status property in the feedparser data. This is what the final conditional of Listing 3-5 does. If the HTTP status code from the Web server is 304 (which stands for "Not Modified"), a message is printed and nothing further is done to process this feed.

 Many other status codes are used by Web servers, some of which have additional significance for feed consumption, such as notifying you that a given feed has been permanently moved (301 Moved Permanently) or is gone entirely (410 Gone). If you want to look into these status codes, perhaps to enhance your aggregator's maintenance of subscriptions, check out this list of HTTP status codes:

```
http://www.w3.org/Protocols/rfc2616/rfc2616-sec10.html
```

Next, you can continue with Listing 3-6 and write the new feed data-processing code.

Listing 3-6: agg02_pollsubs.py Modifications (Part 6 of 8)

```
    else:
        new_entries = 0

        for entry_data in feed_data.entries:

            # Wrap the entry data and get a hash for
            # the entry.
            entry = EntryWrapper(feed_data, entry_data)
            hash  = entry.hash()

            # If the hash for this entry is found in
            # the DB, it's not new.
            if entry_db.has_key(hash): continue

            # Flag entry as seen with the hash key,
            # append to list of new entries.
            entry_db[hash] = 1
            entries.append(entry)
            new_entries += 1

        print "\tFound %s new entries" % new_entries
```

First note that Listing 3-6 starts off with an `else` statement, continuing from the previous conditional, which checked whether the feed had been reported modified by the Web server.

A new variable is introduced, named `new_entries`. This will maintain a count of new entries found for a status message printed at the end of processing a feed. Next, the code begins iterating through feeds found in the feed. In the old `getFeedEntries()` function, all of this was bundled up in a one-line formulation, but here things get a bit more complex, so it's better to spread this out over a few more lines for clarity.

Each entry is wrapped in an `EntryWrapper` object, and a new method named `hash()` is called, which is defined shortly. The `hash()` method examines values found in the feed entry and produces a unique string for this entry. If any of these values in the entry change, this hash changes, thus providing a convenient way to tell whether a particular entry has been seen before.

This hash value is then used to check against the entry database using its `has_key()` method. If this entry has been seen before, there will be a record in the entry database corresponding to this hash key. If the entry database does contain this hash, you can conclude that the entry has been seen, and skip further processing.

However, if this entry has *not* been seen before, flag it in the entry database as having been seen, append it to the list of new entries, and increment the new entry counter. Then, after all feed entries have been processed, print a status message reporting how many new entries were seen.

After this, you can wrap up the getNewFeedEntries() function with the code in Listing 3-7.

Listing 3-7: agg02_pollsubs.py Modifications (Part 7 of 8)

```
        # Finally, update the notes remembered for this feed.
        feed_db[uri] = {
            'last_poll' : time.time(),
            'etag'      : feed_data.get('etag', None),
            'modified'  : feed_data.get('modified', None)
        }

    except:
        raise
        print "Problem polling %s" % uri

entries.sort()
return entries
```

With the processing of entries done for the current feed, you can update the feed database with the latest values for last_poll, etag, and modified, using the current time and the feed-parser's results for ETag and Last-Modified headers, respectively. The shelve module allows you to access the feed database just like a normal Python dictionary, storing a new dictionary containing the record values keyed on the feed's URI. Going full circle here, this database update allows the program to retrieve these values during the next program run.

The remainder of this function is just like getFeedEntries(): Finish off the try/except statement trapping errors for the current feed. Then after all feeds are processed, sort the entries and return the list.

There's one last change you need to make, and that's adding the hash() function to your EntryWrapper class, shown in Listing 3-8.

Listing 3-8: agg02_pollsubs.py Modifications (Part 8 of 8)

```
def hash(self):
    """
    Come up with a unique identifier for this entry.
    """
    if self.entry.has_key('id'):
        return self.entry['id']
    else:
        m = md5.md5()
        for k in ('title', 'link', 'issued', 'modified',
                  'description'):
            m.update(self.entry.get(k,'').encode(UNICODE_ENC))
        return m.hexdigest()
```

Again, although the order doesn't matter, you can tack this new method onto the end of the `EntryWrapper` class definition, after the definition of the `__getitem__()` method.

This method starts by checking whether this entry has a property named `id`. There have been efforts in both the RSS and Atom camps toward including unique identifiers in feed entries—with the `<guid>` element in RSS and the `<id>` element in Atom used to supply the value. In an effort to normalize access to data from both RSS and Atom feeds, the `feedparser` module makes both the `<guid>` and `<id>` tags available in the `id` property of feed entries.

On the Web You can read about the `<guid>` element in the RSS 2.0 specification here:

```
http://blogs.law.harvard.edu/tech/
rss#ltguidgtSubelementOfLtitemgt
```

Alternately, you can check out the details of Atom's `<id>` element here:

```
http://www.mnot.net/drafts/draft-nottingham-atom-
format-02.html#rfc.section.4.13.5
```

Also, look here for some good further discussion about unique IDs in Atom feed entries:

```
http://diveintomark.org/archives/2004/05/28/
howto-atom-id
```

The basic idea in both RSS and Atom is that these elements provide a globally unique identifier for a particular feed entry, meaning that the value found here should be different for any entry in any feed. No two feeds should contain entries with identical values here, unless the feeds actually happen to both include the same item (such as in the case of topical feeds containing subsets of a larger body of entries).

Unfortunately, the idea of a globally unique identifier is relatively new in feed format specifications, so you're very likely to encounter feeds that don't include this value. In this case, the code switches to an alternate (admittedly "hackish") approach using the `md5` module.

This code starts by creating a new `md5()` object using the `md5` module. It then iterates through a few feed entry properties, using the `md5` object's `update()` method to feed it new data. The approach used to extract each property from the feed entry results in an empty string if the property is missing, and ensures that any Unicode data is encoded properly.

Finally, the result of the `md5` object's `hexdigest()` method is returned. The `hexdigest()` method processes all the data in the order it was supplied via the `update()` method and generates a string of hexadecimal digits representing a unique "fingerprint" value for the data. The idea in using this approach is that, should any of the specified data in an entry change (that is, the title, link, issued date, modified data, or description), a different value will be returned by the `hash()` function.

On the Web More details about the `md5` module in Python are available here:

```
http://docs.python.org/lib/module-md5.html
```

Also, you can find a description of the `md5` algorithm itself here:

```
http://www.faqs.org/rfcs/rfc1321.html
```

This implementation of hash() works as a practical compromise based on what you'll find in existing feeds using a variety of feed formats and versions and should perform well enough. It tries to honor the unique identifiers used by feeds that offer them, whereas trying an alternate approach for those that do not.

You may want to play with the list of entry properties included in creating the md5 hash, if it seems like your aggregator is repeating items. Removing the description property, for example, causes the aggregator to ignore any small changes made to feed entries (for example, through the course of a series of small edits made by a blog author). Or, sometimes, entry descriptions contain a count of the number of comments a blog posting has received, so you might see the same entry appear over and over again, just because that count has changed.

On the other hand, some aggregators pay attention only to the title of a feed entry, and so they sometimes miss new entries that might use the same title for a series of entries. So, as with any hack, this is an approximate solution. Your mileage may vary.

But, with that, you're finished with this round of changes to your aggregator. A sample program run might look like this:

```
# python agg02_pollsubs.py
Polling http://xml.metafilter.com/atom.xml
        Found 20 new entries
Polling http://rss.cnn.com/rss/cnn_topstories.rss
        Found 8 new entries
Polling http://www.nytimes.com/services/xml/rss/nyt/HomePage.xml
        Found 6 new entries
Polling http://rss.news.yahoo.com/rss/tech
        Found 12 new entries
Polling http://www.wired.com/news_drop/netcenter/netcenter.rdf
        Found 3 new entries
Polling http://www.decafbad.com/blog/atom.xml
        Found 15 new entries
Polling http://slashdot.org/index.rss
        Found 10 new entries
```

And, if you look in the current directory, you should have a new file named something like aggregator-20050130-163916.html, based on whatever the time was when you ran the aggregator.

If you were to immediately run the program again, you should see something like the following:

```
# python agg02_pollsubs.py
Polling http://xml.metafilter.com/atom.xml
        Feed already polled within the last hour.
Polling http://rss.cnn.com/rss/cnn_topstories.rss
        Feed already polled within the last hour.
Polling http://www.nytimes.com/services/xml/rss/nyt/HomePage.xml
        Feed already polled within the last hour.
Polling http://rss.news.yahoo.com/rss/tech
        Feed already polled within the last hour.
Polling http://www.wired.com/news_drop/netcenter/netcenter.rdf
        Feed already polled within the last hour.
```

```
Polling http://www.decafbad.com/blog/atom.xml
        Feed already polled within the last hour.
Polling http://slashdot.org/index.rss
        Feed already polled within the last hour.
```

Notice that the once-per-hour limit has kicked in, and none of these feeds will have been polled because they have just been checked. Also, because no new entries were found at all, there will be no new HTML page of entries produced by this session. Wait an hour or so, run the program again, and you should see something like this:

```
$ python agg02_pollsubs.py
Polling http://xml.metafilter.com/atom.xml
        Found 2 new entries
Polling http://rss.cnn.com/rss/cnn_topstories.rss
        Found 5 new entries
Polling http://www.nytimes.com/services/xml/rss/nyt/HomePage.xml
        Found 0 new entries
Polling http://rss.news.yahoo.com/rss/tech
        Found 2 new entries
Polling http://www.wired.com/news_drop/netcenter/netcenter.rdf
        Found 0 new entries
Polling http://www.decafbad.com/blog/atom.xml
        Feed unchanged.
Polling http://slashdot.org/index.rss
        Found 2 new entries
```

Here, you'll see a mix of responses. For some feeds, their respective Web servers will have reported the feeds as having been unchanged since their last access, according to the headers produced from the feed database record. Other feeds' servers may not support conditional HTTP GET, and so those feeds will be downloaded, but may result in zero new entries once they've been processed. And, because there were new entries found, you'll have a new HTML file, with a new datestamp, such as aggregator-20050130-192009.html.

You can use this new revision of the aggregator just like the old one, running it manually or by a scheduled task or cron job, and it will periodically generate a series of timestamped HTML pages, each with fresh updates from all of your subscribed feeds.

Creating a Module to Share Reusable Aggregator Parts

At this point, you're up to two revisions of your aggregator, and, although they're a bit different with respect to each other, they have a lot of parts in common. However, the feed aggregators you're going to be building from here on out will have even more in common. You have the basics of simple feed aggregation covered in agg02_pollsubs.py, so maybe it's time you look into a better way to reuse that code than crude copy-and-paste or file duplication.

So, you're going to duplicate things one more time. Make a copy of agg02_pollsubs.py and name it agglib.py. This is going to be the core module behind your programs for the remainder of this part of the book.

Technically, you're finished now: `agglib.py` is a full-fledged, reusable module without any further modification. However, it has a bit of left-over baggage from its former life as a program. In particular, it has some configuration constants and a vestigal `main()` function that you won't necessarily be using again. Also, there's the `writeAggregatorPage()` function and the string template constants whose references have been hardcoded into its implementation—namely, `DATE_HDR_TMPL`, `FEED_HDR_TMPL`, `ENTRY_TMPL`, and `PAGE_TMPL`.

So, to polish up `agglib.py` a little, you want to do two things:

- Strip out the parts that were specific to `agg02_pollsubs.py` (specifically the `main()` function and all configuration constants).

- Rework the `writeAggregatorPage()` function a tad so that its templates are no longer taken from hard-coded references to configuration constants.

This first part is easy—just delete everything from the end of the module's initial docstring down to the definition of the `openDBs()` function. When you're finished, the beginning of your module should look something like Listing 3-9.

Listing 3-9: agglib.py Preamble

```
#!/usr/bin/env python
"""
agglib.py
A reusable module library of things useful for feed aggregators.
"""
import sys, time, feedparser, shelve, md5, time

UNICODE_ENC = "utf-8"

def openDBs(feed_db_fn, entry_db_fn):
```

Now, Listing 3-9 ends just as the definition for `openDBs()` begins, but that's just to show that the chunk of code (the initial constants and the `main()` function) that used to live between the module `imports` and the `openDBs()` function are gone now, with one exception: You can leave the `UNICODE_ENC` constant in this module, because it's something worth leaving common throughout this module and won't need to change between programs in the coming chapters. Along with that, the `openDBs()` function and everything else after it should still be present after this first edit.

The next step in your clean-up operation is to make the `writeAggregatorPage()` function reusable. Take a look at Listing 3-10 to see what changes you need to make. Compare this with the original definition of `writeAggregatorPage()` in `agg02_pollsubs.py` from Listing 2-23.

The only major change shown in Listing 3-10 is that the templates (that is, date_hdr_tmpl, feed_hdr_tmpl, entry_tmpl, and page_tmpl) are no longer constants; they're parameters. To make this change, you can just add the new parameters to the list after the name of the function, and change all their references within the function to lowercase.

Finally, past the end of the writeAggregatorPage() function, clear out the rest of the module that contains the string template constants whose necessity you just obviated. Once you're all finished with that, you're left with a pretty clean module containing a collection of functions, and one class, which you'll be able to use and refine for the next few generations of aggregators you build.

Listing 3-10: agglib.py, writeAggregatorPage() Revised

```
def writeAggregatorPage(entries, out_fn, date_hdr_tmpl, feed_hdr_tmpl,
        entry_tmpl, page_tmpl):
    """
    Given a list of entries and an output filename, use templates to
    Compose an aggregate page from the feeds and write to the file.
    """
    out, curr_day, curr_feed = [], None, None

    for e in entries:
        # If this entry's date is not the current running day, change
        # the current day and add a date header to the page output.
        if e['date'] != curr_day:
            curr_day = e['date']
            out.append(date_hdr_tmpl % curr_day)

            # Oh yeah, and output a reminder of the current feed
            # after the day header if it hasn't changed.
            if e.feed.title == curr_feed:
                out.append(feed_hdr_tmpl % e)

        # If this entry's feed isn't the current running feed, change
        # the current feed and add a feed header to the page output.
        if e.feed.title != curr_feed:
            curr_feed = e.feed.title
            out.append(feed_hdr_tmpl % e)

        # Add the entry to the page output.
        out.append(entry_tmpl % e)

    # Concatenate all the page output collected, fill the page
    # template, and write the result to the output file.
    open(out_fn, "w").write(page_tmpl % "".join(out))
```

Emailing Aggregated Reports of New Items

So, you have your aggregator producing regular reports of just the new items found in feeds. Wouldn't it be nice if it told you when new items were available? After your last batch of tweaks, the program was able to fill up a directory with datestamped HTML pages that you can view in your browser, but you have to remember to view them, and you have to remember where you left off reading in order to know which of the report files themselves are new.

Well, Python just happens to come with a rich set of modules to construct and send email messages. To get started with this next batch of tweaks, start a new file in your editor and call it agg03_emailsubs.py. The beginning of this new program is shown in Listing 3-11.

Listing 3-11: agg03_emailsubs.py (Part 1 of 5)

```
#!/usr/bin/env python
"""
agg03_emailsubs.py

Poll subscriptions and email an aggregate HTML page.
"""
import sys, time, feedparser, shelve, md5, time

from agglib import UNICODE_ENC, openDBs, closeDBs
from agglib import getNewFeedEntries, writeAggregatorPage

import smtplib
from email.MIMEMultipart import MIMEMultipart
from email.MIMEText import MIMEText

FROM_ADDR    = "you@your-address.com"
TO_ADDR      = "you@your-address.com"
SUBJECT      = "New news for you!"
SMTP_HOST    = "localhost"

FEEDS_FN     = "feeds.txt"
HTML_FN      = "aggregator-%s.html"
UNICODE_ENC  = "utf-8"

FEED_DB_FN   = "feeds_db"
ENTRY_DB_FN  = "entry_seen_db"
```

Again, most of Listing 3-11 should look like the familiar preamble to your aggregator. Some standard Python modules are imported, as well as some things you moved into agglib in the last part. Some new Python modules are being brought into play, though:

- `smtplib`—This module defines classes and functions that can be used to communicate with SMTP email servers.

- `email.MIMEText`—This module provides encapsulation for individual parts of a MIME-Multipart message.

- `email.MIMEMultipart`—Email messages containing multiple parts (such as a plain text and HTML version) are encapsulated as a MIME-Multipart message. This module helps build these messages.

Next, some configuration constants define the "From" address to be used in email messages, the address to which the aggregator output should be sent, the subject to use, and, finally, the address to the outgoing SMTP email server to use.

In Listing 3-11, the SMTP server is set to `localhost`, but you may not have an SMTP server available at that address. If you don't know the address to your SMTP server, you may want to check in your favorite email client's preferences to see what you're using there for an outgoing email server with your ISP. The same setting should work here.

Caution

Depending on your ISP's settings on its SMTP server—or your configuration if you run your own main server—you may need to tweak the From and To addresses in email sent from this program, in order to actually get the outgoing mail accepted by the SMTP server, as well as to get it past junk mail filters in your email client. This is another spot where your mileage may vary. For the most part, though, if you use the same outgoing SMTP server as you normally use for email, as well as your own email address for both the From and To addresses, you should be okay.

Your next addition is a `main()` function, as shown in Listing 3-12.

Listing 3-12: agg03_emailsubs.py (Part 2 of 5)

```python
def main():
    """
    Poll subscribed feeds and produce aggregator page.
    """
    feed_db, entry_db = openDBs(FEED_DB_FN, ENTRY_DB_FN)

    feeds   = [ x.strip() for x in open(FEEDS_FN, "r").readlines() ]

    entries = getNewFeedEntries(feeds, feed_db, entry_db)

    if len(entries) > 0:
        out_fn = HTML_FN % time.strftime("%Y%m%d-%H%M%S")
        writeAggregatorPage(entries, out_fn,
            DATE_HDR_TMPL, FEED_HDR_TMPL,
            ENTRY_TMPL, PAGE_TMPL)
        emailAggregatorPage(FROM_ADDR, TO_ADDR, SUBJECT, SMTP_HOST,
            out_fn)

    closeDBs(feed_db, entry_db)
```

The `main()` function defined in Listing 3-12 looks much like the one you used for `agg02_pollsubs.py` in Listing 3-2. There are two main differences here, though:

- `writeAggregatorPage()` is now called with the template constants as parameters, as per revisions made in `agglib`.

- A new function call, to `emailAggregatorPage()`, is introduced.

The `emailAggregatorPage()` function will send out the HTML page generated by `writeAggregatorPage()` as an email. You can start defining it with the code in Listing 3-13.

Listing 3-13: agg03_emailsubs.py (Part 3 of 5)

```
def emailAggregatorPage(from_addr, to_addr, subj, smtp_host, out_fn):
    """
    Read in the HTML page produced by an aggregator run, construct a
    MIME-Multipart email message with the HTML attached, and send it
    off with the given from, to, and subject headers using the
    specified SMTP mail server.
    """
    # Begin building the email message.
    msg = MIMEMultipart()
    msg['To']      = to_addr
    msg['From']    = from_addr
    msg['Subject'] = subj
    msg.preamble   = "You need a MIME-aware mail reader.\n"
    msg.epilogue   = ""
```

The new `emailAggregatorPage()` function definition in Listing 3-13 starts off with the usual parameter list and docstring describing its purpose. Then, it starts constructing a MIME-Multipart message using a `MIMEMultipart` object. The "To," "From," and "Subject" message header fields are filled out from parameter values, and a throwaway preamble and epilogue are set for the message. Your email client shouldn't end up seeing these if it can properly handle MIME-Multipart, as most modern email programs can.

 More details about `MIMEMultipart` objects, as well as `MIMEText` objects, are available here:

> `http://www.python.org/doc/2.4/lib/node569.html`

This code builds the overall shell for your multipart email message. Continuing with the function, you can build the individual parts of the message and send off the whole thing with Listing 3-14.

Listing 3-14: agg03_emailsubs.py (Part 4 of 5)

```
# Generate a plain text alternative part.
plain_text = """
This email contains entries from your subscribed feeds in HTML.
"""
part = MIMEText(plain_text, "plain", UNICODE_ENC)
msg.attach(part)

# Generate the aggregate HTML page, read in the HTML data,
# attach it
# as another part of the email message.
html_text = open(out_fn).read()
part = MIMEText(html_text, "html", UNICODE_ENC)
msg.attach(part)

# Finally, send the whole thing off as an email message.
print "Sending email '%s' to '%s'" % (subj, to_addr)
s = smtplib.SMTP(smtp_host)
s.sendmail(from_addr, to_addr, msg.as_string())
s.close()
```

First, the code in Listing 3-14 builds a simple plain text part for the email message. Because the interesting content is going to be in the HTML part, this just contains a simple message saying as much. A MIMEText object is created using the text message, with a MIME content-type of text/plain (the "text" part is implied) and with a Unicode encoding specified at the beginning of the program.

Next, the code builds the HTML part of the email message. It opens up and reads in the HTML presumably produced beforehand by the writeAggregatorHTML() method. The content read in from this file is then used to create another MIMEText object, this time with a content-type of text/html and, again, with the appropriate Unicode encoding.

And lastly, smtplib is used to fire up a connection to the outgoing SMTP mail server, and the whole MIME-Multipart message is sent off as a string to the given destination email address. After that, the connection is closed, and the function definition is finished.

Now, to finish off this program, Listing 3-15 provides the presentation templates used to produce the email messages.

Listing 3-15: agg03_emailsubs.py (Part 5 of 5)

```
# Presentation templates for output follow:

DATE_HDR_TMPL = """
    <h1 class="dateheader">%s</h1>
"""
```

Continued

Listing 3-15 *(continued)*

```
FEED_HDR_TMPL = """
    <h2 class="feedheader"><a href="%(feed.link)s">%(feed.title)s</a></h2>
"""

ENTRY_TMPL = """
    <div class="feedentry">
        <div class="entryheader">
            <span class="entrytime">%(time)s</span>:
            <a class="entrylink" href="%(entry.link)s">%(entry.title)s</a>
        </div>
        <div class="entrysummary">
            %(entry.summary)s
            <hr>
            %(content)s
        </div>
    </div>
"""

PAGE_TMPL = """
<html>
    <body>
        <h1 class="pageheader">Feed aggregator #1</h1>
        %s
    </body>
</html>
"""


if __name__ == "__main__": main()
```

You may notice that Listing 3-15 is pretty much identical to Listings 2-26 and 2-27 from agg01_pollsubs.py. The only thing missing here are all the CSS styles definitions from Listing 2-27 in the HTML <head/> tag. They're omitted here for the sake of brevity, but you could just go ahead and copy these templates over from agg01_pollsubs.py. Of course, while you're copying them over, you may want to tweak things a bit, because these templates are intended to be used in building an HTML email message—so you may want to format it differently.

And again, don't forget the __name__ trick at the end of the program that calls the main() function—it needs to be at the end, so that everything else gets defined by the time main() is called.

Admittedly, this implementation is a bit of a hack in that it opens up and reads a file that you just wrote to disk. It might seem more efficient to skip the generation of a file and just send the generated HTML straight off as an email. However, this keeps the existing behavior pretty useful, and it makes for an easier addition to the program, so it is left as an exercise for you to figure out how to modify this program and agglib if you want to remove the middleman of a generated file and just handle all the HTML in email.

Running this new program will look much like the previous one:

```
$ python agg03_emailsubs.py
Polling http://xml.metafilter.com/atom.xml
        Found 1 new entries
Polling http://rss.cnn.com/rss/cnn_topstories.rss
        Found 7 new entries
Polling http://www.nytimes.com/services/xml/rss/nyt/HomePage.xml
        Found 1 new entries
Polling http://rss.news.yahoo.com/rss/tech
        Found 0 new entries
Polling http://www.wired.com/news_drop/netcenter/netcenter.rdf
        Found 2 new entries
Polling http://www.decafbad.com/blog/atom.xml
        Feed unchanged.
Polling http://slashdot.org/index.rss
        Found 4 new entries
Sending HTML email to l.m.orchard@gmail.com
```

Note that if no new entries are found (whether due to conditional HTTP GET or all entries having been seen before), no email will be sent out, just as no new HTML file will be written to disk. Once this program run has completed, you should shortly receive a new email message that contains the same HTML content as you've been viewing in your browser from files. Figure 3-1 shows an example of this, as viewed in the Thunderbird mail client.

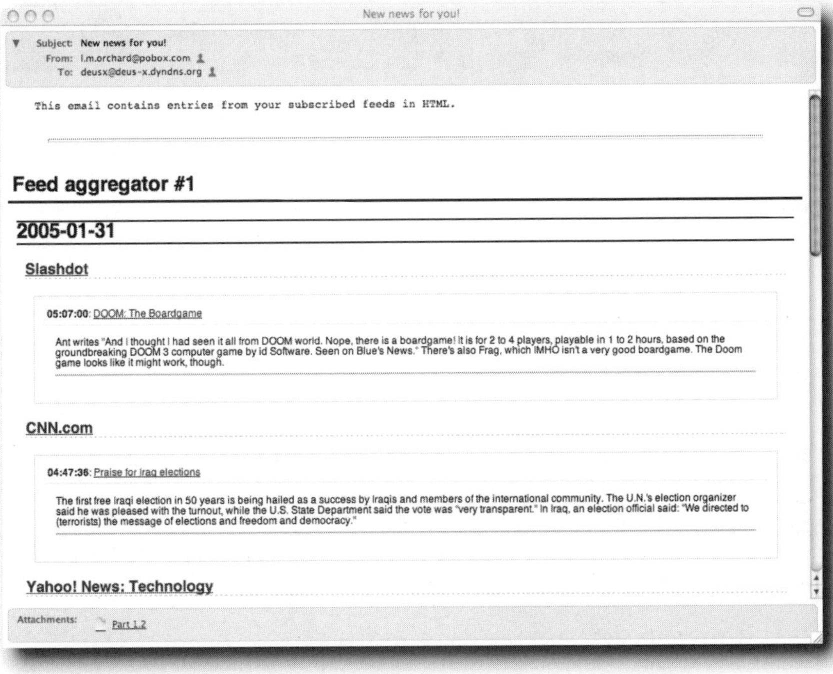

FIGURE 3-1: Aggregated feed entries received as an email message in Mozilla Thunderbird

And with that, this iteration of your aggregator is complete. If you run it on a schedule, you'll start seeing regular updates showing up in your email inbox like a personalized newsletter, driven from your own chosen set of feeds subscriptions.

Emailing New Items as Individual Messages

Making the switch from manually checking for new HTML pages generated by your aggregator to receiving them automatically in your email inbox is a good step forward. Still, though, you're not quite using all the tools your inbox has available with all the feed entries clumped together in aggregate newsletter-like mail messages. The next stage in your aggregator evolution is to move away from building aggregated reports and toward firing off every new entry as it arrives as its own separate email message.

Depending on the number of feeds to which you've subscribed, this could potentially generate a large volume of email coming your way. However, that's not necessarily a bad thing. With each new feed entry split off into its own separate message, you can now use all of the tools your email client offers for managing email—such as filtering messages into folders, marking messages as read, and throwing messages into the trash. As email messages, you can sort, search, and archive feed entries—which are all things that static HTML aggregate reports can't give you.

To get started with this next program, start a new file named agg04_emailsubs.py and check out Listing 3-16 for the preamble to this program.

> **Listing 3-16:** agg04_emailsubs.py (Part 1 of 5)

```
#!/usr/bin/env python
"""
agg04_emailsubs.py

Poll subscriptions and email each new entry as a separate message.
"""
import sys, time, feedparser, shelve, md5, time

from agglib import UNICODE_ENC, openDBs, closeDBs
from agglib import getNewFeedEntries, writeAggregatorPage

import smtplib
from email.MIMEText import MIMEText
from email.MIMEMultipart import MIMEMultipart

FROM_ADDR    = "you@your-address.com"
TO_ADDR      = "you@your-address.com"
SUBJECT      = "[agg04] %(feed.title)s :: %(entry.title)s"
SMTP_HOST    = "localhost"

FEEDS_FN     = "feeds.txt"
UNICODE_ENC  = "utf-8"
```

```
FEED_DB_FN  = "feeds_db"
ENTRY_DB_FN = "entry_seen_db"
```

Everything in Listing 3-16 is the same as in the previous program, with a change to the docstring describing the new program. The one significant change is to the SUBJECT configuration constant. It's now a template string, intended to be filled by values from an EntryWrapper object—namely a feed title and entry title. This string customizes the subject line generated for each feed entry as it's emailed to you, so you can tailor it however you like and insert any additional details from a feed entry.

Next, check out Listing 3-17 for a brief change to your main() function.

Listing 3-17: agg04_emailsubs.py (Part 2 of 5)

```
def main():
    """
    Poll subscribed feeds and email out entries.
    """
    feed_db, entry_db = openDBs(FEED_DB_FN, ENTRY_DB_FN)

    feeds   = [ x.strip() for x in open(FEEDS_FN, "r").readlines() ]

    entries = getNewFeedEntries(feeds, feed_db, entry_db)

    if len(entries) > 0:
        emailEntries(FROM_ADDR, TO_ADDR, SUBJECT, SMTP_HOST, entries)

    closeDBs(feed_db, entry_db)
```

This code in Listing 3-17 replaces the filename generation and the writeAggregatorPage() and emailAggregatorPage() function calls performed in the previous main() function. Now, instead of a single file being generated and then emailed off, the file generation step is skipped altogether and every individual message is shipped off as its own email message.

After this, you can work on defining the emailEntries() function itself, starting with the code in Listing 3-18.

Listing 3-18: agg04_emailsubs.py (Part 3 of 5)

```
def emailEntries(from_addr, to_addr, subj, smtp_host, entries):
    """
    Given a from address, to address, a subject template, SMTP host,
    and a list of entries, construct an email message via template for
    each entry and send it off using the given header values.
```

Continued

Listing 3-18 *(continued)*

```
"""
for entry in entries:

    # Build a subject line for the current feed entry.
    curr_subj = subj % entry

    # Begin building the email message.
    msg = MIMEMultipart()
    msg['To']       = to_addr
    msg['From']     = from_addr
    msg['Subject']  = curr_subj
    msg.preamble    = "You should not see this.\n"
    msg.epilogue    = ""

    # Generate a plain text alternative part.
    plain_text = """
This email contains an entry from your feeds in HTML.
"""
    part = MIMEText(plain_text, "plain", UNICODE_ENC)
    msg.attach(part)
```

In this new function definition for `emailEntries()`, things look an awful lot like the previous `emailAggregatorPage()` function. In fact, if you're careful, you could copy and paste much of it over. This function starts off with a parameter list and a docstring, and begins iterating through the entries passed to it. For each entry, it builds a new subject line by filling in a subject header template passed in as a parameter.

Then, it creates the MIME-Multipart message shell with the usual parts, including the "To" and "From" email addresses, the subject line, and the throwaway preamble and epilogue values. And, as in the previous email code, it builds and attaches a simple plain text message part referring to the HTML content in the next attachment.

Now, you wrap up this function by borrowing a little code from `writeAggregatorPage()` to generate the HTML content for this email, as shown in Listing 3-19.

Listing 3-19: agg04_emailsubs.py (Part 4 of 5)

```
    # Generate the aggregate HTML page, read in the HTML data,
    # attach it as another part of the email message.
    out = []
    out.append(FEED_HDR_TMPL % entry)
    out.append(ENTRY_TMPL % entry)
    html_text = PAGE_TMPL % "".join(out)
    part = MIMEText(html_text, "html", UNICODE_ENC)
    msg.attach(part)

    # Finally, send the whole thing off as an email message.
```

```
print "Sending email '%s' to '%s'" % (curr_subj, to_addr)
s = smtplib.SMTP(smtp_host)
s.sendmail(from_addr, to_addr, msg.as_string())
s.close()
```

Because you're just building HTML for a single feed entry, all of the logic involved in building a presentable aggregate page has disappeared. All that's left is the production via templates of an HTML document containing a feed header and the entry content, wrapped in a page shell template. This content is then used to create the second MIME attachment for the email, which is attached to the email message shell.

And, last but not least, a status message is printed and the completed email message is sent off to your chosen address.

This version of your aggregator is pretty much complete. There is one other thing you might want to do, and that's to revise the set of HTML templates used for generating the email messages. The original set may work just fine, although some simplification as shown in Listing 3-20 might be helpful.

Listing 3-20: agg04_emailsubs.py (Part 5 of 5)

```
FEED_HDR_TMPL = """
    <h2><a href="%(feed.link)s">%(feed.title)s</a></h2>
"""

ENTRY_TMPL = """
    <div>
        <div>
            <span>%(time)s</span>:
            <a href="%(entry.link)s">%(entry.title)s</a>
        </div>
        <div>
            %(entry.summary)s
            <hr>
            %(content)s
        </div>
    </div>
"""

PAGE_TMPL = """
<html>
    <body>
        %s
    </body>
</html>
"""

if __name__ == "__main__": main()
```

Depending on your email client, the CSS styles used in the original aggregator page may not show up or may not appear quite right. This is the part in the recipe where it says, "Salt to taste." Try out these templates and tweak until things appear as you'd like in your email client.

Firing up this version of your aggregator results in output not entirely unlike the previous incarnations, although you'll see some new messages as each email gets sent out:

```
# python agg04_emailsubs.py
Polling http://xml.metafilter.com/atom.xml
        Found 2 new entries
Polling http://rss.cnn.com/rss/cnn_topstories.rss
        Found 1 new entries
Polling http://news.bbc.co.uk/rss/front_page/rss091.xml
        Found 1 new entries
Polling http://www.nytimes.com/services/xml/rss/nyt/HomePage.xml
        Found 1 new entries
Polling http://rss.news.yahoo.com/rss/tech
        Found 0 new entries
Polling http://www.wired.com/news_drop/netcenter/netcenter.rdf
        Found 0 new entries
Polling http://www.decafbad.com/blog/atom.xml
        Found 0 new entries
Polling http://slashdot.org/index.rss
        Found 0 new entries

Sending email '[agg04] NYT > Home Page :: For Many Killed on a
Dark Day in Iraq, the Future Was Bright, and Near' to
'l.m.orchard@gmail.com'

Sending email '[agg04] CNN.com :: Jackson: Truth will vindicate
me' to 'l.m.orchard@gmail.com'

Sending email '[agg04] BBC News | News Front Page | World Edition
:: World leaders praise Iraqi poll' to 'l.m.orchard@gmail.com'

Sending email '[agg04] MetaFilter :: Movie-haulic?' to
'l.m.orchard@gmail.com'

Sending email '[agg04] MetaFilter :: Deity Smoking with Hand of
Squirrel' to 'l.m.orchard@gmail.com'
```

And then, once all of these emails have made it through the Internet ether to land in your inbox, things will look something like they do in Figure 3-2. Here is an inbox with a handful of messages received from the aggregator, and you can see how the subject lines are filled in and how Mozilla Thunderbird, in particular, handles the HTML.

From here, you can play with settings in your email client to figure out how to best manage this new flow of information into your inbox. You might want to play with various forms of subject line and templates for the email message content, along with setting up folders and filter rules to sort incoming feed entries to best suit your personal feed-reading style.

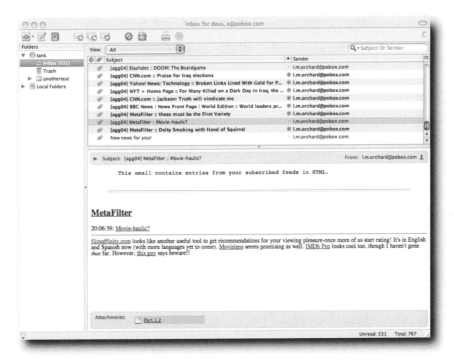

FIGURE 3-2: Individual feed entries received as email in Mozilla Thunderbird

Checking Out Other Options

This section provides other options you might want to explore.

Using rss2email

The rss2email program by Aaron Swartz is another approach to routing RSS and Atom feed items into your inbox. It's written in Python and is available here:

```
http://www.aaronsw.com/2002/rss2email/
```

The aggregator written in this chapter shares some features and simplicity with rss2email, but Aaron Swartz's code is more robust and is better at detecting and reporting errors that might come up in the process of aggregating and emailing feed entries. It also bundles in basic feed subscription-management features, usable from the command line.

Using Newspipe

Yet another feed-to-email bridge is called Newspipe, also implemented in Python, and available here from SourceForge:

```
http://newspipe.sourceforge.net/
```

Newspipe is a much fuller-featured aggregator than the one presented in this chapter. It uses the `feedparser` module to handle feeds, but it goes further to build in options to send individual messages or digests, detects and marks up changes to previously seen feed entries, and downloads images linked from entry content to bundle them into multipart attachments.

Using nntp//rss

Another alternative to managing feed entries in email is to receive them as Usenet newsgroups. The nntp//rss aggregator is a "Java-based bridge between RSS feeds and NNTP clients," found here on SourceForge:

`http://www.methodize.org/nntprss/`

For some people, handling the information flow from feeds may come more naturally within the interface of a Usenet newsreader, and nntp//rss does a good job of this by providing a miniature desktop NNTP server that provides access to the feeds it aggregates.

Summary

Now you have finished a few more revisions to your aggregator, having made it a little smarter in how it deals with feed changes and new entries. Trying out both the aggregate digest and individual message styles of routing feeds to your email inbox should start to give you a feel for what's possible in aggregating entries from RSS and Atom feeds, dealing with them as more than just lists of headlines displayed on Web pages.

In the next chapter, you get even more immediate access to feeds by trading your email inbox for your instant messaging buddy list. You see how to get news delivered to you directly as instant messages, as well as how to build a chatbot with a conversational interface to manage subscriptions and request feed entries on demand.

Adding Feeds to Your Buddy List

So far, your aggregator has been getting increasingly smart and personal. First, it learned how to fetch feeds and produce a composite page of fresh news. Then, you gave it a memory about what it had seen in feeds, so that it could tell new entries from old. And most recently, you gave it the ability to fill your email inbox with fresh feed content. Now it's time to get even more personal. In fact, in this chapter, you'll be able to add your feed aggregator to your Instant Messenger (IM) buddy list.

With the tweaks you make to your aggregator in this chapter, you build a simple chatbot (chat robot) that can send you headlines on two different IM networks. Communicating by instant messenger isn't as informationally dense as an HTML page or an email message, so you can't use it to follow as many feeds with this method. But, what an IM channel lacks in depth, it gains in immediacy and interactivity. You'll be able to create a conversational command interface, allowing you to manage subscriptions and get new headlines from feeds on demand, all from your IM client, from wherever you are.

Using an Instant Messenger Protocol

Quite a few IM networks have sprung up on the Internet, with varying degrees of popularity and hackability. For the purposes of this chapter, you're going to play with one of the original and most popular networks—AOL Instant Messenger—and one of the newest and most hackable networks—the Jabber instant messaging network.

Checking Out AOL Instant Messenger

AOL Instant Messenger (AIM) from America Online (AOL) is one of the most popular IM networks around today, having achieved that popularity by the availability of a desktop client as a free download and (more importantly) access to chat with all the online members of AOL itself. However, although free to use, the AIM network is indeed a proprietary, privately owned service, and thus subject to whatever decisions AOL chooses make with it.

Third-party interoperability with the AIM network has historically been a mixed bag. AIM is accessible via two protocols, named Talk to OSCAR (TOC) and Open System for Communication in Real Time (OSCAR). Specifications were publicly released for the TOC protocol early on in AIM's growth, and the company tolerated the creation of alternative AIM clients for the most part.

 You can check out the AOL specification for the TOC protocol for AIM here:

```
http://www.jamwt.com/Py-TOC/PROTOCOL
```

On the other hand, the track record for the newer and more fully featured OSCAR protocol has been less than welcoming for developers of IM clients and competing networks, because the company has introduced barriers time and again (at one point even requiring a checksum taken from the latest official AIM client binary as a key to access the network via OSCAR).

AOL's resistance to enabling competitors' unwanted inroads into their service is understandable, from a business perspective. However, this means that your freedom to tinker with access to AIM is not assured. But (as of this writing anyway) you still have access to the network via the TOC protocol—although occasionally this route into the network experiences outages for various reasons. But, TOC usually works, and supports the basics of instant messaging you need for this chapter, namely: logging in, sending instant messages, and receiving instant messages.

With all of these caveats in mind, there is a Python module by Jamie Turner called Py-TOC, which makes building AIM chatbots fairly painless. You can download it from this URL:

```
http://www.jamwt.com/Py-TOC/
```

This module has a lot of features to play with, and you may want to read up on the documentation and examples available, but you'll just be using the basics in this chapter. So, grab yourself a copy of Py-TOC—you'll be using it very shortly. You should be looking for a URL to a Python module file named `toc.py`. You can install this module according to the directions on the download page, or simply drop a copy into your project's working directory.

Checking Out Jabber

Jabber is the Open Source alternative to private IM networks. Although not nearly as popular as other IM systems, it is entirely open and free to use and has been formalized by the Internet Engineering Task Force (the group responsible for a great many of the protocols and standards making up the modern Internet). Rather than being hosted in a single company's server farm, Jabber is composed of an interlinked network of servers across many Internet hosts, to which applications such as desktop IM clients connect, all communicating using a streaming, extensible, XML-based protocol called XMPP.

 Read more about the Jabber family of technologies here:

```
http://www.jabber.org/about/overview.shtml
```

Jabber hasn't yet reached the maturity of AOL's instant messenger, and it certainly hasn't amassed anything near the same following, but it is immensely friendlier to tinkerers and third-party developers. In fact, rather than there being any single "official client" for Jabber, a large number of alternative clients of all shapes and sizes are available. And, where chatbots enjoy a dubious status in terms of tolerance on the AIM network, the development of person-to-machine and machine-to-machine conversation via Jabber is very much encouraged.

Although you can install and host your own Jabber server, for now you'll probably just want to visit the Jabber home page (`http://www.jabber.org`), download a client, and check out the list of public servers (`http://www.jabber.org/network/`) to register for an account. In fact, you'll want to register for two accounts if you don't have one of your own already— you'll need one for yourself, and another for the chatbot you're going to build.

A set of Python modules used to access the Jabber IM network, called Xmpppy, is available here on SourceForge:

```
http://xmpppy.sourceforge.net/
```

Take a look at the documentation and examples available for this project and download a copy for yourself. Again, you can follow the instructions in the Xmpppy documentation to get this package installed, or just unpack the archive (named `xmppd-0.2.tar.gz`), look inside the `xmpppy` directory, and copy or move the `xmpp` directory inside *that* into your project's working directory.

Supporting Multiple Instant Messaging Networks

Both the AIM and Jabber networks share a lot of features, which is not too hard to imagine because they're both implementations of instant messaging systems. So, taking just a tiny sub-set of those shared features—specifically connecting and logging in, and sending and receiving plain text messages—you can build a common interface to both of these services. Doing this will help keep your code clean and abstract, without any network-specific dependencies. And, if you feel like it later, you can even add support for other IM networks by following the same interface pattern.

Writing a Test Program for Instant Messenger Connections

You can write the code to handle interactions with the IM networks as a reusable module. To make things easier, build in a test function that will help run the code through its paces.

Create a new file in your editor named `imconn.py` and start it off with the code in Listing 4-1. The code provided there is the preamble for a new combination program and reusable module that will provide consistent interfaces to AIM and Jabber IM network connections. The program part implements an echo chatbot for testing. It connects to AIM and Jabber, and then echoes back every message sent to it. This should help you in getting this code to work properly, as well as showing an example of how to use the rest of the module.

Listing 4-1: imconn.py (Part 1 of 9)

```python
#!/usr/bin/env python
"""
imconn.py

This is a module providing IM server connections
with a built-in echo chatbot for testing.
"""
import sys, os, time, select
from toc import TocTalk
import xmpp

def main():
    AIM_USER, AIM_PASSWD = "someuser", "somepass"
    JAB_USER, JAB_PASSWD = "someuser@jabber.org", "somepass"

    connections = [
        AIMConnection(AIM_USER, AIM_PASSWD, echo),
        JabberConnection(JAB_USER, JAB_PASSWD, echo)
    ]

    for c in connections: c.connect()
    while 1:
        for c in connections: c.runOnce()
        time.sleep(0.1)

def echo(conn, from_nick, msg):
    print "%s | %s: %s" % (conn, from_nick, msg)
    conn.sendIM(from_nick, "Is there an echo in here? %s" % msg)
```

Shortly after the opening docstring describing imconn.py in Listing 4-1 is a series of module imports. You should be familiar with most of them. You've used the first few (sys, os, and time) in previous chapters, and the toc and xmpp modules come from Py-TOC and Xmpppy, respectively, discussed earlier in this chapter. The remaining new module, select, is used in the course of network communications, as is revealed in a little bit.

After the imports is the main() function definition. First thing in this function, a few constants are defined, which contain the username and password for the AIM and Jabber accounts to be used. Next, a list of IM service connection objects is created. The username and password parameters in the object constructor should speak for themselves, but the final parameter is expected to be a reference to a function that will be called when messages arrive on that particular IM service connection. Both of these are supplied with a reference to the echo() function defined at the end of Listing 4-1, which simply accepts a message, prints it to the console, and echoes a message containing the original.

With the connections defined, the `connect()` method is called on each, which establishes the network socket connection to each IM network and performs the respective login steps. Then, the main event loop begins. This simple event loop is a regular feature of networking and multitasking programs. It loops forever and with each step of that loop, every component in the system (the IM connections, in this case) is given a chance to take one trip through its event-handling logic. The loop sleeps for a tiny bit to go easy on CPU consumption, and then it all happens again—rinse, lather, repeat.

This event loop gives each of the IM connections a chance to check for any new communication on their respective network socket connections, to receive messages and other IM protocol events, and to fire off any handlers or callbacks that need firing. Because each `runOnce()` method is expected to run briefly and then return, an illusion of multitasking occurs between the IM connections as they take turns in the execution of the program.

Handling AOL Instant Messenger Connections

This next part, starting with Listing 4-2, is the beginning of an `AIMConnection()` class, which encapsulates connections to the AIM service.

Listing 4-2: imconn.py (Part 2 of 9)

```
class AIMConnection(TocTalk):
    """
    Encapsulate a connection to the AOL Instant Messenger service.
    """

    def __init__(self, user, passwd, recv_func=None):
        """
        Initialize the connection both as a TocTalk subclass.
        """
        TocTalk.__init__(self, user, passwd)
        self._recv_func = recv_func
        self._ready     = False
        self._debug     = 0
```

The `AIMConnection` class in Listing 4-2 starts off as a subclass of the `TocTalk` class, which is a part of the `toc` module. The first method definition is for `__init__()`, the object initializer. It accepts a username and password, as well as the aforementioned function reference to be used when messages are received. The username and password are handled by the `TocTalk` superclass initializer, the message handler is stashed away in an object property, a `_ready` flag is set to false, and a `_debug` property is set to 0. The `_debug` property is part of `TocTalk` and, if you want to see more chatter about what's happening with the AIM service, change this value to 1 or even 2 to unleash more spew.

Next up, you can set up the actual connection to the AIM service, as shown in Listing 4-3.

Listing 4-3: imconn.py (Part 3 of 9)

```
def connect(self):
    """
    Connect to the AIM service.  Overrides the behavior of the
    superclass by waiting until login has completed before
    returning.
    """
    # Start the connection & login process to AIM
    TocTalk.connect(self)

    # Set socket to non-blocking, to be multitasking-friendly
    self._socket.setblocking(0)

    # Process events until login is a success
    while not self._ready:
        self.runOnce()
        time.sleep(0.1)

def start(self):
    """
    This method gets called by the superclass when the connection
    is ready for use.
    """
    self._ready = True
```

Two methods are defined in Listing 4-3: connect() and start().

The first, connect(), overrides that of the parent class and is used to complete the process of connecting to and logging into the AIM service. This is done by calling the superclass's connect() method, which takes care of all the network sockets and starts the connection to AOL's servers.

The next thing that happens, though, is that the network socket is set to non-blocking mode. What this means is that, for example, when an attempt is made to read data from the network connection, the program doesn't wait in place for there to be actual data to read. Instead, if there's nothing to read, the attempt immediately returns empty-handed. This allows you to create network handling code that's friendly with the event loop multitasking in use in this module. You see how this works a little further on.

And last, in the connect() method, a sort of preliminary event loop is established, which ensures that this method processes AIM events and does not return until the login process has completed and the connection is actually ready to be used.

The second method defined, named start(), is called by the superclass once login has been completed at some point during the course of executing runOnce() in the event loop in connect(). The start() method sets the connection's _ready flag to True, thereby signalling that the connection is ready, thus ending the event loop in connect(). Did that all make sense? It's a little twisty, but it works.

Continuing, you can define the runOnce() method, as shown in Listing 4-4.

Listing 4-4: imconn.py (Part 4 of 9)

```
def runOnce(self):
    """
    Perform one processing step of AIM events.
    """
    # Check to see if there's anything to read on the AIM socket,
    # without blocking.  Return if there's nothing yet.
    r, w, e = select.select([self._socket],[],[],0)
    if len(r) > 0:
        # Try receiving an event from AIM, process it if found.
        event = self.recv_event()
        if event: self.handle_event(event)
```

This runOnce() method, defined in Listing 4-4, is where the non-blocking socket and the select module come into play. The original behavior of a method of the TocTalk superclass, named go(), implemented a little private event loop that never shared the CPU with any other task in the program—once called, it took over the entire program for itself. Instead, this new implementation for runOnce() just checks to see if there's any data waiting, and then performs only one event-handling step to read that data from the socket and perform the necessary steps to handle it.

To check whether data is available on the network socket, the select() function defined by the select module is used. (This is one of the imports mentioned earlier in this chapter.) There's a lot to this function, but you're only going to use a bit of it here. Basically, the select() function takes as parameters a list of readable sockets, a list of writable sockets, a list of sockets to check for errors, and a timeout. select() looks through each of these lists, checks the sockets, and then returns a list of sockets with data waiting to be read, a list of sockets available to be written, and a list of sockets that have experienced errors. It's kind of like a filter: You throw in a bunch of sockets, and you get some (or none) back.

 You can find the documentation for the socket and select modules here:

    http://docs.python.org/lib/module-socket.html
    http://docs.python.org/lib/module-select.html

If you'd like to read more about the use of select() in Python network programming, check out this HOWTO document:

    http://www.amk.ca/python/howto/sockets/

In the case of runOnce() method, select() is used to check if any event data is waiting to be handled by passing in a list consisting of just the one socket managed by this connection object. If there is any data waiting, the list of readable sockets will have a length greater than zero. In that case, the recv_event() and handle_event() methods from the TocTalk superclass are used to receive and handle, respectively, the waiting event data.

So, with all of this, runOnce() satisfies the requirement for a step in the program's top-level event loop: check briefly to see if something needs to be done, do it if need be, and then return control back to the event loop as quickly as possible.

And, last but not least, you can wrap up the AOLConnection class with some code to send and receive messages (finally!) in Listing 4-5.

Listing 4-5: imconn.py (Part 5 of 9)

```
def sendIM(self, to_name, msg):
    """
    Given an destination name and a message, send it off.
    """
    self.do_SEND_IM(to_name, msg)

def on_IM_IN(self, data):
    """
    This method is called by the superclass when a new IM arrives.
    Process the IM data and trigger the callback initialized with
    This connection.
    """
    try:
        # This is a quick-and-dirty way to get the first two
        # colon-delimited fields, in case the message itself
        # contains colons
        parts = data.split(':')
        from_nick = parts.pop(0)
        auto_resp = parts.pop(0)
        msg       = ":".join(parts)

    except IndexError:
        # Invalid message format!
        from_nick = None

    if from_nick and self._recv_func:
        self._recv_func(self, from_nick, self.strip_html(msg))
```

The sendIM() and on_IM_IN() methods defined in Listing 4-5 are pretty straightforward.

The sendIM() method just calls the TocTalk superclass method do_SEND_IM() with the destination screen name and the text message as parameters. This method simply serves to adhere to the ad hoc interface scheme devised for this module's connection classes.

The on_IM_IN() method is called by the superclass when incoming messages arrive. In this method, the raw AIM message data is passed in as the parameter data. This contains a colon-delimited string consisting of the screen name from whom the message came, whether or not the message was an auto-response (Y/N), and the message itself.

This data is split apart along the colons, taking care to preserve any colons found in the message part of the data, and then a check is made to see if a message reception callback was registered with this connection object. If so, that function is called, with the message author's screen name, and the message text after having first been stripped of all HTML tags using the strip_html() method of TocTalk. (AIM supports a subset of HTML formatting in messages, but you only want to deal with the plain text contents for this module.)

That concludes the AIMConnection class. It should be all ready to cover the basics of login and simple plain text messages.

Handling Jabber Network Connections

The definition of the JabberConnection class starts in Listing 4-6. You can continue inserting this code directly after the end of the previous class definition.

Listing 4-6: imconn.py (Part 6 of 9)

```
class JabberConnection:
    """
    Encapsulate a connection to the Jabber instant messenger service.
    """

    def __init__(self, user, passwd, recv_func=None):
        """
        Initialize the Jabber connection.
        """
        self._user      = user
        self._passwd    = passwd
        self._recv_func = recv_func
        self._jid       = xmpp.protocol.JID(self._user)
        self._cl        = xmpp.Client(self._jid.getDomain(),debug=[])
```

Whereas the AOLConnection was a subclass of a monolithic AIM connection handler class called TocTalk, things are reversed in the Jabber world via the Xmpppy package. In Listing 4-6, the JabberConnection initializer creates an instance of an XMPP Client connection in an object property, setting it up with an XMPP JID instance created from the passed-in username and password parameters.

Moving along, Listing 4-7 contains the code you need to implement the connect() method for the JabberConnection class.

Listing 4-7: inconn.py (Part 7 of 9)

```
def connect(self):
    """
    Connect to Jabber, authenticate, set up callbacks.
    """
    self._cl.connect()
    self._cl.auth(self._jid.getNode(), self._passwd)
    self._cl.RegisterHandler('message', self._messageCB)
    self._cl.RegisterHandler('presence', self._presenceCB)
    self._cl.sendInitPresence()
```

Listing 4-7 presents the connect() method definition, which consists of a series of method calls on the Jabber client connection instance. First, a connection is established and authentication is attempted. After that, two event handler callbacks are registered. The two event callbacks, _messageCB() and _presenceCB(), are methods to be defined soon in the JabberConnection class. Finishing up the connect() method is a call to sendInitPresence(), which causes the Jabber server to announce to all interested parties that this Jabber client has become present on the network.

Further definitions for the JabberConnection class continue in Listing 4-8.

Listing 4-8: inconn.py (Part 8 of 9)

```
def _presenceCB(self, conn, pres):
    """
    Respond to presence events.  If someone tries subscribing to
    this connection's presence, automatically respond by allowing
    it.
    """
    if pres.getType() == 'subscribe':
        self._cl.sendPresence(jid=pres.getFrom(), typ='subscribed')

def __del__(self):
    """
    Try cleaning up in the end by signalling that this connection
    is unavailable.
    """
    try: self._cl.sendPresence(typ="unavailable")
    except: pass
```

The first method defined in Listing 4-8 is called _presenceCB(), and was mentioned earlier in the connect() method as a callback used to handle XMPP Presence events. This is where you would handle reacting to notifications that other people and presences in whom and which you've registered interest have become present on the Jabber network.

This isn't all that useful for the purposes of the present project, but one thing that does need to happen here are acknowledgments that other clients can subscribe to this connection's presence announcements (in other words, allow people to add this connection to their buddy list). Basically, what happens is that when someone adds a Jabber ID to their buddy list (or roster), a "subscribe" event is sent out. The Jabber server relays this to the Jabber ID being subscribed, which then acknowledges the request with a "subscribed" event. The implementation of _presenceCB() makes this acknowledgment happen automatically.

The second method defined, called __del__(), tries to follow graceful XMPP behavior, announcing that the connection's presence has changed to "unavailable" just before the connection is disconnected and destroyed.

For more information on how presence and presence subscriptions work in XMPP check out this section of the XMPP protocol specification:

> http://www.xmpp.org/specs/rfc3921.html#rfc.section.5.1.6

Move on to Listing 4-9, where you'll find the JabberConnection versions of the runOnce(), sendIM(), and _messageCB() method definitions.

Listing 4-9: inconn.py (Part 9 of 9)

```python
def runOnce(self):
    """
    Process one event handler loop.
    """
    self._cl.Process(1)

def sendIM(self, to_name, msg):
    """
    Send off an instant message.
    """
    self._cl.send(xmpp.protocol.Message(to_name, msg))

def _messageCB(self, conn, mess):
    """
    Respond to message events.  This method calls the callback
    given at connection initialization to handle the message data.
    """
    if self._recv_func:
        user = mess.getFrom().getStripped()
        text = mess.getBody()
        self._recv_func(self, user, text)

if __name__ == "__main__": main()
```

Unlike the one seen in `AIMConnection`, `JabberConnection`'s `runOnce()` method definition in Listing 4-9 is short and sweet. Unlike the `TocTalk` class from Py-TOC, `Client` objects in the Xmpppy package are already built to accommodate an event loop with the `Process()` method.

And like the `sendIM()` method from `AIMConnection`, the one in `JabberConnection` is a pretty simple call made to conform to the module's ad hoc interface scheme. This implementation passes an XMPP `Message` instance created on-the-fly to the `Client`'s `send()` method.

And, as mentioned earlier in the `connect()` method definition, the `_messageCB()` method definition handles incoming messages as a callback from the `Client` object. If a message reception handler had been passed in when the connection was initialized, this function is called with the data from the incoming XMPP `Message`. The origin user ID is stripped of all extra information (such as Jabber resources, the text is extracted from the body), and both are passed along to the message-handling callback function.

The final line of the `imconn.py` module is the (by now) old familiar trick that allows a reusable module to be run as an executable program that calls the `main()` function.

Trying Out the Instant Messenger Module

Once you've finished the module, you should now be able try it out. First, though, be sure to check the constant pairs at the beginning of the `main()` function, named `AIM_USER`, `AIM_PASSWD` and `JAB_USER`, `JAB_PASSWD`. They should be set to the username and password of the respective accounts on the AIM and Jabber networks you want to use for your chatbot. You shouldn't use your *own* account details here, because you'll want to use those yourself to talk to the chatbot once it's online.

Also, note that if you don't want to use both networks (say, for example, you only want to play with Jabber), you can just comment out the line creating the undesired IM network connection by adding a # before the statement.

You can run the test program by executing the module itself. After sending a few messages back and forth with the bot, a session with the program might look something like this on your console:

```
$ python imconn.py
<__main__.AIMConnection instance at 0x4059b8> || deusx23: Testing
1...2...3...
<__main__.AIMConnection instance at 0x4059b8> || deusx23: Yes,
there is an echo in here, isn't there?
<__main__.AIMConnection instance at 0x4059b8> || deusx23: Echo...
echo... echo
<__main__.JabberConnection instance at 0x405bc0> ||
deusx23@jabber.org: Are you receiving me?
<__main__.JabberConnection instance at 0x405bc0> ||
deusx23@jabber.org: This is a test.  1.. 2.. 3..
<__main__.AIMConnection instance at 0x4059b8> || deusx23: Is it
fun to repeat everything I say?
```

This is pretty raw and ugly output, but what you should be seeing is a string representing the connection object in memory that has received a message, the name of the person sending the message, and the message that was received.

If you use an IM client such as AdiumX for Mac OS X (http://www.adiumx.com/), the dialogue in your IM window will look something like Figure 4-1.

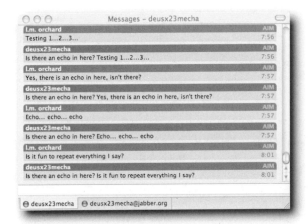

FIGURE 4-1: Echoed instant messages in an AdiumX session

Once you have all of this working, you should be ready to start using it as a component in your feed aggregator.

Sending New Entries as Instant Messages

For this first go at tying feeds to instant messaging, you'll be using just one IM network to send feed updates. This won't be a chatbot, per se, because it will just connect to the network, send you a few messages, and then immediately sign off. It won't be listening for any conversation or commands from you, yet.

Beginning a New Program

Start new file for this program, call it agg05_im_subs.py, and start with the code in Listing 4-10.

Listing 4-10: agg05_im_subs.py (Part 1 of 4)

```
#!/usr/bin/env python
"""

agg05_im_subs.py

Poll subscriptions and send a series of IMs with the latest headlines
"""
```

Continued

Listing 4-10 *(continued)*

```
import time
from agglib import openDBs, closeDBs, getNewFeedEntries
from imconn import AIMConnection, JabberConnection

IM_CLASS   = AIMConnection
IM_TO      = "your_screen_name"
IM_USER    = "bot_screen_name"
IM_PASSWD  = "bot_password"

IM_CHUNK   = 7

FEED_HDR_TMPL = """\n%(feed.title)s - %(feed.link)s\n\n"""
ENTRY_TMPL    = """    * %(entry.title)s - %(entry.link)s\n\n"""
MSG_TMPL      = "%s"

FEEDS_FN      = "feeds.txt"

FEED_DB_FN   = "feeds_db"
ENTRY_DB_FN  = "entry_seen_db"
```

This new program starts off in Listing 4-10 with the usual docstring describing the program, along with a few module imports. In particular, this program needs the `time` module from Python's standard library, but the rest of the imports are coming from your own modules, `agglib` and `imconn`.

The next constants define the following:

- IM_CLASS—This is a reference to which class to use in connecting to an IM network.

- IM_TO—Defined as to whom messages should be sent (that's you).

- IM_USER—This is the username that should be used for logging into the IM network as a bot.

- IM_PASSWD—This is the password for the bot's account.

- IM_CHUNK—To prevent triggering any flood warnings or service denials (on AIM in particular), this constant provides the number of headlines that will be sent in a single instant message before pausing to send more.

Appearing next are the templates used for message formatting. In previous programs, these were full HTML page templates placed at the end of the program, but they've been simplified and moved to the top with the rest of the constants in this iteration of the program. The rest of the constants in Listing 4-10 are the same as what you've used in previous programs.

Defining the main() Function

Next, check out the implementation of the `main()` function, provided in Listing 4-11.

Listing 4-11: agg05_im_subs.py (Part 2 of 4)

```
def main():
    """
    Poll subscribed feeds and send off IMs
    """
    feed_db, entry_db = openDBs(FEED_DB_FN, ENTRY_DB_FN)

    # Create a new IM connection.
    conn = IM_CLASS(IM_USER, IM_PASSWD)
    conn.connect()

    # Read in the subscriptions
    feeds = [ x.strip() for x in open(FEEDS_FN, "r").readlines() ]

    # Iterate through subscribed feeds.
    for feed in feeds:
        # Get new entries for the current feed and send them off
        entries = getNewFeedEntries([feed], feed_db, entry_db)
        if len(entries) > 0:
            sendEntriesViaIM(conn, IM_TO, entries, IM_CHUNK,
                    FEED_HDR_TMPL, ENTRY_TMPL, MSG_TMPL)

    closeDBs(feed_db, entry_db)
```

The new addition to the usual `main()` function in Listing 4-11 is the addition of the IM connection just after opening the databases. Because it uses the constants defined in the preamble, it opens a connection to whichever IM network you've chosen in the configuration constants. Notice that, because this program won't be answering any messages sent its way, it hasn't registered any callback function to accept messages, and has, in fact, left out that parameter altogether when it created the connection.

Next, things are a bit different than in previous incarnations. Instead of loading up all of the new entries for all of the feeds into one aggregated set, this version works its way through the entries, one feed at a time. For each feed, `getNewFeedEntries()` is called with just that feed given as a parameter. And, for any new entries found, `sendEntriesViaIM()` is called to send them on their way to your IM client. Then, after polling the subscribed feeds, `main()` closes the databases and the function definition is finished.

The old approach—that is, collecting all new entries across all subscriptions with one `getNewFeedEntries()` call—would have worked here, technically. However, taking things feed-by-feed produces better results in this context. Sending new headlines for each feed lets you see the progress more immediately, rather than in a single blast. This also goes a little further toward dodging the ire of IM network servers in case they decide that you've been flooding the connection and decide to suspend or ban your bot's account, which can be a danger when using the AIM network, for example.

Sending Feed Entries via Instant Message

Following up on a new function mentioned in main(), Listing 4-12 presents the definition for the sendEntriesViaIM() function.

Listing 4-12: agg05_im_subs.py (Part 3 of 4)

```
def sendEntriesViaIM(conn, to_nick, entries, im_chunk, feed_hdr_tmpl,
        entry_tmpl, msg_tmpl):
    """
    Given an IM connection, a destination name, and a list of entries,
    send off a series of IMs containing entries rendered via template.
    """
    out, curr_feed, entry_cnt = [], None, 0
    for entry in entries:

        # If there's a change in current feed, note it and append a
        # feed header onto the message.
        if entry.feed.title != curr_feed:
            curr_feed = entry.feed.title
            out.append(feed_hdr_tmpl % entry)

        # Append the current entry to the outgoing message
        out.append(entry_tmpl % entry)

        # Keep count of entries.  Every IM_CHUNK worth, fire off the
        # accumulated message content as an IM and clear the current
        # feed title to force a new header in the next batch.
        entry_cnt += 1
        if (entry_cnt % im_chunk) == 0:
            sendIMwithTemplate(conn, to_nick, out, msg_tmpl)
            out, curr_feed = [], None

    # Flush out any remaining content.
    if len(out) > 0:
        sendIMwithTemplate(conn, to_nick, out, msg_tmpl)
```

The implementation of sendEntriesViaIM() in Listing 4-12 has a lot in common with the code used to generate HTML in your other aggregator programs. Here there are no date headers, though, only feed headers, and there is logic to respect the IM_CHUNK constant by sending off a message every time the appropriate number of entries have been seen.

So, this function starts off by initializing a current list of output strings, a variable to remember the current feed, and a count of entries. It then begins iterating through the entries passed in by parameter.

The first order of business in this loop is to append a feed header to the output if the current entry's feed has changed with respect to the previous entry's feed (or if there hasn't been a previous entry yet). Then, the entry itself is appended to the output, rendered via the template defined in the beginning of the program. Next, the count of entries is incremented. If this count is evenly divisible by the value of IM_CHUNK, this fires off an instant message and clears the running list of content and current feed variables. Finally, after all entries have been handled, it fires off one last instant message if any output is still awaiting transmission.

Wrapping Up the Program

To simplify this code a bit, all of the business of sending out instant messages is handled by the sendIMwithTemplate() function, the implementation of which is offered in Listing 4-13. Go ahead and define this function next.

Listing 4-13: agg05_im_subs.py (Part 4 of 4)

```
def sendIMwithTemplate(conn, to_nick, out, msg_tmpl):
    """
    Given an IM bot, a destination name, and a list of content, render
    the message template and send off the IM.
    """
    try:
        msg_text = msg_tmpl % "".join(out)
        conn.sendIM(to_nick, msg_text)
        time.sleep(4)
    except KeyboardInterrupt:
        raise
    except Exception, e:
        print "\tProblem sending IM: %s" % e

if __name__ == "__main__": main()
```

There's not much to sendIMwithTemplate() in Listing 4-13. The list of output content is turned into a block of text via the MSG_TMPL template string. This text is sent off to the appropriate screen name, and a bit of a nap is taken to throttle the message transmission rate in an effort to go easy on the IM network server. This whole process is wrapped in a try/except structure to prevent an individual hiccup in IM transmission from stopping the whole program. (You may eventually want to play with doing more with error conditions here than simply printing a message.)

And, with the end of sendIMwithTemplate(), the call to the main() function is inserted and the program is complete.

Trying Out the Program

If all goes well, you should be able to run the program and see output on your console like this:

```
# python agg05_im_subs.py
Polling http://xml.metafilter.com/atom.xml
        Found 20 new entries
Polling http://rss.cnn.com/rss/cnn_topstories.rss
        Found 7 new entries
Polling http://www.nytimes.com/services/xml/rss/nyt/HomePage.xml
        Found 5 new entries
Polling http://rss.news.yahoo.com/rss/tech
        Found 12 new entries
Polling http://www.wired.com/news_drop/netcenter/netcenter.rdf
        Found 0 new entries
Polling http://www.decafbad.com/blog/atom.xml
        Feed unchanged.
```

However, if you get an exception and a screenful of Python traceback output, you should check the username and password you're using for the program's IM account. If these settings are incorrect, you may see something like this:

```
# python agg05_im_subs.py
...
toc.TOCError: FATAL: Couldn't sign on; Incorrect nickname/password
combination
# python agg05_im_subs.py
...
IOError: Disconnected from server.
```

Once you have this program sending you instant messages, you should start seeing something in your IM client window similar to Figure 4-2.

If these messages are too verbose for you, you can try using some limited HTML in your message templates, such as those appearing in Listing 4-14.

Listing 4-14: agg05_im_subs.py, Alternate Message Templates

```
FEED_HDR_TMPL = """\n<a href="%(feed.link)s"><u>%(feed.title)s</u></a>\n\n"""

ENTRY_TMPL    = """    * <a href="%(entry.link)s">%(entry.title)s</a>\n"""
```

With this tweak to the templates, you can get something a little more concise and, depending on your IM client, you can click on the feed title and entry title links. It should look similar to Figure 4-3.

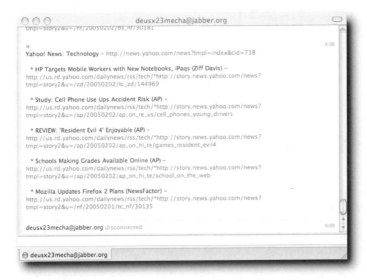

FIGURE 4-2: Feed entry titles and links received in an AdiumX session

FIGURE 4-3: Headlines using alternate HTML templates in an AdiumX session

Remember, the display of these messages is separated out into string templates to make it easier for you to tweak and tailor until they appear as you'd like them. So try out a bunch of different arrangements and see what works best for you.

Creating a Conversational Interface

You've just built an aggregator that fills your IM client window with the latest entries from your subscribed feeds, but that doesn't seem much better than just getting them via email. Wasn't one of the things mentioned at the beginning of this chapter that one of instant messaging's strengths is in its interactivity? So, the next thing is building an aggregator that performs on demand, rather than running according to a schedule.

Updating the Shared Aggregator Module

You're going to reuse some of the functions from the aggregator you just finished working on, so why not add them to the agglib module?

Just copy and paste the function definitions for sendEntriesViaIM() and sendIMwith Template() into agglib.py. It doesn't really matter where they go; the end of the file is fine. Although, a good point might be just before the definition of the EntryWrapper class, just to keep them grouped with the rest of the function definitions in the module. But, the organization of your agglib module is left up to you.

While you're in there, why not add a few more useful functions that you're going to be using shortly? So far, the code here has danced around the topic of subscription management, with a program written early on, called agg01_subscribe.py, which used the feedfinder module to subscribe to feeds, along with the often cut-and-pasted one-liner that fetches the list of subscriptions for main() functions. However, this chatbot will offer a bit more in terms of subscriptions.

So, first, take a look at the Listing 4-15 for the first two subscription-management functions you'll want to add.

Listing 4-15: agglib.py additions (Part 1 of 3)

```
def loadSubs(feeds_fn):
    """
    Load up a list of feeds.
    """
    return [ x.strip() for x in open(feeds_fn, "r").readlines() ]

def saveSubs(feeds_fn, feeds):
    """
    Save a list of feeds.
    """
    open(feeds_fn, "w").write("\n".join(feeds))
```

Pretty simple, so far—the functions defined in Listing 4-15 are loadSubs() and save Subs(), where loadSubs() is just the aforementioned one-liner turned into a function of its own and saveSubs() is its counterpart that writes a list of feeds back to disk.

Next, in Listing 4-16, things get a little more interesting.

Listing 4-16: agglib.py additions (Part 2 of 3)

```
class SubsException(Exception):
    def __init__(self, uri=None):
        self._uri = uri

class SubsNotSubscribed(SubsException): pass

def unsubscribeFeed(feeds, uri):
    """
    Attempt to remove a URI from the give list of subscriptions.
    Throws a SubsNotSubscribed exception if the URI wasn't found in the
    subscriptions.
    """
    if uri not in feeds: raise SubsNotSubscribed(uri)
    feeds.remove(uri)
```

Listing 4-16 defines a function, `unsubscribeFeed()`, and two supporting exception classes, `SubsException` and `SubsNotSubscribedException`. The `SubsException` serves as the parent for all exceptions in subscription management, such as `SubsNonSubscribed Exception`, which is thrown by `unsubscribeFeed()` when it encounters an attempt to unsubscribe from a feed that isn't in the list of subscriptions. These custom exceptions will make it easier in the near future to easily handle problems in subscription management.

Moving on, Listing 4-17 completes the set of tools you'll be using for subscription management.

Listing 4-17: agglib.py additions (Part 3 of 3)

```
class SubsAlreadySubscribed(SubsException): pass
class SubsNoFeedsFound(SubsException): pass
class SubsMultipleFeedsFound(SubsException):
    def __init__(self, uri=None, feeds=[]):
        SubsException.__init__(self, uri)
        self._feeds = feeds

def subscribeFeed(feeds, uri):
    """
    Given a list of feeds and a URI at which to find feeds, try
    adding this feeds to the list.
    """
    feeds_found = feedfinder.getFeeds(uri)
```

Continued

Listing 4-17 *(continued)*

```
if len(feeds_found) == 0:
    raise SubsNoFeedsFound(uri)
elif len(feeds_found) > 1:
    raise SubsMultipleFeedsFound(uri, feeds_found)
else:
    feed_uri = feeds_found[0]
    if feed_uri in feeds:
        raise SubsAlreadySubscribed(feed_uri)
    feeds.append(feed_uri)

return feed_uri
```

The new function defined in Listing 4-17, called `subscribeFeed()`, should look a little familiar to you. It's pretty much the same as the code used in `agg01_subscribe.py` from Listing 2-17, with some changes to raise exceptions rather than printing messages to the console. This allows code using this function to make decisions based on what happens during the subscription attempt, to print a message of its own (or maybe send an instant message), rather than relying on the function do so.

The three new exceptions defined—`SubsAlreadySubscribed`, `SubsNoFeedsFound`, `SubsMultipleFeedsFound`—facilitate this change in error handling.

Oh, and one more thing: Now that you've added code that uses it, don't forget to add an import statement for `feedfinder` at the start of `agglib.py`, which might look something like this:

```
import sys, time, feedparser, feedfinder, shelve, md5, time
```

Building the On-Demand Feed Reading Chatbot

Having finished the addition of some subscription-management tools to `agglib`, you're ready to start building an interactive IM chatbot that will pull everything in this chapter together. Rather than just running on a clock, producing regular updates, this chatbot will listen for your commands to subscribe to and unsubscribe from feeds, poll feeds for new entries, and poll all of your subscriptions for new entries.

Start a new file in your editor and name it `agg06_aggbot.py`. This is one of the longer programs built here, so you might want to attack it across several sittings. When you're ready, take a deep breath, and head into Listing 4-18 for the preamble to this new program.

Listing 4-18: agg06_aggbot.py (Part 1 of 14)

```
#!/usr/bin/env python
"""
agg06_aggbot.py
```

```
Interactive IM bot which manages feed subscriptions and polls feeds
on demand.
"""
import time
from imconn import *
from agglib import *

AIM_USER    = "bot_name"
AIM_PASSWD  = "bot_passwd"
AIM_OWNER   = "your_name"

JAB_USER    = "bot_name@jabber.org"
JAB_PASSWD  = "bot_passwd"
JAB_OWNER   = "your_name@jabber.org"

FEEDS_FN     = "feeds.txt"
FEED_DB_FN   = "feeds_db"
ENTRY_DB_FN  = "entry_seen_db"
```

This start to a program, as shown in Listing 4-18, should look familiar by now. One new thing, if you're not entirely familiar with Python, are the wildcards in the `import` statements—these are basically a lazy convenience that cause the import of everything made available by the two modules.

The purpose of the configuration constants should be fairly self-explanatory. There's a set of user, password, and owner values for both an AIM and a Jabber connection, to be used shortly. The owner value is a crude sort of security feature that establishes to what screen name this bot will respond and whose commands it will obey. You should fill this in with whatever screen name you use in your IM client.

Moving right along, Listing 4-19 offers a definition for the `main()` function.

Listing 4-19: agg06_aggbot.py (Part 2 of 14)

```
def main():
    """
    Create a new bot, add some IM network connections, and fire it up.
    """
    bot = AggBot(FEEDS_FN, FEED_DB_FN, ENTRY_DB_FN)
    bot.addConnection(AIMConnection, AIM_OWNER, AIM_USER, AIM_PASSWD)
    bot.addConnection(JabberConnection, JAB_OWNER, JAB_USER,
        JAB_PASSWD)
    bot.go()
```

The main() function definition in Listing 4-19 simply creates a new instance of a class named AggBot, to be defined shortly. After creation, a method named addConnection() is called to feed the bot details about the IM networks to which it will connect. Note that you can remove any connections you don't want to use, if, for example, you only wanted to use the bot on the AIM network. Or, if you've implemented any new IM network classes, you can add them here as well.

Then, finally, the bot is started up with a call to the go() method. Once started, this method loops forever unless the program is killed or the bot decides to quit.

With the main driver of the program established, continue on to Listing 4-20 to see the beginning of the AggBot class definition.

Listing 4-20: agg06_aggbot.py (Part 3 of 14)

```
class AggBot:
    """
    This is a feed aggregator bot that accepts commands via instant message.
    """

    IM_CHUNK    = 7

    FEED_HDR_TMPL = \
        """\n<a href="%(feed.link)s"><u>%(feed.title)s</u></a>\n\n"""
    ENTRY_TMPL    = """    * <a href="%(entry.link)s">%(entry.title)s</a>\n"""
    MSG_TMPL      = "%s"
```

In AggBot, some of the configuration constants that used to be a part of the main program (namely IM_CHUNK, FEED_HDR_TMPL, ENTRY_TMPL, and MSG_TMPL) have now become class properties. These properties are used throughout the rest of the class, and can be changed in object instances of this class, or subclasses, if need be. Making these properties of the class, versus program constants, can help with reusability, should you decide to move AggBot into its own module.

However, just like their ancestors as program constants in the past, these settings have the same purposes as string templates and their influence on sending instant messages.

Next, define the __init__() and __del__() methods based on the code in Listing 4-21.

Listing 4-21: agg06_aggbot.py (Part 4 of 14)

```
    def __init__(self, feeds_fn, feed_db_fn, entry_db_fn):
        """
        Initialize the bot object, open aggregator databases, load up
        subscriptions.
```

```
    """
    self.feeds_fn    = feeds_fn
    self.feed_db_fn  = feed_db_fn
    self.entry_db_fn = entry_db_fn
    self.connections, self.owners, self.running = [], [], False

def __del__(self):
    """
    Object destructor - make sure the aggregator databases
    get closed.
    """
    try: closeDBs(self.feed_db, self.entry_db)
    except: pass
```

Listing 4-21 shows nothing too radical. The filenames for the subscriptions and databases are stowed away in object properties, and a few other object properties are initialized in the __init__() method. Additionally, the implementation of the __del__() method serves to attempt some last-ditch cleanup, closing the feed databases if for some reason they haven't been closed already.

The next two method definitions, provided in Listing 4-22, deal with connections to IM networks and the limited form of security built into the bot.

Listing 4-22: agg06_aggbot.py (Part 5 of 14)

```
def addConnection(self, conn_cls, owner, user, passwd):
    """
    Given a connection class, owner screen name, and a user /
    password, create the IM connection and store it away along
    with the owner user.
    """
    self.connections.append(conn_cls(user, passwd, self.receiveIM))
    self.owners.append(owner)

def getOwner(self, conn):
    """
    For a given connection, return the owner's screen name.
    """
    return self.owners[self.connections.index(conn)]
```

In Listing 4-22, the addConnection() and getOwner() methods are defined.

The parameters for addConnection() are an IM network connection class, the bot owner's name, and the username and password for the bot on that network. Rather than accept an already-constructed IM connection object, addConnection() wants to be given the necessary parameters to construct one itself. This way, it can register its own receiveIM() method with the connection on initialization in order to process incoming instant messages.

Following addConnection() is the definition of the getOwner() method. This is a convenience method that, when given an IM network connection instance, returns the name of the owner on that network. When IM connections are created in addConnection(), those connections and their owners are appended to parallel lists. So, if you find the index for a connection in one list, you can use that index to find the owner in the other. This is what the implementation of getOwner() does.

Now, build the basic operating methods of the bot with the contents of Listing 4-23.

Listing 4-23: agg06_aggbot.py (Part 6 of 14)

```
def connect(self):
    """
    Cause all the IM connections objects connect to their networks.
    """
    for c in self.connections: c.connect()

def runOnce(self):
    """
    Run through one event loop step.
    """
    for c in self.connections: c.runOnce()

def go(self):
    """
    Connect and run event loop, until running flag set to false.
    """
    try:
        self.feed_db, self.entry_db = openDBs(self.feed_db_fn,
            self.entry_db_fn)
        self.feeds = loadSubs(self.feeds_fn)
        self.running = True
        self.connect()
        while self.running:
            self.runOnce()
            time.sleep(0.1)
    finally:
        try: closeDBs(self.feed_db, self.entry_db)
        except: pass

def stop(self):
    """
    Stop event loop by setting running flag to false.
    """
    self.running = False
```

First in Listing 4-23, the `connect()` and `runOnce()` methods are defined. These call the `connect()` and `runOnce()` methods on all of the bot's connections, respectively.

These two methods are used in the implementation of `go()` that, after opening the aggregator databases and loading up the list of subscriptions, connects to all the IM networks with `connect()` and starts the event loop, repeatedly calling `runOnce()` in between short naps.

One interesting feature of the event loop in `go()` is the `running` flag. This is a property of the object that, while set to `True`, keeps the event loop running. However, should its value ever change to `False`, the event loop will end, as will the `go()` method after first trying to close the aggregator databases.

And that's just what the `stop()` method does. It sets the `running` property in the bot to `False` to bring about an orderly shutdown and halt.

You have just a few more convenience functions to define, found in Listing 4-24.

Listing 4-24: agg06_aggbot.py (Part 7 of 14)

```python
    def getSubscriptionURI(self, sub_arg):
        """
        Utility function which allows reference to a subscription
        either by integer index in list of subscriptions, or by
        direct URI reference.
        """
        try:
            sub_num = int(sub_arg)
            return self.feeds[sub_num]
        except ValueError:
            return sub_arg

    def pollFeed(self, conn, from_name, sub_uri):
        """
        Perform a feed poll and send the new entries as messages.
        """
        entries = getNewFeedEntries([sub_uri], self.feed_db,
            self.entry_db)
        if len(entries) > 0:
            sendEntriesViaIM(conn, from_name, entries, self.IM_CHUNK,
                    self.FEED_HDR_TMPL, self.ENTRY_TMPL, self.MSG_TMPL)
        else:
            conn.sendIM(from_name, "No new entries available.")
```

Listing 4-24 has the two last convenience methods: `getSubscriptionURI()` and `pollFeed()`.

The `getSubscriptionURI()` method will be used later to allow commands to look up feeds either by a numerical index or via a URI directly.

And, last in this listing, pollFeed() encapsulates the functionality of the previous IM-enabled feed aggregator, sending off the new entries found for a feed as instant messages rendered from templates to a given screen name.

Now, you can implement the command shell core of this bot with the receiveIM() method, defined in Listing 4-25.

Listing 4-25: agg06_aggbot.py (Part 8 of 14)

```
def receiveIM(self, conn, from_name, msg):
    """
    Process incoming messages as commands.  Message is space-
    delimited, command is first word found, everything else becomes
    parameters.  Commands are handled by methods with 'cmd_'
    prepended to the name of the command.
    """
    try:
        owner = self.getOwner(conn)
        if from_name != owner:
            # Don't listen to commands from anyone who's not
            # the bot owner.
            conn.sendIM(from_name, "I don't talk to strangers.")
        else:
            if msg == "":
                # Check for empty messages.
                conn.sendIM(from_name, "Did you say something?")
            else:
                # Try to parse the message.  Space-delimited, first
                # part of message is the command, everything else
                # is optional parameters.
                try:
                    fs = msg.index(" ")
                    cmd, args = msg[:fs], msg[fs+1:].split(" ")
                except:
                    cmd, args = msg, []

                # Look for a method in this class corresponding to
                # command prepended with 'cmd_'.  If found,
                # execute it.
                cmd_func  = 'cmd_%s' % cmd
                if hasattr(self, cmd_func):
                    getattr(self, cmd_func)(conn, from_name, args)
                else:
                    conn.sendIM(from_name, "I don't understand.")

    except Exception, e:
        # Something unexpected happened, so make some attempt to
        # say what the exception was.
        conn.sendIM(from_name, "That confused me! (%s)" % e)
```

The `receiveIM()` method in Listing 4-25 looks like it has a lot going on, but it's really pretty simple. It treats incoming messages as potential commands. These are examples of commands it might see:

```
list
unsubscribe 1
subscribe http://www.slashdot.org/
poll 5
pollall
```

This method tries to split up incoming messages by spaces, and treats the first word in the message as the name of a command. The rest of the words in the message (if any) are treated as parameters for the command. Empty messages and messages that haven't come from the bot owner are ignored as commands and given a terse reply.

A bit of Python trickery comes into play when the method to perform the command is located and executed, via the built-in `hasattr()` and `getattr()` functions. First, the name of a potential command method is constructed, using `cmd_` as a prefix on the message's first word. Then, `hasattr()` is used to see if the bot is equipped with a method matching that name. If no such method is found, the bot reports this. However, if such a method is found, the next step is to retrieve that method with `getattr()` and then execute it with the current connection, sender's name, and any parameters found in the message.

This dynamic lookup approach allows the chatbot to be pretty flexible when it comes to adding and implementing commands, because a new command is just a new method following the `cmd_`-prefix naming convention. This means that you could add commands to this bot either by defining new methods in this class directly, or by creating new methods and overriding old ones in a subclass of `AggBot`.

So, speaking of command methods, implement the first one, called `cmd_signoff()`, using the contents of Listing 4-26.

Listing 4-26: agg06_aggbot.py (Part 9 of 14)

```python
def cmd_signoff(self, conn, from_name, args):
    """
    signoff: Command the bot to sign off and exit the program.
    """
    conn.sendIM(from_name, "Okay, signing off now.")
    self.stop()
```

Appropriately enough, the `cmd_signoff()` method in Listing 4-26 causes the bot to sign off from the IM networks and stop running. It notifies the person from whom it received the command, and then calls its own `stop()` method, which should bring everything to a halt once control makes it back to the bot's main event loop.

Having tackled your first bot command, move onto the next in Listing 4-27.

Listing 4-27: agg06_aggbot.py (Part 10 of 14)

```
def cmd_list(self, conn, from_name, args):
    """
    list: List all subscriptions by index and URI.
    """
    out = []
    out.append("You have the following subscriptions:")
    for i in range(len(self.feeds)):
        out.append("   %s: %s" % (i, self.feeds[i]))
    conn.sendIM(from_name, "\n".join(out))
```

Listing 4-27 presents the `cmd_list()` command function, which gathers up the list of subscribed feeds, builds the text of a message listing them out by numerical index, and then sends that message off to the person who issued the command.

These numerical indexes for subscriptions, along with the previously defined `get SubscriptionURI()`, become useful in the next method defined in Listing 4-28, named `cmd_unsubscribe()`.

Listing 4-28: agg06_aggbot.py (Part 11 of 14)

```
def cmd_unsubscribe(self, conn, from_name, args):
    """
    unsubscribe <sub>: Unsubscribe from a feed by index or URI.
    """
    try:
        sub_uri = self.getSubscriptionURI(args[0])
        unsubscribeFeed(self.feeds, sub_uri)
        saveSubs(self.feeds_fn, self.feeds)
        conn.sendIM(from_name, "Unsubscribed from %s" % sub_uri)
    except SubsNotSubscribed:
        conn.sendIM(from_name, "Not subscribed to that feed.")
    except IndexError:
        conn.sendIM(from_name, "Need a valid number or a URI.")
```

The `cmd_unsubscribe()` method in Listing 4-28 provides a command allowing you to remove subscriptions from your list, referring to them either by numerical index (as provided by the list command) or by URI directly. An attempt is made to look up the subscription, remove the subscription, save the changed list of subscriptions, and then notify you that the feed was unsubscribed. If it turns out that the subscription couldn't be found, or that you weren't subscribed to that feed, you'll be notified in either case.

Accompanying this command method is its complement, cmd_subscribe(), as defined in Listing 4-29.

Listing 4-29: agg06_aggbot.py (Part 12 of 14)

```python
def cmd_subscribe(self, conn, from_name, args):
    """
    subscribe <uri>: Use the feedfinder module to find a feed URI
    and add a subscription, if possible.  Reports exceptions such
    as no feeds found, multiple feeds found, or already subscribed.
    """
    try:
        feed_uri = subscribeFeed(self.feeds, args[0])
        saveSubs(self.feeds_fn, self.feeds)
        conn.sendIM(from_name, "Subscribed to %s" % feed_uri)
    except SubsNoFeedsFound:
        conn.sendIM(from_name, "Sorry, no feeds at %s" % args[0])
    except SubsAlreadySubscribed:
        conn.sendIM(from_name, "You're already subscribed.")
    except SubsMultipleFeedsFound, e:
        feeds_found = e.getFeeds()
        out = ['Multiple feeds found, please pick one:']
        for f in feeds_found:
            out.append("    %s" % f)
        conn.sendIM(from_name, "\n".join(out))
```

There's not much real complexity involved with cmd_subscribe() in Listing 4-29. It simply attempts to add a new subscription using subscribeFeed() from agglib, then sends a notification message after having saved the changed subscriptions. The rest of the method is involved in catching the various exceptions thrown by subscribeFeed(), such as when no feeds are found at a URI, when you're already subscribed to the feed, or when a choice of feeds is found. This latter case, finding a choice of feeds, is the most involved because it constructs a message listing all of the alternatives.

Getting close to wrapping up, the next-to-last method is defined in Listing 4-30.

Listing 4-30: agg06_aggbot.py (Part 13 of 14)

```python
def cmd_poll(self, conn, from_name, args):
    """
    poll <index or URI>: Perform an on-demand
    poll of a feed.
    """
```

Continued

Listing 4-30 *(continued)*

```
try:
    sub_uri = self.getSubscriptionURI(args[0])
    self.pollFeed(conn, from_name, sub_uri)
except IndexError:
    conn.sendIM(from_name, \
        "Need a valid number or a URI.")
```

The `cmd_poll()` command method from Listing 4-30 allows you to ask for an on-demand feed poll that, if the feed turns up with new entries, will format them and send you the latest as instant messages (that is, if the parameter to this command is a valid subscription index or feed URI—if not, an error message is sent out).

The final command method for this bot, `cmd_pollsubs()`, is found in Listing 4-31.

Listing 4-31: agg06_aggbot.py (Part 14 of 14)

```
def cmd_pollsubs(self, conn, from_name, args):
    """
    pollsubs: Perform an on-demand poll of all subscriptions.
    """
    conn.sendIM(from_name, "Polling all subscriptions...")
    for feed in self.feeds:
        conn.sendIM(from_name, "Polling %s" % feed)
        self.pollFeed(conn, from_name, feed)

if __name__ == "__main__": main()
```

The `cmd_pollsubs()` command method provided in Listing 4-31 basically duplicates the behavior of the previous, non-interactive aggregator in this chapter: When issued, this command causes the bot to scan all of your subscribed feeds and ship you the new entries found as formatted instant messages.

And, at last, the final line of this program is the call to the `main()` function. With that, your chatbot should be complete and ready to take out for a spin.

Trying Out the On-Demand Feed Reading Chatbot

When you run this program, it shouldn't produce much output if successful. All of its output is devoted to sending instant messages. As mentioned before, this is one of the longer programs, so if you should get any errors when you try to run it, be sure to check things like syntax and indentation level.

However, if everything has worked, you should soon see your new bot appear on the IM networks. You may need to add the bot's screen name to your buddy list first, in order to see it come online.

Once you can see it in your buddy list, try sending it messages. You can send it just about anything, but it'll only tell you that it can't understand you unless you use one of the following commands:

- `signoff`—Causes the bot to sign off and exit.

- `list`—Retrieves a listing of subscribed feeds.

- `unsubscribe [index or URI]`—Given a subscription index (as displayed by the `list` command) or a feed URI, attempts to unsubscribe from that feed.

- `subscribe [URI]`—Given a URI to a site or a feed, attempts to find a feed and add it to the list of subscriptions.

- `poll [index or URI]`—Given a subscription index or a feed URI, polls that feed for new entries.

- `pollsubs`—Goes through all subscribed feeds and polls for new entries.

A short conversation with the chatbot in AdiumX is shown in Figure 4-4. Using the feed polling commands results in feed entries sent to you just as in Figure 4-3, because those commands have borrowed functionality from the previous aggregator.

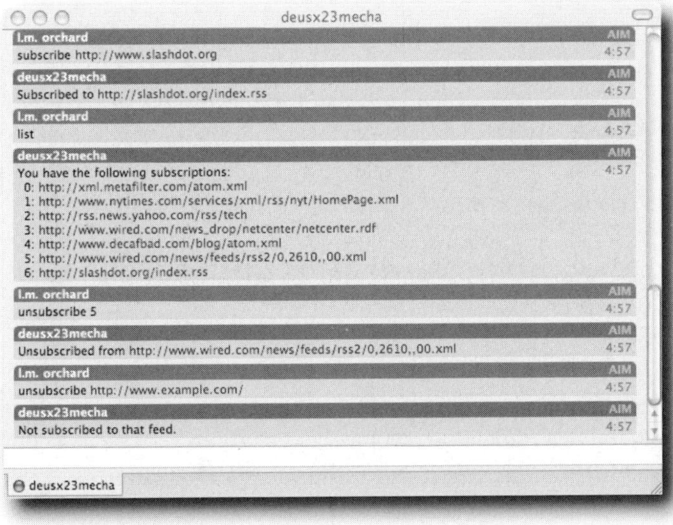

FIGURE 4-4: A sample conversation in an AdiumX session with the chatbot

Checking Out Other Options

This section provides other options you might want to explore.

RSS-IM Gateway

The RSS-IM Gateway is a multi-network IM chatbot, written in Perl, that sends out links and headlines read from RSS feeds. It doesn't really have a command interface, really just offering the top headlines for various sites not unlike the first aggregator built in this chapter.

Check out the home page for RSS-IM here:

```
http://www.duncanlamb.com/sdba/?Projects/RSS-IM+Gateway
```

And, you can download RSS-IM directly from SourceForge here:

```
https://sourceforge.net/project/showfiles.php?group_id=82182
```

rss2jabber

The rss2jabber chatbot is written in PHP, uses MySQL, and works exclusively with the Jabber IM network. It offers a small command interface and can be asked to send new headlines on a scheduled basis.

Take a look at the rss2jabber home page here:

```
http://rss2jabber.berlios.de/
```

JabRSS

JabRSS is another Jabber-only chatbot, written in Python, that serves up feed entries via IM, but is a bit more sophisticated: It offers quite a few commands, help messages, display preferences, and scheduled delivery of new entries.

You can visit the JabRSS home page here:

```
http://cmeerw.org/dev/node/7
```

Summary

So, now you have a personal, interactive feed aggregator listening to your commands from your instant messenger client. It doesn't do much right now, but there's plenty of room to grow. There's certainly a lot more you can do with it, if you want to keep playing.

You could, for example, try some of these projects:

- Build some help messages based on the available commands and their descriptions.
- Include a shortened version of the feed entry summaries to present more information.

- Add some commands to schedule polling of feeds and add a scheduler to the bot's main event loop.

- Figure out how to serve more than just one owner, and manage subscriptions and polling for multiple users.

- Enhance the `agglib` to allow the storage of old news items, rather than just flagging that they've been seen, so you can ask for more than just the latest new entries.

Stay tuned, though, because your feeds are about to get even more personal in the next chapter, when you pack up your subscriptions and take them with you.

Taking Your Feeds with You

O ne of the things I've tried to make a point of showing you in this book is how feeds and feed readers are increasingly becoming a personal technology—your choice of feeds, fetched by your machine, delivered to you. In this chapter, your tinkering is about to get even more personal as you build tools to carry feeds with you on your mobile devices.

Of course, because the screens are smaller and storage is usually more scarce than you're used to on your PC or laptop, you won't be able to follow quite as many feeds—but in exchange, you'll be able to keep up with your "can't miss" news while you're waiting in the doctor's office or the sandwich line at the deli. And, if you can stand the dulcet tones of synthesized speech, you can lose the screen altogether and have your news read to you as you commute to work.

Reading Feeds on a Palm OS Device

The PalmOS family of devices has largely defined personal mobile and wireless computing over the years. You can find PalmOS running in a wide range of devices offering many combinations of processor power, memory, connectivity, and form factors. There are classic stylus-based PDAs with monochrome screens, smartphones with keyboards and wireless Internet access, full-blown personal media players, and there's even been an attempt to squeeze the platform into a wristwatch device. Although competitors have appeared (often packing in more raw computing power or media capabilities), PalmOS devices still tend to set the bar for handheld computing.

Furthermore, one of the factors that havecontributed to the PalmOS success story is the openness of the platform. Development tools exist for just about every platform you could choose, with Mac, Windows, and Linux environments—including compilers, libraries, emulators, and UI builders—available to use in the construction of PalmOS applications. Because of this, there's not only a wealth of commercial and shareware applications available, but you can also find quite a number of Open Source and free packages at your disposal.

Introducing Plucker Viewer and Plucker Distiller

For this chapter, though, the most interesting Open Source package for PalmOS is called Plucker, available at `http://www.plkr.org`. This is how Plucker is described on its home page:

Plucker is an offline Web and e-book viewer for PalmOS based handheld devices and PDAs. Plucker comes with Unix, Linux, Windows, and Mac OS X tools, scripts, and conduits that let you decide exactly what part of the World Wide Web you'd like to download onto your PDA (as long as they're in standard HTML or text format). These Web pages are then processed, compressed, and transferred to the PDA for viewing by the Plucker viewer.

Figure 5-1 shows the Plucker home page and Figure 5-2 shows the Plucker running on a Palm OS Emulator.

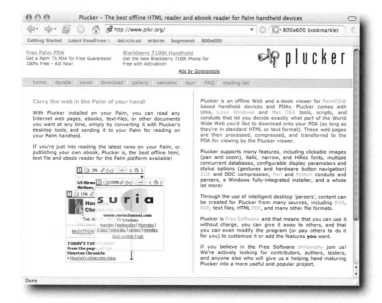

FIGURE 5-1: The Plucker home page at `http://www.plkr.org`

One of the best things about Plucker is that, on the PalmOS side, it works on just about every revision and variation of the platform from the Palm Pilot Professional up to the newest super-high-resolution devices in full color. The best feature for the purposes of this chapter, however, is that there are tools written in Python for creating Plucker documents from HTML pages.

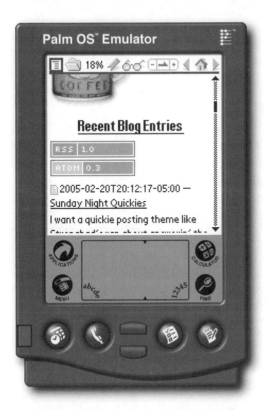

FIGURE 5-2: Plucker running in a Palm OS Emulator

The availability of Python tools means that you will be able to use the library of code you've built up so far for building feed aggregators, just sprinkling in some code to call out to the Plucker Distiller. With this, you can generate documents to read on your PalmOS device from a feed aggregator—and without necessarily needing an Internet connection, because the Plucker Distiller acts as a Web spider following links and folding new pages and images into the file for offline viewing.

Downloading and Installing Plucker Components

If you haven't already, visit the Plucker download page (http://www.plkr.org/dl). You'll find that Plucker is split up into a few components:

- Viewer—This is the core Plucker application for PalmOS devices. Several versions are available targeted at both high- and low-resolution displays, as well as a variety of languages. Choose one of these as appropriate for your personal device.

- `Distiller`—This is the Python code you'll be using to work Plucker support into your feed aggregator. Download this and unpack it into your working project directory.

- `Desktop`—If you'd like a desktop graphical user interface (GUI) to use in generating Plucker documents outside the aggregator you'll build shortly, this is it. Using Plucker Desktop, you can pull down individual Web pages and convert a wide array of other document formats into Plucker documents.

- `Documentation`—It'd be a good idea to download the Plucker documentation, if only to read up on all the features the program offers.

- `Source Code`—Although the Distiller code is all you'll need for this project, the full source code to the PalmOS application and other tools is available here.

- `Extras`—These are optional plugins and fonts for use with the Plucker application.

So, the two components you'll definitely want to grab are the Viewer for your PalmOS device and the Distiller for your tinkering. Depending on which Viewer package you download, you'll have a number of Palm databases to install that include the manual as a Plucker document (`PluckerUserGuide.pdb`), the Viewer itself (`viewer_en.prc`), and a support module that enables compression in Plucker documents (`SysZLib.prc`). It's probably safe to assume you know how to install applications and a database on your PalmOS device, but you'll want to use something like Palm Desktop on Windows or The Missing Sync on Mac OS X from Mark/Space, Inc. (`http://www.markspace.com/`). Figure 5-3 shows the interface for the Missing Sync for PalmOS.

Installing and Using Plucker Distiller

Along with the core Plucker Viewer, you should have also downloaded the Plucker Distiller archive, which consists mainly of a collection of Python modules. When you unpack this archive, downloaded either as a `.zip` or a `.tar.bz` file, locate the `PyPlucker` directory. This contains the guts of what you need to get Plucker built into your aggregator. Copy or move this directory into your working project directory to make it available to your programs. That's about all there is to installing the Plucker Distiller modules.

As for using the Plucker Distiller in your programs, that's pretty easy as well. The Distiller is usually used in a command-line program that offers a large number of options to configure its operation (see Figure 5-4).

Tip The list of options available from the Distiller is far too long to display in one page, but you can bring up a usage list yourself like this from your project directory:

```
python PyPlucker/Spider.py --help
```

This could come in handy if you want to tweak the options you use in calling the Distiller later.

Fortunately, this command-line interface can also be used programmatically, saving you from needing to learn much about how the Distiller works internally. Check out Listing 5-1 for a small example program using the Distiller.

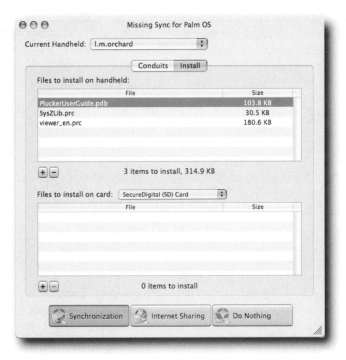

FIGURE 5-3: Installing Plucker on a Palm Device on Mac OS X

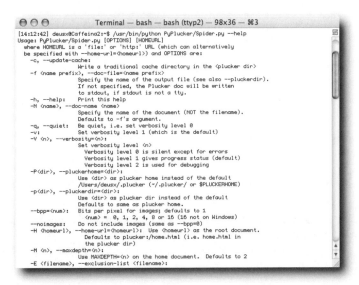

FIGURE 5-4: Plucker Distiller offers quite a few command-line options

Listing 5-1: ch05_plucker_test.py

```python
#!/usr/bin/env python
"""
ch05_plucker_test.py

Take the Plucker Distiller out for a test drive.
"""
import sys, time
import PyPlucker.Spider

HTML_FN       = "http://www.decafbad.com"
PLUCKER_DIR   = "."
PLUCKER_TITLE = "Sample Plucker Document"
PLUCKER_FN    = "plucker-%s" % time.strftime("%Y%m%d-%H%M%S")
PLUCKER_BPP   = 8
PLUCKER_DEPTH = 1

def main():
    """
    Call the Plucker Distiller to output a test document.
    """
    PyPlucker.Spider.realmain(None, argv=[
        sys.argv[0],
        '-P', PLUCKER_DIR,
        '-f', PLUCKER_FN,
        '-H', HTML_FN,
        '-M', PLUCKER_DEPTH,
        '-N', PLUCKER_TITLE,
        '--bpp', PLUCKER_BPP,
        '--title=%s' % PLUCKER_TITLE,
    ])

if __name__ == "__main__": main()
```

The test program, named ch05_plucker_test.py, doesn't do anything spectacularly complex. First, it lays out a few configuration constants:

- HTML_FN—This is the filename or URL from which the Distiller will start building the Plucker document.

- PLUCKER_DIR—Plucker looks for a home directory in which to find configuration files, and this setting uses the current directory.

- PLUCKER_TITLE—You can set a title for the Plucker document, which is displayed in the document listing on the Palm device.

- PLUCKER_FN—The Distiller uses this filename for the Palm database (PDB) file it produces.

- PLUCKER_BPP—Distiller attempts to include any images found in the HTML file or content located via URL, and this setting is the maximum color depth (0, 1, 2, 4, 8, or 16) under which all images are kept. For example, if you have a monochrome or grayscale device, you may want to use a setting of 1 or 2. If you have a color device, try a higher value—but keep in mind that more colorful images require more CPU power to render and move around. Of course, if you don't care to include images at all, use a setting of 0.

- PLUCKER_DEPTH—When parsing an HTML document, Distiller can follow links it finds and recursively download and roll those pages into the Plucker document. This setting determines the number of levels of links deep Distiller will wander. A setting of 1 won't follow any links at all, whereas higher values will go farther.

Caution

Note that increases to the PLUCKER_DEPTH setting will result in exponential growth in the size of Plucker documents, as the Distiller branches out to children of children of children of pages found via links. So, you may not want to go much higher than a setting of 2—and even that will result in some pretty gigantic Plucker documents! In fact, as you're playing with this program and testing it out, you might want to leave it at 0 just to keep from spidering too much at first.

Then, in the main() function definition, the realmain() function of the PyPlucker. Spider module is called. Its first argument can be any file-like object opened to receive the output of the Distiller, but here you can use None and provide a filename as an option to be used for output.

Speaking of options, the next few lines build a list of arguments for the Distiller, which are identical to the options you'd have used if you were running the Distiller by hand from the command line. Each element of the list represents the options and settings that would have been separated by spaces on the command line, but here they are constructed programmatically.

This is just a tad "hackish," but that's okay. It works, and it reuses everything that already works without having to figure out anything else about the Distiller's workings.

If everything goes well, a session with this program should look like Figures 5-5 and 5-6.

The Plucker Distiller provides a lot of output, as it chases down pages and images, both locally and on the Web. And, once it's exhausted all of the links it can spider, it builds the Plucker document as a Palm database. This database will be named something like plucker-20050221-142228.pdb, where the last bit of the filename is the date and time of its generation.

Building a Feed Aggregator with Plucker Distiller

At this point, you have all the pieces you need to build a feed aggregator that automatically produces Plucker documents. And, thanks to the aggregator code you already have socked away, and the simplicity of using the Plucker Distiller in your code, this program will be a relatively short one.

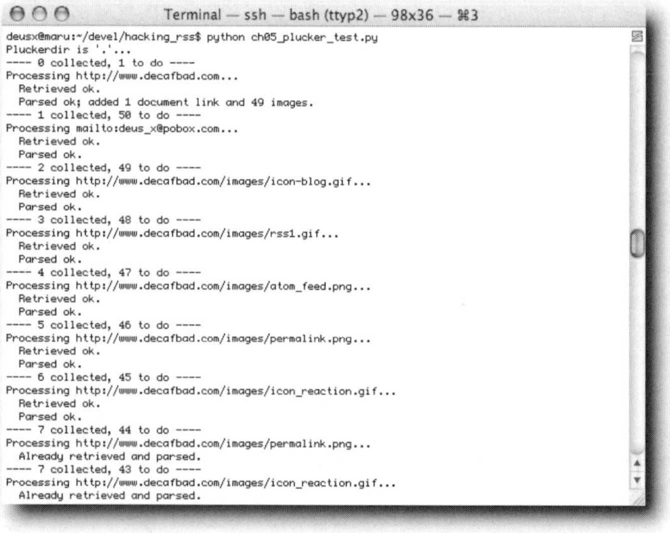

FIGURE 5-5: Trying out `ch05_plucker_test.py`

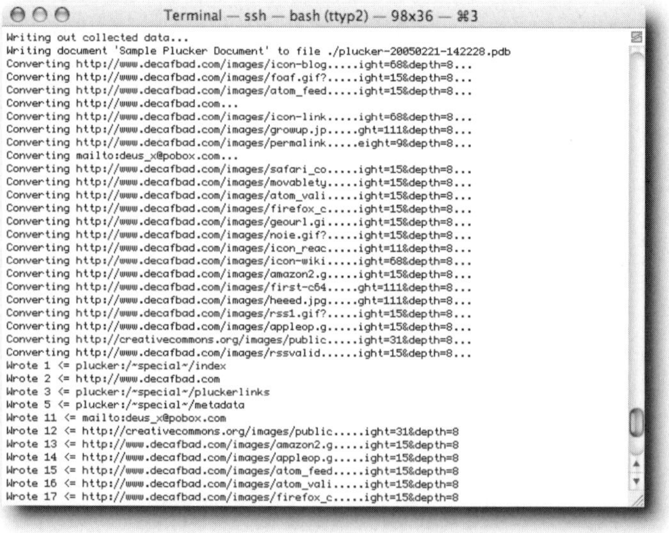

FIGURE 5-6: Watching a run of `ch05_plucker_test.py` **wrapping up**

Start a new program file in your editor and name it ch05_plucker_aggregator.py. Then, take a look at Listing 5-2, which provides the code for the beginning of this file.

Listing 5-2: ch05_plucker_aggregator.py (Part 1 of 4)

```python
#!/usr/bin/env python
"""
ch05_plucker_aggregator.py

Poll subscriptions, produce HTML summaries, wrap up as a plucker document.
"""

import sys, time
from agglib import *
import PyPlucker.Spider

HTML_FN       = "plucker-aggregator-%s.html" % time.strftime("%Y%m%d-%H%M%S")
FEEDS_FN      = "plucker_feeds.txt"
FEED_DB_FN    = "plucker_feeds_db"
ENTRY_DB_FN   = "plucker_entry_seen_db"

PLUCKER_DIR   = "."
PLUCKER_TITLE = "%s News" % time.strftime("%Y%m%d-%H%M%S")
PLUCKER_FN    = "plucker-%s" % time.strftime("%Y%m%d-%H%M%S")
PLUCKER_BPP   = 8
PLUCKER_DEPTH = 1
```

The parts of Listing 5-2 should be old hat by now. The usual suspects are imported, with PyPlucker.Spider appearing as this program's guest star. There are a few standard configuration constants, such as

- The names of an HTML output file for new items.
- Your list of subscriptions—which, if you'll notice, has changed from feeds.txt to plucker_feeds.txt, because you'll probably find it useful to keep your desktop and mobile subscriptions separate.
- The feed and feed entry databases

The next configuration constants are the settings for creating Plucker documents, taken from the program in Listing 5-1.

With that out of the way, you can define the main() function for this program, shown in Listing 5-3.

Listing 5-3: ch05_plucker_aggregator.py (Part 2 of 4)

```
def main():
    """
    Poll subscribed feeds and produce aggregator page.
    """
    feed_db, entry_db = openDBs(FEED_DB_FN, ENTRY_DB_FN)

    feeds   = [ x.strip() for x in open(FEEDS_FN, "r").readlines() ]

    entries = getNewFeedEntries(feeds, feed_db, entry_db)

    if len(entries) > 0:
        out_fn = HTML_FN
        writeAggregatorPage(entries, out_fn, DATE_HDR_TMPL,
            FEED_HDR_TMPL, ENTRY_TMPL, PAGE_TMPL)
        buildPluckerDocument(PLUCKER_DIR, PLUCKER_FN, PLUCKER_TITLE,
            PLUCKER_DEPTH, PLUCKER_BPP, HTML_FN)

    closeDBs(feed_db, entry_db)
```

The code you find in Listing 5-3 is almost identical to what you saw back in Chapter 3, from Listing 3-2. In fact, if you wanted to, you could probably cut and paste that code and work from there. The single new addition is the call to `buildPluckerDocument()`, which does the job of creating the Plucker document from the HTML built from new feed entries.

Note Here's another spot where `writeAggregatorPage()` is used to output an HTML file, which is then reused to feed another function. This is how the email-enabled aggregator in Chapter 3 worked. One potential future improvement for this aggregator might be reworking `writeAggregatorPage()` in your aggregator library to skip the middleman of first writing out to a file.

The definition of `buildPluckerDocument()`, up next in Listing 5-4, is pretty much a duplicate of what you saw in Listing 5-1—the sole difference being that this function takes parameters instead of using the program's configuration constants.

Listing 5-4: ch05_plucker_aggregator.py (Part 3 of 4)

```
def buildPluckerDocument(pdir, pfn, ptitle, pdepth, pbpp, html_fn):
    """
    Given some Plucker settings and an HTML file, attempt to build a
    Plucker document.
    """
```

```
PyPlucker.Spider.realmain(None, argv=[
    sys.argv[0],
    '-P', pdir,
    '-f', pfn,
    '-H', html_fn,
    '-N', ptitle,
    '-M', pdepth,
    '--bpp', pbpp,
    '--title=%s' % ptitle,
])
```

Again, there is not much difference between Listing 5-4 and Listing 5-1. Continuing with this theme, the final stretch of this program presented in Listing 5-5 consists of a few template strings for the aggregator HTML output. These are just simplified versions of what you've already used in previous aggregators, stripped of style sheets and CSS classes because you won't be needing those in Plucker. Take a look at Listing 5-5 to wrap up this newest addition to your family of feed aggregators.

Listing 5-5: ch05_plucker_aggregator.py (Part 4 of 4)

```
# Presentation templates for output follow:

DATE_HDR_TMPL = """
    <h2>%s</h1>
"""

FEED_HDR_TMPL = """
    <h3><a href="%(feed.link)s">%(feed.title)s</a></h2>
"""

ENTRY_TMPL = """
    <div>
        <div>
            <span>%(time)s</span>:
            <a href="%(entry.link)s">%(entry.title)s</a>
        </div>
        <div>
            %(entry.summary)s
            <hr>
            %(content)s
        </div>
    </div>
"""

PAGE_TMPL = """
```

Continued

Listing 5-5 *(continued)*

```
<html>
    <head>
    </head>
    <body>
        <h1>Feed aggregator #1</h1>
        %s
    </body>
</html>
"""


if __name__ == "__main__": main()
```

And that's it—you now have an enhanced feed aggregator that produces Plucker documents. Why not take it for a spin?

Figure 5-7 shows a greatly abbreviated session with the program, with the PLUCKER_DEPTH setting at 0 so that just the aggregator HTML is included and not any linked pages. As noted earlier, with regard to the Distiller test program, you might also want to try this new aggregator with the PLUCKER_DEPTH setting at 0 until you've taken it through a few runs and tested things out.

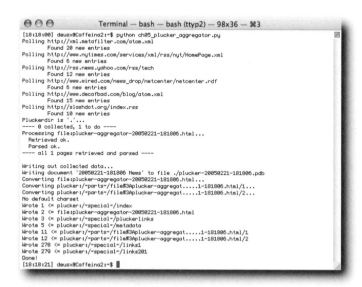

FIGURE 5-7: Watching a short session with
ch05_plucker_aggregator.py

Getting Plucker Documents onto Your Palm OS Device

The final thing that this program needs is some way to get these Plucker documents automatically loaded onto your PalmOS device. However, unlike some other applications that connect to PalmOS devices via HotSync conduits, Plucker relies on plain old installable databases.

This is both good and bad. It's good, because you're not limited by whatever HotSync conduits are available for your operating system from the Plucker authors. The bad part is that although these databases are generally easy to get installed manually—most times it only takes a double-click—it's a little harder to set up the transfer automatically in a way that works everywhere:

- On Mac OS X, there's a utility at /usr/bin/open that does pretty much the same thing from a shell program that a double-click in Finder does. So, issuing a command like this after the Plucker document has been generated could be just what you need, whether you're using Palm Desktop or The Missing Sync:

  ```
  /usr/bin/open plucker-20050221-181806.pdb
  ```

- On Windows, the Palm Desktop and HotSync components usually have a directory set aside where you can put .prc and .pdb files for install at the next sync-up. Copying the finished Plucker document here after generation should cause HotSync to pick up this new file at the next run. Most times, this install directory resides in a directory something like this:

  ```
  C:\Program Files\Palm\<YOUR HOTSYNC NAME>\Install
  ```

- On Linux. . . who knows? Your mileage definitely varies here. There's no official support for syncing PalmOS devices with Linux desktops, but there are lots of unofficial ways to do it. So, if you're already using a PalmOS device with Linux, you probably know more than I do about how your configuration works. However, if you're just starting to look into getting your device working with Linux, you might want to start by visiting the pilot-link community home page here:

  ```
  http://www.pilot-link.org
  ```

Loading Up Your iPod with Feeds

Note This section's program works mainly with the newer generations of the iPod running version 2.0 or later of the iPod firmware. Previous firmware versions and iPod generations either don't offer the Note Reader at all, or provide a version lacking the subset of HTML used for formatting and hyperlinks in this program. You may still be able to benefit from this section, but your mileage may vary.

Introducing the iPod Note Reader

The Note Reader available on Apple's iPod allows you to drop a number of text files into the iPod filesystem for later browsing on its display. This is a relatively recent addition to the iPod firmware, which has been gradually subsuming more and more PDA-like bits of functionality. In fact, in one of the newest revisions of the iPod, these notes support a small subset of HTML usable for a few formatting tweaks and hyperlinks between notes.

This means that you can build fairly complex little webs of documents on your iPod and use the ever-present iPod wheel-and-button interface to scroll through text and select and follow links. A few limitations exist, however: As of this writing, an iPod can only hold up to 1,000 notes and no single note can be over 4 KB in size. Also, don't expect to embed any images. The Note Reader is intended primarily to support text-based notes, with a few rudimentary hypertext features as a bonus.

You can find a complete description of the iPod Note Reader and what sorts of HTML formatting and tags are supported on Apple's developer site here:

        http://developer.apple.com/hardware/ipod/

However, these limitations still haven't stopped quite a few tinkerers from shoehorning all kinds of content into tiny iPod notes. Converters and loaders for weather reports, movie listings, to-do lists, outlines, and word processor documents are available—you can even find a few novels out there, intended for consumption via iPod.

What all this means is that you can take advantage of the Note Reader on your iPod to keep up with syndication feeds. Many feeds out there provide convenient, bite-sized updates on news and events that would fit right into the size constraints of an iPod. Granted, this means that you need to look around a bit for some subscriptions to feeds that aren't heavily dependent on images or fancy HTML layout and rely on decently written entry summaries. Luckily, however, many of the major news sites and many blogs fit this pattern.

Creating and Managing iPod Notes

So, just how do you make notes and how do they make it onto an iPod? Fortunately, the process is incredibly simple, even when compared to using the Plucker Distiller introduced earlier in this chapter. Notes on an iPod are text files that reside in the Notes folder on an iPod—no syncing or conduit loading required.

Simply connect an iPod to your computer with "Enable disk use" turned on, to mount it as a removable hard drive (see Figure 5-8), then look for the Notes folder (see Figure 5-9). That's it. Any text files you drop into the Notes folder will appear in the Note Reader the next time you disconnect your iPod and wander away.

If you haven't already learned about this feature, you can find a tutorial movie guiding you through the process of enabling your iPod to be used as a portable hard drive at Apple's site here:

        http://www.apple.com/support/ipod/tutorial/
        ip_gettingstarted_t11.html

Although this tutorial is Mac-specific, the process is pretty much the same for Windows.

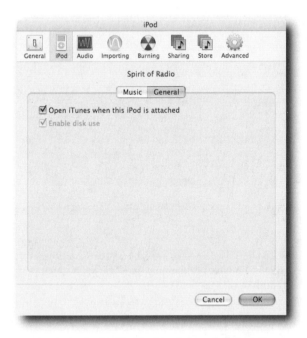

FIGURE 5-8: An iPod with "Enable disk use" activated

FIGURE 5-9: Finding the Notes folder on an iPod under Mac OS X

Again, these notes can be written using a simple (but useful) subset of HTML tags, enabling some basic formatting and (more interesting) inter-note hyperlinks. You'll want to check out the Note Reader docs for specifics, but here's a peek at a sample iPod note:

```
<html>
<head>
    <title>Feeds</title>
    <meta name="ShowBodyOnly" content="true">
    <meta name="HideAllTags" content="true">
    <meta name="LineWrap" content="true">
    <meta name="NowPlaying" content="false">
</head>
<body>
<a href="zz_feeds/123/index.txt">NYT > Home Page</a><br>
<a href="zz_feeds/456/index.txt">Yahoo! News: Technology</a><br>
<a href="zz_feeds/789/index.txt">Wired News</a><br>
<a href="zz_feeds/248/index.txt">BBC News | News Front
Page</a><br>
<a href="zz_feeds/135/index.txt">0xDECAFBAD Blog</a><br>
</body>
</html>
```

This note shows off a few of the pseudo-HTML features available in the Note Reader. If you like, try creating this as a new text file in the Notes folder on your iPod. To see what this would look like being viewed on an iPod, check out Figure 5-10.

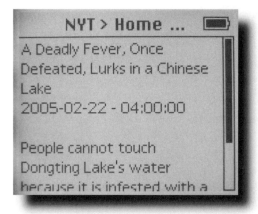

FIGURE 5-10: Sample note displayed on an iPod

Designing a Feed Aggregator with iPod Notes

Now, you have everything you need to build a feed aggregator that will fill up your iPod with plenty of reading material in notes. A few thoughts on the design of this thing are in order, though.

Previous aggregators in this book have mostly relied either on having a Web browser and a relatively large display, or in the case of the Plucker-based aggregator earlier in this chapter, the availability of a flexible and feature-rich document reader.

However, in this case, you'll need to remember the limitations of iPod notes. Specifically, you'll need to work around the simplicity of the scroll-and-click interface, the small size of the screen dimensions, and the 4-KB limit on note length. This means, mainly, that instead of having one big document to browse, you'll need to split up your feeds into a lot of little notes connected by hyperlinks that you can navigate via the scroll wheel and Select button.

This might sound complicated, but it's not really. In fact, the menu system into which this aggregator will structure its notes should feel a lot like the familiar iPod interface itself, with its "drill-down" menu system (see Figure 5-11).

FIGURE 5-11: Drilling down through iPod menus

If you were selecting a particular song, you might browse from "Artists" to "Some Band" to "Some Song." Accordingly, in your notes-based aggregator, you'll use the iPod interface to browse from "Feeds" to "Some Feed" to "Some Entry"—all built from hyperlinked text notes.

The idea is that there's an index linking to all feeds, and for each feed there's an index linking to individual entries for that feed. So, the feeds index is like the "Artists" menu, an index for a feed is like the "Some Band" menu, and each of the entries is like "Some Song."

Building an iPod-based Feed Aggregator

Before you start work on the new program, you need to make a quick tweak to your `agglib` module. So far, all that you've kept track of in the feed database are the `ETag`, modified time, and last poll time for each feed. To make things a little easier for this next aggregator, you're now going to start keeping track of the feed title in the database.

So, open up your copy of `agglib.py`, and find the definition of the `getNewFeedEntries()` function. Scroll down toward the end of that function, and locate the part where the feed database is updated after all the feed entries have been processed.

Now, take a look at Listing 5-6 for a revision to this part.

Listing 5-6: agglib.py Modification

```python
# Finally, update the notes remembered for this feed.
if feed_data.has_key('feed') and feed_data['feed'].has_key('title'):
    feed_title = feed_data['feed']['title']
else:
    feed_title = 'Untitled'

feed_db[uri] = {
    'last_poll' : time.time(),
    'etag'      : feed_data.get('etag', None),
    'modified'  : feed_data.get('modified', None),
    'title'     : feed_title
}
```

The gist here is that an attempt is made to grab the current feed's title from the parsed data, and then the title is squirreled away in the feed database along with the rest of the data you were already storing.

Now, you're ready to start on the aggregator itself. Create a new program file in your editor and name it ch05_ipod_notes_aggregator.py. Take a look at Listing 5-7 for the beginning of this file.

Listing 5-7: ch05_ipod_notes_aggregator.py (Part 1 of 6)

```python
#!/usr/bin/env python
"""
ch05_ipod_notes_aggregator.py

Poll subscriptions, load iPod up with notes.
"""
import sys, os, os.path, shutil, time, md5
from agglib import *

FEEDS_FN        = "ipod_feeds.txt"
FEED_DB_FN      = "ipod_feeds_db"
ENTRY_DB_FN     = "ipod_entry_seen_db"

IPOD_NOTES_PATH      = "/Volumes/Spirit of Radio/Notes"
IPOD_FEEDS_IDX_TITLE = "Feeds"
IPOD_FEEDS_IDX       = "feeds.linx"
IPOD_FEEDS_DIR       = "zz_feeds"
```

For this program, the names of the subscription list and databases have been changed in the initial configuration constant. It's probably best to keep these separate from any other aggregators you might be using, just to keep them from stepping on each other's toes. That, and feed subscriptions that work well elsewhere might not be the best choices for use with your iPod.

The next few configuration constants are new, however, and are related to the addition of the iPod to the mix:

- IPOD_NOTES_PATH—This is the path to your iPod mounted as a hard drive. Mine is named "Spirit of Radio," but you really should replace this with whatever name you've chosen for yours.

- IPOD_FEEDS_IDX_TITLE—Instead of the filename set in the next constant, your iPod displays this setting as the title for the note where all your feed browsing starts.

- IPOD_FEEDS_IDX—The menu of links pointing to feeds gets stored under this filename in the iPod Notes folder. Something interesting to note about this filename (feeds.linx) is that the .linx extension causes the iPod to display this list of links just like one of its own menus, rather than in the smaller font and text layout used for normal notes. This helps maintain the appearance of other iPod applications, though you may want to experiment.

- IPOD_FEEDS_DIR—When the menu structure of linked notes for feeds and feed entries are generated, this is the directory under Notes that contains them. Unfortunately, there's no easy way to hide directories in the Note Reader, and browsing around in this directory isn't nearly as friendly as starting with the feed link index. So, it's best to give this folder a name that will push it as far down the list and out of the way as possible—and starting with "zz_" seems like a good way to do that.

After the configuration constants are established, the next step is to throw together a few string templates that will come in handy when generating iPod notes. These are provided in Listing 5-8.

Listing 5-8: ch05_ipod_notes_aggregator.py (Part 2 of 6)

```
NOTE_TMPL = """
<html>
    <head>
        <title>%(title)s</title>
        <meta name="ShowBodyOnly" content="true">
        <meta name="HideAllTags" content="true">
        <meta name="LineWrap" content="true">
        <meta name="NowPlaying" content="false">
    </head>
    <body>%(content)s</body>
</html>
"""
```

Continued

Listing 5-8 *(continued)*

```
FEED_LINK_TMPL  = """<a href="%(href)s">%(title)s</a><br>\n"""

ENTRY_LINK_TMPL = """* <a href="%(href)s">%(title)s</a><br>\n"""

ENTRY_TMPL      = """<b>%(entry.title)s</b><br>
%(date)s - %(time)s<br>
<br>
%(entry.summary)s
"""
```

The first string template is named NOTE_TMPL, and this is a global template for all notes this aggregator will produce. It defines slots for a title and body content, and the rest is all boiler-plate. If you really want to know what all the <meta> tags do, you should read up on the Note Reader documentation from Apple (mentioned earlier). In a nutshell, these are Note Reader preferences that instruct it to treat this note as much like HTML as possible.

The next two templates, FEED_LINK_TMPL and ENTRY_LINK_TMPL, define how links to feeds and feed entries will be generated, respectively. Both of these take the form of simple HTML hyperlinks followed by line breaks, the only difference being that entry links are pre-ceded by an asterisk as a bullet. The feed links don't really have any formatting, though, because they're displayed differently, as explained in a minute or so.

Last in the set of string templates is ENTRY_TMPL, which is used to generate the body content for individual feed entry notes. Notice that the initial title of the entry is butted up against the first quote of the multi-line string, and that this template doesn't have any other indentation. This is important, because the Note Reader includes any indentation on the screen for body content. So, if any of these lines were indented, that whitespace would appear on the iPod screen and not be ignored as a normal Web browser viewing it would. This wastes valuable screen real-estate, so be careful with this.

The next step is to write the main() function definition for this aggregator, which is shown in Listing 5-9.

Listing 5-9: ch05_ipod_notes_aggregator.py (Part 3 of 6)

```
def main():
    """
    Poll subscribed feeds and load the iPod up with notes.
    """
    # Open the aggregator databases
    feed_db, entry_db = openDBs(FEED_DB_FN, ENTRY_DB_FN)
```

```
# Clean up and recreate feed notes directory
ipod_feeds_path = os.path.join(IPOD_NOTES_PATH, IPOD_FEEDS_DIR)
shutil.rmtree(ipod_feeds_path, ignore_errors=True)
if not os.path.isdir(ipod_feeds_path):
    os.makedirs(ipod_feeds_path)

# Load up the list of subscriptions
feeds = [ x.strip() for x in open(FEEDS_FN, "r").readlines() ]

# Build the notes for all feeds, gathering links to the
# feed indexes
feed_links = buildNotesForFeeds(feed_db, entry_db, ipod_feeds_path,
                                feeds)

# Write the feed index note with links to all feed indexes
index_out = "".join([FEED_LINK_TMPL % f for f in feed_links])
writeNote(filename = os.path.join(IPOD_NOTES_PATH, IPOD_FEEDS_IDX),
          title    = IPOD_FEEDS_IDX_TITLE,
          content  = index_out)

# Close the aggregator databases
closeDBs(feed_db, entry_db)
```

In `main()`, the aggregator databases are first opened, and then the directory for feed notes is wiped out and re-created on the iPod. Doing this keeps things clean and ensures that only fresh notes from the latest run of the aggregator are left on your iPod, preventing any progressive clutter from previous runs.

 Here, in particular, you'll want to be sure that you have the right path set in `IPOD_NOTES_PATH` and `IPOD_FEEDS_DIR`, because this call to `shutil.rmtree()` deletes a directory and all its subdirectories and contents. If this makes you nervous, you may want to comment out this destructive call until you've tested things out a bit. You don't want to accidentally wipe out anything other than old notes.

After that, the list of subscribed feeds is loaded up and passed to a function named `buildNotesForFeeds()`, along with the aggregator databases and the path where feed notes will be stored. This function manages the process of generating notes for new entries found for each subscribed feed, as well as an index note for each feed listing links to all the new entries for each feed.

When it has finished, this function returns a list of titles and links to the feed indexes. These are then used with `FEED_LINK_TMPL` to build a top-level list of links pointing to each of the feed index notes. This list of links is then written out as a top-level note on the iPod with the `writeNote()` function, using a filename defined by the `IPOD_FEEDS_IDX` constant and has a title taken from `IPOD_FEEDS_IDX_TITLE`. This note will be used as the entry point to browsing through all your subscriptions on the iPod.

At this point, the `main()` function suggests a lot of details left to be filled in. But first, you need to add couple of convenience functions, as shown in Listing 5-10.

Listing 5-10: ch05_ipod_notes_aggregator.py (Part 4 of 6)

```
def writeNote(filename, title, content):
    """
    Given a filename, title, and content, write a note to the iPod.
    """
    print "\t\tWrote note: %s" % filename
    fout = open(filename, "w")
    fout.write(NOTE_TMPL % { 'title':title, 'content':content })
    fout.close()

def md5_hash(data):
    """
    Convenience function to generate an MD5 hash.
    """
    m = md5.md5()
    m.update(data)
    return m.hexdigest()
```

The first of these new convenience functions is defined as `writeNote()`. There isn't much to this one. Given a filename, a title, and some content, it prints a message and writes out a note to the desired file after filling out the `NOTE_TMPL` string template with the given title and content. This function exists mostly because this procedure will be reused throughout the program, and making it into a function saves a little bit of effort while adding a bit more clarity.

The next convenience function, named `md5_hash()`, calls upon the `md5` module to generate unique hashes from given data. This is used in the production of filenames for notes, based on things like URLs and titles whose contents might disagree with file and directory name restrictions on the iPod filesystem. It makes for less friendly browsing under the `IPOD_FEEDS_DIR` directory, but you won't need to look around in there anyway thanks to the lists of links this aggregator builds.

Moving on, take a look at Listing 5-11, where you can find the definition of `buildNotesForFeeds()`.

Listing 5-11: ch05_ipod_notes_aggregator.py (Part 5 of 6)

```
def buildNotesForFeeds(feed_db, entry_db, ipod_feeds_path, feeds):
    """
    Iterate through feeds, produce entry notes, feed index notes,
    and return list of links to feed index notes.
```

```
"""
feed_links = []
for feed_url in feeds:

    # Get new entries for the current feed
    entries = getNewFeedEntries([feed_url], feed_db, entry_db)
    if len(entries) > 0:

        # Derive current feed path via md5 hash, create it if needed
        feed_dir_name = md5_hash(feed_url)
        feed_dir      = os.path.join(ipod_feeds_path, feed_dir_name)
        if not os.path.isdir(feed_dir):
            os.makedirs(feed_dir)

        # Get a clean title for this feed.
        feed_title = feed_db[feed_url].get('title', 'Untitled').strip()

        # Build the notes for the new entries, gathering links
        feed_entry_links = buildNotesForEntries(feed_dir, feed_title, \
                                                entries)

        # Write out the index note for this feed, based on entry notes.
        feed_out = "".join([ENTRY_LINK_TMPL % f for f in feed_entry_links])
        writeNote(filename = os.path.join(feed_dir, 'index.txt'),
                  title    = feed_title,
                  content  = feed_out)

        # Include this feed in the top-level index.
        feed_links.append({
            'href'  : '%s/%s/index.txt' % (IPOD_FEEDS_DIR, feed_dir_name),
            'title' : feed_title
        })

return feed_links
```

The `buildNotesForFeeds()` function is the core this aggregator and here's what it does:

- For each feed, it tries to grab new entries. If there are no new entries, it continues onto the next feed.

- If there are new entries, it generates an MD5 hash from the feed URL. This hash is used to come up with the name of a subdirectory for this feed's notes. This feed subdirectory gets created if it doesn't already exist.

- The current feed's title is retrieved from the feed database. Remember that tweak you made earlier to the agglib module? This value is stripped of extra whitespace at the beginning and end, so as to not waste space on the iPod screen.

- A function named buildNotesForEntries() is called with the path to this feed's subdirectory, the feed's title, and the list of entries. This method manages the process of generating notes for all of this feed's new entries. When it is finished, it returns a list of paths and titles to the notes it created for this feed.

- The list of paths and titles returned by buildNotesForEntries() is used with ENTRY_ LINK_TMPL to generate a list of links. This list of links is then used to write out an index note for this feed and its entries.

- Once the index note has been written, a path to it and its title are appended to the running list that is returned at the end of this function.

After this, there's just one function left to be defined, called buildNotesForEntries() and given in Listing 5-12.

Listing 5-12: ch05_ipod_notes_aggregator.py (Part 6 of 6)

```python
def buildNotesForEntries(feed_dir, feed_title, entries):
    """
    Iterate through a set of entries, build a note for each in the
    appropriate feed directory, return list of links to generated
    notes.
    """
    feed_entry_links = []
    for entry in entries:

        # Build note name on MD5 hash, possibly redundant but oh well!
        entry_note_name = '%s.txt' % md5_hash(entry.hash())

        # Get a clean title for the entry note
        entry_title     = entry['entry.title'].strip()

        # Write out the index note for this feed.
        writeNote(filename = os.path.join(feed_dir, entry_note_name),
                  title    = feed_title,
                  content  = ENTRY_TMPL % entry)

        # Include this feed in the top-level index
        feed_entry_links.append({
            'href'  : entry_note_name,
            'title' : entry_title
        })

    return feed_entry_links

if __name__ == "__main__": main()
```

This final function, `buildNotesForEntries()`, is the workhorse of this aggregator. Given a directory for feed notes, the title of the feed, and a list of entries, it dumps out a pile of notes—one for each new entry found in the feed—and returns the list of paths and titles involved.

These notes are built using the `ENTRY_TMPL` string template, with each entry note's filename built from the MD5 hash of that entry's `hash()` method.

Note

All this hashing might sound redundant, because some feed entries are already using MD5 hashes as unique identifiers. However, there's no rule that says they have to. In fact, Atom feeds tend to use the `tag URI scheme`, which, in turn, contains characters that may give the iPod filesystem indigestion. Just to be safe, whatever the entry is using for a hash is turned into an MD5 hex hash—which contains only letters and numbers—so you have a safe filename for the entry note.

And with that, your iPod aggregator is finished. Hopefully you didn't get lost in the levels of note generation, but it should all make sense once you see it running.

Trying Out the iPod-based Feed Aggregator

Before you take your iPod notes aggregator out for a spin, you should probably pick a subset of your normal feeds to use with it. Because of the iPod's small screen, as well as the lack of graphics and the ability to link out to other sites online, you really want to find feeds that are mostly self-contained and offer smaller, more bite-sized pieces of information and news. Here are a few feed URLs that might fit the bill for you:

```
http://www.nytimes.com/services/xml/rss/nyt/HomePage.xml
http://rss.news.yahoo.com/rss/tech
http://www.wired.com/news_drop/netcenter/netcenter.rdf
http://news.bbc.co.uk/rss/newsonline_world_edition/front_page/rss091.xml
```

These sorts of feeds tend to come from more traditional news sites, with feed entry summaries edited and prepared to summarize in a paragraph or two. If you look around, though, you'll probably be able to find some feeds from your favorite blogs or entertainment sites that would be good to read on your iPod.

Once armed with a suitable set of feeds, try running the program. If successful, you should see something like what appears in Figure 5-12. After it finishes, you can take a look in your iPod's Notes folder and see results similar to Figure 5-13. There should be a slew of new files and folders with cryptic MD5-hash names. Don't worry, though. The files and folders under `zz_feeds` aren't meant for your direct perusal—that's why you named this folder `zz_feeds` to begin with, to try to hide it or at least get it out of the way. The important file, your entry point into the whole linked web of notes, is the `feeds.linx` file.

Now, to check out what these notes look like, you'll want to eject and disconnect your iPod using the Eject button in iTunes or the appropriate method for unmounting from the filesystem. (If you watched it, the tutorial on using your iPod as a hard disk mentioned earlier should have explained the proper way to do this.)

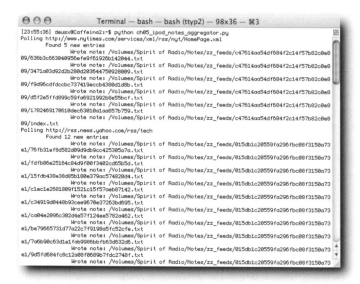

FIGURE 5-12: Running the iPod aggregator

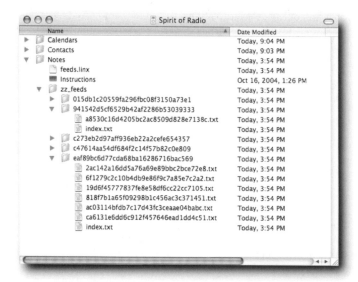

FIGURE 5-13: The aggregator's aftermath in an iPod's Notes folder

Once you have your iPod unmounted and free of your computer, navigate to the Notes option under Extras and take a look. You should see a new "Feeds" item, as well as the zz_feeds folder, as shown in Figure 5-14.

FIGURE 5-14: iPod Notes Reader with the Feeds item

Ignore the zz_feeds folder, and highlight and select the "Feeds" item. Figure 5-15 shows what the next screen should look like: A list of feeds with new entries loaded onto your iPod. This is the contents of the feeds.linx note, but it appears as an item named "Feeds" instead of feeds.linx, thanks to the HTML title tag in the note.

FIGURE 5-15: iPod Notes Reader showing feeds list

From here, drill down into a feed. Figure 5-16 shows you what to expect here: a list of new entries found for this feed. This is the contents of an index.txt file found in one of those obscurely named feed directories, but because you followed a link from "Feeds" to get here, you never need to worry about that directory name. This screen is formatted a bit differently than the "Feeds" screen, though, because the index.txt filenames don't end in the .linx extension. Here, the font is a bit smaller, and an underline is used to highlight links, rather than the iPod standard menu reverse-highlight bar.

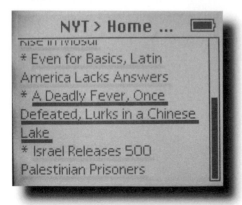

FIGURE 5-16: iPod Notes Reader displaying a list of feed entries

You can navigate and scroll around in this listing of feed entries with the scroll wheel, moving the link highlight until you find an entry you want to read. Click this one, and you'll see the text of the entry displayed as in Figure 5-17. This is the end of the line; no more links to click from here, but you can scroll up and down in the text of this note to read it.

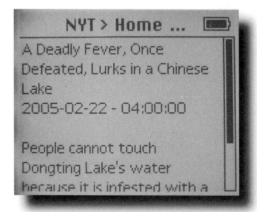

FIGURE 5-17: iPod Notes Reader displaying a feed entry

And, just for the sake of completeness, Figures 5-18 and 5-19 show what you'd see if you browsed into the zz_feeds folder under Notes. It's not a very friendly sight, so for the most part you should just ignore that it's there and enjoy the link-driven menu of notes starting from the "Feeds" item.

FIGURE 5-18: iPod Notes Reader selecting the
`zz_feeds` item

FIGURE 5-19: iPod Notes Reader listing directories
under `zz_feeds`

With this latest program, you should be able to keep yourself equipped not only with all your favorite music, but also with the freshest news whenever you disconnect your iPod and wander away with it. You may want to set up this aggregator to run on a scheduled basis alongside any others you have going, but you may want to do a little homework into how to detect whether the iPod is connected, so that you don't try launching an aggregator run that will try to load notes when the device isn't there. But, that's left as a future project for you.

Using Text-to-Speech on Mac OS X to Create Audio Feeds

The previous aggregator allows you to load up an iPod with a little web of text notes built from your feed subscriptions, which can be convenient while you're out and about and have a few minutes to spend reading. But what about when you're on your daily commute in your car or out doing something else that doesn't give you a chance to safely stare down at a tiny screen for any length of time? Well, the main thing an iPod is best at is playing audio. So, why not build an aggregator that will let your iPod read your news to you with a synthesized voice?

Hacking Speech Synthesis on Mac OS X

Synthesized speech has been a part of the Macintosh experience since its introduction in 1984, so it should be no surprise that the availability of speech continues on in Mac OS X. What is a pleasant discovery, though, is that in carrying speech facilities forward into OS X, Apple has also worked to integrate it with the UNIX-based side of things. This means that, among other things, you can use speech from the command line and in your Python programs.

 On the Web If you'd like to read up a bit on the history of speech on the Mac, consult the Wikipedia for more information:

        http://en.wikipedia.org/wiki/Apple_PlainTalk

Also, you can check out a laundry list of other Mac-flavored additions Apple has made on the UNIX side here, at a page called "Mac OS X Hacking Tools":

        http://www.kernelthread.com/mac/apme/tools/

One of the easiest ways to start hacking with speech synthesis on Mac OS X, then, takes the form of a program at /usr/bin/say. The say command uses whatever Speech preferences you've set in your System Preferences to recite text from the command line, standard input, or a given filename (see Figure 5-20). You can also override the voice set in System Preferences with other command-line options (see Figure 5-21). And, the say command can either play the recitation out loud, or stream it to an AIFF file on disk to be played later or converted to another format.

 On the Web You can find documentation for the say command at Apple's developer site here:

        http://developer.apple.com/documentation/Darwin/
        Reference/ManPages/man1/say.1.html

Here are a few example invocations of the say command to give you a taste:

```
/usr/bin/say "Hello world"
/usr/bin/say -o hello.aiff "Hello world"
/usr/bin/say -v Ralph -o long_speech.aiff -f
long_speech_script.txt
```

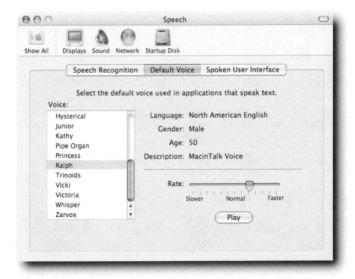

FIGURE 5-20: Speech preference pane on Mac OS X

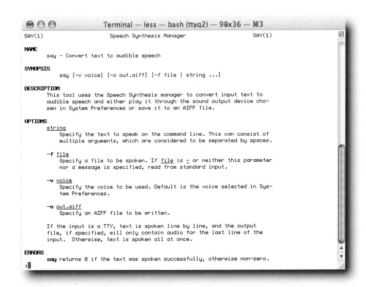

FIGURE 5-21: Man page documentation for /usr/bin/say in a
Terminal window

The first of these simple examples announces "Hello world." The second example results in the
sound of the speech written to a sound file in AIFF format, named hello.aiff. The third
and final example is the most complex. It overrides System Preferences to use the "Ralph"

voice, recording to an AIFF file named `long_speech.aiff`, reading from a text file named `long_speech_script.txt`.

This tool is interesting for your work in Python, thanks to the `os.popen` function, which enables you to launch external processes with piped console input/output. This means that you can call and control `/usr/bin/say` from Python programs, thus gaining access to your Mac's speech synthesis.

You might want to take a minute or two to read up on `os.popen`, with documentation available in the standard Python library under Process Management, here:

> `http://docs.python.org/lib/os-process.html`

Hacking AppleScript and iTunes from Python

Now that you have a tool to make your Mac talk (which even produces audio files), you need a way to get these onto your iPod. To do that, you need to tinker with iTunes, which has the capabilities to convert audio files (that is, from AIFF to MP3) as well as taking charge of managing the contents of your iPod. And, it just so happens that iTunes was built to be scripted and manipulated via AppleScript.

Unfortunately, all of your aggregator code is written in Python, so now you need some way to bridge between iTunes, AppleScript, and Python. Well, you're in luck again, because there's also a command-line tool for dealing with AppleScript, which you can find at `/usr/bin/osascript` (see Figure 5-22).

You can find documentation for the `osascript` command at Apple's developer site here:

> `http://developer.apple.com/documentation/Darwin/`
> `Reference/ManPages/man1/osascript.1.html`

This command allows you to compile and run AppleScript source code on-the-fly from the command line, without using the Script Editor. And, a bit like the `say` command, `osascript` allows the AppleScript code to be fed to it via console input/output, so that Python can speak AppleScript via `os.popen`. It sounds convoluted—and, well, it is—but that's why it's called a hack!

Building a Speaking Aggregator

All the parts are assembled now, so you can start building the last program for this chapter. This aggregator builds a text file as a script for reading, rather than generating HTML. One trick to prevent `/usr/bin/say` from happily reading HTML tags with angle brackets and all, is to be sure all tags are stripped from feed entries. Once prepared, this text file is then run through `/usr/bin/say` to generate an AIFF sound file. After that's done, the sound file is converted to MP3 and imported into iTunes and your iPod, via some AppleScript built on-the-fly and run through `/usr/bin/osascript`.

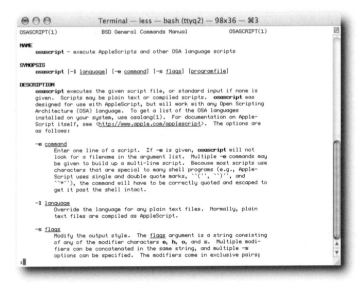

FIGURE **5-22: Man page documentation for** `/usr/bin/osascript` **in a Terminal window**

So, start this new program file under the name `ch05_speech_aggregator.py` and check out Listing 5-13 for the preamble.

Listing 5-13: ch05_speech_aggregator.py (Part 1 of 5)

```python
#!/usr/bin/env python
"""
ch05_speech_aggregator.py

Poll subscriptions, produce plain text script, recite into
a sound file, then attempt to import into iTunes and an iPod.
"""
import sys, os, os.path, time
from agglib import *
from HTMLParser import HTMLParser

FEEDS_FN        = "speech_feeds.txt"
FEED_DB_FN      = "speech_feeds_db"
ENTRY_DB_FN     = "speech_entry_seen_db"

TXT_FN          = "speech-aggregator-%s.txt" % \
                    time.strftime("%Y%m%d-%H%M%S")
```

Continued

Listing 5-13 *(continued)*

```
SOUND_FN       = "speech-aggregator-%s.aiff" % \
                     time.strftime("%Y%m%d-%H%M%S")

DATE_HDR_TMPL = "%s"
FEED_HDR_TMPL = "%(feed.title)s\n%(time)s"
ENTRY_TMPL    = \
    "%(entry.title)s\n\n%(entry.summary)s\n%(content)s"
PAGE_TMPL     = "%s"
```

So far, so good; a few of the usual modules are imported, and some speech-specific filenames are used for the feed subscriptions and the two database files. Then, a datestamp-based filename is generated for both the text script you'll be building, and the AIFF sound file that is used to record speech. Rounding out the end of Listing 5-13 are the set of very simple templates that are to generate the text script for reading.

Continue on to Listing 5-14 for the definition of the main() function.

Listing 5-14: ch05_speech_aggregator.py (Part 2 of 5)

```
def main():
    """
    Poll subscribed feeds and produce aggregator page.
    """
    feed_db, entry_db = openDBs(FEED_DB_FN, ENTRY_DB_FN)

    feeds    = [ x.strip() for x in open(FEEDS_FN, "r").readlines() ]

    entries = getNewFeedEntries(feeds, feed_db, entry_db)

    if len(entries) > 0:
        # Ensure that the summary and content of entries are
        # stripped of HTML
        s = HTMLStripper()
        for e in entries:
            e.entry.summary = s.strip_html(e.entry.summary)
            if e.entry.has_key("content"):
                e.entry.content[0].value = \
                        s.strip_html(e.entry.content[0].value)

        # Write out the text script from new entries, then read into a
        # sound file.  When done reading, convert to MP3 and import
        # into iTunes and iPod.
```

```
    writeAggregatorPage(entries, TXT_FN, DATE_HDR_TMPL,
        FEED_HDR_TMPL, ENTRY_TMPL, PAGE_TMPL)
    speakTextIntoSoundFile(TXT_FN, SOUND_FN)
    importSoundFile(SOUND_FN)

    closeDBs(feed_db, entry_db)
```

In this program's `main()` function, things start off with the databases getting opened and the list of feeds read in. Then, new entries are fetched from all the feeds with a call to `getNewFeed Entries()`.

The first interesting thing that comes up is the use of a new class named `HTMLStripper`. An instance of `HTMLStripper` is created and then used to filter through all the summaries and content of the new entries, stripping all HTML tags from each, attempting to ensure that only plain text is left. The process is a hack, and not perfect, but should greatly reduce the amount of markup crud and tag soup that `/usr/bin/say` will attempt to pronounce.

Next, the simple string templates are used with a call to `writeAggregatorPage()` to produce the text script from all of the new feed entries. Then, the text script is read, with the recitation recorded to the appropriate filename with a call to `speakTextIntoSoundFile()`. Once the recitation has completed, this sound file is converted to MP3 and imported into iTunes and your iPod with a call to `importSoundFile()`.

Press ahead to Listing 5-15, where you'll find the definition for `speakTextIntoSoundFile()`.

Listing 5-15: ch05_speech_aggregator.py (Part 3 of 5)

```python
def speakTextIntoSoundFile(txt_fn, sound_fn):
    """
    Use Mac OS X text-to-speech to make a speech recording of a
    given text file
    """
    print "Reciting text '%s' to file '%s'..." % (txt_fn, sound_fn)
    say_cmd = "/usr/bin/say -o '%s' -f '%s'" % (sound_fn, txt_fn)
    p = os.popen(say_cmd, "w")
    p.close()
```

The definition for `speakTextIntoSoundFile()` is not all that complex. A message is printed, and then an invocation of `/usr/bin/say` is constructed, using the text script filename and sound filename to fill out a string template. Then, `os.popen` is used to launch and execute this invocation. And, that's it; that's all it takes to integrate speech into this aggregator.

However, the next part, with the definition of `importSoundFile()` in Listing 5-16, is a tiny bit more involved.

Listing 5-16: ch05_speech_aggregator.py (Part 4 of 5)

```
IMPORT_APPLESCRIPT = """
property arguments : "%s"

-- Derive a Mac-style path from a given POSIX path.
set track_path to arguments
set track_file to POSIX file track_path

-- Launch iTunes as hidden, if not already running.
tell application "System Events"
    if not (exists process "iTunes") then
        tell application "iTunes"
            launch
            set visible of front window to false
        end tell
    end if
end tell

tell application "iTunes"
    -- Convert the AIFF track (which might take awhile)
    with timeout of 300000 seconds
        set converted_track to item 1 of (convert track_file)
    end timeout

    -- Set the track genre
    set the genre of converted_track to "Speech"

    -- This might fail if no iPod is connected, but try to
    -- copy converted track.
    try
        set the_iPod to some source whose kind is iPod
        duplicate converted_track to playlist 1 of the_iPod
    end try
end tell
"""

def importSoundFile(sound_fn):
    """
    Given a sound filename, import into iTunes and an iPod.
    """
    print "Converting and importing sound file '%s'..." % sound_fn
    f = os.popen('/usr/bin/osascript', "w")
    f.write(IMPORT_APPLESCRIPT % os.path.abspath(sound_fn))
    f.close()
```

The bulk of Listing 5-16 is made up of a stretch of AppleScript source presented as a Python string template. The single slot to be filled in appears on the first line of the AppleScript source, intended to be populated with the full UNIX-style path to an AIFF file.

The script converts this path to the more classic Mac path style and attempts to see if iTunes is currently running, launching it into the background if necessary.

Once iTunes has been verified as running, the AppleScript tells it to convert the AIFF file containing the spoken audio to MP3 format and import that into your Library as a track. Once imported, the track's genre is set to "Speech" and an attempt is made to copy the track onto your iPod.

Finally, back in Python, driving this whole procedure is the importSoundFile() function. This function prints a message and then forks off a process running /usr/bin/osascript. This process is fed the aforementioned AppleScript source, after it's been populated with the sound file path. The osascript tool then compiles and runs this AppleScript, thus converting and importing the spoken audio file.

And, with one last detail to fill in, you're just about finished with this program. Check out Listing 5-17 for the HTMLStripper class definition.

Listing 5-17: ch05_speech_aggregator.py (Part 5 of 5)

```python
class HTMLStripper(HTMLParser):
    """
    Parses HTML to extract the page title and description.
    """
    CHUNKSIZE = 1024

    def strip_html(self, data):
        self.reset()
        self.feed(data)
        return self.data

    def reset(self):
        HTMLParser.reset(self)
        self.data = ""

    def handle_data(self, data):
        self.data += data
    def handle_entityref(self, data):
        self.data += ' '
    handle_charref = handle_entityref

if __name__ == "__main__": main()
```

The `HTMLStripper` class is an `HTMLParser` subclass that does just one thing: Gather text content from potential streams of HTML data and throw out everything else, including entities and tags. The `strip_html()` method accepts a string of data as a parameter, gets to work parsing, and then returns the accumulated text data when finished parsing.

And, with that, your speech-enabled aggregator should be complete and ready to use.

Trying Out the Speaking Aggregator

Despite the convolutions introduced by calling out the other commands to manipulate Speech and iTunes, this is one of the simpler programs in this book. Taking it out for a run should result in output as shown in Figure 5-23. And, if you take a look in iTunes toward the end of the process, you should see conversion and import progress happening, as in Figure 5-24.

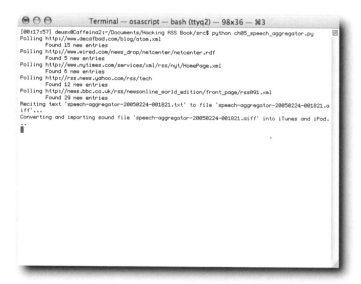

FIGURE 5-23: Running the speaking aggregator in a Terminal window

FIGURE 5-24: Progress converting and importing the sound file in iTunes

You will definitely want to experiment with your selection of feeds for use with this aggregator. Although there is an HTML stripper in this program, its operation is not foolproof. And, not all feeds make the transition to spoken script all that well anyway. But, if you can find a good set of feeds containing some medium-sized clips of information, you'll be well on your way.

Checking Out Other Options

The programs in this chapter are very specific to PalmOS, the iPod, and Mac OS X. But these platforms just represent a slice of what's available for mobility in syndication feeds.

Checking Out iPod Agent

If you have an iPod and use Windows, you might want to check out iPod Agent, available here:

```
http://www.ipodsoft.com/softwaredetail.aspx?sid=1
```

This program offers not only RSS feeds and things like movie listings and weather reports, but also syncs up your Outlook schedule, contacts, tasks, and notes.

Checking Out AvantGo

AvantGo is a very good commercial alternative to Plucker, available here:

```
http://www.avantgo.com/frontdoor/index.html
```

You'll find that AvantGo offers versions for many mobile-computing platforms beyond the PalmOS. Also, one of its great features is that it can download content for reading off the Web right on the mobile device, so you don't need to run a desktop app to build document bundles.

Checking Out QuickNews

QuickNews is a PalmOS-specific feed aggregator, available here:

```
http://standalone.com/palmos/quick_news/
```

Like AvantGo, QuickNews can use wireless connections offered by some devices to download feed updates directly. Also, it supports integration with other applications on the device (such as your email program) to forward links to yourself and others. And, if you have an audio player installed, QuickNews can actually download podcasts and other files while you're on the run.

Summary

The programs in this chapter allow you to take your feeds with you, in the form of readable documents or computerized news shows over your headphones. With or without wireless Internet connectivity, you can still keep in touch.

However, these implementations are certainly not the only way to go—especially if you're not a PalmOS user, don't own an iPod, or don't work on a Mac. You should be able to adapt these ideas to whatever device and operating system you're using, though:

- PalmOS devices certainly don't have a monopoly on portable document readers. Check out the handheld software listings at Handango for a few suggestions on Plucker alternatives:

  `http://www.handango.com/`

- On Windows, you may want to check out the Windows Speech API and investigate how it can tie into Python. The Sayz Me project on SourceForge may give you a few clues toward this end:

  `http://sayzme.sourceforge.net/`

- On Linux, you can check out the Festival Speech Synthesis System, which offers source code for many operating systems:

  `http://www.cstr.ed.ac.uk/projects/festival/`

If do have an iPod, though, keep it handy: You use it again in the next chapter, where you'll be playing with multimedia content delivered via syndication feeds, building your own podcast tuner using direct downloads and BitTorrent technology.

Subscribing to Multimedia Content Feeds

O ne of the most powerful applications of syndication feeds combines automated feed polling and aggregation with fresh downloads of multimedia content. In particular, *podcasting*, which combines RSS feeds and MP3 audio files, has been seeing explosive growth.

With podcasting, amateurs and professionals alike can produce episodic audio content like radio—but rather than tying down listeners with scheduled time slots or by requiring Internet access for streaming audio, podcast receivers can load new shows right onto the portable audio players of listeners, to be enjoyed whenever or wherever. Podcasting brings mobility and time-shifting to Internet radio and, by aggregating this content into playlists, it's like you have your own privately programmed station.

In this chapter, you build a podcast receiver of your own. This program will use the feed aggregator features you've built so far to find new entries with enclosures in RSS feeds. Then it will use standard HTTP and BitTorrent protocols to gather up content. Toward the end of this chapter, if you're a Mac OS X user with an iPod, you learn how to get this stuff automatically loaded as it arrives.

Finding Multimedia Content using RSS Enclosures

RSS feeds are the driving force behind podcasting. Although the pieces may eventually come together for Atom feeds, this chapter is all about the <enclosure> tag in RSS. So, for starters, Listing 6-1 shows what an RSS feed entry with an enclosure looks like.

Listing 6-1: An Example RSS Feed Entry with an Enclosure

```
<item>
    <title>RasterWeb! Audio 2005-01-04 "Evil Brain Mash Up"</title>
    <link>http://rasterweb.net/raster/audio/</link>
    <description>
        RasterWeb! Audio 2005-01-04, Evil Brain Mash Up, A Dam
        12 Days of Podcasting...
    </description>
    <pubDate>Tue, 04 Jan 2005 05:00:00 -0600</pubDate>
    <guid isPermaLink="false">
        tag:rasterweb.net,2005-01-04:/audio/rwaudio20050104.mp3
    </guid>
    <enclosure
        url="http://rasterweb.net/raster/audio/rwaudio20050104.mp3"
        length="569188" type="audio/mpeg" />
</item>
```

Most of this XML should look familiar. There's the title, link, and description found in most feed entries, along with the publication date and the GUID. The new thing here, as you've undoubtedly guessed, is the `<enclosure>` element.

You may have also already figured out how all the `<enclosure>` attributes are used. Just in case you haven't, here's a synopsis:

- `url`—The URL at which this entry's content can be found.
- `length`—How big that content will be, made available so that you can make some decisions ahead of time before downloading.
- `type`—The MIME content type of the content offered by this enclosure.

 You can read about the `<enclosure>` element in the RSS 2.0 specification here:

```
http://blogs.law.harvard.edu/tech/
rss#ltenclosuregtSubelementOfLtitemgt
```

Additionally you can read some early writing on RSS enclosures here:

```
http://www.thetwowayweb.com/payloadsforrss
```

It's important to note that although RSS enclosures are similar in concept to attachments in email, there's a crucial difference. Whereas attachments on email messages are generally MIME-encoded and stuffed into the email message along with everything else, RSS enclosures are formed *by reference via URL*. This allows you to decide what you want to download and how you want to download it. Because an RSS feed tends to contain a list of older entries, it doesn't make sense to continually download a large wad of encoded multimedia content every time you want to poll the feed.

But, now that you know what an enclosure looks like in an RSS feed, you can pretty much forget that you ever saw it—that is, unless you're working on improving your own feed parser from Chapter 2. Otherwise, the `feedparser` module handles enclosure data much like any other RSS feed element. Take a look at Listing 6-2 for an example program named `ch06_enclosure_finder.py` to see how this works.

Listing 6-2: ch06_enclosure_finder.py

```python
#!/usr/bin/env python
"""
ch06_enclosure_finder.py

Given the URL to a feed, list the URLs of enclosures found.
"""

import sys, feedparser

def main():
    feed_url = sys.argv[1]
    feed     = feedparser.parse(feed_url)
    enc_urls = getEnclosuresFromEntries(feed.entries)
    print "\n".join(enc_urls)

def getEnclosuresFromEntries(entries):
    """
    Given a set of entries, harvest the URLs to enclosures.
    """
    enc_urls = []
    for entry in entries:
        enclosures = entry.get('enclosures',[])
        enc_urls.extend([ en['url'] for en in enclosures ])
    return enc_urls

if __name__ == "__main__": main()
```

The `feedparser` module provides the data for any enclosures it finds in entries under the key `enclosures`. One thing to note is that, although RSS 2.0 feeds generally contain only one enclosure per feed entry, earlier versions of RSS explicitly allowed for multiple enclosures. So, in Listing 6-2, the `getEnclosuresFromEntries()` function iterates through every entry, and then every entry's enclosures, to gather one flat list of URLs from the feed.

Downloading Content from URLs

You have almost all the pieces you need to build an enclosure-powered feed aggregator, except a way to download the actual content to which the enclosures refer. Sure, you could just use the `urllib2` module introduced in earlier chapters to grab the content, but why not build in a few more bells and whistles—like, say, a progress display so you have something to look at while things download? Also, it would be nice to build in a little flexibility to easily switch between content transports (for example, HTTP or BitTorrent).

So, start a new file in your editor and name it `downloaders.py`. This will be a shared module that might just be useful beyond the scope of this present project. Check out Listing 6-3 for the beginning of this new module.

Listing 6-3: downloaders.py (Part 1 of 5)

```python
#!/usr/bin/env python
"""
downloaders.py

Provides means to download content by URL.
"""
import sys, os.path, urllib2, time
from urlparse import urlparse

def main():
    """
    Test a downloader.
    """
    url = "http://homepage.mac.com/adamcurry/Default/podcastDefaultWelcome.mp3"
    dl   = HTTPDownloader()
    files= dl.downloadURL(".", url)
    print "\n".join(files)
```

After the usual preamble and module imports, the `main()` function is pretty straightforward. It creates an instance of a class named `HTTPDownloader`, then calls its `downloadURL()` method to grab the given URL (a sort of "test pattern" for podcast clients) and store it in the current working directory. The `downloadURL()` method returns a list of paths to files it downloaded, and these are printed out at the end of `main()`.

To make this test function work, move on to defining the `HTTPDownloader` class, beginning with Listing 6-4.

Listing 6-4: downloaders.py (Part 2 of 5)

```python
class HTTPDownloader:
    """
    This provides a simple HTTP content downloader.
    """
    PERC_STEP  = 10
    CHUNK_SIZE = 10*1024
    PROG_OUT   = sys.stdout
```

```
def _print(self, msg):
    """Output an immediate message."""
    self.PROG_OUT.write(msg)
    self.PROG_OUT.flush()
```

The HTTPDownloader class starts off with a few constants:

- PERC_STEP—Defines what percentage intervals of completed download will cause a progress notice to be displayed.
- CHUNK_SIZE—Defines how much data will be read at one time while pulling down data from a Web server.
- PROG_OUT—Establishes a default output channel for status messages.

The first method defined is _print(), which writes a message out to the output channel (STDOUT, by default) and calls flush(), to ensure that the message is printed immediately, rather than the default behavior of waiting for a certain amount of data or a line break. This will let you print gradual status messages as data is downloaded.

Next, start the downloadURL() method definition with the code in Listing 6-5.

Listing 6-5: downloaders.py (Part 3 of 5)

```
def downloadURL(self, dest_path, url):
    """
    Given a destination path and URL, download with a
    progress indicator.
    """
    files = []

    # Dissect the given URL to extract a filename,
    # build output path.
    url_path  = urlparse(url)[2]
    url_fn    = os.path.basename(url_path)
    fout_path = os.path.join(dest_path, url_fn)
    files.append(fout_path)
    self._print("\t\t%s" % (url_fn))
```

The downloadURL() method takes two parameters: a destination path for downloaded files and a URL from which to download content. It first initializes an empty list in which to collect files that are downloaded. Then, urlparse() is used to extract the file path from the URL, and methods from the os.path module are used to find an appropriate filename for the download and construct a full path using the given destination path. Finally, this full path is appended to the list of files reported as downloaded, and a status message with the filename is printed.

It might seem a little superfluous at the moment to keep a *list* of files around when this `HTTPDownloader` class will result in one file downloaded, at most. But, this will come in handy in a little bit, when you implement another downloader class.

But, before getting too far ahead, continue writing the `downloadURL()` method with Listing 6-6.

Listing 6-6: downloaders.py (Part 4 of 5)

```
# Open the file for writing, initialize size to 0.
fout      = open(fout_path, "w")
fout_size = 0

# Open the URL for reading, try getting the content length.
fin          = urllib2.urlopen(url)
fin_size_str = fin.headers.getheader("Content-Length", "-1")
fin_size     = int(fin_size_str.split(";",1)[0])
self._print(" (%s bytes): " % (fin_size))

# Initialize variables tracking download progress
perc_step, perc, next_perc = self.PERC_STEP, 0, 0
perc_chunk = fin_size / (100/self.PERC_STEP)
```

The code in Listing 6-6 sets the stage for the download. The output file whose path was just constructed is opened for writing. After that, `urlopen()` from the `urllib2` module is used to start a connection for downloading from the given URL.

The next couple of lines are a bit "hackish," but the idea is to extract the value of the `Content-Length` header returned by the URL's Web server. Occasionally, this header will contain a semicolon, which causes a bit of a hiccup in converting the size from a string to an integer. Once the content length is found, this is printed as a status message, directly after the previously displayed filename.

Following the status message is a bit of quick initialization of variables to be used in presenting the percentage of progress during the download. The logic of the progress display will be explained along with the actual content download loop, presented in Listing 6-7.

Listing 6-7: downloaders.py (Part 5 of 5)

```
while True:
    # Read in a chunk of data, breaking from loop if
    # no data returned
    data = fin.read(self.CHUNK_SIZE)
    if len(data) == 0: break
```

```
        # Write a chunk of data, incrementing output file size
        fout.write(data)
        fout_size += len(data)

        # If the current output size has exceeded the next
        while fout_size >= next_perc:
            self._print("%s " % perc)
            perc      += perc_step
            next_perc += perc_chunk

    # Close input & output, line break at the end of progress.
    fout.close()
    fin.close()
    self._print("\n")

    return files

if __name__ == "__main__": main()
```

The content download loop appears to be an infinite loop. However, the first thing done is to attempt to read in a chunk of data from the Web server. If this attempt comes up empty handed, it's assumed that the download is complete and the loop is ended. After a chunk of data is downloaded, this is written to the output file, and a running count of its size is incremented.

The next nested loop handles presenting a display of the progress of download completion. The next_perc variable contains a target output file size at which the next notice of percent progress perc will be displayed. As long as the current output file size is greater than this target, a percent mark is printed out, perc is incremented a step, and the next percentage mark target next_perc is incremented by perc_chunk, which represents a perc_step proportion of the anticipated length of the download.

In a nutshell, this loop implements a rising threshold for percentage-progress display. Each time data is downloaded, this loop prints percentages until it has caught up with the current download length with respect to the total length reported by the Web server.

Finally, after the download loop has completed, the input and output streams are closed, a line break is printed, and the list of files downloaded is returned. You should be able to run this module as a test program now, resulting in a session something like this:

```
# python downloaders.py
            podcastDefaultWelcome.mp3 (613146 bytes): 0 10 20 30 40 50 60 70
80 90 100
./podcastDefaultWelcome.mp3
```

When you run the program, the numbers representing percent completion should appear gradually as the file arrives locally.

Gathering and Downloading Enclosures

Now that you have a decent way to download enclosures, you can get to work building a new feed aggregator using it. Start another new file in your editor named ch06_podcast_tuner.py and take a look at Listing 6-8 for the opening lines.

Listing 6-8: ch06_podcast_tuner.py (Part 1 of 4)

```
#!/usr/bin/env python
"""
ch06_podcast_tuner.py

Poll subscriptions and download new enclosures.
"""
import sys, time, os.path
from agglib      import *
from downloaders import *

FEEDS_FN        = "podcast_feeds.txt"
FEED_DB_FN      = "podcast_feeds_db"
ENTRY_DB_FN     = "podcast_entry_seen_db"
DOWNLOAD_PATH   = "enclosures/%s" % time.strftime("%Y-%m-%d")
NEW_FEED_LIMIT  = 1
```

This new aggregator program starts off importing modules, including a few of your own. Then, it establishes some familiar configuration constants with FEEDS_FN, FEED_DB_FN, and ENTRY_DB_FN. Notice that the usual filenames have changed. You probably want to keep your podcast-based subscriptions and tracking databases separate from those used for general feed aggregation.

The two new constants are DOWNLOAD_PATH and NEW_FEED_LIMIT.

The value of DOWNLOAD_PATH defines where downloaded enclosures will be stashed. In the previous code, this is a directory named enclosures with a subdirectory whose name is constructed based on today's date. This will allow you to keep track of podcasts and other downloaded media organized by the time of download.

Next, the value of NEW_FEED_LIMIT provides a bit of a sanity check when downloading enclosures from a feed that hasn't been polled before. Just about every feed lists a number of older entries, and podcast feeds are no different. So, when you first poll a feed, there may be as many as 15 enclosures waiting for you. However, you're most likely just interested in the first (or the first few) new enclosure. So, NEW_FEED_LIMIT establishes how many enclosures to skim off the top when polling a feed for the first time. Once a feed has been seen, it will be assumed you're interested in all new enclosures from that point on.

Next, check out Listing 6-9 for the main program driver.

Listing 6-9: ch06_podcast_tuner.py (Part 2 of 4)

```
def main():
    """
    Poll subscribed feeds, find enclosures, download content, and
    try importing audio files into the MP3 player.
    """
    feed_db, entry_db = openDBs(FEED_DB_FN, ENTRY_DB_FN)

    # Create current download path, if need be
    if not os.path.isdir(DOWNLOAD_PATH):
        os.makedirs(DOWNLOAD_PATH)

    # Read in the list of subscriptions
    feeds = [ x.strip() for x in open(FEEDS_FN, "r").readlines() ]

    for feed in feeds:
        # Has this feed been seen before?
        new_feed = not feed_db.has_key(feed)

        # Get new entries for feed, skip to next feed if none.
        entries = getNewFeedEntries([feed], feed_db, entry_db)
        if not len(entries) > 0: continue

        # Collect all the enclosure URLs found in new entries.
        enc_urls = getEnclosuresFromEntries(entries)
        if not len(enc_urls) > 0: continue

        # If this is a new feed, only grab a limited number of
        # enclosures.  Otherwise, grab all of them.
        down_limit = new_feed and NEW_FEED_LIMIT or len(enc_urls)

        # Download the enclosures.
        print "\tDownloading enclosures..."
        files = downloadURLs(DOWNLOAD_PATH, enc_urls[:down_limit])

    closeDBs(feed_db, entry_db)
```

The main() function in Listing 6-9 looks much like a few of the others that have popped up in this book so far. Databases are opened, and the subscriptions are loaded up. One new feature is the directory to which enclosures will be downloaded, so this directory is created if it doesn't already exist.

Next, a loop iterates through the feed subscriptions. To facilitate the NEW_FEED_LIMIT used a few lines further on, the new_feed flag is set by checking the database to see if this feed has been seen before. Then, new entries are gathered using getNewFeedEntries() from agglib. After that, the getEnclosuresFromEntries() function is called to extract a list of enclosure URLs from the new entries.

Using the `new_feed` flag set at the beginning of the loop, a download limit is set either to the `NEW_FEED_LIMIT` value if the feed is new, or to the total number of all enclosures if the feed has been seen before. This download limit is then used to call the `downloadURLs()` function with the current `DOWNLOAD_PATH` and a constrained list of enclosure URLs.

Moving right along, check out Listing 6-10 for a modified version of the `getEnclosures FromEntries()` function presented back at the beginning of this chapter.

Listing 6-10: ch06_podcast_tuner.py (Part 3 of 4)

```
def getEnclosuresFromEntries(entries):
    """
    Given a set of entries, harvest the URLs to enclosures.
    """
    enc_urls = []
    for e in entries:
        enclosures = e.entry.get('enclosures',[])
        enc_urls.extend([ en['url'] for en in enclosures ])
    return enc_urls
```

This new function in Listing 6-10 is identical to that in Listing 6-2, with one exception. Because this new function expects to be fed new entries as produced by the `getNewFeedEntries()` function of `agglib`, it must account for the fact that these entries will actually be `EntryWrapper` objects, instead of data straight from the `feedparser` module. This is just a matter of referring to `e.entry` instead of `entry` itself.

Now, you can wrap up this first revision of your podcast tuner with Listing 6-11.

Listing 6-11: ch06_podcast_tuner.py (Part 4 of 4)

```
def downloadURLs(download_path, urls):
    """
    Given a set of URLs, attempt to download their content.
    """
    for url in urls:
        try:
            dl = HTTPDownloader()
            return dl.downloadURL(download_path, url)
        except KeyboardInterrupt:
            raise
        except Exception, e:
            print "\n\t\tProblem downloading %s: %s" % (url, e)

if __name__=="__main__": main()
```

The downloadURLs() function provided in Listing 6-11 is not all that complex. Given a list of URLs, it iterates through each and attempts to use an HTTPDownloader instance to download to the appropriate directory. KeyboardInterrupt exceptions are left unhandled to allow the program to be interrupted, but all other exceptions are trapped and reported without killing the whole program.

The next thing you need to take this thing for a spin is a list of subscriptions. There are a number of directories listing new podcast feeds by topic and popularity, such as:

- http://www.ipodder.org/—iPodder.org, the original directory

- http://www.podcastalley.com/—Podcast Alley, a podcast directory with voting and rating

- http://www.podcast.net/—Podcast.net, yet another podcast directory

However, if you'd just like a list to get running, I've included a random assortment of my favorites in Listing 6-12.

Listing 6-12: podcast_feeds.txt Example

```
http://radio.weblogs.com/0001014/categories/ipodderTestChannel/
rss.xml
http://www.evilgeniuschronicles.org/audio/directmp3.xml
http://www.itconversations.com/rss/recentWithEnclosures.php
http://science.nasa.gov/podcast.xml
http://leoville.tv/tlr/rss.xml
http://www.evilgeniuschronicles.org/audio/directmp3.xml
http://rasterweb.net/raster/feeds/rwaudio.rss
http://www.toeradio.org/index.xml
http://podcast.resource.org/rf-rfc/index.xml
```

Then, once you've got a set of podcast subscriptions, you should see something like this when you finally run the program:

```
# python ch06_podcast_tuner.py
Polling http://radio.weblogs.com/0001014/categories/ipodderTestChannel/rss.xml
        Found 1 new entries
        Downloading enclosures...
                podcastDefaultWelcome.mp3 (613146 bytes): 0 10 20 30 40 50 60 70
80 90 100
Polling http://www.evilgeniuschronicles.org/audio/directmp3.xml
        Found 5 new entries
        Downloading enclosures...
                egc-2005-02-13.mp3 (20103862 bytes): 0 10 20 30 40 50 60 70 80
90 100
```

```
Polling http://www.itconversations.com/rss/recentWithEnclosures.php
        Found 21 new entries
        Downloading enclosures...
                ITC-Web2.0-2004-JamesCurrier.mp3 (6974255 bytes): 0 10 20 30 40
50 60 70 80
```

And, when the aggregator has finished its run, you will end up with a directory structure of new files, something like this:

```
# tree enclosures/
enclosures/
`-- 2005-02-16
    |-- ITC-Web2.0-2004-JamesCurrier.mp3
    |-- TLR20050215-1.mp3
    |-- egc-2005-02-13.mp3
    |-- podcastDefaultWelcome.mp3
    |-- rwaudio20050104.mp3
    `-- story.mp3
```

Every day that you run this podcast tuner, a new directory will be created and filled with new enclosure downloads. If you want to keep up with new arrivals in podcast feeds, you'll probably want to schedule runs of this program alongside your text/HTML-based feed aggregator with separate subscriptions and databases.

Enhancing Enclosure Downloads with BitTorrent

There've been a handful or so mentions of BitTorrent in this chapter so far, so now's a good time to follow up on that and give you a formal introduction before showing how you can improve your podcast tuner to use it.

With all the press (both good and bad) that BitTorrent has been getting lately, you probably know at least something about this technology. In a nutshell, BitTorrent is a peer-to-peer file transfer protocol that exploits *swarming* to ease the pain and expense of offering and acquiring large binary files on the Internet.

The swarming part is where peer-to-peer comes in. An offering of one or more files made available via BitTorrent is chopped up into many smaller tagged chunks. To prime the pump, complete sets of these chunks are offered for download by BitTorrent peers called *seeders*. To coordinate things, a central *tracker* maintains notes on the peers in the swarm and which chunks of the offering each peer holds.

When you start a BitTorrent download, your peer joins the swarm via the tracker and works to acquire chunks from other swarm peers. Once you've acquired at least one complete chunk, your peer then offers up that chunk for download by other swarm peers. The more chunks you've acquired, the more you offer for download. Finally, when you've acquired all the chunks, your download is done—but it's polite at this point for your peer to stick around and become a seeder itself for a while.

In short, BitTorrent is kind of like trading baseball cards—except that once you've acquired a card, you never lose it: you simply make copies of it to trade with your friends. Eventually, everyone should end up with a complete set, and because everyone's cooperating in copying and trading, the person who originally offered up the set of cards doesn't get overwhelmed by the process. And, if everything goes right, the trading process should go faster with all the pairs of hands involved than if just one person was trying to satisfy everyone's requests.

On the Web There's a lot to BitTorrent that this description glosses over. You can check out the protocol specification and other documentation at the official site here:

```
http://bittorrent.com/protocol.html
```

Although many enhanced clones and reimplementations have shown up on various operating systems, written in a number of languages and frameworks, the original BitTorrent software package was written in Python. This means that a very good implementation of BitTorrent is readily available to be used in enhancing your podcast tuner.

So, you'll want to grab the BitTorrent source code from the official site, here:

```
http://bittorrent.com/download.html
```

Although versions are listed for a few operating systems, skip those and click the SourceForge-hosted link to the source code. Look for a file labeled as "Platform-Independent." As of this writing, the following are URLs to the latest version of the source code:

```
http://prdownloads.sourceforge.net/bittorrent/BitTorrent-3.4.2.tar.gz?download
http://prdownloads.sourceforge.net/bittorrent/BitTorrent-3.4.2.zip?download
```

You can choose either `.zip` or `.tar.gz`, depending on your operating system or preference, but be sure to check that you're getting the latest version of the source code, and not a full program distribution for some operating system.

Once you've downloaded the archive, unpack it. Inside, you'll find various command-line programs and examples, as well as Mac OS X GUI client. Check these out if you like, but all you're interested in for this project is the `BitTorrent` directory. You can read the documentation included to get things installed on your system, but if you like, you can skip all of that and just copy the `BitTorrent` directory into your working project folder. This contains all the core Python modules you'll need to build BitTorrent support into your podcast tuner.

After getting the BitTorrent modules installed or copied to your project directory, it's time to get back to work. You're going to revise `downloaders.py` to add a new downloader class, similar in use to `HTTPDownloader`, but implemented using BitTorrent. Listing 6-13 shows the first of your additions, to be inserted just after the first batch of module imports, before the definition of `main()`.

Listing 6-13: downloaders.py Additions (Part 1 of 7)

```
from threading import Event
from BitTorrent.bencode import bdecode
import BitTorrent.download
```

The first import pulls in the Event class from the standard library threading module, which will be used in sending a signal to the BitTorrent downloader. The next two imports bring in core BitTorrent pieces—BitTorrent.bencode.bdecode is used to parse the .torrent metadata files used to describe torrent swarms for joining peers, and BitTorrent.download is a simple interface onto initiating BitTorrent sessions.

Continue on to the code in Listing 6-14 for the beginning of the BitTorrentDownloader class, which you should begin adding to the module after the end of the HTTPDownloader class definition, but before the final line that calls the main() function.

Listing 6-14: downloaders.py Additions (Part 2 of 7)

```
class BitTorrentDownloader:
    """
    This provides a simple BitTorrent downloader, with an optional
    post-download seeding function.
    """
    PERC_STEP     = 10
    START_TIMEOUT = 15
    SEED_TORRENT  = True
    SEED_TIME     = 20 * 60 # 20 minutes
    PROG_OUT      = sys.stdout

    def _print(self, msg):
        """Print an immediate status message."""
        self.PROG_OUT.write(msg)
        self.PROG_OUT.flush()
```

So far, this new BitTorrentDownloader class is following in the footsteps of HTTPDownloader. There's the _print() method, which will be used to display progress messages. Preceding this method are a few class constants:

- PERC_STEP—As before, establishes how much download progress is made in between displaying percentage messages.

- START_TIMEOUT—Number of seconds the downloader will wait for transfer to start before giving up.

- SEED_TORRENT—After downloading is complete, whether or not to stick around to share the completed file set.

- SEED_TIME—Maximum number of seconds to spend on seeding.

- PROG_OUT—Default channel for status and progress messages.

Forging ahead, you can find the full definition for the downloadURL() method in Listing 6-15.

Listing 6-15: downloaders.py Additions (Part 3 of 7)

```
def downloadURL(self, dest_path, url):
    """
    Given the URL to a BitTorrent .torrent, attempt to download
    the content.
    """
    # Initialize some state attributes.
    self._stop        = Event()
    self._init_time   = time.time()
    self._start_time  = None
    self._finish_time = None
    self._next_perc   = 0.0
    self._dest_path   = dest_path

    # Get the list of files and total length from torrent
    name,files,total_length = self._getTorrentMeta(dest_path, url)

    # Display name of file or dir in torrent, along with size
    self._print("\t\t%s (%s bytes): " % (name, total_length))

    # Run the BitTorrent download
    BitTorrent.download.download(['--url', url], self._choose,
            self._display, self._fin, self._error, self._stop, 80)

    # Finish off the progress display, return the list of files
    self._print("\n")
    return files
```

The downloadURL() method expects a destination path and URL, following the lead of
HTTPDownloader. However, in this case, the URL is expected to point to a .torrent
metadata file, rather than the actual content.

The BitTorrent download code is event-driven and integrated with your code via registered
callbacks, not unlike the way in which various event-driven parsers presented in previous chapters worked. So, the downloadURL() method prepares the BitTorrentDownloader
instance by first initializing some private attributes:

- self._stop—An Event instance from the threading module that will be used to
  signal the BitTorrent download event loop that it should stop.

- self._init_time—Contains the time when this download was initiated.

- self._start_time—Initialized to None for now, but will contain the time when the
  download actually starts transferring.

- self._finish_time—Initialized to None for now, but will contain the time when
  the download finally completes.

- `self._next_perc`—Tracks the next target percentage of completion to reach before displaying a new progress message

- `self._dest_path`—Set to the path where files are to be downloaded.

After these initializations, the `_getTorrentMeta()` is used to download and parse the `.torrent` file, returning a name for the torrent (which will be either a file or directory name), the list of files to be expected, as well as a total length in bytes expected for the download.

The name and length are used to output the start of the progress display, and then the BitTorrent download is initiated. The `BitTorrent.download.download()` function is a simplified way to start using BitTorrent. Its expected parameters are, in order:

- The URL where the `.torrent` file resides, in a list formatted as command-line arguments.

- A callback function used to choose a filename when saving downloaded data.

- A callback function to handle status messages meant for display during the download.

- A callback function triggered when the download has completed.

- An `Event` instance which, when triggered, will cause the download to·shut down.

- The number of columns in the display, used to constrain the size of status messages.

With this central method written, you can continue working to fill in the blanks, with the definition of `_getTorrentMeta()` in Listing 6-16.

Listing 6-16: downloaders.py Additions (Part 4 of 7)

```python
def _getTorrentMeta(self, dest_path, url):
    """
    Given the download destination path and URL to the torrent,
    extract the metadata to return the torrent file/dir name,
    files to be downloaded, and total length of download.
    """
    # Grab the torrent metadata
    metainfo_file = urllib2.urlopen(url)
    metainfo = bdecode(metainfo_file.read())
    metainfo_file.close()

    # Gather the list of files in the torrent and total size.
    files = []
    info = metainfo['info']
    if not info.has_key('files'):
        # Get the length and path of the single file to download.
        total_length = info['length']
        files.append(os.path.join(dest_path, info['name']))
```

```
else:
    # Calculate the total length and find paths of all files
    # to be downloaded.
    total_length = 0
    files_root   = os.path.join(dest_path, info['name'])
    for file in info['files']:
        total_length += file['length']
        file_path = os.path.join(*(file['path']))
        files.append(os.path.join(files_root, file_path))

return info['name'], files, total_length
```

This method expects to be given a destination path and the `.torrent` URL, which it will use to figure out what files are being offered for download and the total size of the download.

First off, the method uses `urlopen` from `urllib2` and `bdecode` from `BitTorrent.bencode` to download and decode the `.torrent` metadata. This results in a Python data structure based on the BitTorrent specification. After getting this data, the method looks up the `info` key, where details about the file or files to be downloaded can be found.

Next, the `info` key is checked for a `files` sub-key. If this is not found, then it's certain that the download offers only a single file. So, the `length` key is looked up under `info` and used for the total download length to be returned, and the `name` sub-key of `info` is joined to the destination path and used for the full file path.

However, if the `info` structure contains a `files` key, this download represents a collection of files. Accordingly, the details for each of these files are contained in a list under the `files` key. So, the method first comes up with the root directory for the download as a whole by joining the destination path with the `name` key of `info`. Then, it iterates through the values under `files`, each of which are data structures representing a file to be downloaded. The `length` for each of these is used to increment the total download size, and the `path` for each is joined together with the root download path and added to the list of files to be reported as downloads.

Then, after all that, the name of the download (which is either the sole file downloaded or the name of the download's directory) is returned, along with the list of files and the expected total length of the download.

Now you can fill in a few of the callback methods given in Listing 6-17.

Listing 6-17: downloaders.py Additions (Part 5 of 7)

```
def _fin(self):
    """Handle the completion of file download."""
    if not self.SEED_TORRENT:
        # Stop if not opting to seed the torrent.
        self._stop.set()
```

Continued

Listing 6-17 *(continued)*

```
    else:
        # Note the finish time and print notification of seeding.
        self._finish_time = time.time()
        self._print("SEEDING")

def _choose(self, default, size, saveas, dir):
    """Prepend the destination path onto the download filename."""
    return os.path.join(self._dest_path, default)

def _error(self, message):
    """Handle displaying errors."""
    self._print("[ ERROR: %s ]" % message)
```

Three new methods are given in Listing 6-17: _fin(), _choose(), and _error().

The first of these, _fin(), is called when BitTorrent has finished downloading the file. Here, if you've not opted to seed after downloading (by setting SEED_TORRENT to False), the Event instance in the downloader's _stop attribute is triggered, which will bring the download to an end. However, if you have chosen to seed, the download completion time is noted, and a status message is printed.

The _choose() method is given details that could be used to pop up a file dialog to get input on the filename under which to save a file downloaded. However, this implementation just joins the default choice onto the destination path, which matches up to the file paths gathered from the metadata in _getTorrentMeta().

The last of these callbacks, _error(), is called to display an error message whenever one occurs.

The final callback method is _display(), which begins in Listing 6-18.

Listing 6-18: downloaders.py Additions (Part 6 of 7)

```
def _display(self, disp):
    """
    Display status event handler.  Takes care of tracking stalled
    and started downloads, progress indicator updates, as well as
    seeding the torrent after download.
    """
    # Check download rate to detect download start.
    if disp.has_key('downRate'):
        if not self._start_time and disp['downRate'] > 0.0:
            self._start_time = time.time()

    # Check to see if the download's taken too long to start.
    if not self._start_time:
```

```
        init_wait = (time.time() - self._init_time)
        if init_wait > self.START_TIMEOUT:
            self._print("timeout before download start")
            self._stop.set()

    # Handle progress display, if fractionDone present.
    if disp.has_key('fractionDone'):
        perc_done = disp['fractionDone'] * 100.0
        while perc_done > self._next_perc:
            self._print("%d " % self._next_perc)
            self._next_perc += self.PERC_STEP
```

The `_display()` callback implements the smarts of this downloader. Although it seems mostly intended for the use of updating a GUI, this is a convenient place to make some decisions on what information comes up. The sole parameter of this method is `disp`, a dictionary that contains updates on the course of the BitTorrent session.

The first piece of information tracked appears under the `downRate` key, which is a report of the current rate of data transfer for downloading. Here, if no start time for the download has been recorded yet and the download rate is greater than zero, the current time is noted as the start of the download.

Following this, the time before download start is checked to make sure it's still below the `START_TIMEOUT` value set as a class constant. If the download still hasn't started before then, the `_stop` event is triggered to abort the session.

Then, the `fractionDone` key of the display data is checked to maintain the progress display. Because BitTorrent actually provides a measure of completion as a fraction, the current length of the download doesn't need to be tracked as it was in `HTTPDownloader`. So, target steps along the way to 100 percent completion are tracked and progress messages are displayed appropriately.

The final piece of the `_display()` callback is given in Listing 6-19, which implements the decisions made if and when seeding starts.

Listing 6-19: downloaders.py Additions (Part 7 of 7)

```
    # Handle completed download and seeding conditions.
    if self._finish_time:
        # Stop if no one's downloading from us.
        if disp.has_key('upRate') and not disp['upRate'] > 0.0:
            self._stop.set()

        # Stop if we've uploaded as much or more than we downloaded.
        if disp.has_key('upTotal') and disp.has_key('downTotal') and \
                disp['upTotal'] >= disp['downTotal']:
            self._stop.set()
```

Continued

Listing 6-19 *(continued)*

```
    # Stop if we've been seeding for too long.
    seed_time = time.time() - self._finish_time
    if seed_time >= self.SEED_TIME:
        self._stop.set()
```

So, this code only comes into play once there's been a download finish time recorded. These decisions will also only be considered if seeding is enabled, because otherwise the BitTorrent session would have been ended when the download completed.

However, if seeding is enabled, this code stops if any of three conditions come about:

- No one is downloading from you.
- You've uploaded as much or more than you downloaded.
- You've been seeding for longer than the duration in SEED_TIME.

This seems like a pretty reasonable set of criteria to use for seeding, because it allows you to give back a bit, but not wait around all day so that you can get back to downloading the rest of your enclosures.

This wraps up your additions to the downloaders module. Now you can make a small tweak to your podcast tuner to begin grabbing BitTorrent-enabled podcasts. Check out Listing 6-20 for this change.

Listing 6-20: ch06_podcast_tuner.py Modification

```
def downloadURLs(download_path, urls):
    """
    Given a set of URLs, attempt to download their content.
    """
    for url in urls:
        try:
            if url.endswith(".torrent"):
                dl = BitTorrentDownloader()
            else:
                dl = HTTPDownloader()
            return dl.downloadURL(download_path, url)
        except KeyboardInterrupt:
            raise
        except Exception, e:
            print "\n\t\tProblem downloading %s: %s" % (url, e)
```

The only real addition here is code to switch between `HTTPDownloader` and `BitTorrent Downloader`, based on whether the URL to be downloaded ends with `.torrent`. You could probably find other ways to decide what is a BitTorrent download and what is plain HTTP, but this seems to work for most podcast feeds. Then, because both downloaders offer the same interface for use, the rest of this method is unchanged.

Because nothing else has changed in the podcast tuner program, a session with this new version looks pretty much the same:

```
# python ch06_podcast_tuner.py
Polling http://content.downloadradio.org/sdr-rss.xml
        Found 1 new entries
        Downloading enclosures...
                SDR15FEB.mp3 (14333280 bytes): 0 10 20 30 40 50 60 70 80 90 100
SEEDING
```

The only difference here is the "SEEDING" message that appears after the download has completed, if seeding is left enabled. With this version of the tuner, it's best to schedule runs in the background on a computer that has Internet access most of the time. Downloads may take a little longer than you have patience to wait (if you're sitting and watching the program progress), so it's probably best to just be happily surprised when they show up in the download directory. (Or, maybe you can come up with a few more tweaks to make this program *tell* you when new downloads arrive.)

Importing MP3s into iTunes on Mac OS X

One big piece is missing from your podcast tuner, though, and that's the iPod. Most of the podcast tuners available commercially and as Open Source have some facility for automatically loading new podcasts onto a portable media player, so why shouldn't this one?

To polish off this project, then, you'll be able to build a quick hack of a conduit to shepherd fresh podcasts onto an iPod using iTunes and AppleScript under Mac OS X. If you don't happen to have this particular combination of software and hardware, it still might be instructive to follow along, in case you'd like to do some research and adapt this to another portable media device.

To start, create a new shared module in your editor called `mp3players.py` and begin with the code in Listing 6-21.

Listing 6-21: mp3players.py (Part 1 of 3)

```
"""
mp3players

Contains objects encapsulating methods to manage adding tracks
to audio players.
"""
import sys, os, popen2, os.path, re
```

Continued

Listing 6-21 *(continued)*

```
def main():
    p = iTunesMac()
    p.addTrack(sys.argv[1])
```

There's nothing shocking so far: a few modules imported, and a simple `main()` function to test out the rest of this module—namely an instance of the `iTunesMac` class and its `addTrack()` method. This test program will accept a path to an MP3 and then add the MP3 to your iTunes library and your iPod.

Brace yourself for the next part, though. Listing 6-22 presents the beginning of the `iTunesMac` class and a sizeable amount of AppleScript used to do the real work here.

Listing 6-22: mp3players.py (Part 2 of 3)

```
class iTunesMac:
    OSASCRIPT = '/usr/bin/osascript'

    ADD_TRACK_SCRIPT = """
property arguments : "%s"

-- Derive a Mac-style path from a given POSIX path.
set track_path to arguments
set track_file to POSIX file track_path

-- Launch iTunes as hidden, if not already running.
tell application "System Events"
    if not (exists process "iTunes") then
        tell application "iTunes"
            launch
            set visible of front window to false
        end tell
    end if
end tell

tell application "iTunes"
    -- Import the new track into main library.
    set this_track to add track_file to playlist "library" of source
"library"
    set the genre of this_track to "Podcast"

    -- Create the "Podcasts" playlist if needed, add new track to it.
    if not (exists user playlist "Podcasts" of source "library") then
        make new playlist of source "library" with properties
{name:"Podcasts"}
```

```
        end if
        duplicate this_track to playlist "Podcasts" of source "library"

        -- This might fail if no iPod is connected
        try
            -- Find an iPod
            set the_iPod to some source whose kind is iPod

            -- Copy the new track to the iPod main library
            duplicate this_track to playlist 1 of the_iPod

            -- Create the "Podcasts" playlist if needed, add new track to it.
            if not (exists user playlist "Podcasts" of the_iPod) then
                make new playlist of the_iPod with properties {name:"Podcasts"}
            end if
            duplicate this_track to playlist "Podcasts" of the_iPod
        end try

    end tell

    """
```

AppleScript is a fairly verbose language, so this script is a tad long, although it doesn't do a lot of work. It might seem a bit confusing, because until now, you've been working in Python. But, this is where things become a tad "hackish," because this run of AppleScript source is actually a Python string template into which you can insert the path to an MP3. It needs to be done this way because it's one of the simpler ways to communicate between AppleScript and Python, and thus AppleScriptable applications on OS X.

I won't go blow-by-blow into this AppleScript, but here's a brief outline:

- iTunes is launched as a hidden window if it isn't already running.
- The audio file is added to the main library of iTunes, and its Genre is set to "Podcast."
- A playlist named "Podcasts" is created in iTunes if it doesn't already exist.
- The audio file is added to the "Podcasts" playlist in iTunes.
- An attempt is made to find an iPod attached to the computer.
- If an iPod is found, the audio is imported to it, a "Podcasts" playlist is created (if necessary), and the audio file is duplicated there as well.

So, in short, this AppleScript automatically imports a given MP3 into iTunes and an iPod, as well as into a playlist named "Podcasts" on both.

The rest of this class (which actually executes the AppleScript) is shown in Listing 6-23.

Listing 6-23: mp3players.py (Part 3 of 3)

```
    def _executeAppleScript(self, script):
        """
        Given the text of an AppleScript, attempt to execute it.
        """
        fi = os.popen(self.OSASCRIPT, "w")
        fi.write(script)
        fi.close()

    def addTrack(self, fn):
        abs_fn = os.path.abspath(fn)
        self._executeAppleScript(self.ADD_TRACK_SCRIPT % abs_fn)

if __name__=='__main__': main()
```

First in Listing 6-23 is a method called `_executeAppleScript()`, which accepts the source of an AppleScript as a string. Its implementation uses the `os.popen()` method to fork a process running `/usr/bin/osascript`, which will run AppleScript source fed to it on-the-fly. The `popen()` call allows you to pipe data to the forked process, so this method feeds `osascript` the AppleScript source to run it, and then returns.

The final method of this class is `addTrack()`, which accepts the file path to an audio file to be added to iTunes and an iPod.

Now, you have a few more tweaks to make to the podcast tuner in order to use this new code, so open up `ch06_podcast_tuner.py` and check out Listing 6-24.

Listing 6-24: ch06_podcast_tuner.py Additions (Part 1 of 3)

```
from mp3players  import *

MP3PLAYER       = iTunesMac()
VALID_AUDIO_EXT = ( ".mp3", ".mp4", ".m4p", ".wav", ".aiff" )
```

This first small change imports the `iTunesMac` class from the module you just wrote, and establishes a few new configuration constants:

- `MP3PLAYER`—Used to switch between audio player import code, should you implement alternatives to `iTunesMac` in the future.
- `VALID_AUDIO_EXT`—Contains a list of file extensions that, when matched, are automatically added to the audio device.

Next, you need to work at importing into the main feed polling loop. Take a look at Listing 6-25 for the code you need to add.

Listing 6-25: ch06_podcast_tuner.py Additions (Part 2 of 3)

```
# Download the enclosures.
print "\tDownloading enclosures..."
files = downloadURLs(DOWNLOAD_PATH, enc_urls[:down_limit])

# Import downloaded files into audio player
print "\tImporting the enclosures..."
importAudioFiles(MP3PLAYER, VALID_AUDIO_EXT, files)
```

The pre-existing code for downloading enclosures is presented in Listing 6-25 for context, but the final two lines are what you need to insert at the end of the feed polling loop. It's pretty simple. A function named importAudioFiles() is called, with the MP3PLAYER and VALID_AUDIO_EXT constants supplied as parameters, as well as a list of the files just downloaded.

So, to finish up the additions to your podcast tuner, the implementation of importAudioFiles() appears in Listing 6-26.

Listing 6-26: ch06_podcast_tuner.py Additions (Part 3 of 3)

```
def isValidAudioFile(valid_exts, file):
    """
    Given the path to a file, determine whether it is a
    valid audio file.
    """
    if not os.path.exists(file): return False
    for ext in valid_exts:
        if file.endswith(ext): return True
    return False

def importAudioFiles(player, valid_exts, files):
    """
    Given an MP3 player and list of files, attempt to import any
    valid audio files.
    """
    files = [f for f in files if isValidAudioFile(valid_exts, f) ]
    for file in files:
        try:
            print "\t\t%s" % file
            player.addTrack(file)
        except KeyboardInterrupt:
            raise
        except Exception, e:
            print "\n\t\tProblem importing %s: %s" % (file, e)
```

Before you define `importAudioFiles()`, though, you need to define a helper function named `isValidAudioFile()`. This function takes the list of valid extensions and the path to a file as parameters, then returns `True` or `False` depending on whether or not the given file is an audio file.

So, with that helper in place, the implementation of `importAudioFiles()` starts. It accepts as parameters an audio player handler instance (`iTunesMac`, for this project), the list of valid audio file extensions, and a list of files.

The first thing done in the function is to filter the file list using `isValidAudioFile()` so that it only has to deal with audio files. Then, it iterates through these files, calling the `addTrack()` method of audio player handler for each. This will get each newly downloaded audio file imported into the library. Exceptions are trapped and reported, but `KeyboardInterrupt` is allowed to be raised in order to let this loop be interrupted manually.

Again, because this has really only been a small tweak to the podcast tuner itself, a session with this final revision is not changed much. Here's what a sample run looks like now:

```
# python ch06_podcast_tuner.py
Polling http://podcast.wfmu.org/SD/SD.xml
        Found 1 new entries
        Downloading enclosures...
                sd050216.mp3 (48868039 bytes): 0 10 20 30 40 50 60 70 80 90 100
        Importing the enclosures...
                enclosures/2005-02-16/sd050216.mp3
```

Notice that the new addition comes after the download, where a list of files imported are displayed. After each run of this tweaked podcast tuner, you should not only end up with downloaded enclosures in your chosen directory, but also automatically appearing in iTunes and on your iPod.

Checking Out Other Options

The number and variety of enclosure-based feed aggregators is expanding, and undoubtedly by the time you read this there will be many other choices out there. In fact, audio may soon be giving way to video, and these forms of feed aggregators will probably look very different. Also, the authors of many other feed aggregators (presented in previous chapters) are working on incorporating enclosure-downloading features. But for now, here are a few choices for podcast reception.

Looking at iPodder

You can find iPodder here, hosted at SourceForge:

```
http://ipodder.sourceforge.net/index.php
```

This is a cross-platform podcast receiver, with versions available for Mac OS X (see Figure 6-1) and Windows (see Figure 6-2). It's implemented in Python, so you might just be able to pick up a few tricks for your own podcast tuner from this chapter, if you're so inclined. Or, better yet, contribute back to the project, since it's Open Source.

FIGURE 6-1: iPodder running on Mac OS X

FIGURE 6-2: iPodder running on Windows

Looking at iPodderX

iPodderX is a shareware podcast receiver built just for Mac OS X, available here:

`http://ipodderx.com/`

Along with downloading podcasts in enclosures, iPodderX also does video and integrates with iPhoto to pull images into your photo libraries automatically. In addition, iPodderX integrates with a podcast directory, so you can find new feeds right from the program's interface (see Figure 6-3).

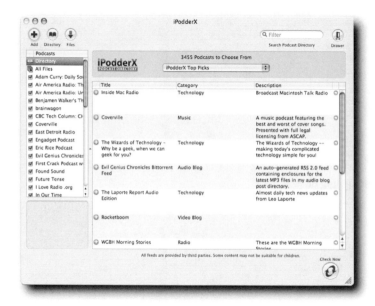

FIGURE 6-3: iPodderX running on Mac OS X

Looking at Doppler

Doppler is a podcast receiver just for Windows, available here:

`http://www.dopplerradio.net`

Although Doppler appears to be a mostly no-frills podcast tuner so far, it does seem to be under active development and, being Windows-specific, it offers a lot of promise on the Windows side of things for the mostly Mac-centric world of podcasting (see Figure 6-4).

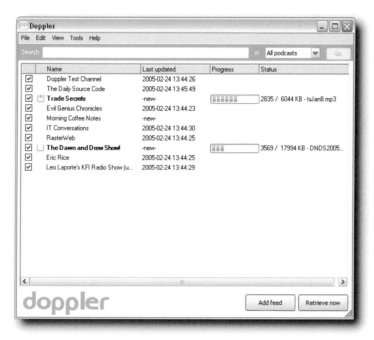

FIGURE 6-4: Doppler running on Windows

Summary

So, it doesn't have a flashy graphical interface or multithreaded concurrent downloads, but the program in this chapter works as a podcast tuner. With the added BitTorrent support, it can come in handy when syndication feeds start getting used for even richer media downloads.

However, this thing has loads of room for improvement before its much competition for other offerings out there:

- Why *not* build a nice GUI for this thing, or check out what it would take to speed up enclosure downloads with multiple processes or threads?

- How about borrowing some of the code you used in previous chapters for email or instant messaging to notify you when new podcasts arrive?

- The combination of Mac OS X, iTunes, and the iPod is not the only viable platform for podcasts. Why not find out how other hardware/software combinations work and build new handlers in mp3players.py?

With this chapter, you've reached the end of the first part of the book on consuming feeds. This next third of the book is devoted to producing feeds, so in Chapter 7 you take a first stab at generating a feed from HTML metadata and content.

Producing Feeds

Building a Simple Feed Producer

By this point, you've had a good run at exploring the possibilities for consuming syndication feeds. Now, you shift gears a bit and take a look at producing syndication feeds. Just as you built a simple feed aggregator near the beginning of the previous part of the book, in this chapter you build a simple feed producer that should give you a taste of what's involved in creating syndication feeds and get you ready for what's to come in the next chapters.

Producing Feeds from a Collection of HTML Files

As you read in the Chapter 1, most RSS and Atom feeds are the product of a template, plug-in, or add-on module for an existing content-management system (CMS) or blogging software package. However, for the purposes of this book, it's a bit too large of an undertaking to build a complete CMS tool from scratch, and getting tied to one particular existing product or tool and its specific scheme for generating feeds doesn't help you learn or tinker with the technology itself.

So, this chapter offers a bit of a compromise. Given a collection of HTML pages, the tools you build here will generate syndication feeds from that collection. The HTML files could be produced from a CMS to which you have access, or they could be hand-maintained from your own personal home page or documentation. (Often, /usr/share/doc offers a large selection of HTML with which to play.) Either way, this chapter's code will build feeds from HTML pages.

Extracting Metadata from HTML

Before you get into the work of producing feeds, though, you need to build a few tools to squeeze some useful data out of raw HTML pages to create feed entries.

So, start a new file in your editor and call it htmlmetalib.py. This is going to be another shared module, starting with the code presented in Listing 7-1.

Listing 7-1: htmlmetalib.py (Part 1 of 7)

```
#!/usr/bin/env python
"""
htmlmetalib.py

Provides HTMLMetaDoc, an easy way to access metadata in
HTML files.
"""
import sys, time, os, os.path
from HTMLParser import HTMLParser, HTMLParseError

def main():
    """
    Test everything out by finding all HTML in a path given as
    a command line argument.  Get metadata for all HTML found
    and print titles, paths, and descriptions.
    """
    docs = findHTML(sys.argv[1])
    tmpl = "%(title)s (%(path)s)\n\t%(description)s"
    print "\n".join([tmpl % x for x in docs])
```

This new module starts off in Listing 7-1 with the standard features: a docstring describing its purpose, and a few module imports.

The main() function defined is intended to test what you'll build in the rest of this module. The first thing it does is call a function called findHTML() that searches a given directory recursively for HTML documents and wraps each in an instance of the HTMLMetaDoc class, which extracts metadata (such as the title and description).

Then, this list of objects is rendered via template and printed. The output will include the titles, paths, and descriptions of the HTML documents found.

To make this work, you next need a definition for the findHTML() function, shown in Listing 7-2.

Listing 7-2: htmlmetalib.py (Part 2 of 7)

```
def findHTML(path):
    """
    Recursively search for all files ending in .html and .htm
    in at a given path.  Create HTMLMetaDoc objects for all and
    return the bunch.
    """
    docs = []
    for dirpath, dirnames, filenames in os.walk(path):
```

```
        for fn in filenames:
            if fn.endswith(".html") or fn.endswith(".htm"):
                fp  = os.path.join(dirpath, fn)
                doc = HTMLMetaDoc(fp)
                docs.append(doc)
    return docs
```

The `findHTML()` function uses the `os.walk()` function from the Python standard library to recursively search from the given directory for files and deeper directories.

For more information on the `os.walk()` function, check out the Python documentation here:

> `http://docs.python.org/lib/os-file-dir.html#l2h-1625`

Once the search is completed, the results are iterated and filenames ending in `.html` or `.htm` are sought. For each of these found, the full path to the file is built using `os.path.join()`, and an `HTMLMetaDoc` object is created using this path. That object is then appended to a list returned at the end of the function after all files have been processed.

Take a look at Listing 7-3 for the `HTMLMetaDoc` class.

Listing 7-3: htmlmetalib.py (Part 3 of 7)

```
class HTMLMetaDoc:
    """
    Encapsulates HTML documents in files, extracting metadata
    on initialization.
    """
    def __init__(self, filepath):
        self.title       = ''
        self.content     = ''
        self.description = ''

        self.path = filepath

        s = os.stat(filepath)
        self.modified = s.st_mtime

        parser = HTMLMetaParser()
        parser.parse_file(self, open(filepath))

    def __getitem__(self, name):
        """
        Translate map-like access into attribute fetch for templates.
        """
        return getattr(self, name)
```

Continued

Listing 7-3 *(continued)*

```
def __cmp__(self, other):
    """
    Compare for sort order on modified dates.
    """
    return other.modified - self.modified
```

There's not much to the `HTMLMetaDoc` class—it's mostly a holder for attributes harvested from HTML files.

Upon initialization, `__init__()` sets default values for its title, content, and description proper-ties. The path property is set to the file path passed in as a parameter. Then, the `os.stat()` function is used to grab the modification time for the file at the given path for the object's `modified` property. Finally, an `HTMLMetaParser` is created and its `parse_file()` method is called with the `HTMLMetaDoc` object and the HTML as an opened file as parameters. This is where the actual metadata from the HTML file is harvested.

The `__getitem__()` method turns map-like access on this object into attribute access, which makes this object easier to use in string templates. And, finally, the `__cmp__()` object facilitates sorting lists of these objects.

Now, move on to the code in Listing 7-4, where the work toward HTML parsing commences.

Listing 7-4: htmlmetalib.py (Part 4 of 7)

```
class _HTMLMetaParserFinished(Exception):
    """
    Private exception, raised when the parser has finished with
    the HTML <head> contents and isn't interested in any more data.
    """
    pass

class HTMLMetaParser(HTMLParser):
    """
    Parses HTML to extract the page title and description.
    """
    CHUNKSIZE = 1024

    def reset(self):
        """
        Initialize the parser state.
        """
        HTMLParser.reset(self)
        self.curr_doc  = None
        self.curr_attrs = {}
```

```
        self.curr_val   = ''
        self.in_head    = False
        self.in_body    = False
        self.parse_body = True

    def reset_doc(self, doc):
        """
        Reset the parser and set the current doc to me populated.
        """
        self.reset()
        self.curr_doc = doc

    def parse_file(self, doc, fin):
        """
        Parse through the contents of a given file-like object.
        """
        self.reset_doc(doc)
        while True:
            try:
                data = fin.read(self.CHUNKSIZE)
                if len(data) == 0: break
                self.feed(data)
            except _HTMLMetaParserFinished:
                break
```

The first thing defined in Listing 7-4 is a new exception, named _HTMLMetaParserFinished. The leading underscore suggests that this exception is private to this class, and it doesn't really have any use anywhere else. It will be thrown within the parser when it's gotten through parsing the <head> section of an HTML document, because it's not really interested in anything else. This is a bit of an improvement on the parsing done back in Chapter 2 for the minifeedfinder module, because it downloaded the HTML page and parsed the entire thing.

Speaking of the minifeedfinder, the HTMLParser from which the HTMLMetaParser class is derived should look a bit familiar. This subclass defines a reset() method, which sets some default values for state variables maintained through the course of parsing. The reset_doc() resets the parser, as well as setting a current HTMLMetaDoc object to be populated with metadata found in an HTML document parsed with the next method, parse_file().

The parse_file() method resets the parser with a new HTMLMetaDoc instance given as a parameter, then continually feeds the parser with data read in chunks from the file-like object given as a parameter, until the file has run out of data or the _HTMLMetaParserFinished exception has been thrown. This parsing loop tries to ensure that only as much as needed is read and processed from the HTML file, which should cut down on processing time for large files and large collections of files.

Next, Listing 7-5 begins the tag handling that implements the real parsing of this class.

Listing 7-5: htmlmetalib.py (Part 5 of 7)

```
def handle_starttag(self, tag, attrs_tup):
    """
    Handle start tags, watch for and flag beginning of <head>
    section, process <meta> tags inside <head> section.
    """
    curr_val = self.decode_entities(self.curr_val.strip())
    self.curr_val = ''
    attrs = dict(attrs_tup)

    if tag == 'head':
        self.in_head = True

    elif tag == 'body':
        self.in_body = True

    elif self.in_head:
        if tag == "meta":
            meta_name    = attrs.get('name', '').lower()
            meta_content = attrs.get('content', '')
            if meta_name == "description":
                self.curr_doc.description = meta_content

    elif self.in_body:
        attrs_str = ' '.join([ '%s="%s"' % x for x in attrs_tup ])
        self.curr_doc.content += '%s<%s %s>' % \
                                ( curr_val, tag, attrs_str )
```

In Listing 7-5's definition for handle_starttag(), several things are tracked:

First, when the start of the <head> or <body> tag is encountered, the in_head and in_body flags are flipped to manage what's done with each part of the HTML document. In the <head> section, <meta> tags are handled—in particular, the "description" meta tag's content attribute will be extracted. On the other hand, all tags found in the <body> section are simply reconstituted in the document's content attribute.

The next thing to handle in parsing are the end tags, with handle_endtag() as defined in Listing 7-6.

Listing 7-6: htmlmetalib.py (Part 6 of 7)

```
def handle_endtag(self, tag):
    """
    Handle end tags, watch for finished <title> tag inside <head>,
    and raise an exception when the end of the <head> section is
    found.
    """
```

```
        curr_val = self.decode_entities(self.curr_val.strip())
        self.curr_val = ''

        if self.in_head:
            if tag == "title":
                self.curr_doc.title = curr_val

        if tag == 'head':
            self.in_head = False
            if not self.parse_body:
                raise _HTMLMetaParserFinished()

        if tag == 'body':
            self.curr_doc.content += curr_val
            raise _HTMLMetaParserFinished()

        if self.in_body:
            self.curr_doc.content += '%s</%s>' % ( curr_val, tag )
```

The definition of handle_endtag() checks for the completion of the <title> tag in the <head> section, the value of which is stowed away into the HTMLMetaDoc object. Next, if the end of the head section is detected, the in_head flag is flipped to False and, if capturing <body> content isn't actually desired, an _HTMLMetaParserFinished exception is thrown to stop parsing early. However, if this is the end of the <body> tag, the current accumulation of character data is appended to the content attribute. And, again, parsing is stopped via throwing an exception. For the end of any other tag, the accumulated character data, as well as the end tag, are appended to the content attribute.

And now, to wrap up this parser, check out the last few methods defined in Listing 7-7.

Listing 7-7: htmlmetalib.py (Part 7 of 7)

```
    def handle_data(self, data):
        self.curr_val += data
    def handle_entityref(self, data):
        self.curr_val += '&' + data + ';'
    handle_charref = handle_entityref

    def decode_entities(self, data):
        data = data.replace('&lt;', '<')
        data = data.replace('&gt;', '>')
        data = data.replace('&quot;', '"')
        data = data.replace('&apos;', "'")
        data = data.replace('&amp;', '&')
        return data

if __name__ == "__main__": main()
```

These methods are pretty much the same as what you used for the `minifeedparser` in Chapter 2. `handle_data()` is used to accumulate the data inside tags, `handle_entityref()` takes care of entity references, and `decode_entities()` decodes a limited set of entities into normal characters.

Finally, the module is wrapped up with the standard trick to run as a program, to fire up the tests in `main()` defined at the beginning of the module.

Testing the htmlmetalib Module

So, of course, this module and its test program aren't very useful without a set of HTML documents on which to try it out. If you don't already have at least a few documents laying around, you should take this opportunity to build a few before you move on to testing things. Check out Listing 7-8 for an example HTML page to use as a basis.

Listing 7-8: test01.html

```
<html>
    <head>
        <title>Test Page #1</title>
        <meta name="description"
            content="This is a sample page description for #1" />
    </head>
    <body>
        <h1>This is a sample page #1</h1>
        <p>
            Lorem ipsum dolor sit amet, consectetur adipisicing elit.
        </p>
    </body>
</html>
```

The two most important parts to notice about this HTML document are the `<title>` tag and the `<meta>` tag description. In its present state, these are the only parts of HTML this parser harvests. To put this thing through its paces, be sure that your documents provide these pieces of information.

And, once you have all of this assembled, a session running the module as a test program might look like this:

```
# python htmlmetalib.py ./
Test Page #1 (./test01.html)
        This is a sample page description for #1
Test Page #2 (./test02.html)
        This is a sample page description for #2
```

```
Test Page #3 (./test03.html)
        This is a sample page description for #3
And now for something completely different (./test04.html)
        Number 23 is the Larch.
```

For this run, there were four HTML files in the current directory. For each, the title was printed, along with the path to the file. Then, on the next line after a tab, the HTML file's metatag description was printed. Try this test program out on your own existing or new HTML files and see what it turns up. Because this parser is built with expandability in mind, you might want to see what else your HTML documents contain that you might want to harvest for inclusion in syndication feeds.

Generating Atom Feeds from HTML Content

Now that you have a source of metadata harvested from HTML files, you can get to work generating syndication feeds. For now, you can start building an Atom feed producer, though once the groundwork is laid, RSS feeds won't be a very difficult addition.

Create a new file with your editor and call it ch07_feedmaker.py. This is a new program, starting out with code provided in Listing 7-9.

Listing 7-9: ch07_feedmaker.py (Part 1 of 6)

```python
#!/usr/bin/env python
"""
ch07_feedmaker.py

Create an RSS feed from a collection of HTML documents
"""
import sys, time, urlparse, urllib, htmlmetalib
from xml.sax.saxutils import escape

BASE_HREF   = 'http://www.example.com'
TAG_DOMAIN  = 'example.com'
MAX_ENTRIES = 15

FEED_META = {
    'feed.title'        : 'A Sample Feed',
    'feed.tagline'      : 'This is a testing sample feed.',
    'feed.link'         : 'http://www.example.com',
    'feed.author.name'  : 'l.m.orchard',
    'feed.author.email' : 'l.m.orchard@pobox.com',
    'feed.author.url'   : 'http://www.decafbad.com'
}
```

Here's a standard program preamble, including your new htmlmetalib module in the imports.

First in the configuration constants is BASE_HREF, which should be set to the URL at which your collection of HTML documents can be accessed. All URLs created to point at these documents will start with the value of BASE_HREF.

Next is TAG_DOMAIN, which needs to be a domain that you control, ideally the same domain as what is used in the BASE_HREF. This will be used in the creation of globally unique IDs for feed items this program will generate.

And one more constant, MAX_ENTRIES, will control how many entries will be included in the feed when it is generated.

Then comes FEED_META, a dictionary that establishes a few bits of information used to describe the feed to be generated itself:

- feed.title—Human-readable title of feed, used in listings and headings.
- feed.tagline—A secondary description of the feed, often displayed in feed directories or listings.
- feed.link—Human-readable Web page alternate for the feed.
- feed.author.name—Full name of the feed's author.
- feed.author.email—Email address for feed's author.
- feed.author.url—URL for feed's author, usually a home page or blog.

Continuing in Listing 7-10 are the string templates this program will use to generate Atom feeds.

Listing 7-10: ch07_feedmaker.py (Part 2 of 6)

```
ATOM_FEED_TMPL = """<?xml version="1.0" encoding="utf-8"?>
<feed version="0.3" xmlns="http://purl.org/atom/ns#">
    <title>%(feed.title)s</title>
    <link rel="alternate" type="text/html"
          href="%(feed.link)s" />
    <tagline>%(feed.tagline)s</tagline>
    <modified>%(feed.modified)s</modified>
    <author>
        <name>%(feed.author.name)s</name>
        <email>%(feed.author.email)s</email>
        <url>%(feed.author.url)s</url>
    </author>
    %(feed.entries)s
</feed>
"""


ATOM_ENTRY_TMPL = """
    <entry>
        <title>%(entry.title)s</title>
```

```
        <link rel="alternate" type="text/html"
              href="%(entry.link)s" />
        <issued>%(entry.modified)s</issued>
        <modified>%(entry.modified)s</modified>
        <id>%(entry.id)s</id>
        <summary type="text/html" mode="escaped">
            %(entry.summary)s
        </summary>
    </entry>
"""
```

The principles in this program are much the same as the first aggregator you built—one template for the feed, which will be populated by many copies of the entry template populated by HTML metadata.

One thing to notice is that the first line of ATOM_FEED_TMPL, the XML declaration, butts right up against the opening quotation marks for the template. Whereas in other templates this wasn't quite as important, this XML declaration *must* occur as the first thing in the output for the feed to be valid, coming in even before any whitespace or carriage returns that might appear later in the feed.

Another thing to note, as well, is that these templates by no means represent all the features available in the Atom feed format. However, Listing 7-10 represents a useful subset to get you started tinkering, at least.

 You can check out the Atom 0.3 specification at this URL:

```
        http://www.atomenabled.org/developers/syndication/
        atom-format-spec.php
```

Now that the initial configuration and templates are out of the way, define the program's main() function using Listing 7-11.

Listing 7-11: ch07_feedmaker.py (Part 3 of 6)

```
def main():
    """
    Find all HTML documents in a given path and produce a
    syndication feed based on the pages' metadata.
    """
    FEED_TMPL   = ATOM_FEED_TMPL
    ENTRY_TMPL  = ATOM_ENTRY_TMPL
    doc_wrapper = AtomTemplateDocWrapper

    # Find all the HTML docs.
    docs = htmlmetalib.findHTML(sys.argv[1])
```

Continued

Listing 7-11 *(continued)*

```python
# Bundle all the HTML doc objects in template-friendly wrappers.
entries = [ doc_wrapper(BASE_HREF, TAG_DOMAIN, d) for d in docs ]
entries.sort()

# Build a map for the feed template.
data_out = {}
data_out.update(FEED_META)
data_out['feed.modified'] = \
        time.strftime("%Y-%m-%dT%H:%M:%SZ", time.gmtime())
entries_out = [ENTRY_TMPL % e for e in entries[:MAX_ENTRIES] ]
data_out['feed.entries'] = "".join(entries_out)

# Handle optional parameter to output to a file
if len(sys.argv) > 2:
    fout = open(sys.argv[2], "w")
else:
    fout = sys.stdout

# Fill out the feed template and output.
fout.write(FEED_TMPL % data_out)
```

The main() function is built with a bit of flexibility in mind, anticipating that you'll be tweaking it to produce another feed format, very shortly after you have it working. So, the first thing that happens is that the Atom feed templates are assigned to the generic variables FEED_TMPL and ENTRY_TMPL. Later on, you can change these at the top of the function—or better yet, switch them based on a command-line parameter.

Next, findHTML() from htmlmetalib is used to find all the HTML documents at a path given on the command line. The HTMLMetaDoc objects produced by this search are then wrapped in instances of another class referred to by doc_wrapper—which in this configuration is AtomTemplateDocWrapper. This wrapper class is intended to make the data in HTMLMetaDoc objects easier to use in the ENTRY_TMPL when generating the feed content. After building this new list, it gets sorted into reverse-chronological order by file modification date.

The dictionary that will be used to populate the feed template gets built in the next segment of code. The FEED_META values are copied into the data_out dictionary, and then the current date and time in World Wide Consortium Date-Time Format (W3CDTF) is tucked away into the feed.modified key. Completing the dictionary, the list of the HTMLMetaDoc-based feed entry objects is rendered into XML using the ENTRY_TMPL string template and stowed away in the feed.entries key.

Notice that the number of entries rendered via template is limited by the MAX_ENTRIES configuration constant. This causes only the newest few HTML docs to be included in the feed.

The W3CDTF format for date and time values is used throughout the Atom format, and is detailed here:

```
http://www.w3.org/TR/NOTE-datetime
```

The next bit allows a bit of output flexibility. If only one argument is given at the command line to this program, that will be handled as the path at which to search for HTML files and the feed data produced will be written out to the console. However, if a second path is given, the feed output will be written to a file at that location.

Finally, all of the data prepared earlier is used to populate the FEED_TMPL string template and then written out.

With the program's main driver written, you can move on to filling in some of the details with Listing 7-12.

Listing 7-12: ch07_feedmaker.py (Part 4 of 6)

```python
class TemplateDocWrapper:
    """
    This class is a wrapper around HTMLMetaDoc objects meant to
    facilitate easy use in XML template strings.
    """
    UNICODE_ENC  = "UTF-8"
    MODIFIED_FMT = "%Y-%m-%dT%H:%M:%SZ"

    def __init__(self, base_href, tag_domain, doc):
        """Initialize the wrapper"""
        self._base_href  = base_href
        self._tag_domain = tag_domain
        self._doc        = doc

    def __cmp__(self, other):
        """Use the docs' comparison method."""
        return cmp(self._doc, other._doc)
```

The TemplateDocWrapper class defined in Listing 7-12 is the base class for the AtomTemplateDocWrapper mentioned in the main() function. The purpose of this class is to wrap up HTMLMetaDoc objects and make them more usable in the context of the feed templates.

The first couple of methods are nothing special: __init__() prepares the instance with base_href, tag_domain, and doc attributes as passed into the method. And, the __cmp__() method passes off the responsibility for sort order down to the HTMLMetaDoc object being wrapped, which defines its own __cmp__() for reverse-chronological order by file modification date.

Continuing on to Listing 7-13, you can see the core of this class in the __getitem__()
method, which facilitates use as a map-like object in templates.

Listing 7-13: ch07_feedmaker.py (Part 5 of 6)

```python
def __getitem__(self, name):
    """
    Translate map-like access from a template into proper values
    based on document attributes.
    """
    if name == "entry.title":
        # Return the document's title.
        val = self._doc.title

    elif name == "entry.summary":
                # Return the document's description
        val = self._doc.description

    elif name == "entry.content":
        # Return the document's content
        val = self._doc.content

    elif name == "entry.link":
        # Construct entry's link from document path and base HREF
        val = urlparse.urljoin(self._base_href, self._doc.path)

    elif name == "entry.modified":
        # Use the class modified time format to create the string
        val = time.strftime(self.MODIFIED_FMT,
                time.gmtime(self._doc.modified))

    elif name == "entry.id":
        # Construct a canonical tag URI for the entry GUID
        ymd = time.strftime("%Y-%m-%d",
                time.gmtime(self._doc.modified))
        val = "tag:%s,%s:%s" % (self._tag_domain, ymd,
                urllib.quote(self._doc.path,''))

    else:
        # Who knows what the template wanted?
        val = "(undefined)"

    # Make sure the value is finally safe for inclusion in XML
    return escape(val.encode(self.UNICODE_ENC))
```

Like the `EntryWrapper` class defined in Chapter 2, this `__getitem__()` method is a bit of a convenience hack. It allows this wrapper object to be used like a Python dictionary, and can be used for populating the `ENTRY_TMPL` string template. It handles the following keys:

- `entry.title`—Returns the value of the HTML document title.

- `entry.summary`—Returns the value of the HTML document description metadata.

- `entry.content`—Returns the HTML document body content.

- `entry.link`—Uses `urljoin` from the `urlparse` module to join the wrapper's `base_href` and the HTML doc's file path.

- `entry.modified`—Uses the object's `MODIFIED_FMT` to return the HTML file modification time in the proper format for the feed.

- `entry.id`—Uses the `tag_domain` property, along with the HTML document modified date and file path values, to build and return a reasonable GUID for this entry.

If an attempt is made to find a key that this wrapper doesn't know about, it just shrugs and returns "(undefined)." And finally, the value produced is encoded into the Unicode encoding of the class and escaped to make it safe for inclusion into the XML template.

Now, it's time to wrap the program up with one final class in Listing 7-14.

Listing 7-14: ch07_feedmaker.py (Part 6 of 6)

```
class AtomTemplateDocWrapper(TemplateDocWrapper):
    """Template wrapper for Atom-style entries"""
    MODIFIED_FMT = "%Y-%m-%dT%H:%M:%SZ"

if __name__ == "__main__": main()
```

The `AtomTemplateDocWrapper` class, a subclass of `TemplateDocWrapper`, was mentioned a little bit earlier. There's not much to it, because all it really does is define a date format for the wrapper. You'll see shortly that this is useful when you tweak the program to generate RSS, because it requires a different date format, but most everything else can remain the same.

Testing the Atom Feed Generator

You should have a collection of HTML documents, either some you had on hand at the start of this chapter, or a set built based on Listing 7-8 to test the `htmlmetalib` module. A session with the program on the same set of HTML used earlier in this chapter would look something like Listing 7-15.

Listing 7-15: An Example Atom Feed Output by ch07_feedmaker.py

```
# python ch07_feedmaker.py ./
<?xml version="1.0" encoding="utf-8"?>
<feed version="0.3" xmlns="http://purl.org/atom/ns#">
    <title>A Sample Feed</title>
    <link rel="alternate" type="text/html"
        href="http://www.example.com" />
    <tagline>This is a testing sample feed.</tagline>
    <modified>2005-02-08T01:44:11Z</modified>
    <author>
        <name>l.m.orchard</name>
        <email>l.m.orchard@pobox.com</email>
        <url>http://www.decafbad.com</url>
    </author>

    <entry>
        <title>And now for something completely different &amp; special</title>
        <link rel="alternate" type="text/html"
            href="http://www.example.com/test04.html" />
        <issued>2005-02-07T01:58:16Z</issued>
        <modified>2005-02-07T01:58:16Z</modified>
        <id>tag:example.com,2005-02-07:.%2Ftest04.html</id>
        <summary type="text/html" mode="escaped">
            Number 23 is the Larch.
        </summary>
    </entry>

    <entry>
        <title>Test Page #3</title>
        <link rel="alternate" type="text/html"
            href="http://www.example.com/test03.html" />
        <issued>2005-02-07T01:04:51Z</issued>
        <modified>2005-02-07T01:04:51Z</modified>
        <id>tag:example.com,2005-02-07:.%2Ftest03.html</id>
        <summary type="text/html" mode="escaped">
            This is a sample page description for #3
        </summary>
    </entry>

    <entry>
        <title>Test Page #2</title>
        <link rel="alternate" type="text/html"
            href="http://www.example.com/test02.html" />
        <issued>2005-02-07T01:04:36Z</issued>
        <modified>2005-02-07T01:04:36Z</modified>
        <id>tag:example.com,2005-02-07:.%2Ftest02.html</id>
        <summary type="text/html" mode="escaped">
            This is a sample page description for #2
        </summary>
    </entry>

    <entry>
```

```
        <title>Test Page #1</title>
        <link rel="alternate" type="text/html"
              href="http://www.example.com/test01.html" />
        <issued>2005-02-07T01:04:14Z</issued>
        <modified>2005-02-07T01:04:14Z</modified>
        <id>tag:example.com,2005-02-07:.%2Ftest01.html</id>
        <summary type="text/html" mode="escaped">
            This is a sample page description for #1
        </summary>
    </entry>

</feed>
```

Once you've reached to the point where you see this successful feed output, you're ready to move onto the next task.

Generating RSS Feeds from HTML Content

The feed generation program you just built was loosely designed to allow it to be easily tweaked to produce feeds of different formats. In particular, your next tweaks will switch the program to producing RSS feeds. The first part of this is to introduce new templates into the program, which are provided in Listing 7-16. You don't need to remove the Atom feed templates, though, so you can just add these below the existing ones.

Listing 7-16: ch07_feedmaker.py Modifications (Part 1 of 3)

```
RSS_FEED_TMPL = """<?xml version="1.0" encoding="utf-8"?>
<rss version="2.0">
    <channel>
        <title>%(feed.title)s</title>
        <link>%(feed.link)s</link>
        <description>%(feed.tagline)s</description>
        <webMaster>%(feed.author.email)s</webMaster>
        %(feed.entries)s
    </channel>
</rss>
"""

RSS_ENTRY_TMPL = """
        <item>
            <title>%(entry.title)s</title>
            <link>%(entry.link)s</link>
            <pubDate>%(entry.modified)s</pubDate>
            <guid isPermaLink="false">%(entry.id)s</guid>
            <description>%(entry.summary)s</description>
        </item>
"""
```

These new templates are just like those given in Listing 7-10, used to generate Atom feeds. They use almost all of the same data keys with the exception of a few, such as `feed.modified`, `feed.author.name`, and `feed.author.url`. Other than that, the information is pretty much all the same, just represented in a different way.

Following this, you need to make a few changes to the `main()` function, in order to make the program use these new templates. This is illustrated in Listing 7-17.

Listing 7-17: ch07_feedmaker.py Modifications (Part 2 of 3)

```
def main():
    """
    Find all HTML documents in a given path and produce a
    syndication feed based on the pages' metadata.
    """
    FEED_TMPL   = RSS_FEED_TMPL
    ENTRY_TMPL  = RSS_ENTRY_TMPL
    doc_wrapper = RSSTemplateDocWrapper
```

The changes themselves are pretty simple—all you really have to do is replace every instance of "Atom" and "ATOM" with "RSS" in the first few lines of `main()`.

And then, the final part is in Listing 7-18, which provides the definition for the `RSSTemplateDocWrapper` class.

Listing 7-18: ch07_feedmaker.py Modifications (Part 3 of 3)

```
class RSSTemplateDocWrapper(TemplateDocWrapper):
    """Template wrapper for RSS-style entries"""
    MODIFIED_FMT = "%a, %d %b %Y %H:%M:%S %z"
```

`RSSTemplateDocWrapper` subclasses `TemplateDocWrapper`, just like `AtomTemplateDocWrapper` from Listing 7-14. And, just like that previous class, this one provides a new date format (based on RFC 822 dates) required by the RSS feed specification.

On the Web
The RFC 822 format for date and time values is used throughout the RSS format, and is detailed here:

    http://www.w3.org/Protocols/rfc822/#z28

You can find some discussion on why RSS uses RFC 822 dates here:

    http://blogs.law.harvard.edu/tech/2004/05/16

Again, when adding this class, there's no need to remove the original `AtomTemplateDoc` `Wrapper` class. In fact, you might want to keep all of the previous code from Atom feed generation around in case you'd like to improve this program further to make the feed formats switchable on demand.

Testing the RSS Feed Generator

Again, you should still have your collection of HTML documents, so fire up the program again. This time, you should get an RSS feed as output, similar to Listing 7-19.

Listing 7-19: An Example RSS Feed Output by ch07_feedmaker.py

```
# python ch07_feedmaker.py ./
<?xml version="1.0" encoding="utf-8"?>
<rss version="2.0">
    <channel>
        <title>A Sample Feed</title>
        <link>http://www.example.com</link>
        <description>This is a testing sample feed.</description>
        <webMaster>l.m.orchard@pobox.com</webMaster>

        <item>
            <title>And now for something completely different &amp;
special</title>
            <link>http://www.example.com/test04.html</link>
            <pubDate>Mon, 07 Feb 2005 01:58:16 +0000</pubDate>
            <guid isPermaLink="false">tag:example.com,2005-02-07:
.%2Ftest04.html</guid>
            <description>Number 23 is the Larch.</description>
        </item>

        <item>
            <title>Test Page #3</title>
            <link>http://www.example.com/test03.html</link>
            <pubDate>Mon, 07 Feb 2005 01:04:51 +0000</pubDate>
            <guid isPermaLink="false">tag:example.com,2005-02-07:
.%2Ftest03.html</guid>
            <description>This is a sample page description for #3</description>
        </item>

        <item>
            <title>Test Page #2</title>
            <link>http://www.example.com/test02.html</link>
            <pubDate>Mon, 07 Feb 2005 01:04:36 +0000</pubDate>
            <guid isPermaLink="false">tag:example.com,2005-02-07:
.%2Ftest02.html</guid>
            <description>This is a sample page description for #2</description>
        </item>
```

Continued

Listing 7-19 *(continued)*

```
        <item>
            <title>Test Page #1</title>
            <link>http://www.example.com/test01.html</link>
            <pubDate>Mon, 07 Feb 2005 01:04:14 +0000</pubDate>
            <guid isPermaLink="false">tag:example.com,2005-02-07:.%2Ftest01.html
</guid>
            <description>This is a sample page description for #1</description>
        </item>

    </channel>
</rss>
```

And, with that working, you have a simple feed producer that can be applied to any pile of HTML you have lying around. Hopefully, you can find a few uses for this program, or at least you've been given some ideas toward how you might further tweak it to handle other kinds of documents—or how it might extract even more information out of HTML docs.

You'll be coming back to this program in future chapters, though, so keep it handy.

Testing and Validating Feeds

The idea of the program you've just built is that it can produce Atom and RSS feeds. But, how do you know that it's doing so—because I told you so in this book? Don't take my word for it. What if I'm wrong, or if I've misread the feed specifications? Or, what if you made a typo or two in the feed templates when you were first typing them in or tinkering later?

Well, remember back in Listing 7-10, when I mentioned that the XML declaration in the feed templates had to be the first thing in the output *for the feed to be valid?* That's an important clue—you need to be sure that any particular feed you've produced (whether of Atom or RSS format) is what it claims to be and contains what everyone else expects it will. If they're valid, you can be reasonably sure that feed aggregators can understand your feeds, some of which may be less forgiving than the `feedparser` module you used in Chapter 2 for your own aggregator.

So, you need a *feed validator*, which will test a feed for you and tell you if the feed is valid. If your feed is not valid, ideally the validator should not only tell you as much, it should also give you some hints as to where you've gone astray.

Luckily, there exists just such a beast: It's called the Feed Validator and you can find it at `http://feedvalidator.org/` (a creative name, I know, but at least it's straightforward and to the point). The Feed Validator has a very simple user interface, as shown in Figure 7-1. It provides a form with a single text field, into which you paste the URL of a feed. Submit the form, and the validator will fetch the feed and check it for validity. If you've done everything right, you should see a page very similar to Figure 7-2.

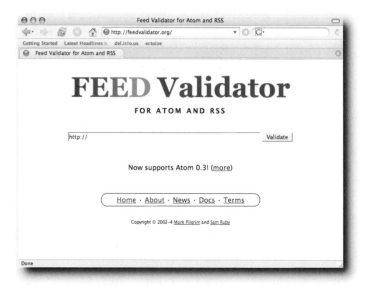

FIGURE 7-1: The Feed Validator

FIGURE 7-2: The Feed Validator successfully validating a feed

However, should your feed contain a few rough edges or errors, the validator will throw you a page telling you so, as well as offer a few suggestions as to what you can do to fix them. Check out Figure 7-3 for an example of what you might see in this case.

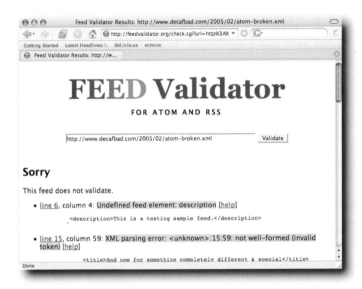

FIGURE 7-3: The Feed Validator reporting problems in an invalid feed

Now, using this public feed aggregator requires that you post your feeds somewhere accessible via URL. This may or may not be a pain to you during the course of your development and tinkering. If you find that it's annoying to have to constantly FTP files around, or do whatever convoluted things your Web hosting situation may require, you should know that the source code for the Feed Validator is available here on SourceForge:

```
http://sourceforge.net/projects/feedvalidator/
```

The code is only available as a checkout from the project CVS repository, so fetching it and setting it up in your development environment may or may not be worth the trouble to you—your mileage may vary. So, check it out if you like—setting up a local feed validator is left as an exercise for you.

In any case, I cannot stress the value of having access to a validator for your feeds, *and using it*. It's really the only way to get a sort of independent opinion on how clean and well put-together your feeds are, and the only way feed aggregators and producers can try to follow standards and escape a tag soup mess like the haphazard HTML that has plagued Web development throughout its history.

So, throughout this part of the book, you should not only check to see that your programs run without error, when they produce feeds, you should also ensure that your programs have *run correctly* and produce *valid* feeds.

Checking Out Other Options

The ways things were done in this chapter aren't the only ways to go. Why not take a look at some other options you have available for creating RSS and Atom feeds?

Looking at atomfeed

`atomfeed` is a Python module for generating Atom feeds, and you can find it here on SourceForge:

`http://atomfeed.sourceforge.net/`

As of this writing, the `atomfeed` module is fairly new and sparsely documented, but it does have quite a few unit tests (45, to be exact).

This module takes a much different approach than was used with string templates in this chapter. `atomfeed` uses the `xml.dom.minidom` module in Python to build Atom feeds in a more formal and sometimes more flexible way, using the DOM interface to create and append XML nodes in the feed document. This approach automatically handles escaping values, as well as Unicode handling, and unlike the string templates, this approach can be used to add or remove optional feed elements on the fly.

Looking at PyRSS2Gen

`PyRSS2Gen` is a Python module for generating RSS feeds, and you can find it here:

`http://www.dalkescientific.com/Python/PyRSS2Gen.html`

Similar in spirit to the `atomfeed` module, `PyRSS2Gen` uses the `xml.sax.saxutils.XMLGenerator` class to more cleanly and flexibly generate RSS feed data by building XML elements and attributes from Python data structures.

Looking at Blosxom and PyBlosxom

Blosxom is a very simple blogging package written as a single Perl script, and you can find it here:

`http://www.blosxom.com/`

PyBlosxom is a more object-oriented Python clone of Blosxom, and you can find it here:

`http://pyblosxom.sourceforge.net/`

What both Blosxom and PyBlosxom have in common with the program built in this chapter is that they work from a set of simple files to produce feeds. In the case of Blosxom and PyBlosxom, though, instead of HTML files, these programs work from simple text files to publish an HTML Web log from templates, as well as RSS and Atom feeds.

These packages might prove more interesting than the simple feed producer you built in this chapter.

Looking at WordPress

WordPress is a personal publishing system written in PHP, and you can find it here:

`http://wordpress.org/`

Along with the full array of blogging features it offers, WordPress provides a range of templates for generating syndication feeds in RSS and Atom formats. Check out this system if you want to see an example of how syndication feeds have usually been generated.

Summary

In this chapter, you built a simple feed producer, and got a taste for what makes up a feed and how to ensure that your feeds are valid. Although not the most sophisticated system for feed content publishing, this program can serve as the basis for a lot of future projects:

- In this chapter's tweaks, you swapped out one feed format for another by changing the code around. Why not make this available as a command-line option, or, better yet, wrap it all up as a module or reusable class?

- The code for parsing metadata from HTML was built with flexibility in mind. You might want to throw in some more code to harvest even more metadata and content out of your pages.

- The use of string templates to generate the feed XML is only one way to do it, and a hackish way at that. Take a look at the `xml.dom` and `xml.sax` modules in Python to check out other ways to generate XML documents.

With this code as a base, you'll soon be exploring how to produce feeds from other sources of data, in the coming chapters. But first, Chapter 8 takes a bit of a quick detour away from generating feeds to explore a few issues involved in publishing these feeds to the Web efficiently and less expensively.

Taking the Edge Off Hosting Feeds

Once you've started producing feeds, you'll want to make them available for consumption by feed readers and aggregators. If you're just building feeds for your own private use, leaving them on your hard drive is probably good enough, because many aggregators will allow you to subscribe to local file URLs.

If you want to make your feeds available to the outside world, however, you'll need to get them hosted on a Web server—and that's where things get a lot more interesting. You see, syndication feeds themselves are a bit of a hack.

The Web has become a pretty efficient means for serving up and navigating between interlinked documents and resources. It's basically a *pull* technology, though. If you want something, you have to find it and ask for it when you want it. But, syndication feeds want to be a *push* technology—meaning that you should be able to register interest in something once and then get updates sent to you in the future, without having to remember to look or ask for it again.

Syndication feeds, then, are an attempt to build *push* on top of *pull*. This sort of thing is called an *impedance mismatch*, which comes with a host of problems and annoyances—but sometimes there are enough benefits to make it worth putting up with. In the case of syndication feeds, the ubiquity of Web servers and HTTP, as well as the relative simplicity of serving up XML data, are what make it so attractive.

So, simulating push using pull requires a lot of *polling*. You don't need to remember to check the feed resource for new items yourself, but your aggregator does. This means asking over and over again for the same thing to see if anything has changed—like a kid in the backseat chanting, "Are we there yet? Are we there yet?"

When this question is asked nonstop by hordes of feed aggregators on an hourly basis or worse, this can start to have an impact on bandwidth and hosting bills. When you're facing hundreds of subscribers, multiplied by 24 hours in a day, multiplied by 30 days a month—even a tiny little 10-KB feed can start to be a pain. So, you need ways to make answering this question more efficient, as well as trying to help aggregators ask the question less often.

This chapter is a little different from the others. Rather than offering a set of complete projects and programs for you to try out, this is more of a grab bag of pointers, ideas, and best practices to use in addressing feed hosting issues. These things are general tweaks that you can make to your Web server and pre-existing publishing software, as well as small changes you can apply to programs you build from this book. Think of this chapter as showing places where you can apply a tune-up or tighten up a bolt in your feed publishing engines.

One caveat, though: Although these suggestions can all provide dramatic relief in the strain on servers hosting particularly popular feeds, their support in feed aggregators is varied at best— one aggregator supports HTTP compression, whereas another supports obeying update schedule hints in the feed itself.

If all aggregators implemented all of the things presented in this chapter, quite a lot of the growing pains of syndication feeds would be assuaged. But, until that happens, it's best to take care of one end of the chicken-and-egg problem, and be sure that your feeds are served up with as many of these tweaks for your feeds as possible.

Baking and Caching Feeds

One of the first improvements you can make in answering requests for feeds is to reduce the amount of thought that goes into coming up with an answer. Some content management systems generate feeds fresh for every incoming request, and if you really wanted to, many of the programs in this book could be reworked as CGI programs that run on demand.

But, although this ensures that subscribers see the latest information as it becomes available, it's the least-efficient approach from a feed publisher's perspective. For the most part, the schedule by which subscribers request a feed does not match up very well with the schedule by which the feed is updated. Regenerating a feed with every request results in a lot of wasted and redundant effort, because it's really not all that likely for new information to be posted between requests.

To put this in perspective, consider that even if you were posting every thought as it occurred to you in a manic rush to your Web log, you'd still probably average less than a post or two (maybe three!) per minute. Whereas, if you have a popular site with a lot of feed subscribers, when aggregators wake up to make their hourly rounds, they'll hit your site with something more like a request or two every *second*.

With updates happening on the order of minutes and requests happening more on the scale of seconds, tying the activity of feed generation to the publishing of new content makes much more sense. And, in some content management packages, such as Movable Type (`http://www.movabletype.com`), this is the case. Feeds are static files rebuilt from templates at the same time as other HTML content resulting from a new entry being posted.

Feeds built and served fresh on demand are *fried*, whereas feeds built ahead of time and served statically are *baked*. Fried feeds are often easier to build and are tastier because, ideally, they'll have the newest stuff sooner. Baked feeds take a bit more up-front preparation and may not taste as great, but they're healthier because they go easier on system resources and conserve effort.

This baked-versus-fried notion is convenient to use in describing Web publishing processes, but I didn't come up with it. You can read up on some of the origins of this jargon at these URLs:

Slides for Ian Kallen's "Industrial Strength Web Publishing"

```
http://www.arachna.com/edu/talks/iswp/slides/
baking_versus_frying.html
```

"Bake, Don't Fry" by Aaron Swartz

```
http://www.aaronsw.com/weblog/000404
```

Baking on a Schedule

Sometimes, you can't tie into the actual publishing process or trigger feed generation directly from the availability of new information. In this case, a decent compromise is to bake on a regular schedule, which keeps the feeds fairly fresh without the demands of rebuilding for every request.

If you're generating feeds using some of the programs in this book, you're baking already. Really, the only two things you need are a feed generation program that can write its results out to a file, and a crontab or scheduled task to run the program periodically. And, if you happen to have access to run the program directly on your Web server, you can just schedule the program to write the feed directly somewhere in the file hierarchy of your Web site.

For example, a crontab entry I might use on my server to schedule runs of ch07_feed-maker.py from the previous chapter looks something like this:

```
0 * * * * /usr/bin/python $HOME/local/bin/ch07_feedmaker.py
$HOME/docs $HOME/www/www.decafbad.com/feeds/sample_feed.xml
```

This would fire off a run of ch07_feedmaker.py at the top of every hour, scanning the docs directory in my home for HTML pages and generating a baked feed called sample_feed.xml under the feeds path on my Web site. There's not much more to it than that, if your feed generation can already generate static files.

 If you need a refresher on how to schedule program runs, you may want to revisit the discussion of scheduling aggregator runs in Chapter 2, under "Using the Simple Feed Aggregator."

Baking with FTP

Unfortunately, not everyone has access to a Web host that provides a shell or the capability to run programs on the server—other than maybe CGI scripts, PHP, or ASP pages. With these environments, though, you usually have the capability to upload files via FTP.

Luckily, Python just happens to have ftplib in its standard library. With this module, you can use a machine of your own (such as the one you've been using to play with the programs from this book) to build feeds and have them shipped up to your Web server automatically. The ftplib module isn't all that difficult to use. Take a look at Listing 8-1 for a utility program you can use to upload a file to an FTP server.

Listing 8-1: ch08_ftpupload.py

```python
#!/usr/bin/env python
"""
ch08_ftpupload.py

Given a remote filename and an optional local filename, upload a
file to an FTP server.
"""
import sys
from ftplib import FTP


FTP_HOST   = "localhost"
FTP_USER   = "youruser"
FTP_PASSWD = "yourpassword"
FTP_PATH   = "/www/www.example.com/docs"

def main():
    # Grab the remote filename as the final command line argument.
    remote_fn = sys.argv.pop()

    # If there's another argument, treat it as a filename to upload.
    if len(sys.argv) > 1:
        # Open the given filename, replace STDIN with it.
        local_fn  = sys.argv.pop()
        sys.stdin = open(local_fn, 'r')

    # Log into the FTP server, change directories, upload everything
    # waiting on STDIN to the given filename, then quit.
    ftp = FTP(FTP_HOST, FTP_USER, FTP_PASSWD)
    ftp.cwd(FTP_PATH)
    ftp.storbinary("STOR %s" % remote_fn, sys.stdin)
    ftp.quit()

if __name__ == '__main__': main()
```

With ch08_ftpupload.py, you can specify the details of your FTP server account in the configuration constants at the beginning of the program. Then, if you're using a UNIX-based shell, you can run it in combination with another program like so:

```
# python ch07_feedmaker.py html_docs | python ch08_ftpupload.py
feeds/sample_feed.xml
```

Invoked like this, ch08_ftpupload.py accepts the output of another program piped to it and, using the account details in the configuration constants, automatically logs in and uploads that program's output to a path specified as a command-line argument.

If you're not using a shell with pipes, or already have a file on disk you'd like to upload, you can invoke the program like this:

```
# python ch07_feedmaker.py html_docs local_file.xml
# python ch08_ftpupload.py local_file.xml feeds/sample_feed.xml
```

When two arguments are supplied, ch08_ftpupload.py treats the first as a local filename to be uploaded. It opens this file for reading in place of standard input and, as before, uses the final argument on the command line as the upload path.

Armed with this utility, you should be able to automate the baking and uploading of any feed generated by programs in this book. If you really feel like getting fancy, though, you could try tweaking other programs to redirect their output to FTP uploads automatically, rather than saving things to local files or writing to standard output.

Caching Dynamically Generated Feeds

If you have a fried feed currently generated on the fly, you can turn it into a baked feed by downloading it periodically and caching it to a static file on your Web server.

Again, although doing this with a schedule isn't as good as hooking directly into the publishing process and baking the feed when (and only when) there's new information to be had, it's a decent compromise to lighten some load on your server—and at least you can control the caching schedule. (Then again, if you *do* know how to hook into your content management system's publishing process, you might consider adapting some form of bakery into it based on what's presented here.)

Although you could use Python's standard library offerings to download feed content, how about revisiting a tool introduced in Chapter 2—namely, httpcache.py, available here:

```
http://bitworking.org/projects/httpcache/
```

If you've been following along, you already have a copy of httpcache.py installed or available in your project directory. If not, you should get it now. As of this writing, the module is available for download here:

```
http://bitworking.org/projects/httpcache/httpcache.py.txt
```

Download that to your project directory as httpcache.py, and you're good to go. Check out Listing 8-2 for a refresher on how to use this module.

Listing 8-2: ch08_feed_fetch.py

```
#!/usr/bin/env python
"""
ch08_feed_fetch.py

Fetch a feed and print to standard output.
"""
import sys
from httpcache import HTTPCache
```

Continued

Listing 8-2 *(continued)*

```
def main():
    """
    Given a feed URL as an argument, fetch and print the feed.
    """
    feed_uri     = sys.argv[1]
    cache        = HTTPCache(feed_uri)
    feed_content = cache.content()

    print feed_content

if __name__ == "__main__": main()
```

The program in Listing 8-2 is pretty simple. Given a URL as a command-line argument, it fetches the data at that URL and prints it to standard output. You could use this utility to grab the content for a dynamically generated feed like so:

```
# python ch08_feed_fetch.py http://www.example.com/mysite/backend.php?sect=
foo&format=rss
```

This would then use the `httpcache` module to fetch this feed and dump it to standard output. If you like, you can pipe this command to `ch08_ftpupload.py` to publish this data as a static file on your server. Like many things in this book, this is definitely a hack, but it might be a convenient way to turn a fried feed into a more server-friendly baked feed.

Saving Bandwidth with Compression

Having conserved some of the processing involved, you can next improve handling requests for feeds by reducing the amount of data transferred in answering requests. One way to do this is through applying compression to transfers.

HTTP 1.1 allows for content coding, meaning that data transferred via HTTP can be first passed through some form of transformation (such as gzip or LZW compression) on the way to being delivered. The details of this transformation are included in HTTP headers, which prompt the client on the other end to first apply the inverse of the transformation (that is, decompress the data). So, using compression in content coding allows data to take up less bandwidth during transfers, which, when applied to feeds, can speed up delivery, lighten the load across the network, and reduce server bills.

On the Web The specification for HTTP/1.1 describes how compression can be used in content coding for transfers, available at this URL:

```
http://www.w3.org/Protocols/rfc2616/rfc2616-sec3.
html#sec3.5
```

To really get a sense for what compression can save, you might need to do a little math. Because feeds are mostly text, with a few bits of punctuation and angle brackets thrown in, applying something like gzip compression can often reduce feed data by as much as 66 percent. Take a look at Table 8-1, where I use this assumption to do a little bit of hypothetical math.

Table 8-1   Feed Bandwidth Savings with Compression

	Without Compression	With gzip Compression
Feed size	35,000 bytes	12,500 bytes (66 percent reduction)
Daily bandwidth for 1,000 hourly subscribers	840 MB	300 MB
Estimated monthly transfer	25 GB	9 GB

Now, this is by no means precise or scientific—and you're doing pretty well if you have a thousand subscribers to your feed—but Table 8-1 should give you some idea of the magnitude of the impact a 66 percent compression rate can have on your server.

In fact, glancing around at a few Web hosting plans available today, requiring a 9 GB monthly transfer versus 25 GB can be the difference between paying $10 and $30 per month in hosting, and that's not accounting for any charges incurred when you go over your monthly limit. This math isn't complicated, but it can be surprising how big an impact a little feed can make.

Enabling Compression in Your Web Server

The best place to enable HTTP compression is in your Web server configuration. When turned on at this level, using compression with your feeds becomes pretty much transparent. Unfortunately, if you aren't in direct control of the Web server hosting your feeds, this may not be an option for you. If you're lucky, though, and your hosting company is smart, they already have this turned on or will gladly do it for you upon request.

On the other hand, if you do have control of the configuration of your Web hosting server, you should be somewhat familiar with its care and feeding. Because this is a pretty big topic beyond the scope of this book, I'll just give you a few pointers toward available modules and documentation.

If you're administering an Apache 1.3 server, you'll want to check out mod_gzip, available here:

```
http://sourceforge.net/projects/mod-gzip/
```

Getting this module built and enabled isn't too difficult, but you should be familiar with Apache server configuration. The following pages linked from the mod_gzip project may help:

```
http://www.schroepl.net/projekte/mod_gzip/install.htm
http://www.schroepl.net/projekte/mod_gzip/config.htm
```

On the other hand, if you've migrated to Apache 2.0 and above, you may want to check out `mod_deflate`, documented here:

```
http://httpd.apache.org/docs-2.0/mod/mod_deflate.html
```

Depending on how your Apache 2.0 server was built and installed, you should probably already have this module available, if not already enabled. But, you should check out this documentation for more information.

If you're in charge of a server running Microsoft's Internet Information Server (IIS), version 6.0 or higher, check out this URL for instructions:

```
http://www.microsoft.com/resources/documentation/iis/6/all/
proddocs/en-us/comp_intro.mspx
```

This part of the IIS documentation should lead you through all the steps necessary to enable HTTP compression.

Enabling Compression using cgi_buffer

If you don't have administrative access to alter the configuration of the Web server hosting your feeds—or if maybe you'd just like to get a little more hands-on with this aspect of feed hosting for curiosity's sake—there's another option available, using Mark Nottingham's `cgi_buffer` libraries, available at this URL:

```
http://www.mnot.net/cgi_buffer/
```

As of this writing, the package is available for direct download at this URL:

```
http://www.mnot.net/cgi_buffer/cgi_buffer-0.3.tgz
```

Unpack this archive, and you should find everything you need under the `python` directory inside the top-level `cgi_buffer` directory. Copy everything from that directory that ends with `.py` into your CGI directory. Leave out the example programs—although you might want to keep those around to make sure things are working. Take a look at Listing 8-3 for a simple example of how `cgi_buffer` is used.

Listing 8-3: ch08_feedfilter.py

```python
#!/usr/bin/env python
"""
ch08_feedfilter.cgi

Filter a feed through cgi_buffer.
"""
import cgi_buffer

FEED_FN   = "sample_rss.xml"
FEED_TYPE = "rss"

def main():
    print "Content-Type: application/%s+xml" % FEED_TYPE
```

```
    print
    print open(FEED_FN, 'r').read()

if __name__=='__main__': main()
```

The CGI program in Listing 8-3 named ch08_feedfilter.py does just one thing: It opens a file named in FEED_FN and outputs it with an appropriate Content-Type header based on the value of FEED_TYPE, which should be either atom or rss.

Because of a bit of Python magic performed in the cgi_buffer module, there's nothing more you need to do. Code in cgi_buffer will capture the output of your CGI program and automatically tweak things to support HTTP compression, among other things. An additional tweak enables conditional GET in HTTP transfers using ETag and If-None-Match headers, which you'll see more about in just a minute.

Patching cgi_buffer 0.3

Well, it's almost that easy. Turns out, there's an issue with cgi_buffer 0.3 and Content-Type header values such as application/atom+xml and application/rss+xml—to enable compression, it expects all Content-Type headers to start off with text.

You could use text/xml as a Content-Type header in the previous program and compression would start working, but this is a Content-Type that's deprecated for use with feeds.

Although it might be fixed by the time you read this, you can hack cgi_buffer.py yourself to address this issue. Just open up the file in your editor and cursor down to code near line 62, which reads like this:

```
### content encoding
if env.has_key('HTTP_ACCEPT_ENCODING') and compress_content and \
zlib and headers.content_type[:4] == 'text':
```

To patch this issue, just remove everything between zlib and the colon at the end of line 64, ending up with code like this:

```
### content encoding
if env.has_key('HTTP_ACCEPT_ENCODING') and compress_content and \
zlib:
```

You'll want to mind the indentation and keep a backup copy of cgi_buffer.py around, but this tweak should get compression working for these feeds.

Minimizing Redundant Downloads

After you've reduced the amount of thought and the length of the conversation involved in answering requests for feeds, what's left is to enable the client requesting feeds to ask for less and ask less frequently. Although these tweaks require the cooperation of the feed reader or aggregator, most modern clients implement some (if not all) of the features necessary to help out in this regard.

Enabling Conditional GET

Asking for less can be accomplished via HTTP/1.1's conditional GET facilities, whereby your server and its clients can collaborate to keep notes tracking when things have changed.

Using HTTP conditional GET can cut feed transfer requirements dramatically—often even more so than the 66 percent reduction promised by compression. This is because, no matter how big the feed is, the amount of data transfer involved in telling a client that nothing has changed remains constant at a few hundred bytes, if that.

Once you have conditional GET enabled, you should only get hit once by each well-behaved subscriber for the full amount of the feed when you post an update to your site. Then, for every further request throughout the day where you haven't posted anything new, every subscriber simply receives a message of around 250 bytes or so telling the subscriber to check back later with an HTTP status code of 304.

When a client requests a resource from a server via HTTP, the server includes a few special pieces of information about the document in response headers. These bits of data are retained by the client, which are included in headers when the resource is requested again.

The server can then use these values to determine whether or not anything has changed in the resource since the last time the client came asking about it. If, indeed, nothing has changed, the server can then opt to tell the client as much, in lieu of sending the resource data over again. This saves both bandwidth and processing, because nothing is transferred by the server, and the client doesn't have to do any work to parse updates.

Conditional GET is facilitated in two main ways via HTTP headers used in requests and responses:

- Last-Modified and If-Modified-Since headers can be used to track resource modification dates.

- ETag and If-None-Match headers can be used to track the content itself using whatever other method the server chooses to implement, such as creating hashes of resource data.

Which method is used depends on what makes the most sense given the content management system on the server—well-behaved clients should be able to handle any or both of these.

On the Web   The HTTP/1.1 specification describes conditional GET at this URL:

        http://www.w3.org/Protocols/rfc2616/rfc2616-sec9.
        html#sec9.3

The Last-Modified, If-Modified-Since, ETag, and If-None-Match headers are described here in Section 14 of the HTTP/1.1 specification:

        http://www.w3.org/Protocols/rfc2616/rfc2616-sec14.html

So, let's do some rough math again. Suppose that you generally update your site five times in a day, spaced out across a few hours between updates. This means that, in a day of 24 hours of hits from aggregators, 5 of those hours will yield new content and 19 of them will offer nothing new. Check out Table 8-2 for a quick estimation of bandwidth used for a feed hosted with conditional GET enabled.

Table 8-2   Feed Bandwidth Savings with Conditional GET

	Without compression	With conditional GET
Feed size	35,000 bytes	35,000 bytes
Daily bandwidth for 1,000 hourly subscribers	840 MB	175 MB of updated feed data + 5 MB of "come back later" responses = 180 MB
Estimated monthly transfer	25 GB	6 GB

These are rough numbers, but they suggest that using conditional GET can get you bandwidth savings of almost 75 percent—which is even better than what you get when using compression. Whereas compression operates on the data that gets sent, conditional GET actually removes the need for data to be sent altogether in many cases. In our hypothetical case, using conditional GET would reduce feed traffic to a trickle for 19 out of 24 hours' worth of daily assault by feed aggregators.

But, there's no reason why you can't use both conditional GET *and* compression. Compression applies to the body of a request. So, because the "come back later" responses are fully expressed as HTTP headers, you can only apply it to the 175 MB of updated feed data. But, even with that constraint, your bandwidth savings are significant, potentially bringing the transfer requirement down to around 2 GB per month, according to a calculation I just did here on a napkin. Again, rough numbers, but you get the gist.

Enabling Conditional GET in Your Web Server

Again, the best place to enable conditional GET compression is in your Web server configuration, where its use becomes mostly seamless. And, you'll either need to administrate your own server or have the help of a bright Web-hosting provider to help you out.

Fortunately, for both Apache 1.3 and 2.0 servers, ETag generation is standard core functionality, so you shouldn't need to do anything to get this working with your baked feeds. On the other hand, to take advantage of the Last-Modified side of conditional GET, you may need to get an optional module installed.

If you're dealing with an Apache 1.3 server, take a look at mod_expires, documented here:

```
http://httpd.apache.org/docs/mod/mod_expires.html
```

Apache 2.0 servers have their own updated version of mod_expires, which you can read about here:

http://httpd.apache.org/docs-2.0/mod/mod_expires.html

This is a pretty common module, so you might already have it installed on your server.

As for Microsoft IIS servers, much of this functionality already works out of the box, although you may want to look into a product such as Port80's CacheRight for finer control over caching and conditional GET headers:

http://www.port80software.com/products/cacheright/

Enabling Conditional GET using cgi_buffer

As mentioned earlier, the cgi_buffer module (http://www.mnot.net/cgi_buffer/) supports conditional GET via the ETag and If-None-Match headers for use with CGI programs that generate content dynamically, including the feed filter program in Listing 8-3. Again, there's nothing special that you need to do to get this functionality working—just simply import the module in a program, and it will do its magic to trap the output of the program.

However, notice that cgi_buffer doesn't offer support for Last-Modified and If-Modified-Since headers. The proper place to figure out modification timestamps is in the code that actually manages the content and, therefore, knows when things have been modified. All that cgi_buffer has access to is the final output of the program, so the best it can do is run a hash of that output to produce an ETag header.

Still, though, an ETag is still sufficient to enable conditional GET. The only drawback is that the program still goes through the effort of generating the content, calculating the hash, and only figuring out that the content isn't worth sending right at the end of the process. The tradeoff here is between server CPU and network bandwidth, and sometimes it's worth burning processor power to save a few gigs of transfer.

Using Expiration and Cache Control Headers

Although usually used for providing instruction to HTTP caches and browsers, the Expires and Cache-Control headers can both be used to supply some update timing information to aggregators.

On the Web You can find a description of the Expires header here in the HTTP/1.1 specification:

> http://www.w3.org/Protocols/rfc2616/rfc2616-sec14.
> html#sec14.21

And, the Cache-Control header is described here:

> http://www.w3.org/Protocols/rfc2616/rfc2616-sec14.
> html#sec14.9

If you have mod_expires installed on your Apache Web server, you can configure it to produce headers like the ones in Listing 8-4. And if you're using Microsoft IIS, you can tweak content expiration for directories, but you'll need something like CacheRight to get finer-grained control.

Listing 8-4: Expires and Cache-Control Headers Example

```
Expires: Mon, 28 Mar 2005 14:00:00 GMT
Cache-Control: max-age=10800, must-revalidate
```

What the headers in Listing 8-4 tell an HTTP client is that whatever it just fetched will become stale in an hour, or by Monday, March 28, 2005, at 2:00PM GMT, whichever is sooner. The client can cache this resource until it's reached the maximum age or the specified time has passed, at which point it will need to fetch the URL again to have the freshest version.

If you have your feed generator running on a schedule (say, every 3 hours), you could configure things to produce headers like these. And, if you have a cooperative subscriber, the feed aggregator should be paying attention to these headers to possibly vary the time at which it plans to make a fresh poll to your feed.

For a very good and detailed tutorial on HTTP caching in general, take a look here:

```
http://www.mnot.net/cache_docs/
```

Providing Update Schedule Hints in Feed Metadata

Now that you've seen just about every flip and twist you can take to improve performance on the delivery side of feed polling, it's time to take a look at a few of the things you can add to the metadata of feeds themselves to attempt to offer hints to feed consumers about when your feeds are actually updated.

For example, if someone's subscribed to your blog's RSS feed, it might not make a whole lot of sense for the aggregator to ask for updates every single hour—at least, not if you're generally in bed from midnight to 6 a.m. and it's highly likely that your feed will almost *never* update during that time. Or, if you have a business blog that only ever sees posts from 9-to-5, Monday through Friday, it'd be nice to have some way to hang a sign with your business hours on it.

Well, there just happen to be some facilities for this for RSS 1.0 and 2.0 feed formats.

Offering Hints in RSS 2.0 Feeds

In RSS 2.0, the following elements for use as feed metadata in the <channel> element are given as optional:

- <ttl>—Specifies how long (in minutes) the feed can be cached before it can be assumed stale.
- <skipHours>—Contains up to 24 <hour> child elements, each supplying a numeric value between 0 and 23 for an hour of the day in GMT time when the feed should not be checked.

- `<skipDays>`—Contains up to 7 `<day>` child elements, each supplying a string naming a day of the week during which the feed should not be checked. These string values are defined as one of the following: Monday, Tuesday, Wednesday, Thursday, Friday, Saturday, or Sunday.

For example, if you wanted to announce in your feed that you'll only be blogging during normal 9-to-5 business hours on weekdays, your feed metadata might look like Listing 8-5.

Note If these hours look like they're a little off, remember that they're meant to be expressed in GMT. And because I'm subject to Eastern Standard Time in the U.S., 9:00 for me is 14:00 in GMT. So, the hours skipped are between 1:00 and 13:00, GMT.

Listing 8-5: Schedule Hints in an RSS 2.0 Feed

```
<rss version="2.0">
    <channel>
        <description>Sample feed</description>
        <link>http://www.example.com/</link>
        <title>Scripting News</title>
        <skipHours>
            <hour>1</hour><hour>2</hour>
            <hour>3</hour><hour>4</hour>
            <hour>5</hour><hour>6</hour>
            <hour>7</hour><hour>8</hour>
            <hour>9</hour><hour>10</hour>
            <hour>11</hour><hour>12</hour>
            <hour>13</hour>
        </skipHours>
        <skipDays>
            <day>Saturday</day>
            <day>Sunday</day>
        </skipDays>
        <item>
            <title>Sample entry</title>
        </item>
    </channel>
</rss>
```

Also, you can use the `<ttl>` element to provide finer-grained control. There's no reason why you can't vary the value from one feed generation to the next.

So, if when you generate a feed, you know that the next scheduled run of the generator isn't for another 4 hours, you can set the `<ttl>` to 240 minutes. Then, 4 hours later, if you know that the feed generator is about to kick into high gear and build every half-hour, start publishing with a `<ttl>` of 30 minutes. Listing 8-6 shows a few example `<ttl>` values.

Listing 8-6: Schedule Hints using <ttl>

```
<ttl>240</ttl>    <!-- 4 hours -->
<ttl>30</ttl>     <!-- 1/2 hour -->
<ttl>10080</ttl> <!-- 7 days, going on a vacation? -->
```

Offering Hints in RSS 1.0 Feeds

Although this book focuses on RSS 2.0 and Atom, it might be useful to mention that for RSS 1.0 there's an extension available that defines the following feed metadata elements used in describing the update period and frequency of a feed:

- <updatePeriod>—Provides the period in which a channel is updated, with values including the following: hourly, daily, weekly, monthly, yearly.

- <updateFrequency>—Gives the number of updates that are expected to occur within the period.

- <updateBase>—Supplies a starting time from which to make calculations using the period and frequency in coming up with a feed polling schedule.

The specification for this extension is available at the following URL:

http://purl.org/rss/1.0/modules/syndication/

For example, the tags in Listing 8-7 offer values used to specify a feed that updates every two hours starting from midnight on March 26, 2005, in the GMT timezone.

Listing 8-7: Schedule Hints in an RSS 1.0 Feed

```
<sy:updatePeriod>hourly</sy:updatePeriod>
<sy:updateFrequency>2</sy:updateFrequency>
<sy:updateBase>2005-03-26T12:00+00:00</sy:updateBase>
```

Checking Out Other Options

Although this chapter has pretty much been nothing but one big summary of options, I still have a few remaindered pointers for you dig into.

Using Unpolluted to Test Feeds

There's a Feed Validator for checking the validity and quality of your feeds, so why not a program to test out how your feeds are getting served up? Check out Unpolluted, a tool written in Python to do just that, at this URL:

```
http://www.kafsemo.org/hacks/#unpolluted
```

Unpolluted will download a feed at a given URL and test for the availability of compression, conditional GET, and caching directives.

Using SFTP to Upload Baked Feeds

If you've taken on the strategy of building feeds on a machine at home and then using FTP to automatically ship them off to your Web server, you might want to check out how to switch to using Secure FTP with the paramiko module found here:

```
http://www.lag.net/paramiko/
```

This module provides support for the Secure Shell (SSH) v2 protocol for use in building encrypted tunnels for file transfers, among other things.

Investigating RFC3229 for Further Bandwidth Control

All of the tweaks in this chapter deal with compressing feeds, deciding whether or not to send the feed, and figuring how out to send hints to feed consumers about when to expect updates to the feed. What all of these have in common, though, is that the feed is always all-or-nothing—that is, the feed itself is treated as an indivisible blob; it all gets sent or not sent.

But, another approach to optimizing feed polling and delivery is to get a finer-grained control and actually acknowledge that a feed is divisible into individual entries. And each of these entries, ideally, has its own metadata (like dates and GUIDs), which can all be used in determining just what new data needs to be sent to a feed consumer.

You can get an introduction to this concept through Bob Wyman's blog post, "Using RFC3229 with Feeds," located here:

```
http://bobwyman.pubsub.com/main/2004/09/using_rfc3229_w.html
```

Summary

This chapter tried to give you an overview of what options are available for streamlining the process of serving up feeds. Every little byte shaved off every request quickly adds up, and the more cooperation there exists between the server providing feeds and the client consuming feeds, the better.

One problem you may find with some of these suggestions, though, is the lack of universal support for everything presented in this chapter in all feed aggregators. The best thing to do, though, is to try to apply as many of these improvements as you can—because most aggregators support at least some subset of the tweaks here.

Even though the neverending polls of a push technology shoehorned into a pull technology will never be a perfect situation, there is definitely a lot of room for improvement, and the sheer inexpensive ubiquity of HTTP and XML is what has made syndication feeds grow so explosively, despite whatever rough edges there might be.

In Chapter 9, you get back to generating syndication feeds. In Chapter 9, you advance to extracting information from existing Web sites by using several useful techniques that will allow you to build feeds where none would otherwise be available.

Scraping Web Sites to Produce Feeds

Once you've become addicted to using feeds to manage how you peruse the Web, it'll start to become painfully obvious that a lot of sites out there have yet to join the party. For a growing number of modern "inforvores," the lack of an available syndication feed is reason enough to leave a site behind and never look back.

But occasionally, you'll find some site bereft of feeds that you just can't drop from your daily rounds—it might be a Web comic that hasn't come around yet, or a favorite niche news site that's just behind the times. Well, instead of grumbling every time you feel the need to leave your aggregator's home base and wander through bookmarks, why not do yourself a favor and brew up some private feeds for all those antiquated sites?

Web pages built with HTML can usually be treated as just another XML format—and you've already seen and built parsers for XML and HTML formats in earlier chapters. In the worst case scenario, an older Web page might not be much more than messy tag soup, but you can even cope with this by using regular expressions and other means of text wrangling available in Python.

So, why not build parsers for your favorite legacy sites that produce feeds for your own private consumption? These parsers are called "scrapers," after the practice used by developers dealing with legacy mainframe applications where data is figuratively "scraped" from character-based forms on green-screen terminal displays and stuffed into more modern data structures and APIs. In the same spirit, you can shoehorn "legacy" Web content into feeds consumable by your favorite aggregator.

Introducing Feed Scraping Concepts

Before you get into writing code for this chapter, it might help to bring up a few considerations of just what it means to scrape a syndication feed from another document format.

Scraper Building Is Fuzzy Logic and Pattern Recognition

There's no simple formula to building a feed scraper, and there's no sure way to automate it. Out of everything presented in this book, this is one activity that most definitely qualifies as hacking: You must be prepared to personally paw through the source code of Web pages and be ready to work through many cycles of trial-and-error before you get a satisfactory result.

Even after all of that, you might never get a wholly satisfying feed out of the process. And once you at least have *something* working, there's no guarantee that it will keep working the day after tomorrow. Webmasters and content managers rework HTML templates, layouts get refreshed from time to time, and data formats change. It might not be intentional, but then again it could be. Some site owners would just rather not have their content used in ways that they don't control, whether you agree with it or not.

Given all that, though, building feed scrapers can be great fun—albeit fun only a hacker could love. Every scraper is an exercise in fuzzy logic and pattern recognition. You'll need to find the shape and boundaries of repeating patterns in data; decide how to pry useful information out of those patterns; what tools to use; and how to express the solution in working code. Sometimes the solution is quickly found and neatly wrapped up, but sometimes you'll need to be a bit more creative.

But, at the end of the day, a working feed scraper will save you time and help you keep up with things you might have otherwise missed in your busy schedule. This is the best result of hacking: a neat trick that brings you repeated and direct personal benefit through automation.

Scraping Requires a Flexible Toolkit

Mainly, you'll be concerned with Web pages—and that means, roughly speaking, HTML and XHTML. However, the resources from which you might be interested in deriving feeds might include relatively more exotic things such as text-based log files, a custom XML schema, or even horribly broken HTML-esque data that just barely passes muster for display in a Web browser. Any of these sources of data can offer interesting information you might like to pull into your aggregator.

So, it would help to have a flexible toolkit at hand that can handle just about anything that comes along, yet allow you to do so in the easiest, most maintainable way possible. No single tool or technique can cover all possibilities you'll run into, so in this chapter you get a chance to play with several approaches:

- Liberal HTML parsing and extraction via Python's `HTMLParser` class
- Text munging via regular expressions
- HTML/XHTML cleansing with HTML Tidy and data extraction using XPath

Building a Feed Scraping Foundation

To accommodate building scrapers for a wide variety of resources, constructing a flexible underlying foundation would be a good place to start. In Chapter 7, you can find some of the pieces for this in the templated approach to generating RSS and Atom feeds. So, this first part is a bit of an evolution from that first simple feed producer.

To get to work, start a new file named `scraperlib.py` in your editor. This will be a shared module in which you'll put the basic parts used for building feed scrapers. Take a look at Listing 9-1 for the opening lines.

Listing 9-1: scraperlib.py (Part 1 of 13)

```
"""
scraperlib

Useful base classes and utilities for HTML page scrapers.
"""
import sys, time, re, shelve
from urllib import quote
from urllib2 import urlopen
from urlparse import urljoin, urlparse
from xml.sax.saxutils import escape

UNICODE_ENC = "UTF8"
```

From the initial module imports here, you can get some sense of what's coming. There are some of the old standby tools for URL manipulation and downloading data from the Web. There's also the `shelve` module for maintaining state in an on-disk database, as well as the `escape` function used in Chapter 7 for ensuring data is safe to include in an XML template.

Encapsulating Scraped Feed Entry Data

Next up is the definition of a class named `FeedEntryDict`, which is kind of a more general and abstract version of Chapter 7's `TemplateDocWrapper`. This class will be used to encapsulate the data representing a feed entry extracted from the scraped data source, doing all the escaping and encoding necessary for its use with an XML string template. Take a look at Listing 9-2 for the beginning of this class.

Listing 9-2: scraperlib.py (Part 2 of 13)

```
class FeedEntryDict:
    """
    This class is a wrapper around HTMLMetaDoc objects meant to
    facilitate easy use in XML template strings.
    """
    UNICODE_ENC = "UTF-8"
    DATE_KEYS   = [ 'modified', 'issued' ]
```

Continued

Listing 9-2 (continued)

```
def __init__(self, init_dict={}, date_fmt='%Y-%m-%dT%H:%M:%SZ'):
    """
    Initialize the feed entry dict, with optional data.
    """
    self.data = {}
    self.data.update(init_dict)
    self.date_fmt = date_fmt
```

Here, you have the familiar Unicode encoding constant, and a couple of feed entry attributes called out. These will contain date values, and will be given special attention later because of the varied date formats used by RSS and Atom. Next is the object instance initializer, which accepts populated dictionary for initialization, as well as a date/time format string that will be used when the aforementioned date attributes are used in the XML template.

In Listing 9-3, you can find two further method definitions for __cmp__() and __setitem__().

Listing 9-3: scraperlib.py (Part 3 of 13)

```
def __cmp__(self, other):
    """Reverse chronological order on modified date"""
    return cmp(other.data['modified'], self.data['modified'])

def __setitem__(self, name, val):
    """Set a value in the feed entry dict."""
    self.data[name] = val
```

The definition for __cmp__() will allow lists of FeedEntryDict objects to be easily sorted by reverse chronological order on their modification dates. The __setitem__() method definition enables instances of this class to be treated like Python dictionaries for the purposes of setting values. Moving on, the __getitem__() method defined in Listing 9-4 provides the complement to __setitem__().

Listing 9-4: scraperlib.py (Part 4 of 13)

```
def __getitem__(self, name):
    """Return a dict item, escaped and encoded for XML inclusion"""
    # Chop off the entry. prefix, if found.
    if name.startswith('entry.'):
        name = name[6:]
```

```
# If this key is a date, format accordingly.
if name in self.DATE_KEYS:
    date = self.data.get(name, time.time())
    val  = time.strftime(self.date_fmt, time.gmtime(date))

# Otherwise, try returning what was asked for.
else:
    val = self.data.get(name, '')

# Make sure the value is finally safe for inclusion in XML
if type(val) is unicode:
    val = val.encode(self.UNICODE_ENC)
return escape(val.strip())
```

In `__getitem__()`, dictionary-style access to `FeedEntryDict` data is enabled. Whenever a key starting with a prefix of `entry.` is encountered, this prefix is stripped, making keys such as `entry.title` and `title` equivalent. This adds just a little convenience for use in string templates.

In the next part of the method, date attributes (as identified in the class constant `DATE_KEYS`) are handled appropriately based on the feed date format specified in the initializer. Finally, any other keys are retrieved with a blank default, and then the value is Unicode-encoded if necessary, whitespace stripped, and escaped for use in an XML string template.

And that's the end of the `FeedEntryDict` class. Next up is an `Exception` class named `_ScraperFinishedException`, shown in Listing 9-5, similar to what was used in Chapter 7 to reduce the amount of parsing done on HTML files once everything interesting had already been gathered.

Listing 9-5: scraperlib.py (Part 5 of 13)

```
class _ScraperFinishedException(Exception):
    """
    Private exception, raised when the scraper has seen all it's
    interested in parsing.
    """
    pass
```

Again, the code in Listing 9-5 doesn't really do anything—it's just a simple exception thrown by scrapers when they've reached the end of anything worth processing.

Reusing Feed Templates

Listing 9-6 provides string templates used to produce an Atom feed. These will be used very shortly in the upcoming definition of the `Scraper` class.

Listing 9-6: scraperlib.py (Part 6 of 13)

```
ATOM_DATE_FMT = "%Y-%m-%dT%H:%M:%SZ"

ATOM_FEED_TMPL = """<?xml version="1.0" encoding="utf-8"?>
<feed version="0.3" xmlns="http://purl.org/atom/ns#">
    <title>%(feed.title)s</title>
    <link rel="alternate" type="text/html"
        href="%(feed.link)s" />
    <tagline>%(feed.tagline)s</tagline>
    <modified>%(feed.modified)s</modified>
    <author>
        <name>%(feed.author.name)s</name>
        <email>%(feed.author.email)s</email>
        <url>%(feed.author.url)s</url>
    </author>
    %(feed.entries)s
</feed>
"""

ATOM_ENTRY_TMPL = """
    <entry>
        <title>%(entry.title)s</title>
        <link rel="alternate" type="text/html"
            href="%(entry.link)s" />
        <issued>%(entry.modified)s</issued>
        <modified>%(entry.modified)s</modified>
        <id>%(entry.id)s</id>
        <summary type="text/html" mode="escaped">
            %(entry.summary)s
        </summary>
    </entry>
"""
```

These Atom feed string templates are taken verbatim from Listing 7-10 of Chapter 7, with the only addition being ATOM_DATE_FMT, defining the Atom feed date format. And, finishing off the definitions used by the Scraper class, are the RSS feed string templates in Listing 9-7.

Listing 9-7: scraperlib.py (Part 7 of 13)

```
RSS_DATE_FMT = "%a, %d %b %Y %H:%M:%S %z"

RSS_FEED_TMPL = """<?xml version="1.0" encoding="utf-8"?>
<rss version="2.0">
    <channel>
        <title>%(feed.title)s</title>
        <link>%(feed.link)s</link>
```

```
        <description>%(feed.tagline)s</description>
        <webMaster>%(feed.author.email)s</webMaster>
        %(feed.entries)s
    </channel>
</rss>
"""

RSS_ENTRY_TMPL = """
        <item>
            <title>%(entry.title)s</title>
            <link>%(entry.link)s</link>
            <pubDate>%(entry.modified)s</pubDate>
            <guid isPermaLink="false">%(entry.id)s</guid>
            <description>%(entry.summary)s</description>
        </item>
"""
```

In Listing 9-7, the RSS_DATE_FMT constant provides the RSS feed date format. And again, the string templates in Listing 9-7 should look familiar, because they were copied from Listing 7-16.

So, at this point, you have the initial bits of the scraperlib module, based on your initial work with feed production in Chapter 7. The FeedEntryDict class provides an abstract encapsulation of scraped data used in populating feed templates, and the Scraper class provides a foundation for all the scrapers throughout this chapter, providing the ability to produce both RSS and Atom feeds, as well as taking care of some basic defaults like consistent entry datestamps and GUIDs.

Building the Base Scraper Class

Some basic similarities exist between all scrapers, so the next step is to bring those together in a parent class. This class, named Scraper, begins in Listing 9-8.

Listing 9-8: scraperlib.py (Part 8 of 13)

```
class Scraper:
    """
    Base class containing a few methods universal to scrapers.
    """
    FEED_META = {
        'feed.title'        : 'A Sample Feed',
        'feed.link'         : 'http://www.example.com',
        'feed.tagline'      : 'This is a testing sample feed.',
        'feed.author.name'  : 'l.m.orchard',
        'feed.author.email' : 'l.m.orchard@pobox.com',
        'feed.author.url'   : 'http://www.decafbad.com',
        'feed.modified'     : ''
```

Continued

Listing 9-8 *(continued)*

```
}
BASE_HREF    = ""
SCRAPE_URL   = ""
STATE_FN     = "scraper_state"
MAX_ENTRIES = 15

ATOM_DATE_FMT    = ATOM_DATE_FMT
ATOM_FEED_TMPL   = ATOM_FEED_TMPL
ATOM_ENTRY_TMPL = ATOM_ENTRY_TMPL

RSS_DATE_FMT     = RSS_DATE_FMT
RSS_FEED_TMPL    = RSS_FEED_TMPL
RSS_ENTRY_TMPL  = RSS_ENTRY_TMPL
```

All scrapers in this chapter inherit from the `Scraper` class, which contains all the basic machinery. The code in Listing 9-8 should look very similar to Listing 7-9, because the default `FEED_META` data structure and presence of the `MAX_ENTRIES` setting should look just about the same. This contains the values that will be used for the top-level elements describing the feed this scraper will produce.

The `BASE_HREF` and `SCRAPE_URL` constants are blank by default, but should be overridden in subclasses. The `STATE_FN` constant should also be overridden in subclasses, but starts off with a default of `"scraper_state"`. This constant contains the filename for a database that will maintain scraper state between runs, the importance of which is explained in a little bit.

The last bit of Listing 9-8 looks a little redundant, but it serves to pull the module-level string template constants into the class as constants that can later be overridden in subclasses. This will come in handy later in the book.

Listing 9-9 continues the `Scraper` class with the definitions of the entry point methods used to produce Atom and RSS feeds.

Listing 9-9: scraperlib.py (Part 9 of 13)

```
def scrape_atom(self):
    """Scrape the page and return an Atom feed."""
    self.FEED_META['feed.modified'] = \
        time.strftime(ATOM_DATE_FMT, time.gmtime(time.time()))
    return self.scrape(ATOM_ENTRY_TMPL, ATOM_FEED_TMPL,
        ATOM_DATE_FMT)

def scrape_rss(self):
    """Scrape the page and return an RSS feed."""
    return self.scrape(RSS_ENTRY_TMPL, RSS_FEED_TMPL, RSS_DATE_FMT)
```

Both the `scrape_atom()` and the `scrape_rss()` methods each call the `scrape()` method, supplying the appropriate entry and feed string templates, as well as a date format. The `scrape_atom()` also generates a current modification time in the feed metadata, which is not used in RSS.

Next, Listing 9-10 offers the beginning of the `scrape()` method.

Listing 9-10: scraperlib.py (Part 10 of 13)

```
def scrape(self, entry_tmpl, feed_tmpl, date_fmt):
    """
    Given an entry and feed string templates, scrape an HTML
    page for content and use the templates to return a feed.
    """
    self.date_fmt = date_fmt
    self.state_db = shelve.open(self.STATE_FN)

    # Scrape the source data for FeedEntryDict instances
    entries = self.produce_entries()

    # Make a polishing-up run through the extracted entries.
    for e in entries:

        # Make sure the entry link is absolute
        e['link'] = link = urljoin(self.BASE_HREF, e['link'])
```

The `scrape()` method is the core of the `Scraper` class. It accepts an entry and feed string template, as well as a date format, and parameters. It first saves the date format in an object attribute, for convenient use throughout processing. Next, it opens up the scraper's state database.

Then, the method gathers a list of `FeedEntryDict` objects by calling the `produce_entries()` method—this does the real work of scraping in subclasses. The rest of this method does some "polishing up" for the list of entries that's applicable for just about any scraper.

The first thing that's done to every entry is that `link` values are made into absolute URLs by using `urljoin()` with the current `BASE_HREF` value. Next, in Listing 9-11, is where the scraper state database comes in.

Listing 9-11: scraperlib.py (Part 11 of 13)

```
        # Try to get state for this URL, creating a new record
        # if needed.
        if not self.state_db.has_key(link):
            self.state_db[link] = {}
        entry_state = self.state_db[link]
```

Continued

Listing 9-11 *(continued)*

```
# Manage remembered values for datestamps when entry data
# first found, unless dates were extracted.
for n in ('issued', 'modified'):
    if e.data.get(n, '') != '':
        continue
    if not entry_state.has_key(n):
        entry_state[n] = time.time()
    e[n] = entry_state[n]
```

First, an attempt is made to find a scraper state record for this entry, using its `link` as the key. If none is found, a blank dictionary is created and stored in the database as a new record. If there's anything you'd like to recall between scraper runs for entries, you can stash these bits of data away in this record in your own code.

In the base class, the state database is mainly used for maintaining datestamps when the scraper subclass doesn't provide them. When data for a particular entry identified by `link` is first found, a current datestamp is generated and stashed away in the state record. The next time this entry's `link` value is encountered, the previously generated datestamps are used. This should ensure that, as long as the entries have consistent values for `link`, the datestamps will be preserved between scraper runs.

The next thing provided by the base class is GUID generation, in Listing 9-12.

Listing 9-12: scraperlib.py (Part 12 of 13)

```
# Construct a canonical tag URI for the entry if none set
if not len(e.data.get('id', '')) > 0:
    (scheme, addr, path, params, query, frag) = \
        urlparse(link)
    ymd = time.strftime("%Y-%m-%d",
            time.gmtime(e.data['modified']))
    e['id'] = "tag:%s,%s:%s" % (addr, ymd, quote(path,''))

# Update the state database record
self.state_db[link] = entry_state
```

If the scraper subclass doesn't provide GUID values for entries, the base class attempts to generate one in Listing 9-12. This is built as a tag: URI with the link domain, modified date, and link path, using the same approach as in Listing 7-13 from Chapter 7. And, finishing up this iteration through the loop, the entry's state record is saved back to the database.

After the end of the entry finalizing loop, Listing 9-13 finishes up the `scrape()` method, as well as the class.

Listing 9-13: scraperlib.py (Part 13 of 13)

```
# Close the state database
self.state_db.close()

# Sort the entries, now that they all should have dates.
entries.sort()

# Build the entries from template, and populate the feed data
entries_out = [entry_tmpl % e for e in
                    entries[:self.MAX_ENTRIES]]
feed = { 'feed.entries' : "\n".join(entries_out) }

# Add all the feed metadata into the feed, ensuring
# Unicode encoding happens.
for k, v in self.FEED_META.items():
    if type(v) is unicode:
        v = v.encode(self.UNICODE_ENC)
    feed[k] = v

# Return the built feed
return feed_tmpl % feed
```

In Listing 9-13, the scraper state database is closed, and then the list of entries extracted is sorted.

Then, the feed production begins. A number of entries up to the MAX_ENTRIES limit are processed through the entry template for the feed format. These are then joined together into a single string and stashed into the feed data structure. This data structure is then updated from the values set in the FEED_META data structure constant for the class. And, at last, the feed data is used to populate the feed template, the results of which are returned as the final scraped feed.

Scraping with HTMLParser

Now that you have a foundation for feed scraping in place, it's time to build your first `Scraper` subclass. But first, you need to find a source for scraping and a plan for extracting the data.

Take a look at the Web site for the United States Library of Congress. In particular, check out the news archive page at http://www.loc.gov/today/pr/, shown in Figure 9-1. Here's a regularly updated, public, government-run page that doesn't have any syndication feeds to go along with it. Looking at the page, you can tell that it has repeating items that could make fine feed entry candidates. You might even find the information here worth watching, so maybe this will be worth a hack for you.

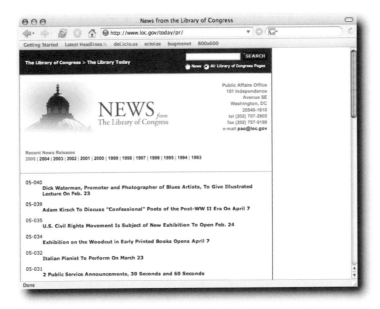

FIGURE 9-1: News from The Library of Congress in Mozilla Firefox

Planning a Scraper for the Library of Congress News Archive

Note   As with any page on the Web, the news archive for the Library of Congress may have changed by the time you read this. But, hopefully, the approach taken here will make enough sense that you can adapt to whatever changes you might find—or to building a scraper for any other page, which is the ultimate goal of this chapter.

Just looking at a page rendered in your browser won't get you very far, though. It's time to dig into the source code for the page. So, open up the View Source window in your browser. If you're using Firefox, you'll see something like Figure 9-2.

Your task from here is to map from the HTML source code to boundaries defining feed entries, and within each, map from HTML tags to individual feed entry attributes.

The first thing you want to find is some landmark indicating the start of interesting things to parse. In the case of this Web page, there's an HTML comment just before the markup for news items:

```
<!-- START PR LIST -->
```

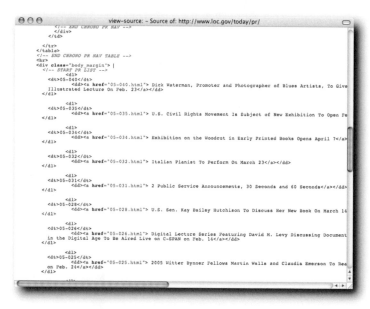

FIGURE 9-2: Start of HTML news items in Firefox's View Source window

Next, you'll want to skim through and try to make some sense of what makes up a repeating collection of markup that can be combed for feed entry data. In this page's source, a run of items looks like this:

```
<dl>
<dt>05-040</dt>
    <dd><a href="05-040.html"> Dick Waterman, Promoter and
Photographer of Blues Artists, To Give
    Illustrated Lecture On Feb. 23</a></dd>
</dl>

<dl>
<dt>05-035</dt>
    <dd><a href="05-035.html"> U.S. Civil Rights Movement
Is Subject of New Exhibition To Open Feb. 24</a></dd>
</dl>

<dl>
<dt>05-034</dt>
    <dd><a href="05-034.html"> Exhibition on the Woodcut
in Early Printed Books Opens April 7</a></dd>
</dl>
```

This HTML is pretty clean, so what should pop out at you is that each item is presented as a `<dl>` element. This, then, is how you'll determine the start and end of each feed entry.

Now, you can move on to working out the individual elements of a feed entry. Within each `<dl>` element is a `<dt>` element containing an identifier and a `<dd>` element containing the `<a>` hyperlink to the news item. You can harvest the title for a feed entry from the contents of `<a>`, extract the `href` attribute for the link, and then maybe use the text from the whole `<dl>` element for an entry summary. There are no dates here, so those will need to be generated in some other way.

Now, scroll down a bit through the source code and find a landmark at which you can stop parsing. Take a look at Figure 9-3 to see what you should be looking for.

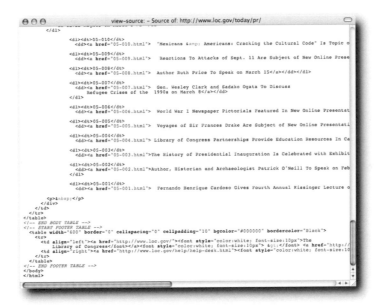

FIGURE 9-3: End of HTML news items in Firefox's View Source window

The final landmark can be anything, really, but one thing that sticks out is this HTML comment:

```
<!-- END BODY TABLE -->
```

And with this, you should have a good idea of the structure of this news archive page, as well as some thoughts on how to lift these details out of the page. To review, these are the steps taken to dissect the Library of Congress news archive source code:

1. Find a landmark in the source to identify the beginning of interesting data for scraping.

2. Find the repeating pattern or tags making up individual news items on the page.

3. Within each repeating block, map from HTML markup to feed entry attributes (such as title, link, and summary).

4. Find a landmark in the source where the news items end and parsing can stop.

Building the HTMLParser Scraper Base Class

Now you're a few steps closer to building your first working scraper, but the Scraper class won't do much on its own. It has most of the parts to generate a feed, but you have to supply the parsing logic in a subclass that implements the produce_entries() method.

To build a scraper for the Library of Congress news archive page, you can start with something based on HTMLParser. The HTML on this page is relatively clean and not all that difficult to process using parser event handlers.

However, using HTMLParser and its liberal HTML parsing engine to scrape pages seems like it'd be a pretty useful approach for quite a few scrapers you might write in the future, so before you get into writing the specific code to scrape the news archive, how about writing a more generally useful HTMLParser scraper class?

You can add this new code to your scraperlib module right where you left off in the previous part. Take a look at Listing 9-14 for the opening lines of the HTMLScraper class.

Listing 9-14: scraperlib.py, HTMLScraper Additions (Part 1 of 3)

```
from HTMLParser import HTMLParser, HTMLParseError

class HTMLScraper(HTMLParser, Scraper):
    """
    Base class for HTMLParser-based feed scrapers.
    """
    CHUNKSIZE   = 1024

    def produce_entries(self):
        fin = urlopen(self.SCRAPE_URL)
        return self.parse_file(fin)

    def reset(self):
        """Initialize the parser state."""
        HTMLParser.reset(self)
        self.feed_entries = []
        self.in_feed      = False
        self.in_entry     = False
        self.curr_data    = ''
```

First, the HTMLParser class is imported, along with HTMLParserError. Then begins the definition of the HTMLScraper class, which inherits from both the HTMLParser and Scraper classes. The first method defined is produce_entries(), which opens up a file-like object to retrieve data from the URL to be scraped. This is then fed to the parse_file() method, which fires off the HTMLParser and returns the results, which will be a list of FeedEntryDict objects.

Next, define some basic feed production methods in Listing 9-15.

Listing 9-15: scraperlib.py, HTMLScraper Additions (Part 2 of 3)

```
def start_feed(self):
    """Handle start of feed scraping"""
    self.in_feed = True

def end_feed(self):
    """Handle end of all useful feed scraping."""
    raise _ScraperFinishedException()

def start_feed_entry(self):
    """Handle start of feed entry scraping"""
    self.curr_entry = FeedEntryDict({}, self.date_fmt)
    self.in_entry   = True

def end_feed_entry(self):
    """Handle the detected end of a feed entry scraped"""
    self.feed_entries.append(self.curr_entry)
    self.in_entry = False
```

Four methods are defined in Listing 9-15: start_feed(), end_feed(), start_feed_entry(), and end_feed_entry(). These aren't a part of HTMLParser, but they will be called during the course of parsing when, as their names suggest, the start and end of the feed and individual entries are encountered.

When start_feed() is called, a flag is set to indicate that parsing has entered the range of elements subject to extraction. When end_feed() is called, _ScraperFinishedException is raised to halt parsing, because there's nothing of interest left to parse.

Upon a call to start_feed_entry(), a new instance of FeedEntryDict is created as the current entry under construction and a flag indicating that an entry is under construction is set. And, finally, when end_feed_entry() is called, the current running feed entry is appended to the list collected so far and the flag indicating an entry is under construction is set to False.

The gist of all of this is that HTMLScraper is an event-driven state machine, both in the process of parsing and in the process of building feed entries. At any particular point, the scraper will be maintaining the state of a particular feed entry under construction, as well as the list of entries completed so far.

The HTMLScraper class is wrapped up in Listing 9-16.

Listing 9-16: scraperlib.py, HTMLScraper Additions (Part 3 of 3)

```
def handle_data(self, data):
    self.curr_data += data
def handle_entityref(self, data):
    self.curr_data += '&' + data + ';'
handle_charref = handle_entityref
```

```
    def decode_entities(self, data):
        data = data.replace('&lt;', '<')
        data = data.replace('&gt;', '>')
        data = data.replace('&quot;', '"')
        data = data.replace('&apos;', "'")
        data = data.replace('&amp;', '&')
        return data

    def parse_file(self, fin):
        """Parse through the contents of a given file-like object."""
        self.reset()
        while True:
            try:
                data = fin.read(self.CHUNKSIZE)
                if len(data) == 0: break
                self.feed(data)
            except _ScraperFinishedException:
                break
        return self.feed_entries
```

Most of Listing 9-16 should be familiar, because it's pretty much been boilerplate functionality for `HTMLParser` use so far. Character data is accumulated, and select entities are
decoded. The `parse_file()` method parses through all the data in chunks, watching for
`_ScraperFinishedException` to be thrown to end parsing early, finally returning the
accumulated list of `FeedEntryDict` objects when everything's done.

Building a Scraper for the Library of Congress News Archive

Now that you have something to scrape, a plan on how to do it, and an `HTMLParser`-based
scraper class, it's time to get started. You can build this scraper as a separate program that uses
`scraperlib`. Start a new program file and name it `ch09_loc_scraper.py`. Listing 9-17
shows the start of this program.

Listing 9-17: ch09_loc_scraper.py (Part 1 of 5)

```
#!/usr/bin/env python
"""

ch09_loc_scraper.py

Use HTMLScraper to produce a feed from loc.gov news
"""
import sys, time, shelve
from urlparse import urljoin
from scraperlib import HTMLScraper
```

Continued

Listing 9-17 *(continued)*

```
def main():
    """
    Given an argument of 'atom' or 'rss' on the command line,
    produce an Atom or RSS feed from the loc.gov news page.
    """
    scraper = LOCScraper()
    if len(sys.argv) > 1 and sys.argv[1] == 'rss':
        print scraper.scrape_rss()
    else:
        print scraper.scrape_atom()
```

In Listing 9-17, you can see some initial imports, as well as the program's `main()` function definition. The `main()` function creates an instance of the `LOCScraper` class, then looks for a command-line argument to decide whether to produce an RSS or an Atom feed. This lets you choose at run-time which format you want to use in building the feed.

Move on to Listing 9-18, where you'll find the beginning of the `LOCScraper` class definition.

Listing 9-18: ch09_loc_scraper.py (Part 2 of 5)

```
class LOCScraper(HTMLScraper):
    """
    Parses HTML to extract the page title and description.
    """
    # Filename of state database
    STATE_FN   = "loc_scraper_state"

    # URL to the Library of Congress news page.
    SCRAPE_URL = "http://www.loc.gov/today/pr/"

    # Base HREF for all links on the page
    BASE_HREF  = SCRAPE_URL

    # Metadata for scraped feed
    FEED_META = {
        'feed.title'        : 'News from The Library of Congress',
        'feed.link'         : SCRAPE_URL,
        'feed.tagline'      : 'Press releases scraped from loc.gov',
        'feed.author.name'  : 'Library of Congress',
        'feed.author.email' : 'pao@loc.gov',
        'feed.author.url'   : SCRAPE_URL,
    }
```

There's no parsing happening yet. Listing 9-18 establishes the initial class constants setting up the scraper:

- STATE_FN—Sets a new filename for the state database.
- SCRAPE_URL—Establishes the URL to the Library of Congress news archive.
- BASE_HREF—Reuses the SCRAPE_URL as the base for all links.
- FEED_META—Lays out the top-level properties for the feed.

Next, in Listing 9-19, parsing starts by watching for the start and end of the area of interest for scraping.

Listing 9-19: ch09_loc_scraper.py (Part 3 of 5)

```
def handle_comment(self, data):
    """
    Look for HTML comments that mark start &
    end of extraction.
    """
    if 'START PR LIST' in data: self.start_feed()
    if 'END BODY TABLE' in data: self.end_feed()
```

The handle_comment() parsing event handler is defined in Listing 9-19. Here, the implementation is watching for the two HTML comments you saw in the source code for the Web page. When a comment containing START PR LIST is seen, this indicates the start of interesting data—so, call the Scraper start_feed() method. Then, when END BODY TABLE is seen in a comment, call the Scraper end_feed() method.

Now, define the handle_starttag() parsing event handler, as shown in Listing 9-20.

Listing 9-20: ch09_loc_scraper.py (Part 4 of 5)

```
def handle_starttag(self, tag, attrs_tup):
    """Handle start tags."""
    attrs = dict(attrs_tup)

    # Use <base> to get the correct base HREF
    if tag == 'base':
        self.BASE_HREF = attrs['href']

    # Use <dl> as signal of entry start.
    if self.in_feed:
```

Continued

Listing 9-20 *(continued)*

```
        if tag == 'dl':
            self.start_feed_entry()

    # Harvest links from <a href="">
    if self.in_entry:
        if tag == "a":
            self.curr_entry['link'] = attrs.get("href", "")
```

The `handle_starttag()` method first watches for the `<base>` tag and if found, uses its `href` attribute to set the current `BASE_HREF` value.

Note

This didn't come up during the first pass through the source code detailed earlier, but you might want to look through it again. Personally, I didn't catch the fact that this page had a `<base>` tag establishing a new base URL for links, and had to figure this out after a few trial runs of this scraper came up with incorrect links. This is a good thing to check for in any `HTMLScraper` subclass, but I though it was worth mentioning as part of the scraper hacking process. Remember that a scraper may take a few tries to get right.

Then, the beginning of a `<dl>` tag is handled, which will signal the start of a new feed entry. After that, `<a>` tags are watched to extract the entry link. Continuing on to Listing 9-21, you'll find the definition of the `handle_endtag()` parsing event handler.

Listing 9-21: ch09_loc_scraper.py (Part 5 of 5)

```
def handle_endtag(self, tag):
    """Handle end tags."""

    # If started scraping a feed...
    if self.in_feed:
        # ...</dl> ends it.
        if tag == 'dl':
            self.end_feed_entry()

    # If in an entry...
    if self.in_entry:
        # ...the end of </a> provides title string.
        if tag == "a":
            self.curr_entry['title'] = self.curr_data.strip()

        # ...accumulate plain text data for the summary.
        self.curr_entry['summary'] += self.curr_data
```

```
        # Clear the tag character data accumulation.
        self.curr_data  = ''

if __name__=="__main__": main()
```

In the definition of `handle_endtag()`, `</dl>` tags are handled to indicate the end of a feed entry and the end of an `<a>` tag is used to extract the entry title. Also, all along the way through extracting a feed entry, text data is accumulated for the entry summary. Wrapping up this handler, character data accumulated for this tag is cleared. And, after the end of the method, the standard trick to call the `main()` function appears, wrapping up the program.

Trying out the Library of Congress News Archive Scraper

You have a fully functioning feed scraper for the Library of Congress news archive at this point. As mentioned earlier, you can supply an option on the command line to choose a feed format when you run it. When you try it out, your output should look something like Figure 9-4 or Figure 9-5, depending on whether you ask it to produce Atom or RSS.

FIGURE 9-4: Running the Library of Congress scraper with Atom feed output

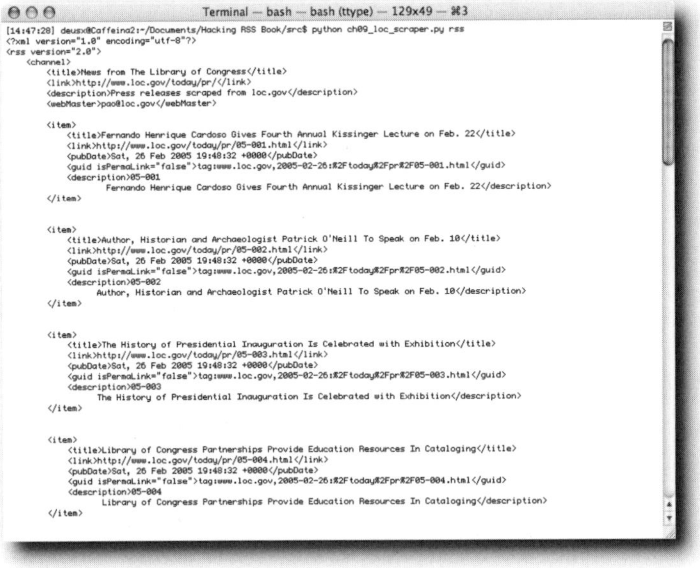

FIGURE 9-5: Running the Library of Congress scraper with RSS feed output

Scraping with Regular Expressions

Working with `HTMLParser` on the Library of Congress news archive page was good for a first stab at building a scraper. The source code for that page was fairly clean and well-structured, and so building a parsing machine wasn't all that involved or difficult. However, very few pages you find will offer such niceties, and the `HTMLParser` approach to scraping will rapidly become cumbersome and require increasingly verbose piles of code as you find yourself adding and tracking state variables with lots of strange and special-case parsing.

Take a look at another public government site, this time for the Federal Communications Commission news headlines at `http://www.fcc.gov/headlines.html`, shown in Figure 9-6.

Again, you should be able to see that this page presents a series of news items that could make good feed entries. Although there don't seem to be any clear candidates for single links per entry from what you see here, there are date headings you can use for the feed entry issued dates. Now, open up the View Source window and take a peek at the guts of this page. Figure 9-7 shows you what things look like after you've scrolled down a bit and found the start of the news headlines.

Figure 9-6: Looking at news headlines from the Federal Communications Commission

Figure 9-7: Finding the start of news headlines in the FCC page source code

The HTML you'll see for this page isn't actually that bad, although it is somewhat more complex than what you saw at the Library of Congress page. You could try building an HTMLParser-based scraper for this one, but now would be a good time to introduce a new tool for scraping.

Introducing Regular Expressions

Consider the worst-case scenario, that a particular Web resource from which you want to build a feed is the nastiest, most unparseable stream of characters pretending to be an HTML document. They probably have tags no one's ever heard of sprinkled around in there, along with a few holdovers from browsers long gone extinct. So, if you want to make sense of this data, you have your work cut out for you. On the other hand, you might want to build a feed based on some data format that's not HTML at all—such as a server log file or some custom format.

In either case, HTMLParser isn't quite the sort of tool you need. The sort of tool you'll need should combine the versatility of a pocket multitool with the leverage of a crowbar. And, there just happens to be such a tool for dealing with streams of text: *regular expressions*.

You might already know all about regular expressions. They're a family of little languages used in expressing recipes for pattern matching and data extraction in text data. They've received a mixed reputation throughout the years, in part because they tend to be write-only because of their hard-to-understand punctuation-character-based syntax. If you walk away from some intricate regular expression and come back to it weeks or years later, sometimes it's easier to just write a new one from scratch, versus comprehending what you were thinking at the time. There are also a slew of variations on regular expression syntax, as well as varying implementations and feature sets.

But, sometimes a regular expression is the most convenient, quick-and-dirty thing to liberate some useful data from an obtuse stream of data. Given that, it would make a lot of sense to add them to your feed scraping repertoire.

 On the Web A complete tutorial on regular expressions is beyond the scope of this book and, indeed, such tutorials have filled volumes all on their own. This chapter spends time showing you how to build a scraper that uses regular expressions, but not how to build regular expressions. For that information, check out one of the many books on the subject, and this Python Regular Expression HOWTO:

```
http://www.amk.ca/python/howto/regex/
```

Planning a Regex-based Scraper for the FCC Headlines Page

Take a look at the HTML source code for this page again, as shown in Figure 9-7. The strategy for building the previous scraper using HTMLParser involved planning how various tags would be handled and how the implementation of parsing event-handlers would work.

However, in using regular expressions, the approach changes quite a bit. Here you should be thinking more along the lines of reverse-engineering a string template, instead of paying attention to the structure of the markup. For example, a news item from this page appears like so:

```
<p><span class="headlinedate">2/3/05</span><br>
FCC To Hold Open Commission Meeting Thursday, February 10,
2005.<br>
Public Notice: <a
HREF="http://hraunfoss.fcc.gov/edocs_public/attachmatch/
DOC-256544A1.doc" title="News Release on FCC To Hold Open
Commission Meeting Thursday, February 10, 2005, Word
Format">Word</a> | <a
HREF="http://hraunfoss.fcc.gov/edocs_public/attachmatch/
DOC-256544A1.pdf">Acrobat</a></p>
```

Forget about seeing this data in terms of tags and parsing. Instead, try reframing this bit of data as a template, with blanks for the data you want to extract:

```
<p><span class="headlinedate">[ENTRY.DATE]</span><br>
[ENTRY.TITLE]<br>
[ENTRY.SUMMARY]</p>
```

Now, this is just sort of a pseudo code-ish way to look at the patterns here. Expressing the reverse-engineered template as a real regular expression looks like this:

```
<p><span class="headlinedate">(?P<date>.*?)</span><br>
(?P<title>.*?)<br>
(?P<summary>.*?)</p>
```

Again, because this HTML source isn't really all that messy, the regular expression can be fairly simple. You have some HTML in the pattern, establishing context for the matches. Then, there are the three named groups expressed as non-greedy wildcard matches in the spaces where the data you want to extract will appear.

Although a proper introduction to regular expressions will tell you more about *greedy* versus *non-greedy*, in a nutshell this means that the wildcard matching will be limited to the smallest run before the next bit of context provided in the pattern. For example, the (?P<date>.*?) pattern will end when the next </span> string is encountered, the (?P<title>.*?) will end at the next <br> tag.

If you want to read up on the Python's named groups feature for regular expressions (which can be a little confusing, because they look like HTML tags themselves), check out this section of the Regular Expression HOWTO:

```
http://www.amk.ca/python/howto/regex/regex.html#
SECTION000530000000000000000
```

Building the RegexScraper Base Class

One benefit using regular expressions has over the previous HTMLParser method is that your code will be more succinct and to the point. The tradeoff is that your code may end up less readable, but that's not necessarily the most important thing when you're pulling off a hack like a feed scraper. So, this new RegexScraper class will end up being much simpler than HTMLScraper.

To start adding this new scraper class to your `scraperlib` module, check out Listing 9-22.

Listing 9-22: scraperlib.py, RegexScraper Additions (Part 1 of 2)

```
class RegexScraper(Scraper):
    """
    Base class for regex-based feed scrapers.
    """
    # Default regex extracts all hyperlinks.
    ENTRY_RE = """(?P<summary>""" + \
        """<a href="(?P<link>.*?)">(?P<title>.*?)</a>)"""

    def __init__(self):
        """Initialize the scraper, compile the regex"""
        self.entry_re = re.compile(self.ENTRY_RE,
            re.DOTALL | re.MULTILINE | re.IGNORECASE)
```

The first constant introduced in the definition of the `RegexScraper` class is `ENTRY_RE`, which is a regular expression that looks for hyperlinks in an HTML page. One thing that might be a bit confusing (even if you *do* understand regular expressions) is the Python-specific construction of *named groups*. Unfortunately, these look a lot like HTML tags themselves, so it's easy to get mixed up. This particular expression uses three of them:

- `(?P<summary>)`
- `(?P<link>)`
- `(?P<title>)`

These named groups in regular expressions make it easy to pull out and tag extracted data by key names, which dovetails in nicely with the main occupation of this scraper—namely, building dictionaries and initializing `FeedEntryDict` objects.

If you were to build a scraper inheriting from this class, without composing your own regular expression, this default value for `ENTRY_RE` would at least harvest all the hyperlinks and link titles from an HTML page for you, so it could be a good place to start.

The last bit of Listing 9-22 is the definition of the object initializer, which compiles the scraper's regular expression for more efficient use later. Note that three flags are used here to simplify things a bit:

- `re.DOTALL`—Wildcard matches in regular expressions include newlines.
- `re.MULTILINE`—Matching is not limited to a single line of text.
- `re.IGNORECASE`—Matching is made case-insensitive, so things like <br> and <BR> are equivalent.

On the Web Check out this section of the Regular Expression HOWTO for information on these compilation flags:

> http://www.amk.ca/python/howto/regex/regex.html# SECTION000450000000000000000000

Move on to Listing 9-23 to see the definition of produce_entries(), where the regular expression is used to extract data and build FeedEntryDict objects.

Listing 9-23: scraperlib.py, RegexScraper Additions (Part 2 of 2)

```
def produce_entries(self):
    """Use regex to extract entries from source"""
    # Fetch the source for scraping.
    src = urlopen(self.SCRAPE_URL).read()

    # Iterate through all the matches of the regex found.
    entries, pos = [], 0
    while True:

        # Find the latest match, stop if none found.
        m = self.entry_re.search(src, pos)
        if not m: break

        # Advance the search position to end of previous search.
        pos = m.end()

        # Create and append the FeedEntryDict for this extraction.
        entries.append(FeedEntryDict(m.groupdict(), self.date_fmt))

    return entries
```

In the implementation of produce_entries(), data at the SCRAPE_URL is downloaded and repeated attempts to match the regular expression against this data are made. When there's no match, the loop ends. If there is a match, a character position pointer is set to the end of this new match, so that the next iteration will advance further through the string of data.

When matches are made, a new FeedEntryDict object is initialized via the match result's groupdict() method. This gathers the extracted data for all the named groups specified in the regular expression into a dictionary structure, which is where the feature becomes really convenient—despite the confusing syntax in the expression. This new FeedEntryDict is appended to the running list and, once the loop has finished, this list of objects is returned.

And that ends the definition of the RegexScraper class. Now, it's time to apply it to the FCC headlines page.

Building a Regex-based Scraper for the FCC Headlines Page

Start a new program file, named `ch09_fcc_scraper.py`. Use the code presented in Listing 9-24, which is almost identical to the beginning of the previous program with an implementation of `main()` that selects between feed formats.

Listing 9-24: ch09_fcc_scraper.py (Part 1 of 4)

```python
#!/usr/bin/env python
"""
ch09_fcc_scraper.py

Use RegexScraper to produce a feed from fcc.gov news
"""
import sys, time, shelve, md5, re
from urlparse import urljoin
from scraperlib import RegexScraper

def main():
    """
    Given an argument of 'atom' or 'rss' on the command line,
    produce an Atom or RSS feed.
    """
    scraper = FCCScraper()
    if len(sys.argv) > 1 and sys.argv[1] == 'rss':
        print scraper.scrape_rss()
    else:
        print scraper.scrape_atom()
```

With the familiar `main()` driver function in place, you can move onto defining the scraper class for the FCC news headlines page. Take a look at Listing 9-25 for the beginning of the FCCScraper class.

Listing 9-25: ch09_fcc_scraper.py (Part 2 of 4)

```python
class FCCScraper(RegexScraper):
    """Use regexes to scrape FCC news headlines"""

    # Filename of state database
    STATE_FN  = "fcc_scraper_state"

    # URL to the Library of Congress news page.
    SCRAPE_URL = "http://www.fcc.gov/headlines.html"
```

```
# Base HREF for all links on the page
BASE_HREF  = SCRAPE_URL

# Metadata for scraped feed
FEED_META = {
    'feed.title'         : 'FCC News',
    'feed.link'          : SCRAPE_URL,
    'feed.tagline'       : 'News from the FCC',
    'feed.author.name'   : 'Federal Communications Commission',
    'feed.author.email'  : 'fccinfo@fcc.gov',
    'feed.author.url'    : 'http://www.fcc.gov/aboutus.html'
}
```

Again, things look very similar to the LOCScraper class, because these are all class constants established by the underlying Scraper class. The STATE_FN provides the filename for the state database to be used by this scraper, and the SCRAPE_URL and BASE_HREF are set to the URL of the FCC news headlines page. Then, the top-level feed metadata is built in the FEED_META constant.

The first parts that are new to the RegexScraper subclass show up in Listing 9-26.

Listing 9-26: ch09_fcc_scraper.py (Part 3 of 4)

```
# Regex to extract news headline paragraphs
ENTRY_RE = '<p>' + \
    '<span class="headlinedate">(?P<date>.*?)</span><br>' + \
    '(?P<title>.*?)<br>' + \
    '(?P<summary>.*?)</p>'

# Regex used in cleaning up HTML tags
HTML_RE = re.compile('<(.*?)>')
```

In Listing 9-26, the first thing is the ENTRY_RE constant, which has been given the regular expression composed during the planning stage of this scraper. The way this string is put together in the Python source code is a little strange. Rather than using a multi-line string, this one is built from a series of concatenated strings.

This is a tradeoff to retain some clarity in the Python source code, yet to keep errant whitespace and carriage returns out of the regular expression. Although there is a re.VERBOSE compilation flag that's supposed to help out with this, it didn't seem to work very well when used here. You may want to tinker with this in your own code.

Things get a little interesting in Listing 9-27, where this class gets wrapped up.

Listing 9-27: ch09_fcc_scraper.py (Part 4 of 4)

```
def produce_entries(self):
    """Parse and generate dates extracted from HTML content"""
    # Extract entries using superclass method
    entries = RegexScraper.produce_entries(self)

    # Finish up entries extracted
    for e in entries:

        # Delete all HTML tags from the title attribute
        e.data['title'] = self.HTML_RE.sub('', e.data['title'])

        # Turn the extracted date into proper issued /
        # modified dates
        dp   = [int(x) for x in e['date'].split('/')]
        dtup = (2000+dp[2], dp[0], dp[1], 0, 0, 0, 0, 0, 0)
        date = time.mktime(dtup)
        e['issued']   = date
        e['modified'] = date

        # Create an ID for the extracted entry
        m = md5.md5()
        m.update(e['title'])
        ymd = time.strftime("%Y-%m-%d", time.gmtime(date))
        e['id'] = "tag:www.fcc.gov,%s:%s" % (ymd, m.hexdigest())

    # Return the list of entries.
    return entries

if __name__=="__main__": main()
```

In Listing 9-27, there's a definition for the produce_entries() method, which overrides the one implemented in the RegexScraper superclass. The reason for this method is, simply, because regular expressions can mostly only extract data. They can't do much to further process or translate what they extract. So, this produce_entries() method fires off the regular expression scraping, then takes a pass through the FeedEntryDict objects produced for a round of polishing up.

The first tweak made is to entry titles. The feed formats do not allow HTML in an entry title, but some of the chunks harvested by regular expression for titles may end up with HTML in them. So, this part uses a regular expression to strip out anything that looks like an HTML tag in entry titles.

The next tweak handles turning the text dates extracted into seconds-based datestamps used by the date formatting code employed when the feed string templates are populated.

And the final tweak produces a GUID for each item. Remember that there weren't any easy candidates for entry links in this page, so the regular expression didn't extract any. Now, this is still valid for the feed—not all entries need to have unique URLs and, in the case of this scraper, the link provided just points back to the FCC news headlines page.

However, GUIDs *do* need unique values and are based, by default in the `Scraper` class, on the entry URL. So, to make up for the lack of unique URLs, this final tweak runs the title of each entry through an MD5 hash and builds a GUID based on that. Although it seems like titles are unique enough for this scraper, you could add some more information from the entry to build a more reliably unique MD5 hash.

Trying out the FCC News Headlines Scraper

This scraper program works just like the last one, so you can try running it with a command-line argument of either "atom" or "rss" to see the results in Figure 9-8 and Figure 9-9.

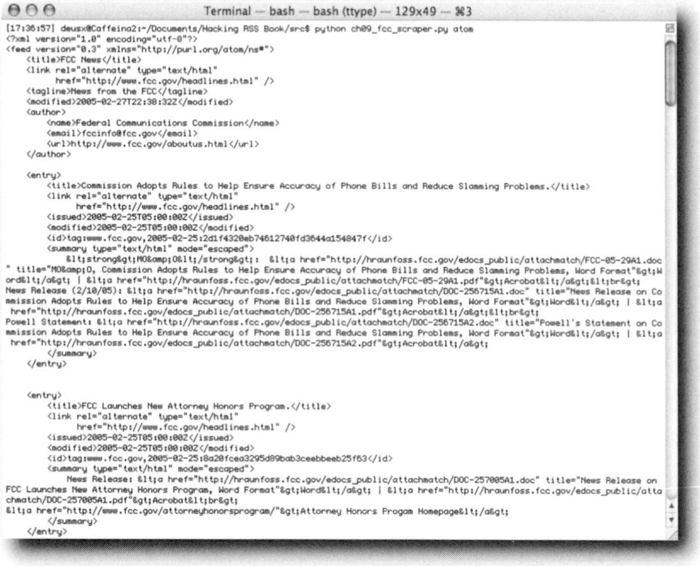

FIGURE 9-8: Running the FCC headline scraper with Atom feed output

FIGURE **9-9: Running the FCC headline scraper with RSS feed output**

Scraping with HTML Tidy and XPath

Working with `HTMLParser` and regular expressions, you have just about everything you need to slice and dice most Web pages and data sources into syndication feeds. But, I'll show you one more technique that, when you know you're working something at least close to HTML or XML, can be more concise than regular expressions, but even easier to understand. The only catch is that this trick requires the installation of a few pieces that Python doesn't offer out of the box, and you may have mixed results getting these parts working.

For this final scraper, take a look at the home page for The White House at `http://www. whitehouse.gov`, shown in Figure 9-10.

Caution Oh yeah, and mind your `.gov` in that URL—accidentally swapping it for `.com` might give you a nasty surprise that's not safe for work or mixed company.

Glancing at The White House home page in your browser, you can see that there's a column of news items available. If you want to keep up with these headlines, scraping them for a feed would be a fine project. So, open up the View Source window and dig beneath the surface. The HTML you'll find here is significantly more complex than what you saw on either the Library of Congress or Federal Communications Commission pages. In fact, you'll need to scroll about halfway down through the source code to get a look at the news items shown in Figure 9-11.

FIGURE 9-10: The White House home page as shown in Firefox

FIGURE 9-11: HTML source code for White House news items

Introducing HTML Tidy

One of the motivations for using something like regular expressions to hack and slash away at an HTML page is that the adherence to standards and the validity of the page source may be questionable at best. Well, rather than surrendering to it and bringing out a hacksaw, another way to approach this mess is to clean it up.

The HTML Tidy Library Project (http://tidy.sourceforge.net) just happens to be an attempt at providing tools to clean up errant HTML pages. And, one of the nice things about HTML Tidy is that it takes the form of a reusable library that you can pull into your own code. To accomplish just that, a Python wrapper for HTML Tidy, called >Tidylib, is available at http://utidylib.berlios.de/.

You'll want to try installing >Tidylib for best results. If you're using Windows, the >Tidylib download page offers an easy-to-use installer that contains everything you need. As of this writing, the latest version of the installer was available at this URL:

http://download.berlios.de/utidylib/uTidylib-0.2.1.win32.exe

On Linux, you should be able to install HTML Tidy using your package manager or the directions on the project page. And, >Tidylib can be installed like other Python modules by running the setup.py script that comes along with it. Be sure to read the INSTALL.txt file that comes with the >Tidylib archive for instructions. As of this writing, the latest version of the archive was available here:

http://download.berlios.de/utidylib/uTidylib-0.2.zip

On Mac OS X, however, installation of HTML Tidy and >Tidylib is a little tricky. As of this writing, it can be done, but only after a little bit of hackery with >Tidylib itself. So, to skip getting bogged down in that, I'll show you how to work around not having >Tidylib installed.

You can use the HTML Tidy command-line executable directly, for which there is a Mac OS X binary available. The only real tradeoff is that your scraper might be a little bit slower, because it's calling on Tidy as an external program, rather than an imported module. As of this writing, the latest Mac OS X binary was available here:

http://tidy.sourceforge.net/cf/tidy_mosx.tgz

Download that, unpack the archive, and copy the tidy program somewhere convenient (such as your project directory).

Now, to make using HTML Tidy easier, you can wrap up usage of both >Tidylib and the command-line executable in a single reusable module. If >Tidylib is available, it will be used; otherwise, this wrapper will fall back to running HTML Tidy in an external process.

So, start a new file in your editor and call it tidylib.py. Take a look Listing 9-28 for the first half of this module.

Listing 9-28: tidylib.py (Part 1 of 2)

```python
#!/usr/bin/env python
"""
tidylib.py

Utility module/program for running web pages through HTML Tidy.
"""
import sys, popen2
from urllib2 import urlopen

TIDY_CMD  = "/Users/deusx/local/bin/tidy"

TIDY_OPTS = dict(
    output_xhtml=1, force_output=1, numeric_entities=1,
    char_encoding='utf8', indent=1, wrap=0, show_errors=0,
    show_warnings=0
)

def main():
    """Try to tidy up the source of a URL."""
    print tidy_url(sys.argv[1])
```

One of the configuration constants set in Listing 9-28 is TIDY_CMD. You should change this value to point at the location of your tidy executable, which is wherever you copied it after downloading it. Again, this is optional, because if you've successfully installed >Tidylib it will be used instead of the executable.

The TIDY_OPTS constant is a series of options that will be fed to HTML Tidy. You shouldn't need to do much tweaking with it, but it's there in case you would like to. This module is concluded in Listing 9-29, where the choice is made whether to use >Tidylib or the HTML Tidy executable in a separate process.

Listing 9-29: tidylib.py (Part 2 of 2)

```python
try:
    # Attempt to import utidylib.  If present, use it for
    # HTML Tidy access.
    from tidy import parseString
    def tidy_string(src):
        return str( tidy.parseString(src, **TIDY_OPTS) )
except:
    # If there was a problem importing utidylib, try using an
    # external process calling on the command line version.
    def tidy_string(src):
```

Continued

Listing 9-29 *(continued)*

```
        opts = " ".join([ "--%s %s" %
                          (k.replace('_','-'), v)
                          for k,v in TIDY_OPTS.items() ])
        cmd = "%s %s" % (TIDY_CMD, opts)
        (o, i, e) = popen2.popen3(cmd)
        i.write(src)
        i.flush()
        i.close()
        return o.read()

def tidy_url(url):
    """Given a URL, return a tidied version of its source."""
    src = urlopen(url).read()
    return tidy_string(src)

if __name__=="__main__": main()
```

There's a little trick used in Listing 9-29. An attempt is made to import the >Tidylib module, and if it succeeds, the `tidy_string()` function is defined to use it. However, if >Tidylib is not installed, trying to import it will cause an exception to be thrown. In this case, this is caught and the `tidy_string()` function is defined to use the `popen2.popen3()` function to launch the `tidy` executable in an external process.

If you'd like to try out this module now, it's set up to be used as a program, as well as a reusable module. Take a look at Figure 9-12 to see what this will look like when applied to The White House home page.

Introducing XPath

Once you have some properly constructed XHTML (as provided by running a source of dubious quality through HTML Tidy), you can apply some of the tools available from the XML family of technologies. For the purposes of this scraper, the most interesting technology is XPath.

XPath started out as a URL and filesystem-inspired path notation for identifying nodes and data within XML documents, originally for use in the XSL and XPointer technologies. However, XPath has proven useful as a technology for dealing with XML in general, so you can find a few implementations of it for Python available for use separately from XSL.

 On the Web You can find the W3C Specification for XPath here, if you'd like a deeply detailed description of this technology:

    http://www.w3.org/TR/xpath

Figure 9-12: Tidied HTML source code for White House home page

Unfortunately, XPath isn't one of the tools included with Python out of the box, so you'll need to install it. One of the most easily installed packages for Python that provides XPath is called 4Suite, available at `http://4suite.org/`. At that URL, you'll be able to find downloads that include a Windows installer and an archive for installation on Linux and Mac OS X.

As of this writing, this is a URL to the latest version of the Windows installer:

`ftp://ftp.4suite.org/pub/4Suite/4Suite-1.0b1.win32-py2.3.exe`

Once downloaded, simply double-clicking on the installer will get you set up. However, if you want to be guided through the process, check out this Windows installation HOWTO:

`http://4suite.org/docs/howto/Windows.xml`

And, for Linux and Mac OS X, you'll want this archive:

`ftp://ftp.4suite.org/pub/4Suite/4Suite-1.0b1.tar.gz`

Once downloaded, check out this UNIX installation HOWTO:

`http://4suite.org/docs/howto/UNIX.xml`

Basically, you can install this package like most Python modules with a series of commands like the following:

```
$ tar xzvf 4Suite-1.0b1.tar.gz
$ cd 4Suite-1.0b1
$ python setup.py install
```

Planning an XPath-based Scraper for the White House Home Page

Now that you've gathered a few tools, it's back to work building a scraper. Take a look at the HTML source for The White House home page again, as shown in Figure 9-13. Actually, you should use your `tidylib.py` program to look at it, because things may be altered a bit with respect to how they appeared in your browser's View Source window. Figure 9-13 shows the output from `tidylib.py` reflecting this. (Comparing this to what you saw back in Figure 9-11 should show quite a difference.)

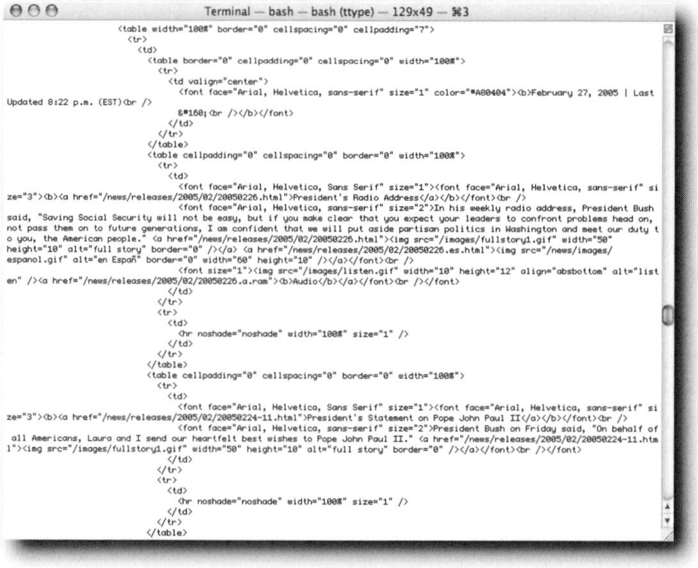

FIGURE 9-13: Tidied HTML source for news items on White House home page.

Even tidied up, though, this page still has a pretty convoluted and tangled run of HTML laying it out. It'd probably be a really bad idea to approach this with an `HTMLParser`-based scraper, and although a regular expression might do okay, using XPath can work out even more nicely.

With `HTMLParser`, you needed to consider the HTML source in terms of parsing events. And, with regular expressions, you needed to think of the page as a string template in need of reverse-engineering.

Well, with XPath, think of this HTML markup as sort of a cross between a database and a directory structure. You can walk through the parsed structure of an HTML document like you would files and directories on your hard drive. And, you can use some very powerful pattern matching and navigation axes to find your way. For example, to get to the data in all table cells in this page, you might write a path like the following:

```
//xhtml:table/xhtml:tr/xhtml:td/text()
```

The double-slash (//)at the beginning of the path signifies that this pattern of `table/tr/td` can be matched at any level of the document, even in the most deeply nested tables.

Because of this, you can think of scraping with XPath as navigating directories and using pattern matching to find document nodes. Take a look at this abridged source snippet for one of the news items lifted from the tidied source:

```
<table cellpadding="0" cellspacing="0" border="0" width="100%">
    <tr>
        <td>
            <font face="Arial, Helvetica, Sans Serif"
size="1"><font face="Arial, Helvetica, sans-serif" size="3"><b>
<a href="/news/releases/2005/02/20050226.html">President's Radio
Address</a></b></font><br />
            <font face="Arial, Helvetica, sans-serif" size="2">
In his weekly radio address, President Bush said...</font><br />
</font>
        </td>
    </tr>
    <tr>
        <td>
            <hr noshade="noshade" width="100%" size="1" />
        </td>
    </tr>
</table>
```

This HTML table is repeated over and over to lay out each news item, deeply nested within the complex markup that sets up the overall page design. However, the way to handle digging this out with XPath is to think in terms of queries, anchors, and navigation.

First, you need to think of a repeating node that, when found, you can treat as a kind of "current directory" from which you can branch out and collect the rest of the data you want to map into a feed entry. So, a good place to start in finding the repeating news items on the page is with an XPath like this:

```
//xhtml:b/xhtml:a[contains(@href,'/news/releases')]
```

This XPath tells the processor to find every <a> tag inside a <b> tag, whose `href` attribute contains the string `/news/releases`. Again, this is kind of like a structured database query as applied to the HTML document tree.

From here, you can loop through every <a> node that matches the previous XPath query. These will be deeply nested within the structure of the HTML page, but you can use each one of these nodes as an anchor, or current directory. Starting from each of these <a> nodes, you can find data to populate a feed entry with the XPaths described in Table 9-1.

Table 9-1   Entry Attributes Mapped to XPaths

Entry Attribute	XPath
Title	`./text()`
Link	`./@href`
Summary	`../../../xhtml:font[2]/text()`

Notice that the title and link XPaths are very simple. They're just using the text and href attributes contained in the <a> nodes used as anchors. However, finding the entry's summary is a little more complicated. It jumps up three parent nodes from the hyperlink, to the <td> node containing the news item. Then, it finds the second <font> node and extracts the text from there.

So, to sum up, this is the benefit of using XPath over HTMLParser and regular expressions. Instead of trying to handle parsing through some frustratingly complex HTML, or coming up with an obfuscated regular expression to reverse-engineer a template, you can just find one repeating aspect in the document structure and express it as an XPath that will drill down to it, and then you can branch out from there to find the values you need to construct a feed entry.

Building the XPathScraper Base Class

Now that you have a taste for scraping with XPath, you can build a `Scraper` subclass that will enable you to actually use XPath. Because most of the power for this scraper is already built into the 4Suite XPath processor, this scraper base class will be very short—which might seem a bit anticlimactic after all the lengthy preamble and explanation getting to this point.

Check out Listing 9-30 for the first of two parts you'll be adding to `scraperlib.py`.

Listing 9-30: scraperlib.py, XPathScraper Additions (Part 1 of 2)

```
from tidylib import tidy_string
from Ft.Xml.Domlette import NonvalidatingReader

class XPathScraper(Scraper):
    """
    Base class for XPath-based feed scrapers.
    """
    NSS = { 'xhtml':'http://www.w3.org/1999/xhtml' }

    # Default xpaths extract all hyperlinks.
    ENTRIES_XPATH = "//xhtml:a"
    ENTRY_XPATHS = {
        'title'   : './text()',
```

```
    'link'     : './@href',
    'summary'  : './text()'
}
```

Listing 9-30 starts off by importing the `tidy_string()` function you defined earlier in your `tidylib` module. After that, the `NonvalidatingReader` class is imported from `Ft.Xml.Domlette` provided by the 4Suite package.

After the imports, the `XPathScraper` class definition begins. A class constant defining the XHTML namespace is set up which will be later used by the XPath processor.

Next is a default set of scraping XPaths. The `ENTRIES_XPATH` value will be used to find the anchors from which the `ENTRY_XPATHS` values will be used to find attributes for feed entries. And, notice that the `ENTRY_XPATHS` constant is constructed as a dictionary map, from feed entry attribute name to XPath value. These defaults will (if left unmodified) extract all the hyperlinks from an HTML page. You can compare these with the regular expression in Listing 9-22, which does basically the same thing.

This class is concluded in Listing 9-31.

Listing 9-31: scraperlib.py, XPathScraper Additions (Part 2 of 2)

```python
def produce_entries(self):
    """
    Use XPaths to extract feed entries and entry attributes.
    """
    # Fetch the HTML source, tidy it up, parse it.
    src      = urlopen(self.SCRAPE_URL).read()
    tidy_src = tidy_string(src)
    doc      = NonvalidatingReader.parseString(tidy_src,
                 self.SCRAPE_URL)

    # Iterate through the parts identified as feed entry nodes.
    entries = []
    for entry_node in doc.xpath(self.ENTRIES_XPATH, self.NSS):

        # For each entry attribute path, attempt to
        # extract the value
        data = {}
        for k,v in self.ENTRY_XPATHS.items():
            nodes = entry_node.xpath(v, self.NSS)
            vals  = [x.nodeValue for x in nodes if x.nodeValue]
            data[k] = " ".join(vals)

        # Create and append the FeedEntryDict for this extraction
        entries.append(FeedEntryDict(data, self.date_fmt))

    return entries
```

The definition of the `produce_entries()` method appears in Listing 9-31. Here is where the XPaths are used to scrape entries out of the HTML document. First, the method downloads the data for the scraper's target URL, passes the data through HTML Tidy, then uses 4Suite's `NonvalidatingReader` to parse the tidied source.

Once a properly parsed document tree is obtained, the `ENTRIES_XPATH` value is used to search for nodes on which to anchor searches for feed entry data. For each of these nodes found, the XPaths defined in `ENTRY_XPATHS` are applied, building up values in a dictionary named `data`.

For the results found for each mapping in `ENTRY_XPATHS`, the `nodeValues` are concatenated into a single string. With this, you can be a little general in your XPaths, allowing for lists of nodes, rather than always nailing down to a single node. That may or may not make sense now, but it will come in handy as you tinker with XPaths.

After all of the XPaths for the entry have been searched, the accumulated values in `data` are used to construct a new `FeedEntryDict`, which is appended to the running list of feed entries. Finally, after all the nodes found by `ENTRIES_XPATH` have been processed, the method returns the list of `FeedEntryDict` objects accumulated.

That's it for XPathScraper—continue on to see how to apply it.

Building an XPath-based Scraper for the White House Home Page

This final scraper program starts off just like the other two in this chapter. Create a new program file named `ch09_whitehouse_scraper.py` and take a look at Listing 9-32 for the opening lines.

Listing 9-32: ch09_whitehouse_scraper.py (Part 1 of 3)

```python
#!/usr/bin/env python
"""
ch09_whitehouse_scraper.py

Use XPathScraper to produce a feed from White House news
"""
import sys
from scraperlib import XPathScraper

def main():
    """
    Given an argument of 'atom' or 'rss' on the command line,
    produce an Atom or RSS feed.
    """
    scraper = WhitehouseScraper()
    if len(sys.argv) > 1 and sys.argv[1] == 'rss':
        print scraper.scrape_rss()
    else:
        print scraper.scrape_atom()
```

After the module imports comes the `main()` function, which should be old hat by now. It accepts an argument from the command line to switch between RSS and Atom feed formats. Moving on, check out Listing 9-33 for the start of the `WhitehouseScraper` class.

Listing 9-33: ch09_whitehouse_scraper.py (Part 2 of 3)

```
class WhitehouseScraper(XPathScraper):
    """
    Parses HTML to extract the page title and description.
    """
    # Filename of state database
    STATE_FN = "whitehouse_scraper_state"

    # URL to the Library of Congress news page.
    SCRAPE_URL = "http://www.whitehouse.gov/"

    # Base HREF for all links on the page
    BASE_HREF  = "http://www.whitehouse.gov/"

    # Metadata for scraped feed
    FEED_META = {
        'feed.title'        : 'News from The White House',
        'feed.link'         : SCRAPE_URL,
        'feed.tagline'      : 'News releases from whitehouse.gov',
        'feed.author.name'  : 'The White House',
        'feed.author.email' : 'info@whitehouse.gov',
        'feed.author.url'   : SCRAPE_URL,
    }
```

Again, more `Scraper` boilerplate configuration constants in Listing 9-33 at the start of the `WhitehouseScraper` class. Now, you can complete this new scraper with the code in Listing 9-34.

Listing 9-34: ch09_whitehouse_scraper.py (Part 3 of 3)

```
    # XPaths for extracting content from the page
    ENTRIES_XPATH = "//xhtml:b/xhtml:a[contains(@href,'/news/releases')]"
    ENTRY_XPATHS = {
        'title'   : './text()',
        'link'    : './@href',
        'summary' : '../../../xhtml:font[2]/text()'
    }

if __name__=="__main__": main()
```

Listing 9-34 wraps up the `WhitehouseScraper` class with the XPaths discussed in the planning stages of this scraper. With that, the scraper class is completed. Finishing off the program is the usual call to the `main()` driver function.

Because of the power available from the XPath processor, there's no parsing logic that needs to be implemented here—everything's encapsulated in the class constants defining XPaths. Also, because you're not doing anything here with dates or other things that need post-processing as in the FCC headline scraper, no methods are defined by this scraper class. Note, however, that if for some reason you do need to do some post-processing, you can still override the `produce_entries()` method, just like the FCC headline scraper did.

Trying Out the White House News Scraper

Like the other two, this scraper program works with a command-line argument of either "atom" or "rss" to see the results in Figure 9-14 and Figure 9-15.

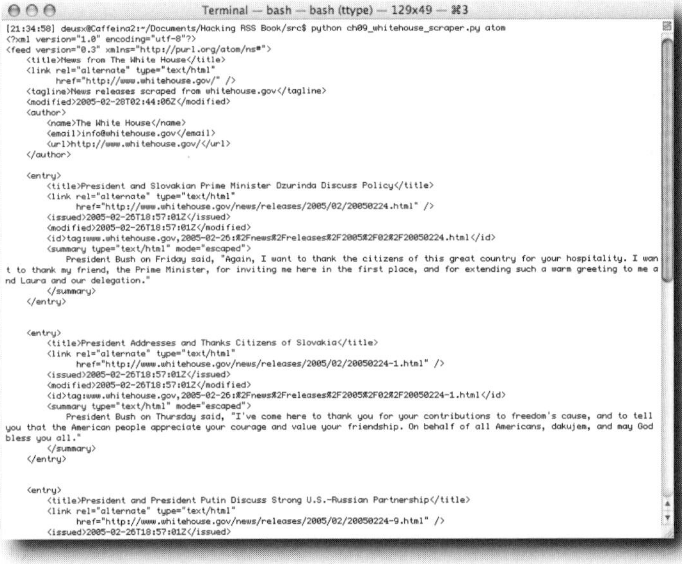

FIGURE 9-14: Running the White House headline scraper with Atom feed output

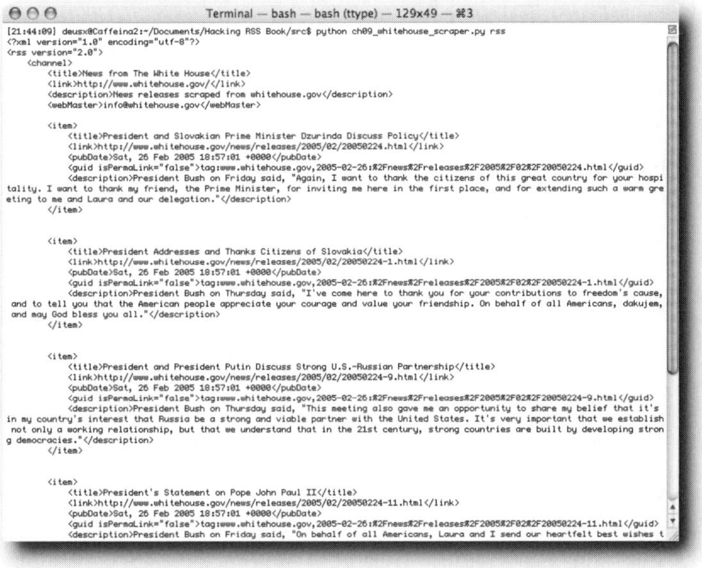

FIGURE 9-15: Running the White House headline scraper with RSS feed output

Checking Out Other Options

If you don't want to write your own scraper, or you'd like to try another approach than what's presented in this chapter, there are a few other options you can look into.

Searching for Feeds with Syndic8

Don't forget to check if a scraped feed (or even an official feed you missed) is already being provided, by making a few searches at Syndic8.com:

```
http://www.syndic8.com
```

Making Requests at the Feedpalooza

Carlo Zottmann runs a site called "Carlo's Bootleg RSS Feedpalooza" which, as of this writing, is accepting requests for creating scraped feeds. You might want to check him out if you don't feel like writing your own scrapers:

```
http://bootleg-rss.g-blog.net/
```

Using Beautiful Soup for HTML Parsing

Beautiful Soup is a Python module that gives you something like a cross between `HTMLParser` and XPath, with a more Pythonic approach. You may want to check it out for the basis of yet another scraper base class. It's available here:

```
http://www.crummy.com/software/BeautifulSoup/
```

Summary

The three techniques presented in this chapter—liberal HTML parsing, regular expression extraction, and XPath navigation—should provide you with a rich arsenal for coaxing full syndication feeds out of even the worst sources of information available. And, where even these approaches fail, you can at least fall back to the `Scraper` base class, which encapsulates the basics of feed production. From there, you can build your own completely custom and specialized data scraper.

There are also a number of improvements you could look into for the scrapers in this chapter:

- The `Scraper` base class defined in this chapter uses string templates for the generation of syndication feeds, but this is not the only (or necessarily the best) approach. Take a look at atomfeed (`http://atomfeed.sourceforge.net/`) and PyRSS2Gen (`http://www.dalkescientific.com/Python/PyRSS2Gen.html`) for other options, as well as maybe generating XML documents using 4Suite.

- When you scraped the Library of Congress news page, all you got were headlines. But, behind each of these headline links is a press release article. Who says a scraper needs to be limited to a single page? Spider a level further and scrape each of these press releases to enrich your feed with full content. However, try to be polite. Use the state database to track whether you've already spidered down to a particular press release and cache the content.

- 4Suite is one of the faster XML packages available for Python, but the Python bindings for libxml2 (`http://xmlsoft.org/`) are even faster (albeit sometimes frustrating to use). You could swap this in for use in XPath scraping.

Next up in Chapter 10, you see a different way of generating feeds, this time from system log files. With these hacks, you'll be able to monitor what's going on with your Web server or other machines you administer, right in your news aggregator. It'll be a bit like scraping, but there will be a few very significant differences.

Monitoring Your Server with Feeds

If you're in charge of administrating your own server, chances are you're well acquainted with the logs and alerts generated by all the bits and pieces you have running at any given time. Or, at least, you should be—these streams of information all have important things to say about the status of your server.

Admittedly, though, all the access logs, error logs, warnings, and just plain chatter coming in from all directions can be a bit overwhelming. And, not every single line spewed into every log is equally important.

But when a system message is important, it's usually vital—like the death knell of a critical server or an intrusion warning. For these, you can find decent monitoring applications with intelligent filtering that can fire off an email, instant message, or pager message to make sure you get the message ASAP and react quickly.

Other messages tend to get lost, though. Below the threshold of screaming emergencies, you don't want to get bothered with constant emails and pages. So, useful, but non-critical, events and informative messages remain lost in the rest of the noise because there's not a very good lesser-urgency channel by which to deliver them.

Well, that's not quite true. Many good system-monitoring solutions will also deliver daily and weekly email reports summarizing recent activity. But, these periodic reports can present information that's become stale and eventually they get ignored as useless spam.

So, as you've probably guessed, this chapter offers a few ways to funnel system log messages and events into syndication feeds. Delivering this information as feed entries strikes a good balance between the drop-everything nature of a pager at your belt and the usual boring report generated every midnight in your email inbox.

Caution

It's worth saying that the feeds generated in this chapter can potentially contain very sensitive information about your server. So, you really don't want these feeds available to the general public. Please consider placing feeds built by programs in this part behind password-protected directories, and, if you're able, access them only via HTTPS.

Note The programs in this chapter are pretty UNIX-centric, dealing with mostly text-based log files and commands. Logging on Windows can be a little different, requiring the use of APIs to access the Event Log. This chapter won't deal much with the Event Log, but you may still find the techniques in this chapter useful even if you're not a UNIX fan.

Monitoring Logs

In general, a log is a stream of events in chronological order. On UNIX systems, logs tend to take the form of text files, with one event per line, which grow over time as new things get appended to the tail end. On Windows, there's the Event Log, a central system service that can accumulate messages and alerts from a number of other system services and running software. And then, depending on what software you're using, there are all sorts of custom variations involving database tables and other schemes—but the idea generally remains the same: a stream of events in chronological order.

At this point, you might be thinking that a log sounds just like a feed, other than the fact that feeds tend to be a stream of entries in *reverse* chronological order. With this in mind, it wouldn't be too difficult to imagine building a scraper that simply translates log events straight into feed entries.

The problem with this solution, though, is that it doesn't do much to help you out with information overload. Logs tend to present a jumbled stream of machine consciousness, with contexts and urgencies all tangled together in a rush to just get it all recorded. Simply telegraphing this chaos into a syndication feed doesn't add much value, and leaves you with a noisy subscription you'll end up ignoring or deleting.

Because the goal is to arrive at a solution somewhere between the immediacy of a beeping pager and the stale summary of a midnight email, you'll want to filter and chunk events in a way that makes sense for useful inclusion in feed entries. You're going to need tools to help you filter events, track new events, and maybe even summarize or analyze things. So, the next few sections take you through a few tools and techniques that will come in handy in this chapter.

Filtering Log Events

Filtering in Python is easy. Take a look at Listing 10-1 for a bare-bones impersonation of tail and grep, two of a UNIX system administrator's best friends.

Listing 10-1: ch10_pytailgrep.py

```
#!/usr/bin/env python
"""

ch10_pytailgrep.py

Simple, naive implementation of a tail with grep.
"""
```

```
import sys, re

def main():
    num_lines = int(sys.argv[1])
    filename  = sys.argv[2]
    pattern   = re.compile(sys.argv[3])

    lines     = open(filename, 'r').readlines()[-num_lines:]
    filtered  = [ x for x in lines if pattern.match(x) ]

    print "".join(filtered)

if __name__ == '__main__': main()
```

Basically, `ch10_pytailgrep.py` can be used to extract a number of lines from the end of a file, filtering for lines that match a given regular expression before dumping them to standard output. For example, here's what it looks like when I run it on my Web server access log, searching for lines that contain the string "atom":

```
# python ch10_pytailgrep.py 100 www/decafbad.com/logs/access.log '.*atom.*'
192.168.123.100 - - [24/Mar/2005:15:01:34 -0500] "GET /images/atom_feed.png
HTTP/1.0" 200 265 "http://www.decafbad.com/links/comics/index" "Mozilla/4.0
(compatible; MSIE 6.0; Windows NT 4.0)"
192.168.123.100 - - [24/Mar/2005:15:01:34 -0500] "GET /images/atom_valid.png
HTTP/1.0" 200 275 "http://www.decafbad.com/links/comics/index" "Mozilla/4.0
(compatible; MSIE 6.0; Windows NT 4.0)"
192.168.123.100 - - [24/Mar/2005:15:02:18 -0500] "GET /atom.xml HTTP/1.1" 304 -
"-" "RssBandit/1.3.0.26 (.NET CLR 1.1.4322.573; WinNT 5.1.2600.0;
http://www.rssbandit.org)"
```

With this sort of code, you can lift out the most recent log events at the end of the file, filtered on criteria in a regular expression. In a Web server access log like this one, you could look for specific filenames, HTTP status codes, and user agents. And, even if you're targeting a log event source other than the standard UNIX log file, this same sort of logic can be pretty easily adapted for use with lists of objects or structured data instead of files of formatted strings.

Tracking and Summarizing Log Changes

A major bit of functionality missing from Listing 10-1's crude version of the UNIX tools that inspired it is the ability to pipe in live streams of events or to follow the tail-end of an actively growing log file. (As you know, staring at carefully filtered lines scrolling by in a terminal window is a favorite pastime of sysadmins everywhere.)

But, this omission is intentional. Feeds are more pull than push, and don't exactly lend well to a constant trickle or rush of real-time updates. Again, this sort of immediacy is really better suited for a stared-at window, an instant message, or a belt-mounted pager. Feed generation, at least in this book, involves regularly scheduled baking for consumption by regularly polling subscribers. The sweet spot for feed entries, then, is at a level of reporting granularity somewhere between end-of-day reports and raw lines scrolling past.

The best approach to take with respect to building feeds from logs is to perform bite-sized bits of analysis throughout a day. Load up each feed entry with incremental reports on what's changed since the last time the feed was built. For less frequently updated logs, this could simply take the form of interesting new events having arrived since the last check.

Take a look at Listing 10-2 for the start of a new program that improves upon the previous one.

Listing 10-2: ch10_bookmark_tailgrep.py (Part 1 of 2)

```python
#!/usr/bin/env python
"""
ch10_bookmark_tailgrep.py

Stateful tail, remembers where it left off reading.
"""
import sys, os, re, shelve

def main():
    """
    Run the bookmark_tailgrep function as a command.
    Usage: ch10_bookmark_tailgrep.py <input file> [<regex>]
    """
    filename = sys.argv[1]

    if len(sys.argv) > 2:
        pattern = re.compile(sys.argv[2])
        pattern_filter = \
            lambda x: ( pattern.match(x) is not None )
        new_lines = bookmark_tailgrep(filename, pattern_filter)
    else:
        new_lines = bookmark_tailgrep(filename)

    sys.stdout.write("".join(new_lines))
```

This program's `main()` driver function in Listing 10-2 handles accepting a filename and an optional `regex` for filtering. If there's a `regex` supplied, `main()` builds a filter function and calls the `bookmark_tailgrep()` function. Otherwise, without a `regex`, `bookmark_tailgrep()` is called without a filter. The lines returned by this function are then dumped to standard output.

Now, onto the `bookmark_tailgrep()` function itself, in Listing 10-3.

Listing 10-3: ch10_bookmark_tailgrep.py (Part 2 of 2)

```python
class BookmarkInvalidException(Exception): pass

def bookmark_tailgrep(tail_fn, line_filter=lambda x: True,
        state_fn="tail_bookmarks", max_initial_lines=50):
    """
    Stateful file tail reader which keeps a line number
    bookmark of where it last left off for a given filename.
    """
    fin       = open(tail_fn, 'r')
    state     = shelve.open(state_fn)
    last_num = state.get(tail_fn, 0)

    try:
        # Fast forward through file to bookmark.
        for idx in range(last_num):
            # If EOF hit before bookmark, it's invalid.
            if fin.readline() == '':
                raise BookmarkInvalidException

    except BookmarkInvalidException:
        # In case of invalid bookmark, rewind to start of file.
        last_num = 0
        fin.seek(0)

    # Grab the rest of the lines in the file as new.
    new_lines = fin.readlines()

    # Advance the bookmark index.
    state[tail_fn] = last_num + len(new_lines)

    # If rewound to beginning of file, limit to the tail-end.
    if last_num == 0:
        new_lines = new_lines[-max_initial_lines:]

    # Pass the new lines through the given line filter
    return [ x for x in new_lines if line_filter(x) ]

if __name__ == '__main__': main()
```

The `bookmark_tailgrep()` function in Listing 10-3 can be used to fetch lines at the tail-end of a file, and by attempting to keep a bookmark in a database, it will try to fetch only new lines found since the last time it was called. These are the steps it takes:

1. Open the file for examination.

2. Open the bookmark database and attempt to grab a saved index for this filename.

3. Attempt to fast-forward through the lines in the file until the bookmark index reached.

4. If an end-of-file occurs before the bookmark is reached, invalidate the bookmark and rewind the file. (This partially accounts for log files that have been rotated since the last check.)

5. Read in the remainder of the file as new lines.

6. Update and save the bookmark index for this file.

7. If the bookmark was at the beginning of the file, constrain the list of new lines to just a number of lines at the end of the file. (This prevents dumping potentially hundreds or thousands of lines from a log visited for the first time.)

8. Run all the new lines through the filter and return the resulting list.

You can use this program with an invocation like the following:

```
python ch10_bookmark_tail.py www/www.decafbad.com/logs/access.log '.*rss.*'
```

By default, the first run of this program will output the last 50 lines of a file. Repeated runs of this program should only produce fresh lines added since the previous run. The logic implemented in this function should help you track log entries that appear in between feed generation runs.

Caution   You might want to bump that 50-line limit for the start-of-file bookmark handling up to something like 500 or 5,000, in case you use this on particularly active logs. Although the limit exists to prevent a full dump of stale log data, you don't want it to arbitrarily omit genuinely new data if there've really been more than 50 new lines since a log was rotated.

Building Feeds Incrementally

For the most part, the scrapers and feed generators presented in this book do their work all at once and without much of a memory. All the useful data is harvested from a Web page or data source by some means, and a feed is built based on those results.

The entries that appear in a feed built this way are driven by the data available at the time of the latest program run and the feed history is contained entirely in that source data. Although there is some state maintained between scraper runs, this is mostly limited to a few notes taken to supplement the feed with dates and other things not made available by the source data.

However, the feed generators in this chapter need to be able to build feeds incrementally. That is, whenever the program runs, it only comes up with new data and new entries. If you want to keep any entries from previous program runs in the feed, you won't be able to rely on the source data to provide any history. So, you need to build a feed generator that can manage a collection of entries, retaining data from previous runs, as well as tossing out data when it goes stale.

To get started building an incremental feed generator, check out Listing 10-4, which offers the start of a new module named `monitorfeedlib`.

Listing 10-4: monitorfeedlib.py (Part 1 of 5)

```python
#!/usr/bin/env python
"""
monitorfeedlib.py

Utilities for building feeds from system logs and reports.
"""
import sys, os, os.path, time, md5, difflib, gzip
from cPickle import dump, load
from scraperlib import FeedEntryDict, Scraper

def main():
    """
    Test out LogBufferFeed by maintaining a random number feed.
    """
    # Construct the feed generator
    f = LogBufferFeed('random_feed')
    f.FEED_META['feed.title']   = 'Random Number of the Moment'
    f.FEED_META['feed.tagline'] = \
        'Serving your random number needs.'
    f.MAX_ENTRIES = 4
    f.MAX_AGE     = 10 * 60 # 10 minutes

    # Construct and append a new entry
    import random
    num = random.random() * 1000
    entry = FeedEntryDict({
        'title'   : 'Random number %s' % num,
        'link'    : '',
        'summary' : \
            'Here is another random number for you: %s' % num
    })
    f.append_entry(entry)

    # Output the current feed entries
    if len(sys.argv) > 1 and sys.argv[1] == 'rss':
        print f.scrape_rss()
    else:
        print f.scrape_atom()
```

The monitorfeedlib module starts off with a main() function as a test and demonstration—it produces a mostly useless toy feed whose every entry reports a new random entry.

The main() function first creates and configures an instance of a yet-to-be-defined class named LogBufferFeed. The object is initialized with a parameter value of 'random_feed', which is the name of a directory this object will use to manage entries it retains between runs.

After creation, the object instance is tweaked with new values for the feed metadata, as well as settings for a maximum number of entries and the maximum age for entries before they're considered stale.

Next, a new FeedEntryDict is constructed using a random number to come up with a title and a summary. This new entry is added to the feed with a call to the LogBufferFeed's append_entry() method. Then, the feed is generated and output in the format of choice, depending on the optional command-line argument.

Listing 10-5 continues with the beginning of the LogBufferFeed class.

Listing 10-5: monitorfeedlib.py (Part 2 of 5)

```
class LogBufferFeed(Scraper):
    """
    Implements a log-style buffered feed, where new entries can
    be added and kept in the feed until they become stale.
    Generated feeds will include buffered entries from previous
    program runs.
    """
    TAG_DOMAIN  = 'decafbad.com'
    MAX_ENTRIES = 50
    MAX_AGE     = 4 * 60 * 6 # 4 hours

    def __init__(self, entries_dir):
        """Initialize object with the path to pickled
           entries."""
        if not os.path.exists(entries_dir):
            os.makedirs(entries_dir)
        self.entries_dir = entries_dir
        self.STATE_FN    = os.path.join(entries_dir, 'state')

    def produce_entries(self):
        """Load up entries and fix up before producing feed."""
        # Load up all the pickled entries
        entries = [load(open(x, 'rb'))
                   for x in self.get_entry_paths()]

        # Tweak each loaded entry to use proper date format.
        for entry in entries:
            entry.date_fmt = self.date_fmt

        # Return the fixed entries.
        return entries
```

The LogBufferFeed class inherits from Scraper, which you defined in the previous chapter. This allows this new class to reuse all of the feed generation machinery encapsulated in the parent class, so you can focus on just the new functionality.

Several class attributes are defined at the start of the class:

- TAG_DOMAIN—Provides a domain name for use in building tag URIs for entry GUIDs.

- MAX_ENTRIES—A new value for the maximum number of entries is defined here, which you will probably want to tweak in log monitoring programs to suit the volume of log activity.

- MAX_AGE—Defines how old (in seconds) an entry can be before it is considered stale.

Following these definitions is the __init__() method, which initializes a new instance of this object. It accepts the path to a directory to be used in maintaining the state and entries for this feed. If the directory doesn't exist yet, this method creates it.

Then comes the produce_entries() method, which is used by the Scraper parent class to come up with entries it needs to populate feeds it generates. The first line of this method packs a big punch, so it may require a little extra attention in explanation.

The LogBufferFeed class relies on the cPickle module, which provides an easy way to serialize just about any Python data structure in the form of a flat data stream suitable for a file on disk or in some other form of external storage. The dump() function, which will be used shortly, provides the method to go from Python to data stream. The load() function, used here, deserializes from flat data stream back to reconstituted Python object.

On the Web Check out the documentation for the Pickle and cPickle modules here:

```
http://docs.python.org/lib/module-pickle.html
http://docs.python.org/lib/module-cPickle.html
```

So, in this class, pickled FeedEntryDict objects are each stored in individual files under the directory given at initialization. The first line of produce_entries() uses a method named get_entry_paths() to grab the paths to all of these entries and then builds a list of deserialized entries from the results of opening and de-pickling each of these files.

After loading up all the FeedEntryDict objects, the method takes a run through them to tweak their date formats to match the current feed format being generated. And, finally, this list of entries is returned to be baked into a feed.

Up next, in Listing 10-6, comes the definition of the append_entry().

Listing 10-6: monitorfeedlib.py (Part 3 of 5)

```python
def append_entry(self, entry):
    """Add a given entry to the buffer."""
    # Clean up entries before adding a new one.
    self.clean_entries()

    # Update entry's modified timestamp.
    entry['modified'] = time.time()
```

Continued

Listing 10-6 *(continued)*

```
# Build an ID for this new entry.
hash = self.hash_entry(entry)
ymd  = time.strftime("%Y-%m-%d", time.gmtime())
entry['id'] = "tag:%s,%s:%s.%s" % \
    (self.TAG_DOMAIN, ymd, self.entries_dir, hash)

# Build entry's file path based on a hash.
entry_fn   = "entry-%s" % hash
entry_path = os.path.join(self.entries_dir, entry_fn)

# Pickle the entry out to a file.
dump(entry, open(entry_path, 'wb'))
```

The `append_entry()` method is used to add entries to the set maintained by `LogBufferFeed`. First thing in this entry is a call to `clean_entries()`, which keeps the entries folder clean by deleting any stale entries. Next, the entry to be added gets an updated modified date. Then, a GUID is built for it using the tag domain, current time, and a hash of the entry contents built using the `hash_entry()` method. Finally, a filename is generated for the entry's pickle file, and then `dump()` from `cPickle` is used to serialize the `FeedEntryDict` object out to disk.

Keep going, on to Listing 10-7, which offers the definition of `clean_entries()`.

Listing 10-7: monitorfeedlib.py (Part 4 of 5)

```
def clean_entries(self):
    """Delete entries older than the maximum age."""
    # Get entry file paths and iterate through them.
    entry_paths = self.get_entry_paths()
    for entry_path in entry_paths:

        # Load up the current entry.
        entry = load(open(entry_path, "rb"))

        # Delete the entry if it's gotten too old.
        entry_age = time.time() - entry.data['modified']
        if entry_age > self.MAX_AGE:
            os.unlink(entry_path)
```

What `clean_entries()` does is pretty simple. It visits each serialized entry currently present in the directory managed by this object and checks the entry's age. If it's older than the maximum allowed, the method deletes this entry file. This keeps stale data out of the feed.

Listing 10-8 finishes up this module with a pair of utility methods.

Listing 10-8: monitorfeedlib.py (Part 5 of 5)

```
def get_entry_paths(self):
    """Get paths to all the pickled entry files."""
    return [ os.path.join(self.entries_dir, x)
             for x in os.listdir(self.entries_dir)
             if x.startswith('entry-') ]

def hash_entry(self, entry):
    """Produce a filename-safe hash of an entry's
       contents."""
    m = md5.md5()
    for k in entry.data.keys():
        v = entry.data[k]
        if not type(v) is unicode:
            m.update('%s' % v)
        else:
            m.update(v.encode(entry.UNICODE_ENC))
    return m.hexdigest()

if __name__ == '__main__': main()
```

The `get_entry_paths()` method packs a lot into a single list comprehension, but, put simply, it looks through the entry folder for files whose names start with `'entry-'` and returns a list of all of these files with the folder path prepended to each. And then there's the `hash_entry()` method, which walks through all the data contained in a given `FeedEntryDict` and returns an MD5 hash built from it.

Now, you can try out this module. Figure 10-1 shows a sample session in a terminal window running the module a few times to demonstrate the incremental growth of the feed. Figure 10-2 shows the results in Mozilla Thunderbird.

When you first run the module as a program, you'll get a feed with a single entry offering a random number. With each successive program run, a new entry appears at the beginning of the feed with a random number. Then, if you wait 10 minutes (the value of MAX_AGE), you'll see these entries disappear because they've gone stale. This provides the feed with a limited window of events over time and prevents it from getting cluttered up with old data.

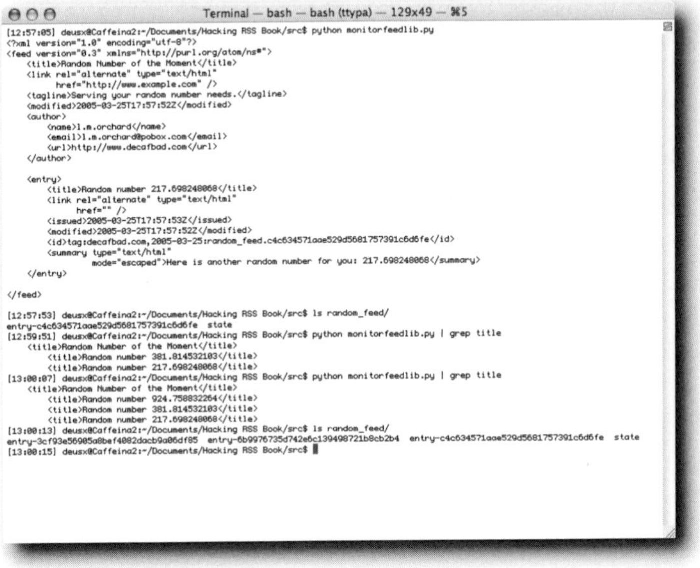

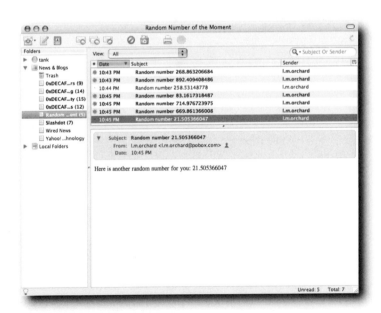

FIGURE 10-1: Running `monitorfeedlib.py` for the first few times

FIGURE 10-2: A feed produced by `monitorfeedlib.py` viewed in Thunderbird

Keeping an Eye Out for Problems in Apache Logs

Now, you have the basic tools to build your first log monitoring feed. This first one will target the error log for an Apache Web server—which should, hopefully, be a relatively low-volume log file. Depending on whether you have some persistently buggy or chatty software (such as Perl CGI scripts that constantly spew semi-useless warnings about uninitialized variables), this log should mostly consist of real problems that need fixing at some point or another.

So, for this feed, you can pretty much just slap together the parts you played with in the first part of this chapter—namely, the `bookmark_tail()` function and `LogBufferFeed`. Entries you'll see in this feed are direct dumps of updates to the error log. Start off this new program, named `ch10_apache_error_feed.py`, with Listing 10-9.

Listing 10-9: ch10_apache_error_feed.py (Part 1 of 3)

```python
#!/usr/bin/env python
"""
ch10_apache_error_feed.py

Provide a periodic tail of the Apache error log.
"""
import sys, os, re, shelve
from xml.sax.saxutils import escape
from scraperlib import FeedEntryDict
from monitorfeedlib import LogBufferFeed
from ch10_bookmark_tailgrep import bookmark_tailgrep

SITE_NAME     = "My Example"
ERROR_LOG     = "www/www.example.com/logs/error.log"
FEED_NAME_FN  = "www/www.example.com/docs/errors.%s"
FEED_DIR      = "error_feed"
```

The configuration constants in this program provide the following:

- `SITE_NAME`—Human-readable name for the site owning this error log, used in the feed title.

- `ERROR_LOG`—Path to the Web server error log to watch for updates.

- `FEED_NAME_FN`—Filename string template to which feeds should be written. This program will generate both RSS and Atom feeds, and so this template will be populated with `'rss'` and `'atom'`, respectively.

- `FEED_DIR`—Provides the path to the directory needed by `LogBufferFeed` for entry management.

The `main()` function for this programs starts in Listing 10-10.

Listing 10-10: ch10_apache_error_feed.py (Part 2 of 3)

```
def main():
    """
    Report new errors found in Apache logs.
    """
    # Construct the feed generator
    f = LogBufferFeed(FEED_DIR)
    f.MAX_AGE = 24 * 60 * 60 # 1 day
    f.FEED_META['feed.title']   = \
        '%s Apache Errors' % SITE_NAME
    f.FEED_META['feed.tagline'] = \
        'New errors from Apache on %s' % SITE_NAME

    # If there were new referrers found, insert a new entry.
    new_lines = bookmark_tailgrep(ERROR_LOG,
                                    max_initial_lines=3000)
```

So far, the definition of main() in Listing 10-10 looks a lot like the demo usage in Listing 10-4.

The LogBufferFeed object is created, and its MAX_TIME set to allow entries of up to a day in age. Then, the FEED_META title and tagline are built using the SITE_NAME title provided in the program configuration constants.

At the end of Listing 10-10 is where bookmark_tailgrep() comes in. It's used to grab the new lines from the end of the Apache error log every time this feed generator is run, with a maximum of 3,000 lines if there's no valid bookmark.

Listing 10-11 wraps up this function and the program.

Listing 10-11: ch10_apache_error_feed.py (Part 3 of 3)

```
    if len(new_lines) > 0:
        # Construct and append a new entry
        esc_lines = [escape(x) for x in new_lines]
        entry = FeedEntryDict({
            'title'   : '%s new lines of errors' % \
                        len(new_lines),
            'link'    : '',
            'summary' : """
                <div style="font-family:monospace">
                    %s
                </div>
            """ % "<br />".join(esc_lines)
        })
        f.append_entry(entry)
```

```
    # Output the current feed entries as both RSS and Atom
    open(FEED_NAME_FN % 'rss', 'w').write(f.scrape_rss())
    open(FEED_NAME_FN % 'atom', 'w').write(f.scrape_atom())

if __name__ == '__main__': main()
```

If there are new lines resulting from the call to `bookmark_tailgrep()`, the code at the start of Listing 10-11 builds a new feed entry. The entry's title will report the number of new lines found in the error log, and the summary of the entry will contain the new lines, which are slightly massaged into rough HTML formatting in a monospace font. Note that, as part of this, the log lines are run through `xml.sax.saxutils.escape()`, to catch any errant angle brackets in errors.

When run, this program doesn't produce anything on standard output, but it does result in two feeds written out to files. Run with configuration constants in Listing 10-9, these files are:

- `www/www.example.com/docs/errors.atom`
- `www/www.example.com/docs/errors.rss`

For an example of the sort of feed produced by this program, check out Figure 10-3 and Figure 10-4.

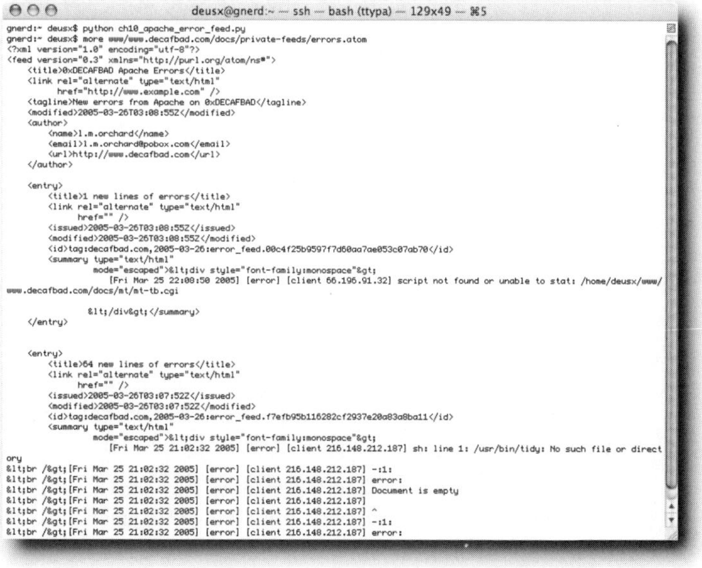

FIGURE 10-3: An Atom feed resulting from an Apache error log

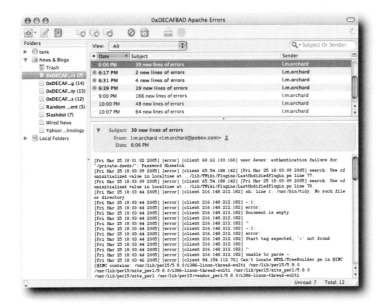

FIGURE 10-4: Viewing the errors feed in Mozilla Thunderbird

If you schedule this program to run on a periodic basis, it should feed you a regular stream of updates from your error log, to be read in your aggregator at your leisure. And, just maybe seeing these things start showing up in your aggregator will remind you to fix some things and tighten a few loose bolts.

Also, keep in mind that you can use this program for more than Web server errors. Depending on how much you want flooding into your aggregator, you can point this at just about any log file you'd ordinarily watch with a pipe to `tail` and `grep`.

Watching for Incoming Links in Apache Logs

Now that you have Apache error logs arriving in your aggregator, how about watching the access logs? The challenge here, though, is that access logs are so much more active, jumbled, and noisy than error logs. But, one thing they have going for them is that each line (more or less) follows a format that you can parse into component fields. Once parsed, you can then use the values of one or many fields to filter and analyze what's happening on your Web server.

For this program, you're going to play with a little light log analysis. As opposed to the last program, dumping log lines straight into feed entries with something this chaotic and active is just not useful. So, to tame things a bit, this program focuses on extracting out one facet of the access log: the referrer field. Despite the spam and trash that's been showing up in access log referrer fields lately, watching this part of the log can still be somewhat useful in finding out how people are getting to your site. You'll see backlinks to other sites and Web logs, and you can see what search terms people are using to arrive at your site.

So, start a new file in your editor and name it `ch10_apache_referrer_feed.py`. Listing 10-12 provides the start of this program.

Listing 10-12: ch10_apache_referrer_feed.py (Part 1 of 8)

```
#!/usr/bin/env python
"""
ch10_apache_referrer_feed.py

Scan the Apache access log for new referring links, build
mini-reports in feed entries.
"""
import sys, os, re, shelve
from scraperlib import FeedEntryDict
from monitorfeedlib import LogBufferFeed
from ch10_bookmark_tailgrep import bookmark_tailgrep

SITE_NAME    = "0xDECAFBAD"
SITE_ROOT    = "http://www.decafbad.com"
ACCESS_LOG   = "www/www.decafbad.com/logs/access.log"
FEED_NAME_FN = "www/www.decafbad.com/docs/referrers.%s"
FEED_DIR     = "referrer_feed"
REFER_SEEN   = "%s/referrer_seen" % FEED_DIR
```

After the module imports, Listing 10-12 establishes the following configuration constants:

- `SITE_NAME`—A label for the Web site used in the feed title.
- `SITE_ROOT`—Base URL for resolving links to the site.
- `ACCCESS_LOG`—File path to the Web server access log.
- `FEED_NAME_FN`—String templates used to create the feed filenames based on feed format.
- `FEED_DIR`—Directory used by `LogBufferFeed` to manage entries and state.
- `REFER_SEEN`—Name of a database that will be used to keep track of referring URLs the program has already seen, and won't display again; presently stashed away inside the `FEED_DIR`.

The program continues in Listing 10-13 with a few more configuration constants.

Listing 10-13: ch10_apache_referrer_feed.py (Part 2 of 8)

```
EXCLUDE_EXACT = {
    'referrer' : [ '', '-' ],
    'path'     : [ '/', 'http://www.decafbad.com' ]
}
EXCLUDE_PARTIAL = {
    'referrer' : [ 'decafbad.com', 'porn', 'xxx', 'hardcore',
                   'incest', 'sex', 'viagra', 'poker', 'casino' ],
    'path'     : [ '/images/', '.rss', '.rdf', '.xml' ]
}
```

As part of the log analysis, this program implements a bit of filtering. As mentioned earlier, there's spam showing up in access logs these days—because, at one point in the history of blogs, people discovered they could assemble backlinks to a post by analyzing referrers and publishing the list of reciprocal links seemed like a nice idea. Well, it was fun for a while, until spammers started loading bogus URLs into the referrer field pointing not back to further discussion, but to their own porn, gambling, and erectile dysfunction offers.

So, these two configuration constants, EXCLUDE_EXACT and EXCLUDE_PARTIAL, will be used in exact and partial matching, respectively, on access log fields to decide which hits in the log should be omitted from any analysis. During the course of your experience with this program, I'm sure your list will continue to grow from this initial blacklist collection.

There's a lot of grumbling out there about referrer spam. Here are a couple of pointers for your perusal:

```
http://en.wikipedia.org/wiki/Referer_spam
http://www.kuro5hin.org/story/2005/2/14/02558/3376
```

In the previous examples, you can see a few common spam keywords—but there's also my domain name in there. You'll probably want to swap this for your own domain or URL. Although your site is probably not spam, this keeps you from flooding the analysis with links between pages of your own site.

Move on to Listing 10-14 for the last of the configuration constants.

Listing 10-14: ch10_apache_referrer_feed.py (Part 3 of 8)

```
SUMMARY_TMPL = """
    <p>Found %(count)s new referring links:</p>
    %(links)s
"""


LINK_TMPL = """
    <table style="margin: 2px; padding: 2px; border: 1px solid #888">
```

```
        <tr style="background: #fff">
            <th>From:</th>
            <td><a href="%(referrer)s">%(referrer)s</a></td>
        </tr>
        <tr style="background: #eee">
            <th>To:</th>
            <td><a href="%(SITE_ROOT)s%(path)s">%(path)s</a></td>
        </tr>
    </table>
"""
```

The string templates in Listing 10-14 are showing off a bit, but they're an attempt to try to build some presentation into the bare listing of referrer links that will be included in feed entry summaries as a result of the rest of this program. The SUMMARY_TMPL string template defines the overall shell for the summary, whereas LINK_TMPL is populated with the details of each new referral link found in the log.

Now, getting into the swing of things, Listing 10-15 is where the program's main() function starts.

Listing 10-15: ch10_apache_referrer_feed.py (Part 4 of 8)

```
def main():
    """
    Scan Apache log and report new referrers found.
    """
    # Construct the feed generator
    f = LogBufferFeed(FEED_DIR)
    f.MAX_AGE = 24 * 60 * 60 # 1 day
    f.FEED_META['feed.title']   = '%s Referring Links' % SITE_NAME
    f.FEED_META['feed.tagline'] = \
        'New referring links from Apache access.log on %s' % SITE_NAME

    # Load up tail of access log, parse, and filter
    new_lines = bookmark_tailgrep(ACCESS_LOG,
                                  max_initial_lines=100000)
    all_events = parse_access_log(new_lines)
    events     = [ x for x in all_events if event_filter(x) ]
```

There's a pattern here. Listing 10-15 is mostly like Listing 10-10 from the previous program. The LogBufferFeed object is created with the FEED_DIR path, the MAX_AGE is set, and the FEED_META title and tagline are generated. Then, bookmark_tailgrep() is used to fetch the latest lines from the log.

The similarities end here, however, because the next thing done is to run all the log lines through a function named `parse_access_log()`, which results in a list of dictionaries of fields parsed from each log line. These are then filtered by the criteria defined in constants at the start of the program, using the `event_filter()` function. Both of these will be defined shortly, but for now, continue on to Listing 10-16 for a bit of no-frills log analysis.

Listing 10-16: ch10_apache_referrer_feed.py (Part 5 of 8)

```
# Scan through latest events for new referrers
referrers_seen = shelve.open(REFER_SEEN)
new_referrers  = []
for evt in events:
    k = '%(referrer)s -> %(path)s' % evt
    if not referrers_seen.has_key(k):
        referrers_seen[k] = 1
        new_referrers.append( (evt['referrer'],
                               evt['path']) )
referrers_seen.close()
```

In short, the code in Listing 10-16 scans through the new log lines and tries to pick out any referrer URL/Web site path pairs it hasn't seen before. The `shelve` database in `referrers_seen` is used to keep track of these pairs. As each log event is visited, any previously unseen pair is appended to a list for inclusion in a new feed entry, and the pair is noted as having been seen in the database.

Speaking of inclusion in a feed entry, Listing 10-17 presents the construction of an entry for any new referrer links found.

Listing 10-17: ch10_apache_referrer_feed.py (Part 6 of 8)

```
# If there were new referrers found, insert a new entry.
if len(new_referrers) > 0:

    # Build a list of hyperlinks for referrers
    links_out = [
        LINK_TMPL % {
            'SITE_ROOT' : SITE_ROOT,
            'referrer'  : x[0],
            'path'      : x[1],
        }
        for x in new_referrers
    ]

    # Build a summary for this entry.
    summary = SUMMARY_TMPL % {
```

```
        'count' : len(new_referrers),
        'links' : "\n".join(links_out)
    }

    # Construct and append a new entry
    entry = FeedEntryDict({
        'title'   : '%s new referrers' % \
                    len(new_referrers),
        'link'    : '',
        'summary' : summary
    })
    f.append_entry(entry)

# Output the current feed entries as both RSS and Atom
open(FEED_NAME_FN % 'rss', 'w').write(f.scrape_rss())
open(FEED_NAME_FN % 'atom', 'w').write(f.scrape_atom())
```

If there are, in fact, any new referrers found on this run, a new feed entry is built and inserted into the feed. The LINK_TMPL is applied to format all of the elements of new_referrers found in Listing 10-16, and this is used along with the count of new links to populate the SUMMARY_TMPL template. Finally, this string is used as the summary for the new entry.

Then, wrapping up the main() function comes the two lines that each build the two formats of the feed. Keep going on to Listing 10-18, which provides one of the convenience functions left to define.

Listing 10-18: ch10_apache_referrer_feed.py (Part 7 of 8)

```
def event_filter(event):
    """Filter events on exact and partial exclusion criteria"""
    for field, blst in EXCLUDE_PARTIAL.items():
        ev_val = event[field]
        for bl_val in blst:
            if ev_val.find(bl_val) != -1: return False

    for field, blst in EXCLUDE_EXACT.items():
        ev_val = event[field]
        for bl_val in blst:
            if ev_val == bl_val: return False

    return True
```

The event_filter() function is defined in Listing 10-18. The EXCLUDE_PARTIAL and EXCLUDE_EXACT data structrures defined at the top of the program each define a mapping between the name of a log record field and a list of strings. For the partial search, each specified field is checked for the presence of any of the given strings in the list, which results in the record being rejected. For the exact search, each of the fields is matched against each of the strings exactly, again causing rejection if any match succeeds. Finally, if the record has cleared all of these criteria, it is allowed to pass.

Now, at last, this program is concluded with the code in Listing 10-19, the core of access log parsing.

Listing 10-19: ch10_apache_referrer_feed.py (Part 8 of 8)

```
ACCESS_RE = re.compile(\
    '(?P<client_ip>\d+\.\d+\.\d+\.\d+) '
    '(?P<ident>-|\w*) '
    '(?P<user>-|\w*) '
    '\[(?P<date>[^\[\]:]+):'
    '(?P<time>\d+:\d+:\d+) '
    '(?P<tz>.\d\d\d\d)\] '
    '"(?P<method>[^ ]+) '
    '(?P<path>[^ ]+) '
    '(?P<proto>[^"]+)" '
    '(?P<status>\d+) (?P<length>-|\d+) '
    '"(?P<referrer>[^"]*)" '
    '(?P<user_agent>".*")\s*\Z'
)

def parse_access_log(log_lines):
    """Parse Apache log file lines via regex"""
    matches = [ ACCESS_RE.search(y) for y in log_lines ]
    return [ x.groupdict() for x in matches if x is not None ]

if __name__ == '__main__': main()
```

The definition of ACCESS_RE is pretty nasty, but that's a regular expression for you. This regex can be used to match and extract fields from the Apache common format in the access log. It provides for a pretty pain-free parser implementation in the parse_access_log() function, which simply uses list comprehensions to match the regex on all given log lines, then extracts and returns the dictionaries of field values.

And, with that, this program is complete. As before, when run, this feed generator doesn't print anything to standard output, resulting instead in a couple of feeds written to files. Take a look at Figure 10-5 and Figure 10-6 to see what a sample feed looks like.

Although this program will need occasional tweaking to update its filters in order to remain useful and relatively spam-free, it can help out a lot in showing you who's talking about your site. Sometimes it can be downright spooky when you just "magically" appear to comment like Kibo on someone's site who just mentioned you a little while ago.

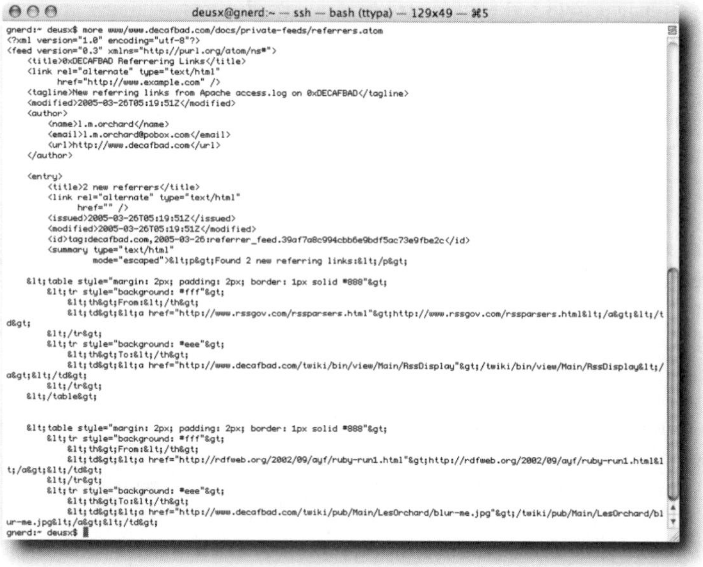

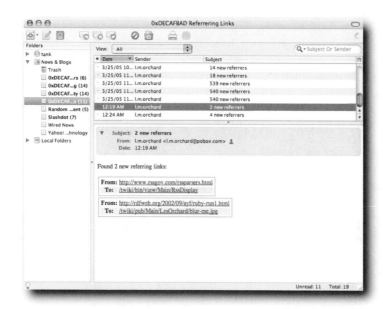

FIGURE 10-5: Atom feed output by `ch10_apache_referrer_feed.py`

FIGURE 10-6: Viewing the referrers feed in Mozilla Thunderbird

Kibo is a figure from the depths of Net mythology with "an uncanny, machine-assisted knack for joining any thread in which his nom de guerre is mentioned," according to this Wikipedia article:

```
http://en.wikipedia.org/wiki/Kibo
```

Watching your Web server logs for referrers is just one of many ways in which you can strive to be like Kibo.

And, after you've had fun with this for a while, you might want to think about how the parts of this program can be repurposed toward other access log analysis. Furthermore, think about what other logs you can parse, filter, and analyze like this.

Monitoring Login Activity on Linux

Watching the tail-end of a log file works great when there's something chattering away to fill a log in the first place. But, sometimes, you have to be a bit more proactive and ask questions to find out what's going on. You may need to run a database query, take a snapshot of current system activity, or make a summary anaysis of a set of accumulated information. And, to generate useful notifications, it would help to keep track of how the answer changed between the last time you asked the question and now.

Two Python modules will come in quite handy for this sort of thing:

- popen2, which you can use to capture the output of programs
- difflib, which can compare lists of strings and report on differences between them

You can find the documentation for the popen2 and difflib modules at the following respective URLs:

```
http://docs.python.org/lib/module-popen2.html
http://docs.python.org/lib/module-difflib.html
```

For the final program of this chapter, you're going to use these two modules to track login activity on a UNIX machine, by way of the "last" command. This will be pretty easy, so go ahead and start into a new program with Listing 10-20, named ch10_logins_feed.py.

> **Listing 10-20:** ch10_logins_feed.py (Part 1 of 5)

```python
#!/usr/bin/env python
"""
ch10_logins_feed.py

Provide reports of login activity.
"""
import sys, os, difflib, gzip
from xml.sax.saxutils import escape
from popen2 import popen4
```

```
from scraperlib import FeedEntryDict
from monitorfeedlib import LogBufferFeed

SITE_NAME    = "0xDECAFBAD"
COMMAND      = "/usr/bin/last -a"
FEED_NAME_FN = "www/www.decafbad.com/docs/private-feeds/logins.%s"
FEED_DIR     = "logins_feed"

TITLE_TMPL   = "Command output update (%(changes)s changes)"

SUMMARY_TMPL = """
    <p>Changes:</p>
    <div style="font-family: monospace">%(changes_lines)s</div>

    <p>All lines:</p>
    <div style="font-family: monospace">%(diff_lines)s</div>
"""
```

Again, following module imports, Listing 10-20 establishes some configuration constants:

- SITE_NAME—A label for the Web site used in the feed title.
- COMMAND—The command to be run and whose output is to be captured.
- FEED_NAME_FN—String templates used to create the feed filenames based on feed format.
- FEED_DIR—Directory used by LogBufferFeed to manage entries and state.
- TITLE_TMPL—A string template that will be used for building feed entry titles.
- SUMMARY_TMPL—A string template that will be used in generating feed entry summary content.

Note You may want to play with the previous setting for COMMAND. The command last -a works on Linux, serving to display a log of recent login activity, with the -a option to place the users' full incoming hostname at the end of each line. On Mac OS X, the last command works but the -a option doesn't. And, of course, this command doesn't actually exist under Windows as such.

Now, move on to Listing 10-21 for the definition of the main() method.

Listing 10-21: ch10_logins_feed.py (Part 2 of 5)

```
def main():
    """
    Detect login activity changes and report in feed.
    """
    # Construct the feed generator
```

Continued

Listing 10-21 *(continued)*

```
f = LogBufferFeed(FEED_DIR)
f.MAX_AGE = 24 * 60 * 60 # 1 day
f.FEED_META['feed.title']   = '%s Login Activity' % SITE_NAME
f.FEED_META['feed.tagline'] = \
    'Summary of login activity on the %s server' % SITE_NAME

# Call the command and capture output
(sout, sin) = popen4(COMMAND)
new_lines   = [ x for x in sout.readlines()
                  if x.find('reboot') == -1 ]

# Attempt load up output from the previous run.
old_lines = None
old_output_fn = os.path.join(FEED_DIR, 'old_output.gz')
if os.path.exists(old_output_fn):
    old_lines = gzip.open(old_output_fn, "r").readlines()
```

Just like the other programs using LogBufferFeed in this chapter, the main() function starts off by creating an instance of the class. It then tweaks the MAX_AGE setting and builds a title and tagline for the feed based on the SITE_NAME constant.

Then, the popen4() method of the popen2 module is used to execute the command specified as the value of the COMMAND constant. The output of this command is slurped in, with any lines containing the string "reboot" omitted. (These lines don't tend to provide useful user login details, so they just clutter up the feed.)

Next, an attempt is made to load up output from the last time this program ran COMMAND. As you'll see toward the end of main(), the data slurped into new_lines is always saved at the end of the program for the comparison coming up in Listing 10-22.

Listing 10-22: ch10_logins_feed.py (Part 3 of 5)

```
# If there is previous output, check for changes...
if old_lines:

    # Run a diff on the previous and current program output.
    diff_lines = [ x for x in difflib.ndiff(old_lines, new_lines) ]

    # Extract only the lines that have changed.
    changes_lines = [ x for x in diff_lines
                      if x.startswith('-') or x.startswith('+') ]
```

If there isn't any old command output to be found, this code in Listing 10-22 (and Listing 10-23) gets skipped. (This usually only happens the first time the program gets run.)

However, given old command output, the ndiff() function from difflib is used to compare the old output with the new output. The ndiff() function then returns a list of strings of its own. Wherever it finds new lines have been added with respect to the previous output, these are prepended with a "+" character. And wherever it looks like lines have disappeared between the previous command run and now, these lines are included with a "-" character prefix. And, finally, lines that appear unchanged are prefixed with a few spaces.

On the Web

To get straight to the description of ndiff() in the Python difflib documentation, visit this URL:

```
http://docs.python.org/lib/module-difflib.html#12h-913
```

So, in order to pluck out just the changes, the results of ndiff() are filtered for just the "+" and "-" lines. Then, if there actually have been any changes, it's time to build a feed entry to report on these changes. You can find this in Listing 10-23.

Listing 10-23: ch10_logins_feed.py (Part 4 of 5)

```python
# Construct and append a new entry if there were changes
if len(changes_lines) > 0:
    esc_changes_lines = [escape(x) for x in changes_lines]
    esc_diff_lines    = [escape(x) for x in diff_lines]
    entry = FeedEntryDict({
        'link'    : '',
        'title'   : TITLE_TMPL % {
            'changes' : len(changes_lines)
        },
        'summary' : SUMMARY_TMPL % {
            'changes_lines' : "<br />".join(esc_changes_lines),
            'diff_lines'    : "<br />".join(esc_diff_lines)
        }
    })
    f.append_entry(entry)
```

In Listing 10-23, if changes have been detected, an entry is built and inserted into the feed. Just about all of the action here depends on the TITLE_TMPL and SUMMARY_TMPL constants defined at the beginning in Listing 10-20.

First, the title is generated by populating TITLE_TMPL with the count of changed lines. Then, the summary is created by filling out the SUMMARY_TMPL template with the list of changes and the full ndiff() results. Notice that both of these lists are run subject to XML escaping to catch anything unsavory, and then they are joined with HTML line breaks for some crude formatting.

Finally, this entry is inserted into the feed, and the program concludes in Listing 10-24.

Listing 10-24: ch10_logins_feed.py (Part 5 of 5)

```
# Save output from the current run for use next time.
gzip.open(old_output_fn, "w").write("".join(new_lines))

# Output the current feed entries as both RSS and Atom
open(FEED_NAME_FN % 'rss', 'w').write(f.scrape_rss())
open(FEED_NAME_FN % 'atom', 'w').write(f.scrape_atom())

if __name__ == '__main_': main()
```

First up in Listing 10-24, the current command output generated for this run is saved to disk for use next time. Note the usage of the `gzip` module—this saves a little room in case the command's output is really verbose.

There's not much to it here, but if you want more information on the `gzip` module, check here:

http://docs.python.org/lib/module-gzip.html

Then, the feed is generated and written out once for each format. And, with that, this program is finished. Check out Figure 10-7 and Figure 10-8 for what this program's feed output looks like in raw form, and when viewed in an aggregator.

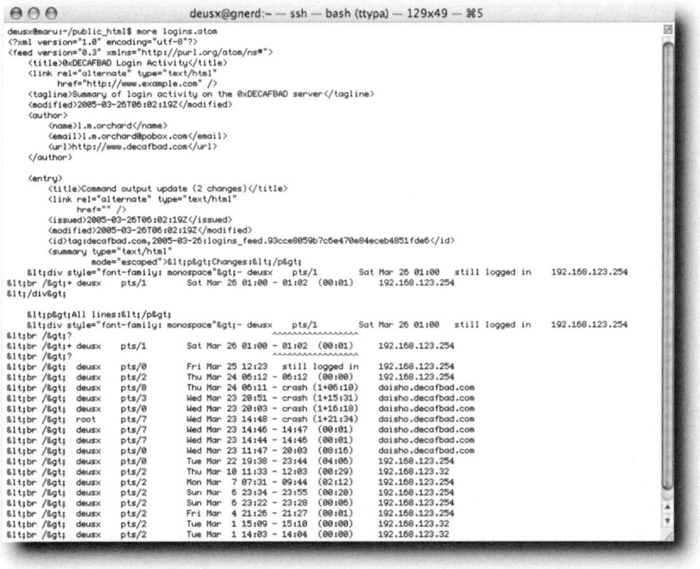

FIGURE **10-7: Atom feed output by** ch10_logins _feed.py

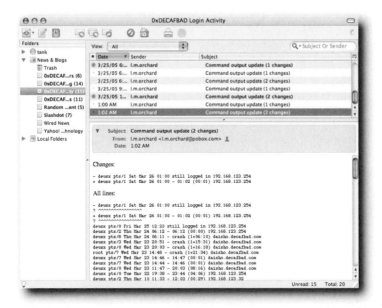

FIGURE 10-8: Viewing the logins feed in Mozilla Thunderbird

Again, although this program as presented is useful for tracking changes in login activity on a Linux box, the code here can be tweaked to track changes in the output of just about any program. So, you might want to give some thought to what other commands you might want to run on scheduled basis to track system status.

Checking Out Other Options

System monitoring via RSS and Atom feeds seems to be a relatively new idea, and finding examples of other projects taking advantage of this channel for delivering timely information seems to be all but absent from packages available as of this writing. But, there are still a few things out there worth looking into.

Tracking Installed Perl Modules

Login activity isn't the only thing worth watching on your server. Check out Ben Hammersley's little RSS hack to keep track of installed Perl modules, located here:

```
http://www.benhammersley.com/code/listing_installed_perl_
modules_in_rss.html
```

This might even be a nifty hack to think about adapting for installed Python modules or software packages installed using `apt-get` or `rpm`.

Windows Event Log Monitoring with RSS

The programs in this chapter have been pretty UNIX-centric, at least with respect to the expectation that logs are text files. But, on Windows, one of the most important system services is its central Event Log, which is most decidedly not a plain text file.

If you'd like to play around with building feeds from this, check out Greg Reinacker's work here:

`http://www.rassoc.com/gregr/weblog/archive.aspx?post=570`

And, if you'd like to stay in Python, take a look at the `win32all` extensions, particularly the `win32evtlog` module:

`http://starship.python.net/crew/mhammond/win32/`

Looking into LogMeister and EventMeister

Although not free or Open Source, at least two system-monitoring packages for Windows support RSS feeds, called LogMeister and EventMeister. They're available here:

`http://www.tlhouse.co.uk/LogMeister/`

One of the interesting features about LogMeister in particular is that it supports both consuming RSS feeds as event sources, as well as publishing log events (such as from the Windows Event Log) out as RSS feeds.

Summary

With this chapter, you should now have a decent set of tools to hack system monitoring into your feed aggregator with log analysis and tracking changes in the output of reports from programs. Again, be sure to pay attention to where you host these feeds, though. Because they're reporting on your server, you really should password-protect them as appropriate for your Web server (that is, with `.htaccess` and `.htpasswd` on Apache) and access them via HTTPS.

But, of course, these hacks are just starting points. Here are some of the things you could look into to continue improving these tools:

- The `bookmark_tailgrep()` hack used in this chapter doesn't necessarily handle log rotation well. Although it does check to see if the bookmark has gone invalid, it can miss new log lines that have appeared since the last check, but before the rotation. You might want to improve this algorithm to make it look in the rotated log to pick up the last few lines. Or, you could try scheduling tasks in synch, so that the feed generation happens before log rotation.

- In the referrer link feed generator, only partial and exact match exclusion is implemented. You could take a look at adding exclusion by regular expression for even more control.

- Instead of looking for referrer links, you could search for hits in the Apache access log that have an HTTP status code of 404—these are usually good indicators of broken links.

- Think of other programs whose output is worth watching in a feed. You could monitor the status of a server's disk space, periodically sample load and running processes, and maybe even run checks of the filesystem directory structure for modified or added files.

- Take a look at the reports you get via email now. How could you break them up in a relevant way for more bite-sized deliveries?

Next up in Chapter 11, you see how you can use feeds to track the day-to-day changes in the source code repositories for Open Source projects.

Tracking Changes in Open Source Projects

If you're reading this book, chances are you're a bit of an alpha geek. And, like many of us alpha geeks, you likely have your eye on a few Open Source projects via channels such as mailing lists and syndication feeds provided by developer blogs. If you're really on the cutting edge, you might keep up with downloads of the latest nightly builds, or grab snapshots of the latest sources to run builds of your own. And, if you're actually *defining* the cutting edge, you may even be a contributor on one or more of these projects.

In any case, you know that the place where things really happen in these projects—where bugs get squashed and features added—is in the code itself. It isn't until later, after the dust settles, that someone has time to fire off an email to the list or post on the home page documenting what's been done. By that point, one or several members of the team have likely already gone through several rounds of changes and revisions have been made to the project source.

So, the real story is found among the check-ins and commits made to a project's revision control system. If you want to put a finger right on a project's pulse, this is where to do it. Granted, keeping up with things at this level in any busy project is just like drinking from a firehose. But you're probably already guzzling from a few informational torrents in your aggregator—so, why not add a few more?

This chapter shows you how to tap into CVS and Subversion repositories to monitor the latest additions and revisions to project source code, and how to funnel those events into syndication feed entries.

Watching Projects in CVS Repositories

Although it's aging a bit and its shortcomings have been well chronicled by many, many frustrated developers, the Concurrent Versions System (CVS) is the main choice in use for tracking changes in and facilitating collaboration on a great many Open Source projects' source code.

On the Web In case you're not already intimately acquainted with CVS in daily usage, here are a few URLs you can visit to take a crash course:

```
https://www.cvshome.org/
http://cvsbook.red-bean.com/
```

To the uninitiated, CVS can seem pretty confusing and convoluted, but the essential functionality boils down to three activities:

- *Check-out*—Fresh source code files are downloaded locally from a shared repository.

- *Update*—Locally checked-out source files are updated with changes submitted to the shared repository.

- *Commit*—Changes made to locally checked-out files are submitted back to the shared repository.

Just about all of the other capabilities of CVS (and revision control systems in general) exist to deal with what happens when multiple people need to do these three things to the same source code at the same time.

Sometimes developers need to attack problems in the same neighborhoods without trampling on each others' work, and on occasion, developers need to branch off to try things without disturbing the main progress of the project. CVS manages these activities with conflict-mediating tools (with respect to source code, at least) that allow developers to record descriptions of their changes, as well as tracking the differences between one commit to the next automatically.

For the purposes of this chapter, though, your main interest lies in the chronicle of committed changes made to a project. As a team fixes bugs and progresses through project goals, CVS tracks everything—it keeps a history log of additions, updates, removals, conflicts, and whatever other activities it makes available to its users. It's from this history log that you can harvest entries for a syndication feed.

Finding a CVS Repository

One of the biggest collections of active Open Source projects in the world lives at SourceForge. At SourceForge, a single developer or a team of collaborators can request resources for their project, free of charge. There is an approval process, though the terms of use generally hinge on the project being made available under an acceptable Open Source license and that the SourceForge.net resources are used for the project's purposes and not for commercial gain.

Included among the resources offered by SourceForge is a CVS repository. This is used by quite a few of the projects hosted there—so if a project you're interested in is hosted on SourceForge.net, it's likely you'll find associated CVS activity.

For this chapter, take a look at the iPodder project mentioned back in Chapter 6—you can find the project page as shown in Figure 11-1 hosted on SourceForge.net at this URL:

```
http://sourceforge.net/projects/ipodder/
```

Visit this project page, then find and click the CVS link, which takes you to the page shown in Figure 11-2 at following URL:

```
http://sourceforge.net/cvs/?group_id=118306
```

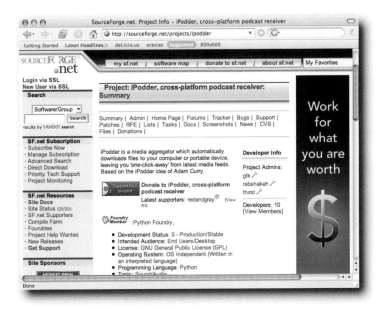

FIGURE 11-1: iPodder project page on SourceForge.net

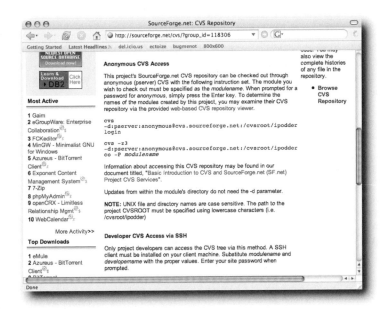

FIGURE 11-2: iPodder project CVS access details on SourceForge.net

This page gives you all the details you need to use CVS at a command line to make an anonymous check-out of the iPodder project. This consists of two commands, one to log in as an anonymous user and another to perform the checkout:

```
cvs -d:pserver:anonymous@cvs.sourceforge.net:/cvsroot/ipodder login
cvs -z3 -d:pserver:anonymous@cvs.sourceforge.net:/cvsroot/ipodder co -P iSpider
```

If you run these commands, you should end up with your own copy of the latest from the iPodder project. However, only the first line performing login is necessary for the rest of this chapter, because you're going to be making remote queries on the CVS repository.

Making Sure You Have CVS

Before you go much farther, though, you should make sure you have CVS installed. Because CVS is pretty much the *de facto* standard for revision control, you likely have it if you're working on Linux and have installed development tools.

And, if you don't have it installed, it usually only takes an `apt-get install cvs` under Debian Linux to get things up to date—your Linux distribution mileage may vary.

Under Windows, you'll need to fetch a binary package to use. My answer to just about all the UNIX-based tools used in this book for Windows is, "Install Cygwin," which you can find here:

```
http://www.cygwin.com/
```

However, you can also find Windows-native CVS tools for download here:

```
http://www.cvsnt.org/
```

If you're using Mac OS X, you should have the Developers Tools installed and you have a version of CVS available as `/usr/bin/cvs`. Unfortunately, though, this is a pretty aged version of CVS—v1.10, as of this writing in Panther—which won't quite work for this chapter. You should take a look at the Fink project for updated tools:

```
http://fink.sourceforge.net
```

In writing this section, I used version 1.11.17, so you should have at least this version or newer, for best results.

Remotely Querying CVS History Events and Log Entries

Most CVS operations require, reasonably enough, that you run them from inside a set of checked-out sources. However, a few can use the networked "pserver" protocol to query information remotely without first having downloaded anything. Luckily, two of these operations just happen to be useful for this chapter's project:

- `history`—Used to retrieve a list of recent CVS activity. This includes additions, modifications, and removals, which are the events most interesting for keeping up to date with a project in feeds.

- rlog—Used to request detailed information on a particular revision of a file in the CVS repository.

Trying Out CVS history

In lieu of making you pore over CVS documentation, I'll give you a command to try right away:

```
cvs -z3 -d:pserver:anonymous@cvs.sourceforge.net:/cvsroot/ipodder history -xMAR
-a -z +0000 -D2005-03-15
```

Here's a simple dissection of what the command does:

- cvs—The CVS command itself.

- -z3—Specifies the compression level to be used on the network.

- -d—The value of this option specifies the CVS user and repository root.

- history—This is the CVS history command.

- -xMAR—Shows modifications, additions, and removal events in the CVS history.

- -z +0000—All times reported should be in the GMT time zone.

- -D2005-03-15—Searches for CVS history events since March 15, 2005.

 In case you are, in fact, interested in poring over CVS documentation, you can find some on the CVS history operation here:

> https://www.cvshome.org/docs/manual/cvs-1.11.19/cvs_16.
> html#SEC138

The output from this command should appear something like what's shown in Figure 11-3. This is a pretty raw output format, but it packs a lot of information into each line. These are some relevant elements that appear:

- Type of event

- Event time stamp

- User responsible for the event

- Revision of the file affected

- Filename

- Path within the repository

Trying Out CVS rlog

Next, you can check out the CVS rlog command, with an invocation like the following:

```
cvs -z3 -d:pserver:anonymous@cvs.sourceforge.net:/cvsroot/ipodder rlog -r1.150
iSpider/iPodderGui.pyw
```

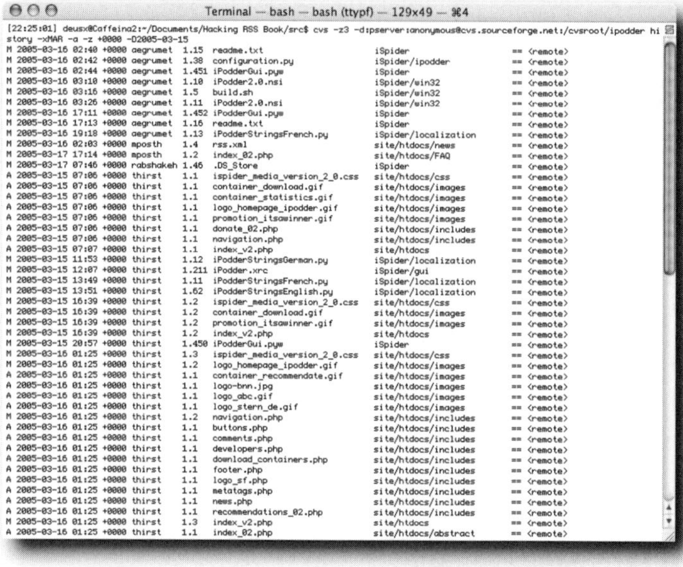

Figure 11-3: CVS history output from the iPodder project

Some things should look familiar in this command, but here's a dissection:

- cvs—The CVS command itself.

- -z3—Specifies the compression level to be used on the network.

- -d—The value of this option specifies the CVS user and repository root.

- rlog—This is the CVS rlog command.

- -r1.150—Asks for details on revision 1.150.

- iSpider/iPodderGui.pyw—This is the path and filename in the repository.

On the Web You can find documentation about the CVS rlog operation here:

```
https://www.cvshome.org/docs/manual/cvs-1.11.19/cvs_16.
html#SEC144
```

Again, output from this command is shown in Figure 11-4. This time things are a bit more suitable for human consumption, so I won't go into a detailed explanation. The part of greatest interest in this chapter appears toward the end of the output—namely, the log entry description.

```
000              Terminal — bash — bash (ttypf) — 129x49 — ⌘4
[20:40:49] deusx@Caffeina2:~/Documents/Hacking RSS Book/src$ cvs -z3 -d:pserver:anonymous@cvs.sourceforge.net:/cvsroot/ipodder rl
og -r1.150 iSpider/iPodderGui.pyw

RCS file: /cvsroot/ipodder/iSpider/iPodderGui.pyw,v
head: 1.452
branch:
locks: strict
access list:
symbolic names:
        v2_0: 1.452
        v_2_rc3: 1.424
        v_2_rc2: 1.390
        v_2_rc1: 1.384
        v_2_beta_3: 1.376
        v_2_beta_2: 1.354
        v_2_beta_1_1: 1.294
        v_2_beta_1: 1.291
        v1_1_4: 1.123
        v1_1_3: 1.118
        v1_1_2: 1.118
        v1_1macfix: 1.109.0.2
        v1_1: 1.109
        v1_1b3: 1.97
        v1_1b2: 1.90
        v1_1_0o0: 1.87
        v1_0_0: 1.34
keyword substitution: kv
total revisions: 453;    selected revisions: 1
description:
----------------------------
revision 1.150
date: 2004/11/27 01:42:15;   author: aegrumet;  state: Exp;  lines: +1 -0
More work on integrating the tree
============================================================================
[20:40:57] deusx@Caffeina2:~/Documents/Hacking RSS Book/src$ ▌
```

FIGURE 11-4: CVS `rlog` output on a file from the iPodder project

---

> **Note**
>
> If you happen to get an error message such as, "Warning: the rlog command is deprecated," when you try the previous command, this means that your version of CVS is really outdated.
>
> You can find out what version you have with `cvs --version`. In this book, I'm using CVS 1.11.17. For example, if it reports something like version 1.10, you could be using the version that comes with Mac OS X as `/usr/bin/cvs`.
>
> In this case, you may want to check out the Fink project (`http://fink.sourceforge.net/`) for updated tools on Mac OS X, such as CVS.

Automating Access to CVS History and Logs

Now that you have some acquaintance with making queries to remote CVS repositories for history events and log entries, you can work toward automating things and parsing the output from the CVS command.

Rather than spending much more time on preamble, you can start writing a new reusable module named `cvslib.py` with the code in Listing 11-1.

Listing 11-1: cvslib.py (Part 1 of 6)

```python
#!/usr/bin/env python
"""
cvslib.py

Common parts for use in querying CVS repositories.
"""
import sys, os
import time, calendar
from popen2 import popen4

CVS_BIN   = '/sw/bin/cvs'

def main():
    PROJECT  = (len(sys.argv) > 1) and sys.argv[1] or 'ipodder'
    CVS_ROOT = ":pserver:anonymous@cvs.sourceforge.net:/cvsroot/%s" % \
               PROJECT

    client = CVSClient(CVS_ROOT, cvs_bin=CVS_BIN)

    events = client.history()
    print '\n'.join(['%(event)s %(revision)s %(path)s' % x
            for x in events[:5]])
    print
    print client.rlog('1.54', 'site/htdocs/index.php').description
```

So far, Listing 11-1 just defines a main() function to test out the rest of this module. When run as a program, main() accepts the short name of a SourceForge project or, if none is given, it defaults to iPodder. Next, it creates a CVSClient instance. With this object, it calls the history() method and prints some information on the first few events returned. Then, it attempts to look up some log information on a version of a file in the project and prints out the description.

Speaking of CVSClient, you can start defining it with the code in Listing 11-2.

Listing 11-2: cvslib.py (Part 2 of 6)

```python
class CVSClient:
    """
    Interface around bits of CVS functionality.
    """

    def __init__(self, root, cvs_bin='/usr/bin/cvs'):
        """
```

```
Initialize the client object with a CVS root and
executable path.
"""
self.root    = root
self.cvs_bin = cvs_bin
```

First up in `CVSClient` is a definition of the `__init__()` method, which stashes away a CVS repository root and the path to a CVS executable. By default, the path to the executable is `/usr/bin/cvs`, but if you have installed CVS elsewhere, you'll want to change this. For example, if you're using Mac OS X and have installed a newer version of CVS using Fink, it will appear at `/sw/bin/cvs`.

Continue on to Listing 11-3 for code that starts actually using CVS.

Listing 11-3: cvslib.py (Part 3 of 6)

```
def _cvs(self, rest):
    """
    Execute a given CVS command, return lines output as a result.
    """
    cmd = "%s -z3 -d%s %s" % (self.cvs_bin, self.root, rest)
    (sout, sin) = popen4(cmd)
    return sout.readlines()

def rlog(self, revision, path):
    """
    Query CVS repository log entries for given revision and path.
    """
    cmd = "rlog -r%s %s" % (revision, path)
    return CVSLogEntry(self._cvs(cmd))
```

The definition of the `_cvs()` method in Listing 11-3 provides a general wrapper for running the CVS executable. It accepts a partial CVS command in the parameter `rest`, and uses this to construct a full CVS command invocation using the object's binary path and repository root. It then uses `popen4()` from the `popen2` module to actually execute the command. The lines output from this command are captured and returned.

Next is the definition of the `rlog()` method, which constructs an `rlog` command invocation for a given revision and path in the repository. The lines returned from the `_cvs()` method executing this command are used in creating a `CVSLogEntry` object, which will be explained shortly.

Move on to Listing 11-4, which defines a slightly more complex CVS command.

Listing 11-4: cvslib.py (Part 4 of 6)

```
DEFAULT_HISTORY_TIME = (7 * 24 * 60 * 60) # 1 week

def history(self, since=None, event_types="MAR"):
    """
    Query CVS repository for a list of recent events, defaults to
    last week of commit events.
    """
    # If no time for since given, calculate a default.
    if since is None:
        since = time.time() - self.DEFAULT_HISTORY_TIME

    # Build & execute the CVS history command, wrapping each
    # line of the results with history event objects.  Return
    # the sorted list.
    cmd = "history -x%s -a -z +0000 -D'%s'" % \
        (event_types,
         time.strftime('%Y-%m-%d', time.localtime(since)))
    try:
        events = [CVSHistoryEvent(x) for x in self._cvs(cmd)]
        events.sort()
        return events
    except:
        # Most common exception stems from no history events
        # available for time range.  Should try to account for
        # others though.
        return []
```

Listing 11-4 provides the definition of the `history()` method, which encapsulates the CVS history operation. It accepts two optional parameters, those being a time from which to start the event query and a list of event types to search for. When no values are supplied, the default behavior is to search for modifications, additions, and removals within the last week.

The history command invocation is constructed via template, using the same sorts of options you used earlier in this chapter. Then, this command is executed using the `_cvs()` method, and the lines returned are each used to create a list of `CVSHistoryEvent` objects.

Because this is a bit of a quick-and-dirty hack, note that there's only a half-hearted attempt here to check for errors, opting simply to punt and return no events when things go pear-shaped. The most common issue that happens is that no events are returned—if there's nothing to be found by the query, CVS reports "No records selected." This will throw an exception in the course of creating a `CVSHistoryEvent` object.

In Listing 11-5, you'll find the definition of the `CVSLogEntry` class.

Listing 11-5: cvslib.py (Part 5 of 6)

```
class CVSLogEntry:
    """
    Encapsulate a parsed CVS log entry.
    """
    def __init__(self, lines):
        """Parse CVS log entry and initialize the object"""
        self.full_entry  = ''.join(lines)
        self.description = ''

        # Parse through the lines of the log entry, capturing just the
        # description for now.
        in_description = False
        for line in lines:
            if line.startswith('-----'): in_description = True
            elif line.startswith('====='): in_description = False
            elif in_description:
                self.description = '%s%s' % (self.description, line)

    def __getitem__(self, name):
        """Facilitate dictionary-style access to attributes."""
        return getattr(self, name)
```

Instances of the CVSLogEntry class encapsulate the results of a CVS rlog command. This is done in the __init__() method, where the lines output by the rlog command are parsed.

In this implementation, however, only the description portion of the rlog output is extracted and the rest is tossed. You might want to further refine the parsing in this method, but a description will suffice for feed entries. And, once the object has been created from the parsed data, the __getitem__() method allows dictionary-style access to the object's attributes.

After this comes the definition of the CVSHistoryEvent class, in Listing 11-6.

Listing 11-6: cvslib.py (Part 6 of 6)

```
class CVSHistoryEvent:
    """
    Encapsulate a parsed CVS history event line.
    """
    HISTORY_EVENTS = {
        "M" : "Commit",
        "A" : "Addition",
        "R" : "Removal",
    }
```

Continued

Listing 11-6 *(continued)*

```python
    def __init__(self, line):
        """Parse the CVS event line into object attributes"""
        (evt, tm, dt, tz, usr, rev, fn, dn) = line.split()[:8]

        tm_tup = \
            time.strptime("%s %s" % (tm, dt), "%Y-%m-%d %H:%M")

        self.path        = '%s/%s' % (dn, fn)
        self.user        = usr
        self.revision    = rev
        self.event       = evt
        self.event_label = self.HISTORY_EVENTS.get(evt, evt)
        self.time_tup    = tm_tup
        self.time        = calendar.timegm(tm_tup)

    def __cmp__(self, other):
        """Facilitate reverse-chron order in lists."""
        return cmp(other.time, self.time)

    def __getitem__(self, name):
        """Facilitate dictionary-style access to attributes."""
        return getattr(self, name)

if __name__ == '__main__': main()
```

Again, the CVSHistoryEvent class implements an __init__() method that parses output from the CVS command. In this case, a single line is passed into the initializer, which splits up the parts of the history event line into its component parts. These are then used to populate the object with a file path, user name, revision, event type, and time stamp.

Special attention is given to the event type, mapping it to a more readable label as defined in the class constant HISTORY_EVENTS. Also, the timestamp is parsed and converted into a tuple, which is then converted into a time as seconds. This will make this data more easily handled when building feed entries.

Finally, the __cmp__() method is useful in sorting lists of CVSHistoryEvent objects, and the __getitem__() method provides dictionary-style access to object attributes.

This concludes the CVSHistoryEvent class, as well as the cvslib module. If you'd like, now is a good time to try running it to see the test code in main() working. This should produce output like Figure 11-5.

FIGURE 11-5: Example `cvslib` test output

Scraping CVS History and Log Entries

Now that you have some code in place to encapsulate CVS history and `rlog` operations and parse their results, you can start building a feed scraper that uses this module. Jump on into Listing 11-7 for the start of a new program, named `ch11_cvs_history_scraper.py`.

Listing 11-7: ch11_cvs_history_scraper.py (Part 1 of 4)

```python
#!/usr/bin/env python
"""
ch11_cvs_history_scraper.py

Build a feed from recent commit history queries
from a remote CVS repository.
"""
import sys
from urllib import quote
from cvslib import CVSClient
from scraperlib import Scraper, FeedEntryDict

CVS_BIN   = '/sw/bin/cvs'
```

Continued

Listing 11-7 *(continued)*

```python
def main():
    """
    Given an argument of 'atom' or 'rss' on the command line,
    produce an Atom or RSS feed.
    """
    project = (len(sys.argv) > 2) and sys.argv[2] or 'ipodder'

    cvs_root = \
        ":pserver:anonymous@cvs.sourceforge.net:/cvsroot/%s" % project
    cvs_client = CVSClient(cvs_root)

    scraper = CVSScraper(cvs_client)

    scraper.LINK_TMPL = \
        "http://cvs.sourceforge.net/viewcvs.py/%s/" % project + \
        "%(path)s?rev=%(revision)s&view=auto"

    scraper.TAG_PREFIX = 'decafbad.com,2005-03-20:%s' % project

    scraper.FEED_META['feed.title'] = \
        "SourceForge CVS changes for '%s'" % project
    scraper.FEED_META['feed.link']    = \
        "http://%s.sourceforge.net" % project
    scraper.FEED_META['feed.tagline'] = ""

    if len(sys.argv) > 1 and sys.argv[1] == 'rss':
        print scraper.scrape_rss()
    else:
        print scraper.scrape_atom()
```

The `main()` function defined in Listing 11-7 is a bit more complex than the typical definition used to drive scrapers in this book. The reason for this is to try to keep all the SourceForge-specific code out of the `CVSScraper` class you're about to define. Although this chapter is using SourceForge for its large collection of projects using CVS, it's not the only place using CVS repositories. So, there's no reason to clutter up `CVSScraper` itself with special cases for SourceForge.

That said, the first thing `main()` does is to construct a CVS repository root using the name of a SourceForge project given as the second argument on the command line, defaulting to iPodder. This is then used to construct a `CVSClient` instance, which is, in turn, used to create an instance of the `CVSScraper` class.

The `CVSScraper` instance is then tweaked a bit, to tailor it for the SourceForge project. There's a Web application named ViewCVS made available for every SourceForge project, which allows

Web-based exploration of CVS repositories. So, for every file path and revision in the project, a link can be constructed to ViewCVS, allowing you to build a decent LINK_TMPL template for feed entry links.

 ViewCVS is a pretty flexible and widely used package for providing Web access to CVS and Subversion repositories. You might want to check it out for use in your own projects. Here's the URL to the ViewCVS home page, on SourceForge of course:

```
http://viewcvs.sourceforge.net/
```

Next, the project name is used to build an entry GUID prefix, as well as some feed metadata values like the title and link. Finally, the selected feed format is generated usng the first argument on the command line, defaulting to Atom.

Now that the main() function is defined, you can start in on the CVSScraper class in Listing 11-8.

Listing 11-8: ch11_cvs_history_scraper.py (Part 2 of 4)

```
class CVSScraper(Scraper):
    """
    Using a CVSClient object, scrape a feed from recent history
    events.
    """
    TAG_PREFIX  = 'decafbad.com,2005-03-20:cvs_scraper'
    STATE_FN    = 'cvs_scraper_state'
    TITLE_TMPL  = \
        "%(event_label)s (r%(revision)s) by %(user)s: %(path)s"
    LINK_TMPL   = ""

    def __init__(self, client):
        """Initialize with the given CVS client."""
        self.client = client
```

The CVSScraper class starts off with a few configuration constants:

- TAG_PREFIX—Default value used for constructing feed entry GUIDs.

- STATE_FN—Filename for scraper state database.

- TITLE_TMPL—String template to be used in building feed entry titles, meant to be populated using a CVSHistoryEvent object.

- LINK_TMPL—String template to be used in building feed entry links, meant to be populated using a CVSHistoryEvent object (which is blank by default).

After the constants comes the definition of the __init__() function, which stores away a CVSClient instance in the object on initialization. Now, keep going on to Listing 11-9, which starts the definition of the produce_entries() method.

Listing 11-9: ch11_cvs_history_scraper.py (Part 3 of 4)

```
def produce_entries(self):
    """
    Build feed entries based on queried CVS history events.
    """
    events  = self.client.history()

    entries = []
    for event in events[:self.MAX_ENTRIES]:
        # Build a GUID for this entry
        cvs_id   = '%(path)s:%(revision)s' % event
        entry_id = 'tag:%s%s' % (self.TAG_PREFIX, quote(cvs_id))

        # Attempt to grab an existing state record for this
        # entry ID.
        if not self.state_db.has_key(entry_id):
            self.state_db[entry_id] = {}
        entry_state = self.state_db[entry_id]

        # If this entry's state doesn't already have a description
        # cached, query CVS for the log entry and grab the it.
        if not entry_state.has_key('description'):
            log_entry = self.client.rlog(event.revision,
                                          event.path)
            entry_state['description'] = log_entry.description
        description = entry_state['description']
```

The produce_entries() method in Listing 11-9 starts off by making a query for history events using the CVSClient object.

Once a list of events has been fetched, each event is processed to build feed entries. Note that the list of events is limited to the number specified by MAX_ENTRIES. Because you'll be doing further CVS queries based on these events, there's no sense in processing more than will be used anyway.

In the processing loop, a GUID for the entry is built. This comes handy in the next bit, where the scraper state database and CVS rlog operations are used together to manage feed entry descriptions.

To get more information into feed entries, you can use the rlog query to fetch further details about the revision affected by the history event under consideration. However, making a query for each CVS history event can start to slow things down and waste some effort and resources, especially if this scraper gets run regularly on a schedule—it will constantly run into events that it's seen before.

Well, this sounds like a job for the scraper state database. The rest of the code in Listing 11-9 caches descriptions fetched via CVS `rlog` for the revision and file found in the current history event. So, the next time this same event is seen again, the state database is consulted, rather than re-running the query.

To do this caching, an attempt is made to find a record in the state database for the current entry GUID. If none exists, a new empty dictionary is created. Next, the entry record is searched for a cached description which, if found, is used in the construction of the entry. If none exists, only then is an `rlog` query made using the `CVSClient` for the current event's revision and file. Once fetched, the description from the `rlog` query is stashed away in the entry's state database record for use next time around.

Listing 11-10 wraps things up with the actual construction of a feed entry.

Listing 11-10: ch11_cvs_history_scraper.py (Part 4 of 4)

```python
        # Build the feed entry based on the CVS event
        # and log entry
        entry = FeedEntryDict(init_dict={
            'id'          : entry_id,
            'title'       : self.TITLE_TMPL % event,
            'link'        : self.LINK_TMPL % event,
            'author.name' : event.user,
            'modified'    : event.time,
            'issued'      : event.time,
            'summary'     : '<pre>%s</pre>' % description
        }, date_fmt=self.date_fmt)

        # Append the completed entry to the list, and save
        # the entry state.
        entries.append(entry)
        self.state_db[entry_id] = entry_state

    return entries

if __name__ == '__main__': main()
```

Building a feed entry in Listing 11-10 is pretty easy at this point, because all the work has been done up front in defining the GUID and fetching the description. The CVS history event is used to populate the entry title and link templates. The event's user is mapped to the entry's author name, and the event's timestamp is mapped to the entry's issued and modified times. And, finally, the description is stuffed into the entry summary, wrapped in HTML <pre> tags for a little hackish formatting. (You may want to play with this bit.)

The entry is wrapped up, appended to the end of the accumulated list, and the entry's state record is saved. Finally, this list is returned and the `produce_entries()` method is concluded—and that also finishes up this program.

Running the CVS History Scraper

You should now have a working feed scraper that can harvest history events from CVS repositories, specifically tailored to dig up news from SourceForge projects. Again, by default, this program queries events for the iPodder project, so when you run it you should get output similar to Figure 11-6 and Figure 11-7.

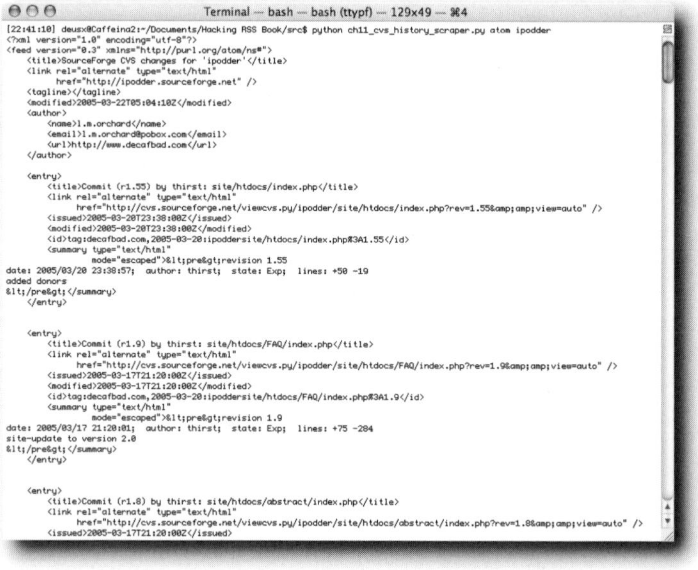

FIGURE 11-6: Scraping an Atom feed from iPodder CVS history

Additionally, this program accepts the "short name" of a project, which you can most easily find used in links to the project page on SourceForge. For example, here's the URL to Azureus, a Java-based BitTorrent client in development on SourceForge:

```
http://sourceforge.net/projects/azureus/
```

From this URL you can pluck out the short name of "azureus" and supply it to the CVS scraper with an invocation like the following:

```
# python ch11_cvs_history_scraper.py atom azureus
```

This command should give you a feed like the one shown in Figure 11-8.

FIGURE 11-7: Scraping an RSS feed from iPodder CVS history

FIGURE 11-8: Scraping an Atom feed from Azureus CVS history

Watching Projects in Subversion Repositories

As mentioned at the beginning of the chapter, CVS has its share of critics and frustrated users. So, many developers have been exploring alternatives. Among the handful or so of CVS replacements getting recent attention, a package named Subversion has been picking up a lot of steam.

 On the Web You can find the Subversion home page here:

        http://subversion.tigris.org/

If you'd like to read a free book about Subversion, check out *Version Control with Subversion* here:

        http://svnbook.red-bean.com/

Subversion has a lot of buzz going for it, because it addresses many of the gripes developers have had with CVS. It introduces things like atomic commits to prevent partially checked-in changes that extend across several files, and directory versioning to help track changes to a project that go beyond just source code changes.

Also, Subversion can be layered atop some other technologies such as HTTP and WebDAV, giving it the ability to piggyback on things such as Apache's compression, authentication, and authorization modules. And, it's worth mentioning that a fresh code base can do a lot to draw the interest of hackers tired of the same old thing.

However, because Subversion is a newer beast, it's not yet as ubiquitous as CVS—so it's likely you'll need to install the client executables on your machine. You can tinker around with installing your own server, as well, but that's not necessary for this chapter. If you're using Debian Linux, or have installed Fink under Mac OS X, your installation process might be as simple as typing this command:

```
apt-get install svn-client
```

If you're on Windows or some other Linux platform, check out the following URL for downloads of the command-line binaries:

```
http://subversion.tigris.org/project_packages.html
```

Finding a Subversion Repository

As of this writing, SourceForge does not yet offer Subversion repositories as a service, so you'll need to look elsewhere to find projects using it. The managers of SourceForge have mentioned that research into offering Subversion hosting is on their agenda, so this may change in the near future.

But for now, I'll point you toward one of my favorite projects that's made the transition from CVS to Subversion. It's Colloquy, an Internet Relay Chat (IRC) client written for Mac OS X. Take a look at this project's developer page shown in Figure 11-9, found at this URL:

```
http://colloquy.info/developers.html
```

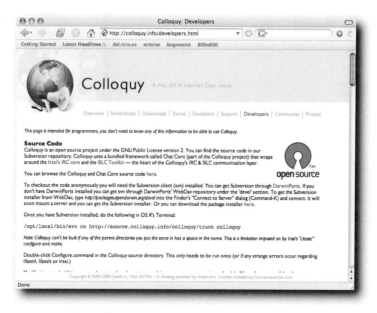

FIGURE 11-9: The Colloquy project's developer page

This page mentions the following command for use in checking out a copy of the Colloquy sources:

```
svn co http://source.colloquy.info/colloquy/trunk colloquy
```

As you can probably tell, the developers of Subversion have tried to make their command-line client work a lot like CVS. In this command, the Subversion repository is identified by a URL rather than the `pserver` protocol repository path used to find iPodder in the previous section.

Again, as with CVS earlier in this chapter, note that you don't really have to check out all source code for Colloquy to build a scraper—you really just need to make a note of the repository URL, which is:

```
http://source.colloquy.info/colloquy/trunk
```

Remotely Querying Subversion Log Entries

If you want to get a view of a week in the Colloquy project, try the following command, whose output is shown in Figure 11-10:

```
svn log -v -r'{2005-03-14}:{2005-03-21}'
http://source.colloquy.info/colloquy/trunk
```

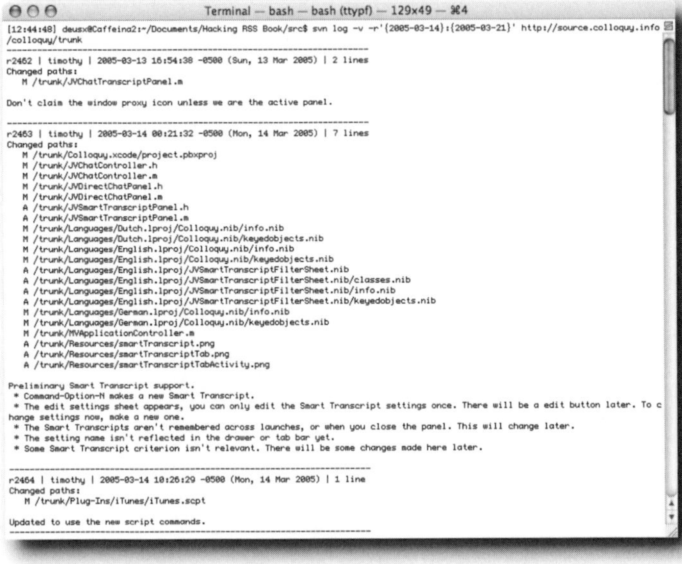

FIGURE 11-10: A week in the life of Colloquy

Here's a breakdown of the options used in this command:

- svn—The Subversion command-line client itself.
- log—This is the Subversion log command.
- -v—Selects verbose log output, which includes the paths of changed files.
- rlog—This is the CVS rlog command.
- -r—Searches for history events in a given range of dates or revisions.
- The final argument to the command is the repository URL.

On the Web You can find a full description of the Subversion log command here:

```
http://svnbook.red-bean.com/en/1.0/ch03s06.html#
svn-ch-3-sect-5.1
```

From the way things worked for CVS, you be might starting to think about how to parse this text output. Well, there's one more option you can throw into this mix to make things a little easier (see Figure 11-11):

```
svn log --xml -v -r'{2005-03-14}:{2005-03-21}'
http://source.colloquy.info/colloquy/trunk
```

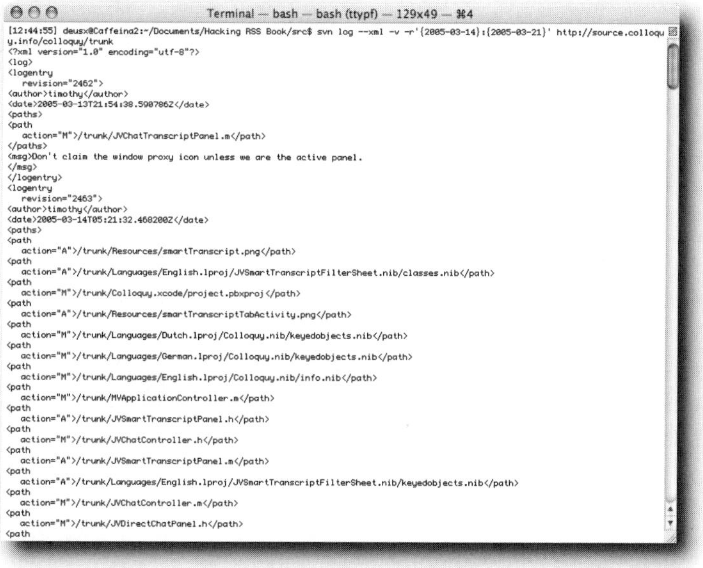

FIGURE 11-11: A week in the life of Colloquy, XML style

With this flag added, all of the output from the log command is presented as XML. So, rather than trying to deal with an odd line-based text format, you can call upon some of the XML scraping techniques presented in Chapter 9.

Scraping Subversion Log Entries

Rather than spending time building a parser for Subversion output, you can just go straight into building the feed scraper using the XPath tools from 4Suite you played with in Chapter 9. Listing 11-11 provides you with the beginning of a new scraper program, named ch11_svn_log_scraper.py.

Listing 11-11: ch11_svn_log_scraper.py (Part 1 of 6)

```
#!/usr/bin/env python
"""

ch11_svn_log_scraper.py

Scrape a feed from log events for a Subversion repository
"""
import sys, time, calendar
```

Continued

Listing 11-11 *(continued)*

```
from urllib import quote
from urlparse import urljoin, urlparse
from popen2 import popen4
from Ft.Xml.Domlette import NonvalidatingReader
from scraperlib import FeedEntryDict, Scraper

SVN_TITLE = "Colloquy"
SVN_URL   = 'http://source.colloquy.info/colloquy/'

def main():
    """
    Given an argument of 'atom' or 'rss' on the command line,
    produce an Atom or RSS feed.  Also optionally accepts a URL
    to a Subversion repository.
    """
    svn_title = (len(sys.argv) > 2) and sys.argv[2] or \
                SVN_TITLE
    svn_uri   = (len(sys.argv) > 3) and sys.argv[3] or SVN_URL
    scraper   = SVNScraper(svn_uri)

    scraper.FEED_META['feed.title'] = \
        "Subversion history for %s" % svn_title
    scraper.FEED_META['feed.link']  = svn_uri

    if len(sys.argv) > 1 and sys.argv[1] == 'rss':
        print scraper.scrape_rss()
    else:
        print scraper.scrape_atom()
```

A slew of modules are imported at the beginning of Listing 11-11, but nothing too exotic. After the imports, the URL for the Colloquy repository is set as the value of a configuration constant named SVN_URL.

Next comes the definition of the main() function, which drives the scraper. This function will accept three optional arguments from the command line:

- Feed format
- Project title
- Project Subversion repository URL

If these aren't supplied, the default is to produce an Atom feed for the Colloquy project repository.

Moving on, the definition of the SVNScraper class begins in Listing 11-12.

Listing 11-12: ch11_svn_log_scraper.py (Part 2 of 6)

```
class SVNScraper(Scraper):
    """
    Base class for XPath-based feed scrapers.
    """
    SVN_BIN    = '/usr/bin/svn'
    LOG_PERIOD = 7 * 24 * 60 * 60 # (1 week)
    STATE_FN   = 'svn_scraper'

    def __init__(self, url):
        """Initialize with URL to Subversion repository"""
        self.url = url

        # Come up with a tag prefix based in svn URL and
        # current time
        (scheme, addr, path, params, query, frag) = \
            urlparse(url)
        ymd = time.strftime("%Y-%m-%d", time.gmtime())
        self.TAG_PREFIX = "%s,%s:" % (addr, ymd)
```

The definition of SVNScraper in Listing 11-12 starts off with the following class constants:

- SVN_BIN—Sets to the path where the Subversion command-line client is found.

- LOG_PERIOD—Defines a timespan (in seconds) that will be used in working out how far back to look in log history queries, set to one week in the previous code.

- STATE_FN—Provides a filename for this scraper's state database.

Note Be sure that you have the right value for SVN_BIN—the location in the previous listing is probably okay for many Linux installations, but it's likely to be different on Mac OS X or Windows or in any situation where you've installed Subversion yourself by hand. Just to be safe, you might want to try the command which svn to locate the exact path to your copy of the Subversion client.

After the class constants comes the definition of the __init__() method, which stows away the repository URL and uses the domain name from that URL and today's date to build a prefix for use in generating GUIDs in feed entries.

Moving right along, Listing 11-13 begins the central produce_entries() method.

Listing 11-13: ch11_svn_log_scraper.py (Part 3 of 6)

```
def produce_entries(self):
    """Use xpaths to extract feed entries and entry attributes."""
    entries = []

    # Iterate through the parts identified as log entry nodes.
    for entry_node in self.svn_log().xpath('//logentry'):

        # Extract a few basic elements from the log entry
        revision = self.xpval(entry_node, './@revision')
        author  = self.xpval(entry_node, './author/text()')
        msg     = self.xpval(entry_node, './msg/text()')
```

With Listing 11-13, the `produce_entries()` method is pretty simple so far, and looks a lot like what you did in Chapter 9. This scraper almost could have been a subclass of the `XPathScraper` from that chapter, but a few kinks in this process make it just as easy to do it this way.

A utility method named `svn_log()` is used to execute the Subversion query and parse its results, to which an XPath is applied to find all the individual log entries. Each of these log entry nodes is processed and mapped onto `FeedEntryDict` objects. But first, a little bit of preparation is in order, starting with the simple extraction of the revision, author, and change description text. After this, things get a little more involved in Listing 11-14.

Listing 11-14: ch11_svn_log_scraper.py (Part 4 of 6)

```
        # Extract and parse the date for the log entry
        date_str   = self.xpval(entry_node, './date/text()')
        date_tup   = time.strptime(date_str[:19],
                                    '%Y-%m-%dT%H:%M:%S')
        entry_time = calendar.timegm(date_tup)

        # Extract and process the list of affected file paths
        paths_changed = []
        for path_node in entry_node.xpath('./paths/path'):
            action = self.xpval(path_node, './@action')
            path   = self.xpval(path_node, './text()')
            paths_changed.append("%s %s" % (action, path))

        entry_id = 'tag:%s%s' % (self.TAG_PREFIX, revision)
```

Because `FeedEntryDict` objects require datestamps in seconds, a few lines of code are spent extracting the current log entry node's date value and converting it first to a time tuple and then to a time in seconds. After this has been completed, all of this entry's affected paths are extracted.

And, finally in Listing 11-14, a GUID for this entry is generated using the TAG_PREFIX and the current revision number. The produce_entries() method is concluded in Listing 11-15.

Listing 11-15: ch11_svn_log_scraper.py (Part 5 of 6)

```
        # Build the feed entry based on log entry information
        entry = FeedEntryDict(init_dict={
            'id'       : entry_id,
            'title'    : 'Revision %s by %s' % (revision, author),
            'link'     : self.url,
            'issued'   : entry_time,
            'modified' : entry_time,
            'summary'  : "<pre>%s\n\nFiles affected:\n%s</pre>" %
                         (msg, '\n'.join(paths_changed))

        }, date_fmt=self.date_fmt)
        entries.append(entry)

    return entries
```

Again, because just about everything was prepared in previous listings, the construction of a feed entry in Listing 11-15 is pretty straightforward. The GUID, link, and datestamps map over directly, and the title is built from the revision and author name. A little more complicated is the construction of the entry summary, which includes the log entry message, as well as a list of file paths affected by the revision.

With the completion of the current feed entry, it gets appended to the list. And, after processing all log entry nodes, this list of feed entries is returned. This program is concluded in Listing 11-16, with the definition of a few utility methods.

Listing 11-16: ch11_svn_log_scraper.py (Part 6 of 6)

```
def svn_log(self):
    """
    Make a log query to the Subversion repository,
    return parsed XML document of query output.
    """
    # Calculate the start and end times for log query
    now  = time.time()
    then = now - self.LOG_PERIOD

    # Format the start/end times for use in svn command
    start_time = time.strftime("%Y-%m-%d",
                               time.localtime(then))
    end_time   = time.strftime("%Y-%m-%d",
                               time.localtime(now))
```

Continued

Listing 11-16 *(continued)*

```
        # Build the svn command invocation, execute it,
        # and return the XML results in a parsed document.
        cmd = '%s log --xml -v -r "{%s}:{%s}" %s' % \
            (self.SVN_BIN, start_time, end_time, self.url)
        (sout, sin) = popen4(cmd)
        return NonvalidatingReader.parseStream(sout, self.url)

    def xpval(self, node, xpath):
        """Given a node and an xpath, extract all text
           information"""
        vals = [x.nodeValue for x in node.xpath(xpath)
                if x.nodeValue]
        return " ".join(vals)

if __name__ == '__main__': main()
```

The `svn_log()` method defined in Listing 11-16 is used to construct and execute an invocation of the Subversion client. It builds the start and end times based on the `LOG_PERIOD` time span, with the range starting in the past and ending at the present date. A string template is used to construct the command invocation, using the path to the binary, the dates, and the repository URL. Then, the `popen4()` from the `popen2` module is used to execute the command and trap the output. Finally, this output is parsed with 4Suite's `NonvalidatingReader` and the resulting document object is returned.

Note that there's no error checking going on here—if there's an issue in getting XML-formatted log entries from the Subversion repository, the whole program halts with an exception. You may want to play around here with more graceful exits in case of problems, but as a hack this works okay.

The final method in the class, `xpval()`, is just a convenience method used to wrap up the extraction of text values from a given XPath search applied to a node.

With the end of this method, the `SVNScraper` class is finished, and so is the program.

Running the Subversion Log Scraper

If everything's come together correctly, you now have a feed scraper you can apply to Subversion repositories. You can run this program with two optional arguments: the first to define feed type and the second to supply the URL to a Subversion repository. If you don't supply either, it defaults to scraping an Atom feed from the Colloquy repository.

Take a look at Figure 11-12 and Figure 11-13 to see some output produced by this program.

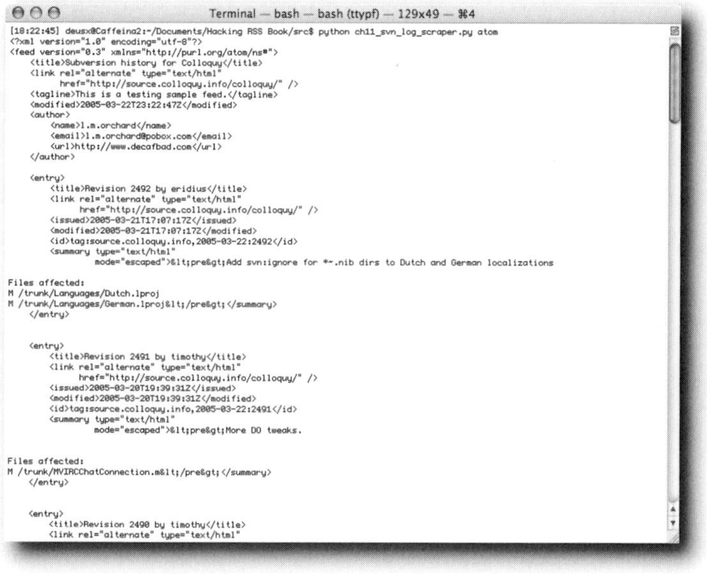

FIGURE 11-12: Scraping an Atom feed from Colloquy's history

FIGURE 11-13: Scraping an RSS feed from Colloquy's history

For the sake of completeness, I'll toss in another of my favorite Open Source projects that uses Subversion. Here's the URL to the repository hosting the source code for Growl, a global notification system for Mac OS X:

```
http://src.growl.info/growl/trunk
```

You can use this URL with the Subversion scraper like so:

```
# python ch11_svn_log_scraper.py atom Growl http://src.growl.info/growl/trunk
```

This should give you output as shown in Figure 11-14.

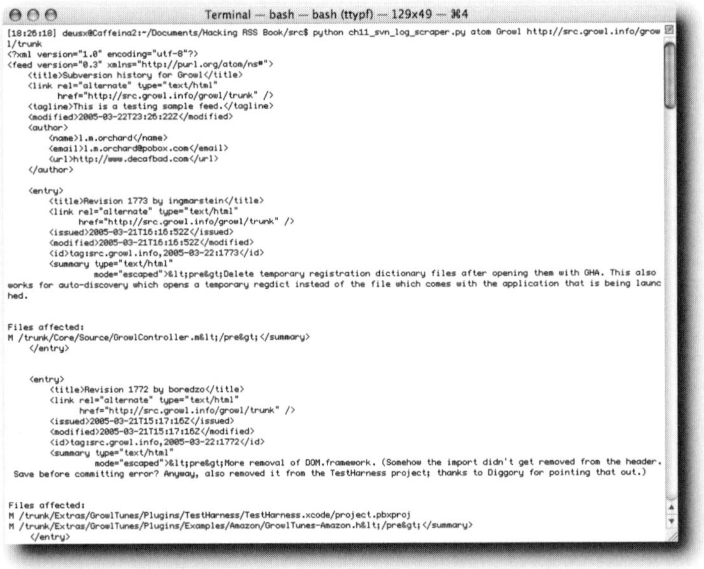

FIGURE 11-14: Scraping an Atom feed from Growl's history

> **Note** If you see any errors related to XML parsing during the course of this program, it's likely that there's something amiss with the XML output from the SVN client or that the SVN client location in SVN_BIN is incorrect. There's no effort in this program to catch or deal with these things, so that's one of the improvements you can make at some point.

Checking Out Other Options

The scrapers presented in this chapter are, of course, not the only options out there. Here are a few other projects and hacks you might want to check out.

Generating RSS Feeds via CVS Commit Triggers

Don't like scraping the output of the CVS history and `rlog` commands? If you control your CVS repository, try hooking feed generation straight into the commit process with this Python Cookbook recipe:

`http://aspn.activestate.com/ASPN/Cookbook/Python/Recipe/310322`

The gist of this recipe is that CVS provides hooks where you can specify programs to be executed when a commit is completed. Typically, this has been used for things like posting to a newsgroup or sending off messages to mailing lists, but pushing entries into a syndication feed is a great usage for these hooks as well. However, unlike the scraper in this chapter, this solution requires that you are in control of the CVS repository.

Considering WebSVN

If you have a Subversion server of your own, you might want to check out WebSVN, found here:

`http://websvn.tigris.org/`

WebSVN is a PHP Web application that offers quite a few browser-based access options for your Subversion server, including RSS feeds built from the repository history. No scraper needed here, but this does appear to require administrative access to a Subversion repository.

Using XSLT to Make Subversion Atom Feeds

If the scraper in this chapter seems a bit too dirty of a hack and you're more of an XSLT fan, check out Norman Walsh's XSLT stylesheet for transforming Subversion client XML output into an Atom feed. The stylesheet is available here:

`http://norman.walsh.name/style/svnlog2atom.xsl`

Also, be sure to read this blog entry about the stylesheet:

`http://norman.walsh.name/2005/02/12/svnfeed`

Using the CIA Open Source Notification System

According to its home page, CIA is "a system for tracking Open Source projects in real-time." Check it out here:

`http://cia.navi.cx/`

CIA is a sort of über-aggregator of happenings in Open Source project development—projects feed CIA from sources like CVS and Subversion commits, and CIA pools all the events together in one place. You can subscribe to RSS feeds for projects here, as well as track what individual developers are doing, and more.

Summary

This chapter presented you with feed scrapers usable with both CVS and Subversion revision control repositories, giving you tools to track software projects on an almost obsessive level, watching every change as it rolls in. And, unlike some other solutions out there, these scrapers do their work remotely, without needing administrative access to the repository, and without actually needing to have any sources checked out locally.

Of course, these programs are really just the beginning. Here are a few suggestions for improvement:

- Just listing out the files affected in a change committed doesn't *really* tell you what happened. Think about what you would need to add to a CVS or Subversion feed scraper to get automatic diffs inserted into feed entries for each revision.

- Think about how you might combine these feeds with the instant messenger feed bot from Chapter 4 to get a more immediate or conversational grasp on project changes.

- Neither the CVS nor Subversion scrapers make much effort at all to cope with errors—if something goes wrong during the scraping process (which is usually rare), things break down without much grace. You might want to take a look at making this more robust.

- The CVS scraper only tracks modifications, additions, and removals, but the CVS history log records quite a few events beyond these three. You may be interested in tracking these if, for example, you are a contributor on a project and really want to keep track.

Next in Chapter 12, you see the inverse of Chapter 3: turning email into syndication feeds. With these new hacks, you'll be able to route messages from IMAP and POP3 email inboxes into syndication feeds, pulling mailing lists and newsletters into your favorite aggregator.

Routing Your Email Inbox to Feeds

In Chapter 3, you built feed aggregators with the capability to send new entries off to your email inbox, both in newsletter-style reports and as individual messages. In this chapter, you're going to use the feed generation and scraping tools you built in Chapter 9, along with a few handy modules from the Python library, to funnel your email messages into syndication feeds.

If you wanted to, you could use the tools in this chapter to keep up with everything that arrives in your email inbox right alongside all your other feed subscriptions. Of course, your feed aggregator is most likely missing most of the basic tools an email client provides (for example, composing new email messages and replies to messages you've received). So, you might not want to entirely abandon your everyday inbox just yet.

However, it still might be useful to move *some* of your email into feeds. In this chapter, you'll be able to selectively filter email messages from your inbox, based on just about whatever criteria you choose. You might have a few announcement-only mailing list subscriptions or get email newsletters sent to you periodically—basically, things that show up in your inbox meant for reading, but not necessarily calling for any sort of response. So, why not shift these kinds of messages out of your cluttered inbox and into your feed reader?

Fetching Email from Your Inbox

First of all, you'll need to get access to your inbox. Of course you can already do this from your favorite email client—but now you're going to do it from a Python program. The Python standard library comes with a set of modules for dealing with email messages, servers, and protocols. In particular, two of the most useful for this chapter are poplib and imaplib.

Accessing POP3 Mailboxes

Although POP3 (which stands for Post Office Protocol, Version 3) is one of the oldest protocols used for accessing email mailboxes, and often considered obsolete, it's still just about the most widespread method offered by ISPs and email providers for access to your inbox. For the most part, POP3 is used to fetch messages from an email server to be stored locally, after which they are deleted from the remote server.

Deletion is optional, and the messages can be left to remain on the server, but that's about where the sophistication of POP3 ends. You can't manage any folders or collections on the server, archive any messages, or do anything other than listing, fetching, and downloading messages. But, for the most part, this feature set is all you need for casual email use.

On the Web In the Python standard library, the `poplib` module deals with the POP3 protocol and mailboxes that support it. You can read all about it in the Python library reference documentation located here:

```
http://docs.python.org/lib/module-poplib.html
```

And, if you'd happen to like to read about the POP3 standard itself, check out RFC 1725:

```
http://www.faqs.org/rfcs/rfc1725.html
```

To jump right into things, take a look at Listing 12-1, which features an example borrowed from the Python documentation that fires up `poplib` and prints out all the messages in a POP3 mailbox, without deleting them.

Listing 12-1: ch12_poplib_example.py

```
"""
ch12_poplib_example.py

Program which fetches and prints out all your
email waiting at a POP3 server.
"""
import poplib

HOST   = "mail.example.com"
PORT   = 110
USER   = "your_account_name"
PASSWD = "your_password"

M = poplib.POP3(HOST, PORT)
M.user(USER)
M.pass_(PASSWD)
numMessages = len(M.list()[1])
for i in range(numMessages):
    for j in M.retr(i+1)[1]:
        print j

M.quit()
```

You'll need to replace the values in the initial configuration constants with the settings from your own email account, which you can probably dig out of the preferences for your usual email program if you already know where to find them. After you do that, you'll see some output such as what's shown in Figure 12-1.

FIGURE 12-1: Sample run of the `poplib` example program

There is one bit of caution, though: If you have a lot of email waiting on your server, be ready to halt the program, because it will print *all* of your email if you let it. You may even want to tweak this program to stop after the first few messages.

Now, if you've never looked under the hood of your email before, this all probably looks like a lot of somewhat nonsensical spew. But every part of it makes sense to something somewhere along the path that email took to get delivered. Usually, your email client hides most of those headers from you, because all you usually care about are maybe the message subject, its date, and the body content. And, as you'll see in a little bit, you can let Python take care of most of this stuff, too.

Accessing IMAP4 Mailboxes

The Internet Mail Access Protocol version 4 (or IMAP4) is a bit newer than POP3 and much more fully featured. You can list, fetch, and download messages with IMAP4. But you can also leave all your messages on the server, organize them into folders, as well as keep track of a number of informational flags (such as whether a message is new, deleted, read, or even if it's an in-progress draft reply, among other things).

Whereas POP3 use tends to be focused on downloading and managing messages on your local machine, the IMAP4 model centers around a connected client/server model. The messages may be cached locally, but they're largely managed on the remote IMAP4 server, and you can access them from a variety of computers and locations. You're not limited to the machine from where you last downloaded mail.

On the Web The `imaplib` module from Python's standard library handles access to IMAP4 mailboxes, and is documented here in Python's library reference:

> `http://docs.python.org/lib/module-imaplib.html`

IMAP4rev1 is also described in RFC 2060:

> `http://www.faqs.org/rfcs/rfc2060.html`

Although usage does differ a bit from that of POP3, take a look at Listing 12-2 for another example program along the same lines as that found in Listing 12-1.

Listing 12-2: ch12_imaplib_example.py

```
"""
ch12_imaplib_example.py

Program which fetches and prints out all your
email waiting at a IMAP4 server.
"""
import imaplib

HOST   = "mail.example.com"
PORT   = 143
USER   = "your_account_name"
PASSWD = "your_password"

M = imaplib.IMAP4(HOST, int(PORT))
M.login(USER, PASSWD)
M.select()
numMessages = M.search(None, "UNDELETED")[1][0].split()
for i in numMessages:
    print M.fetch(str(i), "RFC822")[1][0][1]

M.close()
M.logout()
```

Again, if you try it out, be ready to stop it if you have a lot of email waiting, because it will fetch and display every message. This program's output should be identical to the previous program's, if you happen to have both POP3 and IMAP4 access to the same mailbox. But, just for the sake of completeness, Figure 12-2 shows a sample.

The program in Listing 12-2 glosses over the majority of IMAP4 features, in order to be easily compared to the POP3 example. In addition, you won't be taking advantage of many of those advanced features in this chapter. However, that doesn't preclude you from exploring them on your own and figuring out how you might improve on the code presented here later.

```
Terminal — bash — bash (ttypf) — 129x49 — ⌘4
[21:02:44] deusx@Caffeina2:~/Documents/Hacking RSS Book/src$ python ch12_imaplib_example.py
Return-Path: <SRS@=CfiB=PX=lists.ofdoom.com=ipm-friends-bounces@bounce2.pobox.com>
Delivered-To: deusx@deus-x.dyndns.org
Received: (qmail 24973 invoked from network); 9 Jan 2005 00:55:36 -0000
Received: from gretel.pobox.com (208.58.1.197)
    by tank2.decofbad.com with SMTP; 9 Jan 2005 00:55:36 -0000
Received: from boggle.pobox.com (boggle.pobox.com [208.58.1.193])
    by gretel.pobox.com (Postfix) with ESMTP id 757F54919F7
    for <deusx@deus-x.dyndns.org>; Sat, 8 Jan 2005 18:10:40 -0500 (EST)
Received: from boggle (localhost [127.0.0.1])
    by boggle.pobox.com (Postfix) with ESMTP id 027091029D7
    for <deusx@deus-x.dyndns.org>; Sat, 8 Jan 2005 18:10:40 -0500 (EST)
Received-SPF: pass (boggle.pobox.com: domain of ipm-friends-bounces@lists.ofdoom.com designates 216.29.181.214 as permitted sende
r)
X-SPF-Guess: pass (seems reasonable for ipm-friends-bounces@lists.ofdoom.com to mail through 216.29.181.214)
Received: from overmind.ofdoom.com (ofdoom.com [216.29.181.214])
    by boggle.pobox.com (Postfix) with ESMTP id CBCCF102705
    for <deus_x@pobox.com>; Sat, 8 Jan 2005 18:10:39 -0500 (EST)
Received: (qmail 85128 invoked from network); 8 Jan 2005 23:10:56 -0000
Received: from unknown (HELO overmind.ofdoom.com) (216.29.181.214)
    by overmind.ofdoom.com with SMTP; 8 Jan 2005 23:10:56 -0000
Delivered-To: mailman-ipm-friends@lists.ofdoom.com
Received: (qmail 85059 invoked from network); 8 Jan 2005 23:10:53 -0000
Received: from unknown (HELO pop-7.dnv.wideopenwest.com) (64.233.207.25)
    by overmind.ofdoom.com with SMTP; 8 Jan 2005 23:10:53 -0000
Received: from balthasar.digitalangel.com (d149-67-20-56.try.wideopenwest.com
    [67.149.56.20])
    by pop-7.dnv.wideopenwest.com (8.12.8/8.12.8) with ESMTP id
    j08N0VMD027670
    for <ipm-friends@lists.ofdoom.com>; Sat, 8 Jan 2005 17:16:35 -0500
Message-Id: <5.1.2.0.0.20050108180709.0de93dc0@ofdoom.com>
X-Sender: macross@ofdoom.com
X-Mailer: QUALCOMM Windows Eudora Version 6.1.2.0
Date: Sat, 08 Jan 2005 18:09:19 -0500
To: ipm-friends@lists.ofdoom.com
From: Bob Perye <macross@digitalangel.com>
Mime-Version: 1.0
Content-Type: text/plain; charset="us-ascii"; format=flowed
X-Antivirus: avast! (VPS 0501-1, 01/07/2005), Outbound message
X-Antivirus-Status: Clean
X-Virus-Scanned: ClamAV 0.80/655/Fri Jan  7 07:54:13 2005
    clamav-milter version 0.80j on pop-7.dnv.wideopenwest.com
X-Virus-Status: Clean
Subject: [IPM-Friends] LOST -M- FOUND?
X-BeenThere: ipm-friends@lists.ofdoom.com
X-Mailman-Version: 2.1.5
Precedence: list
Reply-To: DJs and peanut gallery IPM people <ipm-friends@lists.ofdoom.com>
List-Id: DJs and peanut gallery IPM people <ipm-friends.lists.ofdoom.com>
```

FIGURE 12-2: Sample run of the `imaplib` example program

There is something to notice here. Regardless of the protocol used to fetch them, the email messages retrieved are all constructed in exactly the same way. This means that (at least with respect to POP3 and IMAP4, by way of `poplib` and `imaplib`) you should be able to freely interchange email protocols, given that you wrap a common interface around each of them. This will come in handy shortly.

Handling Email Messages

Speaking of how email messages are constructed, it's time to take a look at the Internet Message Format (RFC 2822) and Multipurpose Internet Mail Extensions (or MIME).

 On the Web   If you want to read about the Internet Message Format and MIME from the original standards documents, the following RFCs may help enlighten you:

```
http://www.faqs.org/rfcs/rfc2822.html
http://www.faqs.org/rfcs/rfc2045.html
```

You may already know what RFC 2822 and MIME are and what they're used for. However, if this is your first time reading about these standards, you got a taste in Figure 12-1 and Figure 12-2. RFC 2822 establishes the basic structure of email messages: the envelope and its content. The envelope provides information about the contents in the form of headers, and the content represents the message itself.

Messages following the specifications in RFC 2822 are flat structures consisting of a number of envelope headers and some content data—and the content data is defined as plain old US-ASCII. The purpose of MIME is to provide richness and structure to the message content, specifying how character sets beyond ASCII can be used, as well as how to build and encode nested structures of text and multimedia content. In a way, MIME turns an email message into a sort of miniature filesystem.

In Python, this family of standards can all be handled with the `email` package. Take a look at Listing 12-3 for an enhanced version of the `poplib` example that, instead of printing out entire messages, just prints the subject lines from the parsed messages.

On the Web You can find further reading on the email package here:

```
http://docs.python.org/lib/module-email.html
```

Listing 12-3: ch12_poplib_email_example.py

```python
"""
ch12_poplib_email_example.py

Program which fetches and prints out subject lines of your
email waiting at a POP3 server.
"""
import poplib, email

HOST   = "mail.example.com"
PORT   = 110
USER   = "your_account_name"
PASSWD = "your_password"

M = poplib.POP3(HOST, PORT)
M.user(USER)
M.pass_(PASSWD)
numMessages = len(M.list()[1])
for i in range(numMessages):
    msg_txt = "\n".join(M.retr(i+1)[1])
    msg     = email.message_from_string(msg_txt)
    print msg['Subject']

M.quit()
```

The only change needed from the first example program to start using the `email` package is a simplification of the inner loop to concatenate all the lines of a message into a single string, which is then fed to `email.message_from_string()`. This utility method of the `email` package parses and decodes a message constructed using RFC 2822 and MIME, returning an `email.Message` object. This object, among other things, allows dictionary-style access to the envelope header values (such as the "Subject" header printed out previously). Figure 12-3 shows the sort of output in which this program results.

FIGURE 12-3: Sample run of the `poplib` + `email` example program

With the `email` package, you can easily access any envelope header or content part in the message. It handles all the parsing and navigation of the message structure, as well as decoding and extraction of multimedia and binary parts.

Building Feeds from Email Messages

At this point, you've had an introduction (albeit brief) to most of the tools you'll need to start producing feeds from messages sitting in your inbox. With either `imaplib` or `poplib`, you can fetch messages. And with the `email` package, you can then parse those messages and access their envelopes and contents.

From the other end of things, you can revisit Chapter 9 for the feed generation tools collected in the `scraperlib` module (both the `Scraper` and `FeedEntryDict` classes will prove useful). The only remaining piece still missing is to find a way to bridge between `email.Message` objects and `FeedEntryDict` objects to pull everything together.

To get started, create a new module file named `mailfeedlib.py` and consult Listing 12-4 for the opening lines.

Listing 12-4: mailfeedlib.py (Part 1 of 9)

```
"""
mailfeedlib

Utilities for generating feeds from mail messages.
"""
import sys, time, shelve, md5, re
from urllib import quote
from urlparse import urlparse
import email, email.Utils
from xml.sax.saxutils import escape
from scraperlib import FeedEntryDict, Scraper
```

Many of the modules imported in the beginning of `mailfeedlib.py` have been used more than once in previous chapters, but the `email` and `email.Utils` modules are new.

Building Generic Mail Protocol Wrappers

As previously mentioned, the examples showing how to handle communications with both POP3 and IMAP4 mail servers result in the same message formats being fetched. So, you can easily interchange the two if you build wrappers around them that provide the same common interface.

Well, that's what you're about to do. Take a look at Listing 12-5 for the complete definition of `POP3Client`, a wrapper for `poplib` usage.

Listing 12-5: mailfeedlib.py (Part 2 of 9)

```
import poplib

class POP3Client:
    """
    Generic interface to fetch messages from a POP3 mailbox.
    """
    def __init__(self, host='localhost', port=110,
                       user=None, passwd=None):
        """Initialize POP3 connection details."""
        self.host   = host
        self.port   = port
        self.user   = user
        self.passwd = passwd

    def fetch_messages(self, max_messages=15):
        """
```

```
    Fetch messages up to the maximum, return
    email.Message objects.
    """
    # Connect to the POP3 mailbox
    mailbox = poplib.POP3(self.host, self.port)
    mailbox.user(self.user)
    mailbox.pass_(self.passwd)

    # Look up messages, establish a window for fetching
    nums = range(len(mailbox.list()[1]))
    end_pos   = len(nums)
    start_pos = max(0, end_pos - max_messages)

    # Fetch and accumulate Messages
    msgs = []
    for i in nums[start_pos:end_pos]:
        try:
            msg_txt = "\n".join(mailbox.retr(i+1)[1])
            msg     = email.message_from_string(msg_txt)
            msgs.append(msg)
        except KeyboardInterrupt:
            raise
        except:
            pass

    # Log out of mailbox
    mailbox.quit()

    return msgs
```

You should notice a lot of similarity between Listing 12-5 and Listing 12-3. The POP3Client class is pretty much the same code, just reworked into the form of an object, and given some more robust error handling. Well, actually, it's more like error ignorance, but this is just to try to keep things running in the case of any small hiccups. You may want to explore the issue of error handling to greater detail and come up with code to actually be attentive to errors.

The other major change made for this class (with respect to the original example code) is that a limit to the number of messages downloaded has been imposed. In case you happen to have hundreds or thousands of older messages sitting on the server, this limit should ensure that you only fetch the top few newest available.

So, all of this culminates in the single core method of this class: fetch_messages(). This method connects to the POP3 server, fetches a number of messages, parses them into email.Message objects, and returns the list of messages found.

The next class definition in Listing 12-6, for IMAP4Client, implements an identical interface for use with IMAP4 mail servers.

Listing 12-6: mailfeedlib.py (Part 3 of 9)

```python
import imaplib

class IMAP4Client:
    """
    Generic interface to fetch messages from a IMAP4 mailbox.
    """
    def __init__(self, host='localhost', port=110,
                       user=None, passwd=None):
        """Initialize IMAP4 connection details."""
        self.host   = host
        self.port   = port
        self.user   = user
        self.passwd = passwd

    def fetch_messages(self, max_messages=15):
        """
        Fetch messages up to the maximum, return email.Message objects.
        """
        # Connect to the IMAP4 mailbox
        mailbox = imaplib.IMAP4(self.host, int(self.port))
        mailbox.login(self.user, self.passwd)
        mailbox.select()

        # Look up undeleted messages, establish a window for fetching
        nums = mailbox.search(None, "UNDELETED")[1][0].split()
        end_pos   = len(nums)
        start_pos = max(0, end_pos - max_messages)

        # Fetch and accumulate Messages
        msgs = []
        for i in nums[start_pos:end_pos]:
            try:
                msg_txt = mailbox.fetch(str(i), "RFC822")[1][0][1]
                msg     = email.message_from_string(msg_txt)
                msgs.append(msg)
            except KeyboardInterrupt:
                raise
            except:
                pass

        # Log out of mailbox
        mailbox.close()
        mailbox.logout()

        return msgs
```

Again, a lot of similarities exist between `IMAP4Client` in Listing 12-6 and the example in Listing 12-2. This is the IMAP4 fetching code adapted to work as an object, and with use of `email.message_from_string()` rolled in. As in `POP3Client`, the `fetch_messages()` method of this class attempts to fetch the top recent messages, parses them, and returns the list of `email.Message` objects that result from parsing.

This is where the interchangeability of these two classes comes in: `fetch_messages()` exists in both of them, and its usage is identical for each. So, code that will need to download email messages doesn't need to care about which protocol is used to access your inbox. You can just swap in an instance of either of these two classes.

Generating Feed Entries from Mail Messages

Now you get to the heart of this chapter: You're going to build `MailScraper`, a `Scraper` subclass that employs one of the email protocol classes to build `email.Message` objects from your inbox, constructing `FeedEntryDict` objects based on those messages, and then generating your choice of Atom or RSS feed as a result.

Continue to Listing 12-7 to catch the opening act of the `MailScraper` class definition.

Listing 12-7: mailfeedlib.py (Part 4 of 9)

```
class MailScraper(Scraper):
    """
    Use an email client to download messages on which to base
    a feed.
    """
    TAG_DOMAIN  = "mail.example.com"
    STATE_FN    = "mail_scraper_state"

    ATOM_ENTRY_TMPL = """
        <entry>
            <title>%(entry.title)s</title>
            <author>
                <name>%(entry.author.name)s</name>
            </author>
            <link rel="alternate" type="text/html"
                href="%(entry.link)s" />
            <issued>%(entry.issued)s</issued>
            <modified>%(entry.modified)s</modified>
            <id>%(entry.id)s</id>
            <summary type="text/html"
                    mode="escaped">%(entry.summary)s</summary>
        </entry>
    """

    def __init__(self, client, max_messages=15):
        """Initialize with a given mail client."""
        self.client = client
        self.max_messages = max_messages
```

There's one thing that's a bit "hackish" and odd going on in this new `Scraper` subclass, right from the start. For the most part, RSS and Atom feeds are intended for use as pointers to and representations of Web-based resources—and those resources all have URLs. Although RSS feeds can contain entries that do not have links, the Atom feed standard requires that entries have at least one link attached.

However, Web-based mail services notwithstanding, email messages are not included in URL space—so you're going to have to fake it a bit. The `TAG_DOMAIN` constant defined at the start of `MailScraper` can pretty much be anything, and it will be used for the construction of stand-in URLs for Atom feeds. Also, it will be used in the generation of feed-entry GUIDs.

Another thing to notice about the beginning of `MailScraper`, though, is that there's a new `ATOM_ENTRY_TMPL` string template. This revised template now offers a spot for a named author, which will be filled with the "From" header extracted from email messages.

The final thing to say about this listing is that the `__init__()` object initializer accepts an instance of one of the two previously defined mail server access classes, as well as a maximum number of messages to be downloaded for any session, which will later be passed along to the mail client object when `fetch_messages()` is called.

Moving on, Listing 12-8 provides the definition of two new methods, `produce_entries()` and `filter_messages()`.

Listing 12-8: mailfeedlib.py (Part 5 of 9)

```
def produce_entries(self):
    """
    Fetch messages using email client, return a list of
    entries.
    """
    msgs = self.client.fetch_messages\
        (max_messages=self.max_messages)
    filtered_msgs = self.filter_messages(msgs)
    return self.entries_from_messages(filtered_msgs)

def filter_messages(self, msgs):
    """Return filtered list of messages for inclusion in
        feed."""
    return msgs
```

Both of the methods shown in Listing 12-8 are fairly simple.

The `produce_entries()` method overrides the core method used by `Scraper` to build `FeedEntryDict` objects before using them to populate feed templates. In `MailScraper`, `produce_entries()` uses the email client instance given at initialization to fetch a number of email messages.

These messages are then passed through `filter_messages()`, which has the opportunity to preprocess and sift through the fetched messages. This filtered list is then handed to the `entries_from_messages()` method (defined shortly), which does the work of building `FeedEntryDict` instances.

Note that previous definition of `filter_messages()` does nothing. This is intended to be easily overridden in subclasses that can implement their own message filtering rules.

And now, if you check out Listing 12-9, you'll see the definition for `entries_from_messages()`.

Listing 12-9: mailfeedlib.py (Part 6 of 9)

```python
def entries_from_messages(self, msgs):
    """
    Given a list of email.Message, attempt to build a list
    of FeedEntryDict objects
    """
    entries = []

    for msg in msgs:

        entry = FeedEntryDict(date_fmt = self.date_fmt)

        # Set the 'dummy' link for the entry from feed.link
        entry['link']  = self.FEED_META['feed.link']

        # Use message Subject for entry title.
        entry['title'] = msg.get('Subject', '(Untitled)')

        # Use From header for entry author email.
        entry['author.name'] = msg['From']

        # Convert message Date into seconds, use for modified
        # and issued
        msg_time_raw = email.Utils.parsedate(msg['Date'])
        msg_time     = time.mktime(msg_time_raw)
        entry.data['modified'] = entry.data['issued'] = msg_time

        # Summarize the email for the entry.
        entry['summary'] = self.extract_summary_from_message(msg)

        # Get a GUID for this entry.
        entry['id']      = self.build_guid_for_message(msg, entry)

        # Stuff the new entry into the running list.
        entries.append(entry)

    # Finally, return what was accumulated
    return entries
```

The `entries_from_messages()` method accepts a list of `email.Message` objects and iterates through them, building a list of `FeedEntryDict` objects based on those messages.

Each entry's link attribute is based on the stand-in URL used for the feed, because email messages are not identified by URLs. The message's "Subject" header is used for the entry's title and its "From" header is used for the entry's named author attribute.

And, the message's "Date" header is parsed into a tuple using the `email.Utils.parsedate()` utility method, then converted into seconds using `time.mktime()`. This value is then used to supply modification and issued timestamps for the entry.

Wrapping up this method, the entry's GUID is set as the result of the `build_guid_for_message()` method, and the entry's summary attribute is extracted from the message using `extract_summary_from_message()`.

Continue on to Listing 12-10 for the `build_guid_for_message()` method definition.

Listing 12-10: mailfeedlib.py (Part 7 of 9)

```
def build_guid_for_message(self, msg, entry):
    """
    Build an entry GUID from message ID or hash.
    """
    # Try getting the Message-ID, construct an MD5 hash
    # if unavailable.
    if msg.has_key('Message-ID'):
        msg_id = msg['Message-ID']
    else:
        m = md5.md5()
        m.update(entry.data['title'])
        m.update(entry.data['summary'])
        msg_id = m.hexdigest()

    # Build an entry GUID from message ID or hash.
    entry_time = entry.data['modified']
    ymd = time.strftime("%Y-%m-%d", time.gmtime(entry_time))
    id_quote = quote(msg_id)
    return "tag:%s,%s:%s" % (self.TAG_DOMAIN, ymd, id_quote)
```

Many email messages have a "Message-ID" header upon which you can base a GUID for the feed entry—however, some do not. The `build_guid_for_message()` method attempts to cover the bases by first looking for a "Message-ID" header and using its value, or if that's missing, it falls back to generate an MD5 hash of the entry's title and summary text. Then, it builds and returns a tag URI based upon the ID fetched or generated.

Moving forward, things get interesting with the `extract_summary_from_message()` method defined in Listing 12-11, where the MIME structures of the email message are explored to build summary content for the feed entry.

Listing 12-11: mailfeedlib.py (Part 8 of 9)

```python
def extract_summary_from_message(self, msg):
    """
    Walk through all the message parts, collecting content
    for entry summary.
    """
    body_segs = []
    parts = [ m for m in msg.walk() if m.get_payload(decode=True) ]
    for part in parts:

        # Grab message type, character encoding, and payload
        content_type = part.get_content_type()
        charset      = part.get_content_charset('us-ascii')
        payload      = part.get_payload(decode=True)

        # Sometimes, parts marked as ISO-8859-1 are really CP1252.
        # see: http://manatee.mojam.com/~skip/python/decodeh.py
        if charset == 'iso-8859-1' and \
                re.search(r"[\x80-\x9f]", payload) is not None:
            charset = 'cp1252'
```

Because MIME-based email messages can contain nested levels of contained content, the `walk()` method of an `email.Message` object is provided to recursively visit every message part. If you remember using it, this `walk()` method is akin to the `os.walk()` function used back in Listing 7-2 in Chapter 7, albeit simpler in use.

In the code from Listing 12-11, a list comprehension is used to filter a walk through the message with `get_payload()` to retrieve only those parts that contain payloads, sort of equivalent to the files in the structure as opposed to the directories or folders.

Next, each part filtered out of the message structure is visited. Three things for each message part are important and extracted here:

- `content_type`—This is an identification of what sort of content is contained by this message part, as defined by MIME (that is, text/plain, text/html, image/jpeg, and so on).

- `charset`—This is what encoding was used for the content of this message part (that is, US-ASCII, UTF8, ISO-8859-1).

- `payload`—This is the actual data making up the content for this message part.

And, there's one little hack here, covering for an issue I ran into across many email messages from Windows users. Sometimes, when an email message identifies parts as using ISO-8859-1 for their encoding, they've actually been encoded as CP1252, and the previous regular expression detects this situation.

This will all become important in Listing 12-12, where the payload content is decoded into Unicode strings.

Listing 12-12: mailfeedlib.py (Part 9 of 9)

```
    # Only handle text parts here.
    if content_type.startswith('text/'):

        # Decode the email payload into Unicode, wimp out
        # on errors.
        try:
            body = payload.decode(charset, 'replace')
        except Exception, e:
            body = "[ ENCODING ERROR: %s ]" % e

        # Include this text part wrapped in <pre> tags
        # and escaped
        if content_type == 'text/plain':
            body_segs.append(u"<pre>\n%s</pre>" % escape(body))

    return "\n<hr />\n".join(body_segs)
```

The code in Listing 12-12 concludes the extract_summary_from_message() method, as well as the MailScraper class.

The only message content type handled here is text/plain. Any other images or media types, as well as HTML email payloads (of type text/html), are ignored. One improvement you may wish to explore with this part of the code is how to best handle HTML-formatted email content.

An attempt is made here to decode message payload data into a Unicode string, using the reported character set. However, even with the little hack toward the end of Listing 12-11, this code probably doesn't catch every encoding mishap, so this attempt is wrapped in a try/except block that reports errors, rather than stopping the whole feed-generation process. This is another spot where you might want to look into improving things, at least with regard to how Unicode decoding and errors are handled.

If this payload was reported as text/plain data, it is wrapped in HTML <pre> tags and appended to the list of body segments being collected. Then, after all message content parts are processed, this running list of body segments is joined into one string, with each part separated by HTML <hr /> tags.

This all combines to offer a primitive sort of formatting to summarize all the text message data found in the email message—one more area in which you can tinker and salt to taste. Finally, this summary is returned, which will be used as the summary content for an entry.

Filtering Messages for a Custom Feed

At this point, you have everything you need to start producing feeds from your email inbox—so, it's time to put it all to use. Start a new program file in your editor and call it ch12_mailing_list_feed.py. Because the results of this program depend on the contents of your particular inbox, it'll call for some tweaking, but you can start with the code in Listing 12-13.

Listing 12-13: ch12_mailing_list_feed.py (Part 1 of 2)

```python
#!/usr/bin/env python
"""
ch12_mailing_list_feed.py

Use MailScraper to produce a feed from mailing list messages
"""
import sys
from mailfeedlib import MailScraper, POP3Client, IMAP4Client

MAIL_CLIENT = POP3Client(
    host   = '127.0.0.1',
    port   = '110',
    user   = 'your_account',
    passwd = 'your_password'
)

def main():
    """
    Given an argument of 'atom' or 'rss' on the command line,
    produce an Atom or RSS feed.
    """
    scraper = FooListScraper(client=MAIL_CLIENT)

    if len(sys.argv) > 1 and sys.argv[1] == 'rss':
        print scraper.scrape_rss()
    else:
        print scraper.scrape_atom()
```

The first thing in this program you'll need to change are the values initializing the MAIL_CLIENT constant at the beginning. First, you can use either POP3Client as shown in Listing 12-13, or you can swap it for an IMAP4Client instance. Then, you'll need to supply your own server and account details in the initialization parameters for that instance.

The `main()` function should appear very familiar from the feed scraper programs you built in Chapter 9. It checks for an argument given on the command line to switch between RSS and Atom formats, before firing up an instance of `FooListScraper` to produce a feed.

Listing 12-14 provides the definition for the `FooListScraper` class.

Listing 12-14: ch12_mailing_list_feed.py (Part 2 of 2)

```
class FooListScraper(MailScraper):
    FEED_META = {
        'feed.title'        : 'My Mailing List Feed',
        'feed.link'         : 'http://www.example.com',
        'feed.tagline'      : 'This is a testing sample feed.',
        'feed.author.name'  : 'l.m.orchard',
        'feed.author.email' : 'l.m.orchard@pobox.com',
        'feed.author.url'   : 'http://www.decafbad.com',
    }

    STATE_FN    = "mylist_scraper_state"

    def filter_messages(self, msgs):
        """Return filtered list of messages for inclusion in
            feed."""
        return [ m for m in msgs
                if 'foo-list@example.com' in m.get('To','') ]

if __name__=="__main__": main()
```

The `FooListScraper` class is a `MailScraper` subclass. It defines the `FEED_META` data expected by the `Scraper` parent class, as well as a `STATE_FN`. Take a look back to Chapter 9 if you need a refresher about the purposes for these constants.

Now, the interesting part of this subclass is the `filter_messages()` method definition overriding the one defined in `MailScraper`:

In Listing 12-14, `filter_messages()` selects messages whose `To` header contain `foo-list@example.com` using a list comprehension. You can provide any implementation here that returns a list of messages, presumably based on the list of messages passed in as a parameter.

If you want to see a feed built from all of your inbox messages, go ahead and omit or comment out this method definition. However, if you would like to build a feed consisting of just messages received from a particular mailing list, or messages whose subject lines contain a specific pattern, here's where you can do it. `MailScraper` does most of the work, but this method can be overridden to provide the filter rules tailoring the list of messages included in the feed.

For example, in Listing 12-15 is an alternate implementation of `filter_messages()` that could be used to catch emails received from the `cron` process on a server.

Listing 12-15: Alternate filter_messages() Implementation

```
def filter_messages(self, msgs):
    """Return filtered list of messages for inclusion in
        feed."""
    return [ m for m in msgs
                if 'Cron ' in m.get('Subject','') ]
```

Note that you don't *have* to use a list comprehension to filter messages. It's just one of the easiest ways to do it for a simple message-selection rule. Take a look at Figure 12-4 to see some sample output from this filter in use.

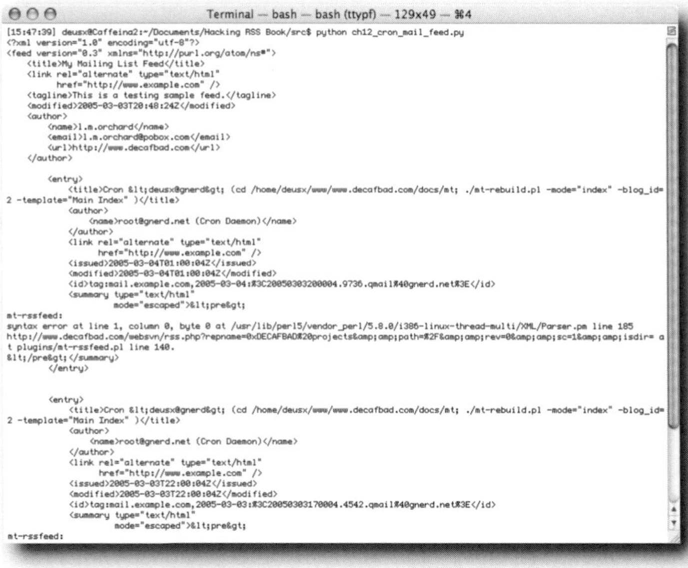

FIGURE 12-4: Atom feed built from `cron` daemon email messages

Furthermore, you can even modify the messages before passing them on, as shown in Listing 12-16.

Listing 12-16: Another alternate filter_messages() Implementation

```python
def filter_messages(self, msgs):
    """Return filtered list of messages for inclusion in feed."""
    msgs_out = []
    for m in msgs:
        if 'Cron ' in m.get('Subject',''):
            subj = m['Subject'].replace('Cron <deusx@gnerd> ','')
            m.replace_header('Subject', subj)
            msgs_out.append(m)
    return msgs_out
```

You'll probably want to check out the documentation for Python's email module, just to see all the options available to you in manipulating Message objects. Peek at Figure 12-5 to see how this filter has tweaked the subject lines of messages used in the feed.

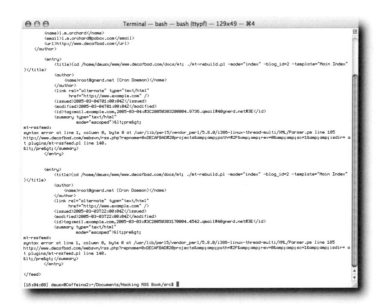

FIGURE 12-5: Atom feed built from tweaked cron daemon email messages

Although many email programs include the ability to filter and move messages into folders, as well as other actions, the expressiveness offered in these rule systems are often limited. But, with the full power of Python expressions at your disposal, you should be able to concoct whatever set of selection criteria and message-tweaking code you'd like in the filter_messages() method.

Checking Out Other Options

Of course, the tools provided in this chapter are not your only choices available if you want to turn email into feeds. Consider the following options available to you.

Checking Out MailBucket

MailBucket is a free service that can capture email to syndication feeds. Check it out here:

`http://www.mailbucket.org/`

Using MailBucket is extremely simple—just get email sent to `foobar@mailbucket.org` and subscribe to `http://www.mailbucket.org/foobar.xml` for an RSS feed where these messages will land, where the `foobar` can be just about anything you want—unless it's already been used by someone else, in which case the two will get all mixed up.

You can use MailBucket email addresses in newsletter subscription forms or when signing up for mailing lists, and instead of the emails arriving in your inbox, they'll be received and provided as a feed by MailBucket. Also, the ten latest emails will be rendered as HTML pages, thus offering something URLs in feed entries and pages to read in your browser.

There is one caveat, though. There's absolutely no guarantee of privacy on MailBucket. Although there's no catalog or listing of the feeds MailBucket provides, there's no promise that a particular feed you've created won't be discovered by someone, eventually—which may or may not be a good thing, depending on what you've used the service for.

Checking Out dodgeit

dodgeit is another free email service that, like MailBucket, offers RSS feeds built from emails sent to some arbitrary address you choose from `@dodgeit.com`. Take a look here:

`http://dodgeit.com`

One of the important differences between dodgeit and MailBucket, though, is that dodgeit has just recently begun offering the option to make a donation to password-protect a particular feed and email address to make it private.

Checking Out Gmail

If you have an account on Google's Gmail Web-based email service, you can access your inbox as an Atom feed with a subscription to a URL like the following:

`https://USER_NAME:PASSWD@gmail.google.com/gmail/feed/atom`

Note that you'll need to replace `USER_NAME` and `PASSWD` with your Gmail username and password, respectively. This feed is a little limited, though, because the links in each entry just go directly to the Gmail home page (or your inbox, if you're already logged in). And, the summaries in each entry a just contain the first sentence or so of the message. However, this feed could prove useful as a general means of keeping track of your Gmail inbox.

Summary

You should now have a pretty good idea of some things you can do to unload some of the regular clutter from your email inbox and shift it into your aggregator, where you can manage email newsletters and mailing list announcements more like every other information source to which you've subscribed. However, like most projects in this book, there's plenty of room for further improvement:

- So far, the `MailScraper` class only handles message parts of `text/plain` type. However, if you played with the MailBucket service, you'd have seen that it offers HTML versions of the latest few emails received. Why not improve `MailScraper` to include HTML content in the feed?

- How about generating HTML pages to which feed entries can link? You could even work on handling other media types such as images and file attachments to create your own alternative feed-based Web email inbox.

- The `MailScraper`, `POP3Client`, and `IMAP4Client` classes fetch email messages without deleting them. If you'd *really* like to clean out your inbox and shift messages into feeds, rework the email server classes to delete successfully processed email messages.

Coming next in Chapter 13, you see how you can access a few popular sites' Web service offerings to build syndication feeds out of search results, news items, and details tracked on products.

Web Services and Feeds

I n Chapter 9, you coaxed feed entries out of data and resources not usually fit for consumption by machines—other than human-guided Web browsers, that is. Accomplishing this feat required a set of tools ranging from blunt instruments to nimble scrapers to account for all the variations and messes found out in the wild.

But no matter how good the tools, one day's successful extraction strategy could turn into the next day's broken feed. Because you have no cooperation or assurances from whomever is providing the content, feed scraping can never be a sure thing.

Sometimes, though, the task can be a lot easier. Many sites and companies are starting to offer Web service APIs to access their applications and resources via HTTP and XML technologies. Although they can introduce issues of their own, Web services at least give you more officially sanctioned and supported means by which to interact with other people's servers and data.

This chapter shows you how you can interact with Web service APIs offered by Google, Yahoo!, and Amazon. From these three companies' popular and powerful Web offerings, you'll be able to build syndication feeds based on product and wish list updates, news keyword searches, and persistent Web index searches.

Building Feeds with Google Web Services

In the spring of 2002, Google launched what's become one of the most popular and most tinkered-with set of Web services available for public use. With the release of Google Web APIs, the company exposed its search engine functionality for use in third-party clients and applications via a SOAP-based interface.

If, for some reason, you haven't heard of SOAP Web services before now, this Wikipedia article might give you a decent starting point for further reading:

```
http://en.wikipedia.org/wiki/Simple_Object_Access_
Protocol
```

Google's Web APIs have remained free to use for developers, but through the use of per-developer assigned license keys, usage of the API is currently limited to 1,000 queries per day and 10 results returned per query. For just about all personal use, however, this limit is usually generous enough—it's just when you want to move into heavy-duty commercial use of the Google Web APIs that limits tend to get reached and issues of licensing and cost come into play. For this chapter, though, you shouldn't need to worry about the query limit.

You'll probably want to visit the Google Web APIs home page to get all the details. Here, you'll find the developer kit, documentation, and the registration form used to obtain a developer license key:

```
http://www.google.com/apis/
```

Anyway, where Google searches tie into syndication feeds is with the idea of persistent searches. Normally, when you want to find something interesting on the Web, you might go to a search engine (such as Google) and type in a few keywords to start looking. Then, days or weeks later, you might come back to the search engine and try the same keywords again, just to see if maybe there's anything new to find. Well, this can be a bit tedious and troublesome because, after all, you have to remember to keep looking for things. Why not automate this and funnel the results into your feed aggregator as they appear?

With the Google Web API and a little bit of Scraper glue, you'll be able to build persistent searches in syndication feeds that can run on a scheduled basis and repeat searches for you, supplying you with feed updates whenever something new shows up.

Working with Google Web APIs

To start working with Google Web APIs, you first need to acquire a license key—all queries to Google's Web services require one. So, hop on over to the aforementioned Google Web APIs home page and look for the "Create a Google Account" link. This page has a registration form as shown in Figure 13-1. After signing up, you'll get an email with instructions as to how to proceed to verify your address and get a license key generated, as shown in Figure 13-2.

Once you've gone through the process of signing up for a Google account, you should shortly see an email arrive in your inbox containing a new license ID. This ID is a string of letters and numbers, something like this:

```
KJNAojOIJOI2kjnkjKINUILlkmMKLASDJ8
```

Note, however, that this is just a fake example and not a valid subscription ID—you'll need to use your own.

FIGURE 13-1: Google Web APIs account creation page

FIGURE 13-2: Google Web APIs license ID is generated

The next thing you need is some way to access Google's SOAP interface from Python. Well, there just happens to not only be SOAP modules for Python, but there's also a way atop those SOAP modules to wrap Google Web APIs for convenient use. Check out the `pygoogle` package here:

`http://pygoogle.sourceforge.net/`

If you read the `pygoogle` README file, though, you'll soon see that it depends upon another package, namely the aforementioned SOAP modules, available here:

`http://pywebsvcs.sourceforge.net/`

Deeper down the dependency rabbit hole, however, you'll find that *this* package in turn requires the installation of the following two packages:

`http://pyxml.sourceforge.net/`

`http://research.warnes.net/projects/RStatServer/fpconst/`

That's the end of the chain, though, so you'll want to check out and install each of these dependencies before you're ready to move on. It's not really all that bad though, because each of these packages follows the conventional pattern for installing Python modules. That is, a set of commands for downloading and installing these packages goes something like this:

```
# curl -sO http://research.warnes.net/~warnes/fpconst/fpconst-0.7.2.tar.gz
# curl -sO http://umn.dl.sourceforge.net/sourceforge/pyxml/PyXML-0.8.4.tar.gz
# curl -sO http://umn.dl.sourceforge.net/sourceforge/pywebsvcs/SOAPpy-
0.11.6.tar.gz
# curl -sO http://umn.dl.sourceforge.net/sourceforge/pygoogle/pygoogle-
0.6.tar.gz
# ( tar -zxf fpconst-0.7.2.tar.gz; cd fpconst-0.7.2; sudo python setup.py
install )
# ( tar -zxf PyXML-0.8.4.tar.gz; cd PyXML-0.8.4; sudo python setup.py install )
# ( tar -zxf SOAPpy-0.11.6.tar.gz; cd SOAPpy-0.11.6; sudo python setup.py
install )
# ( tar -zxf pygoogle-0.6.tar.gz; cd pygoogle-0.6; sudo python setup.py install
)
```

If you're on Windows, you probably want to check out the binary installer available for PyXML, however. But, after you have yourself hooked up with the `pygoogle` module, you're ready to start building persistent search feeds.

Persistent Google Web Searches

So, how about jumping right into using `pygoogle` to build a feed? Check out Listing 13-1 for the start of `ch13_google_search_scraper.py`, a new program that does just that.

Listing 13-1: ch13_google_search_scraper.py (Part 1 of 3)

```
#!/usr/bin/env python
"""
ch13_google_search_scraper.py
```

```
Produce a feed from a Google web search.
"""
import sys
from scraperlib import Scraper, FeedEntryDict
from pygoogle import google

GOOGLE_LICENSE_KEY  = "XXXXXXXXXXXXXXXXXXXXXXXXXXXXX"
GOOGLE_SEARCH_QUERY = "Doctor Who"

def main():
    """
    Given an argument of 'atom' or 'rss' on the command line,
    produce an Atom or RSS feed.
    """
    scraper = GoogleSearchScraper(GOOGLE_LICENSE_KEY,
                                  GOOGLE_SEARCH_QUERY)

    if len(sys.argv) > 1 and sys.argv[1] == 'rss':
        print scraper.scrape_rss()
    else:
        print scraper.scrape_atom()
```

This is pretty standard feed generation program material so far, but note the two configuration constants defined:

- GOOGLE_LICENSE_KEY—Replace this value with your license key string.

- GOOGLE_SEARCH_QUERY—Here's where you supply the terms for the persistent search query.

You can see that the search query is pretty simple. However, Google packs a lot of search options into that query string, so you'll get to see a little more about this later on. For now though, continue on to Listing 13-2 where the definition of the GoogleSearchScraper class starts.

Listing 13-2: ch13_google_search_scraper.py (Part 2 of 3)

```
class GoogleSearchScraper(Scraper):
    """
    Generates feeds from lists of products from Google Web
    Services queries.
    """
    FEED_META = {
        'feed.title'        : 'Google Search Results',
        'feed.link'         : 'http://www.google.com',
        'feed.tagline'      : 'Search results from Google.com',
        'feed.author.name'  : 'l.m.orchard',
```

Continued

Listing 13-2 *(continued)*

```
            'feed.author.email' : 'l.m.orchard@pobox.com',
            'feed.author.url'   : 'http://www.decafbad.com',
    }

    STATE_FN   = "google_search_state"

    def __init__(self, license_key, search_query):
        """Initialize the Google search scraper"""
        self.license_key  = license_key
        self.search_query = search_query

        self.FEED_META['feed.title'] = \
            'Google web search results for "%s"' % search_query
```

This new `GoogleSearchScraper` class starts off with a definition of `FEED_META` to be used in populating the feed's metadata elements when it gets generated. Next is `STATE_FN`, the name of the database file to be used in maintaining scraper state between runs.

After the class constants comes the definition of the `__init__()` method. Here, the license key and search query terms are stored in instance attributes, and the `FEED_META` title is updated to include the search terms provided. This helps distinguish between multiple `GoogleSearchScraper`-produced feeds later, if you happen to use this to maintain more than one persistent search.

You can wrap up this program now, finishing with the code in Listing 13-3.

Listing 13-3: ch13_google_search_scraper.py (Part 3 of 3)

```
    def produce_entries(self):
        """
        Produce feed entries from Google product item data.
        """
        # Start off with an empty list for entries.
        entries = []

        # Execute the Google search
        data = google.doGoogleSearch(self.search_query,
                license_key=self.license_key)

        # Run through all fetched items, building entries
        for result in data.results:

            # Map the web search result data to feed entry properties
            entry = FeedEntryDict(date_fmt=self.date_fmt, init_dict={
                'title'    : result.directoryTitle or '(untitled)',
                'link'     : result.URL,
```

```
        'summary'   : result.snippet,
    })

    # Append completed entry to list
    entries.append(entry)

    return entries

if __name__ == "__main__": main()
```

Here in Listing 13-3 is the core `produce_entries()` method expected by the Scraper parent class. Using the pygoogle interface is not all that difficult, which hopefully makes it worth installing all those dependencies. All you need to do is call `google.doGoogleSearch()` with the search query string, and (among other things) the search results are returned.

For this program, however, the search results are really all you're concerned with, so the next thing to do is to iterate through the Google search results contained in `data.results` and map search result attributes to feed entry attributes to build a new `FeedEntryDict` object for each. The title of each entry is taken from the `directoryTitle` attribute, or "(untitled)" is used if the current result happens not to have a title. Then the entry link comes from the result's URL, and the summary comes from the snippet Google has prepared for this search hit.

Once you have this program put together, try it out. An example Atom feed resulting from this will look something like Figure 13-3 and an RSS feed will resemble Figure 13-4.

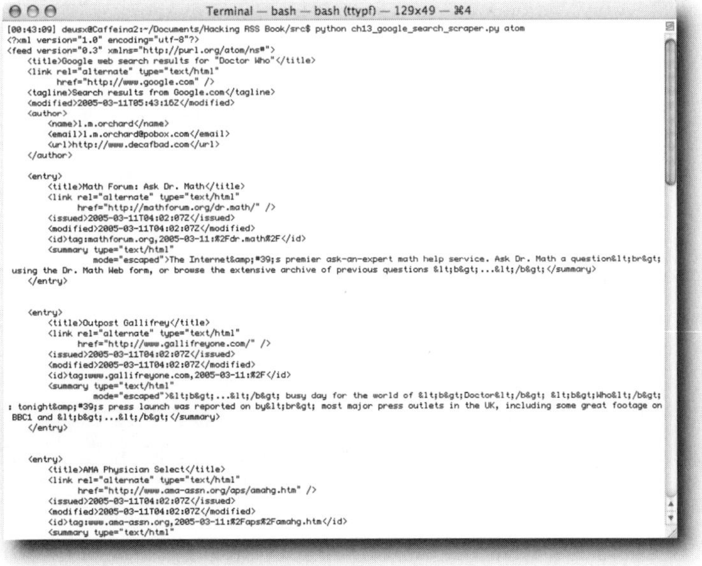

FIGURE 13-3: Atom feed produced from Google search results

Figure 13-4: RSS feed produced from Google search results

Refining Google Web Searches and Julian Date Ranges

At this point, it would really help to read some of the documentation in the Google Web APIs developer's kit—in particular, check out the section on "Search Request Format." The previous program just used a very simple search query consisting of a couple of words, but Google offers many, many more options for refining and narrowing a search.

For example, although you may experience mixed results with this, one of the special query terms allowed in a search query is `daterange:`, which allows you to specify a range of dates in Julian format within which to limit searches on Web pages. To try to make sure your search hits only the freshest stuff, you could work out how to come up with a `daterange` for the last day or so and supply that as a search term. For example, you could use the following:

```
"Doctor Who" daterange:2453440-2453441
```

Calculating Julian dates in Python isn't the most convenient thing with the tools out of the box, however, so here's a handy module that does that for you in Listing 13-4.

Listing 13-4: julian.py

```
"""
julian.py

Calculate Julian date format. Borrowed from:
    http://www.pauahtun.org/julian_period.html
"""
```

```python
import os, sys, math, time

def main():
    print now()

def now():
    """Return today's date in Julian format"""
    return julian_from_tuple(time.localtime(time.time()))

def julian_from_tuple(tup):
    """Turn a 9-tuple of time data into Julian Format"""
    iyyy, mm, id = tup[0], tup[1], tup[2]

    tm = 0.0
    if mm > 2 :
        jy = iyyy
        jm = mm + 1
    else :
        jy = iyyy - 1
        jm = mm + 13

    jul = int ( math.floor ( 365.25 * jy ) + \
        math.floor ( 30.6001 * jm ) + ( id + 1720995.0 + tm ) )
    ja  = int ( 0.01 * jy )
    jul = int ( jul + ( 2 - ja + ( int ( 0.25 * ja ) ) ) )

    return jul

if __name__=='__main__': main()
```

Using this, you could construct a date range query term like so:

```python
import julian
```

```python
tdy = julian.now()
yst = tdy - 1
GOOGLE_SEARCH_QUERY = '"Doctor Who" daterange:%s-%s' % (yst, tdy)
```

This would produce a query something like this:

```python
'"Doctor Who" daterange:2453440-2453441'
```

The rest of the more advanced search query options are a bit simpler to use, though, so be sure to read through the Google Web APIs documentation to see what's available.

Building Feeds with Yahoo! Search Web Services

Google's Web APIs have recently received some stiff competition with the release of Yahoo! Search Web Services in early 2005. As opposed to Google's SOAP interface, Yahoo! Search has provided a simpler REST-style interface to its Web services—basically plain old HTTP GET and XML data—and have gone a few steps further with what functionality is exposed, with respect to Google's offering. Through Yahoo! Search Web Services, you can access images, local yellow pages, news, video, and, of course, Web searches.

 On the Web

Visit the Yahoo! Search Web Services home page here:

>   http://developer.yahoo.net/web/V1/webSearch.html

Also, you can read a bit about the REST style of Web services in this Wikipedia article:

>   http://en.wikipedia.org/wiki/Representational_State_
>   Transfer

Working with Yahoo! Search Web Services

To use these Web services, you're going to have to fill out another form. In this case, though, it's not for a developer-specific license key, because Yahoo! tracks Web service usage *per application*. For the most part, the idea is the similar. You'll need to supply this ID with every access you make to the Web service, but the intent behind this ID isn't to identify *you* so much as it is intended to identify the program using the services. So, ideally, rather than just registering one ID for yourself, you'll register an ID for each major program you write that uses the Yahoo! Search Web Services.

So, to get started, take a visit to this URL:

    http://api.search.yahoo.com/webservices/register_application

If you don't already have a personal Yahoo! ID, you'll need to sign up and login. This isn't your application ID yet. It's just your personal username and password used across the Yahoo! network of sites. Next, once you're logged in, you should see the Yahoo! Search Application ID request form, as shown in Figure 13-5.

Now, the thing about this process, as opposed to that of Google Web APIs, is that you get to choose your own application ID. So, go ahead and think something up and enter it into the "Requested application id" text field. The page should offer some rules as to what characters make up a legal ID. After submission, the site will tell you whether the ID you entered is now legal to use (see Figure 13-6), or whether it contained invalid characters or even whether it was already claimed by another developer (see Figure 13-7).

Once you have an application ID, it's time to find the tools to access the Yahoo! Search Web Services from Python. Well, luckily enough, as opposed to the small tangle of dependencies required to access Google Web APIs from Python, everything you need for Yahoo!'s services is available in the developer kit. And, the module Yahoo! provides depends only upon the standard Python library.

So, pay a visit to the SDK download page here, and click through the licensing agreements:

    http://developer.yahoo.net/download/

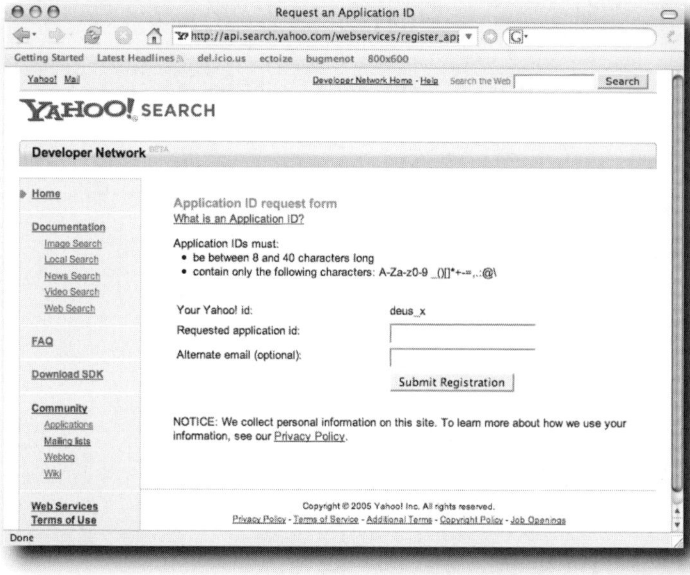

FIGURE 13-5: Yahoo! Search Application ID request form

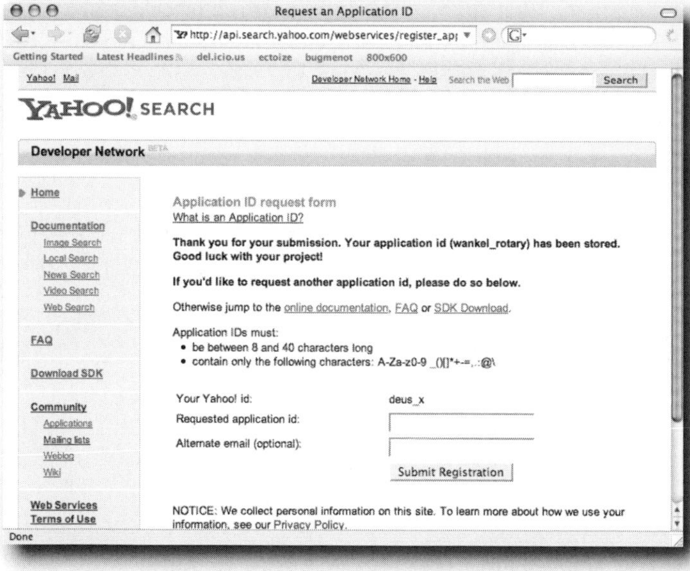

FIGURE 13-6: Successful Yahoo! Search Application ID registration

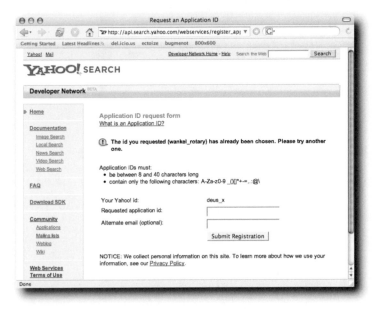

FIGURE 13-7: Unsuccessful Yahoo! Search Application ID registration

You'll be able to download the SDK as either a ZIP file or a tarball. Installation of the Yahoo! Python module is simple. You can find it in the archive inside the `python` directory, in a further directory named `pYsearch-1.3`. Inside *that*, you'll find a `yahoo` directory. You can run the `setup.py` program present there to properly install it.

Persistent Yahoo! Web Searches

You're all set to start using Yahoo! Search Web Services now, so start in on this new program in Listing 13-5, named `ch13_yahoo_search_scraper.py`.

Listing 13-5: ch13_yahoo_search_scraper.py (Part 1 of 3)

```python
#!/usr/bin/env python
"""
ch13_yahoo_search_scraper.py

Produce a feed from a Yahoo! web search.
"""
import sys
from scraperlib import Scraper, FeedEntryDict
from yahoo.search.webservices import WebSearch

YWS_APP_ID       = "hacking_rss"
YWS_SEARCH_QUERY = "Doctor Who"
```

```
def main():
    """
    Given an argument of 'atom' or 'rss' on the command line,
    produce an Atom or RSS feed.
    """
    scraper = YahooSearchScraper(YWS_APP_ID, YWS_SEARCH_QUERY)

    if len(sys.argv) > 1 and sys.argv[1] == 'rss':
        print scraper.scrape_rss()
    else:
        print scraper.scrape_atom()
```

There are no surprises in Listing 13-5, which looks quite a bit like Listing 13-1. You'll need to supply your own application ID in the YWS_APP_ID constant, and you can insert your own search terms in YWS_SEARCH_QUERY. After that, the main() function simply instantiates the YahooSearchScraper class and uses it to produce an Atom or RSS feed.

Moving along, check out Listing 13-6 for the start of YahooSearchScraper.

Listing 13-6: ch13_yahoo_search_scraper.py (Part 2 of 3)

```
class YahooSearchScraper(Scraper):
    """
    Generates feeds from lists of products from Yahoo! Web
    Services queries.
    """
    FEED_META = {
        'feed.title'        : 'Yahoo! Search Results',
        'feed.link'         : 'http://www.yahoo.com',
        'feed.tagline'      : 'Search results from Yahoo.com',
        'feed.author.name'  : 'l.m.orchard',
        'feed.author.email' : 'l.m.orchard@pobox.com',
        'feed.author.url'   : 'http://www.decafbad.com',
    }

    STATE_FN   = "yahoo_search_state"

    def __init__(self, app_id, search_query):
        """Initialize the Yahoo search scraper"""
        self.app_id       = app_id
        self.search_query = search_query

        self.FEED_META['feed.title'] = \
            'Yahoo! web search results for "%s"' % search_query
```

Again, another FEED_META data structure is defined in Listing 13-6, along with the STATE_FN database filename. Then, an __init__() method is defined, which stows away the application ID and search terms. It also updates the FEED_META title to reflect the search terms to be used in generating the feed.

Listing 13-7 finishes up the YahooSearchScraper class, as well as the program itself.

Listing 13-7: ch13_yahoo_search_scraper.py (Part 3 of 3)

```python
def produce_entries(self):
    """
    Produce feed entries from Yahoo! product item data.
    """
    # Start off with an empty list for entries.
    entries = []

    # Create a new Yahoo! API web search
    search = WebSearch(self.app_id, query=self.search_query,
                       results=50)

    # Execute the query and gather results.
    results = [ r for r in search.parse_results() ]

    # Sort the results in reverse-chronological order by
    # modification date
    results.sort(lambda a,b: \
        cmp(b['ModificationDate'], a['ModificationDate']))

    # Run through all fetched items, building entries
    for result in results:

        # Map the web search result data to feed entry properties
        entry = FeedEntryDict(date_fmt=self.date_fmt, init_dict={
            'title'    : result['Title'],
            'link'     : result['ClickUrl'],
            'summary'  : result['Summary'],
            'modified' : int(result['ModificationDate']),
            'issued'   : int(result['ModificationDate']),
        })

        # Append completed entry to list
        entries.append(entry)

    return entries

if __name__ == "__main__": main()
```

Using the Yahoo! Search Web Services module is pretty easy—just supply your application ID, search terms, and a maximum count of results (up to 50) to create an instance of `yahoo.search.webservices.WebSearch`. This object's `parse_results()` method is called and dumped into a list and then it's sorted in reverse-chronological order.

Oh yeah, and this is an improvement over Google's API. Search results returned by Yahoo! Search each contain a `ModificationDate` in seconds since the UNIX epoch, which is a little easier to deal with than Julian date. Not only that, but you can handle the sorting and date range logic in your own program, rather than constructing a special search query term.

Modification dates really are the key to extracting decent feeds from search results. Although ordering by relevancy is important when you're searching in person, it's more important to get fresh results back when you're running persistent and repeated searches.

So, armed with a set of sorted search results, the method loops through to build `FeedEntryDict` objects, initializing each with a mapping from Yahoo! Search result data to feed entry attributes. This mapping is pretty painless. In each search result record, there's a title, a link, a summary, and a modification date, all of which carries into a feed entry nicely.

 To see all of the attributes available with each search result, be sure to check out the WebSearch documentation, available here:

```
http://developer.yahoo.net/web/V1/webSearch.html
```

Finally, to see this thing in action, check out Figures 13-8 and 13-9, which show an Atom feed and an RSS feed produced by this program, respectively.

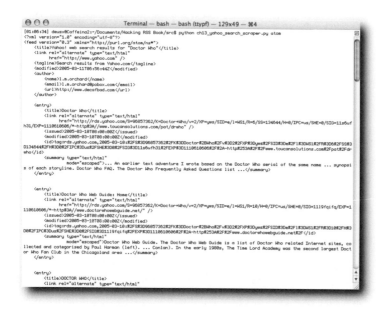

Figure 13-8: Atom feed produced from Yahoo! Search results

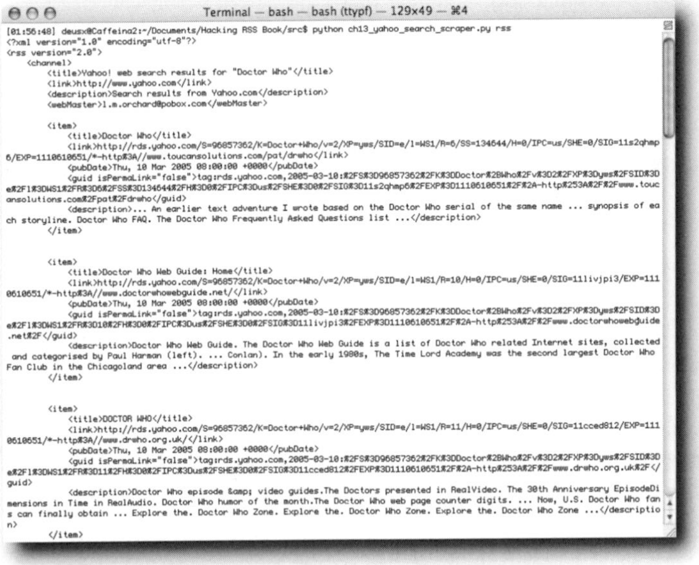

FIGURE 13-9: RSS feed produced from Yahoo! Search results

Generating Feeds from Yahoo! News Searches

Besides providing modification dates in search results, another thing Yahoo! Search Web Services have over Google's offering comes in the form of the News Search functionality. Although Google does offer a human-readable news service called (appropriately enough) Google News, its Web service interface doesn't expose any access to it.

That's where Yahoo! Search Web Services step in. With pretty much the same interface used for searching the Web, you can search up-to-date news stories. So, without further ado, jump into Listing 13-8 to see the next scraper program, named ch13_yahoo_news_scraper.py.

> **Listing 13-8:** ch13_yahoo_news_scraper.py (Part 1 of 3)

```
#!/usr/bin/env python
"""
ch13_yahoo_news_scraper.py

Produce a feed from a Yahoo! web search.
"""
import sys
from scraperlib import Scraper, FeedEntryDict
from yahoo.search.webservices import NewsSearch
```

```
YWS_APP_ID        = "hacking_rss"
YWS_SEARCH_QUERY = "syndication feeds"

def main():
    """
    Given an argument of 'atom' or 'rss' on the command line,
    produce an Atom or RSS feed.
    """
    scraper = YahooNewsScraper(YWS_APP_ID, YWS_SEARCH_QUERY)

    if len(sys.argv) > 1 and sys.argv[1] == 'rss':
        print scraper.scrape_rss()
    else:
        print scraper.scrape_atom()
```

With the exception of swapping the word "News" wherever "Web" appears, Listing 13-8 is identical to Listing 13-5. Continue on to Listing 13-9 for the beginning of the YahooNewsScraper class.

Listing 13-9: ch13_yahoo_news_scraper.py (Part 2 of 3)

```
class YahooNewsScraper(Scraper):
    """
    Generates feeds from lists of products from Yahoo! Web
    Services queries.
    """
    FEED_META = {
        'feed.title'        : 'Yahoo! News Search Results',
        'feed.link'         : 'http://www.yahoo.com',
        'feed.tagline'      : 'Search results from Yahoo.com',
        'feed.author.name'  : 'l.m.orchard',
        'feed.author.email' : 'l.m.orchard@pobox.com',
        'feed.author.url'   : 'http://www.decafbad.com',
    }

    STATE_FN  = "yahoo_search_state"

    ATOM_ENTRY_TMPL = """
        <entry>
            <title>%(entry.title)s</title>
            <author>
                <name>%(entry.author.name)s</name>
                <link>%(entry.author.link)s</link>
            </author>
            <link rel="alternate" type="text/html"
                href="%(entry.link)s" />
            <issued>%(entry.issued)s</issued>
```

Continued

Listing 13-9 *(continued)*

```
            <modified>%(entry.modified)s</modified>
            <id>%(entry.id)s</id>
            <summary type="text/html"
                    mode="escaped">%(entry.summary)s</summary>
        </entry>
    """

    def __init__(self, app_id, search_query):
        """Initialize the Yahoo search scraper"""
        self.app_id       = app_id
        self.search_query = search_query

        self.FEED_META['feed.title'] = \
            'Yahoo! news search results for "%s"' % \
            search_query
```

In Listing 13-9, the usual FEED_META structure is defined along with the STATE_FN file-name. One change is the new replacement template for Atom feed entries. This one has an author name and link added, because you'll be able to fill these with the names and links of news sources from the search results coming up next.

Also, notice the __init__() method again tailors the feed title in FEED_META to reflect the search query. Now, you can finish all this up by checking out Listing 13-10.

Listing 13-10: ch13_yahoo_news_scraper.py (Part 3 of 3)

```
def produce_entries(self):
    """
    Produce feed entries from Yahoo! product item data.
    """
    # Start off with an empty list for entries.
    entries = []

    # Create a new Yahoo! API web search
    search = NewsSearch(self.app_id, query=self.search_query,
                        sort='date', results=50)

    # Run through all fetched items, building entries
    for result in search.parse_results():

        # Map the web search result data to feed entry properties
        entry = FeedEntryDict(date_fmt=self.date_fmt, init_dict={
            'title'      : '[%s] %s' % \
                (result['NewsSource'], result['Title']),
            'link'       : result['ClickUrl'],
            'summary'    : result['Summary'],
```

```
                'author.name' : result['NewsSource'],
                'author.link' : result['NewsSourceUrl'],
                'modified'    : int(result['ModificationDate']),
                'issued'      : int(result['PublishDate']),
            })

            # Append completed entry to list
            entries.append(entry)

    return entries

if __name__ == "__main__": main()
```

This simple News Search usage is practically identical to the Web Search you used previously. Supply the application ID, the query terms, a sort type (by date), and a maximum number of results.

In produce_entries(), the query is made and results are parsed. The list of result records is looped through, and FeedEntryDict objects are constructed. Again, the mapping is fairly straightforward, with one exception. It's a bit of a hack, but I prefer seeing the news source included in the title of the feed entry. Also notice that the news source and its URL are included in the author section for the entry.

Finally, to see this code in action, check out Figures 13-10 and 13-11 for Atom and RSS feed generation, respectively.

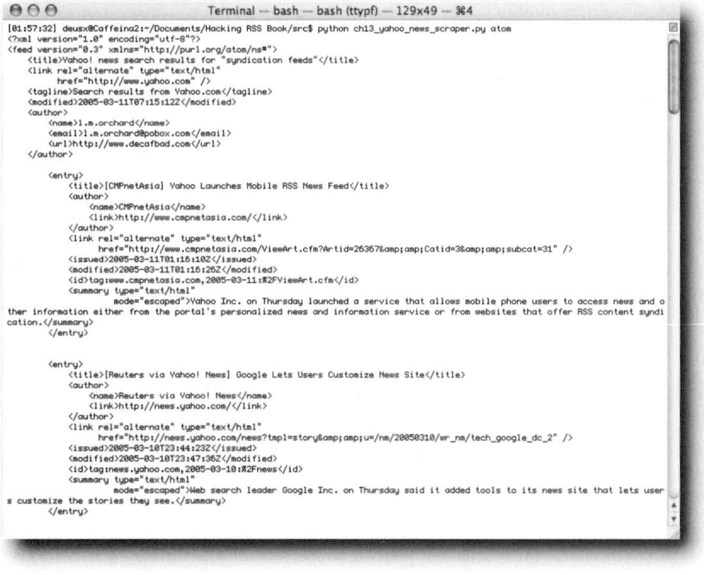

FIGURE 13-10: Atom feed produced from Yahoo! News Search results

FIGURE 13-11: RSS feed produced from Yahoo! News Search results

Using this News Search, you can create custom topical searches and keep up with all the matches that flow through news at Yahoo! News. And, with these two Yahoo! Search Web Services scrapers under your belt, you should easily be able to apply these examples to the other kinds of search available, such as image and video searches, as well as the local yellow pages.

Building Feeds with Amazon Web Services

Since their introduction, Amazon Web Services have gone through several phases of improvements—approaching the point where nearly everything you could do on Amazon.com via Web browser can now be done programmatically or via alternate interfaces or clients. Product searches, shopping carts, and wish lists are all at your disposal, giving you access to a very wide range of functionality. Whereas Google and Yahoo! provide interfaces to perform various kinds of searches, Amazon provides a fairly rich and interactive API enabling all sorts of searches and transactions with the Amazon catalog.

Working with Amazon Web Services

To get started using Amazon Web Services (or AWS), you'll first need to visit the AWS home page here:

```
http://www.amazon.com/webservices/
```

At this page, you'll be able to find documentation and code examples showing you what's possible and how to use AWS.

Registering as an AWS Developer

However, before you can actually do anything with AWS, you'll need to register as a developer. If you haven't registered already, you should be able to find a link to the registration form labeled "Register for AWS." If you have trouble finding the link, you should be able to register at the following URL:

```
http://www.amazon.com/gp/aws/registration/registration-form.html
```

Follow the process outlined there to obtain an AWS subscription ID, and you should soon see a new ID delivered to you via email. This process should be old hat to you now, after dealing with Google and Yahoo! APIs.

Although using Amazon's Web services doesn't currently cost anything, all AWS functionality requires that you supply a valid subscription ID so that Amazon can identify and track usage of its services. Accordingly, all of the code using AWS in this chapter will require you to supply this ID.

In fact, you should sock this ID away in a file in your working directory. Name it `amazon-key.txt`, and its contents should consist solely of the subscription ID you received, like so:

```
15BB79YKBY39KCAK46RJ
```

This is, of course, a made-up AWS subscription ID—you should be sure to get your own.

Using Amazon Web Services

Amazon Web Services offers two main approaches for use: SOAP and REST-based. Although many technologies and tools are centered around the SOAP way of doing things, this chapter focuses on accessing AWS via the REST-based approach. And, whereas with Google and Yahoo! Web services you downloaded ready-made API wrappers for use in your Scrapers, you're going to build your own wrapper for Amazon Web Services here.

So, the version of Amazon Web Services you'll use in this chapter consists of HTTP GET requests that return XML data. You should already know how to perform HTTP GET queries, using `urllib` or `HTTPCache`. As for the XML, back in Chapter 9 you used 4Suite, HTML Tidy, and XPath to extract data from HTML tag soup. So, you might reach for those tools at first. However, AWS promises to serve up valid XML, so you can employ a much simpler bit of hackery here.

Aaron Swartz has made available a module called `xmltramp`, which provides an interface for accessing XML data structures in a way that looks very much like accessing plain old Python data structures. Though you'll likely want to stick with 4Suite for more formal operations using XML, `xmltramp` provides a hack sufficiently useful here for processing Amazon Web Services data.

So, you should check out `xmltramp` at its home page here:

```
http://www.aaronsw.com/2002/xmltramp/
```

And, at the time of this writing, you can download the module directly from this URL:

`http://www.aaronsw.com/2002/xmltramp/xmltramp.py`

So, without further ado, jump into a program that makes a call to Amazon Web Services using `xmltramp` with the code in Listing 13-11. This is the start of a new utility program you can use to search for wish lists, named `ch13_amazon_find_wishlist.py`.

Listing 13-11: ch13_amazon_find_wishlist.py (Part 1 of 2)

```
#!/usr/bin/env python
"""
ch13_amazon_find_wishlist.py

Given search terms as a command line argument, look for wishlists.
"""
import sys, urllib, xmltramp
from httpcache import HTTPCache

AWS_ID  = open("amazon-key.txt", "r").read().strip()
AWS_URL = "http://webservices.amazon.com/onca/xml"
```

Listing 13-11 offers a pretty uneventful preamble to this program: From the imports, you can see that it will be using the `urllib` and `xmltramp` modules, as well as the `HTTPCache`. After these imports, two configuration constants are defined: `AWS_ID` and `AWS_URL`.

One thing to note, however, is that this program will attempt to load up your AWS subscription ID into `AWS_ID` from the text file you created earlier. (You did put your AWS ID in `amazon-key.txt`, right? Just checking.) And, lastly in Listing 13-11, the value of `AWS_URL` points to the base URL for all AWS HTTP GET queries.

Continue on to Listing 13-12 for the final half of this first program.

Listing 13-12: ch13_amazon_find_wishlist.py (Part 2 of 2)

```
def main():
    """
    Search for wishlists using command line arguments.
    """
    # Leaving out the program name, grab all space-separated
    # arguments.
    name   = " ".join(sys.argv[1:])

    # Construct the list of arguments for the AWS query
    args = {
        'Service'       : 'AWSECommerceService',
        'Operation'     : 'ListSearch',
```

```
            'ListType'       : 'WishList',
            'SubscriptionId' : AWS_ID,
            'Name'           : name
    }

    # Build the URL for the API call using the base URL
    # and params.
    url = "%s?%s" % (AWS_URL, urllib.urlencode(args))

    # Perform the query, fetch and parse the results.
    data = HTTPCache(url).content()
    doc  = xmltramp.parse(data)

    # Print out the list IDs found.
    lists = [ x for x in doc.Lists if 'List' in x._name ]
    for list in lists:
        print '%15s: %s' % ( list.ListId, list.CustomerName )

if __name__=="__main__": main()
```

The main() function for this program is defined in Listing 13-12.

This function collects search terms from program arguments and joins them with spaces—so everything given on the command line after the name of the program will be used in the wish list search.

After this, the arguments that will be used in the request to AWS are established in a map named args:

- Service—This is a parameter that must be included in every AWS GET query.

- Operation—This specifies what operation is being requested in the query, in this case a search for lists.

- ListType—A list search operation requires an indication of what type of list to look for, in this case it's wish lists.

- SubscriptionId—This gets filled out with your AWS subscription ID.

- Name—Finally, this parameter contains the name of a person with which to search for wish lists.

Again, you should read up on the Amazon Web Services documentation for exact details of how all of these arguments are used and what they are.

With the arguments established, the urlencode function from the urllib module is used to convert this map of arguments into a properly composed and escaped URL query string, which is then tacked onto the end of the AWS base URL.

The `urlencode` function from `urllib` is very useful for composing queries for HTTP GET based Web services. Check it out in the Python documentation here:

> `http://docs.python.org/lib/module-urllib.html#l2h-3178`

This constructed URL is then fetched with `HTTPCache`. The result of the query is expected as valid XML, so it can be (and is) parsed using `xmltramp`. Then, as you can see from the last two lines of `main()`, you can access this XML almost just like plain objects in Python—albeit with just a little spot of weird gymnastics. Sample output from this program might look like this:

```
# python ch13_amazon_find_wishlist.py leslie michael orchard
  1QWYI6P2JF3Q5: leslie michael orchard
# python ch13_amazon_find_wishlist.py alexandra arnold
  35OIOYWQ9XQAE: Alexandra Arnold
  1HZ4UNUQZRY4Z: Alexandra Arnold
```

Again, you can find full documentation on all the operations and parameters used with Amazon Web Services in the documentation available at its site. You'll see a few of them used in this chapter, but by no means will a full account be presented. So, check out those pages to get a sense of the full range of AWS capabilities—you might want to take a little bit of time to play with this first example program, try out a few different operations, and see how things work.

Building Feeds with the Amazon API

Now that you've seen a first stab at working with Amazon Web Services, how about some reusable code with which you can more easily generate feeds from AWS queries? Start a new module file called `amazonlib.py` and take a look at Listing 13-13 for the opening lines.

Listing 13-13: amazonlib.py (Part 1 of 5)

```python
#!/usr/bin/env python
"""
amazonlib

Tools for generating feeds from Amazon Web Service requests.
"""
import md5, urllib, xmltramp
from scraperlib import FeedEntryDict, Scraper

class AmazonScraper(Scraper):
    """
    Generates feeds from lists of products from Amazon Web
    Services queries.
    """
    AWS_URL = "http://webservices.amazon.com/onca/xml"

    ITEM_TRACK = (
        'ASIN',
```

```
        'ItemAttributes.ListPrice.FormattedPrice'
)

TAG_DOMAIN = "www.decafbad.com"
TAG_DATE   = "2005-03-06"
STATE_FN   = "amazon_feed_state"
```

Again, in Listing 13-13, you see the appearance of `urllib` and `xmltramp`, just as in the previous program. However, now the `scraperlib` has been thrown into the mix. After the imports comes the beginning of the `AmazonScraper` class, which leads off with a few class constants:

- `AWS_URL`—As in the wish list search program, this constant establishes the base URL for Amazon Web Services queries.

- `ITEM_TRACK`—When items are found via an AWS query, the properties listed here will be used to determine uniqueness for inclusion in the feed—in this case, the item's inventory ID and its price are used, so that new feed entries will be included when prices change for items.

- `TAG_DOMAIN`—This offers a domain name to use when generating feed entry tag URIs as GUIDs.

- `TAG_DATE`—This offers a date to be used in generating feed entry tag URIs as GUIDs.

- `STATE_FN`—This is the filename that will be used for storing feed generation state.

Keep going on to Listing 13-14 for a few string templates that will be used to format AWS data when it arrives from queries.

Listing 13-14: amazonlib.py (Part 2 of 5)

```
ATOM_ENTRY_TMPL = """
    <entry>
        <title>%(entry.title)s</title>
        <author>
            <name>%(entry.author.name)s</name>
        </author>
        <link rel="alternate" type="text/html"
            href="%(entry.link)s" />
        <issued>%(entry.issued)s</issued>
        <modified>%(entry.modified)s</modified>
        <id>%(entry.id)s</id>
        <summary type="text/html"
                mode="escaped">%(entry.summary)s</summary>
    </entry>
"""
```

Continued

Listing 13-14 *(continued)*

```
TITLE_TMPL = \
    "[%(ItemAttributes.ProductGroup)s] " + \
    "(%(ItemAttributes.ListPrice.FormattedPrice)s) " + \
    "%(ItemAttributes.Title)s - %(ItemAttributes.Author)s"

SUMMARY_TMPL = """
    <b>%(ItemAttributes.Title)s</b><br />
    <i>%(ItemAttributes.Author)s</i></br />
    <img src="%(MediumImage.URL)s" /><br />
"""
```

The first string template defined in Listing 13-14 is ATOM_ENTRY_TMPL. This replaces the Atom feed entry template used in the Scraper base class, with the primary change being the addition of an author name to the entry. There's no RSS counterpart to this template in this class because the RSS 2.0 specification requires that per-entry authorship information be provided as an email address, something that AWS items don't provide. On the other hand, the Atom 0.3 format distinguishes between name, email, and URL for person constructs, with the name being the only required attribute. So, why not include it where you can?

Following this template are two more string templates: TITLE_TMPL and SUMMARY_TMPL.

The TITLE_TMPL string template is used to construct feed entry titles based on AWS item data. Notice that this string is built using concatenated strings over several lines—this is so that the template can be nicely formatted in the source code, but without introducing unnecessary line breaks in the actual template.

And, the SUMMARY_TMPL string template is used to build the summary content for feed entries. In contrast to TITLE_TMPL, a few line breaks are no problem here, so this string is included as a multi-line Python string.

Continue forward to Listing 13-15, which offers the definition of the produce_entries() method.

Listing 13-15: amazonlib.py (Part 3 of 5)

```
def produce_entries(self):
    """
    Produce feed entries from Amazon product item data.
    """
    entries = []

    all_items = self.fetch_items()

    # Run through all fetched items, building entries
    for item in all_items:
```

```
# Wrap the item in a template-friendly object
tmpl_item = TrampTmplWrapper(item)

# Build an empty entry object
entry = FeedEntryDict(date_fmt=self.date_fmt)

# Generate an ID for this entry based on
# tracked data
m = md5.md5()
for k in self.ITEM_TRACK:
    m.update(tmpl_item[k])
entry['id'] = state_id = "tag:%s,%s:%s" % \
    (self.TAG_DOMAIN, self.TAG_DATE, m.hexdigest())
```

The `produce_entries()` method in Listing 13-15 provides feed entries in the form of `FeedEntryDict` objects for the superclass's feed generation machinery. However, notice that one of the first things it does is call a method named `fetch_items()`.

This method won't be defined in the present class: Analogous to `produce_entries()`, it will be defined in further subclasses to implement the actual AWS search queries that result in product data items. Because AWS uses the same data structures for products found by just about any operation, the rest of this `produce_entries()` can abstract the rest of the feed generation details away from subclasses.

And, after the call to `fetch_items()`, it goes about doing just that. Each item of product data found by the subclass is visited, first getting wrapped in an instance of `TrampTmplWrapper`, a class that will be defined shortly. Then, a new `FeedEntryDict` is created and a GUID is constructed for it using the product attributes listed in the `ITEM_TRACK` class constant defined a little while ago.

The `produce_entries()` method and the `AmazonScraper` class are wrapped up in Listing 13-16.

Listing 13-16: amazonlib.py (Part 4 of 5)

```
# Use the item detail URL for entry link
entry['link'] = tmpl_item['DetailPageURL']

# Use the author, artist, or actor name for item
# and entry author
authors = []
for k in ( 'Author', 'Artist', 'Actor' ):
    v = tmpl_item['ItemAttributes.%s' % k]
    if v: authors.append(v)
entry['author.name'] = ", ".join(authors)
```

Continued

Listing 13-16 *(continued)*

```
        # Build entry title and summary from
        # string templates
        entry['title']   = self.TITLE_TMPL % tmpl_item
        entry['summary'] = self.SUMMARY_TMPL % tmpl_item

        # Append completed entry to list
        entries.append(entry)

    return entries
```

In Listing 13-16, the AWS product data is formatted and copied into the current
`FeedEntryDict`. The entry link is taken from the product's `DetailPageURL`, and the
author field is built up from the product's author, artist, and actor properties—any one or none
of which may be provided by a particular item. Then, the `TITLE_TMPL` and `SUMMARY_TMPL`
templates are combined with the `TrampTmplWrapper` object, to build the entry title and
summary content, respectively.

Finally, the finished entry is appended to the running list and, after all product items have been
processed, this list is returned at the end of the method.

Now, there's just one thing left to this module: The definition of the `TrampTmplWrapper`
class in Listing 13-17.

Listing 13-17: amazonlib.py (Part 5 of 5)

```
class TrampTmplWrapper:
    """
    Wrapper to provide dictionary-style access to xmltramp
    nodes with dotted paths, for use in string templates.
    """
    def __init__(self, node):
        """
        Initialize with an xmltramp node.
        """
        self.node = node

    def __getitem__(self, path):
        """
        Walk through xmltramp child nodes, given a dotted path.
        Returns an empty string on a path not found.
        """
        try:
            # Walk through the path nodes, return end node
            # as string.
```

```
        curr = self.node
        for p in path.split('.'):
            curr = getattr(curr, p)
        return str(curr)

    except TypeError:
        # HACK: Not intuitive, but this is what xmltramp
        # throws for an attribute not found.
        return ""
```

There's not much to `TrampTmplWrapper` in Listing 13-17. Basically, this class just serves to wrap an `xmltramp` node parsed from XML data, providing dictionary-style access to the character data of the node and its children in order to make it easier to build string templates.

So, for example, you can use the following sorts of slots in `TITLE_TMPL` and `SUMMARY_TMPL` in Listing 13-14 to access AWS product data attributes:

- `%(ASIN)s`
- `%(DetailPageURL)s`
- `%(MediumImage.URL)s`
- `%(MediumImage.Width)s`
- `%(OfferSummary.TotalNew)s`
- `%(ItemAttributes.Title)s`
- `%(ItemAttributes.ListPrice.FormattedPrice)s`

You should consult the Amazon Web Services documentation and play around with what `xmltramp` parses out of AWS data to get a sense for the full range of values available for use with this technique. It's important to note, though, that this wrapper facilitates access only to *character data* inside XML tags, and not tag attributes. Luckily, this isn't much of a limitation for AWS data, but you should keep this in mind.

And, with that, this module is finished. It's time to take a look at actually building some feeds.

Using Amazon Product Search to Generate a Feed

This first use you'll see for `AmazonScraper` is in building feeds out of product search results. With these feeds, you can track new releases by a favorite author or artist, maybe even watch for changing prices. Rather than needing to remember to return to Amazon to search for things you're interested in, you can use a feed to revisit searches for you and let the results come to you in your aggregator.

Listing 13-18 provides you with the first half of a new program to accomplish this, called `ch13_amazon_search_scraper.py`.

Listing 13-18: ch13_amazon_search_scraper.py (Part 1 of 3)

```python
#!/usr/bin/env python
"""
ch13_amazon_search_scraper.py

Produce a feed from a given Amazon product search.
"""
import sys, urllib, xmltramp
from amazonlib import AmazonScraper
from httpcache import HTTPCache

AWS_ID       = open("amazon-key.txt", "r").read().strip()
AWS_INDEX    = "Books"
AWS_KEYWORDS = "ExtremeTech"

def main():
    """
    Given an argument of 'atom' or 'rss' on the command line,
    produce an Atom or RSS feed.
    """
    scraper = AmazonSearchScraper(AWS_ID, AWS_INDEX, AWS_KEYWORDS)

    if len(sys.argv) > 1 and sys.argv[1] == 'rss':
        print scraper.scrape_rss()
    else:
        print scraper.scrape_atom()
```

This program follows the familiar scraper program pattern—a few modules get imported, and some configuration constants are defined along with the `main()` function, which provides logic to switch between feed formats.

The configuration constants include the following:

- `AWS_ID`—As in the wish list search program, this constant gets filled with your subscription ID, read in from the file `amazon-key.txt`.

- `AWS_INDEX`—Selects which product index will be searched. You'll want to read through the AWS documentation under the section "Search Index Values" for the complete list, but this case-sensitive constant can contain values such as "Books," "DVD," "Electronics," and "SoftwareVideoGames."

- `AWS_KEYWORDS`—Defines the keywords that will be used in searching the index selected by the value of `AWS_INDEX`.

Given all these values, the `main()` function creates an instance of the `AmazonSearchScraper` class with the constants. This instance is then used to produce the feed. Up next, Listing 13-19 continues the program with the definition of the `AmazonSearchScraper` class.

Listing 13-19: ch13_amazon_search_scraper.py (Part 2 of 3)

```
class AmazonSearchScraper(AmazonScraper):
    """
    Produce feeds from Amazon product searches.
    """
    FEED_META = {
        'feed.title'        : 'Search Feed',
        'feed.link'         : 'http://www.amazon.com',
        'feed.tagline'      : 'Search results from Amazon.com',
        'feed.author.name'  : 'l.m.orchard',
        'feed.author.email' : 'l.m.orchard@pobox.com',
        'feed.author.url'   : 'http://www.decafbad.com',
    }

    STATE_FN = 'amazon_search_state'

    def __init__(self, id, index, keywords):
        """
        Initialize with AWS id and wishlist id.
        """
        self.aws_id   = id
        self.index    = index
        self.keywords = keywords

        self.FEED_META['feed.title'] = \
            'Amazon.com search for "%s" in %s' % \
            (self.keywords, self.index)
```

`AmazonSearchScraper` is a subclass of the recently defined `AmazonScraper` class. As a class property, it defines `FEED_META` data structure, which is used by the `Scraper` parent class to populate the overall metadata for the feed. Following that is the filename of the database that is used by the scraper to maintain state between runs.

Moving on to the `__init__()` method definition, note that it accepts an AWS subscription ID, search index, and keywords as initializing parameters. The subscription ID, search index, and keywords are stowed away in instance properties. After that, a new feed title is constructed for `FEED_META`, based on the index and keywords supplied. You don't really *need* do to this, but it does help tailor the feed a little bit to describe the search results.

This class and program gets wrapped up in Listing 13-20, with the definition of the `fetch_items()` method.

Listing 13-20: ch13_amazon_search_scraper.py (Part 3 of 3)

```python
def fetch_items(self):
    """
    Grab search result items for given index and keywords.
    """
    # Construct the list of arguments for the AWS query
    args = {
        'Service'        : 'AWSECommerceService',
        'Operation'      : 'ItemSearch',
        'ResponseGroup'  : 'Medium',
        'SearchIndex'    : self.index,
        'Keywords'       : self.keywords,
        'SubscriptionId' : self.aws_id,
    }

    # Build the URL for the API call using the base URL
    # and params.
    url = "%s?%s" % (self.AWS_URL, urllib.urlencode(args))

    # Perform the query, fetch and parse the results.
    data = HTTPCache(url).content()
    doc  = xmltramp.parse(data)

    # Fetch first page of items.
    return [ x for x in doc.Items if 'Item' in x._name ]

if __name__ == "__main__": main()
```

Reminiscent of the wish list search program, the definition of fetch_items() in Listing 13-20 starts off with a dictionary of arguments to be used in a call to the Amazon Web Services:

- Service—This is a parameter that must be included in every AWS GET query.

- Operation—This specifies what operation is being requested in the query, in this case a search for product items.

- ResponseGroup—Specifies which data sets should be returned for each item—in this case the query will ask for a default set of attributes defined as "Medium," which includes things like the price, item title and author, as well as thumbnail images.

- SearchIndex—This will select which product index is to be searched with the given keywords.

- Keywords—This supplies the keywords to use in searching the specified product index.

- SubscriptionId—This gets filled out with your AWS subscription ID.

These arguments are then formed into an HTTP GET query string and appended to the AWS base URL. The HTTPCache is used to perform the query, and xmltramp is used to parse the results. Once parsed, the results' <Items/> tag is searched for <Item/> tags, which are then returned for processing into a feed by the AmazonScraper parent class. And with that, this program is complete.

Once you have this program working, it will produce an Atom feed like the one shown in Figure 13-12. Alternately, if you tell the program to produce an RSS feed, it'll appear like Figure 13-13.

FIGURE 13-12: Producing an Atom feed from Amazon product search results

Keeping Watch on Your Amazon Wish List Items

Although turning product search results into feeds can be useful for tracking when new things appear, you can get even more personal by turning your Amazon wish list into a feed. Or, if you have a friend or relative on whom you'd like to keep tabs—maybe to stay well prepared for birthdays or holidays—subscribing to their wish lists can be a way to keep up.

Also, because prices on items tend to change from time to time, wish list feeds aren't limited to just notifying you when new things are added—you can also see when information about pre-existing items changes.

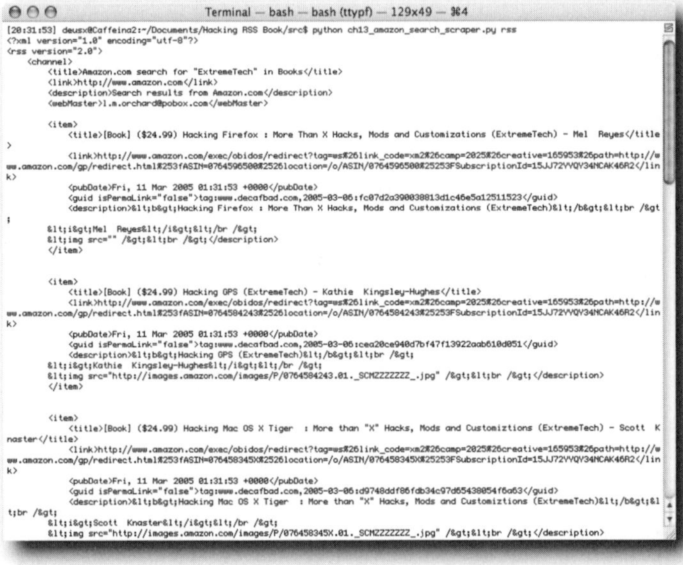

FIGURE **13-13: Producing an RSS feed from Amazon product search results**

The first thing you'll need, however, is a wish list ID. Fortunately, one of the programs in this chapter just happens to be a wish list search utility. You can revisit and use ch13_amazon_find_wishlist.py in Listing 13-11 to search for wish lists using your own name or the names of whomever else you'd like to look up. Once you've found some IDs, you'll have strings that look something like these:

```
1QWYI6P2JF3Q5
35OIOYWQ9XQAE
1HZ4UNUQZRY4Z
```

Pick one, and continue on to Listing 13-21, which provides the start of a new program named ch13_amazon_wishlist_scraper.py.

Listing 13-21: ch13_amazon_wishlist_scraper.py (Part 1 of 3)

```
"""
ch13_amazon_wishlist_scraper.py

Use the Amazon API to look up items for a wishlist.
"""
import sys, urllib, xmltramp
from amazonlib import AmazonScraper
from httpcache import HTTPCache

AWS_ID         = open("amazon-key.txt", "r").read().strip()
AWS_WISHLIST_ID = "1QWYI6P2JF3Q5"
```

```
def main():
    """
    Given an argument of 'atom' or 'rss' on the command line,
    produce an Atom or RSS feed.
    """
    scraper = AmazonWishlistScraper(AWS_ID, AWS_WISHLIST_ID)

    if len(sys.argv) > 1 and sys.argv[1] == 'rss':
        print scraper.scrape_rss()
    else:
        print scraper.scrape_atom()
```

This new program starts off pretty much just like the previous one. Once more, be sure you have your subscription ID in a text file named amazon-key.txt, and set AWS_WISHLIST_ID with one of the wishlist IDs you've looked up. The wishlist ID included in Listing 13-21 belongs to your humble author, so you can go right ahead and look at my items—but you might want to tweak this.

Next, in Listing 13-22, you'll find the definition for AmazonWishlistScraper class, a new AmazonScraper subclass.

Listing 13-22: ch13_amazon_wishlist_scraper.py (Part 2 of 3)

```
class AmazonWishlistScraper(AmazonScraper):
    """
    Produce a feed from Amazon wishlist items
    """
    FEED_META = {
        'feed.title'        : 'Amazon WishList items',
        'feed.link'         : 'http://www.amazon.com',
        'feed.tagline'      : 'Search results from Amazon.com',
        'feed.author.name'  : 'l.m.orchard',
        'feed.author.email' : 'l.m.orchard@pobox.com',
        'feed.author.url'   : 'http://www.decafbad.com',
    }

    STATE_FN = 'amazon_wishlist_state'

    def __init__(self, id, wishlist_id):
        """Initialize with AWS id and wishlist id"""
        self.aws_id      = id
        self.wishlist_id = wishlist_id
```

AmazonWishlistScraper is another subclass of AmazonScraper class. It defines FEED_META data structure with some metadata for the resulting feed. Following that is the filename of the database that is used by the scraper to maintain state between runs.

The __init__() method is defined to accept the AWS subscription ID, as well as a wish-list ID, both of which are socked away in object instance variables. With this beginning behind you, check out Listing 13-23 for the wrap up.

Listing 13-23: ch13_amazon_wishlist_scraper.py (Part 3 of 3)

```
def fetch_items(self):
    """
    Grab search result items for given index and keywords.
    """
    # Construct the list of arguments for the AWS query
    args = {
        'Service'        : 'AWSECommerceService',
        'Operation'      : 'ListLookup',
        'ResponseGroup'  : 'Medium,ListFull',
        'Sort'           : 'LastUpdated',
        'ListType'       : 'WishList',
        'ListId'         : self.wishlist_id,
        'SubscriptionId' : self.aws_id,
    }

    # Build the URL for the API call using the base URL
    # and params.
    url = "%s?%s" % (self.AWS_URL, urllib.urlencode(args))

    # Perform the query, fetch and parse the results.
    data = HTTPCache(url).content()
    doc  = xmltramp.parse(data)

    # Update the feed link and title from search
    # result metadata
    self.FEED_META['feed.link']  = doc.Lists.List.ListURL
    self.FEED_META['feed.title'] = \
        'Amazon.com wishlist items for "%s"' % \
        doc.Lists.List.CustomerName

    # Fetch first page of items.
    return [ x.Item for x in doc.Lists.List
                if 'ListItem' in x._name ]

if __name__ == "__main__": main()
```

And, just like the other two programs making AWS queries in this chapter, Listing 13-23's definition of fetch_items() starts off with a dictionary of query arguments:

- Service—This is a parameter that must be included in every AWS GET query.

- Operation—This specifies what operation is being requested in the query, in this case a search for items belonging to a list.

- ResponseGroup—Specifies which data sets should be returned for each item. Here, the "Medium" group is requested along with the "ListFull" group, which will cause all the list metadata and items to be returned in the search.

- Sort—This defines in what order the items will be returned, in order of the last updated in this case.

- ListType—Defines the list type for the lookup as a wish list.

- ListId—This is filled out with the wish list ID you acquired earlier, to be used in the list lookup.

- SubscriptionId—This gets filled out with your AWS subscription ID.

These parameters are used to build the AWS query URL, which is fetched by HTTPCache and parsed with xmltramp.

Unlike the last program, this one actually uses the metadata returned by the query to update the FEED_META link and title, which is a bit of an improvement. With this extra bit, you can not only see the name of the person to whom the wish list belongs, but when you click the feed's link in your aggregator you'll go straight to their wish list on Amazon.

Also unlike the AmazonSearchScraper, this fetch_items() method has to dig a little deeper for product <Item/> tags, because they're each buried in a <ListItem/> tag. But, once they're extracted and the list of them returned, the AmazonScraper superclass can build them into a feed just the same.

After you have this program working, compare your output with the sample Atom feed in Figure 13-14 and the sample RSS feed in Figure 13-15.

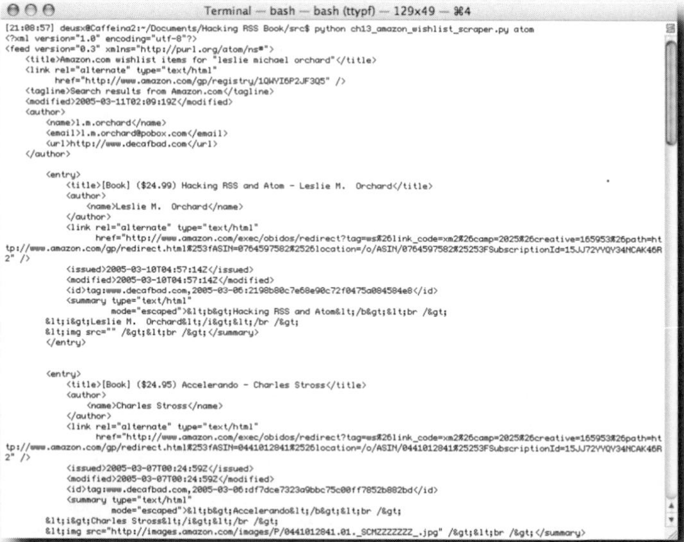

FIGURE 13-14: Producing an Atom feed from an Amazon wish list

FIGURE **13-15**: Producing an RSS feed from an Amazon wish list

Checking Out Other Options

Building feeds from Web services is not the only way to get feeds from the information sources mentioned in this chapter. Take a look at a few alternate approaches.

Using Gnews2RSS and ScrappyGoo

If you have a server with PHP installed, you might be able to use Gnews2RSS, a Google News scraper by Julian Bond with source code available here:

```
http://www.voidstar.com/gnews2rss.php
```

Or, if you'd like to avail yourself of someone else's server, Tim Yang has a version of this script hosted as a service called ScrappyGoo:

```
http://timyang.com/scrappygoo/
```

In either case, you can use one of these solutions as another way to get your Google News fix.

Checking out Yahoo! News Feeds

Although one of the programs in this chapter generates feeds from Yahoo! Search Web Services searches in the news, there's really no need for a scraper if you use Yahoo! News RSS feeds. Check them out here:

```
http://news.yahoo.com/rss
```

However, the program in this chapter can still come in handy for other custom Yahoo! Search feeds.

Transforming Amazon Data into Feeds with XSLT

You can use the programs in this chapter to produce syndication feeds from any number of Amazon Web Services queries, but the AWS API also includes a way to transform the result of queries using XSLT. Check out these sample feeds offered by Amazon by way of this technique:

```
http://www.amazon.com/exec/obidos/subst/xs/syndicate.html
```

Summary

This chapter gave you some starting points for bridging between a few popular Web services and your feed aggregator. It shouldn't be too hard to extend these techniques into other and future Web services as they start popping up from other sites around the Web. There are a few avenues you may want to explore further in particular:

- Take a deeper look at SOAP Web services and how you might pull access to more such APIs into your aggregator.

- The `TrampTmplWrapper` in Listing 13-17 handles only tag character data—you might want to play around with accessing tag attributes for more flexible string templates. This may help you in adapting more REST-based Web services into feeds.

- You could develop the technique of accessing a REST Web service via `xmltramp` into a more general-purpose tool and ease feed generation from these queries even more.

In the next part of the book, things really change directions as you start remixing feeds by converting, filtering, blending, republishing, and extending them. This will combine a lot of what you've done in both consuming *and* producing feeds.

Remixing Feeds

Normalizing and Converting Feeds

By now, you've had a bit of experience tinkering with getting information out of feeds and pushing information into feeds. In this part of the book, you start *remixing* syndication feeds—building programs that clean, convert, filter, blend, republish, and extend feed content. You'll see a few examples of the sorts of components that can make up plumbing in between feed publishers and feed consumers by being a little of both.

But first, you need a few basic tools to lay the groundwork for feed remixing. You see, I've tried so far in this book to be agnostic with respect to competing feed formats and all the versions and variations found out there. Thanks to liberal feed parsing introduced in Chapter 2 and template-based feed generation in Chapter 7, this neutral approach has been easy to maintain.

However, not every application or tool offers this sort of flexibility. The more you start trying to plug various feed producing and consuming tools into each other, the more you'll start to find impedance mismatches and incompatibilities—and the more feed format details start to become important.

In this chapter, you see some of the more tangled bits of feed format interoperability, along with tools for normalization and conversion used to smooth out some of these kinks.

Examining Normalization and Conversion

Normalization is the process of making something normal—that is, removing redundancies, inconsistencies, rough edges, and troublesome bits that trip you up. It's associated with contexts such as mathematics and relational databases, but it all basically boils down to simplifying and cleaning things up.

With respect to syndication feeds, normalization is a process by which you can try to produce consistent and valid feeds where their authors might have taken some liberty with the format or have produced feeds that are invalid altogether. Normalizing feeds before passing them along for further processing allows those tools further down the pipeline to be simpler and more focused, because they won't have to deal with odd edge cases and variations between incoming sources of data.

On the other hand, conversion is a pretty well-known concept—it's how you turn one kind of thing into another. Photovoltaic cells convert sunlight into electricity; using wall plugs in countries other than your own often requires special adaptors; and there are ways to convert cassettes and vinyl records into compact discs.

Applied to syndication feeds, you can convert Atom feeds to RSS, and vice versa, as well as tweak between format versions. This allows you to connect two tools that each have settled on a different feed type and couldn't otherwise be used together. You can also convert feeds into data formats used by tools not ordinarily intended for use with syndications feeds.

Armed with tools for conversion and normalization, you should be able to grease some paths between tools to allow feed format agnosticism where before there'd been none. Something to be aware of, however, is that this flexibility may come at the price of fidelity.

The quality of the conversion depends on both the conversion process and how well the source and result formats match up in the first place. And, because one of the main goals of normalization is simplification, it's often necessarily a lossy process. If you're building a pipeline of tools, any loss of information that happens along the way is cumulative—like a photocopy of a photocopy—and you might not like the result at the end of the line if you're not careful.

These caveats notwithstanding, though, conversion and normalization will be your best friends in remixing feeds.

Normalizing and Converting with XSLT

Because syndication feeds are XML formats, it's useful to consider XSL Transformations (XSLT) for use in normalization and conversion. It's likely you've had some exposure to XSLT if you've been keeping up with XML technologies—though, so far, this book has managed to avoid it. This is because, for the most part, Python offers greater flexibility and conciseness as a general programming language.

On the other hand, because the primary purpose of XSLT is to turn one XML document into another (the activity that makes up the core of feed normalization and conversion), its application would seem particularly apt here. And, if anything, it's a good medium within which to illustrate the nitty-gritty details involved in normalization and conversion.

A Common Data Model Enables Normalization

If you squint hard enough and blur things the right way, all syndication feed formats look a lot alike. Although subtle semantic differences exist among many feed format elements, you can just toss a lot of these fine distinctions aside in order to map mostly equivalent things onto each other. You can fudge together a rough common data model across feeds, regardless of format or version, coming up with a subset of features found. So, although the following should be old news by now, it's worth revisiting:

- Syndication feeds consist of metadata and a collection of entries.

- The top-level metadata in a feed includes such details as

  - Title

  - Publication date

  - Descriptive text

  - Link to a human-readable representation

  - Authorship information

- Each entry contained in a feed is, in turn, a collection of metadata itself, including

  - Title

  - Publication date

  - Link to a human-readable representation

  - Unique ID

  - Summary or blob of content

Of course, a lot of details are passed over by this list, but you can use this to form a serviceable data model onto which most feeds can be mapped. This is the first step toward normalization.

Normalizing Access to Feed Content

Once you have some notion of a common data model, the next task in building the XSL transformation is to come up with XPath expressions to use in accessing the elements of source feeds corresponding to that data model. Rather than reinvent these expressions from scratch, though, you can get a head start from someone else's work.

In an article entitled "Normalizing Syndicated Feed Content" written for his XML.com column "Dive into XML," Mark Pilgrim laid out a set of expressions for use with many variations and complications in feed formats. You can read all about it at this URL:

http://www.xml.com/pub/a/2004/04/07/dive.html

Also, check out the reference documentation for his Universal Feed Parser, which provides XPath expressions to explain how it parses various elements in feeds. These pages go even further than the work presented in the previous article, providing a great deal of coverage between feed formats and versions. Browse around the feedparser reference pages located here:

http://www.feedparser.org/docs/reference.html

The XSLT you see in this chapter borrows heavily from these two resources, so you might want to take some time to check them out for some background on what's coming up.

Normalization Enables Conversion

So far, most of the focus has been on normalization and not conversion. Well, that's because once you have the feed data into a neutral intermediate form (that is, the common data model), conversion is just a matter of outputting the data in your format of choice. Looked at this way, pure normalization itself is just a case of conversion where the output format happens to be the same as the input format.

Building the XSL Transformation

So, you're almost ready to start writing some XSLT code. Here's the plan. Use XPath expressions to map content from a variety of source feed formats to a common data model. Then, use templates to map that data back to a feed format for output.

Take a look at Listing 14-1 for the start of `ch14_xslt_feed_normalizer.xsl`, and I'll explain how things work along the way.

Listing 14-1: ch14_xslt_feed_normalizer.xsl (Part 1 of 12)

```xml
<?xml version='1.0' encoding='utf-8'?>
<!--
    ch14_xslt_feed_normalizer.xsl

    Normalize feed data from Atom and RSS feeds and output
    a new feed in either format, based on 'format' parameter.
-->
<xsl:stylesheet
    version="1.0"
    xmlns:xsl="http://www.w3.org/1999/XSL/Transform"
    xmlns:atom="http://purl.org/atom/ns#"
    xmlns:rdf="http://www.w3.org/1999/02/22-rdf-syntax-ns#"
    xmlns:rss10="http://purl.org/rss/1.0/"
    xmlns:rss09="http://my.netscape.com/rdf/simple/0.9/"
    xmlns:dc="http://purl.org/dc/elements/1.1/"
    xmlns:dcterms="http://purl.org/dc/terms/"
    xmlns:content="http://purl.org/rss/1.0/modules/content/"
    xmlns:l="http://purl.org/rss/1.0/modules/link/"
    xmlns:xhtml="http://www.w3.org/1999/xhtml"
    xmlns:date="http://exslt.org/dates-and-times"
    extension-element-prefixes="date">

    <xsl:import href="http://www.exslt.org/date/functions/format-
date/date.format-date.function.xsl" />

    <xsl:output method="xml" indent="yes" encoding="utf-8" />

    <!-- format parameter expected as 'atom' or 'rss' -->
    <xsl:param name="format" select="'atom'" />
```

```
<!-- Main driver template, switches between
     output formats -->
<xsl:template match="/">
    <xsl:choose>
        <xsl:when test="$format='rss'">
            <xsl:call-template name="rss20.feed" />
        </xsl:when>
        <xsl:otherwise>
            <xsl:call-template name="atom03.feed" />
        </xsl:otherwise>
    </xsl:choose>
</xsl:template>
```

The transformation starts off in Listing 14-1 with a few helpings of XML namespace definitions, as well as a tweak to XSLT formatting options. Then comes a stylesheet parameter named
format, which expects a value of either rss or atom. This is how you can select the output
format. This parameter feeds into the first template of the transformation, which switches
between calling either the template named rss20.feed or the other named atom03.feed,
based on the respective values of the format parameter.

With this established, Listing 14-2 goes on to offer the output templates for the Atom feed
format.

Listing 14-2: ch14_xslt_feed_normalizer.xsl (Part 2 of 12)

```
<!-- Atom 0.3 feed output shell template -->
<xsl:template name="atom03.feed">
    <feed xmlns="http://purl.org/atom/ns#" version="0.3">
        <title><xsl:value-of select="$feed.title"/></title>
        <tagline><xsl:value-of select="$feed.description"/></tagline>
        <link rel="alternate" type="text/html" href="{$feed.link}" />
        <modified><xsl:value-of select="$feed.date" /></modified>
        <xsl:if test="$feed.author.name and $feed.author.email">
            <author>
                <name><xsl:value-of select="$feed.author.name" /></name>
                <email><xsl:value-of select="$feed.author.email" /></email>
            </author>
        </xsl:if>
        <xsl:call-template name="process_entries" />
    </feed>
</xsl:template>

<!-- Atom 0.3 entry output template -->
<xsl:template name="atom03.entry">
    <entry xmlns="http://purl.org/atom/ns#">
        <title><xsl:value-of select="$entry.title" /></title>
        <link rel="alternate" type="text/html" href="{$entry.link}" />
```

Continued

Listing 14-2 *(continued)*

```
            <id><xsl:value-of select="$entry.id" /></id>
            <xsl:if test="$entry.author.name and $entry.author.email">
                <author>
                    <name><xsl:value-of select="$entry.author.name" /></name>
                    <email><xsl:value-of select="$entry.author.email" /></email>
                </author>
            </xsl:if>
            <issued><xsl:value-of select="$entry.date" /></issued>
            <modified><xsl:value-of select="$entry.date" /></modified>
            <summary><xsl:value-of select="$entry.summary" /></summary>
        </entry>
    </xsl:template>
```

Two templates are defined in Listing 14-2: `atom03.feed` and `atom03.entry`. These provide for the production of an Atom 0.3 feed and its entries, respectively. You can see the details of the common feed data model reflected in the variables used to populate the templates. For example, the following XSLT variables are used to provide feed metadata:

- `feed.title`
- `feed.description`
- `feed.link`
- `feed.date`
- `feed.author.name`
- `feed.author.email`

And, to generate each feed entry, these variables come into play:

- `entry.title`
- `entry.link`
- `entry.id`
- `entry.author.name`
- `entry.author.email`
- `entry.date`
- `entry.summary`

You'll see how these variables are supplied with feed data in a little bit, but for now, check out Listing 14-3 for the RSS counterparts to these templates.

Listing 14-3: ch14_xslt_feed_normalizer.xsl (Part 3 of 12)

```
<!-- RSS 2.0 feed output shell template -->
<xsl:template name="rss20.feed">
    <rss version="2.0">
        <channel>
            <title><xsl:value-of select="$feed.title"/></title>
            <description>
                <xsl:value-of select="$feed.description"/>
            </description>
            <link><xsl:value-of select="$feed.link"/></link>
            <pubDate>
                <xsl:call-template name="w3cdtf_to_rfc822">
                    <xsl:with-param name="date" select="$feed.date" />
                </xsl:call-template>
            </pubDate>
            <xsl:if test="$feed.author.email">
                <managingEditor>
                    <xsl:value-of select="$feed.author.email" />
                </managingEditor>
            </xsl:if>
            <xsl:call-template name="process_entries" />
        </channel>
    </rss>
</xsl:template>

<!-- RSS 2.0 entry output template -->
<xsl:template name="rss20.entry">
    <item>
        <title><xsl:value-of select="$entry.title"/></title>
        <link><xsl:value-of select="$entry.link"/></link>
        <pubDate>
            <xsl:call-template name="w3cdtf_to_rfc822">
                <xsl:with-param name="date" select="$entry.date" />
            </xsl:call-template>
        </pubDate>
        <guid><xsl:value-of select="$entry.id" /></guid>
        <description>
            <xsl:value-of select="$entry.summary"/>
        </description>
    </item>
</xsl:template>
```

In Listing 14-3, the templates `rss20.feed` and `rss20.entry` are defined, which are used in building an RSS 2.0 feed and its entries. Just as in Listing 14-2, these templates use variables established by the feed common data model to supply them with content. Comparing the Atom and RSS output templates, you can see what choices have been made with regard to which elements are equivalent.

There is one big difference in these templates for RSS, with respect to the Atom templates. In particular, look at the `<pubDate/>` element in feed metadata and entries. In Atom, timestamps are expressed in W3CDTF format, but in RSS, these timestamps are in RFC 822 format. For the purposes of the common data model, the W3CDTF format was chosen—so, these timestamps will need to be converted for output in RSS feeds. To accomplish this, a template named `w3cdtf_to_rfc822` is employed, which is defined further on in this file.

Cross-Reference If you need a refresher on the RFC 822 and W3CDTF date/time formats, they were first mentioned in this book back in Chapter 7. You may want to flip back there if you want more details.

Moving forward, Listing 14-4 provides the start of building the common data model from the source feed.

Listing 14-4: ch14_xslt_feed_normalizer.xsl (Part 4 of 12)

```
<!-- Extract feed title content -->
<xsl:variable name="feed.title"
    select="/atom:feed/atom:title |
            /rdf:RDF/rss10:channel/rss10:title |
            /rdf:RDF/rss10:channel/dc:title |
            /rdf:RDF/rss09:channel/rss09:title |
            /rss/channel/title |
            /rss/channel/dc:title" />

<!-- Extract feed description -->
<xsl:variable name="feed.description"
    select="/atom:feed/atom:tagline |
            /rss/channel/description |
            /rss/channel/dc:description |
            /rdf:RDF/rss10:channel/rss10:description |
            /rdf:RDF/rdf:channel/rdf:description |
            /rdf:RDF/rdf:channel/dc:description" />

<!-- Extract feed authorship info -->
<xsl:variable name="feed.author.email"
    select="/atom:feed/atom:author/atom:email |
            /rss/channel/managingEditor |
            /rss/channel/dc:creator |
            /rss/channel/dc:author |
            /rdf:RDF/rss10:channel/dc:creator |
            /rdf:RDF/rss10:channel/dc:author |
            /rdf:RDF/rdf:channel/dc:creator |
            /rdf:RDF/rdf:channel/dc:author" />

<!-- Extract feed authorship info -->
<xsl:variable name="feed.author.name"
  select="/atom:feed/atom:author/atom:name |
            $feed.author.email" />
```

Four variables are defined in Listing 14-4, one each for the feed title, description, and author email and name. To pluck this information out of the source feed, XPath expressions borrowed and modified from Mark Pilgrim's work are used to cover Atom 0.3, RSS 2.0, and RSS 1.0 feeds. You can see that a lot of options are involved in each of these data elements, because of feed formats and extensions found in the wild. This is why building a common data model is important—it squashes all the variations down to a few manageable variables.

Here's where some simplification starts, though, as well as information loss.

Although these mappings to identify a feed's author are serviceable, the RSS 2.0 side ignores another potential choice for authorship or ownership cues (that is, the `<webMaster/>` element) and the Atom 0.3 side ignores all contributors and further data available on authors (that is, `<atom:contributor>` and `<atom:url/>` elements).

Each of these things have meanings in the context of their respective formats, but you may or may not need to worry about them—it all depends on what you want out of the feeds and what's significant information for your purposes. In any case, it's important to be aware of where artifacts of the normalization and conversion process start to crop up—here being one of the first places.

Then, a compromise is attempted on name and email address for the author. Whereas RSS feeds generally offer only an email address, Atom has a richer model for its `<author/>` element. In fact, Atom *requires* an author's name, whereas the email address is optional. So, the compromise here is to try to extract both an email address and a name, but if only an email address is available, it will be used for the name.

Continue on to Listing 14-5 for another addition to the feed metadata.

Listing 14-5: ch14_xslt_feed_normalizer.xsl (Part 5 of 12)

```
<!-- Extract various interpretations of feed link -->
<xsl:variable name="feed.link"
    select="/atom:feed/atom:link[@rel='alternate' and
               (@type='text/html' or
                @type='application/xhtml+xml')]/@href |

         /rss/channel/link |
         /rss/channel/dc:relation/@rdf:resource |
         /rss/channel/item/l:link[@l:rel='permalink' and
             (@l:type='text/html' or
              @l:type='application/xhtml+xml')]/@rdf:resource |

         /rdf:RDF/rss09:channel/rss09:link |
         /rdf:RDF/rss10:channel/rss10:link |
         /rdf:RDF/rss10:channel/dc:relation/@rdf:resource |
         /rdf:RDF/rss10:item/l:link[@l:rel='permalink' and
             (@l:type='text/html' or
              @l:type='application/xhtml+xml')]/@rdf:resource" />
```

If you thought there were a lot of options in Listing 14-4 for only three items of data, check out Listing 14-5, which lists a union of eight different XPath expressions in an attempt to locate a link value in the source feed metadata. One way or another, this should hopefully dig up a decent candidate for a feed link in the great majority of cases where one exists at all.

This is where normalization really comes in handy. To support all of these link variants in syndication feeds, a tool would have to implement something as complex as the previous set of XPath expressions. However, if you first run a feed through a normalization transform like what you're building here, all of these potential sources for a link get narrowed down to a single, consistent element, thus allowing the simplification of tools downstream.

Now, move on to Listing 14-6, which attempts to intelligently handle the feed publication date.

Listing 14-6: ch14_xslt_feed_normalizer.xsl (Part 6 of 12)

```
<!-- Extract feed publish date -->
<xsl:variable name="feed.date">
    <xsl:choose>
        <!-- If RSS 2.0 pubDate found, convert from RFC822 -->
        <xsl:when test="/rss/channel/pubDate">
            <xsl:call-template name="rfc822_to_w3cdtf">
                <xsl:with-param name="date"
                    select="/rss/channel/pubDate" />
            </xsl:call-template>
        </xsl:when>
        <!-- All other date formats are assumed W3CDTF/ISO8601 -->
        <xsl:otherwise>
            <xsl:value-of
                select="/atom:feed/atom:modified |
                        /rss/channel/dc:date |
                        /rdf:RDF/rss10:channel/dc:date |
                        /rdf:RDF/rdf:channel/dc:date |
                        /rdf:RDF/rdf:channel/dcterms:modified" />
        </xsl:otherwise>
    </xsl:choose>
</xsl:variable>
```

As mentioned back near Listing 14-3, RSS feeds use the RFC 822 format for dates, whereas the common data model expects to use the W3CDTF format. So, when dates in the RSS 2.0 element <pubDate/> are encountered, you'll need to perform a conversion. You do this using a template named rfc822_to_w3cdtf, which accepts RFC 822 in the parameter date and outputs that as W3CDTF.

With the feed metadata sorted out, it's time to take care of the individual entries. Listing 14-7 offers the start of extracting content from source feed entries in a template named process_entries.

Listing 14-7: ch14_xslt_feed_normalizer.xsl (Part 7 of 12)

```
<xsl:template name="process_entries">

    <!-- Find and process all feed entries -->
    <xsl:for-each
        select="/atom:feed/atom:entry |
                /rdf:RDF/rss10:item |
                /rdf:RDF/rss09:item |
                /rss/channel/item">

        <!-- Extract entry title -->
        <xsl:variable name="entry.title"
            select="atom:title | title | dc:title |
                    rdf:title | rss10:title" />

        <!-- Extract entry GUID -->
        <xsl:variable name="entry.id"
            select="atom:id | @rdf:about |
                    guid[not(@isPermaLink) or @isPermaLink='true']|
                    link"/>

        <!-- Extract entry authorship -->
        <xsl:variable name="entry.author.email"
            select="atom:author/atom:email | dc:creator |
                    dc:author" />
        <xsl:variable name="entry.author.name"
            select="atom:author/atom:name | $entry.author.email" />

        <!-- Extract entry summary content -->
        <xsl:variable name="entry.summary"
            select="atom:summary | description | dc:description |
                    rdf:description | rss10:description" />
```

First off in Listing 14-7's `process_entries` is a `for-each` loop fed by an XPath that matches feed entry nodes in Atom and RSS feeds. Inside this loop are variable definitions extracting entry titles, GUIDs, and summaries, acting as counterparts to the variables defined earlier for feed metadata. Again, each of these elements from source feeds are similar, but just different enough to require slightly different XPath formulations for each. These are mashed together into common data model variables.

Something to notice in the previous discussion is the selection of GUID for entries. Non-permalink GUIDs in RSS are ignored in preference for links. This decision was made because, for inclusion in Atom feeds, entry GUIDs *must* be valid URIs—yet in RSS 2.0, any string value is allowed as a GUID. So, here's a spot where, in order to accommodate two feed formats for output, something that's a requirement of one format (entry GUIDs as URIs) gets used for both.

Also, notice that the same compromise on author details is made here as was done at the feed-level.

Finally, another lossy decision is made here. Feed entry summaries from the Atom format are extracted, discarding elements using its full content model. Also, many content extensions and conventions used by RSS feeds are ignored, such as `<content:encoded/>` and other means to include HTML/XHTML content and enclosures. You may want to think about ways to add handling of these bits of richer content into the normalization process as a future project.

Next, in Listing 14-8, you can find an attempt to harvest links from feed entries.

Listing 14-8: ch14_xslt_feed_normalizer.xsl (Part 8 of 12)

```
<!-- Extract from various candidates for entry link -->
<xsl:variable name="entry.link"
    select="atom:link[@rel='alternate' and
            ( @type='text/html' or
              @type='application/xhtml+xml' )]/@href |

            l:link[@l:rel='permalink' and
              (@l:type='text/html' or
               @l:type='application/xhtml+xml')]/@rdf:resource |

            rss09:link | rss10:link | @rdf:about | comments |
            link | guid[not(@isPermaLink) or @isPermaLink='true']"/>
```

Again, as in Listing 14-5, the XPath expression in Listing 14-8 is fairly complex, because it's an attempt to span many variants to extract feed entry links. Some of these are fairly uncommon, and some of them are just barely different enough to require inclusion (that is, differences in namespaces), but using them all gives an excellent chance of extracting useful information.

There's also a little bit of confusion covered here worth mentioning. Some RSS feeds offer links in their entries with the `<link/>` element, along with generated `<guid/>` values that are not navigable links. Meanwhile, some RSS feeds provide identical values for the `<link/>` and `<guid/>` elements. And, yet other feeds offer the link in a `<guid/>` element and omit `<link/>` altogether. Although the `<guid/>` element specifies an attribute `isPermalink` to help determine semantics, all of this can cause a bit of a teacup tempest of ambiguity that complicates things a little.

There's one last thing left to extract, and it happens in Listing 14-9.

Listing 14-9: ch14_xslt_feed_normalizer.xsl (Part 9 of 12)

```
<!-- Extract entry publish date -->
<xsl:variable name="entry.date">
    <xsl:choose>
        <!-- If RSS 2.0 pubDate found, perform conversion -->
        <xsl:when test="pubDate">
            <xsl:call-template name="rfc822_to_w3cdtf">
                <xsl:with-param name="date" select="pubDate" />
```

```
        </xsl:call-template>
    </xsl:when>
    <!-- All others assumed W3CDTF / ISO8601 -->
    <xsl:otherwise>
        <xsl:value-of
            select="atom:modified | dc:date |
                    dcterms:modified" />
    </xsl:otherwise>
    </xsl:choose>
</xsl:variable>
```

In counterpart to Listing 14-6, the code in Listing 14-9 handles date extraction, using the `rfc822_to_w3cdtf` template to convert RSS entry `<pubDate/>` elements from RFC 822 format to the common data model's W3CDTF format.

And, at last, it's time to build a feed entry from all of this extracted data, in Listing 14-10.

Listing 14-10: ch14_xslt_feed_normalizer.xsl (Part 10 of 12)

```
<!-- Insert the appropriate feed entry format -->
<xsl:choose>

    <xsl:when test="$format='rss'">
        <xsl:call-template name="rss20.entry">
            <xsl:with-param name="entry.title"
                select="$entry.title" />
            <xsl:with-param name="entry.id"
                select="$entry.id" />
            <xsl:with-param name="entry.date"
                select="$entry.date" />
            <xsl:with-param name="entry.summary"
                select="$entry.summary" />
            <xsl:with-param name="entry.link"
                select="$entry.link" />
        </xsl:call-template>
    </xsl:when>

    <xsl:otherwise>
        <xsl:call-template name="atom03.entry">
            <xsl:with-param name="entry.title"
                select="$entry.title" />
            <xsl:with-param name="entry.id"
                select="$entry.id" />
            <xsl:with-param name="entry.date"
                select="$entry.date" />
            <xsl:with-param name="entry.summary"
                select="$entry.summary" />
```

Continued

Listing 14-10 *(continued)*

```
                        <xsl:with-param name="entry.link"
                            select="$entry.link" />
                    </xsl:call-template>
                </xsl:otherwise>

            </xsl:choose>

        </xsl:for-each>

    </xsl:template>
```

There's a lot of verbosity and redundancy in Listing 14-10, but that's mostly because of a limitation in XSLT that prevents the use of a variable in naming a template during a call. So, this code sets up a conditional using the XSLT parameter format, to call either the atom03.entry template defined in Listing 14-2 or rss20.entry defined in Listing 14-3. Both of these calls are supplied with all of the feed entry data model variables extracted in the past few listings.

This wraps up the for-each loop and the process_entries template, all of which results in the harvesting of source feed entries into the common data model variables and the subsequent production of feed entries in the desired result feed format.

What's left in this XSLT code is to finish off the loose ends with the definitions of the w3cdtf_to_rfc822 and rfc822_to_w3cdtf date/time conversion templates. Check out Listing 14-11 for the first of this pair.

Listing 14-11: ch14_xslt_feed_normalizer.xsl (Part 11 of 12)

```
<!--
    w3cdtf_to_rfc822: Accepts a date parameter in W3CDTF format,
    converts and outputs the date in RFC822 format.
-->
<xsl:template name="w3cdtf_to_rfc822">
    <!-- 'date' param, accepts W3CDTF format date/time -->
    <xsl:param name="date" select="'2005-04-08T04:00:00Z'" />

    <!-- Get the timezone and fixup for RFC 822 format -->
    <xsl:variable name="tz_raw"
        select="date:format-date($date, 'z')" />

    <xsl:variable name="tz">
        <xsl:choose>
            <xsl:when test="$tz_raw='UTC'">GMT</xsl:when>
            <xsl:otherwise>
                <xsl:value-of
                    select="concat(substring($tz_raw,4,3),
                                   substring($tz_raw,8,2) )" />
```

```
          </xsl:otherwise>
        </xsl:choose>
    </xsl:variable>

    <!-- Build the RFC 822 date/time string -->
    <xsl:value-of
      select="concat(
      date:format-date($date,'EEE, d MMM yyyy HH:mm:ss '), $tz)" />
</xsl:template>
```

The `w3cdtf_to_rfc822` template in Listing 14-11 uses the EXSLT extensions implemented by many XSLT processors, including the one provided by the 4Suite package you've used in this book. In particular, this template uses the dates and times extension functions, documented here:

`http://exslt.org/date/index.html`

These functions are used to extract and convert parts of a W3CDTF date/time to build components for the RFC 822 format. The time zone handling in this template is notably a bit of a hack, used to force the output of the EXSLT function into a form suitable for inclusion in the RFC 822 format.

And, then, in Listing 14-12, the inverse functionality is implemented in the `rfc822_to_w3cdtf` template.

Listing 14-12: ch14_xslt_feed_normalizer.xsl (Part 12 of 12)

```
<!--
    rfc822_to_w3cdtf: Accepts a date parameter in RFC822 format,
    converts and outputs the date in W3CDTF format.
-->
<xsl:template name="rfc822_to_w3cdtf">
    <!-- 'date' param, accepts RFC822 format date/time -->
    <xsl:param name="date"
        select="'Fri, 08 Apr 2005 04:00:00 GMT'" />

    <!-- Extract the month name -->
    <xsl:variable name="mn" select="substring($date, 9, 3)" />

    <!-- Map month name onto month number -->
    <xsl:variable name="m">
      <xsl:choose>
          <xsl:when test="$mn='Jan'">01</xsl:when>
          <xsl:when test="$mn='Feb'">02</xsl:when>
          <xsl:when test="$mn='Mar'">03</xsl:when>
          <xsl:when test="$mn='Apr'">04</xsl:when>
          <xsl:when test="$mn='May'">05</xsl:when>
          <xsl:when test="$mn='Jun'">06</xsl:when>
          <xsl:when test="$mn='Jul'">07</xsl:when>
```

Continued

Listing 14-12 (continued)

```
            <xsl:when test="$mn='Aug'">08</xsl:when>
            <xsl:when test="$mn='Sep'">09</xsl:when>
            <xsl:when test="$mn='Oct'">10</xsl:when>
            <xsl:when test="$mn='Nov'">11</xsl:when>
            <xsl:when test="$mn='Dec'">12</xsl:when>
        </xsl:choose>
    </xsl:variable>

    <!-- Extract remaining day, year, and time from date string -->
    <xsl:variable name="d" select="substring($date, 6, 2)" />
    <xsl:variable name="y" select="substring($date, 13, 4)" />
    <xsl:variable name="hh" select="substring($date, 18, 2)" />
    <xsl:variable name="mm" select="substring($date, 21, 2)" />
    <xsl:variable name="ss" select="substring($date, 24, 2)" />

    <xsl:variable name="tz_raw" select="substring($date, 27)" />
    <xsl:variable name="tz">
        <xsl:choose>
            <xsl:when test="$tz_raw='GMT'">Z</xsl:when>
            <xsl:when test="$tz_raw='EDT'">-04:00</xsl:when>
            <xsl:when test="$tz_raw='EST'">-05:00</xsl:when>
            <xsl:when test="$tz_raw='CDT'">-05:00</xsl:when>
            <xsl:when test="$tz_raw='CST'">-06:00</xsl:when>
            <xsl:when test="$tz_raw='MDT'">-06:00</xsl:when>
            <xsl:when test="$tz_raw='MST'">-07:00</xsl:when>
            <xsl:when test="$tz_raw='PDT'">-07:00</xsl:when>
            <xsl:when test="$tz_raw='PST'">-08:00</xsl:when>
            <xsl:otherwise>
                <xsl:value-of
                    select="concat(substring($tz_raw,1,3),':',
                                   substring($tz_raw,4))" />
            </xsl:otherwise>
        </xsl:choose>
    </xsl:variable>

    <!-- Build and output the W3CDTF date from components -->
    <xsl:value-of select="concat($y,'-',$m,'-',$d, 'T',
                                 $hh,':',$mm,':',$ss, $tz)" />
</xsl:template>

</xsl:stylesheet>
```

The `rfc822_to_w3cdf` template defined in Listing 14-12 slices and dices RFC 822 format date/times and munges them into W3CDTF format. It's a pretty dirty hack, implementing a somewhat stupid, brute-force parser of RFC 822. In particular, you may want to watch out for (and possibly improve) its handling of time zones. For the most part, though, it seems to work okay for a large enough number of feeds to be useful—but it's certainly not robust by any means.

Using 4Suite's XSLT Processor

You may have a preferred XSLT processor already at your disposal if you do any work with XSLT regularly, and the code so far in this chapter should work fine with it as long as it supports EXSLT extensions. However, if you don't have an XSLT processor at hand, you can use the one supplied by the 4Suite package, which you should have installed back in Chapter 9.

It's pretty easy to set up—take a look at Listing 14-13 for a Python program that runs the XSLT presented in this chapter.

Listing 14-13: ch14_xslt_feed_normalizer.py

```python
#!/usr/bin/env python
"""
ch14_xslt_feed_normalizer.py

Use 4Suite to apply an XSLT to a URL
"""
import sys
from Ft.Xml.Xslt import Processor
from Ft.Xml.InputSource import DefaultFactory

FEED_URL = 'http://www.decafbad.com/blog/index.xml'

def main():
    feed_format = ( len(sys.argv) > 1 ) and sys.argv[1] or 'atom'
    feed_url    = ( len(sys.argv) > 2 ) and sys.argv[2] or FEED_URL

    source      = DefaultFactory.fromUri(feed_url)

    trans_fin = open('ch14_xslt_feed_normalizer.xsl', 'r')
    trans_url = \
        'http://www.decafbad.com/2005/04/ch14_xslt_normalizer.xsl'
    transform = DefaultFactory.fromStream(trans_fin, trans_url)

    processor = Processor.Processor()
    processor.appendStylesheet(transform)

    result = processor.run(source,
                           topLevelParams={'format':feed_format})
    print result

if __name__=='__main__': main()
```

In Listing 14-13, you have a fairly simple program that accepts an optional output feed format argument, as well as a feed to normalize and convert. By default, it produces an Atom feed from the RSS feed at decafbad.com.

Trying Out the XSLT Feed Normalizer

If you take a look at Figure 14-1, you'll see an RSS 2.0 feed before normalization and conversion. Then, check out Figure 14-2 to see this feed rendered in Atom output format. After that, Figure 14-3 shows what RSS feed looks like when normalized back to RSS.

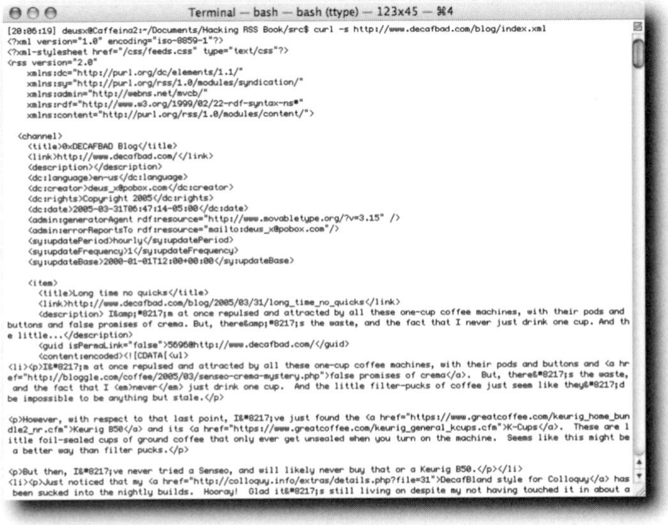

FIGURE 14-1: View of an RSS 2.0 feed before normalization

FIGURE 14-2: RSS 2.0 input feed normalized as an Atom 0.3 feed

FIGURE 14-3: RSS 2.0 input feed normalized as an RSS 2.0 feed

Next, take a look at the example Atom 0.3 feed in Figure 14-4. This feed is normalized back to Atom in Figure 14-5, and then to RSS in Figure 14-6.

FIGURE 14-4: View of an Atom 0.3 feed before normalization

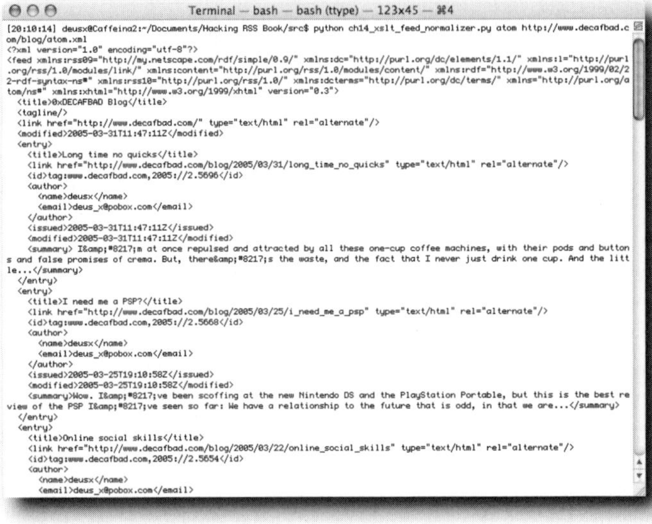

FIGURE 14-5: Atom 0.3 feed normalized as an Atom 0.3 feed

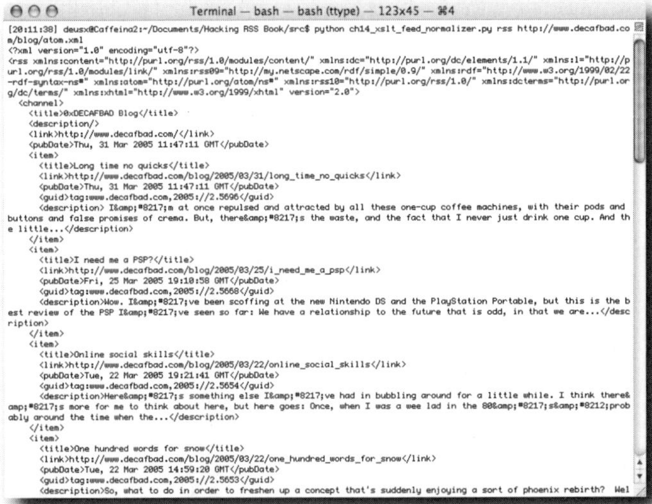

FIGURE 14-6: Atom 0.3 feed normalized as an RSS 2.0 feed

As you can see in these program runs, this XSLT strips a lot of information from the source feeds, resulting in much simpler and more straightforward feeds. These new feeds will be a lot easier to parse and handle in other programs, at the expense of detail.

Normalizing and Converting with feedparser

Now that you've had a chance to dig into the details of feed normalization and conversion using XSLT, it's time to return to Python.

Why? Well, for one, Python is better as a general programming language. So, if you want to do something more than just convert from feed to feed (for example, such as perform a complex filtering algorithm or include data obtained by the use of Web services), you'll find XSLT gets cumbersome pretty fast. (In fact, it already has become a bit awkward, if you consider the kludges employed for converting between date formats.)

The other big reason for returning to Python is that the Universal Feed Parser is there. The XSLT in this chapter borrowed heavily from the XPath expressions found in the feedparser documentation, as well as an article by its author. But, the feedparser goes even further beyond the subset of extraction and normalization steps taken so far in this chapter. In addition, feedparser helps overcome another difficulty you may encounter when trying to handle feeds with XSLT: Namely, that XSLT requires that you supply it with well-formed XML. And, unfortunately, many feeds requiring normalization need it because they're so broken in the first place!

So, this next program combines a few of the tools you already have: the Universal Feed Parser introduced in the first part of this book, and the scraperlib module built in the second. The feedparser module does a great job of making sense of just about anything you can throw at it that even vaguely claims to be a syndication feed. Once you have access to the data structures feedparser produces (analogous to the common data model variables established in the XSLT previously), it won't be hard at all to map them onto scraperlib data structures.

With this in mind, you can start with Listing 14-14, which offers the start of a new program called ch14_feed_normalizer.py.

> **Listing 14-14:** ch14_feed_normalizer.py (Part 1 of 4)

```
#!/usr/bin/env python
"""
ch14_feed_normalizer.py

Use feedparser and scraperlib to normalize feed content.
"""
import sys, calendar, time
import feedparser
from scraperlib import FeedEntryDict, Scraper

def main():
    """
    Given an argument of 'atom' or 'rss' on the command line,
    produce an Atom or RSS feed.
    """
    feed_uri = sys.argv[2]
    scraper  = FeedNormalizer(feed_uri)
```

Continued

Listing 14-14 *(continued)*

```
if len(sys.argv) > 1 and sys.argv[1] == 'rss':
    print scraper.scrape_rss()
else:
    print scraper.scrape_atom()
```

This program's `main()` function expects two arguments to be given on the command line: a feed format and the feed URI to be normalized. An instance of `FeedNormalizer` is initialized with the feed URI, and the appropriate scraper method is called to generate the normalized feed.

Having laid out the driver for this program, you can move on to the definition of the `FeedNormalizer` class, starting in Listing 14-15.

Listing 14-15: ch14_feed_normalizer.py (Part 2 of 4)

```
class FeedNormalizer(Scraper):
    """
    Uses feedparser data to rebuild normalized feeds.
    """
    STATE_FN     = 'normalizer_state'
    FULL_CONTENT = True

    def __init__(self, feed_uri=None):
        """Initialize with the feed URI for parsing."""
        self.feed_uri = feed_uri

    def produce_entries(self):
        """Use normalize_feed() to generate normalized
           entries"""
        feed = feedparser.parse(self.feed_uri)

        self.FEED_META = normalize_feed_meta(feed,
            self.date_fmt)

        entries = normalize_entries(feed.entries,
            self.FULL_CONTENT)

        for e in entries:
            e.date_fmt = self.date_fmt

        return entries
```

The `FeedNormalizer` class in Listing 14-15 is pretty bare-bones. Most of the functionality to normalize the feed metadata and entry content lies in module-level functions to be defined shortly.

`FeedNormalizer` is a subclass of `Scraper`, performing all its work in the `produce_entries()` method. This method fetches and parses the feed using the `feedparser.parse()` function, then it builds feed metadata using the `normalize_feed_meta()` method and uses the `normalize_entries()` method to come up with a list of normalized entries in the form of `FeedEntryDict` objects used by `Scraper`. It then makes a run through these entries, fixing up the date format, and returns the list in the end.

So, moving on, check out the definition of `normalize_feed_meta()` in Listing 14-16.

Listing 14-16: ch14_feed_normalizer.py (Part 3 of 4)

```python
def normalize_feed_meta(feed_parsed, date_fmt):
    """
    Produce normalized feed metadata from a parsed feed.
    """
    feed_in = feed_parsed.feed

    # Build the initial feed metadata map
    feed_meta = {
        'feed.title'        : feed_in.get('title', 'untitled'),
        'feed.link'         : feed_in.get('link', ''),
        'feed.tagline'      : feed_in.get('tagline', ''),
        'feed.author.name'  : 'unnamed',
        'feed.author.email' : 'example@example.com',
        'feed.author.url'   : 'http://www.example.com'
    }

    # Update the output feed's modified time if incoming feed
    # has it
    if feed_in.has_key('modified_parsed'):
        feed_meta['feed.modified'] = \
            time.strftime(date_fmt, feed_in.modified_parsed)
    else:
        feed_meta['feed.modified'] = \
            time.strftime(date_fmt, time.gmtime())

    # Copy incoming feed author details, if any.
    if feed_in.has_key('author_detail'):
        feed_meta['feed.author.name']  = \
            feed_in.author_detail.get('name','')
        feed_meta['feed.author.email'] = \
            feed_in.author_detail.get('email','')
        feed_meta['feed.author.url']   = \
            feed_in.author_detail.get('url','')
```

Continued

Listing 14-16 *(continued)*

```
        # Copy incoming feed author name, if not details.
        elif feed_in.has_key('author'):
            feed_meta['feed.author.name'] = feed_in.author

    return feed_meta
```

The definition of `normalize_feed_meta()` in Listing 14-16 handles building feed-level metadata from the results of `feedparser`'s work. It starts off by building an initial feed metadata map with the feed title, link, and tagline information along with some defaults for author information.

Next, the function checks for the existence of a feed-level modification date. If present, it copies the value over in the appropriate date format given in the function call. The `feedparser` provides the modification timestamp as a standard tuple suitable for use with functions from the `time` module. So, if this key exists, the `stftime` function is used to convert the value to the appropriate date format.

After that, some work is put into copying over the feed author details. The input feed might have provided just an author email in an RSS feed's `<webMaster>` or `<managingEditor>` element, or it may have included the complete set of name/email/URL elements defined in the Atom format. So, the final part of Listing 14-16 attempts to figure out what author details are available, and copies over what it finds.

Continuing on to Listing 14-17, check out the definition of `normalize_entries()`.

Listing 14-17: ch14_feed_normalizer.py (Part 4 of 4)

```
def normalize_entries(entries_in, full_content=True):
    """
    Return a list of normalized FeedEntryDict objects, given a
    list of entries from the feedparser.
    """
    entries = []

    # Process incoming feed entries.
    for entry_in in entries_in:

        # Create the empty new output feed entry.
        entry_out = FeedEntryDict()
        entry_out.orig = entry_in

        # Perform a straight copy of a few entry attributes.
        for n in ('id', 'title', 'link'):
            if entry_in.has_key(n):
                entry_out[n] = entry_in[n]
```

```
        # Convert feedparser time tuples to seconds and
        # copy over.
        for n in ('modified', 'issued'):
            if entry_in.get('%s_parsed' % n, None):
                entry_out[n] = \
                    calendar.timegm(entry_in['%s_parsed' % n])

        # Decide whether to copy only summary or full content.
        if full_content and entry_in.has_key('content'):
            content_list = [ x.value for x in entry_in.content
                             if 'text' in x.type ]
            entry_out['summary'] = ''.join(content_list)
        elif entry_in.has_key('summary'):
            entry_out['summary'] = entry_in.summary

        # Append finished feed to list.
        entries.append(entry_out)

    # Return accumulated output feed entries.
    return entries

if __name__=='__main__': main()
```

In Listing 14-17, with the normalize_entries() function, every incoming feed entry parsed out by feedparser is processed and used to populate a FeedEntryDict object for inclusion in the outgoing feed. The GUID, title, and link from the incoming feed entry (where they exist) are copied over unmodified to the outgoing feed entry. Then, the modified and issued timestamps are provided by feedparser as tuples, so these are each converted to seconds using timegm() from the calendar module and copied into the outgoing entry.

On the Web Note that the use of timegm() is necessary because the feedparser module itself normalizes all times to the UTC time zone. Check out the description of this function here:

> http://docs.python.org/lib/module-calendar.html#12h-1439

Finally, an attempt is made to handle the content or summary provided by the incoming feed entry. Based on the class constant defined at the beginning of the class, this part copies over the feed entry's summary or its full content. This part is definitely a hack, because the summary element of the outgoing feed entry isn't necessarily the best place for full content to be stashed. For the most part, though, this works fine—but you may want to play around with things here.

And that's it for FeedNormalizer, and the program is ready to be used. Take a look at Figure 14-7 to see a feed before normalization. This is actually a valid feed, so it isn't any sort of special case or challenge for the normalizer. Running this feed through the normalizer results in the output shown in Figure 14-8 and Figure 14-9.

FIGURE 14-7: View of an example feed before normalization

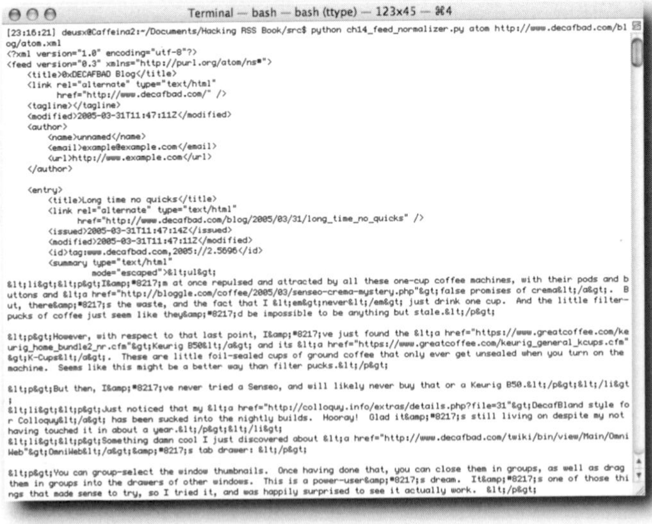

FIGURE 14-8: Input feed normalized as an Atom feed

FIGURE 14-9: Input feed normalized as an RSS feed

You may have noticed that this Python feed normalizer is quite a bit simpler and shorter than the XSLT version—the XSLT took up 12 listings of code, whereas this program fit into only four. The Python version doesn't do significantly less work, so what is it?

Well, in case it isn't obvious, it's because you're not seeing all the code tucked away in the `feedparser` module, and you're reusing all the feed generation code from the previous part of the book. Put all together, the XSLT version is actually simpler and shorter, but less capable. This Python version will be more useful in the coming chapters because you can tap into the middle of the process and tweak the normalized entries on their way to becoming a new feed.

Checking Out Other Options

Although normalization and conversion of syndication feeds is a bit of a new subject, here are a few further resources you can take a look at.

Using FeedBurner

FeedBurner is a service you can use to clean up and normalize feeds, located here:

`http://www.feedburner.com`

With FeedBurner, you can sign up to have feeds you control managed through their servers, redirecting your subscribers to one of their URLs. In exchange for a little loss of control over the hosting of your feeds, you get cleaner feeds tailored to subscribers' news aggregators, as well as a slew of other features.

Finding More Conversions in XSLT

If you'd like some more examples of feed conversion in XSLT, check out these transformations from various feed formats into HTML by Rich Manalang, located here:

`http://manalang.com/archives/2004/06/17/xslts-for-rss-and-atom-feeds/`

Also, take a look at this set of XSLT files for converting Atom to RSS 1.0 and 2.0 by Aaron Straup Cope, found at this URL:

`http://www.aaronland.info/xsl/atom/0.3/`

Playing with Feedsplitter

Feedsplitter is another route to explore in converting feeds to JavaScript includes, hosted here:

`http://chxo.com/software/feedsplitter/`

This project is implemented using PHP, and works as a live and dynamic filter to convert syndication feeds into JavaScript includes.

Summary

In this chapter, you explored what it takes to normalize and convert syndication feeds between formats. In the XSLT version, you saw what decisions were made in squashing various feed elements together, and where data was tossed out altogether. Then, a more Python-friendly version of feed normalization and conversion was offered using the Universal Feed Parser and feed production code from the previous part of the book. This code will come in handy throughout the rest of the book, as source entries are filtered and tweaked on their way to being produced as new feeds.

Plenty of avenues for further development were left open in this chapter:

- The handling of full content and things such as enclosures was left out of the normalization and conversion code in this chapter. You might want to look into these things and see how best to handle them in a cross-format way.

- Date/time handling in the XSLT code is a bit of a hack. Try your hand at improving its robustness.

- Try finding other formats to which conversion of feed data would be useful.

So, now that you've started loosening the bindings between syndication feed data and format, Chapter 15 shows you how to start building some filters and analysis into your feed plumbing.

Filtering and Sifting Feeds

In Chapter 14, you dug into normalization and conversion of feeds by mapping their entries onto a common data model and then generating a new feed based on that data. Any changes that occurred on the way from source feed to the end product came as the result of issues in conversion fidelity or impedance mismatch between feed formats—in other words: unintentional noise in the signal.

Well, in this chapter, you're going to take a different tack by filtering and sifting through feed entries. With filtering, you step into the middle of the conversion process, deciding which entries make it though to the resulting feed. You can take this idea further by introducing a little basic machine learning to try to automate some of this filtering. And, in sifting through feed content, you'll be able to make drastic changes to feeds, even turning them inside out to see what common things people are talking about.

Filtering by Keywords and Metadata

As mentioned previously, one of the things you can do once you have some conversion and normalization machinery for feeds is to intervene in the middle of the process to perform entry filtering. In this first program, you'll be able to use regular expressions matched against properties of feed entries to act as a sieve—entries that match these regexes show up in the feed produced in the end, whereas others are discarded.

Check out Listing 15-1 for the start of this program, named `ch15_feed_filter.py`.

> **Listing 15-1:** ch15_feed_filter.py (Part 1 of 4)

```python
#!/usr/bin/env python
"""
ch15_feed_filter.py

Build a new feed out of entries filtered from a source feed.
"""
import sys, re, feedparser
from scraperlib import FeedEntryDict, Scraper
from ch14_feed_normalizer import normalize_feed_meta, normalize_entries

FEED_NAME_FN = "www/www.decafbad.com/docs/private-feeds/filtered.%s"
FEED_URI     = "http://del.icio.us/rss/deusx/webdev"
FILTER_RE    = {
    'category' : '.*python.*',
}
```

There's nothing shocking yet, with Listing 15-1. The module starts off with a few familiar module imports. The location of the log configuration file is stored in LOG_CONF, and a template for output feed files is supplied in FEED_NAME_FN. Following these is the definition of FEED_URI, a configuration constant supplying the default URI to a feed to be processed in the main() function. At this point, the URI points at a feed of my Web development bookmark postings at del.icio.us.

Next comes the definition of FILTER_RE, which represents the default filter criteria for this program. This is a simple map from feedparser entry dictionary keys to regular expressions—in the coming listings, this map is used to match against the corresponding feed entry attributes to decide whether or not to include a particular entry in the final feed produced by the program.

In Listing 15-1, the definition for FILTER_RE accepts any feed entry whose category attribute contains 'python'. You can tweak this map to filter for any other combination of entry attributes, such as the title, summary, or whatever other attributes are made available by the feedparser module. For example, to filter for feeds whose titles contain 'water pails' and whose authors include 'jack' or 'jill', use something like the following:

```python
FILTER_RE = {
    'title'  : '.*water pails.* ',
    'author' : '(jack|jill)',
}
```

You may want to review both the documentation for the feedparser module and Python's regular expressions to get a feel for what's possible here. Moving on, take a look at Listing 15-2 for the main() function you can use to try out the filter.

Listing 15-2: ch15_feed_filter.py (Part 2 of 4)

```
def main():
    """
    Perform a test run of the FeedFilter using defaults.
    """
    # Build the feed filter.
    f = FeedFilter(FEED_URI, FILTER_RE)
    f.STATE_FN = 'filter_state'

    # Output the feed as both RSS and Atom.
    open(FEED_NAME_FN % 'rss', 'w').write(f.scrape_rss())
    open(FEED_NAME_FN % 'atom', 'w').write(f.scrape_atom())
```

The definition of main() in Listing 15-2 simply serves to apply an instance of the FeedFilter class to the feed located at FEED_URI. The output of this class is written out in both Atom and RSS formats to the appropriate filenames produced by populating the template in FEED_NAME_FN.

Now, Listing 15-3 offers the beginning of the FeedFilter class.

Listing 15-3: ch15_feed_filter.py (Part 3 of 4)

```
class FeedFilter(Scraper):
    """
    Filter feed entries using a regex map.
    """
    def __init__(self, feed_uri, filter_re):
        """Initialize with the feed URI for parsing."""
        # Stow the feed URI and cache
        self.feed_uri   = feed_uri

        # Pre-compile all regexes
        self.filter_re = {}
        for k,v in filter_re.items():
            self.filter_re[k] = re.compile(v,
                re.DOTALL | re.MULTILINE | re.IGNORECASE)
```

Listing 15-3 gives you the definition for the FeedFilter's __init__ method, which accepts a feed URI and entry regex map. The feed URI gets stowed away in the object, but the entry regex map gets preprocessed before storing it in the instance.

A new map is created as an object property with all of the original map's regex strings precompiled into Python regular expression objects. Note that flags are set on these regexes to accept whitespace for wildcard matches, match on multiline strings, and ignore case sensitivity. You may or may not want to tweak these flags in your own use.

Continuing on to Listing 15-4, you can find the definition of the `produce_entries()` method, where the filtering actually takes place.

Listing 15-4: ch15_feed_filter.py (Part 4 of 4)

```python
def produce_entries(self):
    """
    Filter entries from a feed using the regex map, use the
    feed normalizer to produce FeedEntryDict objects.
    """
    # Use the cache to get the feed for filtering.
    feed_data = feedparser.parse(self.feed_uri)

    # Build the output feed's normalized metadata
    self.FEED_META = normalize_feed_meta(feed_data, self.date_fmt)

    # Now, apply the regex map to filter each incoming entry.
    entries_filtered = []
    for entry in feed_data.entries:
        # Initially assume the entry is okay for inclusion.
        ok_include = True

        # Iterate through each entry key and regex pair.
        for k,r in self.filter_re.items():
            # The first time a field of the entry fails to match
            # the regex map criteria, reject it for inclusion.
            if not (entry.has_key(k) and r.match(entry[k])):
                ok_include = False
                break

        # Finally, if the entry passes all the tests, include it.
        if ok_include: entries_filtered.append(entry)

    # Normalize all the filtered entries
    entries = normalize_entries(entries_filtered)
    for entry in entries:
        entry.date_fmt = self.date_fmt

    return entries

if __name__=='__main__': main()
```

The definition of produce_entries() in Listing 15-4 should look a lot like the one in the original Python feed normalizer in Listing 14-15. At least in the beginning, things are similar—in the middle is where the filtering happens.

Each of the entries in the list supplied by feedparser from the original feed is examined. This examination is done by looping through the field name/regular expression pairs that make up the filter map. If a particular attribute is present in the map, but missing from the current entry, the entry is rejected. If the attribute is present, it's matched against the regular expression—failing this match causes the entry to be rejected also.

However, if at the end of the loop, all entry attributes specified in the filter map are present and pass their respective regular expression matches, the entry is appended onto a list of entries for inclusion in the output feed. And finally, at the end of the method, this list of feed entries is passed through the normalize_entries() function from the previous chapter, which does the work of normalizing feedparser entries into FeedEntryDict objects for use in building the output feed.

Trying Out the Feed Filter

Now, if you check out Figure 15-1, you'll see what a sample run of this program looks like. It's not very exciting, because it just writes out the feed in both formats. You can see what this feed might look like as a subscription in Figure 15-2.

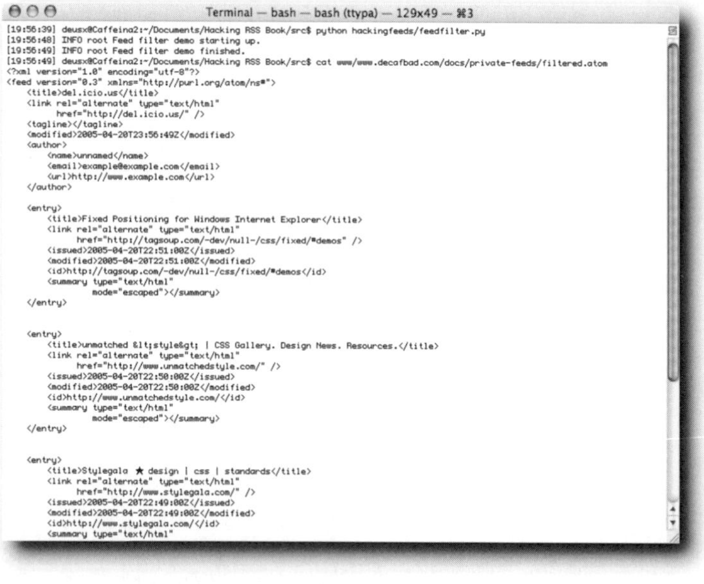

FIGURE 15-1: Sample feed filter program run

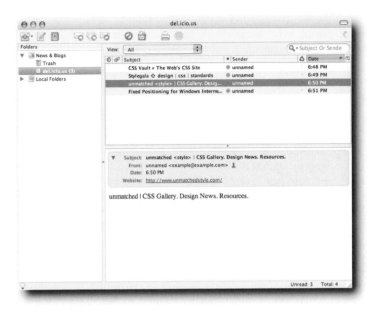

FIGURE 15-2: Filtered feed as a subscription in Thunderbird

Granted, this example might not be the best, because del.icio.us does offer standalone feeds for each tag/category available on the site. But, a lot of sites don't do this, and this filter could come in handy for them. In addition, you might want to consider tweaking this class to accept multiple feeds, but you'll see more on that in Chapter 16.

Filtering Feeds Using a Bayesian Classifier

So, in the program just finished, you were able to filter entries in syndication feeds using criteria tailored to your own design. But, wouldn't it be nice if your computer could automatically figure out what you want filtered, based on watching your example? In this next program, you see how to apply some simple *machine learning* to feeds, which can often help you sift through particularly active feeds for interesting items—but without the need to carefully construct filter rules by hand in advance.

You've probably been exposed to machine learning in the form of Bayesian statistics, even if you don't realize it. As the volume of spam flooding into email inboxes has risen over the past few years, tinkerers have been searching high and low for anything to draft into the fight to block out the unsolicited noise. And, one technique that's proven quite successful and gained great popularity is—you guessed it—filtering using Bayesian statistics. This form of analysis is what's often behind email clients that attempt to learn how to differentiate junk mail from legitimate messages, based on what you've marked as junk as an example.

On the Web The first place I'd ever heard of Bayesian statistics was in Paul Graham's 2002 essay, "A Plan for Spam," located here:

```
http://www.paulgraham.com/naivebayes.html
```

The math involved in a Bayesian classifier is just complex enough to be best explained by someone better grounded in it than your humble author—but I'll take a shot at a quick explanation.

Take two piles of email messages—you could use more than two piles, but stick with two for right now. You can use messages in each of these piles to "train" an automatic classifier based on Bayesian statistics. When given a new document, a Bayesian classifier first chops up a message into words, or tokens. It then works out a probability for each token with respect to its appearing in a given pile. It does this by keeping track of how many times it's seen this particular token in a given pile in past training sessions, as well as how many times it's seen this token in total between all piles.

Later, after you've thrown a large number of known examples at the classifier in training, you can hand it a new message and have it take a guess as to in which pile it belongs. As in training, the classifier will chop up this message into tokens. Then, the classifier will look up the probabilities it's calculated in training for each particular token with respect to piles they've been found in. (So, if you've been training with two piles, the classifier will come up with two probabilities for each token found in this mysterious new message.)

Then—and here's where the math gets dicey for me—it combines all the probabilities found for each token in the new message into a single new probability for each pile it knows about. What you're left with is an educated guess, stated as a set of probability scores, as to how likely it is that your mystery message should be placed in any given pile based on how its content compares with content the classifier has seen before.

I've trampled over a lot of the finer points here, but the gist is that a well-trained Bayesian classifier can make a pretty good guess at how a given message should be classified, based on a statistical analysis of its content. And sometimes, it might even make a better guess than you would on your own—because the probabilities reveal preferences or decisions reflected in your choices of which you weren't even aware. And, of course, sometimes it can seem completely brain-dead and make nonsensical suggestions. But, it's worth checking out.

On the Web If you'd like to dig into much better and more thorough explanations of Bayesian classifiers, you might want to start your search with a Wikipedia article located here:

```
http://en.wikipedia.org/wiki/Naive_Bayes_classifier
```

Introducing Reverend

Luckily, you need not rely on my mathematical prowess to start playing with a Bayesian classifier. Instead take a look at Divmod Reverend, an implementation of a Bayesian classifier in Python, available here:

```
http://www.divmod.org/projects/reverend
```

You'll want to download this package for use in the next program. It provides a set of modules including a class named Bayes, which exposes a pair of methods train() and guess(). All of the math happens under the hood, happily abstracted away for your convenience. It even does rudimentary tokenization out of the box, splitting up text along whitespace-delimited chunks. So, you'll be able to just toss feed entry content at it and see what happens.

Building a Bayes-Enabled Feed Aggregator

The first half of making use of a Bayes classifier is in the training. So, you need some way to provide examples of feed entries to the classifier. One of the easiest places to do this is in a feed aggregator, something that you just happen to have at your disposal, courtesy of Chapter 2.

However, this feed aggregator just produces static HTML files and doesn't provide any interactivity. So, something that you're going to need to enable is a Web server capable of running Python CGI scripts, which will allow you to provide feedback to the classifier via links in the pages the aggregator produces. This shouldn't be too hard to accommodate, though.

So, first off, take a look at Listing 15-5, which offers the beginning of a new feed aggregator, named ch15_bayes_agg.py.

Listing 15-5: ch15_bayes_agg.py (Part 1 of 7)

```
"""
ch15_bayes_agg.py

Bayes-enabled feed aggregator
"""
import sys, time, md5, urllib
import feedparser
from agglib import UNICODE_ENC, EntryWrapper, openDBs, closeDBs
from agglib import getNewFeedEntries, writeAggregatorPage
from reverend.thomas import Bayes

FEEDS_FN        = "bayes_feeds.txt"
FEED_DB_FN      = "bayes_feeds_db"
ENTRY_DB_FN     = "bayes_entry_seen_db"
HTML_FN         = "bayes-agg-%Y%m%d-%H%M%S.html"
BAYES_DATA_FN   = "bayesdata.dat"
ENTRY_UNIQ_KEYS = ('title', 'link', 'issued',
                   'modified', 'description')

def main():
    """
    Build aggregator report pages with Bayes rating links.
    """
    # Create a new Bayes guesser
    guesser = Bayes()
```

```
# Attempt to load Bayes data, ignoring IOError on first run.
try: guesser.load(BAYES_DATA_FN)
except IOError: pass

# Open up the databases, load the subscriptions, get new entries.
feed_db, entry_db = openDBs(FEED_DB_FN, ENTRY_DB_FN)
feeds    = [ x.strip() for x in open(FEEDS_FN, "r").readlines() ]
entries = getNewFeedEntries(feeds, feed_db, entry_db)

# Score the new entries using the Bayesian guesser
entries = scoreEntries(guesser, entries)

# Write out the current run's aggregator report.
out_fn  = time.strftime(HTML_FN)
writeAggregatorPage(entries, out_fn, DATE_HDR_TMPL, FEED_HDR_TMPL,
    ENTRY_TMPL, PAGE_TMPL)

# Close the databases and save the current guesser's state to disk.
closeDBs(feed_db, entry_db)
guesser.save(BAYES_DATA_FN)
```

Listing 15-5 has quite a lot in common with the aggregator in Chapter 2. It imports the usual modules and defines the `main()` function.

This driver function starts off with the creation of a `Bayes` classifier object. The training data maintained by this object is kept on disk, in the file specified by BAYES_DATA_FN—so, this file is loaded up with the classifier's `load()` method at creation. However, because this data may not exist upon first running the program, `IOError` exceptions are ignored. You may need to be careful to ensure that this file exists and is readable after the first run of this program.

Next, aggregator databases are opened and a list of feeds is read in. These are used with the `getNewFeedEntries()` function imported from `agglib` to get a list of new feeds from the subscriptions. These new entries, along with the Bayes `guesser` object, are passed through a to-be-defined function named `scoreEntries()`. These entries are used to build the aggregator page using `agglib`'s `writeAggregatorPage()`, after which the function cleans up by closing the aggregator databases and writing the guesser data to disk.

The program continues with Listing 15-6, with the definition of the `ScoredEntryWrapper` class.

Listing 15-6: ch15_bayes_agg.py (Part 2 of 7)

```
class ScoredEntryWrapper(EntryWrapper):
    """
    Tweak the EntryWrapper class to include a score for
    the entry.
    """
```

Continued

Listing 15-6 *(continued)*

```
def __init__(self, data, entry, score=0.0):
    EntryWrapper.__init__(self, data, entry)
    self.score = score
    self.id    = makeEntryID(entry)

def __getitem__(self, name):
    """
    Include the entry score & id in template output
    options.
    """
    # Allow prefix for URL quoting
    if name.startswith("url:"):
        return urllib.quote(self.__getitem__(name[4:]))

    if name == 'id':           return self.id
    if name == 'feed.url':     return self.data.url
    if name == 'entry.score':  return self.score
    return EntryWrapper.__getitem__(self, name)
```

The `ScoredEntryWrapper` class is a subclass of `EntryWrapper`, and its purpose is simply to add a few new fields to entries. This includes `'id'`, a unique identifier for an entry, and the `'entry.score'` field, which will be populated by guesses from the Bayes classifier. Now, move on to Listing 15-7, where this class starts to see some use.

Listing 15-7: ch15_bayes_agg.py (Part 3 of 7)

```
def scoreEntries(guesser, entries):
    """
    Return a list of entries modified to include scores.
    """
    return [ScoredEntryWrapper(e.data, e.entry, scoreEntry(guesser, e))
            for e in entries]

def scoreEntry(guesser, e):
    """
    Score an entry, assuming like and dislike classifications.
    """
    guess = dict( guessEntry(guesser, e) )
    return guess.get('like', 0) - guess.get('dislike', 0)
```

The `scoreEntries()` function accepts a Bayes guesser and a list of entries as parameters and uses the guesser with `scoreEntry()` method on each entry in the list, rewrapping each in a `ScoredEntryWrapper` instance containing a new score for each.

The scoreEntry() function accepts a guesser and an entry and uses the guessEntry() function on the entry to come up with classifications for the entry. Although you could apply any number of classes in training the Bayes guesser, this program simplifies things by just using a 'like' and a 'dislike' class. So, because only these two are expected here, the 'dislike' probability is subtracted from that of the 'like' probability and this single combined result is returned as the entry's score.

More of the program's blanks get filled next in Listing 15-8.

Listing 15-8: ch15_bayes_agg.py (Part 4 of 7)

```python
def trainEntry(guesser, pool, e):
    """
    Train classifier for given class, feed, and entry.
    """
    content = summarizeEntry(e)
    guesser.train(pool, content)

def guessEntry(guesser, e):
    """
    Make a classification guess for given feed and entry.
    """
    content = summarizeEntry(e)
    return guesser.guess(content)

def summarizeEntry(e):
    """
    Summarize entry content for use with the Bayes guesser.
    """
    # Include the feed title
    content = [ e.data.feed.title ]
    # Include the entry title and summary
    content.extend([ e.entry.get(x,'') for x in ('title', 'summary') ])
    # Include the entry content.
    content.extend([ x.value for x in e.entry.get('content', []) ])
    # Join all the content together with spaces and return.
    return ' '.join(content)
```

As I just mentioned, you could use any labels you want in training entries with the classifier. The three functions defined in Listing 15-8 give you the flexibility to do this.

However, for this chapter, you can get a bit more specific and nail things down to 'like' and 'dislike'—a basic thumbs-up/thumbs-down rating for entries. Then, you can get a guess for an entry, subtract the probability for the 'dislike' classification from the 'like' classification, and get a simple scale that allows for easy sorting and comparison. If an entry is expected to be more liked than disliked, the score will be positive—and vice versa where dislike is more probable.

The `summarizeEntry()` function is the more verbose of the three in Listing 15-8—it extracts the title, summary, and as much content as it can from a given entry. All of this content is then simply joined together into one big blob with spaces and returned. This string of content, then, is what is used in training the classifier and making guesses.

Training is accomplished by passing the name of a category, the feed data, and an entry to the aggregator's `trainEntry()` function. As you can see from the implementation of this function, usage of the Reverend classifier is dead simple. Just get the string of content using the `summarizeEntry()` function of the aggregator and call the guesser's `train()` method. Reverend will take it from there, tokenizing the entry content and analyzing probabilities.

Making guesses about entries is just as simple, in the `guessEntry()` function. The mystery entry's content is summarized, and the results of the classifier's `guess()` method is returned.

Just two more functions need to be defined, in Listing 15-9.

> **Listing 15-9:** ch15_bayes_agg.py (Part 5 of 7)

```
def findEntry(feed_uri, entry_id):
    """
    Attempt to locate a feed entry, given the feed URI and
    an entry ID.
    """
    feed_data = feedparser.parse(feed_uri)
    for entry in feed_data.entries:
        if makeEntryID(entry) == entry_id:
            return ScoredEntryWrapper(feed_data, entry, 0.0)
    return None

def makeEntryID(entry):
    """Find a unique identifier for a given entry."""
    if entry.has_key('id'):
        # Use the entry's own GUID.
        return entry['id'].encode(UNICODE_ENC)
    else:
        # No entry GUID, so build one from an MD5 hash
        # of selected data.
        entry_data = ''.join([
            entry.get(k,'').encode(UNICODE_ENC)
            for k in ENTRY_UNIQ_KEYS
        ])
        return md5.md5(entry_data).hexdigest()
```

The `findEntry()` function defined in Listing 15-9 doesn't actually get used in this program. However, it will be used in the next program to facilitate the user interface for guesser training. It may help simplify that program by defining it here with the other aggregator-related functions.

At any rate, this function accepts a feed URI and an entry ID and attempts to locate the entry in question, loading the feed with the `feedparser` and using `makeEntryID()` to find entry IDs.

Though it generally works, this implementation is very inefficient at the moment. In the absence of any real database or persistence of feed entries, it re-fetches the feed every time it wants to find an entry. To improve things, you might want to check out the `FeedCache` class offered in Appendix A, or think about your own more efficient way to look up feed entries.

And, finally, in Listing 15-9 is the definition of the `makeEntryID()` function. This returns the entry's own GUID, if it has one. Otherwise, it uses the fields listed in `ENTRY_UNIQ_KEYS` to derive an MD5 hash of selected bits of the entry's contents.

Listing 15-10 offers the first part of the revised aggregator string templates.

Listing 15-10: ch15_bayes_agg.py (Part 6 of 7)

```
DATE_HDR_TMPL = """
    <h1 class="dateheader">%s</h1>
"""


FEED_HDR_TMPL = """
    <h2 class="feedheader"><a href="%(feed.link)s">%(feed.title)s</a></h2>
"""


ENTRY_TMPL = """
    <div class="feedentry">
        <div class="entryheader">
            [ %(entry.score)0.3f ]
            [ <a
href="javascript:ratepop('ch15_bayes_mark_entry.cgi?feed=%(url:url:feed.url)s&en
try=%(url:url:id)s&like=1')">++</a> ]
            [ <a
href="javascript:ratepop('ch15_bayes_mark_entry.cgi?feed=%(url:url:feed.url)s&en
try=%(url:url:id)s&like=0')">--</a> ]
            <span class="entrytime">%(time)s</span>:
            <a class="entrylink" href="%(entry.link)s">%(entry.title)s</a>
        </div>
        <div class="entrysummary">
            %(entry.summary)s
            <hr>
            %(content)s
        </div>
    </div>
"""
```

In Listing 15-10, you can see three string templates defined that should look familiar from the original aggregator. `DATE_HDR_TMPL` provides the header for dates inserted into runs of entries, and `FEED_HDR_TMPL` offers the presentation of feed titles and links.

The major departure from the original aggregator comes with the new ENTRY_TMPL. Here, most everything is the same, including the entry title, summary, link, and content. However, there is now an additional section for the entry's guessed score, as contained in the ScoredEntryWrapper object, along with two new links. These links form the "user interface" for the aggregator, with the [++] link used to train the aggregator that you like a particular entry and the [--] link used to signal dislike.

These links pass the entry's ID and feed URL, along with an indication of like or dislike, to a CGI program named ch15_bayes_mark_entry.cgi, opened up in a pop-up window with a JavaScript function named ratepop(). This program will be provided shortly.

Note   It might look a little strange, but the url:url: prefix used to doubly URL-encode the feed URL and entry ID in Listing 15-10 is intentional. This seems to work best with the CGI program coming up, because communication with this program can mangle more complex URLs on occasion without the double encoding.

Listing 15-11 wraps up this new aggregator with a final tweak to the overall page template.

Listing 15-11: ch15_bayes_agg.py (Part 7 of 7)

```
PAGE_TMPL = """
<html>
    <head>
        <style>
            body {
                font-family: sans-serif;
                font-size: 12px;
            }
            .pageheader {
                font-size: 2em;
                font-weight: bold;
                border-bottom: 3px solid #000;
                padding: 5px;
            }
            .dateheader    {
                margin: 20px 10px 10px 10px;
                border-top: 2px solid #000;
                border-bottom: 2px solid #000;
            }
            .feedheader    {
                margin: 20px;
                border-bottom: 1px dashed #aaa;
            }
            .feedentry     {
                margin: 10px 30px 10px 30px;
                padding: 10px;
                border: 1px solid #ddd;
            }
```

```
        .entryheader {
            border-bottom: 1px solid #ddd;
            padding: 5px;
        }
        .entrytime {
            font-weight: bold;
        }
        .entrysummary {
            margin: 10px;
            padding: 5px;
        }
    </style>
    <script>
        function ratepop(url) {
            window.open(url, 'rating',
'width=550,height=125,location=no,menubar=no,status=no,toolbar=no,
scrollbars=no,resizable=yes');
        }
    </script>
</head>
<body>
    <h1 class="pageheader">Bayes feed aggregator</h1>
    %s
</body>
</html>
"""

if __name__ == "__main__": main()
```

The only change here from the original aggregator page template comes toward the end, with the inclusion of the ratepop() JavaScript function used to pop up the rating feedback window. That, and the page title has been changed to reflect this new aggregator.

Building a Feedback Mechanism for Bayes Training

Creating a new aggregator with a Bayes classifier is only half the battle, though. As mentioned earlier, this aggregator only produces static HTML pages, so you need something to handle the interactivity of feedback given on feed entries displayed. That's where this next CGI program comes in handy.

If you're viewing the pages produced by the aggregator on a Web server, you're probably all set to start using this program. If not, you may want to check out how to get CGIs working on your local machine or remote Web server. Short of building a full-blown standalone GUI application, this is the easiest way to build a simple user interface to your new browser-based Bayesian feed aggregator. But, if you are not easily able to get this up and running, it'll still be instructive to see how to enable training to complete the feedback loop.

Take a look at Listing 15-12 for the start of ch15_bayes_mark_entry.cgi.

Listing 15-12: ch15_bayes_mark_entry.cgi (Part 1 of 5)

```
#!/usr/bin/env python
"""
ch15_bayes_mark_entry.cgi

Train a Bayes classifier to like or dislike a chosen feed entry.
"""
import sys; sys.path.append('lib')
import cgi, os, logging
import cgitb; cgitb.enable()

from ch15_bayes_agg import ScoredEntryWrapper, findEntry
from ch15_bayes_agg import guessEntry, scoreEntry, trainEntry
from reverend.thomas import Bayes

BAYES_DATA_FN = "bayesdata.dat"
```

The start of this new program in Listing 15-12 has a lot in common with the start of the aggregator in Listing 15-5—that's because this CGI is really just an extension of that aggregator. It uses the same classifier data file as the aggregator, necessarily so because here's where the training will be done, in counterpart to the guessing and scoring done in the aggregator.

Caution One "gotcha" that often comes up when using a CGI like this in coordination with another program—at least, on operating systems like Linux and Mac OS X—is that the Web server and the user account under which you run the aggregator are usually different, and so you may find conflicting permissions become a problem.

So, you'll need to be sure both accounts have permission to read and write the shared files, which mostly applies to the bayesdata.dat file. You may want to place your user account and the Web server account both in the same group and enable group read / write of all these files.

Take a look now at Listing 15-13, where the definition of main() starts taking care of training.

Listing 15-13: ch15_bayes_mark_entry.cgi (Part 2 of 5)

```
def main():
    """
    Handle training the aggregator from a CGI interface.
    """
    # Load up and parse the incoming CGI parameters.
    form     = cgi.FieldStorage()
    feed_uri = form.getvalue('feed')
    entry_id = form.getvalue('entry')
```

```
like      = ( form.getvalue('like')=='1' ) and \
            'like' or 'dislike'

# Create a new Bayes guesser, attempt to load data
guesser = Bayes()
guesser.load(BAYES_DATA_FN)
```

Like the standalone aggregator program, this CGI fires up and creates an instance of
`cgi.FieldStorage()` to take input from the Web browser making a request to the CGI.
The feed URI, entry ID, and whether the entry was liked or disliked are all expected in the
incoming parameters. Note that the 0/1 value of the `'like'` parameter is converted into the
literal strings `'like'` or `'dislike'`, to be used in training.

Finally in Listing 15-13, a Bayes `guesser` is created and its training data gets loaded. Notice
this time, though, that any exceptions that happen in the course of loading this data are allowed
to crash the program. By this point, the guesser data should already exist, and any errors in trying to load it may be helpful in the course of getting this CGI working.

Next, in Listing 15-14, these parameters are used to attempt to find the entry in question and
perform some classifier training.

Listing 15-14: ch15_bayes_mark_entry.cgi (Part 3 of 5)

```
# Use the aggregator to find the given entry.
entry = findEntry(feed_uri, entry_id)

# Print out the content header right away.
print "Content-Type: text/html"
print

# Check if a feed and entry were found...
if entry:

    # Take a sample guess before training on this entry.
    before_guess = guessEntry(guesser, entry)
    before_score = scoreEntry(guesser, entry)

    # Train with this entry and classification, save
    # the data.
    trainEntry(guesser, like, entry)

    # Take a sample guess after training.
    after_guess = guessEntry(guesser, entry)
    after_score = scoreEntry(guesser, entry)

    # Save the guesser data
    guesser.save(BAYES_DATA_FN)
```

The `findEntry()` function imported from `ch15_bayes_agg.py` comes in handy here to locate the entry identified by the feed URI and entry ID. Of course, it's important to note that it's possible this entry has disappeared from the feed data by the time you get around to rating a particular entry. So, this condition is checked midway through Listing 15-14 before any training begins.

In the happy case that the entry data is still available, a sample guess and score is made before next training the classifier with this entry and the given like/dislike rating. Then, a guess and score is taken after the training. Listing 15-15 then provides code to report the results of this training back to the user in HTML form.

Listing 15-15: ch15_bayes_mark_entry.cgi (Part 4 of 5)

```
# Report the results.
print """
<html>
    <head><title>Feed entry feedback processed</title></head>
    <body>
        <p>
            Successfully noted '%(like)s' classification
            for [%(feed.title)s] %(entry.title)s
        </p>
        <p style="font-size: 0.75em">
            Before: %(before_score)s %(before_guess)s
        </p>
        <p style="font-size: 0.75em">
            After: %(after_score)s %(after_guess)s
        </p>
    </body>
</html>
""" % {
    'like'          : like,
    'feed.title'    : entry['feed.title'],
    'entry.title'   : entry['entry.title'],
    'feed.uri'      : entry['feed.uri'],
    'entry.id'      : entry['id'],
    'before_guess'  : before_guess,
    'before_score'  : before_score,
    'after_score'   : after_score,
    'after_guess'   : after_guess
}
```

Listing 15-15 presents a simple inline string template to build a bare-bones bit of HTML to be displayed in the pop-up window launched from the aggregator. It reports on the successful training done for this entry, as well as the before and after results from the classifier to show you what effect your feedback had on the classifier's consideration of this entry's content. And, finally, this CGI completed in Listing 15-16.

Listing 15-16: ch15_bayes_mark_entry.cgi (Part 5 of 5)

```
    else:
        # Couldn't find a corresponding entry, report the bad news.
        print """
        <html>
            <body>
                <p>
                    Sorry, couldn't find a matching entry for this
                    feed URI and entry ID:
                </p>
                <ul>
                    <li>Feed: %(feed.uri)s</li>
                    <li>Entry: %(entry.id)s</li>
                </ul>
            </body>
        </html>
        """ % {
            'feed.uri'    : feed_uri,
            'entry.id'    : entry_id,
        }

if __name__=='__main__': main()
```

In case no feed entry corresponding to the CGI's parameters is found, the HTML message in Listing 15-16 is provided to present the unfortunate news. In this case, no training is done because there's no content available for the entry in question.

Using a Trained Bayesian Classifier to Suggest Feed Entries

Now there's just one last piece to this puzzle: a feed filter that uses the classifier to find candidates for interesting entries. This program will be a bit of a bridge between the Bayes-enabled feed aggregator and a generated feed, because it will use the aggregator machinery to get and score entries and will use the Scraper machinery for producing a feed of entries scored above a given threshold. You'll be able to subscribe to the feed this program produces to get what the Bayesian classifier considers the cream of the crop, based on what feedback you've supplied during training.

Jump right into Listing 15-17 for the beginning of a new module and program named ch15_bayes_filter.py.

Listing 15-17: ch15_bayes_filter.py (Part 1 of 5)

```
#!/usr/bin/env python
"""
ch15_bayes_filter.py

Build a new feed out of entries filtered from a source feed
above a given Bayesian classifier threshold.
"""
import sys, os, time, ch15_bayes_agg
from agglib import openDBs, closeDBs, getNewFeedEntries
from scraperlib import Scraper
from ch14_feed_normalizer import normalize_feed_meta, normalize_entries
from reverend.thomas import Bayes

FEED_TITLE     = 'Bayes Recommendations'
FEED_TAGLINE   = 'Entries recommended by Bayesian-derived ratings'
FEED_NAME_FN   = "www/www.decafbad.com/docs/private-feeds/bayes-filtered.%s"
FEEDS_FN       = "bayes_feeds.txt"
FEED_DB_FN     = "bayes_filter_feeds_db"
ENTRY_DB_FN    = "bayes_filter_entry_seen_db"

BAYES_DATA_FN = "bayesdata.dat"
```

The introduction to this new program also shares a lot of the same modules with the two previous programs, though now the feed generation modules are included. The configuration constants include a filename template, FEED_NAME_FN, where the generated feeds will be saved—along with the constants FEED_TITLE and FEED_TAGLINE which will be used to define metadata for the generated feed.

Also notice that this program uses different entry and feed databases than ch15_bayes_agg.py. This can be handy because you may have overlooked certain entries in the context of the "training" aggregator that this "recommendations" feed will call out for you.

Now, check out Listing 15-18 for the main() function that will drive this module as a program.

Listing 15-18: ch15_bayes_filter.py (Part 2 of 5)

```
def main():
    """
    Perform a test run of the FeedFilter using defaults.
    """
    # Create a new Bayes guesser, attempt to load data
    guesser = Bayes()
    guesser.load(BAYES_DATA_FN)

    # Open up the databases, load the subscriptions, get
    # new entries.
```

```
feed_db, entry_db = openDBs(FEED_DB_FN, ENTRY_DB_FN)
feeds    = [ x.strip() for x in open(FEEDS_FN,
                                      "r").readlines() ]
entries = getNewFeedEntries(feeds, feed_db, entry_db)

# Build the feed filter.
f = BayesFilter(guesser, entries)
f.FEED_META['feed.title']   = FEED_TITLE
f.FEED_META['feed.tagline'] = FEED_TAGLINE

# Output the feed as both RSS and Atom.
open(FEED_NAME_FN % 'rss', 'w').write(f.scrape_rss())
open(FEED_NAME_FN % 'atom', 'w').write(f.scrape_atom())

# Close the databases and save the current guesser's
# state to disk.
closeDBs(feed_db, entry_db)
```

So, as in the previous aggregator, this program's main() function starts off by creating the Bayes guesser and loading up the data—again, *without* ignoring any IOError exceptions. Then, the aggregator databases are opened, the list of subscribed feeds is read in, and new entries are fetched from the subscriptions.

This is all in preparation to create a BayesFilter object, initialized with the guesser and the list of entries. This object is used to build both RSS and Atom feeds filtered from the entries fetched from the subscriptions. After this, the aggregator databases are closed and the function ends. Because this program doesn't actually do any training with the guesser, notice that the data doesn't get saved here.

Next, in Listing 15-19, it's time to start defining the BayesFilter class.

Listing 15-19: ch15_bayes_filter.py (Part 3 of 5)

```
class BayesFilter(Scraper):
    """
    Filter feed entries using scores from a Bayesian
    classifier.
    """
    STATE_FN    = 'bayes_filter_state'

    def __init__(self, guesser, entries, min_score=0.5):
        """Initialize with the feed URI for parsing."""
        self.guesser         = guesser
        self.entries         = entries
        self.min_score       = min_score
        self.entries_filtered = []
```

In the __init__() method for BayesFilter, several parameters are accepted. These include a Bayes guesser, a list of entries, as well as an optional minimum score threshold for the filter. By default, this score threshold is set to 0.5, but if you'd like to be pickier about what entries get recommended, try setting this higher to 0.75 or even 0.90. Lastly in the initializer, a blank list is created for the filtered feed entries that will be gathered.

Moving on, Listing 15-20 offers a definition for produce_entries().

Listing 15-20: ch15_bayes_filter.py (Part 4 of 5)

```
def produce_entries(self):
    """
    Filter entries from a feed using the regex map, use the
    feed normalizer to produce FeedEntryDict objects.
    """
    # If this hasn't already been done, filter aggregator
    # entries.
    if len(self.entries_filtered) < 1:
        self.filter_aggregator_entries()

    # Normalize all the filtered entries
    entries = normalize_entries(self.entries_filtered)
    for e in entries:
        e.date_fmt = self.date_fmt

    return entries
```

The implementation of the produce_entries() method is fairly basic. The filter_ aggregator_entries() method is called to score and filter all the entries supplied at initialization time. Then, the filtered entries are run through the normalizer before being returned for inclusion in the output feed. Note that the filter_aggregator_entries() method call is done only once at this point. This is so that the work of producing scores and filtering entries doesn't get redone for both the RSS and Atom feed format output calls.

Now, Listing 15-21 is where the actual Bayesian filtering takes place.

Listing 15-21: ch15_bayes_filter.py (Part 5 of 5)

```
def filter_aggregator_entries(self):
    """
    Process new entries from the aggregator for inclusion in the
    output feed.  This is broken out into its own method in order
    to reuse the new entries from the aggregator for multiple feed
    output runs.
    """
```

```
        # Now, get a score for each entry and, for each entry scored
        # above the minimum threshold, include it in the entries
        # for output.
        for e in self.entries:
            score = ch15_bayes_agg.scoreEntry(self.guesser, e)
            if score > self.min_score:
                # HACK: Tweak each entry's title to include the score.
                e.entry['title'] = u"(%0.3f) %s" % \
                        (score, e.entry.get('title', 'untitled'))
                self.entries_filtered.append(e.entry)

if __name__=='__main__': main()
```

Listing 15-21 offers a definition for the `filter_aggregator_entries()` method of this class. Each new entry is run through the `scoreEntry()` function borrowed from `ch15_bayes_agg.py`, and that score is compared to the filter's minimum score threshold.

Each entry whose score passes the threshold gets appended to the list of filtered entries used by `produce_entries()` to generate the output feed. Notice that there's a little hack employed in the filtering loop, which prepends the entry's score onto its title. This is a bit dirty, but it helps see how the filter is scoring things. And, finally, at the end of this method, the current run time is stored for next time.

Trying Out the Bayesian Feed Filtering Suite

At last, now that you have both the training and the guessing side of the Bayesian feed filter suite filled out, you can give it a trial run. You can see what the aggregator pages will look like now in Figure 15-3.

While browsing around reading feed entries, if you find something you particularly like or dislike, give it a thumbs up or down by clicking the appropriate rating link. For example, if you've just seen too many stories about some topic and would rather have them get dropped from recommendations, Figure 15-4 shows you what a "dislike" rating looks like. Note the before and after score and guess from the Bayesian classifier—registering your dislike should show the rating after training drop lower.

On the other hand, if there's some topic that strikes your fancy, and you'd like to see more things similar to it, go ahead and give it the thumbs up. Figure 15-5 gives you an example of what happens when you register a "like" rating. Again, watch the before and after scores, which should go up in response to this positive feedback.

And finally, Figure 15-6 shows you what the feed produced by the feed filter might look like. Notice the scores tacked onto the beginning of feed titles. Also, something worth noting is that this feed is, in fact, being viewed in another aggregator—you could have just built this filtering into the aggregator used for training the classifier, but this separation of the aggregator from the filter recommending entries allows you the flexibility to use whatever aggregator you like once you've spent some time in training.

FIGURE 15-3: Viewing entries in an HTML page produced by the Bayes-enabled aggregator

FIGURE 15-4: A feedback window popped up in response to dislike rating.

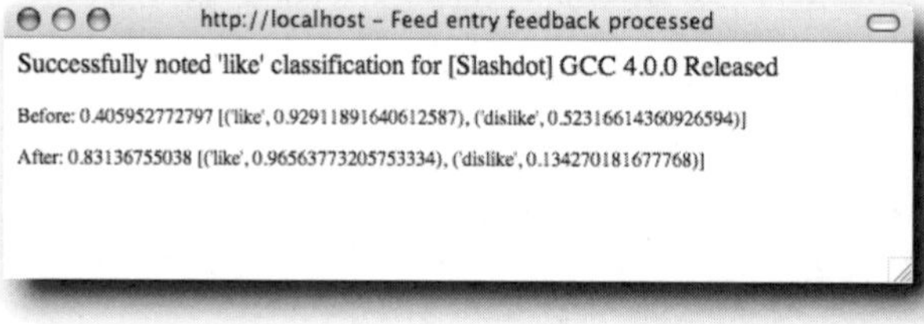

FIGURE 15-5: A feedback window popped up in response to like rating.

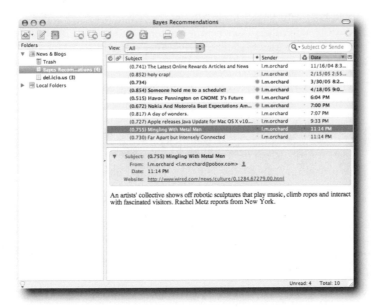

FIGURE 15-6: Sample Bayesian filtered feed viewed in Thunderbird

Hopefully, this suite of programs can help you build a few more smarts into your feed processing machinery.

Sifting Popular Links from Feeds

Shifting gears a bit here, this next program allows you to turn feeds inside out, in a sense. If you've been watching a number of feeds for a while, you've probably noticed the latest meme or breaking news item sweep across your subscriptions as one blogger after another links to the same thing, accompanied by a smart quip or comment. Well, instead of all that distributed redundancy, what if you could just detect when something hot breaks, and collate what everyone's saying about it under one banner?

This next program is a combination of a feed aggregator from the first part of the book and a log-style feed producer as introduced in Chapter 10 in the implementation of `monitorfeedlib.py`. With each program run, it scans through all the entries found in feeds listed as subscriptions, skimming for links in the content of each entry. The URLs for each link found will be used to form an inverse index: feed entries will be gathered together by URLs in their content, thus grouping them together around each link and providing a view on the discussion across all of your subscribed feeds. This inverse index will then be sorted in descending order by the number of entries pointing to each URL, thus providing some measure of how hot some particular link has become.

You can use a cutoff threshold with respect to entry count for each link—for example, you may want to consider only URLs with three or more entries linking to it as worthy of attention. The links above this threshold are then used to produce a feed entry that is included into the output feed, thus providing you with a regular update of what's buzzworthy in your subscriptions.

So, without further ado, take a look at Listing 15-22 for the start of this new program, named ch15_popular_links.py.

Listing 15-22: ch15_popular_links.py (Part 1 of 8)

```
#!/usr/bin/env python
"""

ch15_popular_links.py

Build a feed summarizing link popularity found in a set of feeds.
"""
import sys, re, time, calendar, feedparser

from scraperlib import FeedEntryDict
from monitorfeedlib import LogBufferFeed
from HTMLParser import HTMLParser, HTMLParseError

FEED_TITLE     = 'Popular Links'
FEED_TAGLINE   = 'Links found in feed entries ranked by popularity'
FEED_NAME_FN   = "www/www.decafbad.com/docs/private-feeds/popular.%s"
FEED_DIR       = 'popular-links-feed'
FEEDS_FN       = 'popular-feed-uris.txt'
MIN_LINKS      = 3
MAX_ENTRY_AGE  = 3 * 24 * 60 * 60
LOG_CONF       = "logging.conf"

TITLE_TMPL     = """Popular links @ %(time)s (%(link_cnt)s links)"""
TITLE_TIME_FMT = """%Y-%m-%d %H:%M"""
```

It looks like there's a lot going on in Listing 15-22. After the module imports come the following configuration constants:

- FEED_TITLE—This is the title to be used in the program's output feed.

- FEED_TAGLINE—This is the output feed's description/tagline.

- FEED_NAME_FN—The output feed will be written using this as a template for the filenames.

- FEED_DIR—This is the location of the state directory for the log feed buffer.

- FEEDS_FN—This is the filename of the list of subscribed feed URIs to be processed.

- MIN_LINKS—This is a threshold of how many entries must mention a link before it's included in the report.

- MAX_ENTRY_AGE—This specifies the maximum age for entries in feeds before they're ignored, thus keeping the report fresh.

- LOG_CONF—The logging configuration filename.

- TITLE_TMPL—A template used to define the title for entries in the output feed.

- TITLE_TIME_FMT—A template used to format the date included in the title.

If all of these constants don't make sense now, hopefully they'll make better sense once you get to the point where each of them is used further on in the program. Continuing on to Listing 15-23, you'll find a few string templates that will be employed in the production of content for the output feed.

Listing 15-23: ch15_popular_links.py (Part 2 of 8)

```
CONTENT_TMPL = """
    <div>
        %s
    </div>
"""
LINK_TMPL = """
    <div style="padding: 10px; margin: 10px; border: 1px solid #aaa;">
        <a style="font-size:1.25em" href="%(link)s">
            %(link).80s
        </a>
        <br />
        <i style="font-size:0.75em">(%(link_cnt)s links)</i>
        <ul>
            %(linkers)s
        </ul>
    </div>
"""
LINKER_TMPL = """
    <li>
        <a href="%(entry.link)s">%(entry.title)s</a>
        <br />
        <span style="font-size:0.75em">
            [ <a href="%(feed.link)s">%(feed.title)s</a> ]
        </span>
    </li>
"""
```

The CONTENT_TMPL template will be used as the overall shell wrapped around the list of links making up the content for each new entry. Next, the LINK_TMPL provides what will be populated for each unique link found in your feeds. Then, the LINKER_TMPL is what will be used to render each entry pointing to the unique link—these will be built as a list inserted into the LINK_TMPL in the slot labeled 'linkers'. You'll see how this works shortly.

Move on to the next part, in Listing 15-24, where you'll find the definition of the main() function.

Listing 15-24: ch15_popular_links.py (Part 3 of 8)

```
def main():
    """
    Scan all feeds and update the feed with a new link
    popularity report entry.
    """
    # Construct the feed generator.
    f = LogBufferFeed(FEED_DIR)
    f.MAX_AGE = 1 * 24 * 60 * 60 # 1 day
    f.FEED_META['feed.title']   = FEED_TITLE
    f.FEED_META['feed.tagline'] = FEED_TAGLINE

    # Load up the list of feeds.
    feed_uris  = [ x.strip() for x in
                   open(FEEDS_FN,'r').readlines() ]
```

In Listing 15-24, the definition of main() builds an instance of LogBufferFeed that will be used to generate this program's output feed. Next, it loads up the list of subscriptions from the file specified in FEEDS_FN and creates a FeedCache instance. These feeds start getting processed in Listing 15-25.

Listing 15-25: ch15_popular_links.py (Part 4 of 8)

```
    # Skim for links from each feed, collect feed and entries in an
    # inverted index using link URLs as top-level keys.
    links = {}
    for feed_uri in feed_uris:
        feed_data = feedparser.parse(feed_uri)

        # Grab the feed metadata from parsed feed.
        feed      = feed_data.feed
        feed_link = feed.get('link', '#')

        # Process all entries for their links...
        for curr_entry in feed_data.entries:
```

```
# HACK: Ignore entries without modification dates.
# Maybe improve this by stashing seen dates in a DB.
if curr_entry.get('modified_parsed', None) is None:
    continue

# If the current entry is older than the max allowed age,
# skip processing it.
now = time.time()
entry_time = calendar.timegm(curr_entry.modified_parsed)
if (now - entry_time) > MAX_ENTRY_AGE:
    continue
```

Listing 15-25 presents the start of feed processing—subscribed feeds are loaded up using the feedparser, and then each of the entries in a feed is visited and checked for freshness with respect to MAX_ENTRY_AGE. By only accepting entries within a certain time span, you'll be able to keep this feed fresh, allowing older topics to drop off the list and new ones to float to the top.

There's a little bit of a hack going on here, though. Some feeds offer modification or publication dates for their entries, but some don't. For expediency's sake, this program opts to simply skip over entries that don't offer this date information. You may want to consider making an improvement here to track timestamps when entries were first seen. However, enough feeds include date information nowadays to make this not worth the effort in this context.

For entries that do offer timestamps, however, this value is used to check the age of the entry—any entries older than the duration set in MAX_ENTRY_AGE are skipped. Keep going on to Listing 15-26 to see what's done with entries that pass the freshness test.

Listing 15-26: ch15_popular_links.py (Part 5 of 8)

```
# Build a LinkSkimmer and feed it all summary and
# HTML content data from the current entry.  Ignore
# parse errors in the interest of just grabbing
# what we can.
skimmer = LinkSkimmer()
try:
    skimmer.feed(curr_entry.get('summary',''))
    for c in curr_entry.get('content', []):
        skimmer.feed(c.value)
except HTMLParseError:
    pass

# Process each link by adding the current feed
# and entry under the link's key in the inverted
# index.
for uri, cnt in skimmer.get_links():
```

Continued

Listing 15-26 *(continued)*

```
    if not links.has_key(uri):
        links[uri] = {}
    if not links[uri].has_key(feed_link):
        links[uri][feed_link] = (feed, curr_entry)
```

First up in Listing 15-26, an instance of the `LinkSkimmer` class is created. This will be defined toward the end of the program, but it's useful to note for now that this is an `HTMLParser` subclass.

Any and all content found in the entry is thrown at the `LinkSkimmer`, all done within a `try/except` block to ignore any bumps along the way in the parsing process. Being careful or precise isn't all that much a concern here, because the worst that can happen is you miss a link or two mentioned in someone's messy feed content—don't worry, it'll probably be mentioned by someone else, if it's important! Because mentions of hot topics tend to enjoy redundancy across many of your subscribed feeds, this program can afford to be sloppy.

After parsing, the links found in this entry are added to the inverse index being built. The `links` variable contains a map of topical links pointing to maps of feed links, each of which in turn points to a tuple listing the feed and the entry.

So, in your usual feed aggregator view, the relationship between feed entry and link looks something like this:

- Feed #1/Entry #1
  - http://www.example.com/
  - http://www.sample.org/
- Feed #2/Entry #1
  - http://www.fakesite.com/
  - http://www.example.com/
- Feed #2/Entry #2
  - http://www.fakesite.com/
  - http://www.somecompany.com/pressrelease/
- Feed #3/Entry #1
  - http://www.somecompany.com/pressrelease/
  - http://www.sample.org/
  - http://www.example.com/

These relationships are inverted by this program, so that now they appear organized like so:

- `http://www.example.com/`
    - Feed #1/Entry #1
    - Feed #2/Entry #1
    - Feed #3/Entry #1
- `http://www.sample.org/`
    - Feed #1/Entry #1
    - Feed #3/Entry #1
- `http://www.fakesite.com/`
    - Feed #2/Entry #2
- `http://www.somecompany.com/pressrelease/`
    - Feed #2/Entry #2
    - Feed #3/Entry #1

Also worth noting is that this program only considers one entry per feed mentioning any given unique URL—depending on the order of the feed, this will probably be the latest entry in the feed that links to the URL, but not necessarily.

This behavior occurs because, although the preceding example lists depict the feed/entry pairs associated with each unique link as a simple list, this isn't quite how things are implemented. Stored under each unique URL is *another* map, with feed URIs pointing to feed/entry data pairs. Whenever a new entry for a given feed URI appears for a link, that entry overwrites the one previously captured.

This is reflected in the previous list by the fact that, although Feed #2 mentions `fakesite.com` in two separate entries, only the second of these entries is counted. This feature helps ensure that links reported by this program's feed are, in fact, widely mentioned among many feeds—rather than just repeated over and over in the same feed.

So, after the completion of this scan through subscribed feeds, the collected index of links gets sorted and rendered as a feed entry in Listing 15-27.

Listing 15-27: ch15_popular_links.py (Part 6 of 8)

```
# Turn the inverted index of links into a list of tuples,
# sort by popularity of links as measured by number of
#  linked entries.
links_sorted = links.items()
```

Continued

Listing 15-27 *(continued)*

```
links_sorted.sort(lambda a,b: cmp( len(b[1].keys()),
                                   len(a[1].keys()) ))
# Build the overall entry content from all the links.
links_out = []
for x in links_sorted:

    # Get the link and the list of linkers, skip this link
    # if there aren't enough linkers counted.
    link, linkers = x
    if len(linkers) < MIN_LINKS: continue

    # Build the list of linkers for this link by populating
    # the LINKER_TMPL string template.
    linkers_out = []
    for feed, entry in linkers.values():
        linkers_out.append(LINKER_TMPL % {
            'feed.title'  : feed.get('title', 'untitled'),
            'feed.link'   : feed.get('link', '#'),
            'entry.title' : entry.get('title', 'untitled'),
            'entry.link'  : entry.get('link', '#'),
        })

    # Build the content block for this link by populating
    # the LINK_TMPL string template.
    links_out.append(LINK_TMPL % {
        'link'     : link,
        'link_cnt' : len(linkers),
        'linkers'  : '\n'.join(linkers_out)
    })
```

At the top of Listing 15-27, the map of URL-to-linkers built in the previous listing gets flattened down to a list of URL/linkers tuples. The linkers have been collected in a map of feed URI to feed/entry tuples, so taking a count of all the elements in this map gives you the number of entries found pointing to the unique URL. This count is used to sort the list of URL/linkers tuples, thus placing it in an order of descending popularity. Whew—that's a lot of work for only two lines of code.

Anyway, let's move on. Once the list is sorted, it's time to loop through the list of links and linkers to build the popularity report. For each unique URL, the number of linkers is counted and, if this count is below the MIN_LINKS threshold set at back in Listing 15-22, processing for this URL is skipped. This keeps the noise level down, attempting to ensure that only the most buzzworthy links get included in this run of the program.

However, if this unique URL does have enough entries mentioning it, it's time to build some content for the feed entry. This is done inside out, by first looping through the list of feed/entry pairs making up the linkers—these are each used to populate the LINKER_TMPL string template to build a list of linkers. After that, the link itself is used to populate the LINK_TMPL string template, along with a count of linkers and the list linker content concatenated together by carriage returns. The end result, depending on the templates, is a block of content with the unique URL as a heading and entries linking to the URL in a list below it.

After doing this for all the unique URLs harvested from your subscriptions, Listing 15-28 finishes up the feed entry and adds it to the feed.

Listing 15-28: ch15_popular_links.py (Part 7 of 8)

```
# Complete building the content for this entry by
# populating the CONTENT_TMPL string template.
out = CONTENT_TMPL % '\n'.join(links_out)

# Construct and append a new entry
entry = FeedEntryDict({
    'title'   : TITLE_TMPL % {
        'link_cnt' : len(links_out),
        'time'     : time.strftime(TITLE_TIME_FMT)
    },
    'link'    : '',
    'summary' : out
})
f.append_entry(entry)

# Output the current feed entries as both RSS and Atom
open(FEED_NAME_FN % 'rss', 'w').write(f.scrape_rss())
open(FEED_NAME_FN % 'atom', 'w').write(f.scrape_atom())
```

In Listing 15-28, the list of content blocks built for the unique URLs are joined together with carriage returns and used to populate the CONTENT_TMPL string template. Then, a new FeedEntryDict object is created, using this content, a count of links, and the current date to build the content and title for the feed entry. This entry is then appended onto the feed, and the feed is output in both Atom and RSS formats to the appropriate locations as specified by FEED_NAME_FN.

And, with that, the main program is done. Now, take a look at Listing 15-29 for the definition of the LinkSkimmer class.

Listing 15-29: ch15_popular_links.py (Part 8 of 8)

```python
class LinkSkimmer(HTMLParser):
    """
    Quick and dirty link harvester.
    """
    def reset(self):
        """
        Reset the parser and the list of links.
        """
        HTMLParser.reset(self)
        self.links = {}

    def get_links(self):
        """
        Return the links found as a list of tuples,
        link and count.
        """
        return self.links.items()

    def handle_starttag(self, tag, attrs_tup):
        """
        Harvest href attributes from link tags
        """
        attrs = dict(attrs_tup)
        if tag == "a" and attrs.has_key('href'):
            self.links[attrs['href']] = \
                self.links.get(attrs['href'], 0) + 1

if __name__=='__main__': main()
```

The operation of LinkSkimmer in Listing 15-29 is not all that complicated. It's an HTMLParser subclass that maintains a map of URLs, each associated with a count of how many times it's been seen. The handle_starttag() parsing event handler keeps an eye out for <a/> tags and attempts to grab the href attribute from each of them, incrementing that URL's count in the running list.

After the definition of this class, the program is finished.

Trying Out the Popular Link Feed Generator

You can see a sample run of this program in Figure 15-7. The output to the console consists mainly of log messages, listing out the status of feeds visited using the FeedCache object—the real action happens in the feeds it produces and writes out to disk.

```
Terminal — python2.3 — bash (ttypa) — 129x49 — #3
[13:37:11] deusx@Caffeina2:~/Documents/Hacking RSS Book/src$ python ch15_popular_links.py
[13:37:41] INFO root Popular link feed builder starting up.
[13:37:41] DEBUG root Feed #1/692:
[13:37:41] DEBUG FeedCache Refreshing
[13:37:41] DEBUG FeedCache       Feed already refreshed recently.
[13:37:41] DEBUG root Feed #2/692: http://localhost/~deusx/blend.xml
[13:37:41] DEBUG FeedCache Refreshing http://localhost/~deusx/blend.xml
[13:37:41] DEBUG FeedCache       Feed already refreshed recently.
[13:37:41] DEBUG root Feed #3/692: http://localhost/~deusx/amazon.xml
[13:37:41] DEBUG FeedCache Refreshing http://localhost/~deusx/amazon.xml
[13:37:41] DEBUG FeedCache       Feed already refreshed recently.
[13:37:41] DEBUG root Feed #4/692: http://localhost/~deusx/links.xml
[13:37:41] DEBUG FeedCache Refreshing http://localhost/~deusx/links.xml
[13:37:41] DEBUG FeedCache       Feed already refreshed recently.
[13:37:41] DEBUG root Feed #5/692: http://feeds.feedburner.com/decafbad/blog
[13:37:41] DEBUG FeedCache Refreshing http://feeds.feedburner.com/decafbad/blog
[13:37:41] DEBUG FeedCache       Feed already refreshed recently.
[13:37:42] DEBUG root Feed #6/692: http://www.technorati.com/watchlists/rss.html?wid=13709
[13:37:42] DEBUG FeedCache Refreshing http://www.technorati.com/watchlists/rss.html?wid=13709
[13:37:42] DEBUG FeedCache       Feed already refreshed recently.
[13:37:42] DEBUG root Feed #7/692:
[13:37:42] DEBUG FeedCache Refreshing
[13:37:42] DEBUG FeedCache       Feed already refreshed recently.
[13:37:42] DEBUG root Feed #8/692: http://deus-x.dyndns.org/~deusx/scraped-feeds/ineedcoffee.rss
[13:37:42] DEBUG FeedCache Refreshing http://deus-x.dyndns.org/~deusx/scraped-feeds/ineedcoffee.rss
[13:37:43] DEBUG root Feed #9/692: http://www.dark-roast.com/rss.xml
[13:37:43] DEBUG FeedCache Refreshing http://www.dark-roast.com/rss.xml
[13:37:47] DEBUG root Feed #10/692: http://www.flickr.com/groups/espresso/pool/feed/?format=atom_03
[13:37:47] DEBUG FeedCache Refreshing http://www.flickr.com/groups/espresso/pool/feed/?format=atom_03
[13:37:47] WARNING FeedCache Bozo exception for http://www.flickr.com/groups/espresso/pool/feed/?format=atom_03: xml.sax._excepti
ons.SAXParseException <unknown>:3:-1: Extra content at the end of the document

[13:37:47] DEBUG root Feed #11/692: http://coffeeworks.blogs.com/coffee_and_tea/atom.xml
[13:37:47] DEBUG FeedCache Refreshing http://coffeeworks.blogs.com/coffee_and_tea/atom.xml
[13:37:48] DEBUG root Feed #12/692: http://thecoolkids.us/coffee/index.php?&feed=feed
[13:37:48] DEBUG FeedCache Refreshing http://thecoolkids.us/coffee/index.php?&feed=feed
[13:37:48] WARNING FeedCache Bozo exception for http://thecoolkids.us/coffee/index.php?&feed=feed: xml.sax._exceptions.SAXPar
seException <unknown>:45:-1: EntityRef: expecting ';'

[13:37:52] DEBUG root Feed #13/692: http://www.vancouvercoffee.ca/atom.xml
[13:37:52] DEBUG FeedCache Refreshing http://www.vancouvercoffee.ca/atom.xml
[13:37:54] DEBUG root Feed #14/692: http://www.bloggle.com/coffee/atom.xml
[13:37:54] DEBUG FeedCache Refreshing http://www.bloggle.com/coffee/atom.xml
[13:37:56] WARNING FeedCache Bozo exception for http://www.bloggle.com/coffee/atom.xml: feedparser.CharacterEncodingOverride docu
mented declared as us-ascii, but parsed as windows-1252
[13:37:56] DEBUG root Feed #15/692: http://www.decafbad.com/feeds/ineedcoffee.rss
[13:37:56] DEBUG FeedCache Refreshing http://www.decafbad.com/feeds/ineedcoffee.rss
[13:37:56] WARNING FeedCache Bozo exception for http://www.decafbad.com/feeds/ineedcoffee.rss: feedparser.NonXMLContentType no Co
ntent-type specified
```

FIGURE 15-7: Sample program run with the `ch15_popular_links.py`

Something important to realize about this program is that it works best with a large pool of
feeds to analyze—the more subscriptions the better. Personally, I've use it with a list of around
700 feed subscriptions I've accumulated over the years. This means that the program will tend
to take awhile to run.

Cross-Reference Be sure to check out the `FeedCache` class in Appendix A. Using this, the effort of fetching and
parsing the feeds will be shared with your other programs—so if you're pulling feeds from the
same set of subscriptions used in your aggregator, chances are that things will stream by pretty
quickly because the cache will already have reasonably fresh version of all the shared feeds. And,
if you run this program many times in a row as you attempt to tweak or debug it, the cache
should help speed this process.

In Figure 15-8, you can see an example of the feed this program generates, as a subscription in
Mozilla Thunderbird. Take a look at the URL headings with their accompanying feed entry
linkers. And, Figure 15-9 shows you an entry that comes up later in the feed from a subsequent
program run, demonstrating how things change over time as some URLs gain and lose linking
entries.

You'll probably want to run this program on a schedule. I have it cued up to run every four
hours or so, just to put it through its paces. However, you may want to try a more or less-
frequent schedule based on how many feeds you have and how eager you are to watch every
change in the list. This program can produce interesting results even if you only run it once or
twice a day.

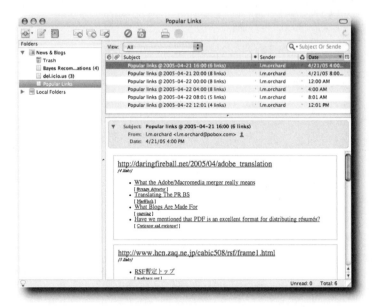

FIGURE 15-8: Popular links feed as a subscription in Thunderbird

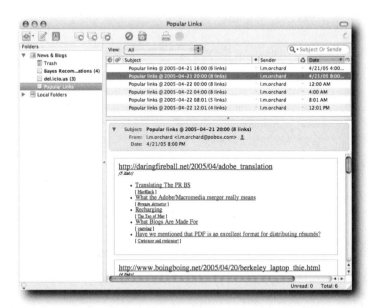

FIGURE 15-9: Viewing a later entry in the popular links feed in Thunderbird

Checking Out Other Options

You may like controlling things yourself with the programs in this chapter. However, it might be worth it to you to check out a few of these other hosted solutions that provide similar features.

Using AmphetaRate for Filtering and Recommendations

AmphetaRate is a centralized rating-and-recommendation service, located here:

`http://amphetarate.newsfairy.com/`

This service can be integrated into an aggregator for training by use of a Web-based API, and it can provide a feed of recommended feed entries based on not only your own training, but also on the interaction recorded from other users of the service. So, you can get some of the features of Bayesian filtering presented here in this chapter, as well as collaborative filtering assisted by other users who read similar things as you.

One negative aspect to this service, though, is that the training side does have to be integrated into an aggregator for you to use it—thus limiting your options. But, that's no different than the Bayesian training aggregator presented in this chapter, really. You could potentially alter it to use AmphetaRate instead of the local instance of Reverend.

Visiting the Daypop Top 40 for Popular Links

Daypop is a "current event search engine," according to its on-site blurbs. Check it out here:

`http://www.daypop.com/top/`

This page is a Top 40 list of hot links, quite similar to the popular links feed in this chapter, only drawn from a much wider array of sources than you're likely to have assembled. On the plus side, this site spans a great number of feeds and sites in its indexing of hot links and topics. And, not only does it provide an HTML view, but there's an RSS feed to which you can subscribe as well. On the minus side, however, you're not in control of the news sources from which it culls the latest links, so what DayPop provides may or may not be tailored well to your interests.

Summary

In this chapter, you've seen three approaches to filtering feeds and sifting through them for information. With regular expressions, you can design handmade criteria through which to pass feed entries. On the other hand, with a trained Bayesian classifier in use, you can train a machine to come up with criteria on its own. And, finally, you can turn feeds inside out—instead of seeing feed entries linking to hot topics, you can see the hot topics themselves gathering discussion from your feeds.

Quite a few avenues are still open for play with these programs, though:

- Right now, the regex feed filter only handles a single input feed at a time, and produces only one feed as output. You could tinker with accepting multiple feeds and applying an array of filters to completely remix things, producing multiple feeds on the other side. For example, such a feed filter could consume your complete list of subscriptions, perform its magic, and spit out neatly organized category- or tag-centric feeds distilled from their entries.

- At present, training a Bayesian classifier requires customizations to your aggregator. Well, the next chapter focuses on making changes to feed entries and blending in information from other sources. In this vein, you could build a feed filter that blends feedback links into every entry of a feed, thereby allowing you to subscribe to it in whatever aggregator you choose, yet still get the benefit of training a Bayesian classifier as you read.

- And, as I mentioned earlier in the chapter, although the classifier here focuses on a thumbs-up/thumbs-down pair of classes for feed entries, there's no reason why you couldn't expand the training. Maybe start teaching your aggregator how to assign categories or tags to feed entries in order to automatically produce feeds that focus on a single topic plucked from your subscriptions. One hint on this one: Try tweaking the `summarizeEntries()` function to actually include the entry category, if it has one.

- In the popular links report, you may find that some people use slightly different URLs in discussion that all actually point to the same thing. For example, one URL might have a trailing slash (for example, `http://www.example.com/`), whereas another does not (for example, `http://www.example.com`)—yet, for all intents and purposes, these URLs are equivalent. So, take a look at normalizing these URLs to the same value in order to better collate discussion.

- And consider one more thought for the popular links feed. All the topics are presented in a single new entry added to the feed on a periodic basis. Why not take a look at breaking these topics out into their own individual entries? You'll need to keep track of a few things, such as entry IDs for the link summary, while providing updates to the URL-centered entries as new discussion appears and drops away. This approach will let you see when new things first pop up as individual entries, although you will lose the overall ranking provided at present.

Coming up next in Chapter 16, you trade filtering and distilling feeds for blending new things into existing feeds. These new hacks will allow you to stir in daily bookmarks, links to products, and related links.

Blending Feeds

So far, your feed "remixing" has been limited to working with the entries of a single feed in the processes of normalization, conversion, and filtering. Well, that covers the "re-" part—the reinterpretation, reconstitution, and recombination of feeds and feed entries. In this chapter, you get around to the "-mixing" part by merging feeds, enhancing entries with related links, mixing in entries with daily links, and inserting relevant products for affiliate credit.

Merging Feeds

To get a sense for what it takes to merge feeds, it's useful to think of them as blocks of wax or soft metal. When delivered as XML, feeds are in solid forms that don't lend very well to combination. So, to get past that, you'll need to melt them down with a feed parser and some normalization.

Parsing liberates the fluid information from the solid form, and *normalization* purifies and renders the feed entries mixable (because Atom and RSS entries might otherwise be like water and oil together). In fact, even entries from two feeds claiming to be the same format could do with some normalization, depending on their respective authors' interpretations of the format. Then, once you have the entries in a fluid and mixable state, you can combine them and then cool them down into a new feed as XML.

Nearly all of this is covered by the functionality of the feed normalizer you built back in Chapter 14. So, the task of building a feed blender mostly consists of reusing the feed normalizer code, throwing in the code to handle multiple feeds, and mixing the entries before feed generation. Hooray for code reuse!

So, getting right into it, check out Listing 16-1 for the start of a new program named ch16_feed_merger.py.

Listing 16-1: ch16_feed_merger.py (Part 1 of 3)

```python
#!/usr/bin/env python
"""
ch16_feed_merger.py

Combine many feeds into a single normalized feed.
"""
import sys, feedparser
from httpcache import HTTPCache
from scraperlib import FeedEntryDict, Scraper
from ch14_feed_normalizer import normalize_entries
```

So far, this is standard stuff. Listing 16-1 starts off with the usual short description, as well as a few familiar imports. There's not much going on here, though, because most of this program's heavy lifting will be done by the feed normalizer.

Move on to Listing 16-2 for the definition of the main() function.

Listing 16-2: ch16_feed_merger.py (Part 2 of 3)

```python
def main():
    """
    merge a handful of link feeds into one mega link feed.
    """
    feeds = [
        'http://blogdex.net/xml/index.asp',
        'http://dev.upian.com/hotlinks/rss.php?n=1',
        'http://del.icio.us/rss/',
        'http://www.daypop.com/top/rss.xml',
        'http://digg.com/rss/index.xml'
    ]

    f = FeedMerger(feeds)
    f.STATE_FN = 'link_merger_state'

    if len(sys.argv) > 1 and sys.argv[1] == 'rss':
        print f.scrape_rss()
    else:
        print f.scrape_atom()
```

The main() function serves to try out an instance of the FeedMerger class by loading it up with a list of feeds from the following sites:

- Blogdex (`http://www.blogdex.net`)—The Web log diffusion index.

- Hot Links (`http://dev.upian.com/hotlinks/`)—A link aggregator with preview thumbnails.

- del.icio.us (`http://del.icio.us`)—The social bookmarking mothership.

- Daypop (`http://www.daypop.com`)—A current events search engine.

- digg (`http://digg.com`)—A collaboratively filtered link and news feed.

Each of these sites is constantly updated with new stories, links, and news, and each of them provides a feed offering a regular flood of entries. So, how better to test the feed blender than to take one big drink from all the firehoses? Listing 16-3 provides the `FeedMerger` class definition that makes this all work.

Listing 16-3: ch16_feed_merger.py (Part 3 of 3)

```
class FeedMerger(Scraper):
    """
    Merge several feeds into a single normalized feed.
    """
    INCLUDE_TITLE = True

    def __init__(self, feed_uris):
        """Initialize with the feed URI for parsing."""
        self.feed_uris = feed_uris

    def produce_entries(self):
        """
        Use normalize_entries() to get feed entries, then merge
        the lists together.
        """
        entries = []

        # Iterate and gather normalized entries for each feed.
        for feed_uri in self.feed_uris:

            # Grab and parse the feed
            feed_data = feedparser.parse(HTTPCache(feed_uri).content())

            # Append the list of normalized entries onto merged list.
            curr_entries = normalize_entries(feed_data.entries)
            for e in curr_entries:
                if self.INCLUDE_TITLE:
                    e['title'] = "["+ feed_data.feed.title + "] " + \
                                 e.data['title']
            entries.extend(curr_entries)

        return entries

if __name__=='__main__': main()
```

As you can see in Listing 16-3, `FeedMerger` is a subclass of `Scraper`, in order to take advantage of the already-built feed generation code. The `__init__()` method accepts a list of feed URIs for object initialization, and the `produce_entries()` method forms the heart of this class.

In `produce_entries()`, each feed is fetched and parsed using the `feedparser`. The `normalize_entries()` function from Chapter 14 is used with the data produced by `feedparser` to extract normalized `FeedEntryDict` objects. Then, if the `INCLUDE_TITLE` flag is true, the feed title is prepended onto each entry title. This helps identify the source of each entry in the merged feed.

After this, the list of entries is tacked onto the end of the master list. And, after all the source feeds have been processed, this master list is returned to be processed by the `Scraper` feed generation.

Trying Out the Feed Merger

Take a look at Figure 16-1 and Figure 16-2 for sample program runs in Atom and RSS feed formats, respectively. And, Figure 16-3 presents what the feed looks like as a subscription in Mozilla Thunderbird.

FIGURE 16-1: Merged feed in Atom output format

```
                        Terminal — bash — bash (ttype) — 129x49 — #4
[13:26:05] deusx@Caffeina2:~/Documents/Hacking RSS Book/src$ python ch16_feed_merge.py rss
<?xml version="1.0" encoding="utf-8"?>
<rss version="2.0">
    <channel>
        <title>A Sample Feed</title>
        <link>http://www.example.com</link>
        <description>This is a testing sample feed.</description>
        <webMaster>l.m.orchard@pobox.com</webMaster>

        <item>
            <title>[HotLinks - Level 1] FuckedGoogle</title>
            <link>http://www.fuckedgoogle.com/</link>
            <guid isPermaLink="false">http://dev.upian.com/hotlinks/archives/2005/04/04/#item33452</guid>
            <description>&lt;a href="http://www.fuckedgoogle.com/"&gt;&lt;img src="http://dev.upian.com/hotlinks/img/2005/04/04/1
112633726-0.png" alt="" /&gt;&lt;/a&gt;
&lt;p&gt;&lt;a href=""&gt;Jeremy Zawodny&lt;/a&gt; : FuckedGoogle - &lt;em&gt;FuckedGoogle: google bashing blog&lt;/em&gt;&lt;/p&
gt;</description>
        </item>


        <item>
            <title>[HotLinks - Level 1] TimeTrax - Timeshifting Software for XM Satellite Radio</title>
            <link>http://www.timetraxtech.com/</link>
            <pubDate>2005-04-04T17:55:26Z</pubDate>
            <guid isPermaLink="false">http://dev.upian.com/hotlinks/archives/2005/04/04/#item33451</guid>
            <description>&lt;a href="http://www.timetraxtech.com/"&gt;&lt;img src="http://dev.upian.com/hotlinks/img/2005/04/04/1
112633718-0.png" alt="" /&gt;&lt;/a&gt;
&lt;p&gt;&lt;a href="">&gt;plasticbag&lt;/a&gt; : TimeTrax - Timeshifting Software for XM Satellite Radio - &lt;em&gt;Apparently r
ecords individual songs as played on the radio as well. Interesting little thing. Love to know how well it works...&lt;/em&gt;&lt
;/p&gt;</description>
        </item>


        <item>
            <title>[HotLinks - Level 1] Replay Music records music off the radio and automatically tags it</title>
            <link>http://www.replay-music.com/</link>
            <pubDate>2005-04-04T17:55:11Z</pubDate>
            <guid isPermaLink="false">http://dev.upian.com/hotlinks/archives/2005/04/04/#item33450</guid>
            <description>&lt;a href="http://www.replay-music.com/"&gt;&lt;img src="http://dev.upian.com/hotlinks/img/2005/04/04/1
112633711-0.png" alt="" /&gt;&lt;/a&gt;
&lt;p&gt;&lt;a href="">&gt;plasticbag&lt;/a&gt; : Replay Music records music off the radio and automatically tags it - &lt;em&gt;U
ses audio fingerprinting to figure out the beginning or end of the songs as well&lt;/em&gt;&lt;/p&gt;</description>
        </item>


        <item>
            <title>[HotLinks - Level 1] Independent developers claim wireless DS tunneling by April 11</title>
            <link>http://www.livejournal.com/community/nintendo_ds/227958.html</link>
```

FIGURE 16-2: Merged feed in RSS output format

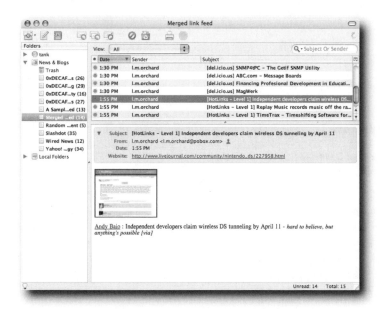

FIGURE 16-3: Merged feed as viewed in Mozilla Thunderbird

Adding Related Links with Technorati Searches

Now that you've had a chance to work with mixing feeds at the granularity of whole entries, it's time to muck around with the entries themselves. In this section, you enhance feed entries by adding related links resulting from searches performed using the Technorati API.

Before getting into the next program, though, you may need a little introduction to the Technorati API. You can find details at the Technorati Developer Center (see Figure 16-4), located here:

```
http://www.technorati.com/developers/
```

FIGURE 16-4: Technorati Developer Center in Firefox

In case you've never before played with the services provided by Technorati, here's the lowdown: Technorati crawls Web logs and harvests links and metadata from them. You can use Technorati to discover which blogs link to which, and you can search for blog entries and links via keywords and phrases. And, not only can you search and browse for these things manually via Web browser, but there's also a REST-style API available and documented at the Developer Center.

Stowing the Technorati API Key

Like many Web services available for public developer use, the Technorati API requires that you sign up for an account at its Web site and acquire an API key to be included with every request. If you visit the aforementioned Developer Center home page, you'll see a link to "API

Key," which should guide you through this process. You should receive a string of letters and numbers something like the following:

```
12345df45b5678c2573024a47e67e8xp
```

Of course, this isn't a real key, so you will need to get your own. After you've done that, create a text file in your project directory named `technorati-key.txt` and paste this string into it—the program you're about to build will read the key from this file for use in search queries.

Searching with the Technorati API

Once you have a key, use of the API is done through simple HTTP GET requests. For example, here's an invocation for making a search from the command line using cURL:

```
# K=`cat technorati-key.txt`
# curl -sD -
"http://api.technorati.com/search?key=$K&limit=5&query=I+like+science+fiction"
```

 cURL is a flexible command-line tool for accessing many resources via URL. It can come in very handy for testing out HTTP GET requests. You can find it here:

> http://curl.haxx.se/

This command-line sequence pulls your stored API key into a shell variable and then uses it to make a search on the Technorati API for the phrase "I like science fiction." The command-line options given to cURL cause it to output the headers, as well as the body of the response in XML. You can see the results of this in Figure 16-5.

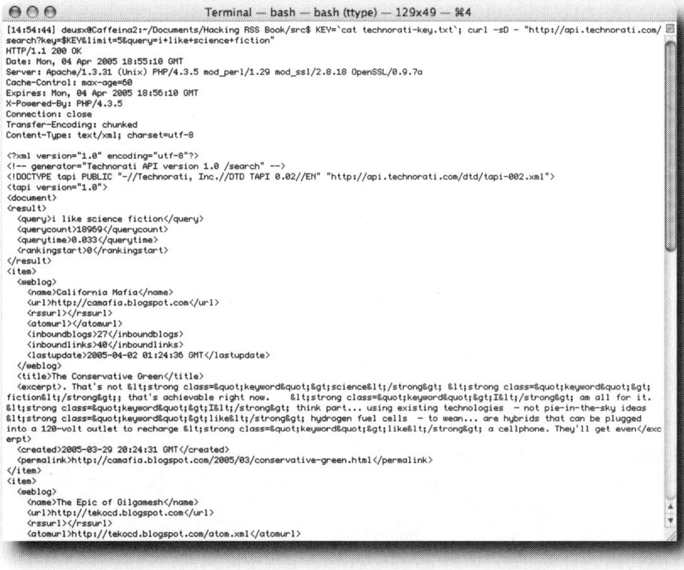

FIGURE 16-5: Results of a Technorati API search

Parsing Technorati Search Results

Now that you've seen the results of a Technorati search, it's time to try it out with a Python program. One of the easiest ways to handle calling the API is with a combination of `HTTPCache` to make the query and a module named `xmltramp` to parse the XML data returned.

 On the Web The `xmltramp` module, by Aaron Swartz, offers a quick-and-dirty way for getting access to XML data such as what's returned by the Technorati API. Check it out here:

> http://www.aaronsw.com/2002/xmltramp/

You need to download a copy of this module to your project directory. It is located at the following URL:

> http://www.aaronsw.com/2002/xmltramp/xmltramp.py

Check out Listing 16-4 for a quick program using `HTTPCache` and `xmltramp` to perform a search using the Technorati API.

Listing 16-4: ch16_technorati_search.py

```python
#!/usr/bin/env python
"""
ch16_technorati_search.py

Perform a search on the Technorati API
"""
import sys, urllib, urllib2, xmltramp
from xml.sax import SAXParseException
from httpcache import HTTPCache

def main():
    key   = open("technorati-key.txt", "r").read().strip()
    query = (len(sys.argv) > 1) and sys.argv[1] or 'test query'
    tmpl  = 'http://api.technorati.com/search' + \
            '?key=%s&limit=5&query=%s'
    url   = tmpl % (key, urllib.quote_plus(query))
    data  = HTTPCache(url).content()

    # HACK: I get occasional encoding issues with Technorati,
    # so here's an ugly hack that seems to make things work
    # anyway.
    try:
        doc = xmltramp.parse(data)
    except SAXParseException:
        data = data.decode('utf8', 'ignore').encode('utf8')
        doc = xmltramp.parse(data)

    items = [ x for x in doc.document if x._name == 'item' ]
```

```
    for i in items:
        print '"%(title)s"\n\t%(permalink)s' % i

if __name__=='__main__': main()
```

The program in Listing 16-4 first loads up the Technorati API key from a file and grabs a query phrase from the command line (with `'test query'` as a default, if none given). It then assembles a URL for use in calling the Technorati API by filling in a template with the key and the query phrase.

This URL is used with `HTTPCache` to fetch the search results, which are parsed using `xml-tramp`. There's a little bit of a hack here, though. Although the Technorati results claim to be encoded as UTF-8, I've occasionally run into issues with some anomalies in the encoding. So, in this case, an attempt is made to try parsing over again after a little bit of crude cleaning up.

When you try running this program, you'll get output something like the following:

```
# python ch16_technorati_search.py 'i like science fiction'
"The Conservative Green"
        http://camafia.blogspot.com/2005/03/conservative-green.html
"Life , the Universe and Everything"
        http://calm.esinner.com/wp/?p=3
"MSNBC story on the Minute Man Project, Friday Evening"
        http://tekocd.blogspot.com/2005/04/msnbc-story-on-minute-man-
project.html
"Srange World. Imagine a world where people read o..."
        http://sitbehind.blogspot.com/2005/04/srange-world.html
"Hiding galaxies, Meteor Crater and inhabitants of Taurus II"
        http://alienlifeblog.blogspot.com/2005/03/hiding-galaxies-meteor-crater-
and.html
```

Adding Related Links to Feed Entries

Now you have all the pieces you need to use Technorati searches to add related links to feed entries. For this next program, you'll be performing a search for each entry using the title of the entry as the query. You'll then be able to use the search results to construct lists of links to tack onto the end of each entry summary.

Listing 16-5 presents the start of this new program, named `ch16_feed_related.py`.

Listing 16-5: ch16_feed_related.py (Part 1 of 4)

```
#!/usr/bin/env python
"""
ch16_feed_related.py

Insert related links into a normalized feed.
```

Continued

Listing 16-5 *(continued)*

```
"""
import sys, urllib, feedparser, xmltramp
from xml.sax import SAXParseException
from httpcache import HTTPCache
from scraperlib import FeedEntryDict, Scraper
from ch14_feed_normalizer import normalize_feed_meta,
normalize_entries

FEED_URL = 'http://www.decafbad.com/blog/index.xml'

def main():
    """
    Use the FeedRelator on a given feed.
    """
    feed_url = ( len(sys.argv) > 2 ) and sys.argv[2] or \
               FEED_URL

    f = FeedRelator(feed_url)
    f.STATE_FN = 'link_related_state'

    if len(sys.argv) > 1 and sys.argv[1] == 'rss':
        print f.scrape_rss()
    else:
        print f.scrape_atom()
```

This program starts off with the familiar preamble of a short description, a series of module imports, a configuration constant, and the main() function. The sole configuration constant is FEED_URL, whose value is used to find the feed to be normalized and enhanced with related links. The main() function creates an instance of the FeedRelator class and uses it to produce the finished feed.

Continue on to Listing 16-6, which provides the start of the FeedRelator class.

Listing 16-6: ch16_feed_related.py (Part 2 of 4)

```
class FeedRelator(Scraper):
    """
    Insert related links found via Technorati search into a
    normalized feed.
    """

    TECHNORATI_KEY  = open("technorati-key.txt", "r").read().strip()
```

```
SEARCH_URL_TMPL = \
    "http://api.technorati.com/search?key=%s&limit=5&query=%s"

INSERT_TMPL = """
    <div style="border: 1px solid #888; padding: 12px;">
        <b><u>Further reading:</u></b><br />
        <ul>
        %s
        </ul>
    </div>
"""
INSERT_ITEM_TMPL = """
    <li>
        [<a href="%(weblog.url)s">%(weblog.name)s</a>]
        <a href="%(permalink)s">%(title)s</a>
    </li>
"""

def __init__(self, main_feed):
    """Initialize with the feed URI for parsing."""
    self.main_feed = main_feed
```

The `FeedRelator` class in Listing 16-6 starts off with a few class constants:

- `TECHNORATI_KEY`—The value of this constant is loaded up with the API key contained in the file named `technorati-key.txt`, which you should have created a little while ago.

- `SEARCH_URL_TMPL`—This constant contains a string template to be used in building a URL for use in performing a search on the Technorati API.

- `INSERT_TMPL`—This contains a string template that will be used to create the block of additional content for related links added to entries.

- `INSERT_ITEM_TMPL`—This string template will be used to render each related link in the list that will populate `INSERT_TMPL`.

Finally, this listing offers an `__init__()` method, which stows away the URL to the feed into which related links will be inserted. Moving on, Listing 16-7 gives the start of the `produce_entries()` method.

Listing 16-7: ch16_feed_related.py (Part 3 of 4)

```
def produce_entries(self):
    """
    Use FeedNormalizer to get feed entries, then merge
    the lists together.
```

Continued

Listing 16-7 *(continued)*

```python
    """
    # Grab and parse the feed
    feed = feedparser.parse(HTTPCache(self.main_feed).content())
    # Normalize feed meta data
    self.FEED_META = normalize_feed_meta(feed, self.date_fmt)
    self.FEED_META['feed.title'] += ' (with related links)'

    # Normalize entries from the feed
    entries = normalize_entries(feed.entries)

    # Run through all the normalized entries...
    for e in entries:

        # Perform a search on the entry title, extract the items
        result = self.technorati_search(e['title'])
        items  = [ x for x in result if x._name == 'item' ]

        # Use each search result item to populate the templates.
        insert_items = []
        for i in items:
            insert_items.append(self.INSERT_ITEM_TMPL % {
                'weblog.name' : i.weblog.name,
                'weblog.url'  : i.weblog.url,
                'title'       : i.title,
                'permalink'   : i.permalink
            })
        insert_out = self.INSERT_TMPL % '\n'.join(insert_items)

        # Append the rendered search results onto the
        # entry summary.
        e.data['summary'] += insert_out.decode('utf-8', 'ignore')

    return entries
```

First off in produce_entries(), the feed is fetched and parsed using feedparser along with HTTPCache. This feed data is then passed to normalize_feed_meta() from Chapter 14 to build metadata for this program's output feed. Then, the normalize_entries() function is used to get a list of normalized entries for manipulation.

Once acquired, each entry in this list is visited. The title of the current entry is used to perform a Technorati API search, via the to-be-defined method technorati_search(). The <item> elements are extracted and each is used to populate the INSERT_ITEM_TMPL string template.

The list of strings generated by populating this template are then joined together and used, in turn, to populate the INSERT_TMPL template. The results of this are then tacked onto the end of the current entry's summary content, thus resulting in the current entry gaining a list of related links courtesy of the Technorati API.

Finally, in Listing 16-8 comes the definition of the technorati_search() method, and the end of this program.

Listing 16-8: ch16_feed_related.py (Part 4 of 4)

```
def technorati_search(self, query):
    """
    Given a query string, perform a Technorati search.
    """
    # Construct a Technorati search URL and fetch it.
    url  = self.SEARCH_URL_TMPL % \
           (self.TECHNORATI_KEY, urllib.quote_plus(query))
    data = HTTPCache(url).content()

    # HACK: I get occasional encoding issues with
    # Technorati, so here's an ugly hack that seems to
    # make things work anyway.
    try:
        return xmltramp.parse(data).document
    except SAXParseException:
        data = data.decode('ascii', 'ignore')
        return xmltramp.parse(data).document

if __name__=='__main__': main()
```

Listing 16-8 reworks what was offered in Listing 16-4, this time as a reusable method for this feed generator. This technorati_search() method accepts a query string, constructs a Technorati API search URL, fetches it using HTTPCache, and then returns the parsed results of the XML data from the query.

Trying Out the Related Link Feed Blender

Now, you should be able to try out this program. By default, it produces an Atom format feed based on the default value in the FEED_URL constant. Like most of the other feed generation programs in this book, you can optionally supply a feed format and a new feed URL. Figure 16-6 and Figure 16-7 show sample runs of this feed generator in Atom and RSS formats, and Figure 16-8 provides an example of what a feed resulting from this program looks like as a subscription in Thunderbird.

FIGURE 16-6: Feed with related links output in Atom format

FIGURE 16-7: Feed with related links output in RSS format

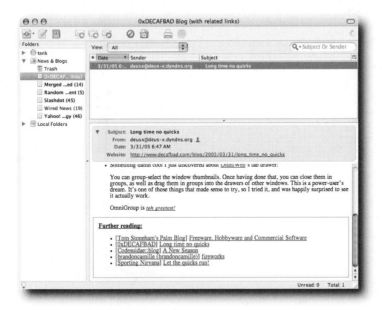

FIGURE 16-8: Feed with Technorati links viewed in Thunderbird

Mixing Daily Links from del.icio.us

In this chapter's first two programs, you merged entries from existing feeds together and tweaked entries to add related links. In this part, you build brand new entries for addition into a feed based on daily summaries of links posted to del.icio.us.

In case you haven't heard of it before, del.icio.us is a social bookmarks manager located, appropriately enough, at this URL:

```
http://del.icio.us
```

Members of this site, via the use of bookmarklets and other utilities, can store and share bookmarks to sites of interest, adding their own comments and quasi-categories called tags. RSS feeds are available for every user's set of bookmarks and every tag—and behind all of this lies a REST-style API.

Using the del.icio.us API

The del.icio.us API, under constant development, is documented at this URL (shown in Figure 16-9):

```
http://del.icio.us/doc/api
```

All API usage requires that you sign up for an account. So, while you're checking out the site and the API documentation, you should get an account of your own. Whereas some sites' APIs require the use of key strings or IDs, the del.icio.us API calls for HTTP authentication.

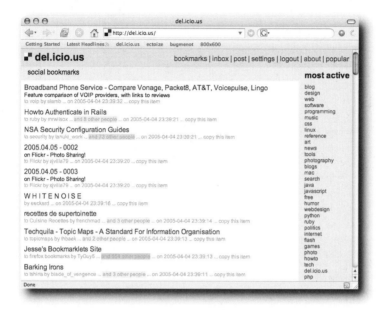

FIGURE **16-9: del.icio.us home page in Firefox**

Once you've signed up for an account, create a file named `delicious-acct.txt` and put your account details into it, like so:

`username:password`

So, for example, if your user name is "foo" and your password is "bar," the contents of this file should be a single line like so:

`foo:bar`

With this file created, you can try out the API using cURL on the command line like so:

```
# AUTH=`cat delicious-acct.txt`
# curl -sD - "http://$AUTH@del.icio.us/api/posts/get?dt=2005-03-31"
```

Example output from this command is shown in Figure 16-10.

You'll probably want to review the API documentation for del.icio.us in further detail, but this post retrieval call is all you'll need to know for this chapter.

Inserting Daily del.icio.us Recaps into a Feed

This next program uses the del.icio.us API to retrieve several days' worth of bookmark postings, building a new feed entry from each. You've already seen the `xmltramp` in action in the previous program, so you can just jump right into this new program. Start a new file named `ch16_feed_delicious_recaps.py`, with the code starting in Listing 16-9.

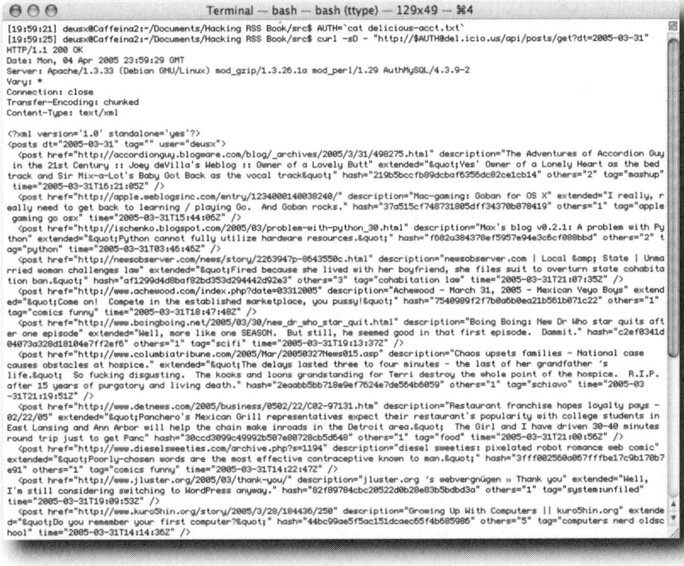

FIGURE 16-10: Output of a post retrieval query on the del.icio.us API

Listing 16-9: ch16_feed_delicious_recaps.py (Part 1 of 5)

```python
#!/usr/bin/env python
"""
ch16_feed_delicious_recaps.py

Insert del.icio.us link recaps into a normalized feed.
"""
import sys, time, urllib2, feedparser, xmltramp
from httpcache import HTTPCache
from xml.sax import SAXParseException
from scraperlib import FeedEntryDict, Scraper
from ch14_feed_normalizer import normalize_feed_meta,
normalize_entries

FEED_URL = 'http://www.decafbad.com/blog/atom.xml'

def main():
    """
    Use the DeliciousFeed on a given feed.
    """
    feed_url = ( len(sys.argv) > 2 ) and sys.argv[2] or \
               FEED_URL
    f = DeliciousFeed(feed_url)
```

Continued

Listing 16-9 *(continued)*

```
f.STATE_FN = 'link_delicious_recaps_state'
f.DEL_USER, f.DEL_PASSWD = \
    open('delicious-acct.txt').read().strip().split(':')

if len(sys.argv) > 1 and sys.argv[1] == 'rss':
    print f.scrape_rss()
else:
    print f.scrape_atom()
```

The new program in Listing 16-9 again starts off with the usual description and imports, as well as a FEED_URL configuration constant with the default URL to a feed to which the recaps will be added.

Next up is the definition of main(), which accepts an optional feed format and feed URL. It creates an instance of the DeliciousFeed class, giving it a new state filename, and reading in the user account details you stored previously in the file delicious-acct.txt.

The definition of the DeliciousFeed class is next, in Listing 16-10.

Listing 16-10: ch16_feed_delicious_recaps.py (Part 2 of 5)

```
class DeliciousFeed(Scraper):
    """
    Insert daily recaps of del.icio.us links as entries
    into a normalized feed.
    """
    DEL_API_URL = "http://del.icio.us/api/posts/get?dt=%s"
    DEL_USER, DEL_PASSWD = "user", "passwd"
    NUM_DAYS = 3

    DEL_ENTRY_TMPL = """
        <ul>
        %s
        </ul>
    """
    DEL_LINK_TMPL = """
        <li>
            <a href="%(href)s">%(description)s</a> (%(tags)s)<br />
            %(extended)s
        </li>
    """
    DEL_TAG_TMPL = """<a href="%(href)s">%(tag)s</a> """
```

```
def __init__(self, main_feed):
    """Initialize with the feed URI for parsing."""
    self.main_feed = main_feed
```

The `DeliciousFeed` class starts off with a series of constants, including the following:

- `DEL_API_URL`—A string template used to build the API query for retrieving posts.

- `DEL_USER`—del.icio.us account user name.

- `DEL_PASSWD`—del.icio.us account password.

- `NUM_DAYS`—How many days into the past should be queried for bookmark posts on which to base recaps in feed entries.

- `DEL_ENTRY_TMPL`—This string template forms the overall shell for content in book-mark post recaps.

- `DEL_LINK_TMPL`—This string template will be populated with each of the bookmark postings found in the results for an API query.

- `DEL_TAG_TMPL`—Each link posted to del.icio.us can be assigned one or more tags, and this string template will be used to construct links to each tag.

After these constants comes the definition of `__init__()`, which records the feed URL that will be normalized and have del.icio.us link recaps inserted. Next up, in Listing 16-11, is the definition of the `produce_entries()` method.

Listing 16-11: ch16_feed_delicious_recaps.py (Part 3 of 5)

```
def produce_entries(self):
    """
    Normalize the source feed, insert del.icio.us
    daily link recaps.
    """
    # Grab and parse the feed
    feed = feedparser.parse(HTTPCache(self.main_feed).content())

    # Normalize feed meta data
    self.FEED_META = normalize_feed_meta(feed, self.date_fmt)
    self.FEED_META['feed.title'] += ' (with del.icio.us links)'

    # Normalize entries from the feed
    entries = normalize_entries(feed.entries)

    # Iterate through a number of past days' links
```

Continued

Listing 16-11 *(continued)*

```
for n in range(self.NUM_DAYS):
    # Calculate and format date for this query
    post_secs = time.time() - ( (n+1) * 24 * 60 * 60 )
    post_time = time.localtime(post_secs)
    post_dt   = time.strftime('%Y-%m-%d', post_time)

    # Prepare for Basic Authentication in calling del API
    auth = urllib2.HTTPBasicAuthHandler()
    auth.add_password('del.icio.us API', 'del.icio.us',
                      self.DEL_USER, self.DEL_PASSWD)
    urllib2.install_opener(urllib2.build_opener(auth))

    # Build del API URL, execute the query, and parse response.
    url  = self.DEL_API_URL % post_dt
    data = urllib2.urlopen(url).read()
    doc  = xmltramp.parse(data)
```

The beginning of `produce_entries()` in Listing 16-11 follows much of the same pattern as Listing 16-7. The feed is fetched and parsed using `feedparser` and `HTTPCache`. This feed data is used with Chapter 14's `normalize_feed_meta()` function to supply the new feed with metadata. Then, the normalized feed entries are obtained using `normalize_entries()`.

However, unlike the previous program, none of the incoming feed entries will be modified. Instead, you'll be adding *new* entries in this program. The purpose of the next loop in this method is to step back through the last few days' postings on del.icio.us.

So, the loop iterates through a number of days. These are each calculated as times in seconds counted from the current time, with the appropriate days' worth of seconds subtracted. This value is then converted into a time tuple, which is in turn formatted into a string for use in the upcoming API call.

Before the HTTP GET to the del.icio.us API can be made, though, you need to prepare the `urllib2` module to use HTTP Basic Authentication. You do this by creating an `HTTPBasicAuthHandler` object, and calling its `add_password()` method with the appropriate account details. This handler is then installed globally in the module with the `install_opener()` function.

Finally, things are ready for you to make a call to the del.icio.us API. So, the `DEL_API_URL` string template is populated with the date string produced at the start of the loop iteration. Then, the API query is made and the XML data is fetched using `urllib2.urlopen()` and parsed with `xmltramp`.

Next, in Listing 16-12, the data retrieved from the del.icio.us API is processed to generate the content for a new feed entry.

Listing 16-12: ch16_feed_delicious_recaps.py (Part 4 of 5)

```
# Skip this day if no posts resulted from the query
if not len(doc) > 0: continue

# Iterate through all posts retrieved, build
# content for entry.
post_out = []
for post in doc:

    # Run through post tags, render links with template.
    tags_out = [ self.DEL_TAG_TMPL % {
        'tag'  : t,
        'href' : 'http://del.icio.us/%s/%s' % \
                 (self.DEL_USER, t)
    } for t in post("tag").split() ]

    # Build content for this link posting using template.
    try:    extended = post('extended')
    except: extended = ''

    post_out.append(self.DEL_LINK_TMPL % {
        'href'        : post('href'),
        'description' : post('description'),
        'extended'    : extended,
        'tags'        : ''.join(tags_out)
    })
```

In Listing 16-12, each of the posts are processed to generate content for the new feed entry. Note that the loop skips ahead if there aren't any posts for this particular day. If there are, the first thing done for each post is to use the DEL_TAG_TMPL template to render each of the post's tags into links. Then, the rest of the attributes of the bookmark post are used to populate the DEL_LINK_TMPL template. There's special treatment for the 'extended' attribute, because it's not a required field in del.icio.us postings.

And, the content generated in this way is appended to the post_out list, to be used in Listing 16-13 to build a new feed entry containing a recap of this day's bookmark postings.

Listing 16-13: ch16_feed_delicious_recaps.py (Part 5 of 5)

```
# Construct and append a new feed entry based on
# the day's links
new_entry = FeedEntryDict(date_fmt=self.date_fmt,
                          init_dict={
    'title'    : 'del.icio.us links on %s' % post_dt,
    'issued'   : post_secs,
    'modified' : post_secs,
    'link'     : 'http://del.icio.us/%s#%s' % \
```

Continued

Listing 16-13 *(continued)*

```
                          (self.DEL_USER, post_dt),
            'summary'   : self.DEL_ENTRY_TMPL % "\n".join(post_out)
        })
        entries.append(new_entry)

        # Pause, because http://del.icio.us/doc/api says so.
        time.sleep(1)

if __name__=='__main__': main()
```

With the code in Listing 16-13, a new `FeedEntryDict` object is constructed with a title based on the date used to retrieve postings; issued and modified timestamps are given the time in seconds; the link is constructed based on the your account's home page; and finally the content built in Listing 16-12 is supplied as the entry's summary content.

This new entry is appended to the normalized feed's entries, and then a pause of 1 second is taken, as per the del.icio.us API documentation's request.

Trying Out the Daily del.icio.us Recap Insertion

This program is ready to insert daily del.icio.us recap entries now. Figure 16-11 shows this program spitting out an Atom feed and Figure 16-12 shows an RSS feed. And, finally, Figure 16-13 offers a screenshot of how a feed produced by this program appears in Mozilla Thunderbird.

FIGURE 16-11: Feed with daily del.icio.us links output in Atom format

FIGURE 16-12: Feed with daily del.icio.us links output in RSS format

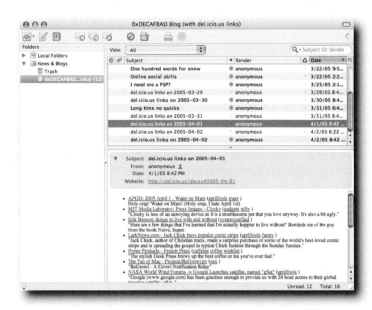

FIGURE 16-13: Feed with del.icio.us recaps viewed in Thunderbird

Inserting Related Items from Amazon

You've seen Amazon Web Services (AWS) in use before, back in Chapter 13 when you built feeds from product search results. But, now that you have the machinery for remixing feeds, how about one more hack that revisits AWS?

The final hack of this chapter allows you to insert links and thumbnails to Amazon products into your feed entries, based on a TextStream search using the summary content of each entry. You can read about TextStream searches in the documentation at the AWS developer site (`http://www.amazon.com/gp/aws/landing.html`), under the section "API Reference," "Operations," "Item Operations," "ItemSearch."

Basically, the idea is that you throw some text at AWS, and it attempts to dig up appropriately relevant products to go along with that text. And, because you can include an Amazon Associate tag in product links produced by AWS calls, this hack can enable you to inject a little unobtrusive affiliate advertising, supporting you and your feed if your readers decide to make purchases based on the products recommended in this way.

Trying Out an AWS TextStream Search

Although you've had exposure to the AWS API in Chapter 13, how about a quick refresher? Like a few of the other Web services you played with in this chapter, AWS requires a key for use in making queries to the service. You should already have one, but if you still need to register with AWS, you can do so at this URL:

`http://www.amazon.com/gp/aws/registration/registration-form.html`

After signup, you should receive an email with the key as a string of characters, something like this:

`27BB61CCSY35NKAC64R5`

Once you have a key, you should make sure there's a copy of it in a text file named `amazon-key.txt`. The program coming up will consult this file for your key.

Although the results in XML (as shown in Figure 16-14) won't be very pretty to human eyes, you can fire up a TextStream item search request to the AWS using cURL like so:

```
# KEY=`cat amazon-key.txt`
# curl -s "http://webservices.amazon.com/onca/xml?
SubscriptionId=$KEY&AssociateTag=0xdecafbad-
20&Service=AWSECommerceService&Operation=ItemSearch&SearchIndex=Books&
ResponseGroup=Medium%2CItemAttributes&TextStream=i+like+science+fiction"
```

The URL used to query the AWS product search stuffs a lot into one little HTTP GET, but it should all make more sense once you've had a chance to read through the documentation a bit. Again, you've probably seen all this back in Chapter 13, but it can't hurt to revisit things and play a bit before moving on.

FIGURE 16-14: XML data spewed from an AWS TextStream search query

Building an Amazon Product Feed Blender

Based on the work done so far in this chapter, accessing the REST-styled API offered by AWS is made simple through the combination of `HTTPCache` and `xmltramp`. You can dive right into this last program, called `ch16_feed_amazon_ads.py`, starting with Listing 16-14.

Listing 16-14: ch16_feed_amazon_ads.py (Part 1 of 4)

```python
#!/usr/bin/env python
"""
ch16_feed_amazon_ads.py

Insert Amazon links into a normalized feed.
"""
import sys, urllib, feedparser, xmltramp
from xml.sax import SAXParseException
from httpcache import HTTPCache
from scraperlib import FeedEntryDict, Scraper
from ch14_feed_normalizer import normalize_feed_meta, 
normalize_entries

FEED_URL = 'http://www.decafbad.com/blog/atom.xml'

def main():
    """
    Use the AmazonAdFeed on a given feed.
```

Continued

Listing 16-14 *(continued)*

```
"""
feed_url = ( len(sys.argv) > 2 ) and sys.argv[2] or \
           FEED_URL

f = AmazonAdFeed(feed_url)
f.STATE_FN = 'link_amazon_ads_state'

if len(sys.argv) > 1 and sys.argv[1] == 'rss':
    print f.scrape_rss()
else:
    print f.scrape_atom()
```

Listing 16-14 provides the preamble for this new program, including a few familiar module imports, the default location of the feed for blending in FEED_URL. There's also the definition of main(), which creates an instance of the AmazonAdFeed class and fires it up to produce a feed in the desired format.

Continue on to Listing 16-15 for the beginning of the definition of this AmazonAdFeed class.

Listing 16-15: ch16_feed_amazon_ads.py (Part 2 of 4)

```
class AmazonAdFeed(Scraper):
    """
    Insert amazon_ads links found via Technorati search into a
    normalized feed.
    """
    AMAZON_KEY     = open("amazon-key.txt", "r").read().strip()
    ASSOCIATE_TAG  = '0xdecafbad-20'
    MAX_ITEMS      = 3

    INSERT_TMPL = """
        <div style="border: 1px solid #888; padding: 12px;">
            <b><u>Possibly Related Amazon Items:</u></b><br />
            <ul>
            %s
            </ul>
        </div>
    """
    INSERT_ITEM_TMPL = """
        <li>
            <img src="%(img)s" align="middle" style="padding: 5px;" />
            <a href="%(url)s">%(title)s</a>
        </li>
    """

    def __init__(self, main_feed):
```

```
    """Initialize with the feed URI for parsing."""
    self.main_feed = main_feed
```

First up in Listing 16-15, your AWS subscription key is loaded up into the class constant AMAZON_KEY, from the text file where you stashed it earlier. Next, an Amazon Associate tag is established in the ASSOCIATE_TAG constant.

The MAX_ITEMS constant defines how many products will be included in every feed entry from the search results.

The final two class constants are string templates. The first, INSERT_TMPL, is the wrapper shell for the list of products that will be injected into your feed's entries. The second template, INSERT_ITEM_TMPL, provides a string template for rendering each product to be included in the entry.

After these constants comes the definition of __init__(), which does the usual job of stowing away the value of the feed URL to blend. Moving forward, you can find the definition of produce_entries() in Listing 16-16.

Listing 16-16: ch16_feed_amazon_ads.py (Part 3 of 4)

```python
def produce_entries(self):
    """
    Use FeedNormalizer to get feed entries, then merge
    the lists together.
    """
    # Grab and parse the feed
    feed = feedparser.parse(HTTPCache(self.main_feed).content())

    # Normalize feed meta data
    self.FEED_META = normalize_feed_meta(feed, self.date_fmt)
    self.FEED_META['feed.title'] += ' (with Amazon items)'

    # Normalize entries from the feed
    entries = normalize_entries(feed.entries)

    # Run through all the normalized entries...
    for e in entries:

        # Perform a search on the entry title, extract the items
        result = self.amazon_search(e['summary'])
        items  = [ x for x in result.Items if 'Item' in x._name ]

        # Use the search results to populate the templates.
        insert_items = [ self.INSERT_ITEM_TMPL % {
            'title' : i.ItemAttributes.Title,
            'url'   : i.DetailPageURL,
            'img'   : i.SmallImage.URL
        } for i in items[:self.MAX_ITEMS] ]
```

Continued

Listing 16-16 *(continued)*

```
        insert_out = self.INSERT_TMPL % '\n'.join(insert_items)

        # Append the rendered search results onto the
        # entry summary.
        e.data['summary'] += insert_out.decode('utf-8', 'ignore')

    return entries
```

Once more with feeling—the `produce_entries()` method in Listing 16-16 takes its cues from Listing 16-11 and Listing 16-7. It uses `feedparser` to grab the feed data and employs `normalize_feed_meta()` to build the metadata for the blended feed under construction. And, again, `normalize_entries()` is used to acquire a list of normalized entries from the source feed.

Each of these entries are visited in a loop, and the `amazon_search()` method is called with the current entry's summary text. This method returns the results of the search, parsed using `xml-tramp`. The product items are then lifted out of the search results with a list comprehension.

These Amazon items are then digested in another list comprehension, producing a list of strings via the `INSERT_ITEM_TMPL` string template. This list of strings is joined together and supplied to the `INSERT_TMPL` string template to generate the content block. And, finally, this content is appended to the current entry's summary.

After each entry has been processed in this way, the loop is over, and the method is ended by returning the list of normalized and blended feed entries.

Listing 16-17 finishes off this program with the definition of the `amazon_search()` method.

Listing 16-17: ch16_feed_amazon_ads.py (Part 4 of 4)

```
def amazon_search(self, query):
    """
    Given a query string, perform a Technorati search.
    """
    # Construct an Amazon search URL and fetch it.
    args = {
        'SubscriptionId' : self.AMAZON_KEY,
        'AssociateTag'   : self.ASSOCIATE_TAG,
        'Service'        : 'AWSECommerceService',
        'Operation'      : 'ItemSearch',
        'ResponseGroup'  : 'Medium,ItemAttributes',
        'SearchIndex'    : 'Books',
        'TextStream'     : query
    }
    url   = "http://webservices.amazon.com/onca/xml?%s" % \
        urllib.urlencode(args)

    # Parse and return the results of the search
```

```
        data = HTTPCache(url).content()
        doc  = xmltramp.parse(data)
        return doc

if __name__=='__main__': main()
```

The `amazon_search()` method defined in Listing 16-17 serves to encapsulate the process of building a URL for the `TextStream` query. It uses `urllib2.urlencode()` to properly encode and join the series of query parameters required by the AWS API, including the subscription key, associate tag, and the query text itself, among other things. An HTTP GET is fired off using `HTTPCache`, and the resulting search results in XML are returned after being parsed using `xmltramp`.

Trying Out the Amazon Product Feed Blender

At this point, you should be ready to try out this program. Like the rest in this chapter, you can execute the program on its own to get a normalized Atom feed from the default feed URL, with Amazon items injected into feed entries. Or, you can supply the optional format and feed URL parameters to change this.

Take a look at Figures 16-15 and 16-16 for sample runs, using Atom and RSS feed formats, respectively. And, you can take a look at Figure 16-17 to see how the added Amazon links appear when viewed as a subscription in Mozilla Thunderbird.

FIGURE 16-15: Feed with Amazon items output in Atom format

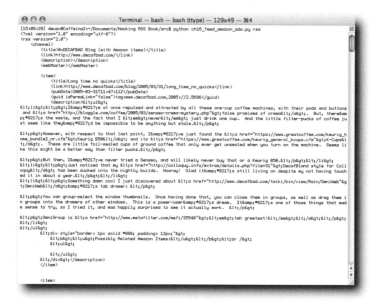

FIGURE 16-16: Feed with Amazon items output in RSS format

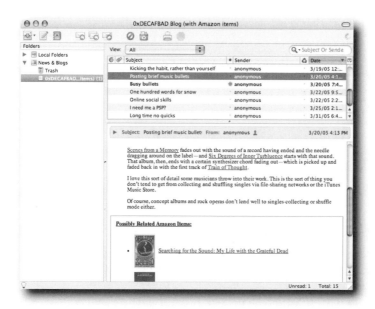

FIGURE 16-17: Feed with Amazon items viewed in Thunderbird

Checking Out Other Options

There's more to blending feeds than this chapter can cover. Here are a few pointers for further exploration.

Looking at FeedBurner

If you'd like to combine the features of most of the programs in this chapter, and then some, take a look at the FeedBurner service at this URL:

```
http://www.feedburner.com
```

You can sign with FeedBurner to set up filters for your syndication feeds, which can inject Amazon product links, add bookmark summaries, and more. The only real downside of this service—and it can be a deal-breaker for some people—is that you need to redirect all of your subscribers to a URL hosted on the FeedBurner servers. The tradeoff is that, in exchange for losing a bit of control over your feed, you won't need to install any software or scripts on your end.

Considering CrispAds

Advertising in syndication feeds has been a bit of a controversial subject, and many people are already looking for ways to block them. Nonetheless, you may be interested in checking out the somewhat unobtrusive text-based ads offered by CrispAds, located here:

```
http://www.crispads.com/
```

One of the downsides of these ads, however, appears to be that they're not contextually related to the surrounding feed content, thus limiting their relevance where they're placed.

Summary

In this chapter, you tinkered with blending feeds together and with other sources of information culled from Web services. This is a relatively fresh application for syndication feeds, so hopefully the programs here can give you a few ideas for further development. A few loose ends are left open in the code provided earlier, however, so you may want to consider the following further directions for tinkering:

- All of the programs in this chapter are very similar. You could rework them a bit to turn them into modules you can pipeline together in the same program, applying all the blending operations.

- If you'd like, this sort of feed pipeline could also be implemented as a CGI program, thus offering a live filter for feeds. Use the URL of a feed as a query parameter to the CGI program, and output the normalized and blended feed.

■ None of these programs cache data fetched from Web services. It might be a good idea to leverage the state database available during feed generation to stash away past query results (such as the daily bookmark postings retrieved from del.icio.us). Although you want to make sure the data stays fresh, this could speed things up and lighten the load on remote Web services. Revisit Chapter 11 and check out how the CVS feed scraper cached `rlog` history queries in `ch11_cvs_history_scraper.py`.

■ You could also possibly use the `LogBufferFeed` class from Chapter 10 to build blended feeds. Track what source feed entries you've seen by ID in the state database, and only add new entries to the feed buffer. This could prevent previously blended entries from changing if search results and data pulled from Web services change.

Next up, in Chapter 17, you play with a few approaches toward republishing feeds. You'll be able to publish a standalone group blog produced from syndication feeds, repost feed entries to an existing Web log, and create JavaScript-based includes that allow you to display headline lists on your own Web sites.

Republishing Feeds

U p to this point in your feed remixing activities, your programs have consumed feeds and produced feeds of one form or another as a result. In this chapter, though, you're going to break out of the bounds of feed formats and work on republishing feeds as HTML on Web pages in the form of group Web logs and sidebar headline lists.

Creating a Group Web Log with the Feed Aggregator

The HTML output from the feed aggregator introduced in Chapter 2 was intended for your own personal consumption—but with a little bit of tweaking, there's no reason it wouldn't make for a decent public feed aggregator. Use it to build a group Web log from your friends' or colleagues' Web logs, or create a topical silo of feeds hand-picked from the blogosphere.

To publish a feed-driven blog page, you need to make things a bit more presentable—maybe improve the template a bit, and include some indication of what feeds drive the page. And, it wouldn't hurt if it took care of itself a bit better—Chapter 2's aggregator just offered HTML files with timestamped filenames that, although marginally fine for your own perusal, don't quite make for a decent public Web site. So, instead, this version will maintain a running history—of, say, around 25 entries—in a single index page.

Getting right down to business, Listing 17-1 gives you the opening of a new program, named ch17_feed_blog.py.

Listing 17-1: ch17_feed_blog.py (Part 1 of 6)

```
#!/usr/bin/env python
"""
ch17_feed_blog.py

Republish feed entries as a static HTML blog.
"""
import sys, os, time, calendar, pickle
from agglib import openDBs, closeDBs
from agglib import getNewFeedEntries, writeAggregatorPage

FEEDS_FN     = "feed_blog_uris.txt"
FEED_DB_FN   = "feed_blog_feeds_db"
ENTRY_DB_FN  = "feed_blog_entry_seen_db"
HISTORY_FN   = "feed_blog_history_db"
BLOG_FN      = "feed_blog.html"
ARCHIVE_FN   = "feed_blog_%Y%m%d_%H%M%S.html"
MAX_ENTRIES  = 25

def main():
    """
    Fire up the feed blog generator, write the static HTML
    to disk.
    """
    # Try to load up entry history, start with an empty list in
    # case of any problems.
    try:    entries = pickle.load(open(HISTORY_FN, 'rb'))
    except: entries = []

    # Open up the databases, load the subscriptions, get
    # new entries.
    feed_db, entry_db = openDBs(FEED_DB_FN, ENTRY_DB_FN)
    feeds   = [ x.strip() for x in open(FEEDS_FN,
                                        "r").readlines() ]
```

So, Listing 17-1 starts off with a few imports from the standard library and from `agglib`, which is followed by a series of configuration constants:

- `FEEDS_FN`—The name of the feed subscriptions file.

- `FEED_DB_FN`—Filename used for the feed database.

- `ENTRY_DB_FN`—Filename used for the seen entries database.

- `HISTORY_FN`—Filename used for a database used to maintain a historical window of entries.

- BLOG_FN—This is the filename where the group aggregator page will be saved.

- ARCHIVE_FN—This is the filename pattern that will be used in saving the current run's aggregator output.

- MAX_ENTRIES—A maximum count of entries to be shown on the group blog page.

After the configuration constants comes the beginning of the definition of the main() function driving the program. Here, the database of feed entries included in the page from the previous program run is opened, with an empty list used by default if there's any problem in reading the file—such as the file not yet existing on the first run of the program. Next, the aggregator databases are opened and the list of feeds is read in.

The next part in Listing 17-2 continues the driver function with the start of feed processing.

Listing 17-2: ch17_feed_blog.py (Part 2 of 6)

```
# Gather new entries from all feeds.
subs_details = []
for feed_uri in feeds:

    # HACK: Grab 'custom' feed record details before
    # agglib update.
    if feed_db.has_key(feed_uri):
        feed_rec   = feed_db[feed_uri]
        feed_link  = feed_rec.get('link',  '#')
        feed_title = feed_rec.get('title', 'untitled')

    # Get new entries, if any.
    new_entries = getNewFeedEntries([feed_uri], feed_db,
                                    entry_db)

    # If there's no record of the feed in the DB, skip it.
    if not feed_db.has_key(feed_uri): continue

    # Update feed record details from fresh feed, if any
    # entries found.
    if len(new_entries) > 0:
        feed       = new_entries[0].data.feed
        feed_link  = feed.get('link',  '#')
        feed_title = feed.get('title', 'untitled')

    # HACK: Update 'custom' feed record details.
    # after agglib update.
    feed_rec = feed_db[feed_uri]
    feed_rec['link']  = feed_link
    feed_rec['title'] = feed_title
    feed_db[feed_uri] = feed_rec
```

Continued

Listing 17-2 *(continued)*

```
# Add details for this feed to the sidebar content.
subs_details.append({
    'feed.link'  :  feed_link,
    'feed.title' :  feed_title,
    'feed.url'   :  feed_uri
})
```

In Listing 17-2, the processing of feeds starts. The main point behind the code here is to gather details in `sub_details` for all of the feeds listed as subscriptions for the group blog, in order to be able to later list them in the page template. The difficulty in doing this is that these feed details aren't always available, because of the way `agglib` is currently built.

When `getNewFeedEntries()` is called, data is returned only when a feed offers new entries. But, when returned, each of the `EntryWrapper` objects carries a reference to the metadata for the feed from which it came. So, from this you can get the title, link, and source URL for the feed just by peeking at the first new entry.

But, in this program, you want to list details for all the feeds making up the group blog, regardless of whether that feed currently offers new entries. So to compensate, you should stash them away in the feed database when these details *are* available. That way, they'll be available the next time through, new entries or no. There's one more problem, though: The current implementation of `getNewFeedEntries()` in `agglib` clobbers any additional fields you add to the record for a feed in the database.

Rather than going back and revisiting `agglib` at this point, however, Listing 17-2 offers a workaround hack. At the start of processing for a feed, the link and title retained for the feed, if any, are fetched from the feed database. Then, `getNewFeedEntries()` is called—and here in the course of its operation, by the way, the retained link and title you just fetched get clobbered. Next, if there are new entries, the first entry is examined for updated feed metadata. After that, the feed details are once more stashed in the feed database, now safe to do because `getNewFeedEntries()` has finished its work with the database for this feed.

And at the end of all of this comes the payoff: The link, title, and URL for the current feed are appended to the `sub_details` list, whether or not new entries were found for the feed.

Of course, one of the main sources for all of these gymnastics can be found in the simplistic one-URI-per-line format of the feed subscriptions file. This wouldn't be an issue if the subscriptions file contained more information for each feed. Alternatively, if `agglib` was smarter about its handling of the feed database—and maybe even maintained a richer cache of these feed metadata fields for itself—a lot of this could be simplified. This is a case of simplicity in one area necessitating complexity in another. You might want to poke around with improving these parts, moving the complexity to where it belongs in the shared code.

Next up in Listing 17-3, the feed processing loop is wrapped up with some last cleanup for new any new entries found.

Listing 17-3: ch17_feed_blog.py (Part 3 of 6)

```
    # Skip ahead if no new entries found.
    if len(new_entries) < 1: continue

    # Make sure entries have a modified date, using now
    # by default.
    for e in new_entries:
        if not e.entry.has_key('modified_parsed'):
            e.entry['modified_parsed'] = time.gmtime()

    # Tack the list of new entries onto the head of
    # the main list.
    entries = new_entries + entries
```

In Listing 17-3, if new entries were found, they're all supplied with the current date if necessary and prepended to the list of entries to be displayed on the output page.

Something to note about this little bit, though, is that the modification date supplied for entries initially missing them will be stored in the HISTORY_FN database. So, this will need to be done only once, and the datestamp assigned for this current program run will be retained for the next program run.

Continue on to Listing 17-4, where the results of the feed processing loop are handled and rendered into HTML.

Listing 17-4: ch17_feed_blog.py (Part 4 of 6)

```
    # Sort the subscription details, build the sidebar content.
    subs_details.sort(lambda a,b: cmp( a['feed.title'],
                                       b['feed.title'] ))
    subs_out = [ SUBSCRIPTION_TMPL % x for x in subs_details ]

    # Sort all the entries, truncate to desired length.
    entries.sort()
    entries = entries[:MAX_ENTRIES]

    # Write out the current run's aggregator report.
    out_fn = time.strftime(ARCHIVE_FN)
    writeAggregatorPage(entries, out_fn, DATE_HDR_TMPL,
        FEED_HDR_TMPL, ENTRY_TMPL, PAGE_TMPL)

    # Build the page template from the template template.
    out = SHELL_TMPL % {
        'subs' : '\n'.join(subs_out),
        'main' : open(out_fn).read()
    }
    open(BLOG_FN, 'w').write(out)
```

Continued

Listing 17-4 *(continued)*

```
# Close the databases and save the entry history back
# out to disk.
closeDBs(feed_db, entry_db)
pickle.dump(entries, open(HISTORY_FN, 'wb'))
```

First in Listing 17-4, the subscription details gathered are sorted by title and rendered into a list of strings using the SUBSCRIPTION_TMPL string template. Then, all the gathered entries are sorted by modification date, after which the list is truncated at the end to fit under the maximum entry count set in MAX_ENTRIES. This truncation ensures that only the newest few entries are used to fill out the blog page, leaving the rest to fall off the end of the list.

Next, the current window of entries is rendered into HTML and written to disk using the writeAggregatorPage() function with string templates to be defined at the end of the program. Note that the filename for the HTML is defined by using the ARCHIVE_FN template filled in with the current date and time. After writing this file, the full current page of entries is produced by reading in the HTML file and using it, along with the list of subscriptions in subs_out, to populate the SHELL_TMPL string template. This content is written out to the filename in BLOG_FN.

And finally, wrapping up the main() function, the aggregator databases are closed and the list of entries displayed in the output is written out to disk using the pickle.dump() function for reference during the next run of the program.

Move on to Listing 17-5 for the first half of the string templates used in this class.

Listing 17-5: ch17_feed_blog.py (Part 5 of 6)

```
# Presentation templates for output follow:

SUBSCRIPTION_TMPL = u"""
    <li>
        [<a href="%(feed.url)s">feed</a>]
        <a href="%(feed.link)s">%(feed.title)s</a>
    </li>
"""


PAGE_TMPL = "%s"

DATE_HDR_TMPL = """
    <h1 class="dateheader">%s</h1>
"""

FEED_HDR_TMPL = """
    <h2 class="feedheader"><a href="%(feed.link)s">%(feed.title)s</a></h2>
"""
```

```
ENTRY_TMPL = u"""
    <div class="feedentry">
        <div class="entryheader">
            <span class="entrytime">%(time)s</span>:
            <a class="entrylink" href="%(entry.link)s">%(entry.title)s</a>
        </div>
        <div class="entrysummary">
            %(entry.summary)s
        </div>
    </div>
"""
```

In Listing 17-5, five string templates are defined:

- SUBSCRIPTION_TMPL—Provides a bit of HTML in which to present subscriptions as site and feed links.

- PAGE_TMPL—This template strips the original aggregator page shell down to a bare slot for inclusion in a bigger shell.

- DATE_HDR_TMPL—Standard aggregator template used to render date separator headers.

- FEED_HDR_TMPL—The usual aggregator template used to render feed headers.

- ENTRY_TMPL—Offers HTML formatting for each displayed entry, much like the original FeedAggregator version.

And, at last, this program is wrapped up with the definition of one more string template in Listing 17-6.

Listing 17-6: ch17_feed_blog.py (Part 6 of 6)

```
SHELL_TMPL = u"""
<html>
    <head>
        <style>
            body {
                font-family: sans-serif;
                font-size: 12px;
            }
            .subscriptions {
                float: right;
                clear: right;
                width: 220px;
                padding: 10px;
                border: 1px solid #444;
```

Continued

Listing 17-6 *(continued)*

```
        }
        .main {
            margin-right: 240px;
        }
        .pageheader {
            font-size: 2em;
            font-weight: bold;
            border-bottom: 3px solid #000;
            padding: 5px;
        }
        .dateheader   {
             margin: 20px 10px 10px 10px;
             border-top: 2px solid #000;
             border-bottom: 2px solid #000;
        }
        .feedheader   {
             margin: 20px;
             border-bottom: 1px dashed #aaa;
        }
        .feedentry    {
            margin: 10px 30px 10px 30px;
            padding: 10px;
            border: 1px solid #ddd;
        }
        .entryheader {
            border-bottom: 1px solid #ddd;
            padding: 5px;
        }
        .entrytime {
            font-weight: bold;
        }
        .entrysummary {
            margin: 10px;
            padding: 5px;
        }
    </style>
</head>
<body>
    <h1 class="pageheader">Feed blog central</h1>
    <div class="subscriptions">
        <b>Subscriptions:</b>
        <ul>
            %(subs)s
        </ul>
    </div>
    <div class="main">
        %(main)s
    </div>
```

```
    </body>
</html>
"""


if __name__=="__main__": main()
```

Listing 17-6 defines the SHELL_TMPL string template, which replaces the old PAGE_TMPL—
now with slots to be filled with the list of subscriptions, as well as the feed entries filtered for display. Be sure to tailor this to fit your site design, adding whatever masthead and header elements
you want.

Trying Out the Group Web Log Builder

This thing should be ready to start building your public feed aggregator page. You'll probably
want to set this to run on a regular schedule, maybe hourly, to keep the page updated with fresh
content. Take a look at Figure 17-1 for what a sample run should look like with console logging
turned on.

And, Figure 17-2 shows you what sort of page this program should generate—not much different
than the plain vanilla aggregator page template from Chapter 2, just with a list of subscriptions
added. The other important difference not noticeable here, though, is that the filename and URL
remain constant as feed entries appear at the top and drop off the end of the page over time.

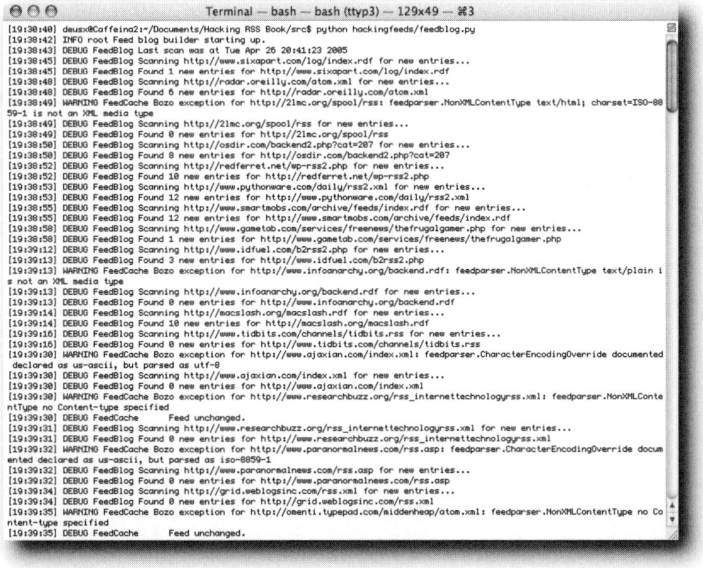

FIGURE 17-1: Sample feed blog program run

FIGURE 17-2: View of the program's HTML output in Firefox

Reposting Feed Entries via the MetaWeblog API

The program you just finished can be used to maintain a single-page blog summarizing the latest and greatest from a list of feeds. But, what if you already have a blog and the software to maintain it—such as an installation of Movable Type (`http://www.movabletype.com`) or WordPress (`http://www.wordpress.org`)? These software packages offer a great deal more flexibility than the single page generated by this chapter's first program (such as better content management, category support, and template management).

Well, something supported by both Movable Type and WordPress (as well as with many other blogging packages) is the MetaWeblog API. This is an XML-RPC-based interface used by many desktop Web log management applications, allowing a developer to programmatically perform such tasks as posting new content, editing existing posts, and even managing the blog templates.

You can find the original description of the MetaWeblog API, as well as pointers to XML-RPC itself, at the following URL:

```
http://www.xmlrpc.com/metaWeblogApi
```

So, instead of building a blog page, you can build a bridge between a feed aggregator and the MetaWeblog API of your favorite blogging software. This next program scans for new entries in a list of subscriptions, reformats, and reposts them to your blog of choice.

Take a look at Listing 17-7 for the start of ch17_feed_reposter.py.

Listing 17-7: ch17_feed_reposter.py (Part 1 of 3)

```python
#!/usr/bin/env python
"""
ch17_feed_reposter.py

Republish feed entries to a metaWeblogAPI server.
"""
import sys, time, xmlrpclib
from agglib import openDBs, closeDBs, getNewFeedEntries

FEEDS_FN    = "reposter_uris.txt"
FEED_DB_FN  = "reposter_feeds_db"
ENTRY_DB_FN = "reposter_entry_seen_db"

API_URI     = "http://www.example.com/mt/mt-xmlrpc.cgi"
API_USER    = "your_username_here"
API_PASSWD  = "your_passwd_here"
API_BLOGID  = 1
```

In Listing 17-7, the program initially defines a handful of configuration constants:

- FEEDS_FN—Name of the file containing feed URIs for reposting.

- FEED_DB_FN—Aggregator feed database filename.

- ENTRY_DB_FN—Aggregator entry database filename.

- API_URL—Change this to point to the URL where your Web log software's MetaWeblog API resides. Movable Type usually offers a CGI named mt-xmlrpc.cgi, whereas WordPress offers a PHP app named xmlrpc.php. Consult your software's documentation for more information.

- API_USER—This is the username used to authenticate for usage of the MetaWeblog API. You should be able to manage this in your Web log's configuration file or control panel pages.

- API_PASSWD—Along with the username, the API requires a password for authentication, and here's where you should put it.

- API_BLOGID—Some blog software, like Movable Type, requires this to identify the particular blog instance to be manipulated with the API—you should be able to work out what a particular blog's ID is from how it's identified in the management screens. On the other hand, because it only manages a single blog per installation, WordPress ignores this value.

If you use some desktop application to manage your blog, such as ecto (`http://ecto.kung-foo.tv/`), it's likely that you already have the API details needed by the preceding configuration constants. Take a look in your preferences and see what you can find.

Next up, the definition of `main()` begins in Listing 17-8 with the start of feed processing.

Listing 17-8: ch17_feed_reposter.py (Part 2 of 3)

```python
def main():
    """
    Process new feed entries and repost to the blog API.
    """
    # Get a handle on the blog API server
    srv = xmlrpclib.ServerProxy(API_URI)

    # Open up the databases, load the subscriptions, get new entries.
    feed_db, entry_db = openDBs(FEED_DB_FN, ENTRY_DB_FN)
    feeds   = [ x.strip() for x in open(FEEDS_FN, "r").readlines() ]
    for e in getNewFeedEntries(feeds, feed_db, entry_db):

        # Get the entry and feed metadata.
        feed, entry = e.data.feed, e.entry


        # Build a blog post title using feed and entry titles.
        title = u'%s &#8212; %s' % ( feed.get('title', u'untitled'),
                                     entry.get('title', u'untitled') )

        # Generate an ISO8601 date using the feed entry modification,
        # with current date/time as default.
        date = time.strftime('%Y-%m-%dT%H:%M:%SZ',
                          entry.get('modified_parsed',
                                    time.gmtime()))

        # Build blog post body content from what's available in the
        # feed entry.
        content_out = []
        if entry.has_key('summary'):
            content_out.append(entry.summary)
        content_out.extend([ c.value for c in entry.get('content', [])
                          if 'html' in c.type ])
        content = '<br />\n'.join(content_out)
```

First up in Listing 17-8's definition of `main()`, an instance of `ServerProxy` from the `xmlrpclib` module is created using the `API_URI` value established in the beginning of the program. This object provides a simple, easy-to-use gateway onto the MetaWeblog API—you'll see it in use in the next listing.

xmlrpclib is a module from Python's standard library that allows you to easily access XML-RPC APIs on the Web. You can find documentation for it here:

> `http://docs.python.org/lib/module-xmlrpclib.html`

After creating the `ServerProxy` object, an instance of `FeedAggregator` is created and then used to fetch new entries from all the subscribed feeds. These are then each processed in a loop.

A title for the blog posting is created by joining the feed title together with the entry title, separated by the HTML entity for an em dash. Next, a date is worked out for the post, using either the entry's supplied modification date or the present time if no date is found in the entry. Then, summary and any content found in the entry are joined together, with HTML line breaks, into one big string.

Continuing on, the program is finished up in Listing 17-9, where the posting is built and sent off to the API.

Listing 17-9: ch17_feed_reposter.py (Part 3 of 3)

```
        # Build the blog post content from feed and entry.
        desc = u"""
            %(content)s
            <br />
            [ <a href="%(entry.link)s">Originally</a> posted
              at <a href="%(feed.link)s">%(feed.title)s</a> ]
        """ % {
            'content'      : content,
            'entry.link'   : entry.get('link', u''),
            'feed.title'   : feed.get('title', u''),
            'feed.link'    : feed.get('link', u''),
        }

        # Build post item data, call blog API via XML-RPC
        post  = {
            'title'             : title,
            'dateCreated'       : date,
            'description'       : desc,
            'category'          : entry.get('category', u''),
            'mt_convert_breaks' : False
        }
        try:
            srv.metaWeblog.newPost(API_BLOGID, API_USER,
                                   API_PASSWD, post, True)
            print "Posted %s" % title
        except KeyboardInterrupt:
            raise
        except:
            print "Problem posting %s" % title

if __name__=='__main__': main()
```

At the top of Listing 17-9, the body of the new Web log post is built, using the entry content harvested in the previous entry, as well as the entry link, feed link, and feed title. Then, a dictionary of MetaWeblog API posting parameters is built. This includes the new post's title, publication date, content, a category, and a little something for Movable Type to disable automatic formatting (because things are already in HTML format).

The keys used in this dictionary are pretty similar to what's used in RSS, as specified in the MetaWeblog API description, though there are a few differences. You'll want to read up on whatever your particular blogging package supports for the MetaWeblog API—for example, the `mt_convert_breaks` key is specific to Movable Type, although WordPress actually honors it as well.

Following the creation of this data structure is the call to the MetaWeblog API itself. The `ServerProxy` object created earlier in the program can be used like a standard Python object—a call to `srv.metaWeblog.newPost()` is proxied into an XML-RPC call to the remote API. This method call is given the blog ID and API authentication details, along with the posting data structure—all of which `xmlrpclib` happily marshalls into XML-RPC data and sends it on its way. This program doesn't care about the return value, so that's ignored.

And with that, this program is complete.

Trying Out the MetaWeblog API Feed Reposter

Now, all you need to put this program to use is a list of feeds and a blog with an available MetaWeblog API implementation. Take a look at Figure 17-3 to see what this program should look like in action.

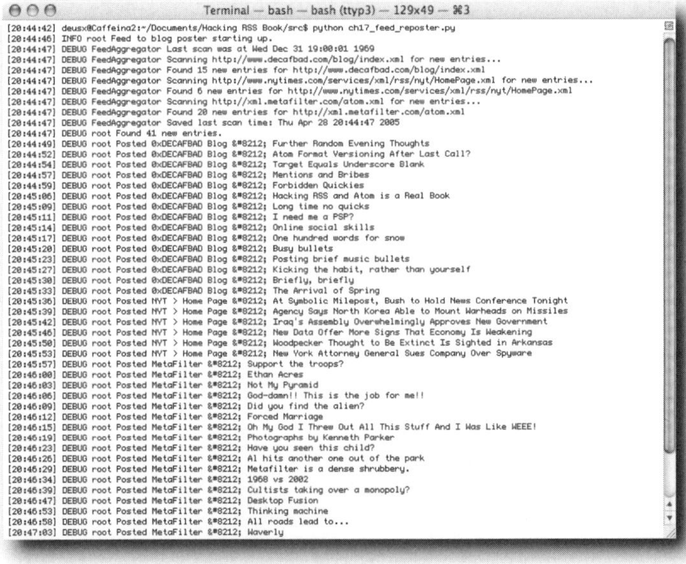

FIGURE 17-3: Feed to Web log API posting program run

My site currently runs on Movable Type, so I set up a new blog instance to receive entries from my feeds. Check out Figure 17-4 to see what these look like when these entries get published on my new blog.

FIGURE 17-4: Reposted feed entries shown in Firefox

This program should help you build a side blog of topics interesting to you and your readers— or you could use it to build a more fully featured group Web log than the first program in this chapter, pulling in the feeds of your group members' blogs and enabling comments and other things offered by a more fully featured Web log engine.

Building JavaScript Includes from Feeds

By this point, you've seen how to build a new single page blog from many feeds, as well as integrating feeds into an existing blog via the MetaWeblog API. But what if you don't really want feeds to entirely take over your site? Maybe you just want a list of headlines in a box somewhere in your site sidebar like you've seen on other sites such as Slashdot (http://www.slashdot.org).

Well, one way to do this is to use server-side includes or some other form of dynamic pages. However, this can be inconvenient on a Web log or site produced as static HTML pages by something like Movable Type. Although many blogging packages (including Movable Type) offer plug-ins that can render and inject feed content into page templates, this isn't always the easiest approach. Quite often, it can result in stale content unless you schedule regular rebuilds of otherwise static pages.

Another solution is to use JavaScript-based client-side includes. Now, this technique is definitely a hack. There's no such thing as client-side includes, really—at least not in any form supported by most browsers. But, what *is* supported by most browsers is a JavaScript tag of the following form:

```
<script src="http://www.example.com/foo.js"></script>
```

What this tag does is cause the browser to load up and interpret the contents of the URL in the src attribute as JavaScript, as if it were included inline in the page like any other script. To make the leap from this feature of JavaScript to a client-side include hack, recall that JavaScript can do the following:

```
document.writeln("Hello world!");
```

This little snippet of JavaScript, when run, injects the phrase "Hello world!" into an HTML page at the location where the code appears in the file.

So, now, put the pieces together. You can build a file full of JavaScript document.writeln() calls with a regularly scheduled program, then you can pull this file into an HTML page using a <script/> tag—thus inventing client-side includes. The trick is just being careful and making sure whatever raw HTML content you want to insert into a page gets safely processed into valid JavaScript source code—which mostly consists of escaping quotes and any other troublesome special characters.

So, this chapter's final program shows you how to render feed entries into a form suitable to use by this client-side include hack. Take a look at Listing 17-10 for the start of ch17_feed_to_javascript.py.

Listing 17-10: ch17_feed_to_javascript.py (Part 1 of 4)

```python
#!/usr/bin/env python
"""
ch17_feed_to_javascript.py

Fetch and parse a feed, render it as JavaScript code suitable
for page include.
"""
import sys, feedparser
from httpcache import HTTPCache
from ch14_feed_normalizer import normalize_entries

FEED_URL = "http://www.decafbad.com/blog/index.xml"
JS_FN    = "feed-include.js"

def main():
    """
    Accepts optional arguments including feed url and
    JavaScript code filename.
    """
    # Produce the JavaScript feed include
```

```
feed_url = (len(sys.argv) > 1) and sys.argv[1] or FEED_URL
js_fn    = (len(sys.argv) > 2) and sys.argv[2] or JS_FN
js_feed  = JavaScriptFeed(feed_url)
out      = js_feed.build()
open(js_fn, "w").write(out)
```

This program starts off with a description and a few imports, then the following two configuration constants:

- FEED_URL—Default URL to a feed for formatting into a JavaScript include.

- JS_FN—Default filename to which the JavaScript include will be written.

These constants are then used in the definition of the main() function, which accepts optional command-line arguments for the feed URL and JavaScript filename. An instance of the JavaScriptFeed class is created, with the feed URL. The build() method of this instance is then called to produce the JavaScript include content, which is saved out to the appropriate file.

Now, Listing 17-11 offers the start of the JavaScriptFeed class definition.

Listing 17-11: ch17_feed_to_javascript.py (Part 2 of 4)

```
class JavaScriptFeed:
    """
    Class which facilitates the formatting of a feed as a
    JavaScript page include.
    """
    UNICODE_ENC = 'UTF-8'

    INCLUDE_TMPL = """
        <b>%(feed.title)s included via JavaScript:</b>
        <ul>
            %(feed.entries)s
        </ul>
    """

    ENTRY_TMPL = """
        <li>
            <b><a href="%(link)s">%(title)s</a></b>:
            <blockquote>
                %(summary)s
            </blockquote>
        </li>
    """

    def __init__(self, feed_url):
        self.feed_url = feed_url
```

The `JavaScriptFeed` class begins with a few configuration constants:

- `UNICODE_ENC`—Establishes the unicode encoding to be used in formatting the content.

- `INCLUDE_TMPL`—Gives an overall HTML shell template with which to format the entries.

- `ENTRY_TMPL`—Provides an HTML template to be populated with the data from each entry parsed from the feed.

And finally, Listing 17-11 ends with the definition of the __init__() method, which stashes away a logging object and the given URL to the feed to be processed. Next, Listing 17-12 contains the definition of the `build()` method.

Listing 17-12: ch17_feed_to_javascript.py (Part 3 of 4)

```python
def build(self):
    """
    Fetch feed data and return JavaScript code usable as an
    include to format the feed as HTML.
    """
    # Fetch and parse the feed
    cache     = HTTPCache(self.feed_url)
    feed_data = feedparser.parse(cache.content())

    # Build a list of content strings by populating
    # entry template
    entries_out = [ self.ENTRY_TMPL % {
        'link'    : entry.get('link',  ''),
        'title'   : entry.get('title', ''),
        'summary' : entry.get('summary', ''),
    } for entry in feed_data.entries ]

    # Build final content by populating the overall
    # shell template
    out = self.INCLUDE_TMPL % {
        'feed.title'   : feed_data.feed.title,
        'feed.entries' : "\n".join(entries_out)
    }

    # Encode the content using the object unicode encoding
    out = out.encode(self.UNICODE_ENC)

    # Return the content wrapped in JavaScript code
    return self.js_format(out)
```

In Listing 17-12, the build() method first caches and parses the feed content. Next, the set of entries found in the feed are filtered through the ENTRY_TMPL string template to render each entry link, title, and summary as HTML. Then, this list of content is used, along with the feed title, to produce one final block of HTML content, by way of the INCLUDE_TMPL string template.

This HTML content is encoded with the appropriate Unicode encoding. Then it's wrapped with JavaScript code for inclusion in a Web page and this final result is returned.

Listing 17-13 completes this class, and the program, with the definition of the js_format() method.

Listing 17-13: ch14_feed_to_javascript.py (Part 4 of 4)

```python
def js_format(self, out):
    """Wrap a string of content in JavaScript code
       for include"""
    lines_out = []
    for line in out.splitlines():
        line = line.replace('\\', '\\\\')
        line = line.replace('"', '\\"')
        line = 'document.writeln("%s");' % line
        lines_out.append(line)

    return "\n".join(lines_out)

if __name__ == "__main__": main()
```

Turning HTML content in to JavaScript code is pretty simple, as implemented in the definition of the js_format() method in Listing 17-13. Basically, the input content is split into lines, and each line is searched for backslashes and quotes. Each of these are escaped with a backslash—so, a \ becomes \\ and a " becomes \". This, then, makes it safe to wrap each line with a JavaScript document.writeln(), which will inject the HTML content into a Web page, including the code.

Trying Out the JavaScript Feed Include Generator

At this point, the program is ready to use. Check out Figure 17-5 for a sample program run—the program accepts the URL to a feed for rendering, followed by a filename where the resulting JavaScript code should be saved. Or, you can just allow the default values to be used.

Now that you have some JavaScript, you need an HTML page in which to include it. Check out Listing 17-14 for a bit of sample HTML that accomplishes this.

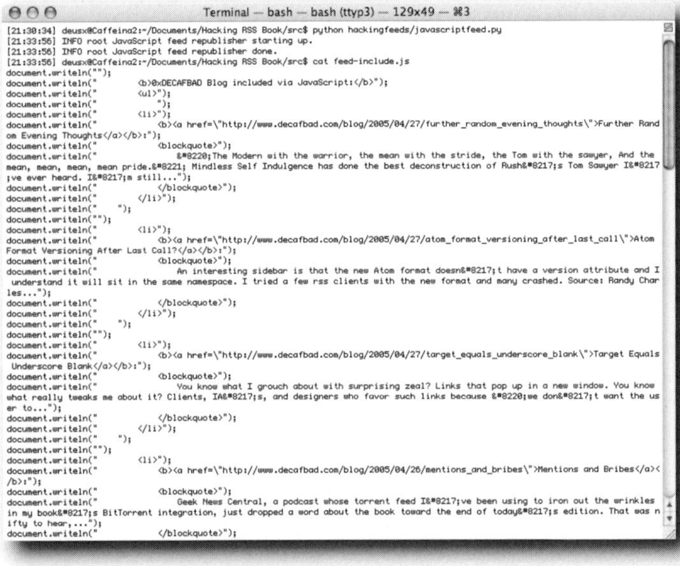

FIGURE 17-5: Sample program run and resulting JavaScript-wrapped HTML

Listing 17-14: feed-include.html

```html
<html>
    <head>
        <meta http-equiv="Content-Type"
            content="text/html; charset=UTF-8" />
    </head>
    <body>
        <h1>Feed include test:</h1>
        <script src="feed-include.js" language="JavaScript"></script>
    </body>
</html>
```

Finally, Figure 17-6 depicts what the HTML in Listing 17-14 looks like in a Web browser. Remember that the bulk of this content has been injected on-the-fly by the JavaScript code and isn't present in the HTML page itself. As you can see, each feed entry is formatted as an item in an unordered list with the title of an entry as a hyperlink, along with the entry summary in a blockquote.

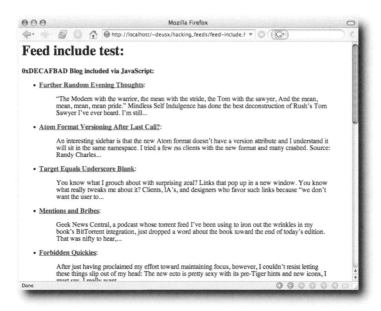

FIGURE 17-6: Feed JavaScript include in a page shown in Firefox

You can use this program to turn just about any feed into a JavaScript include for your own Web pages. If you run it on a schedule, you can keep your site supplied with regularly updated content from other sites without much dynamic code running on the page itself to accommodate the feeds. Just tweak the string templates provided in the `JavaScriptFeed` class in a subclass or instance to make the client-side includes match your site's look and feel.

Checking Out Other Options

Many other projects and services are available that served as inspiration and also as alternatives to the programs presented in this chapter. This section takes a look at a few of them.

Joining the Planet

Planet is a feed aggregator and republisher used by projects such as GNOME (`http://planet.gnome.org/`), Debian (`http://planet.debian.net/`), and Apache (`http://www.planetapache.org/`). You can find the project home page here:

`http://www.planetplanet.org/`

This program uses the Universal Feed Parser like most of the programs in this book, and serves to produce simple group Web logs by contributing members of many Open Source projects.

Running a reBlog

The reBlog package, produced by the Eyebeam group, is a modified personal feed aggregator that allows you to filter and choose feed entries for republication in a blog. Check it out here:

```
http://www.reblog.org/
```

This program links up with a Web log installation by way of plug-ins and API calls to republish chosen feed entries as new blog posts, allowing you to be the curator of your own topical news site and feed.

Using RSS Digest

RSS Digest is a free service that allows you to supply the URL of an RSS feed to produce JavaScript, PHP, or IFrame-style includes for your site. Take a look at this URL:

```
http://www.bigbold.com/rssdigest/
```

Unlike the program in this chapter, this isn't a program whose execution you need to schedule—simply include the URL they supply in your page, and content updates occur automatically. One downside to this service, however, is that it does not support Atom feeds as of this writing.

Summary

This chapter showed you another way to remix feeds through republishing. You saw how to generate a group blog from scratch, how to integrate with an existing Web log package via the use of a Web service API, and finally how to easily include content using a client-side include hack. Hopefully, these tools will come in handy when you have a need to help pull a community's conversations together or to enrich your own site with relevant news sources.

Next up, in the book's concluding chapter, you broaden your feed horizons by extending the formats themselves with new kinds of information.

Extending Feeds

This is the final chapter of the book, so it's as good a place as any to take a look into what might be the future of syndication feeds.

With the notable exception of the podcast tuner in Chapter 6, pretty much every hack in this book assumed that the point of a syndication feed was to deliver little capsules of content formatted as text or HTML. Blog entries, news stories, and log file summaries are all blobs of text and formatting mostly meant for human consumption.

And, at first, this was enough of an advance to make syndication feeds one of the best things to hit the Web since HTML. But what about taking things further, carrying richer data, using more machine intelligence and automation? Those bits of content, though readable by humans, are pretty opaque with respect to programs you might write.

Sure, in Chapter 15, you saw how Bayesian statistics can be used to build a trainable filter to help find items of interest. But however astute it may (or may not) have seemed at making suggestions, that filter was really just fumbling in the dark. Machine smarts are really pretty dumb, so in order to really get something useful, you need to provide some more predigested hints as metadata—and it wouldn't hurt if you gave those blobs of content inside entries a bit more structure, as well. This chapter takes a look at a few approaches to this issue.

Extending Feeds and Enriching Feed Content

Say that you want to write about an upcoming concert in your blog. Your feed will likely contain only the title and date, along with the text of the post itself. Your subscribers might understand the concert announcement, but wouldn't it be nice if maybe their calendaring apps and PDAs understood it, too? Toward that end, you need to add a few more elements to your feed—such as where the concert might be and when doors open (a date and time quite distinct from the blog entry's publication date)—and all of this in a form more suitable for reading by a simple-minded calendaring app.

Adding Metadata to Feed Entries

You should already be familiar with some of the standard bits of metadata that come "out of the box" with feed formats—things like titles, publication dates, and categories. These may or may not be contained in the main content of a feed entry, but are separated out into their own elements so as to be easily identified and extracted by parsers and aggregators.

One place where you can improve the situation for machines trying to understand feed content is by including more metadata. For example, if you publish a concert announcement, you could add a new element in your feed entry (that is, `<startdate />`) that specifies the date and time when doors open. And, it might also be handy to throw in an element describing where the concert's at (that is, `<location />`).

Well, there just happens to be such an extension to the RSS 1.0 feed format, named mod_event. You can check out its specification here:

`http://web.resource.org/rss/1.0/modules/event/`

In short, this RSS 1.0 module adds the following elements to feed entries, under the ev namespace (`http://purl.org/rss/1.0/modules/event/`):

- `ev:startdate`—A W3CDTF date/time specifying the start of an event.

- `ev:enddate`—A W3CDTF date/time specifying when an event is expected to end.

- `ev:location`—A description of the event's location (possibly a URL).

- `ev:organizer`—The name of the organization or person responsible for the event (possibly a URL or a phone number).

- `ev:type`—An indication of the type of event (such as meeting, deadline, or conference).

Take a peek at Listing 18-1 to see what a concert announcement might look like, using these extension elements.

Listing 18-1: Example Feed Entry Using mod_event Elements

```
<item rdf:about="http://example.com/xyzzy/shows/2005/#mi">
    <title>The Flying Xyzzy</title>
    <link>http://example.com/xyzzy/shows/2005/#mi</link>
    <ev:type>concert</ev:type>
    <ev:organizer>Foobar Entertainment</ev:organizer>
    <ev:location>Wankel Rotary Ampitheater, Anytown, MI</ev:location>
    <ev:startdate>2005-05-18T20:00:00-05:00</ev:startdate>
    <ev:enddate>2005-05-18T23:30:00-05:00</ev:enddate>
    <description>
        Come see The Flying Xyzzy at the Wankel Rotary Ampitheater!
        Doors open at 8:00PM on Thursday, May 5!
        Brought to you by Foobar Entertainment!
    </description>
</item>
```

As you can see in Listing 18-1, the mod_event extension adds a few pieces of extra metadata that would allow an aggregator that understood scheduling to do something a bit more intelligent with this entry. Instead of trying to divine what the entry's textual content is saying about the concert, it can just process the cleanly delimited pieces of metadata for what it needs. Once it has this information, an aggregator could communicate with your scheduling application or PDA to place this event on your calendar.

Structuring Feed Entry Content with Microformats

Now, you've just seen an example of how additional metadata can be used to offer more machine-legible parts in your feeds. But, you could consider that this information is not just data describing an entry. In fact, in some sense, this stuff is a part of the entry content itself. So, copying these facts and figures out of the entry's source material (a blog post or Web page, for example) could be seen as a bit redundant.

And worse, if some parts are provided as structured data in a feed and nowhere else (such as the time when the event ends in the previous example) machines will lose the ability to access this information as soon as the entry falls off the end of the feed. Keep in mind that many feed publishers include only the newest 10 to 15 entries, something that is actually a requirement in some versions of RSS. So, when these metadata-rich entries go away, you're possibly left back where you started: with content that's informative to people yet opaque to machines.

Another way to pack more machine-friendly information into feeds is to impose some structure on the actual content carried by the entries. One approach to this doesn't actually have anything to do with feeds specifically, but that's actually a plus.

Microformats are a relatively new way of doing things, centered essentially around specially structured XHTML content. They not only fit nicely into a feed, but also work in a standalone resource like a Web page, thus solving the issue of disappearing data when the feed has long forgotten about this particular document.

Oh, and there's one more potential issue solved through the use of microformat content in feeds: The mod_event extension is designed specifically for the RSS 1.0 feed format. Although this doesn't mean that it can't be adapted for use in Atom 0.3 or RSS 2.0 feeds, it's not explicitly meant for either of those. Using a microformat to construct content in feed entries sidesteps the issue of feed format altogether, because most feed formats support the inclusion of XHTML content without much fuss.

Continuing the theme of calendar events, take a look at the hCalendar microformat specification, under development here:

http://developers.technorati.com/wiki/hCalendar

As this page explains, the hCalendar microformat is based on the iCalendar standard (http://www.ietf.org/rfc/rfc2445.txt). Take a look at Listing 18-2 for a sample Atom feed entry containing the same information as Listing 18-1.

Listing 18-2: Sample Atom Feed Entry with a Concert Announcement

```
<entry>
  <title>The Flying Xyzzy</title>
  <link rel="alternate" type="text/html"
        href="http://example.com/xyzzy/shows/2005/#mi" />
  <issued>2005-04-29T09:39:21Z</issued>
  <modified>2005-04-29T09:39:21Z</modified>
  <id>tag:example.com,2005-01-01:xyzzy.2005</id>

  <content type="application/xhtml+xml" mode="xml">
      <div xmlns="http://www.w3.org/1999/xhtml">
          <span class="vcalendar"><span class="vevent">
              <a class="url" href="http://example.com/xyzzy/shows/2005/#mi">
                  Come see
                  <span class="summary">The Flying Xyzzy</span>
                  at the
                  <span class="location">Wankel Rotary Ampitheater</span>!
                  Doors open at
                  <abbr class="dtstart" title="2005-05-18T20:00:00-05:00">
                      8:00PM on Thursday, May 5
                  </abbr>!
                  <abbr class="dtend" title="2005-05-18T23:30:00-05:00"
                      style="display:none">
                      Over at 11:30PM.
                  </abbr>
                  Brought to you by
                  <span class="organizer">Foobar Entertainment</span>!
              </a>
          </span></span>
      </div>
  </content>

</entry>
```

A reading of the hCalendar spec, as well as RFC 2445, might give you a more complete picture of what's going on here in Listing 18-2. But, notice that the entry metadata consists only of the basic elements supplied by the Atom feed format—all the exciting parts show up within the entry content itself.

This hCalendar microformat provides a scheme by which to turn iCalendar property names into CSS classes and semantic XHTML tags that can be used for both human-readable presentation as well as parseable markup. The content starts off with an XHTML <span/> tag with a CSS class of "vcalendar", containing a child <span/> tag with a CSS class of "vevent". These class attributes can both be used to visually style this content, as well as serving as hints to a parser that this is a block of hCalendar content, and this is the first event.

The rest of the XHTML content inside these tags follows much of the same pattern. The event is described in plain language, but the parts with significance to a parser are marked up with XHTML tags and those tags are given CSS classes mapped to iCalendar properties. For example, when the location of the concert appears (that is, "Wankel Rotary Ampitheater"), it's wrapped in `<span />` tags with a CSS class of `"location"`. Now, keep in mind, though, that you're not limited to `<span/>` tags—you can use just about any HTML tag, because the CSS classes carry the main semantic hints here.

One important departure from this occurs when the event start and end times appear. Here, an XHTML abbreviation tag is used to mark up the human-readable dates, and ISO8601 dates are used for the abbreviation titles. The reasoning given in discussion of the hCalendar specification is that, in some sense, the plain language expression of the date and time are an abbreviation of the fully detailed ISO8601 timestamp—and thus, this could be considered a "semantically appropriate" use of the `<abbr />` tag.

Using Both Metadata and Microformats

So, you've just seen two options for publishing more capsules of content in your syndication feeds: feed entry metadata and feed content microformats. Metadata has the advantage of being cleaner to parse and having fairly clear semantics, whereas microformats offer a few more hoops through which to jump in parsing and interpretation. On the other hand, microformats have a life outside of feeds and so can offer a bit more permanence, and the fact that they're just conventions established for carefully constructed XHTML means that any feed that supports XHTML can carry them.

The thing is, though, there's nothing that says you need to pick one or the other: Both mod_ event and hCalendar have a large amount of overlap, but they live in separate parts of a feed. In fact, you could (and do, in this chapter) construct a feed filter that enhances entry metadata from any microformat data parseable from the entry's own content. A feed containing hCalendar content could be enriched with mod_event metadata to offer the best of both worlds.

Finding and Processing Calendar Event Data

To get started playing with calendar events, you're going to need two things: a source of calendar events and a way to represent and manipulate them in Python.

One common format for calendar event data is described by the iCalendar specification (`http://www.ietf.org/rfc/rfc2445.txt`), on which the hCalendar microformat is based. Many calendar and scheduling applications (including Apple's iCal for Mac OS X and the Mozilla Sunbird project) support data import and export using the iCalendar standard.

One additional piece of calendaring software you may want to check out is PHP iCalendar, available on SourceForge at this URL:

`http://sourceforge.net/projects/phpicalendar/`

You'll need a Web server with PHP installed to use it, but it can come in handy for viewing iCalendar data if you don't happen to have another calendaring application available—or if you don't feel like cluttering up your *real* calendar with bogus events while you play with things in this chapter. Installing this is optional, but you'll see a few examples in this chapter using it to display calendar events.

Next, it'd be a good idea to start looking for sources of calendar events. Export data from your own personal schedule, or take advantage one of the following sites offering calendars for download:

- `http://www.apple.com/macosx/features/ical/library/`
- `http://www.icalshare.com/`
- `http://www.icalx.com/`

The examples in this chapter use the following iCalendar file containing various U.S. holidays:

`http://icalx.com/public/peterpqa/US-Practical.ics`

Download a calendar data file, or export one of your own from your favorite calendaring app. If you have installed PHP iCalendar, you can upload this example data into the calendar, to see something like what's shown in Figure 18-1 for the month view, and Figure 18-2 for what a single event looks like when clicked.

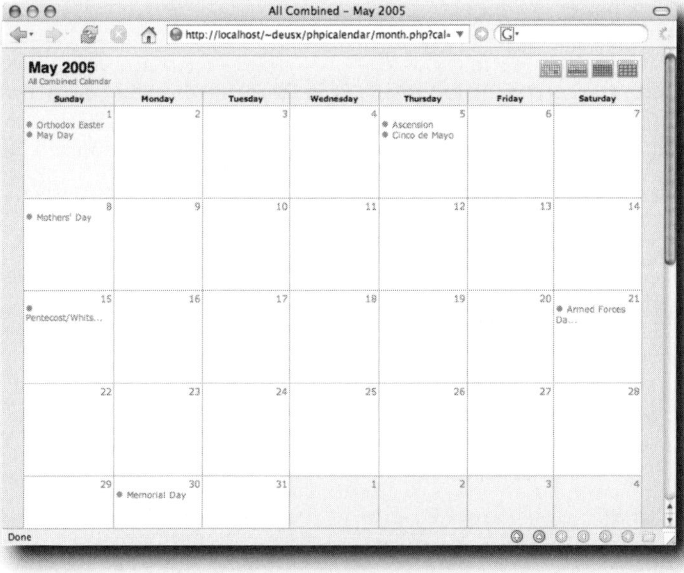

FIGURE 18-1: U.S. holidays for May 2005 shown via PHP iCalendar

FIGURE 18-2: Details shown for Memorial Day in PHP iCalendar

Once you have an iCalendar file with which to tinker, the next thing you need is some support in Python for the actual tinkering. For this, you can employ an Open Source module named, oddly enough, iCalendar. You can find this module's home page here:

`http://codespeak.net/icalendar/`

As of this writing, the following is a direct download link for the package:

`http://codespeak.net/icalendar/iCalendar-0.10.tgz`

Grab yourself a copy of the iCalendar package and install it using the usual `setup.py` script included in the tarball.

Building Microformat Content from Calendar Events

With some calendar data and the code to process it at your disposal, it's time to play. The first task here is to render the iCalendar data as hCalendar-formatted HTML pages. This serves two purposes. First, it can allow you to easily publish your own schedules managed within an iCalendar-compliant calendar app. And, second, you'll see how these calendar events are formatted with the hCalendar format, in case you'd like to build them by hand or with another tool (such as a Web log editor).

Listing 18-3 presents the start of this first new program, named `ch18_ical_to_hcal.py`.

Listing 18-3: ch18_ical_to_hcal.py (Part 1 of 4)

```
#!/usr/bin/env python
"""
ch18_ical_to_hcal.py

Render iCalendar as hCalendar-formatted HTML.
```

Continued

Listing 18-3 *(continued)*

```
"""
import os, sys
from md5 import md5
from httpcache import HTTPCache
from icalendar import Calendar, Event

HTML_DIR = "hcal"
ICS_URL  = "http://icalx.com/public/peterpqa/US-Practical.ics"
```

This program starts off with a few module imports and defines two configuration constants:

- HTML_DIR—The name of a directory where the generated HTML pages will be written.
- ICAL_URL—The URL of an iCalendar data file, which points to the file of U.S. holidays.

Continue on to Listing 18-4 for one more configuration constant.

Listing 18-4: ch18_ical_to_hcal.py (Part 2 of 4)

```
HEVENT_TMPL = u"""
    <html>
        <head>
            <title>%(dtstart:date:%A, %B %d, %Y)s: %(summary)s</title>
            <meta name="description" content="%(description)s" />
        </head>
        <body>
            <div class="vcalendar">
                <div class="vevent" id="%(uid)s">
                    <abbr class="dtstart" title="%(dtstart:encoded)s">
                        %(dtstart:date:%A, %B %d, %Y)s
                    </abbr>:
                    <b class="summary">%(summary)s</b>
                    <blockquote class="description">
                        %(description)s
                    </blockquote>
                    <abbr class="dtend" title="%(dtend:encoded)s"
                        style="display:none" />
                </div>
            </div>
        </body>
    </html>
"""
```

Defined in Listing 18-4 is a string template named HEVENT_TMPL. This is what will be used to build an HTML page for each calendar event found in the data located at ICAL_URL. The

HTML source is constructed to follow the hCalendar microformat, and the format of the template slots will be explained in the definition of a template wrapper class shortly.

Next up, in Listing 18-5, is the definition of the program's main driver.

Listing 18-5: ch18_ical_to_hcal.py (Part 3 of 4)

```python
def main():
    """
    Perform iCalendar to hCalendar rendering.
    """
    # Establish the calendar URL and output file.
    ics_url  = len(sys.argv) > 1 and sys.argv[0] or ICS_URL
    html_dir = len(sys.argv) > 2 and sys.argv[1] or HTML_DIR

    # Get the calendar via URL and parse the data
    cal = Calendar.from_string(HTTPCache(ics_url).content())

    # Create html_dir if it doesn't already exist
    if not os.path.exists(html_dir): os.makedirs(html_dir)

    # Process calendar components.
    for event in cal.walk():

        # Skip this calendar component if it's not an event.
        if not type(event) is Event: continue

        # Summarize the event data, make a hash, build a filename.
        hash_src = ','.join(['%s=%s' % x for x in event.items()])
        hash     = md5(hash_src).hexdigest()
        hcal_fn  = os.path.join(html_dir, '%s.html' % hash)

        # Build the hCalendar content and write out to file.
        hcal_out = HEVENT_TMPL % ICalTmplWrapper(event)
        open(hcal_fn, 'w').write(hcal_out)
```

The definition of main() in Listing 18-5 is where the main action happens. Here, the URL for the iCalendar data is grabbed from an optional command-line argument, or ICS_URL is used as a default. Likewise, the directory where HTML will be stored is taken as an argument, or HTML_DIR is used as a default.

Next, the calendar data is fetched and used to create an instance of the Calendar class imported from the iCalendar package you installed earlier. This class has a walk() method, which is used to visit each of this calendar's Event components.

For each Event component in the Calendar, an MD5 hash is created from a summary of all its properties. This hash is, in turn, used to create a filename where the HTML content will be written. And, finally, the event is wrapped in an instance of ICalTmplWrapper and used to populate the HEVENT_TMPL, the results of which will be written out to disk using the generated filename.

Move on to Listing 18-6, which provides the definition of the `ICalTmplWrapper` class.

> **Listing 18-6:** ch18_ical_to_hcal.py (Part 4 of 4)

```
class ICalTmplWrapper:
    """
    Formatting helper class for iCalendar objects.
    """

    def __init__(self, obj):
        """Initialize wrapper with an iCal obj instance."""
        self.obj = obj

    def __getitem__(self, key):
        """Provides simple formatting options for dates
           and encoding."""
        # Get the name and optional formatting type from format key
        name, fmt = (':' in key) and key.split(':', 1) or (key, None)

        # If no such key in obj, return blank.
        if not self.obj.has_key(name): return ''

        # No special formatting, return decoded value.
        if fmt is None: return self.obj.decoded(name)

        # 'encoded' formatting, return the encoded value.
        elif fmt == 'encoded': return self.obj[name]

        # 'date' formatting, so assume this value is a datetime
        # and return formatted according to supplied option.
        elif fmt.startswith('date:'):
            fmt, date_fmt = fmt.encode().split(":",1)
            data = self.obj.decoded(name)
            return data.strftime(date_fmt)

if __name__=='__main__': main()
```

The `ICalTmplWrapper` provides some basic formatting support for the `HEVENT_TMPL` string template. Here are some examples taken from the template:

- `%(summary)s`—This gets filled with string data decoded from the iCalender format.
- `%(dtstart:encoded)s`—This gets replaced by the original encoded data from the iCalendar data. In particular, this example results in the ISO8601 date string, rather than the parsed date/time.

- %(dtstart:date:%A, %B %d, %Y)s—This slot offers some date formatting based on the parsed version of the date/time from the calendar. This example produces content formatted something like this: "Sunday, May 8, 2005".

Trying Out the iCalendar to hCalendar Program

Now you're ready to use this program to build a set of hCalendar HTML files for use in the rest of this chapter. This thing doesn't really produce much in the way of interesting output on the console, but you can see an example program run in Figure 18-3.

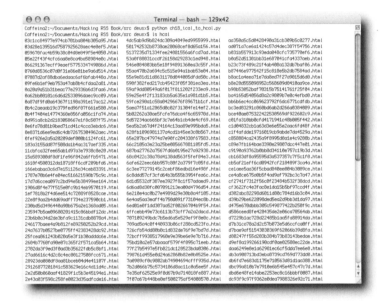

FIGURE 18-3: Sample program run for the hCalendar content builder

And, if you want to see what these files look like once they've been generated, take a look at Figure 18-4 for an example.

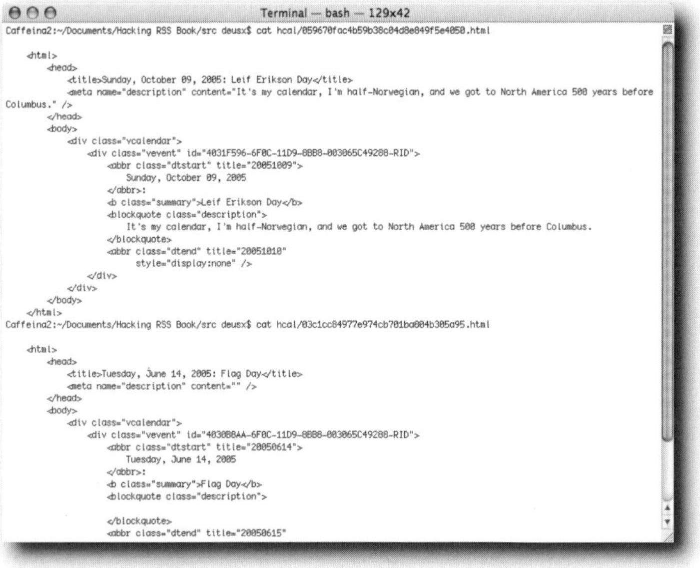

FIGURE 18-4: Example hCalendar content

Building a Simple hCalendar Parser

At this point, you should have a set of HTML documents formatted using the hCalendar microformat. You can use the previous program or build them by hand, but either way you're now going to need a way to interpret these documents. So, the next step is to build a parser module. This will use the same `HTMLParser` class as you saw in scrapers built back in Chapter 9.

Take a look at Listing 18-7 for the start of this new reusable module, named `hcalendar.py`.

> **Listing 18-7:** hcalendar.py (Part 1 of 7)

```python
#!/usr/bin/env python
"""

hcalendar.py

Parse hCalendar-formatted HTML to harvest iCalendar data.
"""
import sys, time, os, os.path
from datetime import datetime
from httpcache import HTTPCache
from HTMLParser import HTMLParser, HTMLParseError
from icalendar import Calendar, Event, TypesFactory

def main():
    """
    Perform iCalendar to hCalendar rendering.
```

```
    """
    html_dir = len(sys.argv) > 1 and sys.argv[1] or 'hcal'
    ics_fout = len(sys.argv) > 2 and open(sys.argv[2], 'w') \
               or sys.stdout

    # Parse a directory of HTML files for hCalendar events.
    hp = HCalendarParser()
    events = []
    for dirpath, dirnames, filenames in os.walk(html_dir):
        for fn in filenames:
            if fn.endswith(".html") or fn.endswith(".htm"):
                fp   = os.path.join(dirpath, fn)
                data = open(fp, 'r').read()
                events.extend(hp.parse(data))

    # Build a calendar from the parsed events and print
    # the data
    cal = Calendar()
    for e in events:
        cal.add_component(e)
    ics_fout.write(cal.as_string())
```

In Listing 18-7, this new module starts off with a few imports, followed by a main() function that will serve to demonstrate the rest of the module. The first thing it does is grab the name of a directory where it should find HTML for processing—with a default of 'hcal', matching up with the previous program—along with an optional filename where it will write iCalendar data harvested from the hCalendar-formatted HTML files.

Next, it creates an instance of the HCalenderParser class, to be defined shortly. The given directory is searched for HTML files, each of which is read in and supplied to the HCalenderParser instance's parse() method. This method returns a list of iCalendar Event instances, one for each event found in hCalendar format in the HTML file. These are gathered into one big list, which is then used to build a Calendar object. This Calendar object is then output as a string to the appropriate output file.

Now, keep going on to Listing 18-8, which offers the start of the HCalenderParser class.

Listing 18-8: hcalendar.py (Part 2 of 7)

```
class HCalendarParser(HTMLParser):
    """
    hCalendar parser, produces iCalendar Event objects.
    """
    CHUNKSIZE       = 1024
    ITEM_CLASS      = "vevent"
    PROPERTY_CLASSES = []

    def __init__(self):
        """Initialize the parser, using iCalendar
```

Continued

Listing 18-8 *(continued)*

```
            properties."""
        self._types = TypesFactory()
        self.PROPERTY_CLASSES = \
            [x.lower() for x in TypesFactory.types_map.keys()]

    def parse(self, data):
        """Parse a string of HTML data, return items."""
        self.reset()
        try:
            self.feed(data)
        except HTMLParseError:
            pass
        self.finish()
        return self.items()

    def parse_uri(self, uri):
        """Parse HTML content at a URI, return items."""
        return self.parse(HTTPCache(uri).content())
```

Listing 18-8 offers the start of the HCalendarParser class and the definition of three methods: __init__(), parse(), and parse_uri().

The __init__() method performs a bit of initialization for HCalendarParser, first creating an instance of the TypesFactory class from the iCalendar package. This instance serves as a utility for handling data types defined in the iCalendar specification, which will come in handy in a little bit.

The next part, though only one line, might need a little explanation. The TypesFactory class contains a mapping of all the property names in the iCalendar format to their respective data types. The specification of the hCalendar microformat declares that all of the CSS class names to be used in the format are lowercase versions of the names of properties in iCalender data. So, __init__() cheats a little to get a list of all the CSS class names by borrowing a lowercase list of properties from the TypesFactory class's property map keys.

Following __init__() is the definition of parse(), which accepts a string of HTML data, resets the instance, and feeds the data through the parser via the feed() method. After all the data is parsed, the finish() method is called, and the final list of parsed Event instances is returned by using the items() method.

Then, parse_uri() offers a convenience method that fetches the content at a given URI using an HTTPCache instance, before returning the results of feeding that data to the parser with the parse() method.

Follow along to Listing 18-9, which gives a definition for the items() method.

Listing 18-9: hcalendar.py (Part 3 of 7)

```
def items(self):
    """Build and return iCalendar Events for hCalendar items
    harvested from HTML content."""

    events_out = []
    for item in self._items:

        # Build a new blank entry to receive the hCalendar data.
        event_out = Event()

        for name, val in item:
            try:
                val = self._types.from_ical(name, val.strip())
                if val: event_out.add(name, val)
            except:
                pass

        # Add the finished entry to the list to be returned.
        events_out.append(event_out)

    return events_out
```

You haven't reached the parsing yet, but this definition of items() shows you how the class comes up with Event instances. In a nutshell, items() processes all the raw data obtained via parsing and converts it all into iCalendar Event instances.

The parsing process generates an internal list of event property sets, which are each in turn lists of name/value tuple pairs. So, this method iterates through the list of event property sets. And, for each of these, an instance of the iCalendar Event class is created.

Each of the properties for the current parsed event are visited. The from_ical() method of the TypesFactory utility is used to convert from the string data obtained during parsing to a proper iCalendar data type. Because the TypesFactory instance has a map of iCalendar property names and respective data types, HCalendarParser doesn't need to know anything about the conversion in particular.

Then, the add() method on the current Event instance is then used to stow this property away in the object. After all the parsed properties have been handled, the finished Event instance is added to the list, which will be returned at the end of the method. Note that, if any problems are encountered while trying to add a property to the event, that property is just skipped.

Following this is Listing 18-10, where you get to see the start of parsing.

Listing 18-10: hcalendar.py (Part 4 of 7)

```python
def reset(self):
    """Initialize the parser state."""
    HTMLParser.reset(self)
    self._parse_stack   = [ [ {}, [], '' ] ]
    self._item_stack    = []
    self._items         = []

def finish(self):
    """After parsing has finished, make sure last items
       get captured."""
    while len(self._item_stack):
        item = self._item_stack.pop()
        if len(item): self._items.append(item)

def handle_starttag(self, tag, attrs_tup):
    """Handle start tags, maintaining tag content stacks
       and items."""
    # Initialize this level of the parsing stack.
    attrs   = dict(attrs_tup)
    classes = attrs.get('class', '').lower().split()
    self._parse_stack.append( [ attrs, classes, '' ] )

    # If this tag is the start of an item, initialize
    # a new one.
    if self.ITEM_CLASS in classes:
        self._item_stack.append([])
```

Now, in Listing 18-10, you're given definitions for the following methods: reset(), finish(), and handle_starttag().

The reset() method simply serves to clear out any previous parser state, including stacks of parsed data, in-progress event items, and the final list of extracted property lists. The initialization of _parse_stack might look a little weird, but it'll be explained in a minute.

The finish() method is called at the end of parsing and works to ensure that any straggling event items left on the stack make their way into the final list of items.

And then there's the handle_starttag() method, which acts as the event handler when the parser encounters opening HTML tags. Here, the list of attributes set on the tag is converted into a straight dictionary map, and the space-delimited CSS classes on this tag are split out into a list.

Then, a list containing the current tag attributes, the CSS classes, and an initially empty string meant for collecting the tag's character data contents is pushed onto the _parse_stack property of the parser. This stack is used to handle the potentially nested tags encountered in the HTML document throughout parsing. You'll see more of its use in the next list.

Finishing off this method and the listing is the following. If the current list of classes contains the value of ITEM_CLASS (that is, 'vevent'), this is taken as a signal that everything inside this current starting tag represents a new calendar event item—so a new, empty property set is pushed onto the _item_stack to accumulate the properties anticipated for this new item.

Next up in Listing 18-11 comes the start of handle_endtag(), where the meat of parsing happens.

Listing 18-11: hcalendar.py (Part 5 of 7)

```
def handle_endtag(self, tag):
    """Handle closing tags, capturing item properties
        as necessary."""
    # Pop the current tag's attributes and classes.
    attr, classes, value = self._parse_stack.pop()

    # Pop the current accumulation of character data from
    # the stack but append it onto the parent's data
    value = self.decode_entities(value)
    self.handle_data(value)

    # Not currently tracking an item?  Skip
    # processing, then.
    if not len(self._item_stack): return
```

Use of the _parse_stack began in handle_starttag(), and here in handle_endtag() is where the information on the stack is actually used. You'll see the handlers that actually do this toward the end of the class, but throughout the processing of the innards of a tag, character data is accumulated. So, by the time the end tag is encountered, the top of the _parse_stack offers the attributes, classes, and complete character data contents for the current tag.

Because this is the end of that tag, the set of parsed information is popped off the top of the stack. In addition, because the character data is also a part of the parent tag, this is passed along for accumulation in the parent tag's entry on the stack. Next, a quick check is made to ensure parsing is currently taking place inside an hCalendar event tag—if not, there's no sense in looking for tags marked up as event properties, so the method returns in this case.

Keep going on to Listing 18-12 to see what's done with tags inside an hCalendar event.

Listing 18-12: hcalendar.py (Part 6 of 7)

```
        # Get the current working item
        curr_item = self._item_stack[-1]

        # If this type supports a uid, look for an id attribute
        if 'id' in attr and 'uid' in self.PROPERTY_CLASSES:
```

Continued

Listing 18-12 *(continued)*

```
            curr_item.append( ('uid', attr['id']) )

    # Is this the end of an item?  If so, pop and add to
    # the list.
    if self.ITEM_CLASS in classes:
        item = self._item_stack.pop()
        if len(item): self._items.append(item)
        return

    # Work through current tag's potential classes.
    for prop_class in classes:
        if prop_class in self.PROPERTY_CLASSES:

            if prop_class=='url' and 'href' in attr:
                prop_val = attr['href']
            elif 'longdesc' in attr:
                prop_val = attr['longdesc']
            elif 'alt' in attr:
                prop_val = attr['alt']
            elif 'title' in attr:
                prop_val = attr['title']
            else:
                prop_val = value

            # Add the property name and value to the item.
            curr_item.append( (prop_class,
                                prop_val.strip()) )
```

First off in Listing 18-12, the event item currently under construction is fetched from the top of the _item_stack. Immediately after, a check is made to see if the current tag has an id attribute value—this can be used for the event's uid property, so it gets appended to the current item's list of properties if it's present.

Then, the current tag's list of CSS classes is searched for the value of ITEM_CLASS (that is, 'vevent'). If present, this is the end of the current event item, so it gets popped from the stack and, if it's not empty, it gets appended to the list of extracted items. Then, because there's no sense in looking for any more properties in this tag, the handler returns.

Finally, if parsing is taking place inside an hCalendar event, and it's not ended yet, it's time to look for potential property values in this current tag.

As established in the __init__() method, the parser's PROPERTY_CLASSES attribute contains a list of CSS classes associated with iCalendar event properties. So, each of the CSS classes found on the current tag are matched up against the list in PROPERTY_CLASSES. It's important to note here that the name of the tag itself doesn't really matter yet—just the CSS classes are significant. (That is, a `<div class="location">...</div>` and `<b class="location">...</b>` tag are both candidates for containing the value for an event's location property.)

Whenever a match is found, it's time to try to harvest content from the HTML for the appropriate calendar event property. Here's where a little bit of heuristics comes into play, in order to accommodate some of the compromises microformats make between making the HTML both presentable and parseable:

- If the current property is named `'url'`, and the current tag has an `'href'` attribute, the `'href'` attribute is used for the property value. This allows the use of a hyperlink like the following to define the URL of an event:

```
<a href="http://www.example.com" class="url">
    <span class="location">Example Dot Com</span>
</a>
```

- Otherwise, if the current tag has a `'longdesc'` attribute, use it for the property value. Rarely used, this can allow you to attach a URL to an image, like so:

```
<img src="http://example.com/foo.gif" class="url"
    longdesc="http://www.example.com" />
```

- Otherwise, if the current tag has an `'alt'` attribute, use it. This option can allow you to use an image in your HTML, yet still supply a title string for a property:

```
<img src="http://example.com/title_bar.gif" class="summary"
    alt="Example Event Title" />
```

- Otherwise, if the current tag has a `'title'` attribute, use it. This is mostly used in conjunction with the `<abbr />` tag when supplying dates in both machine- and human-readable forms—the idea being that the human-target contents of the tag is conceptually an abbreviation of the tag's title:

```
<abbr title="2005-05-07T10:00:00Z">
    Saturday, May 7, 2005 at 10:00 AM
</abbr>
```

- Finally, if none of the above, use the tag's character data as the property value. This covers just about every other common case of property value in markup:

```
<b class="summary">Leif Erikson Day</b>
<blockquote class="description">
    It's my calendar, I'm half-Norwegian, and we got to
    North America 500 years before Columbus.
</blockquote>
<span class="organizer">Foobar Entertainment</span>
```

As you can see, there are a few twists to this notion of making HTML both human- and machine-readable, but it's still a workable proposition. Now, you can find the conclusion of this module in Listing 18-13.

Listing 18-13: hcalendar.py (Part 7 of 7)

```
# Basic character data accumulation handlers.
def handle_data(self, data):
    self._parse_stack[-1][2] += data
def handle_entityref(self, data):
    self._parse_stack[-1][2] += '&' + data + ';'
handle_charref = handle_entityref

# Utility function to resolve a limited set of
# HTML entities.
ENTITIES = [ ('&lt;', '<'), ('&gt;', '>'), ('&quot;', '"'),
             ('&apos;', "'"), ('&amp;', '&') ]
def decode_entities(self, data):
    for f, t in self.ENTITIES: data = data.replace(f, t)
    return data

if __name__ == "__main__": main()
```

As mentioned earlier, the character data found within tags is accumulated as it's found by the parser. Well, these are the event handlers that accomplish this task. They should look familiar, because they're not much different than what was used back in Chapter 9—the biggest difference is that these methods help maintain the _parse_stack information as they go. And, with that, this module is wrapped up.

Trying Out the hCalendar Parser

Now you're all set to try out this module. At this point, you've come full circle. The first program of this chapter converts from iCalendar data to hCalendar HTML documents, whereas this second program goes from hCalendar HTML back to iCalendar data. Check out Figure 18-5 for an example program run.

The important thing to notice here, though, is that the original iCalendar data looks a bit different from the iCalendar data output here. There is a bit of signal loss along the way from iCalendar to hCalendar and back to iCalendar again. However, that's not really the fault of the hCalendar microformat itself. It's just that the code in this chapter doesn't work to exhaustively cover every aspect of both iCalendar and hCalendar. Because that's a little bit beyond the scope of this book, I'll leave those improvements up to you, once you've had some time to play with things.

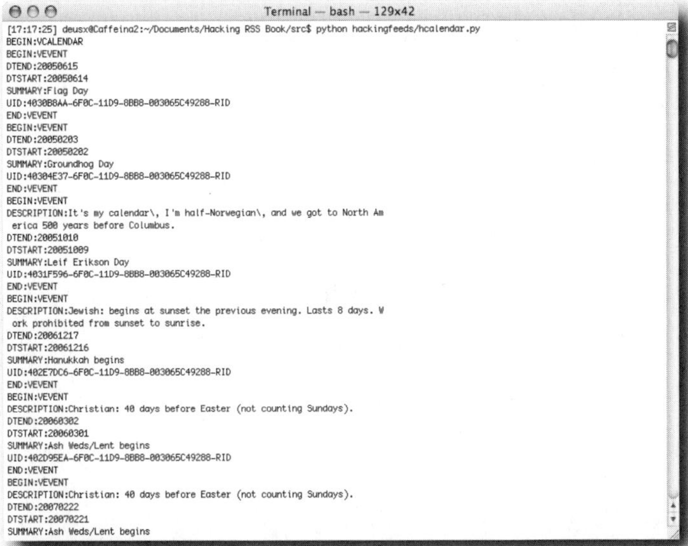

FIGURE **18-5**: Sample program run for the hCalendar content parser

Adding Feed Metadata Based on Feed Content

Well, now that you have a round-trip conversion established between iCalendar and hCalendar, it's time to widen the loop a bit. For this next part, you'll want to dig up the feed maker script from back in Chapter 7.

If you haven't played with this aspect already, you'll want to tweak the feed templates in ch07_ feedmaker.py to include full HTML body content, rather than just the summary description. This entails using %(entry.content)s instead of %(entry.summary)s in the Atom and RSS entry templates. For example, this is how your Atom entry template from Listing 7-10 should look:

```
ATOM_ENTRY_TMPL = """
    <entry>
        <title>%(entry.title)s</title>
        <link rel="alternate" type="text/html"
            href="%(entry.link)s" />
        <issued>%(entry.modified)s</issued>
        <modified>%(entry.modified)s</modified>
        <id>%(entry.id)s</id>
        <summary type="text/html" mode="escaped">
            %(entry.content)s
        </summary>
    </entry>
"""
```

And, your RSS entry template from Listing 7-16 should be changed like so:

```
RSS_ENTRY_TMPL = """
        <item>
            <title>%(entry.title)s</title>
            <link>%(entry.link)s</link>
            <pubDate>%(entry.modified)s</pubDate>
            <guid isPermaLink="false">%(entry.id)s</guid>
            <description>%(entry.content)s</description>
        </item>
"""
```

With these changes made to `ch07_feedmaker.py`, you can run it on a collection of hCalendar-formatted HTML documents. If you use the collection generated by `ch18_ical_to_hcal.py`, this should produce a feed something like what's shown in Figure 18-6. You will end up with feed entries containing hCalendar microformat content. You should store this feed in a file—I used the filenames `hcal.atom` and `hcal.rss`.

FIGURE 18-6: Sample program run of the feed maker on hCalendar documents

Up to this point, this chapter has been covering hCalendar. But, the other half of feed extension described at the beginning was adding metadata to feeds outside entry content itself. So, now that you have a feed whose entries contain hCalendar content, you can build a feed filter that can enhance the feed with new metadata elements based on parsing that content. After running a feed through this filter, you'll be able to have the best of both worlds: calendar event information in feed entry metadata, as well as hCalendar content inside the entries.

This filter program, named ch18_mod_event_feed_filter.py, starts in Listing 18-14.

Listing 18-14: ch18_mod_event_feed_filter.py (Part 1 of 4)

```python
#!/usr/bin/env python
"""
ch18_mod_event_feed_filter.py

Enhance a feed with metadata harvested from entry content
"""
import sys, feedparser
from scraperlib import FeedEntryDict, Scraper
from ch14_feed_normalizer import normalize_feed_meta,
normalize_entries
from hcalendar import HCalendarParser

FEED_IN_URL = "file://./hcal.atom"
FEED_OUT_FN = "www/www.decafbad.com/docs/private-feeds/mod-
event.%s"

def main():
    """
    Run a feed through the filter and produce the mod_event
    enhanced version.
    """
    # Grab the incoming feed URL
    feed_url = ( len(sys.argv) > 1 ) and sys.argv[1] or \
            FEED_IN_URL

    f = ModEventFeed(feed_url)
    f.STATE_FN = 'mod_event_feed_filter'

    # Output the current feed entries as both RSS and Atom
    open(FEED_OUT_FN % 'rss', 'w').write(f.scrape_rss())
    open(FEED_OUT_FN % 'atom', 'w').write(f.scrape_atom())
```

After a few familiar imports from other feed filters, as well as a couple of new ones, Listing 18-14 presents a pair of configuration constants:

- FEED_IN_URL—Default URL pointing to the input feed.

- FEED_OUT_FN—Filename string template where the RSS and Atom output feeds will be written.

You'll want to tweak these constants to point to more appropriate things on your own personal machine or server. After these comes the definition of the main() function, which initializes the logger, gets the URL for the input feed, then drives the feed filter to generate the output feeds.

Getting down to the real business, Listing 18-15 gives you the start of the ModEventFeed class.

Listing 18-15: ch18_mod_event_feed_filter.py (Part 2 of 4)

```
class ModEventFeed(Scraper):
    """
    Enhance feed metadata by parsing content.
    """
    ATOM_FEED_TMPL = """<?xml version="1.0" encoding="utf-8"?>
<feed version="0.3" xmlns="http://purl.org/atom/ns#"
        xmlns:ev="http://purl.org/rss/1.0/modules/event/">
        <title>%(feed.title)s</title>
        <link rel="alternate" type="text/html"
                href="%(feed.link)s" />
        <tagline>%(feed.tagline)s</tagline>
        <modified>%(feed.modified)s</modified>
        <author>
            <name>%(feed.author.name)s</name>
            <email>%(feed.author.email)s</email>
            <url>%(feed.author.url)s</url>
        </author>
        %(feed.entries)s
    </feed>
    """

    ATOM_ENTRY_TMPL = """
        <entry>
            <title>%(entry.title)s</title>
            <link rel="alternate" type="text/html"
                href="%(entry.link)s" />
            <issued>%(entry.issued)s</issued>
            <modified>%(entry.modified)s</modified>
            <id>%(entry.id)s</id>
            <ev:startdate>%(entry.ev_startdate)s</ev:startdate>
            <ev:enddate>%(entry.ev_enddate)s</ev:enddate>
            <summary type="text/html"
                    mode="escaped">%(entry.summary)s</summary>
        </entry>
    """
```

In Listing 18-15, the definition of ModEventFeed begins as a subclass of Scraper, like the other feed filters in this part of the book. And first up in the class definition is a pair of string templates, ATOM_FEED_TMPL and ATOM_ENTRY_TMPL. These override the superclass's versions with new ones—the feed-level template adds the mod_event namespace (http://purl.org/rss/1.0/modules/event/) to the <feed/> tag, and the entry-level template adds the mod_event elements <ev:startdate/> and <ev:enddate/>.

It's important to note that only two of the elements offered by mod_event are added here. This is because, given the other programs in this chapter, the calendar events used as source material in this chapter don't necessarily provide more than a title, a summary, and start and end dates. The list of U.S. holidays won't contain things like a location or an organizer. However, it shouldn't be too hard for you to add more mod_event metadata as the information becomes available in your own feeds, once you have this filter up and running.

Listing 18-16 gives you the RSS equivalents of the previous two templates.

Listing 18-16: ch18_mod_event_feed_filter.py (Part 3 of 4)

```
RSS_FEED_TMPL = """<?xml version="1.0" encoding="utf-8"?>
<rss version="2.0"
     xmlns:ev="http://purl.org/rss/1.0/modules/event/">
    <channel>
        <title>%(feed.title)s</title>
        <link>%(feed.link)s</link>
        <description>%(feed.tagline)s</description>
        <webMaster>%(feed.author.email)s</webMaster>
        %(feed.entries)s
    </channel>
</rss>
"""

RSS_ENTRY_TMPL = """
    <item>
        <title>%(entry.title)s</title>
        <link>%(entry.link)s</link>
        <pubDate>%(entry.modified)s</pubDate>
        <guid isPermaLink="false">%(entry.id)s</guid>
        <ev:startdate>%(entry.ev_startdate)s</ev:startdate>
        <ev:enddate>%(entry.ev_enddate)s</ev:enddate>
        <description>%(entry.summary)s</description>
    </item>
"""
```

As in Listing 18-15, two string templates are given in Listing 18-16: RSS_FEED_TMPL and RSS_ENTRY_TMPL. These are, respectively, used to override the superclass's templates for generating RSS feed metadata and all the entries contained in the feed.

Another thing to note is that these templates define Atom 0.3 and RSS 2.0 feeds—which might seem a little odd, because the mod_event extension is actually for the RSS 1.0 feed format. Well, because this book has really just focused on Atom 0.3 and RSS 2.0, and because those respective feed formats don't outlaw this sort of extension to feed entries, this sort of adaptation of the mod_event specification should work out just fine.

Now, you can finish up this program with Listing 18-17.

```
def __init__(self, main_feed):
    """Initialize with the feed URI for parsing."""
    self.main_feed = main_feed

def produce_entries(self):
    """
    Get a feed, attempt to parse out hCalendar content
    and add mod_event metadata based on it.
    """
    # Grab and parse the feed
    feed = feedparser.parse(self.main_feed)

    # Normalize feed meta data
    self.FEED_META = normalize_feed_meta(feed,
        self.date_fmt)

    # Run through all the normalized entries...
    hp = HCalendarParser()
    entries = normalize_entries(feed.entries)
    for entry in entries:
        events = hp.parse(entry.data.get('summary', ''))
        if events:
            event = events[0]

            if 'dtstart' in event:
                dtstart = event.decoded('dtstart')
                entry.data['ev_startdate'] = \
                    dtstart.strftime('%Y-%m-%dT%H:%M:%SZ')

            if 'dtend' in event:
                dtend = event.decoded('dtend')
                entry.data['ev_enddate'] = \
                    dtend.strftime('%Y-%m-%dT%H:%M:%SZ')

    return entries

if __name__=='__main__': main()
```

Things are pretty simple in Listing 18-17. The __init__() method accepts the URL to the feed for filtering and stows it away in the new instance.

Then, the produce_entries() method does the work of filtering through the source feed. The first thing done is to use the feedparser module to fetch the original feed. Next, normalize_feed_meta() is used to normalize and pass through the original feed metadata to the new feed.

After taking care of the feed metadata, next an `HCalendarParser` instance is created, the entries from the source feed are normalized, and each of them are processed. For each entry, an attempt is made to grab its summary content, which is then run through the `HCalendarParser`. If any events are returned from the parser, only the first one is paid any attention.

The start (`'dtstart'`) and end (`'dtend'`) dates are grabbed from the iCalendar `Event` instance dug up by the parser, both of which are used to set the `mod_event` start and end dates in the normalized entry. These are then used in the templates defined at the start of this class to fill in the appropriate `mod_event` element slots, `<ev:startdate/>` and `<ev:enddate/>`.

This all serves to extract the hCalendar content data out into `mod_event` feed entry metadata. After all the processing, the list of normalized entries gets returned, and the program is finished.

Trying Out the mod_event Feed Filter

Finally, it's time to put this thing to work. If you've been following along so far, you should have produced a feed containing hCalendar content earlier, having built it from HTML files produced via the other programs in this chapter. So, take a look at Figure 18-7 for a sample run and output generated by the `mod_event` feed filter.

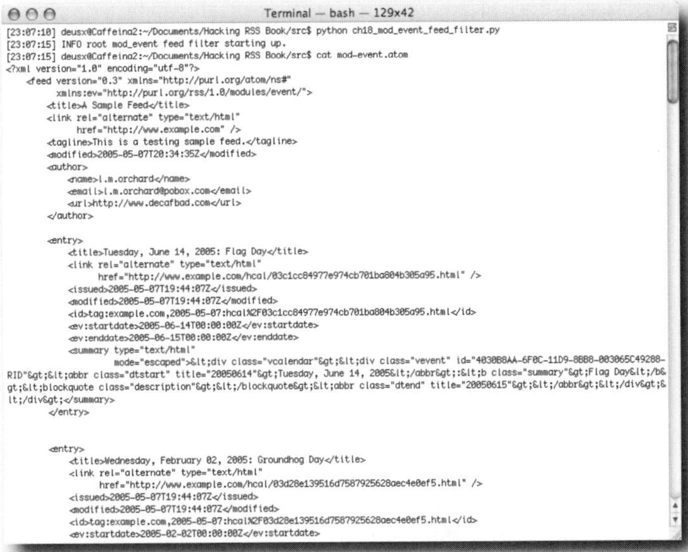

FIGURE 18-7: Sample program run of the mod_event feed filter

As you can see, the feed output isn't much changed, except for the two new `mod_event` elements added to each feed entry. Now, the thing to remember about this filter is that you don't *have* to use it with the other programs in this chapter—you just need a feed with hCalendar-formatted content, which could come from blog entries published in your own pre-existing feed. And, getting hCalendar content into your blog is as simple as using the right CSS classes in the right spots. Just follow the example of the HTML content generated by the programs earlier on, and you should be set.

Harvesting Calendar Events from Feed Metadata and Content

Building up to this point in the chapter, the programs supplied so far have allowed you to progress from iCalendar data to HTML files with hCalendar-formatted content, and from hCalendar content to mod_event-enhanced feeds. Now, in this chapter's final program, you go full circle by converting these enhanced feeds back to iCalendar data using both the mod_event metadata and hCalendar content in entries.

You can see the start of the last program, ch18_feed_to_ical.py, in Listing 18-18.

Listing 18-18: ch18_feed_to_ical.py (Part 1 of 4)

```
#!/usr/bin/env python
"""
ch18_feed_to_ical.py

Produce iCalendar data from a syndication feed.
"""
import os, sys, feedparser
from hcalendar import HCalendarParser
from icalendar import Calendar, Event, TypesFactory

FEED_URL = "http://localhost/~deusx/hackingfeeds/src/mod-
event.atom"
ICS_FN   = "feed_events.ics"
```

The program leads off with a few imports that should be familiar by now, followed by a couple of configuration constants:

- FEED_URL—URL pointing to a feed with mod_event metadata and/or hCalendar entry content.

- ICS_FN—Output filename where iCalendar data will be written.

Continuing forward, check out Listing 18-19 for the start of the main() function.

Listing 18-19: ch18_feed_to_ical.py (Part 2 of 4)

```
def main():
    """
    Process calendar data present in a feed to build
    iCalendar events.
    """
    # Grab the feed for processing
    feed_url = len(sys.argv) > 1 and sys.argv[1] or FEED_URL
    ics_fn   = len(sys.argv) > 2 and sys.argv[2] or ICS_FN

    # Get the feed, create a new calendar and an
    # hCalendar parser.
    feed  = feedparser.parse(feed_url)
    cal   = Calendar()
    hp    = HCalendarParser()
    types = TypesFactory()
```

The definition of main() in Listing 18-19 looks for optional command-line arguments for the feed URL and iCalendar output filename, using the appropriate configuration constants as defaults. Toward the end of the listing, it grabs the input feed, prepares the output Calendar instance, and creates an HCalendarParser and TypesFactory for use as utilities.

Next up, the feed entry processing begins in Listing 18-20.

Listing 18-20: ch18_feed_to_ical.py (Part 3 of 4)

```
    # Scan all the feed entries for calendar events.
    for entry in feed.entries:

        # First, check for any hCalendar events in the
        # feed summary content.
        if 'summary' in entry:
            # Attempt to parse the entry summary for
            # hCalendar events.
            events = hp.parse(entry['summary'])
            if events:
                # Add all the events, then continue on to
                # next entry.
                for e in events: cal.add_component(e)
                continue
```

Each feed entry is visited in a loop. And, first off in this loop, the entry is searched for summary content. If any is present, it gets run through the HCalendarParser instance. If any events are returned by this parser run, they're inserted into the Calendar instance, and the loop skips ahead to the next feed entry. Things are pretty easy here, thanks to the HCalendarParser doing all the hard work.

Now keep going on to Listing 18-21, to see what happens when the HCalendarParser comes up empty-handed.

Listing 18-21: ch18_feed_to_ical.py (Part 4 of 4)

```
# Here's an attempt to map feedparser entry metadata
# to event properties.
entry_to_event = [
    ( 'link',          'url' ),
    ( 'title',         'summary' ),
    ( 'summary',       'description' ),
    ( 'ev_startdate',  'dtstart' ),
    ( 'ev_enddate',    'dtend' ),
    ( 'ev_location',   'location' ),
    ( 'ev_organizer',  'organizer' ),
    ( 'ev_type',       'type' ),
]

# If no events found in entry content, try constructing
# one from feed metadata values.
event = Event()
for entry_key, event_key in entry_to_event:

    # Check to see this metadata key is in the entry.
    if entry_key in entry:
        entry_val = entry[entry_key]

        # HACK: Get rid of date and time field separators to
        # better match iCalendar's time format.
        if event_key.startswith('dt'):
            entry_val = entry_val.replace('-','')
            entry_val = entry_val.replace(':','')

        # Convert the entry metadata value to a event date type
        # and add it to the event.
        val = types.from_ical(event_key,
                              entry_val.encode('UTF-8'))
        event.add(event_key, val)

    # Add the event to the calendar after building it.
    cal.add_component(event)

# Write the iCalendar file out to disk.
open(ics_fn, "w").write(cal.as_string())

if __name__ == '__main__': main()
```

The code wrapping up the program here in Listing 18-21 runs a bit longer than the other portions—but in a nutshell, when the HCalendarParser doesn't find any calendar events in the feed entry contents, the program falls back to mapping feed entry metadata to iCalendar Event properties.

The first part is the definition of a list named entry_to_event: This establishes a mapping from source feed event metadata fields to destination iCalender Event properties. Immediately after this definition, a new blank Event instance is created and then each of the mappings from entry_to_event is checked out.

Wherever the entry has metadata for a given key in the map, that value is extracted from the entry and added to the Entry under the corresponding name in the map. One little hack involved here is to remove dashes and colons separating date and time fields, respectively. Both of the date fields in the Event start with 'dt', and they're meant to contain a simplified version of the ISO8601 date/time format. So, this tweak attempts to ensure that the Event gets data it can handle.

Finally, after all of the candidate metadata fields in the entry are checked for data, the finished Entry is added to the Calendar. And then, at the end of the loop, the iCalendar data is written out to disk.

Trying Out the Feed to iCalendar Converter

At last, it's time to come full circle. If you've been working through all the transformations so far in the chapter, you've seen iCalendar events published as hCalendar-microformatted HTML. These HTML documents were then stuffed into a feed, which you filtered to add mod_event metadata. Now, you're going to turn this feed *back* into iCalendar event data.

Check out Figure 18-8 for a sample run of the program. Although the transformation process hasn't been perfect or comprehensive, you should see a resemblance between this program's end product and the original list of U.S. holidays.

But wait, that's not all. This program wouldn't be all that useful if it were limited to just being the end of the transformation chain established in this chapter. You can use this thing on existing feeds on the Web to turn *their* calendar event metadata and content into iCalendar data. One such site that publishes events and happenings in mod_event-enriched feeds is Protest.Net, a "collective of activists who are working together to create our own media." You can check them out here:

http://protest.net/about_protest_net.html

For example, the following is a feed listing various things going on in New York:

http://protest.net/NYC/rss

Why not try out the feed converter on this feed? Take a peek at Figure 18-9 to see what this should look like. And, calling on PHP iCalendar again, you can see what the calendar data produced from this Protest.Net feed looks like imported into the calendar in Figure 18-10, as well as how the detail view on an event appears in Figure 18-11. Try this program out on other feeds with calendar events, and see what happens!

FIGURE 18-8: Sample program run of the feed to iCalendar converter using the U.S. holidays feed.

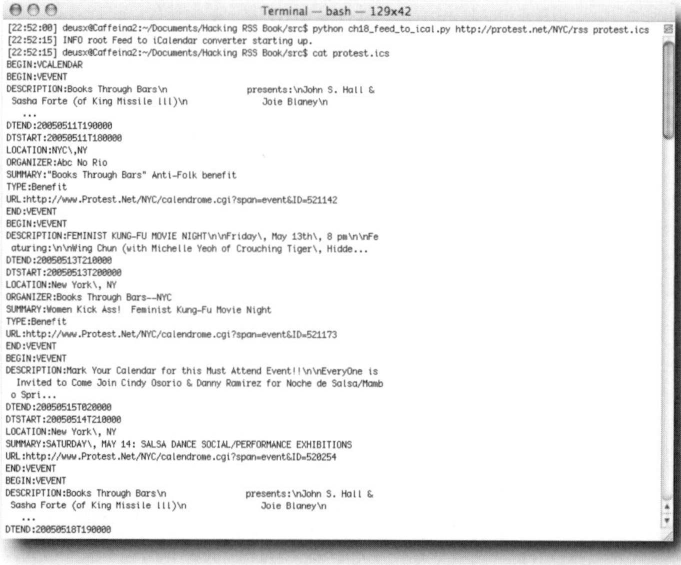

FIGURE 18-9: Sample program run of the converter on a `mod_event`-enriched feed from Protest.Net

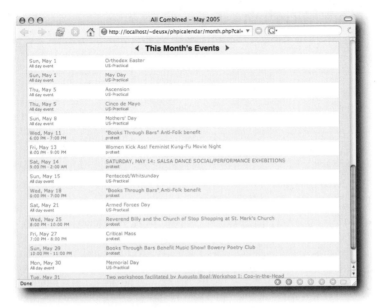

FIGURE 18-10: List of events added to PHP iCalendar for May from the converted Protest.Net RSS feed

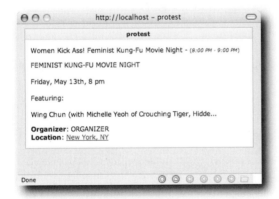

FIGURE 18-11: Detail view on an event from the converted Protest.Net RSS feed

Checking Out Other Options

Extending feeds with new forms of content has been tinkered with for some years now, but it seems to be taking a while to really take off. However, you might be interested in checking out a few of these other efforts.

Trying Out More Microformats

The notion of microformat specifications was pretty fresh at the time of this writing, so there's bound to have been further activity by the time you read this. Check out what's under development here:

```
http://developers.technorati.com/wiki/MicroFormats
```

At last glance, there were budding specifications in play for expressing contact information (hCard) and reviews (hReview) alongside the hCalendar specification—any of these might make good additions to a feed.

Looking at RSSCalendar

Although it doesn't look like it has iCalendar import or export, RSSCalendar does offer calendar events in RSS form and interactive Web-based tools for managing your calendars. Take a look here:

```
http://www.rsscalendar.com/rss/
```

It seems like, at least for the moment, that this service is a work in progress—so it might be worth keeping an eye on as it explores further options surrounding calendar events in syndication feeds.

Watching for EVDB

One more service that looks like it'll be taking off soon is EVDB, the "the Events and Venues Database," located here:

```
http://www.evdb.com/
```

From what details its (as of this writing) beta preview site reveal, you should soon be able to subscribe to calendar events data here in both iCalendar and mod_event-enriched RSS form.

Summary

This chapter took you on a trip through several stages of transforming calendar event data from the iCalendar standard, through the hCalendar microformat, into syndication feeds, and back out again as iCalendar data. Hopefully, you should be able to jump in anywhere in this circuit to figure out how to either publish your own calendar events, or how to subscribe to events published by someone else. Quite a few avenues are left open to additional hacking by this chapter, however:

- The feed filter in this chapter doesn't cover the full range of mod_event elements. You might try tweaking it a bit to conditionally include more information as it's available.

- The feed to iCalendar converter in this chapter isn't an aggregator—check into pulling many calendar feeds together and importing only the new events into your calendar program.

- There are aspects of the hCalendar format that this chapter doesn't cover—such as including hCard-formatted contact information for organizers and attendees in events. These are under development now and may become important very soon, so stay tuned!

- Also, as mentioned, hCalendar isn't the only microformat out there—and mod_event isn't the only feed extension around. Take a look at what's being done for product reviews, as well as other feed metadata such as including geographic locations and other related information in feeds.

Appendix

Implementing a Shared Feed Cache

At the end of Chapter 2, one of the avenues for further hacking I'd mentioned was to separate feed scanning from the production of the output page, storing the results of scans in between program runs. Well, I couldn't resist throwing in a bonus module that does just that.

This appendix offers code for a shared cache of fetched feed data, usable in your programs as a drop-in replacement for feedparser. After working with HTTPCache throughout the book, it seemed like there should be something like this specifically for feeds—so here's an attempt to provide it.

This module can share the effort of feed fetching between programs, minimizing actual feed downloads by supporting the details of conditional HTTP GET and performing downloads at most once per hour. When multiple programs attempt to grab the same feed, or when the same program tries fetching the same feed repeatedly, this cache will serve up data stored locally until it's been determined to be stale. Only at that point will it actually fetch the fresh feed.

This code isn't absolutely necessary to make any hack in this book work. It could help improve things for you, however, especially if you start playing with large numbers of feeds. In particular, this becomes an issue fairly quickly if you amass a large number of feeds for sifting with a hack like the popular links feed generator in Chapter 15. Personally, I'm running that hack on around 700 feeds, and this cache comes in quite handy while trying to tweak the output of that program over multiple trial runs. Also, you can use this in your feed aggregator to speed up program runs while you're playing around with changing templates.

So, without further ado, check out Listing A-1 for the opening lines of this new module, named feedcache.py.

Listing A-1: feedcache.py (Part 1 of 10)

```
#!/usr/bin/env python
"""
feedcache

Implements a shared cache of feed data polled via feedparser.
"""
import sys, os, os.path, md5, gzip, feedparser, time
import cPickle as pickle

def main():
    """
    Either print out a parsed feed, or refresh all feeds.
    """
    feed_cache = FeedCache()
    if len(sys.argv) > 1:
        # In demonstration, fetch and pretty-print a parsed feed.
        from pprint import pprint
        pprint(feed_cache.parse(sys.argv[1]))
    else:
        # Open up the feed cache and refresh all the feeds
        feed_cache.refreshFeeds()
```

Like many of the other reusable modules in this book, Listing A-1 starts off with a main() driver function. It accepts an optional argument on the command line, which is expected to be the URL to a feed. Given this argument, it will fetch the feed and pretty-print the parsed feed data to the console.

However, if no argument is given, the main() function creates a FeedCache instance and calls a method named refreshFeeds(). Where this comes in handy is if you run the module in a crontab or scheduled task, say once per hour. The refreshFeeds() method scans through all the feeds that have been fetched and cached before, thus acting to ensure all the feeds in the cache are fresh before any of your other programs ask for them. Because this scheduled refreshing tends to happen in the background while you're off doing something else, you should get fairly fast responses from your programs that use the cache.

Getting on with the show, take a look at Listing A-2 for the definition of a class named FeedCacheRecord.

Listing A-2: feedcache.py (Part 2 of 10)

```
class FeedCacheRecord:
    """
    Record stored in feed cache.
    """
```

```
def __init__(self, last_poll=0.0, etag='', modified=None,
             data=None):
    """Initialize the cache record."""
    self.last_poll = last_poll
    self.etag      = etag
    self.modified  = modified
    self.data      = data
```

The `FeedCacheRecord` class definition in Listing A-2 is somewhat bare-bones. It mostly consists of just a few properties describing a cached feed, including the feed data and a timestamp when the cache last refreshed this feed, along with the HTTP modification data and `ETag` headers from the last fetch.

Listing A-3 offers the start of the `FeedCache` class.

Listing A-3: feedcache.py (Part 3 of 10)

```
class FeedCache:
    """
    Implements a cache of refreshed feed data.
    """
    CACHE_DIR      = ".feed_cache"
    REFRESH_PERIOD = 60 * 60

    def __init__(self, cache_dir=CACHE_DIR,
                 refresh_period=REFRESH_PERIOD):
        """
        Initialize and open the cache.
        """
        self.refresh_period = refresh_period
        self.cache_dir      = cache_dir

        # Create the cache dir, if it doesn't yet exist.
        if not os.path.exists(cache_dir):
            os.makedirs(cache_dir)
```

In Listing A-3, the `FeedCache` class starts off with a pair of class constants:

- `CACHE_DIR`—This provides the name for a directory in which the cached feed data will be maintained.

- `REFRESH_PERIOD`—This constant establishes a minimum period in seconds between feed refreshes. In this case, the setting ensures that no feed will be refreshed more than once an hour.

Following these is the definition of the __init__() method. Here, the class constants are used as default initializers for object properties. If the cache directory doesn't yet exist, it gets created.

Continuing on, Listing A-4 defines a few more methods.

Listing A-4: feedcache.py (Part 4 of 10)

```
def parse(self, feed_uri, **kw):
    """
    Partial feedparser API emulation, only accepts a URI.
    """
    self.refreshFeed(feed_uri)
    return self.getFeedRecord(feed_uri).data

def getFeedRecord(self, feed_uri):
    """
    Fetch a feed cache record by URI.
    """
    return self._loadRecord(feed_uri, None)
```

The parse() method defined in Listing A-4 is provided for a bit of compatibility with the feedparser module, because it will accept the same feed URI parameter and return the same feed data as feedparser. In doing this, the parse() method trips a refresh of the feed via refreshFeed() and returns the parsed feed data.

You'll see more details about this method soon, but it might help to know this: Even though the refreshFeed() method is called, it obeys the REFRESH_PERIOD and conditional HTTP GET rules. So, you don't need to worry about repeated calls to parse() firing off too many feed fetches—this is just a means of automatically firing off refreshes when they're needed in the course of using feed data.

After this method comes the getFeedRecord() method, which fetches the FeedCacheRecord for a given feed URI, via the _loadRecord() method. This might seem a bit redundant, but it'll be explained in a bit.

Keep going on to Listing A-5 for more FeedCache definition.

Listing A-5: feedcache.py (Part 5 of 10)

```
def refreshFeeds(self):
    """
    Refresh all the feeds in the cache.
    """
    # Load up the list of feed URIs, report how many feeds
    # in cache and start processing.
    feed_uris = self._getCachedURIs()
    for feed_uri in feed_uris:
```

```
try:
    # Refresh the current feed URI
    self.refreshFeed(feed_uri)
except KeyboardInterrupt:
    # Allow keyboard interrupts to stop the program.
    raise
except Exception, e:
    # Soldier on through any other problems.
    pass
```

In Listing A-5, the `refreshFeeds()` method used in `main()` is defined. Here, the `_getCachedURIs()` method is called to dig up a list of all the feed URIs that appear in records stored in the cache directory. For each of these, an attempt is made to refresh the feed using the `refreshFeed()` method. Any exception other than a `KeyboardInterrupt` is silently ignored. This is useful in the context of a scheduled task when you're not there to receive errors, but you may want to consider making this part a bit noisier (that is, by writing to a log file) in order to catch any problems that occur along the way.

Now, in Listing A-6, you have the first half of the definition of `refreshFeed()`.

Listing A-6: feedcache.py (Part 6 of 10)

```
def refreshFeed(self, feed_uri):
    """
    Refresh a given feed.
    """
    # Get the record for this feed, creating a new one
    # if necessary.
    feed_rec = self._loadRecord(feed_uri, FeedCacheRecord())

    # Check to see whether it's time to refresh this feed yet.
    # TODO: Respect/obey TTL, update schedule, cache control
    # headers.
    if (time.time() - feed_rec.last_poll) < self.refresh_period:
        return
```

First off in the definition of `refreshFeed()` of Listing A-6, the cache record for the given feed URI is fetched using the `_loadRecord()` method. Note that this method is called with an empty `FeedCacheRecord` as a default, which is returned if an existing record for this feed URI is not found in the cache. Next, a check is made against the cache record's last refresh timestamp. For a new record, this will be a zero value. If the time between now and the last feed refresh is less than the refresh period, the method returns without doing anything.

The second half of this method is presented in Listing A-7.

Listing A-7: feedcache.py (Part 7 of 10)

```
    else:
        # Fetch the feed using the ETag and Last-Modified notes.
        feed_data = feedparser.parse(feed_uri,\
            etag=feed_rec.etag, modified=feed_rec.modified)
        feed_rec.last_poll = time.time()

        bozo = feed_data.get('bozo_exception', None)
        if bozo is not None:
            # Throw any keyboard interrupts that happen in parsing.
            if type(bozo) is KeyboardInterrupt: raise bozo

            # Don't try to shelve exceptions, it's bad.
            # (TODO: Maybe save this in a text form, for
            # troubleshooting.)
            del feed_data['bozo_exception']

        # If the feed HTTP status is 304, there was no change.
        if feed_data.get('status', -1) != 304:
            feed_rec.etag     = feed_data.get('etag', '')
            feed_rec.modified = feed_data.get('modified', None)
            feed_rec.data     = feed_data

        # Update the feed cache record.
        self._saveRecord(feed_uri, feed_rec)
```

If the `refreshFeed()` method execution reaches the code in Listing A-7, it's been long enough since the last recorded feed refresh. So, the `feedparser.parse()` function is called to poll the feed, supplied with the `ETag` and last modified values recorded from response headers received after the previous poll. This state-keeping allows the cache to support conditional HTTP `GET`, thus making the feed refresh a bit more efficient.

Next, the data returned by `feedparser` is checked for errors in its `bozo_exception` property. In this current implementation, nothing is really done with this information, other than to raise `KeyboardException` errors to facilitate manual program breaks. (You might want to add some logging here to report on errors found in feeds.) And, notice at the tail end of this conditional, the exception data is deleted from the structure. This is done because the complex objects that often appear in parsing exceptions don't agree with being stored in the cache directory as pickled `FeedCacheRecord` objects.

After this brief trip through error handling, the HTTP status of this feed fetch is checked. If the status is `304`, conditional HTTP `GET` has reported that the feed hasn't actually changed. Otherwise, it's time to update the `FeedCacheRecord` with new header values and new fetched feed data. Finally, this method wraps up with a call to `_saveRecord()` to store the updated `FeedCacheRecord` object.

It's getting pretty close to the end of this class, so continue on to Listing A-8.

Listing A-8: feedcache.py (Part 8 of 10)

```
# Watch for subclassable parts below here.

def _recordFN(self, feed_uri):
    """
    Return the filename for a given feed URI.
    """
    hash = md5.md5(feed_uri).hexdigest()
    return os.path.join(self.cache_dir, '%s' % hash)

def _getCachedURIs(self):
    """
    Get a list of feed URIs in the cache.
    """
    uris = []
    for fn in os.listdir(self.cache_dir):
        rec_fn = os.path.join(self.cache_dir, fn)
        data   = pickle.load(open(rec_fn, 'rb'))
        uri    = data['data'].get('url', None)
        if uri: uris.append(uri)
    return uris
```

The first method defined in Listing A-8 is _recordFN(), a utility method that transforms a feed URI to a filename in the feed cache directory. This will be used to manage FeedCacheRecord objects in pickled form.

The next method is _getCachedURIs(), a quick-and-dirty way to find all the URIs of feeds in the cache used by the refreshFeeds() method. It walks through all the files in the cache directory, loads up the picked data, and attempts to extract the feed URI for each. This list of URIs is returned at the end of the method.

Check out Listing A-9 for the conclusion of the FeedCache class.

Listing A-9: feedcache.py (Part 9 of 10)

```
def _loadRecord(self, feed_uri, default=None):
    """
    Load a FeedCacheRecord from disk.
    """
```

Continued

Listing A-9 *(continued)*

```
    try:
        rec_fn = self._recordFN(feed_uri)
        data   = pickle.load(open(rec_fn, 'rb'))
        return FeedCacheRecord(**data)
    except IOError:
        return default

def _saveRecord(self, feed_uri, record):
    """
    Save a FeedCacheRecord to disk.
    """
    rec_fn = self._recordFN(feed_uri)
    pickle.dump(record.__dict__, open(rec_fn, 'wb'))
```

Listing A-9 offers a pair of methods, _loadRecord() and _saveRecord(). These are used, oddly enough, to load and save FeedCacheRecord objects. In this implementation, files in a cache directory are used and the pickle module is used to convert the Python data structures into binary streams in those files.

One thing to notice here: Rather than serializing the FeedCacheRecord objects directly, these methods manipulate the underlying dictionary of properties for the objects. This isn't ideal, but it ended up being useful during development when changes in the FeedCacheRecord class tended to upset things with pickle and this technique seemed to fix things.

The other thing to notice about these last few methods is that they're intended as hooks for customization. For example, say you wanted to trade the cache directory for a SQL database. You should be able to leave most of the class alone, just altering the implementation of FeedCacheRecord management in a subclass.

Finally, Listing A-10 wraps up the feedcache module.

Listing A-10: feedcache.py (Part 10 of 10)

```
def parse(feed_uri, cache=None, **kw):
    """
    Partial feedparser API emulation, only accepts a URI.
    """
    return (cache or FeedCache()).parse(feed_uri, **kw)

if __name__=='__main__': main()
```

This final bit of code in Listing A-10 is module-level function. It serves as one more piece of `feedparser` compatibility: With this, you can pretty much replace any call to `feedparser.parse()` with a call to `feedcache.parse()` in your programs and expect the same results—with the only difference being that things should be "magically" faster and more efficient.

It is important to note, though, that I just wrote "pretty much replace any call," with respect to this `feedparser` API emulation. This function accepts a URI, but not a file or a string as the real `feedparser` does. Also, `feedparser` accepts a number of other parameters—such as an `ETag`, modification date, user agent, and referrer. The `parse()` function in Listing A-10 and the `parse()` method in Listing A-4 both *accept* all of these parameters for the sake of compatibility, but they're all *ignored* during operation.

So, take a look at Listing A-11 for a quick tweak to Chapter 2's `feed_reader.py` from Listing 2-18.

Listing A-11: cached_feed_reader.py

```python
#!/usr/bin/env python

import sys
import feedcache as feedparser

if __name__ == '__main__':
    feed_uri  = sys.argv[1]
    feed_data = feedparser.parse(feed_uri)

    print "============================================================="
    print "'%(title)r' at %(link)r" % feed_data['feed']
    print "============================================================="
    print

    for entry in feed_data['entries']:
        print "-------------------------------------------------------------"
        print "Date:  %(modified)r" % entry
        print "Title: %(title)r" % entry
        print "Link:  %(link)r" % entry

        if not entry.get('summary', '') == '':
            print
            print "%(summary)r" % entry

        print "-------------------------------------------------------------"
        print
```

The only real difference between this program and the one from Chapter 2 is the following line:

```
import feedcache as feedparser
```

This imports the `feedcache` module under the name `feedparser`, allowing it to masquerade as that original module. But, just like the original program, an example session running this test program could look like this:

```
# python cached_feed_reader.py http://www.boingboing.net/atom.xml


===========================================================
'Boing Boing' at http://www.boingboing.net/
===========================================================


-----------------------------------------------------------
Date:   2005-01-18T13:38:05-08:00
Title:  Cory NPR interview audio
Link:   http://www.boingboing.net/2005/01/18/cory_npr_interview_a.html
-----------------------------------------------------------


-----------------------------------------------------------
Date:   2005-01-18T13:12:28-08:00
Title:  Explanation for region coded printer cartridges?
Link:   http://www.boingboing.net/2005/01/18/explanation_for_regi.html
-----------------------------------------------------------
```

Look familiar? It should. Now, if you try running this program over and over again, you might notice that successive runs go quite a bit faster—although this speed up might just get masked by the time it takes your Python interpreter to start up and run the program. The benefits of the feed cache will become much more apparent when you start dealing with large numbers of feeds. Enjoy!

Index

Continued

S

How to take it to the Extreme.

If you enjoyed this book, there are many others like it for you. From *Podcasting* to *Hacking Firefox*, ExtremeTech books can fulfill your urge to hack, tweak and modify, providing the tech tips and tricks readers need to get the most out of their hi-tech lives.